Education Law

Principles, Policies, and Practice

John Dayton, J.D., Ed. D.

Wisdom Builders Press ™

www.wisdombuilderspress.com

First Edition © 2012

ISBN: ISBN-13: 978-1470063214
ISBN-10: 1470063212

To my wife Kathy and our sons Joel, Jared, and Joshua

About the Author

John Dayton, J.D., Ed. D.

John Dayton is a Professor of Education Law and Policy, and the Director of the Education Law Consortium, a non-partisan pro bono research group dedicated to advancing knowledge and practice in education law. Professor Dayton is an internationally recognized expert on law and policy. He is a lawyer with experience in public and private legal practice. He has also served as a judicial clerk, and as a public school teacher and Program Director. In recognition of his academic achievements he was offered academic scholarships from many outstanding law schools including the Indiana University-Bloomington School of Law in his home State. Professor Dayton holds both a law degree and a doctoral degree in educational administration and policy from Indiana University. Dr. Dayton has taught law and policy courses for over two decades including education law; special education law; medical law; and professional ethics. Dr. Dayton is currently a professor at the University of Georgia where he was the first recipient of the Glickman Award for excellence in research and teaching and is a member of the University Teaching Academy. Dr. Dayton is the author of over a 100 law review articles, books, and other publications on law and policy. He is an internationally recognized author and speaker on law and policy issues.

Summary of Contents

Table of Contents

Preface

After decades of teaching education law to thousands of students, I can tell you with great certainty that if you want to acquire a strong working knowledge of education law, this is the book you need. This is the book I always wanted, and now it is available to help you master education law principles, policies, and practice. If you are an administrator, teacher, counselor, social worker, lawyer, or other professional working with schools or students, having a working knowledge of education law is a professional necessity.

As a professional you must know the laws governing your profession for these essential reasons:

1) *Self Preservation*: Ignorance of the law can have dire personal and professional consequences. Career ending legal landmines can only be avoided if you know where they are and how to safely navigate around them;

2) *Professional Confidence*: Professionals who know the law are far more confident and successful. They effectively utilize the law and need never fear it;

3) *Protecting Your Institution and Colleagues*: Employees who do not understand and comply with the law may cause devastating financial liability and serious damage to the reputation of the institution, often with ruinous consequences for their colleagues as well;

4) *Professional Responsibility and Leadership*: Professionals are leaders in their communities. They must know and respect the law, and strengthen and improve their communities by modeling lawful and ethical conduct in practice.

The oldest maxim in law is that: "Ignorance of the law is no excuse." All professionals must know the laws governing their profession. Acquiring a strong working knowledge of the law will give you the knowledge and professional confidence necessary to become an invaluable asset to your institution and community.

From cover to cover, this book is designed to actively engage you in learning education law and to build a strong working knowledge of the law in practice. This book is unique in that it:

- Clearly explains even the most complex principles of law;
- Connects essential principles of law to current policies and practices;
- Provides an optimal balance of case law and instructive commentary;
- Harmonizes complex and contradictory case law into a clear statement of current law;
- Presents thought provoking comments and questions throughout; and
- Provides useful and informative chapter summaries that:
  - Clearly state the most significant points of law;
  - Offer helpful practice tips;
  - Present stimulating discussion questions; and
  - Suggest enrichment activities for further learning and application.

There is nothing like first-hand knowledge. In recognition of this fact, this book provides you with the direct text of the most important primary sources of the law. You do not have to settle for someone's opinion about the law. You can learn the law first-hand through direct experience as this book presents you with the most important cases, statutes, and regulations. You will see for yourself what the Court, Congress, or Administrative Agency said concerning the law.

This book does not, however, leave you on your own to distill the complexities of law and put this knowledge into a working context. Instead, this book follows the most important cases, statutes, and regulations with clear legal analyses and helpful legal tests and summaries derived from the law. These materials provide you with invaluable guidance in translating legal principles and policies into practice.

Law is a complex body of knowledge. To maximize learning and minimize confusion this knowledge must be presented with clarity and without unnecessary distractions. Legal scholars value extensive citations. But after decades of teaching law it became clear that for most students excessive citations and lengthy compilations of contradictory lower court opinions did little but confuse and distract them from mastering core legal principles. For these reasons this book limits citations to only those necessary for readers to easily find further information when needed, and case law to only the most important and illuminating cases, those defining current and well established law. In the age of the Internet, extensive footnotes and citations are unnecessary when readers can easily find additional information through a simple Internet search. A glossary of terms also seemed unnecessary. Most legal terms are defined in the text, but if further definitions are needed a quick Internet search provides abundant information.

Concerning case law, this book focuses on U.S. Supreme Court opinions and only includes lower court opinions if an issue has not been addressed by the Supreme Court and lower court opinions represent a clear majority view. U.S. Supreme Court opinions are binding law in all U.S. states and territories. In contrast trial court opinions are only binding on the parties in the case, a point commonly misunderstood by readers new to legal study, who often mistakenly assume that other jurisdictions' trial or appellate court opinions govern the law in their jurisdiction also. To avoid confusion and give the reader a clear working knowledge of current and binding law, this book focuses on U.S. Supreme Court opinions and other stable, well established law, avoiding confusing, unsettled, and often contradictory lower court opinions. In this way the reader can clearly see the big picture and the essential details, avoiding unnecessary confusion and distractions.

Several reviewers commented on my elective capitalization of "People" and "Rule of Law" in the text. After considerable thought, I decided to leave these capitalized for this reason: I wanted to make it clear with each use of these terms that I was referring to the "People" and not just some people; and the "Rule of Law" and not just some rules of law.

When I use the term the People I am referring to the perpetual inter-generational trust of humanity as represented by those alive in the present and honor-bound to: 1) Respect the sacrifices of past generations; and 2) Create the better world that is possible for future generations. I am referring to the People as the source of all legitimate powers of governance and as the rightful holders and ultimate protectors of inalienable human rights.

When I use the phrase the Rule of Law I am referring to the timeless and compelling ideals of justice and equality embodied by this renowned legal maxim. I am emphasizing the stark contrast between equal justice under the common Rule of Law by mutual consent, and arbitrary rule through corrupted laws illegitimately imposed by powerful men. The Rule of Law commands that no one is ever above the limits of the law or below its protections.

Enduring commitments to democratic governance by the People and the just Rule of Law form essential walls in the legal stronghold against totalitarianism and injustice. These principles may at first seem abstract and highly philosophical. But as this book will demonstrate these concepts form a vital part of your world. Governance by the People and justice under the common Rule of Law are essential to the protection of your personal liberty and safety on a daily basis. History proves that where the People govern and the Rule of Law is strong you find liberty, justice, peace, and prosperity. But where strong men dominate others through self-serving rules of law, the People suffer repression, injustice, discontent, and the powerful prosper at everyone else's expense. Chapter 1 provides a more complete explanation of these principles and their role in educating strong citizens for a strong democracy.

The study of law can play a vital role in the educational process. Law is unique among academic disciplines, combining the intellectual depth and wisdom of philosophy with the power and consequence of practice. Law is founded on abstract philosophical principles. But the law is not just abstract and philosophical. The law governs every aspect of our daily lives from birth through death. A good judge must be guided by philosophical ideals of justice. But the judge must also decide the case in front of him or her in a way that works in the real world; promotes stability and efficiency; and improves citizens' daily lives.

The well-known statue of Lady Justice, with her blindfold, weighing scales, and sword, provides a graphic illustration of the law as an essential bridge between philosophical principles of justice and the application of justice in our daily lives. Under the Rule of Law, the blindfolded Lady Justice pays no heed to who is before her, applying the same principles of justice to all persons on an equal basis. She thoughtfully and carefully weighs principles of justice, applicable laws, and the unique facts in each case. And when she makes a just decision based on the law and the facts, the Sword of Justice symbolizes that Lady Justice fully intends to enforce her decision under the Rule of Law, bringing principles of justice into our daily lives.

As you read through this book, I would like to make the following suggestions to help you achieve the full benefits from your reading: Thoughtfully reflect on what you read, and talk about what you are learning with your professors, fellow students, and colleagues. The law is a system of just and logical dispute resolution developed over thousands of years. Learning the law is not a spectator sport. It requires you to recreate an understanding of the legal system and legal reasoning in your own mind piece by piece. This can only be achieved by actively engaging in critical thought; examining and testing ideas and assumptions; and discovering the essential connections between legal principles and practice in your world.

Legal principles mean nothing if they do not make real differences in our daily lives. There is no value in principles that do not genuinely elevate us, and no honor in holding lofty ideals we do not intend to live by. Thousands of years of human progress demonstrate that just legal principles can uplift us and improve the human condition. This has too often been a tragically slow and painful process, severely testing human morality, justice, and resolve. But as Dr. Martin Luther King, Jr. said: "The arc of the moral universe is long, but it bends toward justice." Just laws remain humanity's best tool for moving toward greater justice in our lives. Your personal understanding of the law contributes to your progress and to human progress through your positive example and influence on others around you.

This book is intended to help the reader achieve both valuable professional knowledge and priceless personal growth. Formal study is a powerful means of acquiring professional knowledge and skills. Better educated people enjoy far greater success and earn significantly more money over the course of their professional careers. Because of its obvious utility and value, learning about the law is an especially potent area of study. Those who know the laws governing their profession will be far more capable, confident, and valuable professionals.

While professional preparation is a very important part of education, and a major objective of this book, it must never be forgotten that the broader goal of education is to not only prepare students for professional success, but to also open their minds to a richer quality of life and the possibility of a better future. Education should broaden and expand students' horizons and their understanding of the world in which they live. Understanding the history and purposes of the law not only helps you to better understand and apply the law in the present, but it also gives you a much broader understanding of the law and your essential role in advancing justice in your community. Rather than only teaching how things are, education must inspire students and give them the intellectual tools to make things better. This book will help you learn the laws governing your profession. But it will also guide you on a voyage to greater personal understanding of your own human history and the world in which you live, leading from professional knowledge to personal wisdom.

Although this book is primarily focused on the laws concerning U.S. public schools, many of the principles and laws are equally applicable to higher education and private schools. Further, while this book is focused on U.S. law, the fundamental principles of law (*e.g.*, human rights, freedoms, due process, etc.) are applicable internationally as well. Consult the laws in your jurisdiction, but foundational legal principles are generally universally applicable.

In this book every effort was made to present you with an accurate academic presentation of the law. Perfect objectivity is impossible. But this book has no agenda other than to explain just principles of law, current policies, and their application in practice. It is important to note, however, that no book can give you legal advice. Legal advice can only be obtained from an attorney licensed to practice law in your jurisdiction and familiar with the unique facts in your case. If you need to seek legal counsel, however, having a solid working knowledge of the law can help you to work more effectively and efficiently with your lawyer.

This book contains nearly a quarter million words and well over a million letters. Given this reality, there will be some typographical errors. Although this book was reviewed by many highly qualified reviewers and a very capable editor, any errors are ultimately my responsibility and my fault alone. My apologies for any errors, and any discovered errors will be corrected in the next addition. Note, however, that if official U.S. Supreme Court citations were not yet available those citations were intentionally left blank for later completion (*e.g.*, ___ U.S. ___).

Enjoy your journey through the unique and fascinating realm of the law. By studying the law it is guaranteed that you will become a more capable professional and a wiser person. You will understand the world around you much better and you can become a more able participant in the promotion of justice, democracy, and the shaping of a better future for yourself and others. Over the years your understanding of this important knowledge and useful skills will continue to grow. This is only the beginning of your journey, and it is a voyage that will change and improve your life and the lives of others around you. I want to give you my very best personal wishes for an enjoyable adventure in learning. It is my great hope that you will find your studies engaging, enlightening, and highly useful in your future.

John Dayton

Chapter 1: Introduction to Law and Governance

Before beginning the study of any area of law, including education law, it is essential to first understand the foundational framework on which that law functions. An understanding of the theoretical and historical framework of U.S. law and governance will prove invaluable to your later comprehension of education law and its application in practice. This knowledge is vital for all professionals working with children, educators, or schools.

> ### *All Professionals Must Know the Essential Laws Governing Their Profession*

It is critically important that educators working in public institutions understand the mandates of the Constitution and the lawful system of democratic governance. Public school educators are government officials legally bound by the limitations of the Constitution and the laws of democratic governance. Article VI of the U.S. Constitution requires that all government officials "both of the United States and of the several States, shall be bound by Oath or Affirmation, to support this Constitution."

As agents of the state government (local public schools are a division of the state government), public school educators are required to pledge an oath of office to support the Constitution of the United States, the constitution of their state, and the laws consistent with these constitutions. The State of New York, for example, requires the following oath from all state officials including public educators:

> I do hereby pledge and declare that I will support the constitution of the United States and the constitution of the State of New York, and that I will faithfully discharge the duties of the position of [Title of Position] according to the best of my ability.

As required by Article VI of the U.S. Constitution, all 50 states mandate similar oaths in which public officials including public educators must pledge, swear, or affirm their support for the federal and state constitutions. Public officials who violate their oaths of office may be subject to dismissal and monetary damages under 42 U.S.C. § 1983 or other applicable laws.

Many public school educators sign these oaths along with other employment documents, taking little notice of what they are swearing to or what the constitutions and laws require of them. One of the oldest maxims in law, however, is that "ignorance of the law is no excuse." If accused of failing to follow the law, professional educators will be held accountable for knowing the laws governing their profession whether they actually know the laws or not.

As a matter of both professional competence and self-protection it is essential that educators understand the laws and governance systems applicable to their profession. This is necessary so that they may perform their professional duties in accordance with the law; protect their own rights; and help protect the legal rights of their students, colleagues, and community. Further, compliance with professional ethics requires not only that educators obey the law, but that they must never be a party to violations of the law or condone unlawful conduct by others.

Schools are the Nurseries of the Democracy. Educators must Teach and Model Respect for the Rule of Law, Justice, and Democratic Governance

Educators who know the law and understand their system of government are far better prepared to teach this essential knowledge to their students. As the U.S. Supreme Court said in *Board of Education v. Pico,* 457 U.S. 853 (1982):

> Indeed, the Constitution presupposes the existence of an informed citizenry prepared to participate in governmental affairs, and these democratic principles obviously are constitutionally incorporated into the structure of our government. It therefore seems entirely appropriate that the State use public schools to . . . inculcate fundamental values necessary to the maintenance of a democratic political system.

Schools are the nurseries of the democracy. Democracy can be lost in a single generation, however, if educators are not prepared to teach the essential lessons of history, democracy, and the Rule of Law to the next generation of citizens. The Rule of Law is a foundational principle of democracy. In a democracy, as Aristotle said "the law should govern."

The common Rule of Law was a central focus in rejecting English Royal Rule and establishing American Democracy. John Adams famously said we must have "a government of laws, not of men." In a genuine democracy it is just and equal laws resulting from a democratic process that decide the lawful rules for all persons. Governance is not left only to the arbitrary and self-interested whims of men with power. Under the common Rule of Law no one is above the limits of the law, and no one is below the protections of the law. The rights of all persons are recognized as equal. As Thomas Jefferson observed:

> The general spread of the light of science has already laid open to every view the palpable truth, that the mass of mankind has not been born with saddles on their backs, nor a favored few booted and spurred, ready to ride them legitimately, by the grace of God.

Our collective future depends on how well we teach these lessons of democracy and the Rule of Law to our children. It cannot be overemphasized that the most powerful way to teach these essential lessons is to act consistently with these principles in performing our professional responsibilities and in our interactions with students, colleagues, and community members. As the U.S. Supreme Court stated in *Bethel v. Fraser*, 478 U.S. 675 (1986):

> The process of educating our youth for citizenship in public schools is not confined to books, the curriculum, and the civics class; schools must teach by example the shared values of a civilized social order. Consciously or otherwise, teachers--and indeed the older students--demonstrate the appropriate form of civil discourse and political expression by their conduct and deportment in and out of class.

Among the most important lessons educators can teach their students is that the enforcement of laws and rules is not just an arbitrary exercise of power and positional authority. Instead, students must see through daily examples that educators are acting in their best interests, fairly

2

and in good faith, as part of a just system of laws and rules essential to achieving the order necessary for the common good.

Simply having the power to make and enforce laws and rules should never be confused with legitimate leadership under the Rule of Law. Leaders serving under the just Rule of Law can achieve great things for the common good by earning broad-based trust, respect, and support. Those who become intoxicated and corrupted by their own petty power, however, inevitably lead the institution to disaster. Legitimate leaders must always remember that the institutional power belongs to the institution and the people it serves and not to the leader personally.

> *"Power Tends to Corrupt, and Absolute Power Corrupts Absolutely." Lord Acton*

History relentlessly confirms Lord Acton's thesis on power. In a fascist state such as Hitler's Germany, for example, power and personal authority quickly became the only things that mattered. The Rule of Law was systematically dismantled and replaced with the rule of power, and democratic governance was supplanted by an authoritarian cult of personality. Laws were increasingly disregarded in favor of allowing arbitrary authority to be exercised by power corrupted government officials. As the disastrous tragedy of Hitler's Germany confirmed, however, iron-fisted authoritarian rule may initially produce quick results, but unchecked powers and cults of personality inevitably lead to corruption and ultimate destruction at terrible costs to everyone. The lawless authoritarian state may quickly rise to power, but it will just as quickly end in the ashes of its own disaster. The only safe repository of public power is the common Rule of Law.

> *"In America the Law is King." Patrick Henry*

Government officials trusted with public power must never forget that they are public servants and not rulers. And if they forget their proper limits and abuse public power, the legal system must hold them accountable to the People. Government officials should have no special rights, privileges, or immunities. Like all other citizens they must pay their fair share of taxes and follow the same common laws.

Government officials are delegated public powers for purposes of performing their public duties and protecting the common good. They are not, however, given any greater rights than other citizens. They have no formal powers beyond those granted by the People for the lawful performance of their public duties. A police officer, for example, is given a badge, a weapon, and powers of arrest in order to protect and serve the People. Exercise of these powers is only lawful when used for legitimate public purposes. Similarly, public school officials are granted public powers to protect and serve students and their communities. We want school officials to fully use their lawful powers to hire, fire, suspend, expel, etc., to protect safety and promote order and excellence in our schools. We do not, however, want their official powers misused for personal profit or vengeance.

Through their elected representatives the People pass laws with which all persons must comply. Our Nation's Founders recognized that the exercise of government power was necessary to protect everyone's life, liberty, and property. But they also recognized that a government with unchecked and excessive powers was the greatest potential threat to individual life, liberty, and property. Totalitarian regimes have killed millions of their own people, imprisoned countless citizens because of their political and religious beliefs, and seized private property when there was no lawful system of checks and balances guarding against such abuses of power.

To guard against these dangers, our Founders established within the U.S. Constitution a dynamic, interactive system of checks and balances to help prevent the accumulation and abuse of governmental power. They created a multifaceted system capable of evolving and adapting to changing circumstances and needs. Nonetheless, no matter how well designed, a governance system can never be better than the people who make it function.

The Founders knew that this system would ultimately fail unless both government officials and the People themselves understood and defended the foundational values of democracy and the Rule of Law, and understood the historical reasons democracy and the common Rule of Law were necessary. As a thorough student of history, Thomas Jefferson recognized: "Those who expect to be both ignorant and free, expect what never was and never will be." In a more ominous warning, the American philosopher George Santayana said: "Those who do not learn from history are doomed to repeat it."

There are two ways of learning these essential lessons: Through direct personal experience, or vicariously through the historical experiences of others. Those who suffered under totalitarian regimes or survived the chaos of revolution and war learned many powerful lessons about the importance of freedom and democracy. But these lessons were learned at great personal costs. We can spare ourselves and our children from this suffering, if we have the wisdom to learn and teach the essential lessons of history, and if we maintain the courage, strength, and determination to demand that our government officials respect fundamental human rights, democratic values, and the just Rule of Law.

Comments and Questions

Ironically, among the greatest dangers to the continuation of freedom and democracy may be the complicity that can set in among those who have always enjoyed the fruits of freedom and democracy in their lives. If you have no real personal knowledge of the horrors of totalitarian rule; constant police state surveillance; government torture; dissenters "disappearing"; and well-founded fears of expressing your sincerely held religious and political beliefs; how well prepared and motivated are you to defend against these dangers?

History shows that a democracy rarely becomes a police state overnight. Citizens' rights and liberties are gradually eroded over time. Like the "slow boiling frog" that would have immediately tried to jump out if tossed in a boiling pot, but passively cooks if the water temperature is only gradually increased, people are inclined to ignore small incremental loses of freedom as government power expands. They continue to go about their daily affairs passively, too busy in their own personal lives to react to these minor but growing expansions of governmental power.

But small incremental loses of rights can accumulate to dangerous loses of liberty over time. And if you have already compromised core principles of liberty and allowed unwarranted governmental expansions of power in the past, what is left of the principle to stand between you and the next intrusions on your liberties? Once the principle has been compromised, how do you stop the accelerating slide down the slippery slope toward the police state? As James Madison famously warned: "It is proper to take alarm at the first experiment on our liberties."

Government officials who do not respect democracy and the Rule of Law will always present seemingly plausible reasons why they need more power, but the People need less rights; why government officials need more secrecy, but the People need to be watched more closely; why the emergencies of the moment justify "temporary" exceptions to the Rule of Law. And these arguments are especially easy to sell when the majority of the People do not know the lessons of history and can be convinced that increased government powers are intended only for others and not for them.

As the Nazis gradually transformed German democracy into a totalitarian nightmare, millions cheered, convinced that this growing government power would only be used against the people they hated anyway, and never against them. As government power grows, however, so does the scope of its targets. Nonetheless, millions of citizens stood by passively because it wasn't them the government was targeting at the time, but they feared it would be if they spoke out against increasing abuses of power:

> They came first for the Communists, and I didn't speak up because I wasn't a Communist.
> Then they came for the trade unionists, and I didn't speak up because I wasn't a unionist.
> Then they came for the Jews, and I didn't speak up because I wasn't a Jew.
> Then they came for me and by that time no one was left to speak up.
>
> Pastor Martin Niemöller (1892–1984)

What can you learn from the experiences of others who have lived under totalitarian regimes, survived civil wars, etc.? What lessons can you teach your students and children so that they can learn from the experiences of others and not have to learn these terrible lessons directly in the future?

If you work for the federal, state, or local government (including public schools) do you recall the oath of office you were required to sign to respect the Constitution and the Rule of Law? Do you take this pledge seriously? Do your colleagues? What does this pledge require of you in your official actions concerning, for example, respect for church/state separation and religious freedom; respecting freedom of speech (even when the comments are unwelcomed); providing fair due process of law (even for those we may believe to be guilty); protecting equality for everyone under the law; and your role in advancing democracy and justice?

History proves that what we don't know can hurt us. Ignorance and indifference are grave dangers to our future. The remedy is education. And by learning the lessons of history, democratic governance, and the Rule of Law, you will be better prepared to teach your children and to actively participate in your own governance under the common Rule of Law.

Fundamental Theory and History of the Anglo-American Legal System

In earliest human history there was only one law: The law of the wild. The most powerful individual prevailed without regard to justice. Beyond the moral evils associated with the purely selfish use of force, however, the resulting violence and chaos were contrary to the common good and economic efficiency. Violence, chaos, and injustice are in no one's longer-term best interests. They cause not only immediate suffering and wasteful destruction, but they also inevitably fuel future rebellion and chaos. Where there is no justice, it is always only a matter of time until there is no peace.

The longer-term pursuit of peace, happiness, and prosperity requires justice, stability, and a reasonable degree of certainty that hard work and investment today will be rewarded in the future. There is no rational incentive to invest significant time and effort in such broadly beneficial activities as planning for the future, education, agriculture, improving property, and building wealth and industry without a system of laws that reasonably protect the individual's investments of time, energy, and resources for the future.

Long-term planning, education, capital improvements, and the production of valuable goods are essential to economic progress. And economic progress can help to create conditions favorable for social progress, resulting in a better future for all. None of this can happen, however, without the stability and mutual trust created by the just Rule of Law. Just laws protect rights of life, liberty, property, and the pursuit of happiness from abuses of power so that free individuals have an opportunity to enhance their own lives and to contribute to the common good of the community.

Good Laws Establish a Just and Efficient System of Problem Resolution

Justice must be the first and primary goal of any legitimate system of laws. The legal maxim *fiat justitia ruat caelum* ("may justice be done though the heavens fall") is engraved at the entrance of many courts or behind the judicial bench as an ever present reminder that justice is the foremost goal of the Rule of Law.

To be sustainable, however, a good legal system must also be efficiently designed and operated. Adequate time, effort, and resources must be provided to assure justice. But these limited resources must be allocated efficiently or the system will result in unnecessary waste and delays in the provision of justice. No matter how well intentioned, an inefficient and unsustainable legal system will eventually fail and collapse. Whether it is the U.S. Supreme Court reviewing constitutional disputes, or a school official administering student discipline, a just result is the essential goal. But the process must also be conducted with reasonable efficiency to avoid unnecessary delays and wastes of resources.

Good Laws Advance the Common Good

In the law and policy making process, good laws and rules should also be motivated by sincere efforts to resolve genuine problems and advance the common good. The People are not authentically helped by empty political grand-standing; culture wars motivated legislative remedies for invented problems; or by laws that use real problems as a pretext for personal profit and advantage. Laws that merely advantage one group's interests over others, or further the goals of powerful special interests at the expense of the common good are all too frequent products of the exercise of political power. They are not, however, good laws. Good laws must establish a just and efficient system of problem resolution aimed at resolving genuine problems for the common good.

Merely having the power to enact and enforce laws does not assure that those laws will be good and just. As Dr. Martin Luther King, Jr., recognized in his *Letter from Birmingham Jail* (1963):

> There are two types of laws: just and unjust . . . One has not only a legal but a moral responsibility to obey just laws. Conversely, one has a moral responsibility to disobey unjust laws. I would agree with St. Augustine that "an unjust law is no law at all" . . . An unjust law is a code that a numerical or power majority group compels a minority group

to obey but does not make binding on itself . . . Sometimes a law is just on its face and unjust in its application. For instance, I have been arrested on a charge of parading without a permit. Now, there is nothing wrong in having an ordinance which requires a permit for a parade. But such an ordinance becomes unjust when it is used to maintain segregation and to deny citizens the First Amendment privilege of peaceful assembly and protest . . . We should never forget that everything Adolf Hitler did in Germany was "legal" and everything the Hungarian freedom fighters did in Hungary was "illegal." It was "illegal" to aid and comfort a Jew in Hitler's Germany. Even so, I am sure that, had I lived in Germany at the time, I would have aided and comforted my Jewish brothers.

From the U.S. Congress to the local school board; from the President of the United States to the local school superintendent; it is only just and efficient laws and policies aimed at resolving genuine problems and promoting the common good that will merit and receive broad-based respect and compliance over time. Rational, moral people respect and obey just and efficient laws because they clearly serve the common good in a fair manner. In contrast, no amount of enforcement will be sufficient to achieve broad compliance with laws or policies that are widely perceived as unwise and unjust.

A lawful system of problem resolution will always be necessary because humans will always have problems, disputes, and competing interests. And while these difficulties have too often been resolved through counter-productive conflict and even violence, it is far more just, and far more efficient to resolve problems through a fair system of laws. A system in which fair rules are known in advance, everyone has a reasonable opportunity to conform their conduct to the common rules, and the same fair rules apply to everyone on an equal basis.

> ### *To Assure Justice: The Powerful Need the Limits of the Law;*
> ### *The Weaker Need the Protections of the Law*

The modern Rule of Law is the product of thousands of years of human experience, thought, and a desire for greater justice, stability, and happiness in peoples' lives. Any serious student of human history quickly learns that the most severe problems among humans occur when there are imbalances in power. Oppression or exploitation of others becomes far easier, and therefore far more likely, when one person or group holds disproportionate power, and those who are relatively weaker are unable to protect their own interests. Nearly 4,000 years ago Hammurabi's Code of Law recognized that the essential purpose of the law was "to bring about the rule of righteousness in the land . . . so that the strong should not harm the weak."

Government power is both an essential human tool, and potentially humanity's most dangerous force. The same government power that can be used to protect the People can also be used to destroy the People. The common government must have sufficient power to protect the life, liberty, and property of the People. In the absence of sufficient government power chaos reigns and everyone suffers, inevitably leading to calls for a strong leader to end the chaos. Order can be imposed by a strong leader, but without sufficient checks and balances on that leader's governance power, as Lord Acton observed, power corrupts and leads to abuses of that power. Every abuse of power and every act of oppression then fuels the inevitable call for rebellion, resulting in a return to chaos, and a yet another call for a strong leader to end the chaos.

Cycle of Suffering Caused by Imbalances in Governance Power

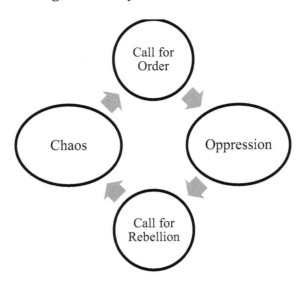

© Dayton

Much of human history reflects this repetitive tale of bloody pendulum swings between unfettered chaos and brutal oppression, both of which leave terrible human suffering and destruction in their wakes. Humanity faced a challenging dilemma in breaking this cycle of suffering: A government with insufficient power resulted in dangerous chaos; but a government with excessive unchecked powers resulted in dangerous abuses of power and oppression.

Magna Carta (1215) marked a significant step forward in the development of the law of human governance by recognizing certain limits on governance power, protecting common rights, and requiring due process of law. The *Magna Carta* declared:

> 𝔍𝔒𝔥𝔑, by the grace of God King of England, Lord of Ireland, Duke of Normandy and Aquitaine, and Count of Anjou, to his archbishops, bishops, abbots, earls, barons, justices, foresters, sheriffs, stewards, servants, and to all his officials and loyal subjects, Greeting. 𝔎𝔑𝔒𝔚 𝔗𝔥𝔄𝔗 𝔅𝔈𝔉𝔒𝔯𝔈 𝔊𝔒𝔇, for the health of our soul and those of our ancestors and heirs, to the honour of God, the exaltation of the holy Church, and the better ordering of our kingdom . . .
>
> 1. In the first place we have granted to God, and by this our present charter confirmed for us and our heirs forever that the English Church shall be free, and shall have her rights entire, and her liberties inviolate; and we will that it be thus observed; which is apparent from this that the freedom of elections, which is reckoned most important and very essential to the English Church, we, of our pure and unconstrained will, did grant, and did by our charter confirm and did obtain the ratification of the same from our lord, Pope Innocent III, before the quarrel arose between us and our barons: and this we will observe, and our will is that it be observed in good faith by our heirs forever. We have also granted to all freemen of our kingdom, for us and our heirs forever, all the underwritten liberties, to be had and held by them and their heirs, of us and our heirs forever . . .

39. No freemen shall be taken or imprisoned or disseised or exiled or in any way destroyed, nor will we go upon him nor send upon him, except by the lawful judgment of his peers or by the law of the land.

40. To no one will we sell, to no one will we refuse or delay, right or justice . . .

45. We will appoint as justices, constables, sheriffs, or bailiffs only such as know the law of the realm and mean to observe it well . . .

63. Wherefore we will and firmly order that the English Church be free, and that the men in our kingdom have and hold all the aforesaid liberties, rights, and concessions, well and peaceably, freely and quietly, fully and wholly, for themselves and their heirs, of us and our heirs, in all respects and in all places forever, as is aforesaid. An oath, moreover, has been taken, as well on our part as on the part of the barons, that all these conditions aforesaid shall be kept in good faith and without evil intent. Given under our hand - the above named and many others being witnesses - in the meadow which is called Runnymede, between Windsor and Staines, on the fifteenth day of June, in the seventeenth year of our reign.

Magna Carta recognized certain limits on the lawful authority of the King. The *Magna Carta* did not, however, reject the "Divine Rights of Kings" theory which held that the King derived his authority from God and was therefore not generally subject to the will of the People. According to the *Magna Carta* the King was "by the grace of God king of England" legitimizing a hierarchy of governance in which the King was the divinely appointed Ruler and the People were rightfully his servants:

Model of Governance in the Magna Carta

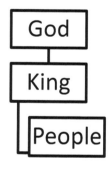

© **Dayton**

The U.S. Declaration of Independence (1776) confronted and reversed the two lower, earthly components of this model of governance, recognizing human equality and the supremacy of the People over their government by declaring:

We hold these truths to be self-evident, that all men are created equal, that they are endowed by their Creator with certain unalienable Rights, that among these are Life, Liberty and the pursuit of Happiness --That to secure these rights, Governments are instituted among Men, deriving their just powers from the consent of the governed.

Model of Governance in the Declaration of Independence

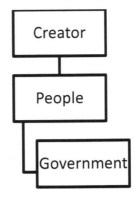

© Dayton

The Declaration held that the fundamental equality of all men was so obvious a truth that it was "self-evident." Contrary to royalist mythology, the King was simply another man also subject to the common laws. And all persons were the King's equals under the law. Therefore the King and his hierarchical government were not legitimate as rulers. Legitimate governments were servants to the People, not rulers. And the only legitimate governments were those that retained the consent of the People and justly served the needs of the People. The legitimate purpose of government was not to advance and protect the self-serving interests of those in power, but to advance the common good, and to dutifully protect the life, liberty, and property of the People.

A government of, by, and for the People was a legal ideal that promised to help limit the terrible cycle of chaos and oppression. Nonetheless, even after the successful revolution against English monarchical rule many remained skeptical that the People could be trusted with their own government. In his first inaugural address Thomas Jefferson responded to these skeptics stating "it is said that man can not be trusted with the government of himself. Can he, then, be trusted with the government of others? Or have we found angels in the form of kings to govern him? Let history answer this question."

As James Madison recognized: "If men were angels, no government would be necessary." Clearly humans are not angels, and some humans are quite the opposite. It is too often the case that the desire for access to government power attracts exactly the people who should not have any power, but who desperately want it for their own selfish purposes. While humans are capable of great good, kindness, and altruism, there is also a darker side to human nature found in varying degrees in all humans. Because of this ever present darker side of human nature, a common government is necessary to protect the People from those in government and the private sphere who would otherwise be tempted to act out on their darker impulses if left unaccountable under the law.

But how do you achieve the ideals of democratic governance when humanity seems to be eternally trapped between the Scylla and Charybdis of chaos and oppression? Our Nation's Founders faced a difficult task in crafting a system of government that would be less likely to fall to these dual afflictions. As thorough students of history, they knew that the government must have sufficient power to protect the People or chaos would reign. But they also knew, some of them from bitter personal experience, that if the government had too much power, corrupted government officials would oppress and exploit the People, not protect and serve them. Constitutional democracy was a promising ideal, but without adequate checks and balances the new democracy would also be vulnerable to the inevitable evils brought about by imbalances in power. Simply substituting majority rule for royal rule did not resolve the fundamental problem of abuse of power. As Lord Acton recognized:

> It is bad to be oppressed by a minority, but it is worse to be oppressed by a majority. For there is a reserve of latent power in the masses which, if it is called into play, the minority can seldom resist. But from the absolute will of an entire people there is no appeal, no redemption, no refuge.

As noted above, much of human history is the story of radical pendulum swings of human societies from chaos to oppression and back again, with tremendous human suffering in this cyclical process. This is not, however, the entire story of humanity. In a fortunate few societies, between these pendulum swings there were sometimes magnificent but all too fleeting periods of peace, prosperity, and democracy.

For a time, ancient Athens enjoyed the benefits of democracy. As the Athenian leader Pericles said concerning Athenian democracy (c. 400 B.C.E.):

> Our constitution . . . favors the many instead of the few; this is why it is called a democracy. If we look to the laws, they afford equal justice to all . . . advancement in public life falls to reputation for capacity, class considerations not being allowed to interfere with merit; nor again does poverty bar the way, if a man is able to serve the state, he is not hindered by the obscurity of his condition. The freedom which we enjoy in our government extends also to our ordinary life. There, far from exercising a jealous surveillance over each other, we do not feel called upon to be angry with our neighbor for doing what he likes . . . But all this ease in our private relations does not make us lawless as citizens. Against this fear is our chief safeguard, teaching us to obey the magistrates and the laws, particularly such as regard the protection of the [weaker] whether they are actually on the statute book, or belong to that code which, although unwritten, yet cannot be broken without acknowledged disgrace . . . instead of looking on discussion as a stumbling-block in the way of action, we think it an indispensable preliminary to any wise action at all.

The philosopher Plato compared the virtues and vices of democracy (rule by the governed), monarchy (rule by an individual), and oligarchy (rule by a small social or corporate elite). While democratic self-governance is also imperfect, the greater dangers of rule by an all-powerful few are obvious. Winston Churchill famously said: "Democracy is the worst form of government, except all those other forms that have been tried from time to time." Imperfect humans cannot create and operate a perfect government, but at least in a democracy, the fate of the People ultimately rests with the People themselves.

> *"In a Democracy, People Get the Government They Deserve."*
> *Alexis de Toqueville*

Successful self-governance requires active participation by an educated and informed citizenry. There is no magical power in the ballot box, and voting alone will not give anyone the better future promised by a just democracy. An uninformed citizenry will make uninformed choices at the ballot box, and the uneducated are dangerously easy to manipulate. When the human mind is not solidly grounded by a thorough education, relevant facts, and the learned power of rational thought, those who would profit from human ignorance can easily inflame the potent human emotions of fear, hate, and prejudice towards their own selfish ends, with disastrous results for the victims of their manipulation.

Unless carefully guarded, even the most virtuous forms of democracy can quickly devolve to chaos or oppression. Our Nation's Founders recognized these patterns in history, and believed that the solution was an educated and empowered citizenry, and a system of government that allowed sufficient power to the government while setting clear limits on the accumulation and exercise of that government power by any individual or group.

Given the experiences of political domination and tyrannical abuses of government powers by monarchies, the drafters of the Constitution rightly feared an unlimited central government. The People did not fight a long and bloody war against royal rule merely to hand their hard won freedoms to yet another all-powerful central government. Instead, the Constitution divides governance powers between the federal and state governments in a governance system known as federalism.

American federalism is a system of governance in which the federal government holds only those powers that are deemed most effectively exercised by a central government, such as the declaration of war and the regulation of inter-state commerce. All powers not delegated to the federal government are reserved to the state governments or the People themselves, as counter-balances guarding against the accumulation and abuse of power by the federal government. The U.S. Constitution further created a system of internal governmental checks and balances by separating powers held by the federal government into three separate and co-equal branches:

Separation of Powers under the U.S. Constitution

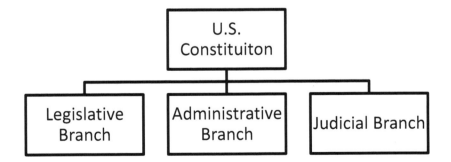

© **Dayton**

The U.S. Constitution is the product of efforts to create an effective system of institutional balances, reconcile competing political interests, and limit dangerous extremes in governance. If

12

one branch of government begins to accumulate and exercise too much power the other branches, the states, or the People are to assert their powers and set appropriate limits consistent with the Constitution and the Rule of Law. The constitutional balances and compromises were also intended to assure that while the will of the majority would prevail, the rights of smaller states, political minorities, and individuals were also reasonably respected and protected. As Thomas Jefferson said: "All, too, will bear in mind this sacred principle, that though the will of the majority is in all cases to prevail, that will to be rightful must be reasonable; that the minority possess their equal rights, which equal law must protect, and to violate would be oppression."

Each branch of government has a unique mission and unique powers to achieve that mission. Among the powers granted to Congress (the federal legislative branch) are the powers to enact federal laws and the "power of the purse" controlling U.S. funds. Given these substantial powers, however, the Founders made Congress the branch of government most directly accountable to the People.

The U.S. Congress is made up of two separate governing bodies: 1) The House of Representatives; and 2) The Senate. Members of Congress represent citizens in their home regions and they are held accountable to these people through periodic elections. Elections occur every two years in the House of Representatives allowing relatively quick turnover if U.S. Representatives fail to retain the trust of the People. U.S. Senators, however, serve six-year staggered terms, assuring greater continuity in governance in the Senate. The House of Representatives provides proportional representation, with more populous states having more representatives and therefore more votes and power in Congress. In contrast each state is allocated only two Senators, regardless of population, to act as a check and balance helping protect states with smaller populations from political domination by the more populous states.

The U.S. Administrative Branch, including the President of the United States and all administrative agencies and agents working under the President, is charged with administering the laws passed by the People's elected representatives in Congress. The Administrative Branch has both regulatory and police powers to achieve this mission. The President of the United States, the chief executive officer of the Administrative Branch, is elected for a four-year term, and is limited to no more than two consecutive terms. The President is also charged with serving as Commander-in-Chief for the U.S. military, assuring publicly accountable civilian control of the military.

The Administrative Branch is the largest branch of government. It is divided into many different agencies charged with regulating specific areas, including the U.S. Department of Education. These administrative agencies are empowered by statute and funded by the Congress to issue administrative regulations, oversee federal funding, and enforce federal laws. The Congress, however, retains the authority and responsibility to oversee these administrative agencies. The Congress can withhold funding or even act to abolish an administrative agency if it is deemed necessary by a majority in Congress.

The Judicial Branch is charged with resolving cases and controversies under the law, and with the important task of interpreting the Constitution. In *Marbury v. Madison*, 5 U.S. 137 (1803), the Court established the Judicial Branch as holding the definitive power to interpret the U.S. Constitution. The Court's interpretation of the Constitution can only be overridden by amending the Constitution itself, which requires the affirmative vote of two-thirds of the Congress and the ratification of three-fourths of the states, making it very difficult to overturn the U.S. Supreme Court's interpretation of the U.S. Constitution.

The Court does not, however, have the direct financial or police powers of the other branches to enforce its decisions. The Court must rely on its powers of persuasion in judicial opinions, and on broad-based respect for the Rule of Law. If the People and the other branches of government fail to respect the Court's opinions and the Rule of Law, however, the Court's decisions can become little more than words on paper. But if this happens, the entire system of constitutional democracy is threatened with collapse, as respect for the common Rule of Law is the foundation for constitutional democracy.

The U.S. system of constitutional democracy established an organic, interactive system to help limit unwise or unlawful actions by any branch of government. If, for example, the U.S. Congress passed a statute that the Administrative Branch deemed unwise, the President could exercise a veto, preventing Congress' bill from becoming a law. In response, if at least two-thirds of the members of Congress disagreed with the President's veto, Congress could vote to override the presidential veto. If the People disagreed with either or both political branches, they could vote elected officials out of office at the next election. Disputes that could not be resolved among the two political branches could be brought to the Judicial Branch for resolution. Any act of government that violated the U.S. Constitution could be declared unconstitutional and therefore voided by the Court.

The constitutional system both allocates powers and guards against the accumulation of powers; makes the system responsive to popular will and guards against the excesses and volatile pendulum swings of popular will or domination of the minority by the majority. To help support these ends, even when they are politically unpopular, the Founders granted federal judges life-time tenure and also prohibited reducing their pay, pending good conduct (*i.e.*, a federal judge who abuses official power or commits a serious crime is still subject to removal), so that federal judges could be reasonable insulated from direct political pressures.

While the other two branches (the political branches) are subject to direct political pressure through periodic elections, the Code of Conduct for United States Judges mandates: "A judge should be faithful to, and maintain professional competence in, the law and should not be swayed by partisan interests, public clamor, or fear of criticism." Judges are to ignore political pressure, and instead maintain fidelity to the Constitution and the Rule of Law.

Under this Constitutional system of checks and balances Congress holds the power of the purse, but Congress cannot withhold judges' pay. The Administrative Branch has broad regulatory and police powers, but cannot unilaterally fire a judge. The President does, however, have the power to make initial nominations to federal judgeships, and the U.S. Senate has the power to confirm or reject these nominees prior to their appointment and tenure as a federal judge. But once on the bench, judges owe their allegiance only to the Constitution and the Rule of Law.

These are merely illustrative examples of the complex system of checks and balances that the Founders created to guard against the accumulation and abuse of governmental powers.

> ### The Constitutional System Requires Cooperation and Persuasion to Govern and Discourages Unilateral Actions and Coercion

The system helps to assure that no one can lawfully act unilateral through the force of power, but must instead achieve their mission and objectives through the power of persuasion, building consensus, and mutual cooperation under the Rule of Law.

Comments and Questions

When the U.S. Declaration of Independence was published, for its signers, it was the equivalent of signing their own death warrants. Declaring British Royal Rule illegitimate and all men the King's equals was revolutionary to say the least. We no longer consider democratic rule and human equality controversial, yet the words of the Declaration still generate controversy: "We hold these truths to be self-evident, that all men are created equal."

In the Declaration, what is the meaning of the term "men" in the phrase "all men are created equal"? In answering this question we start with an initial problem. Exactly determining group intent is an impossible task: 1) Even if a group is able to reach general consensus on a particular point, there is in reality no single, unitary "group intent" that can be unquestioningly attributed to every member of that group. A total of 56 persons signed the Declaration. Some views were more congruent than others, but there were 56 individual intents concerning this document and the exact meaning of its words; 2) Even individual's actions are commonly motivated by multiple and sometimes even internally conflicting intentions. Individual intent is like the layers of an onion: There is the surface intent (what the individual may publicly state), the next layer down (what the individual may tell himself), the next layer down (unacknowledged self-interests), and even deeper layers of motivation beyond the conscious mind of the individual.

Consider the intent of Thomas Jefferson, the drafter of the Declaration. While there is little doubt that some of his contemporaries probably did intend "men" in the text of the Declaration to mean white, property-owning, Anglo, Christian males, was this the intent of Jefferson? As William Cohen stated in *Thomas Jefferson and the Problem of Slavery*:

> It seems paradoxical that Thomas Jefferson, one of the enduring heroes of American democracy, should have been the owner of more than 180 slaves at the very time when he was proclaiming that all men were created equal and that they were "endowed by the Creator" with the "unalienable Rights" of "Life, Liberty and the pursuit of Happiness." Morever, throughout his life he continued to hold that slavery was unjust and immoral. In 1785 he had used the phrase "avarice and oppression" to characterize the slaveholding interest, and he contrasted this with the "sacred side" of emancipation. A year later, he marveled at the fact that American patriots who had endured beatings, starvation, and imprisonment at the hands of their British oppressors could inflict "on their fellow men a bondage one hour of which is fraught with more misery than ages of that which he rose in rebellion to oppose." In the final year of his life, he reiterated his belief that it was unlawful for "one man to appropriate to himself the faculties of another without his consent." Most Jefferson scholars have dealt with this contradiction by ignoring it, or by citing his views on abolition and holding that his role as an owner of men was entailed upon him. Born into a slave system, they argue, he could not in good conscience abandon his black charges; he made the best of a bad situation by behaving as a benevolent and indulgent master. *See* William Cohen, *Thomas Jefferson and the Problem of Slavery*, 56 THE JOURNAL OF AMERICAN HISTORY 503 (1969).

Do humans sometimes sincerely hold one view yet practice another out of perceived necessity? What would have been the real world consequences if Jefferson would have emancipated the more than 180 slaves held by his household at a time and place where slavery was thoroughly embedded in the social, political, legal, and economic systems? What would have happened to the persons Jefferson emancipated? Would they all be able to find adequate food, shelter, safety, and employment in that situation? What would have happened to Jefferson, his family, and Monticello? How would others react to Jefferson's actions? Can we fairly answer these questions from a world view over two centuries after Jefferson's?

Historians use the term "presentism" to describe attempts to judge historically distant persons and cultures through the lens of present experiences. What might persons two centuries in the future say about us? What if, for example, theories of global warming and man-made climate change become proven fact eventually wrecking environmental havoc on a planetary scale, causing droughts, heat waves, super-storms, and flooding; massive crop failures and starvation; triggering social unrest, wars and chaos; and leading to an unprecedented loss of human life? Might this avoidable man-made catastrophe be considered by future generations a massive crime against humanity perpetrated by present generations against future generations? As the evidence of the problem grew, could future generations rightly consider all those that continued to participate in producing the excess environmental carbons to be co-perpetrators in this crime?

But how many of us can actually stop driving our cars; heating and cooling our homes; eating foods grown with fossil fuel-based fertilizers and farm equipment; using fossil fuel manufactured and transported products; or refuse police and fire protection, electricity, etc., because fossil fuels are used in providing these services? Is it possible to live in our world without using fossil fuels? Can over 7 billion people world-wide survive without fossil fuel dependent food and energy?

If you personally decided to refuse to use any fossil fuels, would you still be able to find adequate food, shelter, safety, and employment in that situation? What would happen to you and your family? How would others react to your decision? How many of us would be willing to walk or ride a horse to class or work? Might you be endangering others on the road and be ticketed for obstructing traffic if you did, and where do you park your horse?

Do we have any viable options to participation in our fossil fuel-based society, or are we to a large degree trapped in our own current social, political, legal, and economic systems? Do you sincerely hold one view about the necessity to protect the environment for future generations, but to some degree practice another out of necessity? How is this different from Jefferson's dilemma?

It can be argued that Jefferson clearly intended to send a message to his peers and to the world in his draft of the Declaration, a message concerning his precise intent in using the phrase "all men are created equal." One tool used in legal interpretation is to examine the use of the term in question in other parts of the document, implying common meaning.

Jefferson used the term "men" in another section of his draft of the Declaration, stating in a charge against King George that "he had waged cruel war against human nature itself, violating it's most sacred rights of life & liberty in the persons of a distant people who never offended him, captivating & carrying them into slavery in another hemisphere, or to incur miserable death in their transportation hither, this piratanical warfare, the opprobrium of infidel powers, is the warfare of the **Christian** [emphasis and underline added by Jefferson, presumably to highlight that King George's conduct was not in fact "Christian" conduct] king of Great Britain, determined to keep open a market where **MEN** [emphasis added by Jefferson] should be bought & sold."

Clearly, the "**MEN**" Jefferson is referring to here as being "bought & sold" are not white, property-owning, Anglo, Christian males. The "**MEN**" referred to here were in fact black African men, women, and children; "men" as humans, the collective members of humanity. These "**MEN**" were the victims of King George's slave trade, and the very persons whom some of his colleagues wished to continue to exclude from equality by maintaining the institution of slavery in the new democracy.

Apparently Mr. Jefferson's provocative message concerning slavery and fundamental human equality was received loud and clear by pro-slavery members of the delegation. Mr. Jefferson's statement against slavery was removed from the final draft of the Declaration.

Excerpted from Jefferson's Original Draft of the Declaration

Excerpt from: http://www.princeton.edu/~tjpapers/declaration/declaration3.gif

Slavery remained lawful throughout Mr. Jefferson's life, and it was not abolished until 1865 with the ratification of the 13th Amendment to the U.S. Constitution. But in the wake of the abolition of slavery a system of laws emerged that perpetuated unjust segregation and inequality based on race. Is the law still the law when the law is unjust? Please reconsider Dr. Martin Luther King Jr.'s renowned *Letter from Birmingham Jail* (1963) in which he distinguishes between just and unjust laws:

> Since we so diligently urge people to obey the Supreme Court's decision of 1954 outlawing segregation in the public schools, it is rather strange and paradoxical to find us consciously breaking laws. One may well ask: "How can you advocate breaking some laws and obeying others?" The answer is found in the fact that there are two types of laws: There are just laws and there are unjust laws. I would be the first to advocate obeying just laws. One has not only a legal but moral responsibility to obey just laws. Conversely, one has a moral responsibility to disobey unjust laws. I would agree with Saint Augustine that "An unjust law is no law at all." Now what is the difference between the two? How does one determine when a law is just or unjust? A just law is a man-made code that squares with the moral law or the law of God. An unjust law is a code that is out of harmony with the moral law. To put it in the terms of Saint Thomas Aquinas, an unjust law is a human law that is not rooted in eternal and natural law. Any law that uplifts human personality is just. Any law that degrades human personality is unjust. All segregation statutes are unjust because segregation distorts the soul and damages the personality. It gives the segregator a false sense of superiority and the segregated a false sense of inferiority. To use the words of Martin Buber, the great Jewish philosopher, segregation substitutes an "I-it" relationship for an "I-thou" relationship, and ends up relegating persons to the status of things. So segregation is not

only politically, economically, and sociologically unsound, but it is morally wrong and sinful.

What do you believe is the difference between just and unjust laws? How do people react to laws they perceive as just? What is the reaction to unjust laws? Historically, unjust laws are often motivated by misguided prejudice, fear, or greed. And while these laws may serve the immediate wishes of those in power for the short-term, over the long-term they generally end in disastrous failure.

What is the difference between just governance policies and unjust governance policies? How do people react to governance policies they perceive as just or unjust? Reasonable people would agree, for example, that traffic-lights are necessary and part of a just governance policy (*i.e.*, efficiently and fairly regulating traffic and improving safety), and they will stop for a red-light even when no one is looking. Further, reasonable people would agree that motorists who intentionally or recklessly run a red-light deserve a ticket and that this is a just deterrent to reckless driving.

But what if local government officials install automated ticketing systems at traffic-lights (leased from a company that just happens to be owned by close relatives of city officials); city officials are heard stating that the real purpose of the new policy was increased city revenue and not public safety; fines are dramatically increased; city officials had the yellow-signal shortened so the signal would turn red faster resulting in more tickets/fines; tickets are being issued on a zero tolerance basis (*i.e.*, ticketing for being in the intersection 0.1 seconds after the yellow-signal changed to red); and accidents in the intersection actually increased significantly as motorists began speeding up through the intersection or slamming on their brakes to avoid an expensive ticket? What do you think should or would happen to public respect for this system of law enforcement?

School officials are charged with the important responsibility of maintaining safety and order in schools, so rules prohibiting weapons and fighting in school receive broad support. But should these rules be "zero tolerance" rules? A student who knowingly brings a weapon to school with a clear intent to use it deserves severe punishment. A student who violently and willfully attacks a teacher or another student deserves severe punishment. But what if evidence proves that the student did not know the weapon was in his book bag but was placed there by someone else? What if the "weapon" is a steak knife the student's mother accidently dropped on the back floor of her daughter's car when she was helping her mother move to another apartment over the weekend? What if the "weapon" is actually a chicken "McNugget" an elementary student is playing with as if it were a toy gun? If one student violently attacks another student and the attacked student clearly only acts in self-defense are both students "fighting" under the zero tolerance policy? What are just laws and policies, and unjust laws and policies, and how do you distinguish one from the other?

Operationalizing a Democratic System of Law and Governance

The Founders made clear their purposes in creating our Nation's system of governance. The U.S. Constitution's Preamble declares:

We the people of the United States, in order to form a more perfect union, establish justice, insure domestic tranquility, provide for the common defense, promote the general welfare, and secure the blessings of liberty to ourselves and our posterity, do ordain and establish this Constitution for the United States of America.

While the general goals were clear and constant, under ever-changing circumstances we could only continue to make progress toward these goals if our system of governance was capable of evolutionary adaptation. Accordingly, the Founders designed the constitutional system so that it could evolve with the needs of the People, it could be amended and changed when necessary. The U.S. Declaration of Independence recognized that the duty of any just government was to protect the rights of equal citizens, and that:

Whenever any Form of Government becomes destructive of these ends, it is the Right of the People to alter or to abolish it, and to institute new Government, laying its foundation on such principles and organizing its powers in such form, as to them shall seem most likely to effect their Safety and Happiness. Prudence, indeed, will dictate that Governments long established should not be changed for light and transient causes; and accordingly all experience hath shewn, that mankind are more disposed to suffer, while evils are sufferable, than to right themselves by abolishing the forms to which they are accustomed. But when a long train of abuses and usurpations, pursuing invariably the same Object evinces a design to reduce them under absolute Despotism, it is their right, it is their duty, to throw off such Government, and to provide new Guards for their future security.

Consistent with the ideals of the Declaration, the constitutional system provides a means of changing laws, government structures, and even the Constitution itself. The Founders wanted to assure that there was always a lawful, orderly means for all persons to express their concerns about the laws and the common government, and to persuade others to join them in peacefully changing the laws and government when necessary.

Any citizen with a grievance can turn to the administrative branch to request that existing laws be properly enforced; lobby representatives in the legislative branch for new laws if current laws are inadequate; argue for the amendment or repeal of any law or policy; and turn to the courts for relief if laws are being improperly applied or if they believe laws are unconstitutional. And anytime the government is insufficiently responsive to calls for redress, citizens can use their rights of Free Speech to appeal directly to the People for support in compelling necessary changes in the laws and governance system through peaceful protests and the ballot box. It should be noted that the process of lawful change is intentionally a protracted process to limit the risks of reactionary, rash decisions or the dangers of mob rule. But through the lawful process, even radical change can be achieved over time.

In a nation under the Rule of Law, a constitution can act as the collective conscience of the nation; as a document that codifies the People's higher ideals and attempts to make them a reality through the power and progress possible through law. A democratic system of government is certainly far from perfect. As Winston Churchill said: "No one pretends that democracy is perfect or all-wise." Ultimately, a constitutional democracy can be no better than the People themselves. But constitutional democracy does give the People an opportunity to take responsibility for their own government; to strive to "form a more perfect union"; to "secure the blessings of liberty"; and to work toward greater justice, social progress, and a better future.

As noted above the primary mechanisms for achieving these goals are an educated and informed citizenry; periodic elections; separations of powers; and other constitutional checks and balances. Constitutional checks and balances on government power are essential to democratic governance and the Rule of Law.

Federal Powers, Limits, and Sources of Federal Law

The U.S. Constitution was intended in part as a remedy for the flaws in the prior U.S. Articles of Confederation. The Articles of Confederation resulted in a federal government that was hopelessly under-funded and under-powered. And the inadequacies of what the federal government couldn't do were aggravated by what the states were allowed to do. Allowing states the authority to tax interstate commerce resulted in tariff wars among the states interfering with the free flow of needed goods, services, and productive commerce nationally. Having individual states engaged in the minting of state currency increased confusion and instability in the national economy. States unilaterally entering into treaties with foreign nations caused international confusion over who did and did not speak for the United States in foreign relations.

The new U.S. Constitution sought to remedy these problems while also attempting to not create new problems. It would be no real remedy, for example, to replace a federal government that was too weak with a federal government that was too powerful. The new Constitution sought to bring balance, order, and stability to the new nation through careful delegation of powers, checks and balances against accumulations and abuses of powers, and a clear means of amendment to allow for adaptation to changing circumstances.

Powers had to be carefully delegated to the authority best able to accomplish the necessary mission. Foreign affairs, immigration, war powers, minting of currency, the regulation of interstate commerce and other powers most appropriate for the federal government were delegated to the U.S. government by the Constitution. All other powers, however, were retained by the states or the People themselves, making the federal government a government of limited powers.

> ### *The Federal Government is a Government of Limited Powers*

Under the Tenth Amendment to the U.S. Constitution the federal government may exercise only those powers expressly delegated to the federal government in the text of the U.S. Constitution. The Tenth Amendment declares: "The powers not delegated to the United States by the Constitution, nor prohibited by it to the States, are reserved to the States respectively, or to the people." All powers not expressly delegated to the federal government remain with the states (with their own internal systems of separation of powers and other checks and balances), or ultimately to the People.

Division of Powers under the U.S. System of Law and Governance

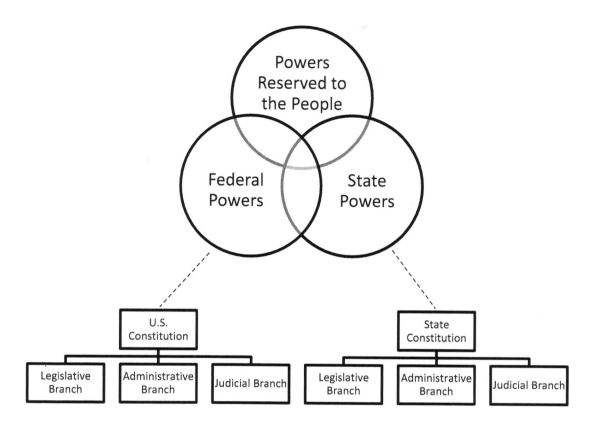

© Dayton

    Rather than relying on government officials to independently respect the limits of their powers, the constitutional system relies on each branch of government to jealously guard its own powers from intrusion, and relies on the People to stand up against government intrusion on their rights when necessary. State governments can contest any federal expansions of power beyond constitutional limits; the federal government can object to any intrusions on federal powers or any state intrusions on the rights of federal citizenship; and citizens can use free speech and the ballot box to protect their rights and help assure that no one is able to accumulate so much power that they become above the law and unaccountable to the People.

    The federal government only has those powers delegated to it through the Constitution. Education is not mentioned in the U.S. Constitution, therefore it is a power reserved to the states and the People. Although public education is a state function, through civil rights legislation under the Fourteenth Amendment (*e.g.*, Title VI, Title VII, Title IX, etc.), federal conditional funding grants (*e.g.*, IDEA, NCLB, etc.), and federal court decisions concerning state public education, the federal government now exerts significant control over the daily operations of public schools. The appropriate balance of federal and state authority over education is a perpetual issue of debate. But the federal government currently exercises significant control over education. Accordingly, those responsible for the daily operation of schools must know and understand applicable federal laws.

Sources of Federal Laws

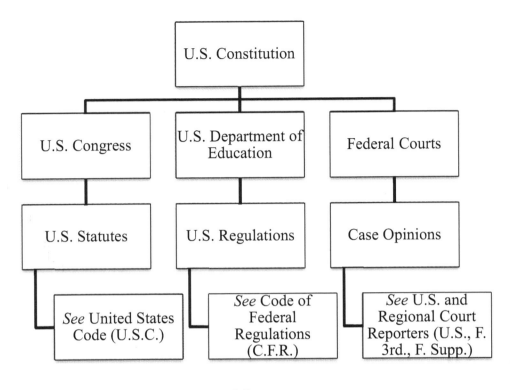

© **Dayton**

Applicable federal laws may take the form of U.S. statutes enacted by Congress. These statutes can be found in the United States Code (U.S.C.). Here is a sample citation:

$$20 \; U.S.C. \; \S \; 4071$$

Number
Title 20

Reporter
U.S. Code

Section or page
Section 4071

   This sample citation is the citation for the Equal Access Act, a federal statute governing meetings of student groups. All legal citations follow the same basic format: 1) Number; 2) Name of the reporter; and 3) Section or page number. This citation tells you that the Equal Access Act can be found in Title 20 of the United States Code at section 4071. The symbol "§" is a section symbol. This citation would be pronounced "twenty U.S.C. section 4071." Two section symbols together (§§) are pronounced "sections" and are merely the plural of the section symbol, referring to multiple sections of a statute.

   The federal administrative branch is charged with administering statutes enacted by Congress. Federal education statutes are administered through the U.S. Department of Education which issues administrative regulations published in the U.S. Code of Federal Regulations (C.F.R.). Here is a sample citation to a federal regulation:

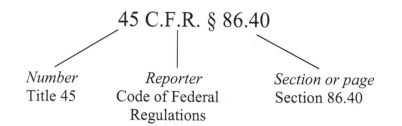

45 C.F.R. § 86.40

Number	*Reporter*	*Section or page*
Title 45	Code of Federal Regulations	Section 86.40

This is a citation to the U.S. Department of Education's regulations prohibiting discrimination based on marital or parental status under Title IX. Congressional statutes provide the fundamental framework of federal law, but federal regulations provide operational details and guidance on interpretation and administration of the statute.

Federal courts issue opinions on cases and controversies under federal law, and review challenges to the constitutionality of federal laws both facially (reviewing the text of the law only) and as applied (reviewing the application of the law). These opinions are published in court reporters. The court reporter for U.S. Supreme Court decisions is the U.S. Reporter. Here is a sample citation to a U.S. Supreme Court decision:

347 U.S. 483 (1954)

Number	*Reporter*	*Page*	*Year*
Volume 347	United States	483	1954

This is the citation to the U.S. Supreme Court's opinion in *Brown v. Board of Education,* 347 U.S. 483 (1954). This citation tells you that you can find the Court's opinion in volume 347 of the U.S. Reporter beginning on page 483. Case citations also include the year the opinion was issued, in this case 1954. Court opinions are decided on a particular date (*e.g.,* May 17, 1954) so the year designation for a case never changes. Formal citations to statutes and regulations should also include a year designation, but because amendments of legislation and regulations are ongoing processes the proper year for citation of legislation and regulations may be the year enacted, the year of a relevant amendment, or the current year depending on what exactly the author intends to reference.

Before cases reach the U.S. Supreme Court they are first heard by lower courts. Federal cases are generally initiated in Federal District Courts, the trial courts in the federal system. Appeals from these decisions are heard in the U.S. Courts of Appeals. Federal district court opinions are published in the Federal Supplement (F. Supp. and F. Supp. 2d, the second and more recent set of reporters). Here is a sample citation for an opinion from a U.S. District Court:

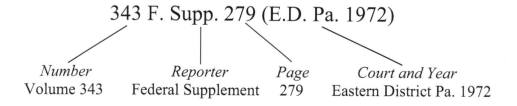

343 F. Supp. 279 (E.D. Pa. 1972)

Number	*Reporter*	*Page*	*Court and Year*
Volume 343	Federal Supplement	279	Eastern District Pa. 1972

U.S. Court of Appeals Decisions are published in the Federal Reporter (F., F.2d, or F.3d):

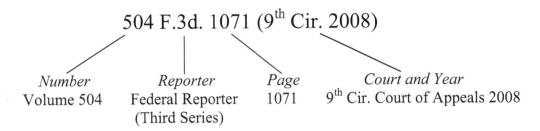

$$504 \text{ F.3d. } 1071 \text{ (9}^{th} \text{ Cir. 2008)}$$

Number	Reporter	Page	Court and Year
Volume 504	Federal Reporter (Third Series)	1071	9th Cir. Court of Appeals 2008

State Powers, Limits, and Sources of State Law

In part, the U.S. Civil War was fought over the constitutional limitations of state powers and the scope of sovereignty retained by the states. The U.S. Constitution primarily imposes limits on federal power. But following the Civil War and the adoption of the Fourteenth Amendment in 1868 it could no longer be credibly argued that the Constitution imposed no limitations on the powers of states. The Fourteenth Amendment declared: "No State shall make or enforce any law which shall abridge the privileges or immunities of citizens of the United States."

Under the Fourteenth Amendment, rights of federal citizenship superseded any state limitations on these rights. This was indicated by the Supremacy Clause of Article VI of the U.S. Constitution prior to 1868, but expressly stated in the Fourteenth Amendment. The Supremacy Clause states:

> This Constitution, and the Laws of the United States which shall be made in pursuance thereof; and all treaties made, or which shall be made, under the authority of the United States, shall be the supreme law of the land; and the judges in every state shall be bound thereby, anything in the constitution or laws of any state to the contrary notwithstanding.

States can protect fundamental rights such as religious freedoms, free speech, due process, equality under the law, etc., at a higher level than is guaranteed by the U.S. Constitution. But states cannot fall below the floor of protection for fundamental rights guaranteed under the U.S. Constitution. As a practical matter, if guarantees of individual rights are to be meaningful those rights must be protected from all agencies of government. It makes little difference to the individual whether their rights are denied by federal, state, or local agents. The infringement on those rights is equally as harmful to the individual regardless of which government is responsible.

Although the U.S. Constitution imposes some limits on state power, states still exercise broad powers in those areas outside of the scope of the U.S. Constitution. Education is a power generally reserved to the state through public systems of education, or the People themselves through private schools and home study programs. There are variations among the 50 U.S. states, but generally concerning public education plenary authority is vested in the legislative branch, the State General Assembly.

The General Assembly has broad authority over education in the state, subject only to the limits of the U.S. Constitution, the state constitution, and the will of the People. All 50 states have different education clauses in their constitutions, but all recognize the importance of education and the role of the state and the General Assembly in supporting education. The Texas Constitution, Article 7, states for example:

> A general diffusion of knowledge being essential to the preservation of the liberties and rights of the people, it shall be the duty of the Legislature of the State to establish and make suitable provision for the support and maintenance of an efficient system of public free schools.

Because education is the largest single item in most state's budgets, however, and the administration of a state-wide system of public education is an enormous, complex, and politically sensitive undertaking, Governors and state Departments of Education are generally very actively involved in the administration of public schools at the state level. Disputes under state laws or the state constitution are resolved by state courts.

Sources of State Laws

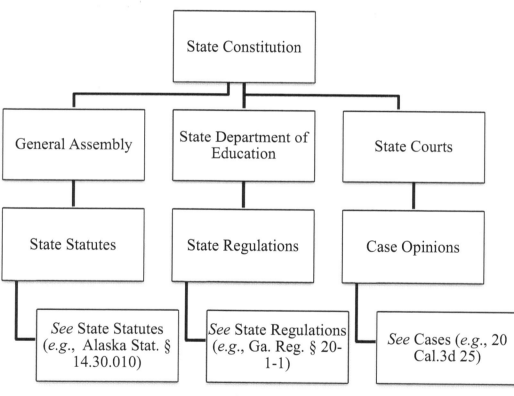

© Dayton

The constitutions of all 50 states make it the responsibility of the state's general assembly to create and support a public system of education. For example, the Kentucky Constitution declares: "The General Assembly shall, by appropriate legislation, provide for an efficient system of common schools throughout the State."

The General Assembly then enacts appropriate legislation necessary to create an efficient system of common schools, including, for example, statutes governing school finance,

25

attendance, curriculum, student discipline, and teacher employment, tenure and dismissals. The administrative branch of state government, including the Governor, the State Board of Education, the State Superintendent, and the State Department of Education establish policies and regulations for the state-level administration of education statutes. Local School Boards are responsible for the local administration of state education laws.

Members of a local Board of Education may be elected by school district residents or appointed by state officials depending on state law. School Board members have no individual authority, and may only exercise legal authority collectively as the School Board. The School Board oversees district level school operations, including the review and approval of school budgets, personnel decisions, and local school district policies.

Oversight and policy establishment at the school district level are the primary functions of the School Board. The School Board hires administrators and teachers to administer the daily operations of schools. Whether they are federal, state, or local public officials, all government officials are bound by applicable federal and state constitutions, statutes, regulations, and case decisions.

The U.S. Judicial System

As impartial arbiters in cases and controversies, judges play a critically important role in the resolution of disputes and the promotion of justice. The American judicial tradition is the product of thousands of years of history. The roots of American law can be traced back to Hebrew, Greek, and Roman law. As former English Colonies, however, the most direct antecedents of U.S. law come from the English Common Law tradition. U.S. federal courts and the courts in 49 of the 50 states follow the English Common Law system.

The Common Law system emerged in England in the Middle-Ages, and was based on judicial development of the law through real world experiences and the application of logic. The Common Law system is in part a grass-roots upwards system of law development. In cases of first impression, where no clear precedent exists, judges attempted to develop just, practical, and logical legal rules to resolve disputes.

When parties objected to the court's decision, the decision could be appealed to a higher court. In the absence of applicable higher binding precedent the appeals court could adopt the lower court's legal reasoning if it was persuasive, or overturn the decision and apply an interpretation of law the higher court determined was superior.

In either case, however, higher court opinions became binding on lower courts under the jurisdiction of the higher courts. This Common Law tradition of *stare decisis* (*i.e.*, standing by the decision) in which the decisions of higher courts are binding on lower courts in the same jurisdiction promotes uniformity and predictability while allowing the law to continue to evolve as necessary.

Because of its French history and tradition, the State of Louisiana followed the Napoleonic Code and the Civil Law system. Although some merger with the dominant U.S. Common Law system was inevitable, Louisiana continues to generally follow the Civil Law tradition. Civil Law is a system of law with its origins primarily in Roman Law and the Justinian Code. Many non-English speaking nations have adopted the Civil Law system.

In the Civil Law tradition statutes are the primary source of law. Judges do not develop judicial law. Nor are judges bound by judicially created precedent. Instead judges are charged with interpreting and applying the Civil Code directly. Both the Common Law and Civil Law traditions have unique strengths. These different legal traditions reflect the history and diversity of the U.S. and contribute to the strength of the American legal system.

Judicial Jurisdiction

Judicial jurisdiction concerns whether a court has the legal authority to decide a particular case. This includes questions of subject matter jurisdiction and geographic jurisdiction. Concerning subject matter jurisdiction, just as the federal government is a government of limited powers, federal courts are courts of limited subject matter jurisdiction. Federal courts generally only have subject matter jurisdiction over federal issues including disputes over federal laws or the U.S. Constitution. Further, under Article III of the U.S. Constitution federal courts may only issue opinions involving actual cases and controversies. They cannot decide cases based on hypothetical questions, nor can they issue advisory opinions or address a question that has become moot and no longer involves an active case or controversy.

In contrast, state courts are courts of general jurisdiction. State courts can hear and decide cases involving both state and federal issues. Further, in some cases, state courts may address hypothetical questions (from members of the state General Assembly or other state government agencies) and issue advisory opinions in answer to those questions. Just as the U.S. Supreme Court has the final word on interpreting the U.S. Constitution, the state's highest court is the final authority on interpreting the state constitution.

There are also special courts created for hearing particular types of cases, and these courts have jurisdiction over cases involving that specific subject matter. For example, federal tax courts hear cases involving questions under the tax code. The special courts most relevant to education are juvenile courts.

Juvenile courts are courts established to address the unique needs of children. In contrast to adult courts, proceedings in juvenile courts are generally treated as confidential and are not open to the public. Even in cases where children have committed crimes there is greater emphasis on rehabilitation efforts. Records of juvenile offenses generally do not follow the child into adulthood, allowing a second chance at good citizenship as an adult.

Juvenile court jurisdiction is defined by state statute and may vary among states. In general, however, juvenile courts are charged with deciding questions involving minor children, including delinquency, child protection, custody, etc., and juvenile judges adjudicate all but the most serious criminal offenses by juveniles. Some serious felonies committed by older children may be subject to adult criminal jurisdiction.

Geographic jurisdiction is the physical area over which a court has jurisdiction. The U.S. Supreme Court, for example, has geographic jurisdiction over the entire U.S., including U.S. possessions and territories. U.S. Courts of Appeals have jurisdiction over multi-state regions in the U.S., and U.S. District Courts only have jurisdiction over the section of the state in which the federal district court is located.

Geographic Boundaries
of United States Courts of Appeals and United States District Courts

From: www.uscourts.gov

Criminal and Civil Law

The U.S. system of laws is divided into two main branches of law: 1) Criminal law; and 2) Civil law. Criminal law concerns the prosecution of acts expressly prohibited by the government, such as murder, theft, child abuse, etc. The primary purpose of criminal law is to deter or punish acts that harm society. Because crimes harm society, crimes are prohibited acts not only against individual victims but also against the People generally. Therefore crimes are prosecuted by the common government and not by individuals.

Due to the element of moral turpitude involved in many criminal acts there is a significant social stigma associated with criminal prosecutions. Further, the punishments for criminal acts can be very severe, ranging from fines and imprisonment to execution in many states. Since criminal punishments significantly impinge on the individual's life, liberty, or property rights, adequate due process of law is essential.

A criminal trial begins with the defendant presumed innocent. The State bears the entire burden of proving guilt "beyond a reasonable doubt." If the State fails to fully meet this burden of proof the defendant is declared not guilty. A finding of guilt generally requires proof of both an *actus reas* (a guilty act) and *mens rea* (a guilty mind).

In contrast, civil law concerns disputes between individuals, such as contract suits, alleged torts, custody rights, etc. The party prosecuting the civil action (the plaintiff) bears the burden of proving the case against the defendant by a "preponderance of the evidence" a much lower burden of proof than is required in a criminal case. In contrast to the punitive nature of criminal law, civil law is generally only corrective in nature. It seeks to avoid injustices and provide restitution for wronged parties.

The Litigation Process

All litigation begins with a dispute and a formal complaint filed with a court having proper jurisdiction. In civil cases the party filing the complaint is the plaintiff, and the party called to respond to the complaint is the defendant (*i.e.*, *Smith v. Jones*). In criminal cases the State acts as the "plaintiff" but is referred to as the State (*i.e.*, *State of New York v. Jones*). While public school officials may be involved in criminal cases as witnesses (and more rarely as victims or defendants), most litigation involving schools is civil litigation. And most frequently the plaintiff is a student, parent, or employee bringing a civil case against the defendant school officials and school district.

There are far more disputes and threats of lawsuits than there is actual litigation. Angry people often threaten litigation. But no one can legitimately file a lawsuit just because they are angry. The plaintiff must have legal standing to bring the case: That is the plaintiff must be a proper party directly affected by the actions of the defendant. In order to survive a motion to dismiss by the defendant, the plaintiff's complaint must state a valid legal cause of action. When viewed in the light most favorable to the plaintiff, the plaintiff's complaint must present credible evidence that the defendant breached the law and that there is a legal remedy the court can provide for this breach of the law. Otherwise the complaint will be dismissed by the court. The court must also have subject matter and geographic jurisdiction over the case and parties.

Before proceeding to litigation, however, both parties should consider alternatives to litigation. Litigation can be very expensive, time consuming, and stressful for all parties. Alternatives to litigation include informal efforts by the parties to find a mutually acceptable resolution, mediation, negotiations, and arbitration. If good faith efforts to resolve the dispute fail, however, litigation may be necessary.

The trial court is the first court to hear the case. The case may be presented to a judge or in many cases a jury may be requested. Both the plaintiff and defendant file pleadings with the court stating their positions on unresolved issues in the case. In the trial parties will make opening statements, enter evidence, present testimony, be subject to cross-examination, and make closing statements.

Trial courts rule on both questions of fact and the application of the law under those facts. After the trial has concluded the trial the court will enter a judgment for either the plaintiff or the defendant. If the plaintiff prevails the judge will also order a remedy for the plaintiff when appropriate, for example monetary damages from the defendant.

The trial court's decision can be appealed, but reviewing courts will only review questions of law, not challenges to factual findings by the trial court. Factual findings by the trail court generally stand as fact in further proceedings. In the appeals process reviewing courts do not rehear the case. They rule only on questions of law based on the record of the proceedings in the trial court.

In the federal system appeals are generally heard by a three judge panel of the Court of Appeals. The most significant and difficult cases, however, may be heard *en banc* by all members of the Court of Appeals. The Courts of Appeals hear appeals from cases in the trial courts in their geographic circuit. Decisions by the Court of Appeals may be appealed to the Supreme Court.

The U.S. Supreme Court receives as many as 10,000 petitions for review each year. It is impossible for the Court to hear this many cases, so the U.S. Supreme Court uses the process of *certiorari* to determine which cases will be heard. Parties seeking review by the Court file a *writ of certiorari* arguing why their case should be heard by the Court. Ultimately the Court will hear less than 100 cases per term. The Court is most likely to hear cases that address important legal issues of national significance, especially when there is a split on the issue of law among the lower courts, and the Court's decision could clarify and unify the law in the U.S.

With the assistance of law clerks the nine U.S. Supreme Court Justices (one Chief Justice and eight Associate Justices) review the petitions and then meet to vote on which cases to hear in the next term (the Court's term begins the first Monday in October and ends in early summer). Concerning granting *certiorari* the Court follows the "rule of four" in which at least four Justices must vote to hear a case or the *writ of certiorari* is denied. If a case is accepted by the Court the parties must prepare briefs for the Court concerning the merits of their case, and prepare for oral arguments in which members of the Court can question the parties on any issues they wish to explore further.

After oral arguments are completed the Justices meet to discuss the case. In order of seniority from most senior to least, the Justices state the basis on which they would decide the case. The Justices take a preliminary vote on which party should prevail. The most senior justice in the majority (or the Chief Justice if the Chief Justice is in the majority) has the right to assign the writing of the draft opinion to him or herself or to another Justice in the majority.

After drafting the opinion the Justice authoring the draft circulates the draft opinion and may receive suggestions for revision from other Justices. The author is not required to accept any of these suggestions for revision, but the other justices may withdraw their vote at any time before the opinion is released if they are dissatisfied with the reasoning in the majority opinion. A 5-4 majority opinion, for example, could become a minority opinion if even one Justice's vote is lost.

A majority opinion is an opinion joined by 5 or more of the 9 Justices. A majority opinion has the force of law regardless of whether it is a 5-4 opinion or a 9-0 opinion. The opinion generally states the name of the author, but if no single author is named it is a *per curium* opinion by the Court. A concurring opinion is an opinion written by a justice in the majority who agrees that the correct party prevailed in the case, but wishes to communicate something not in the majority opinion, for example different legal reasoning concerning the case.

A dissenting opinion is an opinion written by a Justice in the minority who believes that the other party should have prevailed and wants to explain why the other party should have prevailed. Concurring and dissenting opinions help to explain the complexity of views among the Justices, but only the majority opinion has the force of law and establishes legal precedent which must be followed by lower courts.

Chapter Summary

This chapter presented an introduction to law and governance including the theory and history of the U.S. law and governance system, a means for operationalizing a democratic system of governance, and an overview of the U.S. judicial system. After reading this chapter, please consider the following points in review and for further thought and discussion:

I. *Review Points*:

1) All professionals are accountable for knowing the laws that govern their profession.

2) To fully understand the application of the law you must understand the purpose of the law.

3) The Rule of Law is the necessary foundation for democracy.

4) An educated citizenry is essential to democracy: Schools are the nurseries of the democracy.

5) The law is applied philosophy. Our laws must be firmly grounded in our highest ideals of justice, and the legal system must be capable of bringing this justice to citizens' daily lives.

6) Our Constitution is the Nation's collective conscience: It is a legal tool through which we codify our highest common ideals and attempt to make them our collective reality.

7) The greatest tests of our principles come during times of crisis. It is at these times that it is most difficult to remain true to our own Constitution. But these are the times we most need our Constitution as a constant reminder of our own principles and who we are as a People.

8) The Constitution is the Supreme Law of the Land. All laws and all actions of government officials must be consistent with the Constitution.

9) Government power is necessary to protect life, liberty, and property. But the vast power of government must be carefully limited and controlled through adequate checks and balances, and through constant oversight by a vigilant Press informing public oversight of government.

10) No one is above the limits of the law, and no one is below the protections of the law.

11) In a democracy government officials are public servants not rulers.

12) The tragic lessons of history are repeated until they are learned.

13) In a democracy the People get the government they have earned.

14) To have peace we must have justice.

15) Good laws, policies, and administration serve as a just and efficient system of problem resolution.

16) The powerful need the limits of the law; the weaker need the protections of the law.

17) Justice and the common good are the constant unchanging goals. But to realize these goals governance systems, laws, and policies must be capable of adapting to changing circumstances.

18) Totalitarian leaders coerce; democratic leaders persuade. Totalitarian power requires fear; democratic power is based on the free will of the People.

19) The criminal law system punishes and deters harmful conduct; the civil law system compensates for harms and deters future harms.

20) The government prosecutes criminal cases; individual plaintiffs bring civil suits.

21) Legal burdens of proof:

> Civil law: Proof by a preponderance of the evidence.
> Criminal law: Proof beyond a reasonable doubt.

22) For a case to be heard the plaintiff must have legal standing to bring the case and the court must have subject matter and geographic jurisdiction over the case and the parties.

23) Federal courts are courts of limited subject matter jurisdiction hearing disputes concerning federal law. State courts are courts of general subject matter jurisdiction and hear disputes involving state and federal law.

II. *Principles to Practice Tips*:

1) *Learning and Teaching the Lessons of History*: Concerning human nature, there is truly nothing new under the Sun. The most challenging problems are always the human problems. Names, faces, and details change, but the underlying problems of human nature do not. History is a textbook for understanding human nature. For those wise enough to distill its lessons, history teaches us not only what happened, but also what is likely to happen. Learning and teaching the lessons of history can help you and your students to better understand human nature and respond to its challenges more effectively.

2) *Just and Unjust Laws*: Great thinkers from Socrates to Dr. King have written on the distinction between just and unjust laws. This question is not one of theoretical importance only: School officials must apply rules to real people in real circumstances. What should you do if you believe a law, policy, or rule you are asked to enforce may be unjust or illegal? At least since the *Nuremberg Trials* it has been well established law that "following orders" is not a valid legal defense if the order is unlawful. On the other hand, it is insubordination to refuse to follow a lawful order. Quick decisions are often necessary in practice, so to make the right decision under pressure it is critically important to have a solid working knowledge of the law in advance of a crisis. If you know the law you will make the right decision. When the law is unclear, however, whenever possible well considered decisions are in everyone's best interests. Concerning

difficult and important decisions of law and policy, whenever possible review the applicable law thoroughly, and seek the advice of qualified legal counsel when needed, so you can make a lawful decision consistent with good practice and your own conscience. Doing what is right is often not what is easy. But in the longer run you never go wrong by doing what is right.

3) *Avoiding Unnecessary Litigation*: Disputes are inevitable, but litigation is not. To avoid unnecessary litigation know the law and apply it fairly. Even when you must take negative actions, treat others fairly and respectfully. Most people can accept negative consequences if they believe they have been treated fairly and respectfully. And few people really want to be engaged in expensive and stressful litigation if it can be reasonably avoided. In "The Art of War" Sun Tzu advised building a golden bridge for your enemy to retreat on, and said that the greatest victory comes in the battle that was never fought. Look for wise ways to achieve your necessary objectives without unnecessary conflicts.

III. *Questions for Discussion*: Please consider these questions and be prepared to discuss:

1) *Governance and Law*: What are the legitimate purposes of government? What are the legitimate purposes of law? What distinguishes good and bad government; good and bad laws? How should the common government reconcile: Majority rule with minority rights?; Freedom with security?; Individualism with the common good? Did the Founders believe that we could answer these questions definitively? Or was their intention to provoke perpetual public dialogue about how to address these issues under changing circumstances consistent with our foundational values? What do the values evidenced in the Declaration of Independence, the Constitution, and the Bill of Rights suggest to you concerning these issues?

2) *Control of Education Policy*: What is the proper role of the federal government in public education? Should states; local school boards; or parents and students have more or less control over public education?

3) *Judicial Duty and Activism*: If judges neglect their judicial duties justice is denied and the Rule of Law is jeopardized. But if judges overstep their constitutional bounds through judicial activism judges intrude on legislative powers and the Rule of Law is jeopardized. What checks and balances are needed to keep judges from straying out of their constitutional lane in either direction (neglect of judicial duty or judicial activism)? Should judges be granted lifetime tenure? Should judges be appointed or elected? Should judges be subject to popular recall? Should different policies apply to federal and state judges?

4) *Open Forum*: What other related issues or current events would you like to discuss?

IV. *Suggested Activities*:

1) Read the U.S. Constitution (an edited copy is included in the appendix). Discuss what you learned.

2) Find your State's Constitution (available online) and read through your State's Bill of Rights and the sections governing education. Discuss what you learned.

3) Contact your U.S. Senator and your Representative in Congress concerning an issue of importance to you.

4) Contact your State Senator and your State Representative in the State General Assembly concerning an issue of importance to you.

5) Visit a local federal or state courthouse and sit in on part of a trial. Most trials are open to the public and visitors are welcomed to watch the proceedings.

Chapter 2: Children, Families, and the State

Children's Rights

Nearly 4,000 years ago in one of the earliest known codes of law Babylonian King Hammurabi recognized that the purpose of the law was to bring the rule of righteousness to the land so that the strong would not harm the weak. Children are an especially vulnerable group that must be rigorously protected by the law. The Geneva Declaration of the Rights of the Child (1924) recognized "the child, by reason of his physical and mental immaturity, needs special safeguards and care, including appropriate legal protection." Among the rights that must be protected the United Nations Convention on the Rights of the Child (1990) recognized a child's inherent rights to life; liberty; fundamental equality; essentials for survival and human dignity; education; a name; a nationality; family relationships where possible; rights to freedoms of expression, conscience, and religion; and protections from violence, maltreatment, exploitation, neglect and abuse including sexual abuse.

While respecting legitimate family privacy and parental authority, there is a collective social responsibility to protect children and provide necessary services in the best interests of the child. The first right and responsibility to care for and protect the child resides with parents or other legal guardians. If parents fail in these obligations, however, centuries old common law recognizes an obligation for the common government to assume these obligations under the *parens patriae* ("parent of the nation") doctrine. The *parens patriae* doctrine holds that while rights and responsibilities concerning the child are first vested in the parents, the common government also has a role as *parens patriae* when parents fail in their responsibilities to the child.

Parents may also delegate some of their parental authority to school officials or others under the *in loco parentis* ("in place of the parent") doctrine. Under the *in loco parentis* doctrine school officials may exercise reasonable quasi-parental authority while the child is in the care and custody of school officials, subject to the limits of the law and guided by the best interests of the child. When acting *in loco parentis* school officials have a duty to supervise and protect children as a reasonable parent would under the circumstances. And children have a duty to follow the reasonable orders of school officials just as they must follow reasonable orders from their parents.

Children necessarily rely on the protection of adults both at home and at school. It is therefore the responsibility of adults to ensure that homes and schools provide a safe haven for children. Educators must protect the safety and well-being of students in schools so that the students may focus their full attention on learning and growing into well-adjusted, responsible, productive citizens through their studies and healthy social interactions in schools.

Children have legal rights from the moment of their birth, but the degree to which a child may exercise these rights necessarily depends on the maturity of the child. As the child grows closer to maturity, the child increasingly enjoys the full scope of rights belonging to mature adults. For example, children generally have the following rights at these ages:

AGE	EXAMPLE RIGHTS OBTAINED AT EACH MINIMUM AGE*
13	May be left home alone or "baby sit" younger children for a reasonable time
14	May select among otherwise fit and proper custodial parents
15	May obtain a learner's permit to drive
16	May legally consent to sexual contact (in some states)
17	May join the military with parental consent
18	Reaches the age of legal majority and is no longer a minor
21	May legally purchase and consume alcohol

* These are example minimum ages. Laws vary among states.

© Dayton

Parental Rights

Parents have both the legal right and responsibility to care for and make decisions on behalf of their minor children. Parental rights are taken very seriously under U.S. law and are protected by both the U.S. and state constitutions. Parents may, however, voluntarily give up parental rights by consenting to adoption or requesting a termination of parental rights. In order to involuntarily terminate parental rights, however, the state must generally show: 1) Clear and convincing evidence that the parent is unfit; and 2) That it is in the best interests of the child to terminate parental rights. Legal grounds for involuntary termination of parental rights may include child abandonment; neglect; abuse; mental incapacity of the parent; and other acts and conditions inconsistent with performing parental responsibilities, including the commission of serious felonies and resulting long-term incarceration.

Child Protective Services

Child Protective Services are the state agencies responsible for protecting the health, safety, and welfare of children when parents fail in these duties. These agencies act under the *parens patriae* doctrine. They have legal authority to investigate claims of child abuse and neglect; seek remedial court orders; and when necessary remove children from the home and seek termination of parental rights. Child Protective Services agents act under the dual goals of: 1) Pursuing the best interests of the child; and 2) Preserving the family. In practice, however, these dual goals may sometimes conflict and prove mutually impossible when preserving the family is clearly not in the best interests of the child. Child Protective Services agents constantly face the danger of doing too little or too much in their efforts to protect children, either failing to adequately protect the child, or over-stepping their legal authority and intruding on family privacy and parental rights.

In *DeShaney v. Winnebago*, 489 U.S. 189 (1989), for example, Child Protective Services officials had received many complaints that Joshua, a minor child, had been subjected to severe beatings by his father. Nonetheless, state social services agents did not remove the child from the custody of his father. His father eventually beat Joshua so severely that the child suffered permanent brain damage and was left profoundly and permanently mentally impaired. Joshua's mother sued State Child Protective Services on Joshua's behalf. In *DeShaney* the U.S. Supreme Court ruled against Joshua and his mother stating:

> Judges and lawyers, like other humans, are moved by natural sympathy in a case like this to find a way for Joshua and his mother to receive adequate compensation for the grievous harm inflicted upon them. But before yielding to that impulse, it is well to remember once again that the harm was inflicted not by the State of Wisconsin, but by Joshua's father. The most that can be said of the state functionaries in this case is that they stood by and did nothing when suspicious circumstances dictated a more active role for them. In defense of them it must also be said that had they moved too soon to take custody of the son away from the father, they would likely have been met with charges of improperly intruding into the parent-child relationship, charges based on the same Due Process Clause that forms the basis for the present charge of failure to provide adequate protection. The people of Wisconsin may well prefer a system of liability which would place upon the State and its officials the responsibility for failure to act in situations such as the present one. They may create such a system, if they do not have it already, by changing the tort law of the State in accordance with the regular lawmaking process. But they should not have it thrust upon them by this Court's expansion of the Due Process Clause of the Fourteenth Amendment.

In a dissenting opinion, however, Justice Blackmun declared:

> Poor Joshua! Victim of repeated attacks by an irresponsible, bullying, cowardly, and intemperate father, and abandoned by [state social services agents] who placed him in a dangerous predicament and who knew or learned what was going on, and yet did essentially nothing except, as the Court revealingly observes, "dutifully recorded these incidents in [their] files." It is a sad commentary upon American life, and constitutional principles--so full of late of patriotic fervor and proud proclamations about "liberty and justice for all"--that this child, Joshua DeShaney, now is assigned to live out the remainder of his life profoundly retarded. Joshua and his mother, as petitioners here, deserve--but now are denied by this Court--the opportunity to have the facts of their case considered in the light of the constitutional protection that 42 U.S.C. § 1983 is meant to provide.

The Court's ruling in *DeShaney* leaves little or no protection in federal courts for children like Joshua where the direct perpetrator was a private citizen and not an agent of the state. State courts, however, have awarded substantial monetary damages against State Child Protective Services agencies who negligently or knowingly failed to protect children from persons supervised by the state, such as foster parents.

State courts appear to be more willing to hold state officials accountable for protecting children where state officials knew or should have known they were putting children in serious danger, and the state had some supervisory responsibility for the perpetrator. Substantial damages have been awarded in cases involving sexual abuse of children by foster parents licensed and supervised by State agencies, where persons with prior histories and convictions for abuse and sexual offenses against children were nonetheless licensed as foster parents and the children assigned to them were abused. Before state officials place a child in the care of any foster parent or other caretaker state officials should conduct appropriate background checks and adequately monitor child safety and conditions in the home or other care facility.

State officials have legal authority to protect children from abuse. There are, however, constitutional limits to this authority. Due process of law is essential when the State is engaged in so serious an act as the forcible removal of children from the home and the termination of parental rights.

For example, in March 2008 a local domestic abuse hotline reported receiving a call from a 16 year-old girl who identified herself only as "Sarah." The caller claimed physical and sexual abuse at the "Yearning for Zion" (YFZ) Ranch in a rural area near Eldorado, Texas. Four days later Texas Department of Family Protective Services and Texas law enforcement officials conducted a military-style raid on the YFZ Ranch. State agents were armed with automatic weapons, helicopters, and armored vehicles. They were not, however, met with any resistance from residents.

Texas officials were there to forcibly remove children from the YFZ Ranch based on their theory that the religious beliefs of the Fundamentalist Church of Jesus Christ of Latter Day Saints (FLDS) created a danger that children could be indoctrinated in harmful beliefs, and therefore the children must be removed from their parents' homes now for their future safety. The belief system in question allegedly included a history of polygamy involving under-age brides, and a culture of socialization and coercion into under-age marriages.

State officials searched the Ranch and 468 children were taking from their homes and placed in state custody. State officials had not obtained a court order or provided individual parents with due process of law prior to seizing the children. It was later learned that "Sarah" the complainant who provided the basis for this action was not a 16 year-old abused child, but was in fact a much older woman who had prior arrests for false reports in which she impersonated an abused girl. Further, the search of the Ranch and police interviews of children and parents did not produce any credible evidence of mass child abuse. The forced removals caused great emotional distress to FDLS children and parents. And many of the children who were not vaccinated because of sincerely held religious beliefs became sick when exposed to communicable diseases while in state child care facilities. FDLS parents sued state officials for the return of their children.

The Supreme Court of Texas, in *In re Texas Department of Family and Protective Services*, 255 S.W.3d 613 (Tex., 2008), held that the Texas Department of Family and Protective Services' allegations concerning FLDS religious beliefs and a culture of polygamy did not justify emergency removal of all 468 children prior to the provision of adequate due process of law. Individual parents had a right to notice of any charges against them and an individual opportunity to be heard concerning any alleged misconduct involving their child. Mass removals of children from their parents based on little more than unproven theories about their religious beliefs and guilt by association was constitutionally unacceptable. The court of appeals had found:

> There was no evidence that the Department made reasonable efforts to eliminate or prevent the removal of any . . . children. The evidence is that the Department went to the Yearning For Zion ranch to investigate a distress call from a sixteen year-old girl. After interviewing a number of children, they concluded that there were five minors who were or had been pregnant and that the belief system of the community allowed minor females to marry and bear children. They then removed all of the children in the community

(including infants) from their homes and ultimately separated the children from their parents. This record does not reflect any reasonable effort on the part of the Department to ascertain if some measure short of removal and/or separation from parents would have eliminated the risk the Department perceived with respect to any of the children.

The Supreme Court of Texas affirmed the court of appeals decision in favor of parents, and stated:

> On the record before us, removal of the children was not warranted. The Department argues without explanation that the court of appeals' decision leaves the Department unable to protect the children's safety, but the Family Code gives the district court broad authority to protect children short of separating them from their parents and placing them in foster care. The court may make and modify temporary orders "for the safety and welfare of the child," including an order "restraining a party from removing the child beyond a geographical area identified by the court." The court may also order the removal of an alleged perpetrator from the child's home and may issue orders to assist the Department in its investigation. The Code prohibits interference with an investigation, and a person who relocates a residence or conceals a child with the intent to interfere with an investigation commits an offense.

When there is clear and convincing evidence that children are in immediate danger, state officials have the authority to forcibly remove children from their parents on an emergency basis when necessary. This is, however, an extraordinary power that should only be used under extraordinary, emergency circumstances. Further, state officials must comply with state statutes and due process of law in this process.

Mandatory Reporting Statutes for Suspected Abuse or Neglect

All 50 U.S. states have statutes mandating reports to state officials of suspected abuse or neglect of children. These statutes provide criminal sanctions for failure to make a timely report. Under these statutes child care professionals are included as mandated reporters. The list of child care professionals mandated to report generally includes teachers and other educators; social workers; doctors and other health care providers; day-care providers; law enforcement personnel; court officials; and members of the clergy.

Some states also impose a general duty on all citizens to report suspected abuse or neglect of children. In these states child care professionals could be charged with two separate counts of failure to report: One in their professional capacity; and one in their private capacity as a citizen. In addition to mandated reporters, any person may report suspected child abuse or neglect to state officials.

> **If the Facts and Circumstances would have caused a Reasonable Person to Suspect Child Abuse or Neglect, there is a Duty to Report**

Mandatory reporting statutes were enacted in recognition of the general duty of adults, and child services professionals in particular, to protect children. In enacting these statutes lawmakers made a policy decision that it is better to have too many reports rather than too few.

Over-reporting consumes resources, and sometimes causes unnecessary intrusions, but under-reporting presents a serious danger that children will go unprotected. Therefore the legal standard is generally knowledge of "suspected" abuse and not just "known" abuse. There is a legal duty to make a report when a reasonable person would have suspected abuse under the facts and circumstances within the knowledge of the individual.

This is an objective legal standard, not a subjective standard. The "reasonable person" standard is based on the expected conduct of the ordinary person under the circumstance, a person with average knowledge, skills, and judgment. If a reasonable person would have made a report under those facts and circumstances, there is a legal duty to report. Further, the report should be made as soon as practicable avoiding any unnecessary delay that could interfere with the timely provision of help for the child.

Levels of Evidence of Abuse and Neglect and Duty to Report

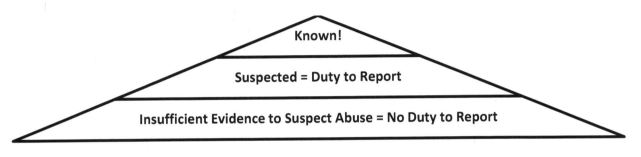

© Dayton

If there is insufficient evidence to cause a reasonable person to suspect abuse there is no duty to report. If there is evidence sufficient to cause a reasonable person to suspect child abuse, there is a legal duty to report and willful failure to do so is generally a misdemeanor that could be punishable by up to a year in jail depending on state law. Known abuse calls for immediate action to protect the child including a referral to law enforcement.

For failing to report suspected abuse or neglect child care professionals could lose their professional licenses and be convicted of a misdemeanor. But if it can be proven that an adult actually knew about child abuse and allowed the abuse to continue by failing to report, that person could be subject to prosecution as an accessory to the crime. In cases of child sexual abuse this could be a felony level prosecution punishable by significantly more than a year in prison.

If abuse or neglect are suspected the witness must comply with state laws for reporting abuse or neglect. These laws are published online or an individual can call state social services for guidance in reporting. Reporting procedures generally include reporting the suspected abuse or neglect to the individual in charge of the institution (*i.e.*, the school principal, the director of the medical facility, etc.), and/or reporting directly to state Child Protective Services or law enforcement personnel. State Child Protection Services personnel will investigate the report and make an initial determination whether the child is in danger or whether the child and family are in need of services.

But what if a report turns out to be unfounded? As long as the report was made in good faith, persons reporting suspected abuse or neglect are generally shielded from any liability under state law by good faith immunity. Knowingly making a false report, however, is a crime. A person who knowingly makes a false report for the purposes of harassing or harming the public reputation of another person could be subject to both criminal prosecution and liability for defamation.

Abusers rarely abuse children in public view. Instead, child care professionals and community members may see signs and behaviors indicating that a child may be abused or neglected. Signs of abuse may include unexplained injuries; difficulty walking or sitting; refusal to disrobe for gym; unusual fears of being touched; fear of parents; fear of going home; sudden changes in behavior; age inappropriate sexual conduct or knowledge; and inappropriate interactions between parents and children. Signs of neglect may include lack of personal hygiene; unclean clothing; unaddressed dental and medical problems; stealing food or money; evidence of drug or alcohol use; excessive absences; or parental indifference, substance abuse, or mental health problems.

Juvenile Law

Children necessarily rely on the protection, support, and guidance of adults. Children, and especially younger children, generally lack the cognitive abilities, experience, and maturity to understand the complexities of the world and to make appropriate daily decisions. For all of these reasons children are generally treated differently than adults under the law, and children are subject to appropriate juvenile laws.

Juvenile laws are primarily defined by state law. In most instances children under the age of 18 are subject to juvenile laws. Juvenile laws allow greater restrictions on the rights of children, restrictions that would be unlawful if applied to competent adults. Children, for example, must obey the lawful orders of their parents and school officials. They are subject to compulsory school attendance and curfew rules. And children are prohibited from engaging in many activities that would be lawful rights if they were adults including driving; living independently; working; marriage; voting; and the purchase of alcohol, tobacco products, and adult literature.

Juvenile laws sometimes restrict children's rights. But they also protect children and generally make them subject to less severe punishments than adults. Although children can commit criminal acts and be held accountable for criminal conduct, criminal culpability requires proof of both *actus reus* (a guilty act) and *mens rea* (a guilty mind). Establishment of *mens rea* for juveniles requires proof that the child understood the consequences of the actions under the circumstances. It must be proven that the child knew the difference between right and wrong, and that the child was capable of conforming behavior to avoid the prohibited acts.

Children under the age of 7 are deemed incapable of sufficiently understanding the criminality of their acts. There is a rebuttable presumption that children ages 7-14 are incapable of sufficiently understanding the criminality of their actions. But this presumption could be rebutted with compelling evidence in a particular case. Children ages 14 and over are presumed capable of understanding the criminality of their actions. But this presumption may be rebutted with evidence that a particular child was incapable of understanding the criminality of his or her actions as a juvenile. For children under the age of 18 the focus of the law is on rehabilitation rather than on punishment.

Although the emphasis of juvenile law is on rehabilitation, consequences for children can still be severe including long-term imprisonment. In some cases children have even been executed for crimes committed when they were a minor. Juvenile courts were created to address the special needs of children and protect them from the harshness of the adult system. But juvenile court systems initially lacked due process requirements present in the adult court system, due process requirements that could help protect children from wrongful convictions or excessive punishments. The informality of an unregulated juvenile system could allow for greater flexibility in dealing with the special needs of children. But the lack of due process also presented serious dangers of errors and abuse of authority.

In *In re Gault*, 387 U.S. 1 (1967), the U.S. Supreme Court addressed a case in which 15 year-old Gerald Gault had been arrested based on a report from one of his neighbors. The neighbor had called police to complain about a phone call made to her in which "the caller or callers made lewd or indecent remarks." In response, a Sheriff's Deputy took Gerald from his family home to the juvenile Detention Center leaving no notification to parents about the location of their son. After considerable anguish over the whereabouts of their son the Gaults discovered Gerald had been taken to the Detention Center by police.

A petition was filed against Gerald, but it was never served to the Gaults. Further, the petition was *pro forma* ("as a formality") only and it was so minimal it did not describe the charges or the evidence against Gerald. No one was sworn in at the hearing and there was no record made of the hearing. The juvenile court judge later testified that Gerald's actions were in dispute. The Deputy recalled Gerald admitting making a lewd statement, as did the judge. But Gerald maintained that he "only dialed Mrs. Cook's number and handed the telephone to his friend, Ronald." Mrs. Gault requested that the accuser Mrs. Cook be present at the formal hearing "so she could see which boy that done the talking, the dirty talking over the phone." The juvenile judge denied this request. At no time did the judge communicate with Mrs. Cook concerning her complaint or the evidence against Gerald.

At the conclusion of the hearing the judge declared Gerald a juvenile delinquent and committed him to the State Industrial School "for the period of his minority (that is, until 21)." Under state law no appeal was permitted in a juvenile case. The Gaults challenged these decisions as unconstitutional. In reviewing this case the U.S. Supreme Court stated:

> Failure to observe the fundamental requirements of due process has resulted in instances, which might have been avoided, of unfairness to individuals and inadequate or inaccurate findings of fact and unfortunate prescriptions of remedy. Due process of law is the primary and indispensable foundation of individual freedom. It is the basic and essential term in the social compact which defines the rights of the individual and delimits the powers which the state may exercise. As Mr. Justice Frankfurter has said: "The history of American freedom is, in no small measure, the history of procedure." But, in addition, the procedural rules which have been fashioned from the generality of due process are our best instruments for the distillation and evaluation of essential facts from the conflicting welter of data that life and our adversary methods present. It is these instruments of due process which enhance the possibility that truth will emerge from the confrontation of opposing versions and conflicting data. "Procedure is to law what 'scientific method' is to science" . . . Ultimately, however, we confront the reality of that portion of the Juvenile Court process with which we deal in this case. A boy is charged with misconduct. The boy is committed to an institution where he may be restrained of liberty for years. It is of no constitutional consequence--and of limited practical meaning--that the institution to which he is committed is called an Industrial School. The fact of the matter is that, however euphemistic the title, a "receiving home" or an

"industrial school" for juveniles is an institution of confinement in which the child is incarcerated for a greater or lesser time. His world becomes a building with whitewashed walls, regimented routine and institutional hours. Instead of mother and father and sisters and brothers and friends and classmates, his world is peopled by guards, custodians, state employees, and delinquents confined with him for anything from waywardness to rape and homicide. In view of this, it would be extraordinary if our Constitution did not require the procedural regularity and the exercise of care implied in the phrase "due process." Under our Constitution, the condition of being a boy does not justify a kangaroo court. The traditional ideas of Juvenile Court procedure, indeed, contemplated that time would be available and care would be used to establish precisely what the juvenile did and why he did it--was it a prank of adolescence or a brutal act threatening serious consequences to himself or society unless corrected? Under traditional notions, one would assume that in a case like that of Gerald Gault, where the juvenile appears to have a home, a working mother and father, and an older brother, the Juvenile Judge would have made a careful inquiry and judgment as to the possibility that the boy could be disciplined and dealt with at home . . . If Gerald had been over 18, he would not have been subject to Juvenile Court proceedings. For the particular offense immediately involved, the maximum punishment would have been a fine of $5 to $50, or imprisonment in jail for not more than two months. Instead, he was committed to custody for a maximum of six years. If he had been over 18 and had committed an offense to which such a sentence might apply, he would have been entitled to substantial rights under the Constitution of the United States as well as under Arizona's laws and constitution. The United States Constitution would guarantee him rights and protections with respect to arrest, search, and seizure, and pretrial interrogation. It would assure him of specific notice of the charges and adequate time to decide his course of action and to prepare his defense. He would be entitled to clear advice that he could be represented by counsel, and, at least if a felony were involved, the State would be required to provide counsel if his parents were unable to afford it. If the court acted on the basis of his confession, careful procedures would be required to assure its voluntariness. If the case went to trial, confrontation and opportunity for cross-examination would be guaranteed. So wide a gulf between the State's treatment of the adult and of the child requires a bridge sturdier than mere verbiage, and reasons more persuasive than cliche can provide. As Wheeler and Cottrell have put it, "The rhetoric of the juvenile court movement has developed without any necessarily close correspondence to the realities of court and institutional routines" . . . We conclude that the Due Process Clause of the Fourteenth Amendment requires that in respect of proceedings to determine delinquency which may result in commitment to an institution in which the juvenile's freedom is curtailed, the child and his parents must be notified of the child's right to be represented by counsel retained by them, or if they are unable to afford counsel, that counsel will be appointed to represent the child . . . . We conclude that the constitutional privilege against self-incrimination is applicable in the case of juveniles as it is with respect to adults. We appreciate that special problems may arise with respect to waiver of the privilege by or on behalf of children, and that there may well be some differences in technique--but not in principle--depending upon the age of the child and the presence and competence of parents. The participation of counsel will, of course, assist the police, Juvenile Courts and appellate tribunals in administering the privilege. If counsel was not present for some permissible reason when an admission was obtained, the greatest care must be taken to assure that the admission was voluntary, in the sense not only that it was not coerced or suggested, but also that it was not the product of ignorance of rights or of adolescent fantasy, fright or despair . . . For the reasons stated, the judgment of the Supreme Court of Arizona is reversed and the cause remanded for further proceedings not inconsistent with this opinion. It is so ordered.

In *Roper v. Simmons*, 543 U.S. 551 (2005), the U.S. Supreme Court held that it was unconstitutional to impose the death penalty on juveniles. In cases involving serious felonies, however, older children may otherwise be subject to prosecution as adults. Except for those cases in which state law allows for the transfer of criminal jurisdiction to adult courts, juvenile courts generally have jurisdiction over proceedings involving children, including hearings on delinquency, abuse, neglect, children in need of services, and child custody.

Comments and Questions

Historically government agents have used threats, intimidation, beatings, and even sexual assaults and torture to coerce confessions to crimes. Not surprisingly persons subjected to coercion and torture will eventually confess to most anything. In addition to the serious human rights violations and crimes against humanity inherent in these abusive tactics, coercion commonly elicits false confessions. The path from coercion to torture is a notoriously slippery slope. To avoid these evils the U.S. Constitution banned coerced confessions through the Fifth Amendment's prohibition against compelling a person to testify against himself in a criminal case, and the Sixth Amendment's right to legal counsel for defense in a criminal case.

School officials commonly need to question students about discipline, safety issues, or possible violations of school rules, and they have a legal duty and legitimate authority to do so. School officials are questioning students about civil matters related to school events, none of which involve criminal interrogations or trigger constitutional protections applicable in criminal cases. But when law enforcement officers question students about their alleged criminal conduct, constitutional protections may apply.

To protect Fifth and Sixth Amendment rights, and to help prevent coerced confessions, the Court requires *Miranda* warnings to inform individuals of their constitutional rights when they are subjected to custodial interrogations. The *Miranda* warning, from *Miranda v. Arizona*, 384 U.S. 436 (1966), is intended to assure informed consent by the suspect, and that any subsequent confession during the custodial interrogation is voluntary and not coerced. A custodial interrogation is criminal questioning when the individual cannot leave or does not reasonably feel free to leave under the circumstances.

Generally, police officers can ask anyone a question, just as any citizen can ask another citizen a question. But the person asked the question is free to answer or not. And unless the person is in police custody, the person is free to leave. If in police custody, however, a *Miranda* warning is required to inform the person of applicable rights prior to police interrogation. No exact wording is required by *Miranda*, but the suspect must be notified of: 1) A right to remain silent; 2) That statements can and will be used against the suspect; 3) The right to have a lawyer before and during questioning; and 4) A lawyer will be provided free of cost for indigent suspects. To determine whether the individual is "in custody" and entitled to a *Miranda* warning the Court has required an objective analysis of the circumstances, testing whether under those circumstances a reasonable person would have believed they were free to leave.

In *J.D.B. v. North Carolina*, ___ U.S. ___ (2011) the Court addressed whether the age of the child questioned must be a factor in this objective test, giving special consideration to the vulnerabilities of children to coercion by adult authority figures:

> J.D.B. was a 13–year–old, seventh-grade student . . . when he was removed from his classroom . . . escorted to a closed-door conference room, and questioned by police . . . neither the police officers nor the school administrators contacted J.D.B.'s grandmother. . . The door to the conference room was closed. With the two police officers and the two administrators present, J.D.B. was questioned for the next 30 to 45 minutes. Prior to the commencement of questioning, J.D.B. was given neither *Miranda* warnings nor the opportunity to speak to his grandmother. Nor was he informed that he was free to leave the room . . . After learning of the prospect of juvenile detention, J.D.B. confessed that he and a friend were responsible for the break-ins. [Police] only then informed J.D.B. that he could refuse to answer the investigator's questions and that he was free to leave . . . We granted certiorari to determine whether the *Miranda* custody analysis includes consideration of a juvenile suspect's age . . . By its very nature, custodial police interrogation entails inherently compelling pressures. Even for an adult, the physical and psychological isolation of custodial interrogation can undermine the individual's will to resist and . . . compel him to speak where he would not otherwise do so freely. Indeed, the pressure of custodial interrogation is so immense that it can induce a frighteningly high percentage of people to confess to crimes they never committed. That risk is all the more troubling--and recent studies suggest, all the more acute--when the subject of custodial interrogation is a juvenile. Recognizing that the inherently coercive nature of custodial interrogation blurs the line between voluntary and involuntary statements, this Court in *Miranda* adopted a set of prophylactic measures designed to safeguard the constitutional guarantee against self-incrimination. Prior to questioning, a suspect "must be warned that he has a right to remain silent, that any statement he does make may be used as evidence against him, and that he has a right to the presence of an attorney, either retained or appointed." And, if a suspect makes a statement during custodial interrogation, the burden is on the Government to show, as a prerequisite to the statement's admissibility as evidence in the Government's case in chief, that the defendant "voluntarily, knowingly and intelligently" waived his rights. Because these measures protect the individual against the coercive nature of custodial interrogation, they are required only where there has been such a restriction on a person's freedom as to render him "in custody" . . . In some circumstances, a child's age would have affected how a reasonable person in the suspect's position would perceive his or her freedom to leave. That is, a reasonable child subjected to police questioning will sometimes feel pressured to submit when a reasonable adult would feel free to go. We think it clear that courts can account for that reality without doing any damage to the objective nature of the custody analysis. A child's age is far more than a chronological fact. It is a fact that generates commonsense conclusions about behavior and perception. Such conclusions apply broadly to children as a class. And, they are self-evident to anyone who was a child once himself, including any police officer or judge. Time and again, this Court has drawn these commonsense conclusions for itself. We have observed that children generally are

less mature and responsible than adults, that they often lack the experience, perspective, and judgment to recognize and avoid choices that could be detrimental to them, that they are more vulnerable or susceptible to . . . outside pressures than adults, and so on. Addressing the specific context of police interrogation, we have observed that events that would leave a man cold and unimpressed can overawe and overwhelm a lad in his early teens . . . these observations restate what any parent knows--indeed, what any person knows--about children generally. In fact, in many cases involving juvenile suspects, the custody analysis would be nonsensical absent some consideration of the suspect's age. This case is a prime example. Were the court precluded from taking J.D.B.'s youth into account, it would be forced to evaluate the circumstances present here through the eyes of a reasonable person of average years. In other words, how would a reasonable adult understand his situation, after being removed from a seventh-grade social studies class by a uniformed school resource officer; being encouraged by his assistant principal to "do the right thing"; and being warned by a police investigator of the prospect of juvenile detention and separation from his guardian and primary caretaker? To describe such an inquiry is to demonstrate its absurdity. Neither officers nor courts can reasonably evaluate the effect of objective circumstances that, by their nature, are specific to children without accounting for the age of the child subjected to those circumstances . . . we hold that so long as the child's age was known to the officer at the time of police questioning, or would have been objectively apparent to a reasonable officer, its inclusion in the custody analysis is consistent with the objective nature of that test.

In *J.D.B.* the Court held that the unique age-related vulnerabilities of children must be considered in determining whether children reasonably believed they were in custody when questioned by police. Provided federal constitutional limits are respected, further details of student questioning rules are governed by state laws and local policies. Consult applicable state laws and local policies, but the following model policy provides a useful guide to understanding the general issues involved in student questioning by state officials.

Student Questioning by State Officials: Model Policy*

School Administrators: School administrators have the responsibility and authority to question students for the purposes of maintaining a safe and orderly school environment. Though it is important to inform parents about issues of significant concern, school officials do not need parental consent to question students about school related events. *Child Protective Services (CPS) Personnel*: Upon a showing of lawful authority, CPS representatives investigating potential child abuse should be granted permission to conduct reasonable interviews and inspections of children. If the investigation involves suspected child abuse by individuals other than those residing in the child's household, parents should be informed of the CPS request. If the subject of the investigation is a parent/caretaker residing with the child, parental permission is not required and interviews may be permitted over the objections of parents when a CPS official is carrying out duties under the Child Abuse Reporting Act. No child should be released into the custody of anyone, including CPS personnel, without proof of identification and verification of a lawful basis for the removal. If CPS officials choose to conduct the interview of the child on school premises a school official should be present to assure that the child is treated age appropriately and in no way abused or coerced. If photographs are taken on school property for purposes of evidence they should be taken in a manner that does not directly reveal the identity of the subject, tagged with a recorded tracking code, and kept in a secure chain of custody. Inspection of children should be left to CPS officials, physicians, or medical staff. School employees should not undress students in an effort to determine whether physical abuse has taken place.

Court Appointed Guardian Ad Litem (GAL): The GAL is appointed by the court to represent the best interests of the minor child in court proceedings. The GAL investigates various aspects of the assigned child's case by interviewing children, parents, and other witnesses. In addition, the GAL may conduct interviews and/or inspect CPS, Juvenile Court, health care, and school records. Any request to inspect or obtain a student's records should be submitted in writing along with lawful documentation establishing the court appointed GAL relationship with the child.

Law Enforcement Officers: School Resource Officers and Probation Officers of the Juvenile Court investigating school related issues may be permitted to reasonably question students at school without prior parental approval. Law enforcement officers from other agencies investigating non-school related matters do not have the right to interview students at school simply for convenience. In such cases, the interrogation of students is not permitted without the consent of the parent unless the officer presents a valid court order or warrant for arrest, or states that the situation involves hot pursuit of a suspect linked to a felony crime.

School/Law Enforcement Cooperation Protocols: Proper boundaries of jurisdiction and authority between the school and law enforcement agencies should be negotiated and respected. All parties should recognize that school administrators are not police officers and police officers are not school administrators. Law enforcement officers should not be unreasonably hindered in the conduct of their official duties. Law enforcement officers, however, should not interfere with the educational process and should recognize that school administrators are charged with full responsible for the control of school property and all students during school hours. School administrators are not subject to charges of interference with law enforcement for reasonably refusing access to a child or interrogation during school hours. Law enforcement personnel should be questioned as to the lawful basis for any proposed interrogation of an in-school student to assure compliance with applicable laws and policies. Arrests or interrogations of students during school hours are to be discouraged in favor of off-campus and after school arrests or interrogations whenever possible. Students may not be released from the school to any officer unless the officer provides proper identification and a lawful reason for taking the child into custody is confirmed. Upon entering school property all persons, including law enforcement officers, must report to the school office immediately to state the purpose of their presence and be cleared for entry to the school unless there is an emergency or the law enforcement officer is in hot pursuit of a felony suspect.

* This model policy provides a general overview of these issues for educational purposes. Consult state laws, local policies, and legal counsel to assure legal compliance in your jurisdiction.

© **Dayton**

State law governs most juvenile law issues, including the age of consent to sexual conduct. Under state law minors in some states can legally consent to sexual contact at age 16. Other states declare age 17 or 18 the lawful age of consent to sexual contact. In a majority of states the age is not absolute and is instead a statutory formula of some specified age of the younger party for lawful consent, age of the older party for liability to criminal prosecution, and the age difference between the two. For example, some states may allow consent to sexual contact as young as 16, but establish an age range between partners that cannot lawfully exceed 5 years. A 16 year old could not then legally consent to sexual contact with anyone over 21 without the older party being subject to potential criminal prosecution.

The goals of these more flexible laws are first to protect children from exploitation and abuse, but also to recognize and not unjustly criminalize common social reality. Ideally minors would not be engaged in sexual activity before they are mature enough to fully understand and take responsibility for the consequences of their behavior. Laws prohibiting sex with minors can help deter older persons from preying on the vulnerabilities of less experienced and immature minors. But if not well written and applied with common sense by prosecutors these laws could also create situations in which more peer-aged boyfriends or girlfriends are prosecuted with statutory rape for relationships that may have been unwise but are not justly regarded as criminal.

In some states with absolute rather than relative age limits, prosecutions have occurred in cases in which minor-aged partners were mere months apart in age but on opposite sides of the designated age line. Although prosecution in these close cases may seem contrary to common sense, the marginally older partners have sometimes been prosecuted and convicted. They are then criminally punished and assigned the status of being a publicly registered sex offender. The consequences of this status includes a life-time of public shame; loss of rights; limitations on employment; prohibitions from living in certain areas; requirements to notify law enforcement officials of any relocation; and prohibitions from being in the presence of minors or within 1,000 feet of schools, bus stops, public recreation areas, parks, libraries, places of worship, or other areas where children commonly congregate.

While these punishments and restrictions are appropriate for any person who poses a credible risk to children, do your state's statutes appropriately separate between dangerous sexual predators and young people who may have made an ill-advised choice in a relationship? Do they both protect children from predators who would take advantage of a young person's vulnerabilities, and also protect young people from becoming subject to felony prosecutions for conduct that is all too common among young people?

What is the age of consent in your state, and what are the circumstances under which that consent is lawful? If you become aware of sexual contact involving a minor, under what circumstances might this suggest a referral to a school counselor, and under what circumstances does this require a report to Child Protective Services or law enforcement agents?

Find your state statute mandating reports for suspected abuse or neglect of children. What constitutes child abuse under the laws of your state? What constitutes child neglect under the laws of your state? Who is required to report? To whom do they report? Are persons who make reports granted good faith immunity under the laws of your state?

What are the proper boundaries between the state's legitimate duty to protect children and family privacy? Can a family's sincerely held religious beliefs ever be the lawful basis of removal of children from the home absent proof of specific criminal acts? Do families with minority religious beliefs sometimes attract disproportionate scrutiny because the religious beliefs they hold are regarded with suspicion or contempt by state officials elected or appointed by the majority?

In the YFZ Ranch case the court of appeals found: "After interviewing a number of children, [Texas Department of Family Protective Services] concluded that there were five minors who were or had been pregnant." If true, that would mean that teen pregnancy rates in the FLDS Community were actually lower than many other communities in Texas. Further, there was no evidence that the FLDS Community had higher rates of child abuse than many other communities in Texas. Why didn't Texas Family Protective Services raid and seize children in communities with the highest rates of teen pregnancy and child abuse instead of raiding the FLDS Community? Was it simply the unpopular religious beliefs of FLDS parents that resulted in the raid on their community? Do teen pregnancy and child abuse present any less danger to children in the absence of these religious beliefs?

Child Custody

Serious situations involving abuse and neglect may result in termination of parental rights and a change in child custody. More commonly child custody changes result from a change of family circumstances including dissolution of marriage. When family circumstances change and these changes affect parent-child relationships and living circumstances, appropriate decisions must be made concerning the continued care and custody of minor children.

Child custody is generally divided into: 1) Physical custody; and 2) Legal custody. Parents with physical custody have the legal authority and responsibility to make daily decisions concerning child care and discipline, and emergency decisions when necessary. Parents with legal custody generally have rights to participate in longer-term decisions for the child including decisions on education, religious instruction, and other non-emergency decisions.

Concerning parental rights regarding students, state laws generally presume custody rights belong to the enrolling parent(s). Others may rebut this presumption, however, by presenting a valid court order, etc. When school officials encounter a dispute between parents over parental rights, access to student records, etc., the party challenging the status quo must document the claim by presenting the court decree concerning child custody, etc. Otherwise, parents must take any unresolved issues to the court for resolution. School officials should comply with a valid court order, but otherwise avoid direct involvement in contentious custody disputes between parents. Child custody disputes are decided by judges, not school officials. Parents must take their dispute to the court for resolution.

Access to Student Records

Educational institutions keep extensive records on students including a student's grades; disciplinary history; family status; health information; etc. These records are often used by school officials in making important decisions concerning the student. Without access to this information, there would be no way for parents and students to know what these school files contained or whether the information school officials relied on in making decisions was accurate. Inaccurate information could have serious negative impacts on the student's future. Higher education institutions, for example, may decide to deny admission based on inaccurate negative information in school records concerning grades or discipline. Further, parents and students have a significant interest in assuring that their educational records and the private information in them are not released to third parties without their knowledge and permission.

In 1974 The Family Educational Rights and Privacy Act (FERPA), 20 U.S.C. § 1232g, was enacted to address these concerns. FERPA applies to all educational institutions that receive federal funds. FERPA provides parents and any age-eligible student access to their own educational records, and prohibits the disclosure of these records to third parties without parent or eligible student permission.

Parents generally hold this right on behalf of their minor children and have a right to access their child's educational records unless there is a court order, etc., concerning child custody that specifically revoked a parent's right to access these records. The right to access educational records transfers to the student who has reached age 18 or who is attending any institution of postsecondary education.

Parents or students have a right to a copy of their own records. School officials may charge a reasonable fee for the production of copies, but they cannot charge a fee for the retrieval of these records. Parents of students have a right to challenge any errors in the record and request amendments.

The educational institution must respond to the request for amendment in a reasonable time. If school officials refuse to amend the record the parent or eligible student must be informed of the right to a hearing to challenge the decision. Parents and students do not have a right to review documents that contain confidential information concerning other students or to access letters of recommendation for which the student waived the right to access.

School officials with a legitimate need to access student records may access these records internally without permission, but only for legitimate educational purposes. They may also share information from these records with other educational institutions or government agencies either with the permission of the parent or eligible student, or consistent with certain exceptions under FERPA including the disclosure of directory information (*i.e.*, student name; phone; address; academic major; dates of attendance; and participation in school activities); health or safety emergencies; or in compliance with a court order or other lawful request from state or federal government officials.

One might reasonable assume that among the reasons Congress enacted FERPA was to avoid students being publicly embarrassed in front of their peers by information in their educational records including grades. FERPA obviously prevents school officials from allowing students to snoop in the files of other students to view their grades. But does FERPA prohibit the practice of "peer grading" in which a student is allowed to grade another student's test, or grades are called out in class for purposes of recording by the teacher?

In *Owasso v. Falvo*, 534 U.S. 426 (2002), the U.S. Supreme Court held that such "peer grading" did not violate FERPA. Although this practice did publicly disclose the grades of individual students (seemingly in violation of the principles of privacy otherwise protected by the Act), the Court defined the statute to more narrowly only protect this information *after* it was recorded by an agent of the school. While this practice may be viewed by many as unwise, inappropriate, or inconsistent with the spirit of FERPA, based on the Court's decision in *Owasso*, "peer grading" is not a violation of FERPA. These practices may, however, violate state law or local policy.

Student records may also contain private health care information falling under the protections of the Health Insurance Portability and Accountability Act (HIPAA), 29 U.S.C. § 1181 (2011). The fundamental purposes of HIPAA are to better protect privacy and personal medical information, and to improve the efficiency and portability of records and medical insurance. If FERPA and HIPAA are in conflict, it is the opinion of the U.S. Department of Health and Human Services that FERPA controls, and that FERPA was not amended or preempted by HIPAA.

Compulsory School Attendance Laws

There is a legitimate public interest in assuring that all children are provided with an opportunity for education. As the U.S. Supreme Court noted in *Brown v. Board of Education*, 347 U.S. 483 (1954):

> Today, education is perhaps the most important function of state and local governments. Compulsory school attendance laws and the great expenditures for education both demonstrate our recognition of the importance of education to our democratic society. It is required in the performance of our most basic public responsibilities, even service in the armed forces. It is the very foundation of good citizenship. Today it is a principal instrument in awakening the child to cultural values, in preparing him for later professional training, and in helping him to adjust normally to his environment. In these days, it is doubtful that any child may reasonably be expected to succeed in life if he is denied the opportunity of an education.

If children grow up unable to read or write, or lack the knowledge necessary for successful employment; military service; informed voting; following public safety signs while driving; etc., their lack of education may have serious negative impacts on others in the community. Therefore the People, as represented by their common government, have a legitimate interest in assuring that all children have an opportunity for education. But how far can the state go in mandating what and where children will learn?

Around the turn of the century and through the early 1900s the U.S. experienced massive immigration through New York's now famous Ellis Island. Many American citizens can trace their family roots to this wave of immigration in the shadow of the Statue of Liberty where a bronze tablet on the Statue's pedestal wall is engraved with the phrase:

> *Give me your tired, your poor,*
> *Your huddled masses yearning to breathe free,*
> *The wretched refuse of your teeming shore.*
> *Send these, the homeless, tempest-tost to me,*
> *I lift my lamp beside the golden door!*

Not everyone was so welcoming to these new immigrants, however. In contrast to earlier patterns of U.S. immigration, many of these turn of the century immigrants were not from Protestant, English-speaking, or Western European Nations. Instead, millions were Catholics, Jews, and others from Southern and Eastern Europe. Some American citizens viewed these new immigrants with suspicion and contempt, fearing that their different beliefs and customs could change and harm the America they knew. A leading member of the Ku Klux Klan declared "somehow these mongrel hordes must be Americanized; failing that, deportation is the only remedy." Some saw public schools as the ideal vehicle for this "Americanization" and they advocated and passed laws requiring all children to attend only public schools, prohibiting private or home school instruction of children. A state statute requiring public school only attendance was challenged in *Pierce v. Society of the Sisters*.

Pierce v. Society of the Sisters
268 U.S. 510 (1925)
Supreme Court of the United States

Mr. Justice McREYNOLDS delivered the opinion of the Court.

The challenged act, effective September 1, 1926, requires every parent, guardian, or other person having control or charge or custody of a child between 8 and 16 years to send him "to a public school for the period of time a public school shall be held during the current year" in the district where the child resides; and failure so to do is declared a misdemeanor . . . the Society's bill alleges that the enactment conflicts with the right of parents to choose schools where their children will receive appropriate mental and religious training . . .

No question is raised concerning the power of the state reasonably to regulate all schools, to inspect, supervise and examine them, their teachers and pupils; to require that all children of proper age attend some school, that teachers shall be of good moral character and patriotic disposition, that certain studies plainly essential to good citizenship must be taught, and that nothing be taught which is manifestly inimical to the public welfare . . .

We think it entirely plain that the [challenged act] unreasonably interferes with the liberty of parents and guardians to direct the upbringing and education of children under their control. As often heretofore pointed out, rights guaranteed by the Constitution may not be abridged by legislation which has no reasonable relation to some purpose within the competency of the state.

The fundamental theory of liberty upon which all governments in this Union repose excludes any general power of the state to standardize its children by forcing them to accept instruction from public teachers only. The child is not the mere creature of the state; those who nurture him and direct his destiny have the right, coupled with the high duty, to recognize and prepare him for additional obligations.

The decrees below are affirmed.

* * * * * * *

Comments and Questions

In *Pierce* the Court ruled that while the State may require the provision of educational opportunity to children, whether children receive this educational opportunity in a public, private, or home school is a decision that belongs to parents and not the State. The State may reasonably regulate education and schools to assure adequacy and safety, but the State may not prohibit private and home school education.

All 50 U.S. states have compulsory school attendance laws making it the duty of parents to assure that children between the designated ages attend school. Parents may satisfy this requirement by having their children attend public, private, or home school programs of study.

States apply differing levels of regulations to private and home schools, ranging from virtually no active regulation to much more detailed requirements concerning teacher qualifications, minimum curriculum requirements, periodic attendance reports, and requirements for periodic standardized testing of children. Failure to comply with attendance requirements may be subject to criminal prosecution including fines or incarceration.

What are the laws governing private and home schools in your state? Do these laws go far enough in assuring that all children are provided with adequate opportunities for learning? Do these laws go too far in intruding on family privacy and the rights of parents to make decisions about the education of their own children?

Viral infections such as small pox, polio, measles, etc., have had devastating impacts on children, killing millions and causing serious injury and life-long impairments to others. The invention of relatively low-cost and effective vaccinations saved the lives of countless children. The common government has a significant interest in protecting public health generally and a compelling interest in protecting children from preventable life-threatening conditions. Schools are places where large numbers of children come in close contact, so schools have proven to be high-risk locations for the transmission of communicable diseases. To protect public health state and local officials require proof of necessary vaccinations prior to school admission.

Exceptions to these otherwise valid vaccination requirements may be allowed or required, however, if vaccination requirements conflict with sincerely held religious beliefs protected under the U.S. Constitution, state constitution, or state law. Parents do not have to prove that their religious beliefs are "true" or even that their religious beliefs are orthodox within their chosen faith. What is generally required to be entitled to an exemption from vaccination requirements is that the belief must be: 1) Religious in nature; and 2) Sincerely held by the parents and/or child.

The law attempts to justly balance the essential rights of individuals with the legitimate safety needs of the majority. In the case of vaccinations to protect public health, if the vast majority of students are already protected through their own vaccinations, the health risk is limited to those few unvaccinated children. Under these circumstances courts have generally been supportive of parents with sincerely held religious objections to vaccinations, finding that the right to free exercise of religion outweighed state interests in health where only small numbers of unvaccinated religious objectors remained unprotected and the overall health risk was low.

That is not to say, however, that the state may never override parental objections to medical treatment. Under the *parens patriae* doctrine the State may intervene on an emergency basis and administer medical treatment when it is necessary to preserve a child's life, even over the religious objections of parents. If a child is likely to die without a shot of penicillin, for example, the state is likely to administer the required medical treatment on an emergency basis. But what if medical treatment is generally needed by the child but there is no emergency? What if the parents refuse treatment but the child wants the treatment? In these cases and in others where the interests of the state, parents, and the child are in conflict, what is the appropriate balance between state authority, parental authority, and the child's rights and freedom of conscience?

Children's Freedom of Conscience and the Limits of State Authority

In ancient Sparta the child was the property of the State. Newborns were inspected by state officials at birth. If the newborn was found physically unfit the infant was taken away to die. Children deemed physically acceptable were removed from their mothers at age 7 and placed in the custody of the State for rigorous military-style training. Young women who survived the rigorous training and passed the final tests of fitness were granted citizenship, assigned a husband, and allowed to return home. Young men who survived this rigorous training and were found fit for service in the military were required to fight for Sparta until age 60 when they could retire and return home. Persons who were physically acceptable but unable to pass the rigorous tests for full citizenship where left to the conduct of trades, farming, commerce and the other necessary work of the State.

Under the Roman legal doctrine of *patria potestas* (paternal powers) the father had absolute ownership and power over the child. Until the father died or freed the child (through voluntary emancipation of sons or marriage of daughters) the father owned everything the child acquired and even held the power of capital punishment over the child.

Under circumstances of such brutal domination by either the state or the parent, the child's free will was given no serious consideration. In time, however, the doctrine of *patria potestas* was weakened under Roman Law, and state ownership of the child gave way to the protective doctrine of *parens patriae* (parent of the nation) with the state protecting children even from their own parents when necessary.

The modern view of children's rights and freedom of conscience is that at birth every child is vested with full human rights, including freedom of conscience, religion, speech, etc. But these rights are more symbolic than functional for very young children, as infants are totally dependent on their parents (or the state when necessary) for care and guidance. Infants and very young children do not have any knowledge of the infinite personal choices they will face in the future concerning religion, politics, justice, morality, etc. Their ability to understand these issues will grow as they mature and their individual personalities and perspectives emerge. As the child matures the child will exercise increasing personal autonomy and freedom of conscience.

The modern view of children's rights is far superior to the abject subjugation of the child under the laws of some ancient nations. In the United Nations Convention on the Rights of the Child (1990), the general statements on children's freedom of conscience declared:

> States Parties shall assure to the child who is capable of forming his or her own views the right to express those views freely in all matters affecting the child, the views of the child being given due weight in accordance with the age and maturity of the child . . . States Parties shall respect the right of the child to freedom of thought, conscience and religion . . . Freedom to manifest one's religion or beliefs may be subject only to such limitations as are prescribed by law and are necessary to protect public safety, order, health or morals, or the fundamental rights and freedoms of others.

But who determines when the child is "capable of forming his or her own views"? Exactly what degree of control over children's freedom of conscience do parents or the state retain?

In November 1935 the Gobitis family decided that for reasons of sincerely held religious belief they could no longer participate in saluting and pledging allegiance to the U.S. flag in school. When others learned of their decision the children were subjected to taunts and attacks by students and faculty, including a teacher grabbing the arm of one child and attempting to physically force the child to salute the flag. Because of their continued refusal to salute the flag the children were expelled from school. The Gobitis family challenged the expulsions in federal court. The trial court and the Third Circuit Court of Appeals ruled in favor of the Gobitis family.

But the decision in favor of the Gobitis family was reversed by the U.S. Supreme Court in *Minersville School District v. Gobitis*, 310 U.S. 586 (1940):

Mr. Justice FRANKFURTER delivered the opinion of the Court.

A grave responsibility confronts this Court whenever in course of litigation it must reconcile the conflicting claims of liberty and authority . . . Lillian Gobitis, aged twelve, and her brother William, aged ten, were expelled from the public schools of Minersville, Pennsylvania, for refusing to salute the national flag as part of a daily school exercise . . . .The Gobitis family are affiliated with "Jehovah's Witnesses", for whom the Bible as the Word of God is the supreme authority. The children had been brought up conscientiously to believe that such a gesture of respect for the flag was forbidden by command of scripture . . . The religious liberty which the Constitution protects has never excluded legislation of general scope not directed against doctrinal loyalties of particular sects . . . The mere possession of religious convictions which contradict the relevant concerns of a political society does not relieve the citizen from the discharge of political responsibilities . . . the question remains whether school children, like the Gobitis children, must be excused from conduct required of all the other children in the promotion of national cohesion. We are dealing with an interest inferior to none in the hierarchy of legal values. National unity is the basis of national security . . . The ultimate foundation of a free society is the binding tie of cohesive sentiment . . . We live by symbols. The flag is the symbol of our national unity, transcending all internal differences, however large, within the framework of the Constitution. This Court has had occasion to say that the flag is the symbol of the nation's power--the emblem of freedom in its truest, best sense. It signifies government resting on the consent of the governed; liberty regulated by law; the protection of the weak against the strong; security against the exercise of arbitrary power; and absolute safety for free institutions against foreign aggression . . . Reversed.

Mr. Justice STONE, dissenting:

I think the judgment below should be affirmed. Two youths, now fifteen and sixteen years of age, are by the judgment of this Court held liable to expulsion from the public schools and to denial of all publicly supported educational privileges because of their refusal to yield to the compulsion of a law which commands their participation in a school ceremony contrary to their religious convictions. They and their father are citizens and have not exhibited by any action or statement of opinion, any disloyalty to the Government of the United States. They are ready and willing to obey all its laws which do not conflict with what they sincerely believe to be the higher commandments of God . . . even if we believe that such compulsions will contribute to national unity, there are other ways to teach loyalty and patriotism which are the sources of national unity, than by compelling the pupil to affirm that which he does not believe and by commanding a form of affirmance which violates his religious convictions . . . The very essence of . . . liberty . . . is the freedom of the individual from compulsion as to what he shall think and what he shall say, at least where the compulsion is to bear false witness to his religion. If these guaranties are to have any meaning they must, I think, be deemed to withhold from the state any authority to compel belief or the expression of it where that expression violates religious convictions, whatever may be the legislative view of the desirability of such compulsion. History teaches us that there have been but few infringements of personal liberty by the state which have not been justified, as they are here, in the name of righteousness and the public good, and few which have not been directed, as they are now, at politically helpless minorities . . . This seems to me no more than the surrender of the constitutional protection of the liberty of small minorities to the popular will . . . The Constitution expresses more than the conviction of the people that democratic processes must be preserved at all costs. It is also an expression of faith and a command that freedom of mind and spirit must be preserved, which government must obey, if it is to adhere to that justice and moderation without which no free government can exist . . .

The Court issued its 8-1 opinion against the Jehovah's Witnesses on June 3, 1940. On June 9, 1940 an angry mob set fire to the Jehovah's Witnesses Kingdom Temple in Kennebunk, Maine. In the wake of the Court's decision in *Gobitis* persecutions of Jehovah's Witnesses intensified nation-wide. Jehovah's Witnesses were arrested, imprisoned, fined, beaten, tortured, and terrorized. In justifying running Jehovah's witnesses out of town a local Sheriff was reported to say: "They're traitors. The Supreme Court says so." In "The Persecution of Jehovah's Witnesses" (1941), the American Civil Liberties Union documented these attacks including affidavits from victims:

```
From an affidavit by Albert Stroebel of Flagstaff, Arizona dated June
26, 1940:

On Wednesday evening June 19th, 1940 my dad and I drove to Ash Fork
from Williams to contact two fellow workers at a friend's house. I
drove up in front of the house and went up on the porch when three men
stepped into the yard up on the porch and said, "Are you looking for
anyone?"-and then, "will you salute the flag?" and when I replied that
I respected the flag but was consecrated to do God's will and did not
salute or attribute salvation to the flag they cried, "Nazi spy!"
knocked me down, beat me badly, and finally knocked me out-then dragged
and pushed me across the street to a service station and again tried to
make me salute the flag. I was dizzy, befuddled and don't clearly
remember anything further except that a considerable crowd had gathered
yelling "Nazi spy!-Heil Hitler!-String him up!-Chop his head off!"
```

The 1940 ACLU report concluded:

Documents filed with the Department of Justice by attorneys for Jehovah's Witnesses and the American Civil Liberties Union showed over three hundred thirty-five instances of mob violence in forty-four states during 1940, involving one thousand four hundred eighty-eight men, women, and children. The cause of this extraordinary outbreak was the "patriotic" fear aroused by the success of the Nazi armies in Europe and the panic which seized the country at the imagined invasion of the United States.

In 1943 the U.S. Supreme Court had an opportunity to reconsider its *Gobitis* decision in the *Barnette* case:

West Virginia State Board of Education v. Barnette
319 U.S. 624 (1943)
Supreme Court of the United States

Mr. Justice JACKSON delivered the opinion of the Court.

Following the decision by this Court on June 3, 1940, in *Minersville School District v. Gobitis*, 310 U.S. 586, the West Virginia legislature amended its statutes to require all schools therein to conduct courses of instruction in history, civics, and in the Constitutions of the United States and of the State "for the purpose of teaching, fostering and perpetuating the ideals, principles and spirit of Americanism, and increasing the knowledge of the organization and machinery of the government." Appellant Board of Education was directed, with advice of the State Superintendent of Schools, to "prescribe the courses of study covering these subjects" for public schools. The Act made it the duty of private, parochial and denominational schools to prescribe courses of study "similar to those required for the public schools."

The Board of Education on January 9, 1942, adopted a resolution containing recitals taken largely from the Court's *Gobitis* opinion and ordering that the salute to the flag become "a regular part of the program of activities in the public schools," that all teachers and pupils "shall be required to participate in the salute honoring the Nation represented by the Flag; provided, however, that refusal to salute the Flag be regarded as an Act of insubordination, and shall be dealt with accordingly."

The resolution originally required the "commonly accepted salute to the Flag" which it defined. Objections to the salute as "being too much like Hitler's" were raised by the Parent and Teachers Association, the Boy and Girl Scouts, the Red Cross, and the Federation of Women's Clubs. Some modification appears to have been made in deference to these objections, but no concession was made to Jehovah's Witnesses. What is now required is the "stiff-arm" salute, the saluter to keep the right hand raised with palm turned up while the following is repeated: "I pledge allegiance to the Flag of the United States of America and to the Republic for which it stands; one Nation, indivisible, with liberty and justice for all."

Failure to conform is "insubordination" dealt with by expulsion. Readmission is denied by statute until compliance. Meanwhile the expelled child is "unlawfully absent" and may be proceeded against as a delinquent. His parents or guardians are liable to prosecution, and if convicted are subject to fine not exceeding $50 and jail term not exceeding thirty days.

Appellees, citizens of the United States and of West Virginia, brought suit in the United States District Court for themselves and others similarly situated asking its injunction to restrain enforcement of these laws and regulations against Jehovah's Witnesses. The Witnesses are an unincorporated body teaching that the obligation imposed by law of God is superior to that of laws enacted by temporal government. Their religious beliefs include a literal version of Exodus, Chapter 20, verses 4 and 5, which says: "Thou shalt not make unto thee any graven image, or any likeness of anything that is in heaven above, or that is in the earth beneath, or that is in the water under the earth; thou shalt not bow down thyself to them nor serve them." They consider that the flag is an "image" within this command. For this reason they refuse to salute it.

Children of this faith have been expelled from school and are threatened with exclusion for no other cause. Officials threaten to send them to reformatories maintained for criminally inclined juveniles. Parents of such children have been prosecuted and are threatened with prosecutions for causing delinquency.

The Board of Education moved to dismiss the complaint setting forth these facts and alleging that the law and regulations are an unconstitutional denial of religious freedom, and of freedom of speech, and are invalid under the "due process" and "equal protection" clauses of the Fourteenth Amendment to the Federal Constitution. The cause was submitted on the pleadings to a District Court of three judges. It restrained enforcement as to the plaintiffs and those of that class. The Board of Education brought the case here by direct appeal.

This case calls upon us to reconsider a precedent decision, as the Court throughout its history often has been required to do. Before turning to the *Gobitis* case, however, it is desirable to notice certain characteristics by which this controversy is distinguished. The freedom asserted by these appellees does not bring them into collision with rights asserted by any other individual. It is such conflicts which most frequently require intervention of the State to determine where the rights of one end and those of another begin. But the refusal of these persons to participate in the ceremony does not interfere with or deny rights of others to do so. Nor is there any question in this case that their behavior is peaceable and orderly. The sole conflict is between authority and rights of the individual. The State asserts power to condition access to public education on making a prescribed sign and profession and at the same time to coerce attendance by punishing both parent and child. The latter stand on a right of self-determination in matters that touch individual opinion and personal attitude.

As the present Chief Justice said in dissent in the *Gobitis* case, the State may "require teaching by instruction and study of all in our history and in the structure and organization of our government, including the guaranties of civil liberty which tend to inspire patriotism and love of country." Here, however, we are dealing with a compulsion of students to declare a belief. They are not merely made acquainted with the flag salute so that they may be informed as to what it is or even what it means. The issue here is whether this slow and easily neglected route to aroused loyalties constitutionally may be short-cut by substituting a compulsory salute and slogan . . .

There is no doubt that, in connection with the pledges, the flag salute is a form of utterance. Symbolism is a primitive but effective way of communicating ideas. The use of an emblem or flag to symbolize some system, idea, institution, or personality, is a short cut from mind to mind. Causes and nations, political parties, lodges and ecclesiastical groups seek to knit the loyalty of their followers to a flag or banner, a color or design. The State announces rank, function, and authority through crowns and maces, uniforms and black robes; the church speaks through the Cross, the Crucifix, the altar and shrine, and clerical regiment. Symbols of State often convey political ideas just as religious symbols come to convey theological ones. Associated with many of these symbols are appropriate gestures of acceptance or respect: a salute, a bowed or bared head, a bended knee. A person gets from a symbol the meaning he puts into it, and what is one man's comfort and inspiration is another's jest and scorn . . .

The *Gobitis* decision, however, assumed, as did the argument in that case and in this, that power exists in the State to impose the flag salute discipline upon school children in general . . . The Fourteenth Amendment, as now applied to the States, protects the citizen against the State itself and all of its creatures--Boards of Education not excepted. These have, of course, important, delicate, and highly discretionary functions, but none that they may not perform within the limits of the Bill of Rights. That they are educating the young for citizenship is reason for scrupulous protection of Constitutional freedoms of the individual, if we are not to strangle the free mind at its source and teach youth to discount important principles of our government as mere platitudes . . .

The very purpose of a Bill of Rights was to withdraw certain subjects from the vicissitudes of political controversy, to place them beyond the reach of majorities and officials and to establish them as legal principles to be applied by the courts. One's right to life, liberty, and property, to free speech, a free press, freedom of worship and assembly, and other fundamental rights may not be submitted to vote; they depend on the outcome of no elections . . .

Lastly, and this is the very heart of the *Gobitis* opinion, it reasons that "National unity is the basis of national security," that the authorities have "the right to select appropriate means for its attainment," and hence reaches the conclusion that such compulsory measures toward "national unity" are constitutional. Upon the verity of this assumption depends our answer in this case.

National unity as an end which officials may foster by persuasion and example is not in question. The problem is whether under our Constitution compulsion as here employed is a permissible means for its achievement. Struggles to coerce uniformity of sentiment in support of some end thought essential to their time and country have been waged by many good as well as by evil men. Nationalism is a relatively recent phenomenon but at other times and places the ends have been racial or territorial security, support of a dynasty or regime, and particular plans for saving souls. As first and moderate methods to attain unity have failed, those bent on its accomplishment must resort to an ever-increasing severity. As governmental pressure toward unity becomes greater, so strife becomes more bitter as to whose unity it shall be.

Probably no deeper division of our people could proceed from any provocation than from finding it necessary to choose what doctrine and whose program public educational officials shall compel youth to unite in embracing. Ultimate futility of such attempts to compel coherence is the lesson of every such effort from the Roman drive to stamp out Christianity as a disturber of its pagan unity, the Inquisition, as a means to religious and dynastic unity, the Siberian exiles as a means to Russian unity, down to the fast failing efforts of our present totalitarian enemies. Those who begin coercive elimination of dissent soon find themselves exterminating dissenters. Compulsory unification of opinion achieves only the unanimity of the graveyard.

It seems trite but necessary to say that the First Amendment to our Constitution was designed to avoid these ends by avoiding these beginnings. There is no mysticism in the American concept of the State or of the nature or origin of its authority. We set up government by consent of the governed, and the Bill of Rights denies those in power any legal opportunity to coerce that consent. Authority here is to be controlled by public opinion, not public opinion by authority.

The case is made difficult not because the principles of its decision are obscure but because the flag involved is our own. Nevertheless, we apply the limitations of the Constitution with no fear that freedom to be intellectually and spiritually diverse or even contrary will disintegrate the social organization. To believe that patriotism will not flourish if patriotic ceremonies are voluntary and spontaneous instead of a compulsory routine is to make an unflattering estimate of the appeal of our institutions to free minds. We can have intellectual individualism and the rich cultural diversities that we owe to exceptional minds only at the price of occasional eccentricity and abnormal attitudes. When they are so harmless to others or to the State as those we deal with here, the price is not too great. But freedom to differ is not limited to things that do not matter much. That would be a mere shadow of freedom. The test of its substance is the right to differ as to things that touch the heart of the existing order.

If there is any fixed star in our constitutional constellation, it is that no official, high or petty, can prescribe what shall be orthodox in politics, nationalism, religion, or other matters of opinion or force citizens to confess by word or act their faith therein. If there are any circumstances which permit an exception, they do not now occur to us.

We think the action of the local authorities in compelling the flag salute and pledge transcends constitutional limitations on their power and invades the sphere of intellect and spirit which it is the purpose of the First Amendment to our Constitution to reserve from all official control. The decision of this Court in *Minersville School District v. Gobitis* and the holdings of those few *per curiam* decisions which preceded and foreshadowed it are overruled, and the judgment enjoining enforcement of the West Virginia Regulation is affirmed.

Affirmed.

* * * * * * *

Comments and Questions

The *Gobitis* decision was an 8-1 decision against Jehovah's Witnesses plaintiffs in 1940. But in 1943, just three years after the *Gobitis* decision, the Court expressly overruled this case with a 6-3 decision in favor of Jehovah's Witnesses plaintiffs in *Barnette*. What could explain such a dramatic shift by the Court in just three years?

Between 1940 and 1943 the Court lost Justices Hughes and McReynolds, and added two new Justices, Justices Jackson and Rutledge, both of whom voted in favor of the plaintiffs in *Barnette*. But that change alone would still result in a 6-3 decision against the plaintiffs, unless a number of sitting Justices changed their minds in just three years.

Justices Black, Douglas, and Murphy voted against the plaintiffs in *Gobitis*, but for the plaintiffs three years later, forming the new 6-3 majority in favor of Jehovah's Witnesses plaintiffs in *Barnette*. Justices make their decisions carefully, and take their decisions seriously. So what could have caused such a dramatic change of mind in just three years?

It can be speculated that the dual specters of nation-wide bigotry and violence against a religious minority in the wake of the Court's *Gobitis* decision, and forced patriotism and persecution of a religious minority in Hitler's Germany, caused grave concern among many Americans regarding the wisdom and justice of forced patriotism.

It is said that "the road to Hell is paved with good intentions." No doubt most advocates of mandatory pledge acts had good intentions. But good intentions do not guarantee good or just results. Did the Court's decision in *Gobitis* in fact trigger the 1940 wave of violence against Jehovah's Witnesses as some suggest? Did Hitler's forced patriotism cause members of the Court to reject any forced patriotism under the U.S. Constitution?

In the *Barnette* opinion the Court devoted considerable attention to the form of salute required of children. Children were required to raise their arms in a manner many saw as disturbingly similar to the Nazi salute. The Court noted that objections to the salute as "being too much like Hitler's" were made by the "Parent and Teachers Association, the Boy and Girl Scouts, the Red Cross, and the Federation of Women's Clubs." A note in the *Barnette* case documented a defense against these charges:

> The National Headquarters of the United States Flag Association takes the position that the extension of the right arm in this salute to the flag is not the Nazi-Fascist salute, "although quite similar to it. In the Pledge to the Flag the right arm is extended and raised, palm Upward, whereas the Nazis extend the arm practically straight to the front

(the finger tips being about even with the eyes), palm Downward, and the Fascists do the same except they raise the arm slightly higher."

Is this a sufficient distinction? Or is it a distinction without any real difference? Does this distinction adequately address the concerns by the Parent and Teachers Association, the Boy and Girl Scouts, the Red Cross, and the Federation of Women's Clubs? Would you be comfortable with this salute, or comfortable having your children required to engage in this salute?

Notice the text of the pledge required in *Barnette* (1943): "I pledge allegiance to the Flag of the United States of America and to the Republic for which it stands; one Nation, indivisible, with liberty and justice for all." The original version of this pledge did not include the phrase "under God." The phrase "under God" was added by the U.S. Congress in 1954 in part to distinguish the U.S. from the atheism of its Communist Cold War adversaries.

In 2002, in *Newdow v. United States Congress*, 292 F.3d 597 (9th Cir. 2002), the U.S. Court of Appeals for the Ninth Circuit held that Congress's insertion of the words "under God" in the Pledge of Allegiance violated the First Amendment's Establishment Clause. The U.S. Supreme Court granted *certiorari*, and in *Elk Grove Unified School District* v. *Newdow*, 542 U.S. 1 (2004), the Court held that Newdow lacked standing because he was not the custodial parent of his public school student daughter, an unusual move that some suggested was motivated by the Court's desire to avoid any substantive decision in this case in an election year.

But in a 2005 district court decision in *Newdow v. Congress of the United States,* 383 F. Supp.2d 1229 (Cal. 2005), a court essentially reinstated the Ninth Circuit decision. In a note following the decision, the judge declared:

> This court would be less than candid if it did not acknowledge that it is relieved that, by virtue of the disposition above, it need not attempt to apply the Supreme Court's recently articulated distinction between those governmental activities which endorse religion, and are thus prohibited, and those which acknowledge the Nation's asserted religious heritage, and thus are permitted. As last terms cases, *McCreary County v. ACLU*, 125 S. Ct. 2722 (2005) and *Van Orden v. Perry*, 125 S. Ct. 2854 (2005) demonstrate, the distinction is utterly standardless, and ultimate resolution depends of the shifting, subjective sensibilities of any five members of the High Court, leaving those of us who work in the vineyard without guidance. Moreover, because the doctrine is inherently a boundary-less slippery slope, any conclusion might pass muster. It might be remembered that it was only a little more than one hundred years ago that the Supreme Court of this nation declared without hesitation, after reviewing the history of religion in this country, that "this is a Christian nation." *Church of the Holy Trinity v. United States*, 143 U.S. 457 (1892). As preposterous as it might seem, given the lack of boundaries, a case could be made for substituting "under Christ" for "under God" in the pledge, thus marginalizing not only atheists and agnostics, as the present form of the Pledge does, but also Jews, Muslims, Buddhists, Confucians, Sikhs, Hindus, and other religious adherents who, not only are citizens of this nation, but in fact reside in this judicial district.

A section from Rev. Dr. Newdow's legal complaint in the pledge case describes his religious motivation for this case as follows:

Plaintiff is a minister, having been ordained more than twenty years ago. His ministry espouses the religious philosophy that the true and eternal bonds of righteousness and virtue stem from reason rather than mythology. It recognizes that it is never possible to prove that something does not exist, but finds that fact to be an absurd justification to accept the unproved. The bizarre, the incredible and the miraculous deserve not blind faith, but rigorous challenge. To plaintiff and his religious brethren, belief in a deity represents the repudiation of rational thought processes, and offends all precepts of science and natural law. Our religion incorporates the same values of goodness, hope, advancement of civilization and elevation of the human spirit common to most others. We, however, feel that all these virtues must ultimately be based on truth, and that they are only hindered by reliance upon a falsehood, which we believe any God to be.

Flag burning is also a highly controversial issue, and Congress periodically attempts to amend the U.S. Constitution to prohibit flag burning. A 2005 proposed amendment stated: "The Congress shall have power to prohibit the physical desecration of the flag of the United States." The proposal passed in the House but did not have the necessary support in the Senate. Any amendment to the U.S. Constitution requires passage by two-thirds of both houses of Congress and subsequent ratification by three-fourths of the states.

Although it is highly offensive to many, flag burning is recognized as within the bounds of free speech protected by the First Amendment. In *Texas v. Johnson*, 491 U.S. 397 (1989) the U.S. Supreme Court ruled 5-4 that flag burning constituted protected political speech under the First Amendment, invalidating state flag desecration statutes. Mr. Johnson had burned a U.S. flag in front of the Dallas City Hall to protest U.S. policies. He was arrested, convicted, and sentenced to a year in jail and a $2,000 fine. In overturning the Texas statute as a violation of the First Amendment, the U.S. Supreme Court stated: "If there is a bedrock principle underlying the First Amendment, it is that Government may not prevent the expression of an idea simply because society finds the idea itself offensive." Is the Court correct?

Chapter Summary

This chapter reviewed the lawful balance of children's rights, parents' rights, and State authority. After reading this chapter, please consider the following points in review and for further thought and discussion:

I. *Review Points*:

1) Children have a right to protection, education, and other necessary provisions for their healthy development into adulthood.

2) As the child develops toward maturity the child increasingly possesses the full scope of rights and responsibilities belonging to mature adults.

3) Parents have the first right and responsibility to care for the child. But under the doctrine of *parens patriae* if parents fail in their responsibilities to the child, the State may assume these duties consistent with the best interests of the child.

4) Child Protective Services agencies act under the dual (and sometimes conflicting) goals of:

    a) Pursuing the best interests of the child; and
    b) Preserving the family.

5) Parental rights are protected under the U.S. and state constitutions. To involuntarily terminate parental rights the State must prove:

    a) Clear and convincing evidence that the parent is unfit; and
    b) That termination is in the best interests of the child.

6) When parents place the child in school they temporarily delegate some of their parental authority to educators. Educators act *in loco parentis*. Educators have a responsibility to supervise and protect the children in their care as a reasonable parent would. And children have a duty to follow the lawful orders of educators while under their authority.

7) Child Protective Services agents must carefully balance between doing too little or too much in their efforts to protect children. They must neither fail to adequately protect the child, nor over-step their legal authority and intrude on family privacy and parental rights.

8) The Court's ruling in *DeShaney* left little protection in federal courts when a child is abused by a private citizen and not an agent of the state. Courts appear to be more willing to hold state officials accountable for protecting children when state officials knew or should have known they were putting children in serious danger, and the state had supervisory responsibility over the perpetrator (*i.e.*, a state approved foster parent, etc.).

9) If there is clear and convincing evidence that children are in immediate danger state officials have the authority to remove children from their parents on an emergency basis. This is an

extraordinary power that should only be used under emergency circumstances and state officials must comply with state statutes and due process of law.

10) All 50 U.S. states have statutes mandating reports to state officials of suspected abuse or neglect of children.

11) Until age 18 children are generally subject to juvenile laws which provide greater protections for children, but also allow for greater restrictions on children.

12) School officials can question students concerning civil matters including potential violations of school codes of conduct. But special care is required in questioning a child about criminal matters. In *In re Gault* the U.S. Supreme Court declared "the condition of being a [child] does not justify a kangaroo court . . . the constitutional privilege against self-incrimination is applicable in the case of juveniles as it is with respect to adults. We appreciate that special problems may arise with respect to waiver of the privilege by or on behalf of children, and that there may well be some differences in technique--but not in principle--depending upon the age of the child and the presence and competence of parents . . . the greatest care must be taken to assure that the admission was voluntary, in the sense not only that it was not coerced or suggested, but also that it was not the product of ignorance of rights or of adolescent fantasy, fright or despair." In all proceedings potentially impinging on their life, liberty, or property, children must be given fair hearings and adequate due process of law.

13) Child custody is divided into:

   a) Physical custody: Right to make daily and emergency decisions; and
   b) Legal custody: Right to participate in longer-term decisions.

14) Educational records are generally confidential. Parents or eligible students have a right to view the record, request amendments, and grant permission to other parties to access the record. School officials may access the records for legitimate institutional purposes.

15) When their children are subject to mandatory school attendance laws, parents have a legal duty to assure school attendance. Parents may satisfy this duty through public, private, or home school attendance by the child.

16) In *West Virginia v. Barnette* the U.S. Supreme Court declared: "If there is any fixed star in our constitutional constellation, it is that no official, high or petty, can prescribe what shall be orthodox in politics, nationalism, religion, or other matters of opinion or force citizens to confess by word or act their faith therein." Children can be asked to participate in school pledges to the flag, and punished for willful disruption or other violations of legitimate codes of student conduct, but they cannot be coerced or punished for declining to participate by word or act (*i.e.*, not standing or saluting). Respectful refusal to participate in public professions of creed is a constitutionally protected right in a free society.

II. *Principles to Practice Tips*:

1) *Protecting Children*: Learn to recognize the signs of child abuse and neglect, and teach your colleagues and other adults to recognize clear signs that children may need help. In most cases of abuse and neglect physical or behavioral signs are present and discernable to a trained observer. Nonetheless, sometimes a bruise is just a bruise; and sometimes unusual behavior is just unusual behavior. If, however, there is a pattern of signs of abuse or neglect, or any serious sign that cannot be reasonably dismissed as benign under the circumstances, a prompt report and appropriate professional intervention are warranted to protect the child.

2) *Protecting the Family*: Willful and intentional abuse or neglect of children must be dealt with appropriately, including removal of the child from the home and filing criminal charges when warranted. Do not, however, assume that all child neglect is willful. Sometimes otherwise loving parents are overwhelmed by financial, health, or other problems and are in need of services themselves. With appropriate assistance and support the parent may be able to improve child care standards to healthy levels for the child. If it is possible to safely allow the child to remain with a parent who loves the child and is capable of providing appropriate care with appropriate assistance, preserving the child's family is a priority both legally and ethically.

3) *Protecting Yourself*: Failure to report suspected child abuse and neglect is a crime in all 50 states. If you must report suspected abuse, also appropriately document your report including the facts and circumstances you reported; who you reported to; the date of your report; and any other relevant information. Most administrators will promptly and responsibly forward and follow up on your report. But be warned: Someone who is unethical enough not to forward your report to the proper authorities is likely also unethical enough to claim that you never made the report if threatened with criminal charges for failing to forward your report. Documentation of your report protects you from any future false claim that you failed to report. Keep your documentation confidential and in a safe location. Also, be very cautious about getting overly involved in any domestic disputes between warring parents, etc. These disputes can be highly emotional, volatile, and even dangerous. An appropriate professional distance is called for, functionally and emotionally. And if there are any threats or other serious signs of danger notify law enforcement authorities to protect yourself and others.

III. *Questions for Discussion*: Please consider these questions and be prepared to discuss:

1) *International Children's Rights*: Only two nations declined to ratify the United Nations Convention on the Rights of the Child (1990), Somalia and the United States. Should the U.S. ratify the United Nations Convention on the Rights of the Child? Why or why not? What is the current status of children's rights in the U.S. and in other nations? Do children have adequate protections for safety and access to clean water, air, and a toxin free environment; food; shelter; clothing; medical care; education; and a chance for a healthy, happy, and productive future? What can be done to improve children's chances for a healthy, happy, and productive future?

2) *Home School and Alternative Education*: Millions of children receive a high quality, highly individualized education through home school studies, and go on to subsequent success in college, work, etc. For some children, however, home schooling is little more than legalized

truancy. State laws governing home schooling range from what some consider far too intrusive on family privacy to what others consider far too lax in protecting children's rights to education. What laws govern your state's home school programs? Are these laws appropriate, too intrusive, or too permissive? Private and home school parents pay school taxes also. Should private and home school students be allowed to participate in public school academic and extra-curricular programs? Why or why not? Public schools were born in the Industrial Age and are based on a factory model with both its strengths and weaknesses. What modifications or alternatives to this increasingly antiquated factory model hold the greatest promise for the future?

3) *Group Solidarity and Individual Free Will*: Children have a right to decline participation in flag salutes and pledges, and they are not required to provide school officials with any explanation for their decision. Further, it would be inappropriate and possibly unlawful for school officials to question a student's religious beliefs related to these activities. If the student volunteered, however, that the refusal to participate was based on political or philosophical objections only, these are lawful topics of discussion with students. Would you want to attempt to persuade the student to participate? What would you say? Is our tolerance for dissent and diversity of belief a national strength or weakness?

4) *Open Forum*: What other related issues or current events would you like to discuss?

IV: *Suggested Activities*:

1) Read the United Nations Convention on the Rights of the Child (available online). Talk with educators or others with international experiences to compare and contrast the realities of children's rights in different nations.

2) Invite a Juvenile Court Judge to visit your class. What are the greatest challenges the Judge faces in helping children? How can educators and the court work together more effectively to help children?

3) Read your state's statute mandating reports of suspected child abuse and neglect. What constitutes child abuse or neglect under your state's laws? Who is required to report? Who do you report to? What are the potential consequences for failing to report? Discuss the application of this statute in protecting children in your school.

4) Although children are commonly asked to say the Pledge, few educators have explained to them what the Pledge means and why it is important. Prepare a lesson explaining the meaning and history of the U.S. Pledge of Allegiance and present it to your students or an interested local civics group.

Chapter 3: First Amendment Freedoms and Religion

First Amendment Freedoms

Freedom of belief and expression are fundamental human rights. Humans are unique in their abilities to think abstract thoughts, formulate complex systems of belief, and communicate these ideals through speech, writing, and other means of expressive communication. To deny these rights of belief and expression to individuals is to deny their rights to be fully human.

Nonetheless, human history is in substantial part a long and tragic tale of powerful individuals, organizations, and governments attempting to deny freedom of belief and expression to those whose ideas might challenge the existing religious or political status quo. Defenders of the status quo have discouraged new beliefs and the communication of new ideas because they knew that ideas can change individuals, and when an idea becomes widely accepted, ideas can change the world.

> ### *New Ideas Change People; and People with New Ideas Change the World*

When the U.S. Declaration of Independence declared "all men are created equal, that they are endowed by their Creator with certain unalienable Rights . . . to secure these rights, Governments are instituted among men, deriving their just powers from the consent of the governed" and "whenever any Form of Government becomes destructive of these ends, it is the Right of the People to alter or to abolish it" those were ideas with the power to change the world. King George and his government had good reason to fear these powerful ideas, but they were ultimately powerless to stop them. Individuals are vulnerable to coercion, imprisonment, or death, but no one can kill an idea. And the more powerful the idea, the harder it is to silence.

> ### *"You Can Kill the Dreamer, But You Can't Kill the Dream."*
> ### *Dr. Martin Luther King, Jr.*

The ideas that came from the pen in Thomas Jefferson's hand were far more dangerous to the King's rule than any sword, and the ideas that Dr. King communicated through his moving and powerful speeches changed the world. Ideals of human equality under the law, unalienable human rights, and government as a servant and not as a master rapidly changed the world views of millions, and ultimately billions of people. These ideas transformed the world in a process of global democratization that still continues.

American Founders understood the human harm and stagnation that resulted from a government that punished free will in thought and the free expression of belief. They knew that the printing press was the remedy for the Dark Ages; free speech was the essential protector of all other freedoms; and a free market-place of ideas was the best guarantee of future prosperity, security, and a better life for all. So they sought to free both the human mind and the human tongue, and let individual people, rather than powerful and self-interested officials, decide which ideas they wished to speak, hear, and accept as their own. They enshrined these principles into the U.S. Constitution, including broad protections for individual rights of belief and expression in the First Amendment. The First Amendment to the *U.S. Constitution* declared:

> Congress shall make no law respecting an establishment of religion, or prohibiting the free exercise thereof; or abridging the freedom of speech, or of the press; or the right of the people peaceably to assemble, and to petition the Government for a redress of grievances.

The First Amendment is not merely a random collection of rights the Founders believed were important, but instead presents a systematic hierarchy of associated rights necessary to the protection of liberty. At the very core of these associated rights is the right to believe whatever the individual chooses to believe, free from governmental coercion or compulsion of belief through official establishment of religion. Under the Establishment Clause, government is prohibited from establishing any preferred religion and using the power of government to coerce adults and indoctrinate children into believing only the officially approved beliefs.

The individual right to believe is the only right that is absolute: Each individual can freely choose to believe anything he or she chooses to believe. Pure belief is protected absolutely. The reason pure belief can be protected absolutely, however, is because one's internal beliefs do not infringe on the rights and safety of others.

> **Individual Freedom of Belief is Protected Absolutely. All other Individual Rights must be balanced against their Impact on the Rights of Others**

Free Exercise of religion is highly protected by the First Amendment. Government should not have the power to wall off free will only within the limits of the mind and prohibit individuals from expressing their beliefs and living their lives in the ways that they believe are mandated by their beliefs. But while free exercise of religion is highly protected, government officials also have a duty to protect the rights and safety of others.

Free Exercise rights are broad indeed, but they reach their limits when government has a compelling interest in protecting the rights and safety of others from real harms presented by the exercise of religious beliefs. For example, a belief in worshipping in a particular manner is generally protected as free exercise of religion. But if the exercise of that belief involves, for example, human sacrifice, government can act to prohibit religious exercise (but not pure belief) where there is a compelling interest in protecting public safety and the rights of others.

Freedom of Speech is very broadly and rigorously protected. But because speech can impact the rights and safety of others, protection for individual free speech cannot be absolute. As Justice Holmes said in *Schenck v. United States*, 249 U.S. 47 (1919): "The most stringent protection of free speech would not protect a man falsely shouting fire in a theater and causing a panic."

The rights of one individual must yield when there is clear and significant harm to the rights of others. Freedom of the Press is protected under the First Amendment. But because of the broader dissemination of the Press, and now broadcast and other mass electronic media, government has a wider interest in assuring that these mass communications respect appropriate boundaries established to reasonably protect legitimate public interests. Individual consenting adults, for example, have a constitutional right to engage in indecent speech (*i.e.*, pornography) as free speech if they choose to, and this speech can be communicated through printed and electronic media. They do not, however, have a right to broadcast indecent speech to the general public including persons who do not choose to engage in this speech, and communication of indecent speech to children is lawfully prohibited.

The Rights of Assembly and Petitioning for a Redress of Grievances are also important and protected rights under the First Amendment. But government officials have significant interests in assuring that mass public assemblies do not unreasonably block traffic, create public dangers, etc., and that public assemblies are safe and orderly with grievances expressed in a reasonable time, place, and manner.

The most vigorous constitutional protections are given to those rights closest to the core of individual free will belief. All First Amendment rights are protected. But the further the right is from the core of individual belief, and the more the individual right potentially impacts the rights and safety of others, the greater government's legitimate need to set reasonable limits on the time, place, and manner of the exercise of that right.

The Core Right of Belief and other Associated 1rst Amendment Rights

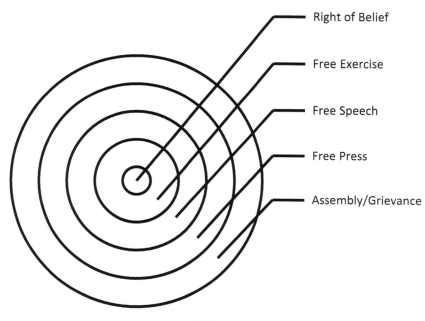

© Dayton

Individual freedom of belief is at the core of the First Amendment and the core of human liberty. But it is the official establishment of religion that has historically posed the greatest danger to both the individual right to believe and the common peace. By definition, religious faith is rooted in individual belief and free will concerning that belief. As James Madison, the author of the First Amendment recognized, efforts to use the force of government to coerce and compel beliefs have caused great pains to individuals throughout human history, and served as the basis of countless conflicts and wars.

In recognition of these concerns, the First Amendment's "Establishment Clause" prohibits government officials from establishing any favored or disfavored religion. The "Free Exercise Clause" mandates that government officials must respect individual free exercise of religion and provide reasonable accommodations for that individual free exercise of religion when necessary.

The First Amendment's religion clauses have been broadly interpreted as requiring official governmental neutrality concerning religion, and establishing a reasonable "wall of separation" between church and state. This symbolic "wall of separation" between church and state has been attributed to Thomas Jefferson, based on a letter he sent to the Danbury Baptist Association in 1802:

Gentlemen:

The affectionate sentiments of esteem and approbation which you are so good as to express towards me, on behalf of the Danbury Baptist association, give me the highest satisfaction. My duties dictate a faithful and zealous pursuit of the interests of my constituents, & in proportion as they are persuaded of my fidelity to those duties, the discharge of them becomes more and more pleasing.

Believing with you that religion is a matter which lies solely between Man & his God, that he owes account to none other for his faith or his worship, that the legitimate powers of government reach actions only, & not opinions, I contemplate with sovereign reverence that act of the whole American people which declared that their legislature should "make no law respecting an establishment of religion, or prohibiting the free exercise thereof," thus building a wall of separation between Church & State. Adhering to this expression of the supreme will of the nation in behalf of the rights of conscience, I shall see with sincere satisfaction the progress of those sentiments which tend to restore to man all his natural rights, convinced he has no natural right in opposition to his social duties.

I reciprocate your kind prayers for the protection & blessing of the common Father and Creator of man, and tender you for yourselves & your religious association, assurances of my high respect & esteem.

Thomas Jefferson (Jan. 1, 1802)

This wall of separation between church and state is not, however, an absolute wall of separation. Religion plays a central role in many peoples' lives, and it has been a driving force throughout much of human history. Religion cannot be banned from the public square without also banning the free expression of people who hold religious beliefs. On the other hand, history shows that few issues are more divisive than whose religion will be officially recognized and favored in the public square.

The purpose of the symbolic wall of separation between church and state is to set appropriate boundaries between private religion and public governmental power. This protects religion from governmental interference. And protects the common government from the disruption and divisiveness of conflict over whose religion should receive official endorsement and have the power to compel others to express belief or face governmental punishment.

First Amendment Wall of Separation between Church and State

© Dayton

The height and strength of the wall of separation increases or diminishes in each case depending on the degree of danger presented by the co-mingling of church and state. For example, the Court has rejected challenges to the use of the phrase "In God We Trust" on coins and "so help me God" in the Presidential oath of office. The passive, benign use of these phrases by government seems to present little real danger that anyone's religious freedom is jeopardized. Therefore the wall of separation is low enough, and flexible enough, to allow for the continued lawful use of these religious terms by government. At the other end of the continuum, however, public school sponsored prayer has been repeatedly rejected by the Court as a genuine danger to individual religious freedom and the essential maintenance of religious neutrality by the common government.

The wall of separation between church and state is at its highest in public schools where highly impressionable children are subject to compulsory attendance laws enforced by criminal sanctions. The Court has recognized that captive audiences of highly impressionable children are vulnerable to state sponsored religious indoctrination. Further, few issues are more potentially divisive and disruptive than battles over whether the political majority should have the authority to compel their religious beliefs and practices on other people's children through compulsory school attendance.

Establishment Clause Limitations on Public Schools

In the wake of World War II there was a growing fear in the U.S. that the ideals of Communism could spread throughout the world. To guard against this perceived danger, many believed it was essential to bolster the foundations of Western Democracy and culture in children through patriotic pledges and prayers. To some, prayer was an essential part of character and citizenship education for children and necessary to distinguish Western Democracy from "Godless Communism."

As a nation of immigrants, many of whom fled from religious oppression in Europe and other places, the U.S. is extremely religiously diverse with thousands of variations of faiths. Most Americans share common democratic values and a desire that children learn good character and

71

citizenship. And most Americans also hold strong personal religious beliefs and family traditions. But if children are to pray together in the common public school, whose prayer would they pray?

What common public school prayer could possibly be as religiously diverse as the people that would be asked to pray this prayer? What prayer could capture the faiths of the many denominations of Protestants, Catholics, Jews, Muslims, Hindus, Native Americans, etc., and yet not be religiously objectionable to any of these faiths? And if you attempted to religiously water-down the common prayer so that it was offensive to no one, wouldn't it become potentially offensive to all religious believers as a compromised, insincere governmental desecration of their genuine religious faith? Who would have the power to decide what the children would pray? Should government officials be involved in composing prayers for other people's children? These were among the issues brought to the Court in *Engel v. Vitale*.

Engel v. Vitale
370 U.S. 421 (1962)
Supreme Court of the United States

Mr. Justice BLACK delivered the opinion of the Court.

The respondent Board of Education . . . acting in its official capacity under state law, directed the School District's principal to cause the following prayer to be said aloud by each class in the presence of a teacher at the beginning of each school day: "Almighty God, we acknowledge our dependence upon Thee, and we beg Thy blessings upon us, our parents, our teachers and our Country." This daily procedure was adopted on the recommendation of the State Board of Regents, a governmental agency created by the State Constitution to which the New York Legislature has granted broad supervisory, executive, and legislative powers over the State's public school system. These state officials composed the prayer which they recommended and published as a part of their 'Statement on Moral and Spiritual Training in the Schools,' saying: "We believe that this Statement will be subscribed to by all men and women of good will, and we call upon all of them to aid in giving life to our program."

Shortly after the practice of reciting the Regents' prayer was adopted by the School District, the parents of ten pupils brought this action in a New York State Court insisting that use of this official prayer in the public schools was contrary to the beliefs, religions, or religious practices of both themselves and their children. Among other things, these parents challenged the constitutionality of both the state law authorizing the School District to direct the use of prayer in public schools and the School District's regulation ordering the recitation of this particular prayer on the ground that these actions of official governmental agencies violate that part of the First Amendment of the Federal Constitution which commands that "Congress shall make no law respecting an establishment of religion" a command which was "made applicable to the State of New York by the Fourteenth Amendment of the said Constitution."

We think that by using its public school system to encourage recitation of the Regents' prayer, the State of New York has adopted a practice wholly inconsistent with the Establishment Clause . . . The petitioners contend among other things that the state laws requiring or permitting use of the Regents' prayer must be struck down as a violation of the Establishment Clause because that prayer was composed by governmental officials as a part of a governmental program to further religious beliefs. For this reason, petitioners argue, the State's use of the Regents' prayer in its public school system breaches the constitutional wall of separation between Church and State. We agree with that contention since we think that the constitutional prohibition against laws respecting an establishment of religion must at least mean that in this country it is no part of the business of government to compose official prayers for any group of the American people to recite as a part of a religious program carried on by government.

It is a matter of history that this very practice of establishing governmentally composed prayers for religious services was one of the reasons which caused many of our early colonists to leave England and seek religious freedom in America. The Book of Common Prayer, which was created under governmental direction and which was approved by Acts of Parliament in 1548 and 1549, set out in minute detail the accepted form and content of prayer and other religious ceremonies to be used in the established, tax-supported Church of England. The controversies over the Book and what should be its content repeatedly threatened to disrupt the peace of that country as the accepted forms of prayer in the established church changed with the views of the particular ruler that happened to be in control at the time. Powerful groups representing some of the varying religious views of the people struggled among themselves to impress their particular views upon the Government and obtain amendments of the Book more suitable to their respective notions of how religious services should be conducted in order that the official religious establishment would advance their particular religious beliefs. Other groups, lacking the necessary political power to influence the Government on the matter, decided to leave England and its established church and seek freedom in America from England's governmentally ordained and supported religion.

It is an unfortunate fact of history that when some of the very groups which had most strenuously opposed the established Church of England found themselves sufficiently in control of colonial governments in this country to write their own prayers into law, they passed laws making their own religion the official religion of their respective colonies. Indeed, as late as the time of the Revolutionary War, there were established churches in at least eight of the thirteen former colonies and established religions in at least four of the other five. But the successful Revolution against English political domination was shortly followed by intense opposition to the practice of establishing religion by law. This opposition crystallized rapidly into an effective political force in Virginia where the minority religious groups such as Presbyterians, Lutherans, Quakers and Baptists had gained such strength that the adherents to the established Episcopal Church were actually a minority themselves. In 1785-1786, those opposed to the established Church, led by James Madison and Thomas Jefferson, who, though themselves not members of any of these dissenting religious groups, opposed all religious establishments by law on grounds of principle, obtained the enactment of the famous "Virginia Bill for Religious Liberty" by which all religious groups were placed on an equal footing so far as the State was concerned.

By the time of the adoption of the Constitution, our history shows that there was a widespread awareness among many Americans of the dangers of a union of Church and State. These people knew, some of them from bitter personal experience, that one of the greatest dangers to the freedom of the individual to worship in his own way lay in the Government's placing its official stamp of approval upon one particular kind of prayer or one particular form of religious services. They knew the anguish, hardship and bitter strife that could come when zealous religious groups struggled with one another to obtain the Government's stamp of approval from each King, Queen, or Protector that came to temporary power. The Constitution was intended to avert a part of this danger by leaving the government of this country in the hands of the people rather than in the hands of any monarch. But this safeguard was not enough. Our Founders were no more willing to let the content of their prayers and their privilege of praying whenever they pleased be influenced by the ballot box than they were to let these vital matters of personal conscience depend upon the succession of monarchs. The First Amendment was added to the Constitution to stand as a guarantee that neither the power nor the prestige of the Federal Government would be used to control, support or influence the kinds of prayer the American people can say--that the people's religions must not be subjected to the pressures of government for change each time a new political administration is elected to office. Under that Amendment's prohibition against governmental establishment of religion, as reinforced by the provisions of the Fourteenth Amendment, government in this country, be it state or federal, is without power to prescribe by law any particular form of prayer which is to be used as an official prayer in carrying on any program of governmentally sponsored religious activity.

When the power, prestige and financial support of government is placed behind a particular religious belief, the indirect coercive pressure upon religious minorities to conform to the prevailing officially approved religion is plain. But the purposes underlying the Establishment Clause go much further than that. Its first and most immediate purpose rested on the belief that a union of government and religion tends to destroy government and to degrade religion. The history of governmentally established religion, both in England and in this country, showed that whenever government had allied itself with one particular form of religion, the inevitable result had been that it had incurred the hatred, disrespect and even contempt of those who held contrary beliefs. That same history showed that many people had lost their respect for any religion that had relied upon the support for government to spread its faith. The Establishment Clause thus stands as an expression of principle on the part of the Founders of our Constitution that religion is too personal, too sacred, too holy, to permit its "unhallowed perversion" by a civil magistrate. Another purpose of the Establishment Clause rested upon an awareness of the historical fact that governmentally established religions and religious persecutions go hand in hand. The Founders knew that only a few years after the Book of Common Prayer became the only accepted form of religious services in the established Church of England, an Act of Uniformity was passed to compel all Englishmen to attend those services and to make it a criminal offense to conduct or attend religious gatherings of any other kind--a law which was consistently flouted by dissenting religious groups in England and which contributed to widespread persecutions of people like John Bunyan who persisted in holding "unlawful (religious) meetings to the great disturbance and distraction of the good subjects of this kingdom." And they knew that similar persecutions had received the sanction of law in several of the colonies in this country soon after the establishment of official religions in those colonies. It was in large part to get completely away from this sort of systematic religious persecution that the Founders brought into being our Nation, our Constitution, and our Bill of Rights with its prohibition against any governmental establishment of religion. The New York laws officially prescribing the Regents' prayer are inconsistent both with the purposes of the Establishment Clause and with the Establishment Clause itself.

It has been argued that to apply the Constitution in such a way as to prohibit state laws respecting an establishment of religious services in public schools is to indicate a hostility toward religion or toward prayer. Nothing, or course, could be more wrong. The history of man is inseparable from the history of religion. And perhaps it is not too much to say that since the beginning of that history many people have devoutly believed that "More things are wrought by prayer than this world dreams of." It was doubtless largely due to men who believed this that there grew up a sentiment that caused men to leave the cross-currents of officially established state religions and religious persecution in Europe and come to this country filled with the hope that they could find a place in which they could pray when they pleased to the God of their faith in the language they chose. And there were men of this same faith in the power of prayer who led the fight for adoption of our Constitution and also for our Bill of Rights with the very guarantees of religious freedom that forbid the sort of governmental activity which New York has attempted here. These men knew that the First Amendment, which tried to put an end to governmental control of religion and of prayer, was not written to destroy either. They knew rather that it was written to quiet well-justified fears which nearly all of them felt arising out of an awareness that governments of the past had shackled men's tongues to make them speak only the religious thoughts that government wanted them to speak and to pray only to the God that government wanted them to pray to. It is neither sacrilegious nor antireligious to say that each separate government in this country should stay out of the business of writing or sanctioning official prayers and leave that purely religious function to the people themselves and to those the people choose to look to for religious guidance . . .

To those who may subscribe to the view that because the Regents' official prayer is so brief and general there can be no danger to religious freedom in its governmental establishment, however, it may be appropriate to say in the words of James Madison, the author of the First Amendment:

> It is proper to take alarm at the first experiment on our liberties. Who does not see that the same authority which can establish Christianity, in exclusion of all other Religions, may establish with the same ease any particular sect of Christians, in exclusion of all other Sects? That the same authority which can force a citizen to contribute three pence only of his property for the support of any one establishment, may force him to conform to any other establishment in all cases whatsoever?

The judgment of the Court of Appeals of New York is reversed and the cause remanded for further proceedings not inconsistent with this opinion.

* * * * * * *

The Court's decision in *Engel v. Vitale* was vigorously opposed by many elected officials and public polling suggested majority support for school prayer. Nonetheless, proposed constitutional amendments overturning the Court's decision in *Engel* failed in the U.S. Congress. In *Engel* the Court held that the Establishment Clause prohibited state officials from composing prayers and requiring students to recite these prayers. The functional separation of church and state was intended to preserve the common government's religious neutrality; the independence of the church; and individual free-will in the exercise of religion, with the Court recognizing "a union of government and religion tends to destroy government and degrade religion."

But were these Establishment Clause concerns sufficiently reduced if government officials were not composing prayers as in *Engel*, but instead simply requiring readings from the Bible? In 1963 the Court addressed this issue in two consolidated cases, *School District of Abington Township v. Schempp* and *Murray v. Curlett*. The plaintiff in the latter case was Madalyn Murray, a professed atheist, a fact that tended to further inflame political supporters of government sponsored school prayer. Nonetheless, the Court again struck down state efforts to conduct religious exercises in public schools, reaffirming its reasoning in *Engel v. Vitale*.

School District of Abington Township v. Schempp
Murray v. Curlett
374 U.S. 203 (1963)
Supreme Court of the United States

Mr. Justice CLARK delivered the opinion of the Court.

Once again we are called upon to consider the scope of the provision of the First Amendment to the United States Constitution which declares that "Congress shall make no law respecting an establishment of religion, or prohibiting the free exercise thereof." These companion cases present the issues in the context of state action requiring that schools begin each day with readings from the Bible. While raising the basic questions under slightly different factual situations, the cases permit of joint treatment. In light of the history of the First Amendment and of our cases interpreting and applying its requirements, we hold that the practices at issue and the laws requiring them are unconstitutional under the Establishment Clause, as applied to the States through the Fourteenth Amendment.

The Facts in Each Case: The Commonwealth of Pennsylvania . . . requires that "At least ten verses from the Holy Bible shall be read, without comment, at the opening of each public school on each school day. Any child shall be excused from such Bible reading, or attending such Bible reading, upon the written request of his parent or guardian." The Schempp family . . . brought suit to enjoin enforcement of the statute, contending that their rights under the Fourteenth Amendment to the Constitution of the United States are, have been, and will continue to be violated unless this statute be declared unconstitutional as violative of these provisions of the First Amendment. They sought to enjoin the appellant school district, wherein the Schempp children attend school, and its officers and the Superintendent of Public Instruction of the Commonwealth from continuing to conduct such readings and recitation of the Lord's Prayer in the public schools of the district pursuant to the statute . . . The appellees . . . are of the Unitarian faith and are members of the Unitarian Church . . .

On each school day at the Abington Senior High School between 8:15 and 8:30 a.m., while the pupils are attending their home rooms or advisory sections, opening exercises are conducted pursuant to the statute. The exercises are broadcast into each room in the school building through an intercommunications system and are conducted under the supervision of a teacher by students attending the school's radio and television workshop. Selected students from this course gather each morning in the school's workshop studio for the exercises, which include readings by one of the students of 10 verses of the Holy Bible, broadcast to each room in the building. This is followed by the recitation of the Lord's Prayer, likewise over the intercommunications system, but also by the students in the various classrooms, who are asked to stand and join in repeating the prayer in unison. The exercises are closed with the flag salute and such pertinent announcements as are of interest to the students. Participation in the opening exercises, as directed by the statute, is voluntary. The student reading the verses from the Bible may select the passages and read from any version he chooses, although the only copies furnished by the school are the King James version, copies of which were circulated to each teacher by the school district. During the period in which the exercises have been conducted the King James, the Douay and the Revised Standard versions of the Bible have been used, as well as the Jewish Holy Scriptures. There are no prefatory statements, no questions asked or solicited, no comments or explanations made and no interpretations given at or during the exercises. The students and parents are advised that the student may absent himself from the classroom or, should he elect to remain, not participate in the exercises . . .

Edward Schempp, the children's father, testified that after careful consideration he had decided that he should not have Roger or Donna excused from attendance at these morning ceremonies. Among his reasons were the following. He said that he thought his children would be "labeled as 'odd balls'" before their teachers and classmates every school day; that children, like Roger's and Donna's classmates, were liable "to lump all particular religious difference(s) or religious objections (together) as 'atheism'" and that today the word "atheism" is often connected with "atheistic communism", and has "very bad" connotations, such as "un-American" . . . with overtones of possible immorality. Mr. Schempp pointed out that due to the events of the morning exercises following in rapid succession, the Bible reading, the Lord's Prayer, the Flag Salute, and the announcements, excusing his children from the Bible reading would mean that probably they would miss hearing the announcements so important to children. He testified also that if Roger and Donna were excused from Bible reading they would have to stand in the hall outside their "homeroom" and that this carried with it the imputation of punishment for bad conduct.

Expert testimony was introduced by both appellants and appellees at the first trial, which testimony was summarized by the trial court as follows: Dr. Solomon Grayzel testified that there were marked differences between the Jewish Holy Scriptures and the Christian Holy Bible, the most obvious of which was the absence of the New Testament in the Jewish Holy Scriptures. Dr. Grayzel testified that portions of the New Testament were offensive to Jewish tradition and that, from the standpoint of Jewish faith, the concept of Jesus Christ as the Son of God was "practically blasphemous." He cited instances in the New Testament which, assertedly, were not only sectarian in nature but tended to bring the Jews into ridicule or scorn. Dr. Grayzel gave as his expert opinion that such material from the New Testament could be explained to Jewish children in such a way as to do no harm to them. But if portions of the New Testament were read without explanation, they could be, and in his specific experience with children Dr. Grayzel observed, had been, psychologically harmful to the child and had caused a divisive force within the social media of the school. Dr. Grayzel also testified that there was significant difference in attitude with regard to the respective Books of the Jewish and Christian Religions in that Judaism attaches no special significance to the reading of the Bible per se and that the Jewish Holy Scriptures are source materials to be studied. But Dr. Grayzel did state that many portions of the New, as well as of the Old, Testament contained passages of great literary and moral value.

Dr. Luther A. Weigle, an expert witness for the defense, testified in some detail as to the reasons for and the methods employed in developing the King James and the Revised Standard Versions of the Bible. On direct examination, Dr. Weigle stated that the Bible was non-sectarian. He later stated that the phrase "non-sectarian" meant to him non-sectarian within the Christian faiths. Dr. Weigle stated that his definition of the Holy Bible would include the Jewish Holy Scriptures, but also stated that the "Holy Bible" would not be complete without the New Testament. He stated that the New Testament "conveyed the message of Christians." In his opinion, reading of the Holy Scriptures to the exclusion of the New Testament would be a sectarian practice. Dr. Weigle stated that the Bible was of great moral, historical and literary value. This is conceded by all the parties and is also the view of the court . . .

The trial court, in striking down the practices and the statute requiring them, made specific findings of fact that the children's attendance at Abington Senior High School is compulsory and that the practice of reading 10 verses from the Bible is also compelled by law. It also found that:

> The reading of the verses, even without comment, possesses a devotional and religious character and constitutes in effect a religious observance. The devotional and religious nature of the morning exercises is made all the more apparent by the fact that the Bible reading is followed immediately by a recital in unison by the pupils of the Lord's Prayer. The fact that some pupils, or theoretically all pupils, might be excused from attendance at the exercises does not mitigate the obligatory nature of the ceremony for [state law] unequivocally requires the exercises to be held every school day in every school in the Commonwealth. The exercises are held in the school buildings and perforce are conducted by and under the authority of the local school authorities and during school sessions. Since the statute requires the reading of the "Holy Bible" a Christian document, the practice prefers the Christian religion. The record demonstrates that it was the intention of the Commonwealth to introduce a religious ceremony into the public schools of the Commonwealth . . .

[In *Murray v. Curlett*] [state law] provided for the holding of opening exercises in the schools of the city, consisting primarily of the "reading, without comment, of a chapter in the Holy Bible and/or the use of the Lord's Prayer." The petitioners, Mrs. Madalyn Murray and her son, William J. Murray III, are both professed atheists. Following unsuccessful attempts to have the respondent school board rescind the rule, this suit was filed . . . It was alleged that William was a student in a public school of the city and Mrs. Murray, his mother, was a taxpayer therein; that it was the practice under the rule to have a reading on each school morning from the King James version of the Bible; that at petitioners' insistence the rule was amended to permit children to be excused from the exercise on request of the parent and that William had been excused pursuant thereto; that nevertheless the rule as amended was in violation of the petitioners' rights "to freedom of religion under the First and Fourteenth Amendments" and in violation of "the principle of separation between church and state, contained therein." The petition particularized the petitioners' atheistic beliefs and stated that the rule, as practiced, violated their rights . . .

It is true that religion has been closely identified with our history and government. As we said in *Engel v. Vitale* . . . "The history of man is inseparable from the history of religion" . . . In *Zorach v. Clauson*, 343 U.S. 306 (1952), we gave specific recognition to the proposition that "we are a religious people whose institutions presuppose a Supreme Being." The fact that the Founding Fathers believed devotedly that there was a God and that the unalienable rights of man were rooted in Him is clearly evidenced in their writings, from the Mayflower Compact to the Constitution itself. This background is evidenced today in our public life through the continuance in our oaths of office from the Presidency to the Alderman of the final supplication, "So help me God." Likewise each House of the Congress provides through its Chaplain an opening prayer, and the sessions of this Court are declared open by the crier in a short ceremony, the final phrase of which invokes the grace of God. Again, there are such manifestations in our military forces, where those of our citizens who are under the restrictions of military service wish to engage in voluntary worship . . . It can be truly said, therefore, that today, as in the beginning, our national life reflects a religious people who, in the words of Madison, are "earnestly praying, as in duty bound, that the Supreme Lawgiver of the Universe guide them into every measure which may be worthy of his (blessing)."

This is not to say, however, that religion has been so identified with our history and government that religious freedom is not likewise as strongly imbedded in our public and private life. Nothing but the most telling of personal experiences in religious persecution suffered by our forebears . . . could have planted our belief in liberty of religious opinion any more deeply in our heritage. It is true that this liberty frequently was not realized by the colonists, but this is readily accountable by their close ties to the Mother Country. However, the views of Madison and Jefferson . . . came to be incorporated not only in the Federal Constitution but likewise in those of most of our States. This freedom to worship was indispensable in a country whose people came from the four quarters of the earth and brought with them a diversity of religious opinion . . .

The conclusion follows that in both cases the laws require religious exercises and such exercises are being conducted in direct violation of the rights of the appellees and petitioners. Nor are these required exercises mitigated by the fact that individual students may absent themselves upon parental request, for that fact furnishes no defense to a claim of unconstitutionality under the Establishment Clause. Further, it is no defense to urge that the religious practices here may be relatively minor encroachments on the First Amendment. The breach of neutrality that is today a trickling stream may all too soon become a raging torrent and, in the words of Madison, "it is proper to take alarm at the first experiment on our liberties . . ."

It is insisted that unless these religious exercises are permitted a "religion of secularism" is established in the schools. We agree of course that the State may not establish a "religion of secularism" in the sense of affirmatively opposing or showing hostility to religion, thus "preferring those who believe in no religion over those who do believe." We do not agree, however, that this decision in any sense has that effect. In addition, it might well be said that one's education is not complete without a study of comparative religion or the history of religion and its relationship to the advancement of civilization. It certainly may be said that the Bible is worthy of study for its literary and historic qualities. Nothing we have said here indicates that such study of the Bible or of religion, when presented objectively as part of a secular program of education, may not be affected consistently with the First Amendment. But the exercises here do not fall into those categories. They are religious exercises, required by the States in violation of the command of the First Amendment that the Government maintain strict neutrality, neither aiding nor opposing religion.

Finally, we cannot accept that the concept of neutrality, which does not permit a State to require a religious exercise even with the consent of the majority of those affected, collides with the majority's right to free exercise of religion. While the Free Exercise Clause clearly prohibits the use of state action to deny the rights of free exercise to anyone, it has never meant that a majority could use the machinery of the State to practice its beliefs. Such a contention was effectively answered by Mr. Justice Jackson for the Court in *West Virginia Board of Education v. Barnette*, 319 U.S. 624 (1943):

> The very purpose of a Bill of Rights was to withdraw certain subjects from the vicissitudes of political controversy, to place them beyond the reach of majorities and officials and to establish them as legal principles to be applied by the courts. One's right to freedom of worship and other fundamental rights may not be submitted to vote; they depend on the outcome of no elections.

The place of religion in our society is an exalted one, achieved through a long tradition of reliance on the home, the church and the inviolable citadel of the individual heart and mind. We have come to recognize through bitter experience that it is not within the power of government to invade that citadel, whether its purpose or effect be to aid or oppose, to advance or retard. In the relationship between man and religion, the State is firmly committed to a position of neutrality. Though the application of that rule requires interpretation of a delicate sort, the rule itself is clearly and concisely stated in the words of the First Amendment.

It is so ordered.

* * * * * * *

In *Engel v. Vitale* and *Abbington v. Schempp* the Court firmly declared state policies requesting students to pray state composed prayers or read passages from the Bible to be violations of the Establishment Clause. But what if the prayers were offered by a religiously diverse, rotating selection of clergymen from the community, and only offered at non-compulsory graduation ceremonies? Further, what if the clergymen were given state approved guidelines for the prayers they were to offer, intended to assure that the prayers were non-sectarian and appropriate for civic occasions? Would these changes in policy and practice be sufficient to survive a challenge under the Establishment Clause?

Lee v. Weisman
505 U.S. 577 (1992)
Supreme Court of the United States

Justice KENNEDY delivered the opinion of the Court.

School principals in the public school system of the city of Providence, Rhode Island, are permitted to invite members of the clergy to offer invocation and benediction prayers as part of the formal graduation ceremonies for middle schools and for high schools. The question before us is whether including clerical members who offer prayers as part of the official school graduation ceremony is consistent with the Religion Clauses of the First Amendment, provisions the Fourteenth Amendment makes applicable with full force to the States and their school districts.

Deborah Weisman graduated from Nathan Bishop Middle School, a public school in Providence, at a formal ceremony in June 1989. She was about 14 years old. For many years it has been the policy of the Providence School Committee and the Superintendent of Schools to permit principals to invite members of the clergy to give invocations and benedictions at middle school and high school graduations. Many, but not all, of the principals elected to include prayers as part of the graduation ceremonies. Acting for himself and his daughter, Deborah's father, Daniel Weisman, objected to any prayers at Deborah's middle school graduation, but to no avail. The school principal, petitioner Robert E. Lee, invited a rabbi to deliver prayers at the graduation exercises for Deborah's class. Rabbi Leslie Gutterman, of the Temple Beth El in Providence, accepted.

It has been the custom of Providence school officials to provide invited clergy with a pamphlet entitled "Guidelines for Civic Occasions," prepared by the National Conference of Christians and Jews. The Guidelines recommend that public prayers at nonsectarian civic ceremonies be composed with "inclusiveness and sensitivity," though they acknowledge that "prayer of any kind may be inappropriate on some civic occasions." The principal gave Rabbi Gutterman the pamphlet before the graduation and advised him the invocation and benediction should be nonsectarian. Rabbi Gutterman's prayers were as follows:

INVOCATION: God of the Free, Hope of the Brave: For the legacy of America where diversity is celebrated and the rights of minorities are protected, we thank You. May these young men and women grow up to enrich it. For the liberty of America, we thank You. May these new graduates grow up to guard it. For the political process of America in which all its citizens may participate, for its court system where all may seek justice we thank You. May those we honor this morning always turn to it in trust. For the destiny of America we thank You. May the graduates of Nathan Bishop Middle School so live that they might help to share it. May our aspirations for our country and for these young people, who are our hope for the future, be richly fulfilled. Amen.

BENEDICTION: O God, we are grateful to You for having endowed us with the capacity for learning which we have celebrated on this joyous commencement. Happy families give thanks for seeing their children achieve an important milestone. Send Your blessings upon the teachers and administrators who helped prepare them. The graduates now need strength and guidance for the future, help them to understand that we are not complete with academic knowledge alone. We must each strive to fulfill what You require of us all: To do justly, to love mercy, to walk humbly. We give thanks to You, Lord, for keeping us alive, sustaining us and allowing us to reach this special, happy occasion. Amen.

The parties stipulate that attendance at graduation ceremonies is voluntary. The graduating students enter as a group in a processional, subject to the direction of teachers and school officials, and sit together, apart from their families . . . the students stood for the Pledge of Allegiance and remained standing during the rabbi's prayers . . .

The District Court held that petitioners' practice of including invocations and benedictions in public school graduations violated the Establishment Clause of the First Amendment, and it enjoined petitioners from continuing the practice . . . On appeal, the United States Court of Appeals for the First Circuit affirmed . . . We granted certiorari, and now affirm.

These dominant facts mark and control the confines of our decision: State officials direct the performance of a formal religious exercise at promotional and graduation ceremonies for secondary schools. Even for those students who object to the religious exercise, their attendance and participation in the state-sponsored religious activity are in a fair and real sense obligatory, though the school district does not require attendance as a condition for receipt of the diploma . . . The government involvement with religious activity in this case is pervasive, to the point of creating a state-sponsored and state-directed religious exercise in a public school. Conducting this formal religious observance conflicts with settled rules pertaining to prayer exercises for students, and that suffices to determine the question before us.

The principle that government may accommodate the free exercise of religion does not supersede the fundamental limitations imposed by the Establishment Clause. It is beyond dispute that, at a minimum, the Constitution guarantees that government may not coerce anyone to support or participate in religion or its exercise, or otherwise act in a way which "establishes a [state] religion or religious faith, or tends to do so." The State's involvement in the school prayers challenged today violates these central principles.

That involvement is as troubling as it is undenied. A school official, the principal, decided that an invocation and a benediction should be given; this is a choice attributable to the State, and from a constitutional perspective it is as if a state statute decreed that the prayers must occur. The principal chose the religious participant, here a rabbi, and that choice is also attributable to the State. The reason for the choice of a rabbi is not disclosed by the record, but the potential for divisiveness over the choice of a particular member of the clergy to conduct the ceremony is apparent.

Divisiveness, of course, can attend any state decision respecting religions, and neither its existence nor its potential necessarily invalidates the State's attempts to accommodate religion in all cases. The potential for divisiveness is of particular relevance here though, because it centers around an overt religious exercise in a secondary school environment where . . . subtle coercive pressures exist and where the student had no real alternative which would have allowed her to avoid the fact or appearance of participation.

The State's role did not end with the decision to include a prayer and with the choice of a clergyman. Principal Lee provided Rabbi Gutterman with a copy of the "Guidelines for Civic Occasions," and advised him that his prayers should be nonsectarian. Through these means the principal directed and controlled the content of the prayers. Even if the only sanction for ignoring the instructions were that the rabbi would not be invited back, we think no religious representative who valued his or her continued reputation and effectiveness in the community would incur the State's displeasure in this regard. It is a cornerstone principle of our Establishment Clause jurisprudence that "it is no part of the business of government to compose official prayers for any group of the American people to recite as a part of a religious program carried on by government," *Engel v. Vitale*, 370 U.S. 421 (1962), and that is what the school officials attempted to do . . .

The First Amendment's Religion Clauses mean that religious beliefs and religious expression are too precious to be either proscribed or prescribed by the State. The design of the Constitution is that preservation and transmission of religious beliefs and worship is a responsibility and a choice committed to the private sphere, which itself is promised freedom to pursue that mission. It must not be forgotten then, that while concern must be given to define the protection granted to an objector or a dissenting nonbeliever, these same Clauses exist to protect religion from government interference. James Madison, the principal author of the Bill of Rights, did not rest his opposition to a religious establishment on the sole ground of its effect on the minority. A principal ground for his view was: "Experience witnesseth that ecclesiastical establishments, instead of maintaining the purity and efficacy of Religion, have had a contrary operation" . . .

The degree of school involvement here made it clear that the graduation prayers bore the imprint of the State and thus put school-age children who objected in an untenable position . . . The lessons of the First Amendment are as urgent in the modern world as in the 18th century when it was written. One timeless lesson is that if citizens are subjected to state-sponsored religious exercises, the State disavows its own duty to guard and respect that sphere of inviolable conscience and belief which is the mark of a free people. To compromise that principle today would be to deny our own tradition and forfeit our standing to urge others to secure the protections of that tradition for themselves.

As we have observed before, there are heightened concerns with protecting freedom of conscience from subtle coercive pressure in the elementary and secondary public schools . . . What to most believers may seem nothing more than a reasonable request that the nonbeliever respect their religious practices, in a school context may appear to the nonbeliever or dissenter to be an attempt to employ the machinery of the State to enforce a religious orthodoxy.

We need not look beyond the circumstances of this case to see the phenomenon at work. The undeniable fact is that the school district's supervision and control of a high school graduation ceremony places public pressure, as well as peer pressure, on attending students to stand as a group or, at least, maintain respectful silence during the invocation and benediction. This pressure, though subtle and indirect, can be as real as any overt compulsion . . . There can be no doubt that for many, if not most, of the students at the graduation, the act of standing or remaining silent was an expression of participation in the rabbi's prayer . . . Finding no violation under these circumstances would place objectors in the dilemma of participating, with all that implies, or protesting. We do not address whether that choice is acceptable if the affected citizens are mature adults, but we think the State may not, consistent with the Establishment Clause, place primary and secondary school children in this position. Research in psychology supports the common assumption that adolescents are often susceptible to pressure from their peers towards conformity, and that the influence is strongest in matters of social convention. To recognize that the choice imposed by the State constitutes an unacceptable constraint only acknowledges that the government may no more use social pressure to enforce orthodoxy than it may use more direct means.

The injury caused by the government's action, and the reason why Daniel and Deborah Weisman object to it, is that the State, in a school setting, in effect required participation in a religious exercise. It is, we concede, a brief exercise during which the individual can concentrate on joining its message, meditate on her own religion, or let her mind wander. But the embarrassment and the intrusion of the religious exercise cannot be refuted by arguing that these prayers, and similar ones to be said in the future, are of a *de minimis* character. To do so would be an affront to the rabbi who offered them and to all those for whom the prayers were an essential and profound recognition of divine authority. And for the same reason, we think that the intrusion is greater than the two minutes or so of time consumed for prayers like these. Assuming, as we must, that the prayers were offensive to the student and the parent who now object, the intrusion was both real and, in the context of a secondary school, a violation of the objectors' rights. That the intrusion was in the course of promulgating religion that sought to be civic or nonsectarian rather than pertaining to one sect does not lessen the offense or isolation to the objectors. At best it narrows their number, at worst increases their sense of isolation and affront . . . While in some societies the wishes of the majority might prevail, the Establishment Clause of the First Amendment is addressed to this contingency and rejects the balance urged upon us. The Constitution forbids the State to exact religious conformity from a student as the price of attending her own high school graduation. This is the calculus the Constitution commands . . .

We do not hold that every state action implicating religion is invalid if one or a few citizens find it offensive. People may take offense at all manner of religious as well as nonreligious messages, but offense alone does not in every case show a violation. We know too that sometimes to endure social isolation or even anger may be the price of conscience or nonconformity. But, by any reading of our cases, the conformity required of the student in this case was too high an exaction to withstand the test of the Establishment Clause. The prayer exercises in this case are especially improper because the State has in every practical sense compelled attendance and participation in an explicit religious exercise at an event of singular importance to every student, one the objecting student had no real alternative to avoid . . .

Our society would be less than true to its heritage if it lacked abiding concern for the values of its young people, and we acknowledge the profound belief of adherents to many faiths that there must be a place in the student's life for precepts of a morality higher even than the law we today enforce. We express no hostility to those aspirations, nor would our oath permit us to do so. A relentless and all-pervasive attempt to exclude religion from every aspect of public life could itself become inconsistent with the Constitution. We recognize that, at graduation time and throughout the course of the educational process, there will be instances when religious values, religious practices, and religious persons will have some interaction with the public schools and their students. But these matters, often questions of accommodation of religion, are not before us. The sole question presented is whether a religious exercise may be conducted at a graduation ceremony in circumstances where, as we have found, young graduates who object are induced to conform. No holding by this Court suggests that a school can persuade or compel a student to participate in a religious exercise. That is being done here, and it is forbidden by the Establishment Clause of the First Amendment.

For the reasons we have stated, the judgment of the Court of Appeals is Affirmed.

Justice SCALIA, with whom THE CHIEF JUSTICE, Justice WHITE, and Justice THOMAS join, dissenting.

Three Terms ago, I joined an opinion recognizing that the Establishment Clause must be construed in light of the "government policies of accommodation, acknowledgment, and support for religion [that] are an accepted part of our political and cultural heritage." That opinion affirmed that "the meaning of the Clause is to be determined by reference to historical practices and understandings." It said that "a test for implementing the protections of the Establishment Clause that, if applied with consistency, would invalidate longstanding traditions cannot be a proper reading of the Clause." *County of Allegheny v. American Civil Liberties Union*, 492 U.S. 573 (1989) (KENNEDY, J., concurring in judgment in part and dissenting in part).

These views of course prevent me from joining today's opinion, which is conspicuously bereft of any reference to history. In holding that the Establishment Clause prohibits invocations and benedictions at public-school graduation ceremonies, the Court--with nary a mention that it is doing so--lays waste a tradition that is as old as public-school graduation ceremonies themselves, and that is a component of an even more longstanding American tradition of nonsectarian prayer to God at public celebrations generally. As its instrument of destruction, the bulldozer of its social engineering, the Court invents a boundless, and boundlessly manipulable, test of psychological coercion . . . Today's opinion shows more forcefully than volumes of argumentation why our Nation's protection, that fortress which is our Constitution, cannot possibly rest upon the changeable philosophical predilections of the Justices of this Court, but must have deep foundations in the historic practices of our people . . . From our Nation's origin, prayer has been a prominent part of governmental ceremonies and proclamations. The Declaration of Independence, the document marking our birth as a separate people, "appealed to the Supreme Judge of the world for the rectitude of our intentions" and avowed "a firm reliance on the protection of divine Providence." In his first inaugural address, after swearing his oath of office on a Bible, George Washington deliberately made a prayer a part of his first official act as President: "It would be peculiarly improper to omit in this first official act my fervent supplications to that Almighty Being who rules over the universe, who presides in the councils of nations, and whose providential aids can supply every human defect, that His benediction may consecrate to the liberties and happiness of the people of the United States a Government instituted by themselves for these essential purposes." Such supplications have been a characteristic feature of inaugural addresses ever since. Thomas Jefferson, for example, prayed in his first inaugural address: "May that Infinite Power which rules the destinies of the universe lead our councils to what is best, and give them a favorable issue for your peace and prosperity." In his second inaugural address, Jefferson acknowledged his need for divine guidance and invited his audience to join his prayer:

> I shall need, too, the favor of that Being in whose hands we are, who led our fathers, as Israel of old, from their native land and planted them in a country flowing with all the necessaries and comforts of life; who has covered our infancy with His providence and our riper years with His wisdom and power, and to whose goodness I ask you to join in supplications with me that He will so enlighten the minds of your servants, guide their councils, and prosper their measures that whatsoever they do shall result in your good, and shall secure to you the peace, friendship, and approbation of all nations.

Similarly, James Madison, in his first inaugural address, placed his confidence "in the guardianship and guidance of that Almighty Being whose power regulates the destiny of nations, whose blessings have been so conspicuously dispensed to this rising Republic, and to whom we are bound to address our devout gratitude for the past, as well as our fervent supplications and best hopes for the future" . . .

In addition to this general tradition of prayer at public ceremonies, there exists a more specific tradition of invocations and benedictions at public school graduation exercises . . . The Court presumably would separate graduation invocations and benedictions from other instances of public "preservation and transmission of religious beliefs" on the ground that they involve "psychological coercion." I find it a sufficient embarrassment that our Establishment Clause jurisprudence regarding holiday displays, *see County of Allegheny v. American Civil Liberties Union*, 492 U.S. 573 (1989), has come to "require scrutiny more commonly associated with interior decorators than with the judiciary." But interior decorating is a rock-hard science compared to psychology practiced by amateurs. A few citations of "research in psychology" that have no particular bearing upon the precise issue here, cannot disguise the fact that the Court has gone beyond the realm where judges know what they are doing. The Court's argument that state officials have "coerced" students to take part in the invocation and benediction at graduation ceremonies is, not to put too fine a point on it, incoherent . . .

The coercion that was a hallmark of historical establishments of religion was coercion of religious orthodoxy and of financial support by force of law and threat of penalty. Typically, attendance at the state church was required; only clergy of the official church could lawfully perform sacraments; and dissenters, if tolerated, faced an array of civil disabilities. Thus, for example, in the Colony of Virginia, where the Church of England had been established, ministers were required by law to conform to the doctrine and rites of the Church of England; and all persons were required to attend church and observe the Sabbath, were tithed for the public support of Anglican ministers, and were taxed for the costs of building and repairing churches.

The Establishment Clause was adopted to prohibit such an establishment of religion at the federal level (and to protect state establishments of religion from federal interference) . . . But there is simply no support for the proposition that the officially sponsored nondenominational invocation and benediction read by Rabbi Gutterman--with no one legally coerced to recite them--violated the Constitution of the United States. To the contrary, they are so characteristically American they could have come from the pen of George Washington or Abraham Lincoln himself.

Thus, while I have no quarrel with the Court's general proposition that the Establishment Clause "guarantees that government may not coerce anyone to support or participate in religion or its exercise," I see no warrant for expanding the concept of coercion beyond acts backed by threat of penalty--a brand of coercion that, happily, is readily discernible to those of us who have made a career of reading the disciples of Blackstone rather than of Freud. The Framers were indeed opposed to coercion of religious worship by the National Government . . .

Our Religion Clause jurisprudence has become bedeviled (so to speak) by reliance on formulaic abstractions that are not derived from, but positively conflict with, our long-accepted constitutional traditions. Foremost among these has been the so-called *Lemon* test, *see Lemon v. Kurtzman*, 403 U.S. 602 (1971), which has received well-earned criticism from many Members of this Court. The Court today demonstrates the irrelevance of *Lemon* by essentially ignoring it, and the interment of that case may be the one happy byproduct of the Court's otherwise lamentable decision. Unfortunately, however, the Court has replaced *Lemon* with its psycho-coercion test, which suffers the double disability of having no roots whatever in our people's historic practice, and being as infinitely expandable as the reasons for psychotherapy itself.

Another happy aspect of the case is that it is only a jurisprudential disaster and not a practical one. Given the odd basis for the Court's decision, invocations and benedictions will be able to be given at public school graduations next June, as they have for the past century and a half, so long as school authorities make clear that anyone who abstains from screaming in protest does not necessarily participate in the prayers. All that is seemingly needed is an announcement, or perhaps a written insertion at the beginning of the graduation program, to the effect that, while all are asked to rise for the invocation and benediction, none is compelled to join in them, nor will be assumed, by rising, to have done so. That obvious fact recited, the graduates and their parents may proceed to thank God, as Americans have always done, for the blessings He has generously bestowed on them and on their country.

The reader has been told much in this case about the personal interest of Mr. Weisman and his daughter, and very little about the personal interests on the other side. They are not inconsequential. Church and state would not be such a difficult subject if religion were, as the Court apparently thinks it to be, some purely personal avocation that can be indulged entirely in secret, like pornography, in the privacy of one's room. For most believers it is not that, and has never been. Religious men and women of almost all denominations have felt it necessary to acknowledge and beseech the blessing of God as a people, and not just as individuals, because they believe in the "protection of divine Providence," as the Declaration of Independence put it, not just for individuals but for societies; because they believe God to be, as Washington's first Thanksgiving Proclamation put it, the "Great Lord and Ruler of Nations." One can believe in the effectiveness of such public worship, or one can deprecate and deride it. But the longstanding

American tradition of prayer at official ceremonies displays with unmistakable clarity that the Establishment Clause does not forbid the government to accommodate it . . .

I must add one final observation: The Founders of our Republic knew the fearsome potential of sectarian religious belief to generate civil dissension and civil strife. And they also knew that nothing, absolutely nothing, is so inclined to foster among religious believers of various faiths a toleration--no, an affection--for one another than voluntarily joining in prayer together, to the God whom they all worship and seek. Needless to say, no one should be compelled to do that, but it is a shame to deprive our public culture of the opportunity, and indeed the encouragement, for people to do it voluntarily. The Baptist or Catholic who heard and joined in the simple and inspiring prayers of Rabbi Gutterman on this official and patriotic occasion was inoculated from religious bigotry and prejudice in a manner that cannot be replicated. To deprive our society of that important unifying mechanism, in order to spare the nonbeliever what seems to me the minimal inconvenience of standing or even sitting in respectful nonparticipation, is as senseless in policy as it is unsupported in law.

For the foregoing reasons, I dissent.

* * * * * * *

Comments and Questions

The Court's public school prayer cases have held that state officials cannot compose and require student prayers; direct students to read daily Bible passages; or invite clergymen to pray at graduation ceremonies. While all of these opinions evidenced differences among the Justices, the Court's decision in *Lee v. Weisman* prompted a scathing dissent from Justice Scalia. Justice Scalia accused the Court's Majority of "social engineering" and inventing a "boundlessly manipulable, test of psychological coercion." Justice Scalia also suggested that graduation prayers could lawfully proceed if proper disclaimers were placed in school graduation programs. Is Justice Scalia correct?

Justice Scalia criticized the "*Lemon* test" in his dissenting opinion in *Lee v. Weisman*. He was referring to a legal test the Court adopted in *Lemon v. Kurtzman*, 403 U.S. 602 (1971). Judicially developed legal tests, like the *Lemon* test, are intended to guide judges in interpreting and applying the law, helping bridge the gap between broad general principles and the application of the law in specific cases. The First Amendment's Establishment Clause, for example, declared that Congress "shall make no law respecting an establishment of religion." While these words articulate a broad general principle, they do little to guide judges or anyone else in determining whether a particular challenged government action violates the Establishment Clause, especially in the closer cases that are most likely to be litigated.

Judicially developed legal tests are an essential part of the Common Law tradition. These legal tests provide a uniform framework for judges to use in deciding cases, thereby promoting essential predictability in the law. Like most other judicially created legal tests, the *Lemon* test was developed over time based on logic and real world experiences in addressing legal questions. Elements of legal tests are added, removed, or modified through an evolutionary process of judicial efforts to better address legal questions, often guided by legal scholarship and the work of lawyers.

As Justice Scalia noted, however, the *Lemon* test has generated considerable judicial and scholarly criticism since its adoption by the Court in 1971. Nonetheless, the test continues to be used by courts in Establishment Clause cases. While no doubt imperfect, the *Lemon* test does provide some useful guidance. Until a better test is devised and adopted by the U.S. Supreme Court, courts are likely to continue using the *Lemon* test in appropriate cases.

Under the *Lemon* test, a government action challenged as violating the Establishment Clause will be constitutionally valid only if it satisfies each of the following conditions:

> 1) *Purpose*: There must a legitimate secular purpose for the challenged government action. The primary purpose underlying the government action cannot be religious in nature.

> 2) *Effect*: The primary effect of the government action must be religiously neutral. It must neither advance nor inhibit religion.

> 3) *Entanglement*: The government action must not foster excessive entanglement between church and state.

If a government action is found to have violated any of the three-prongs of the *Lemon* test, the challenged statute, regulation, policy, or practice is declared unconstitutional. Government officials have no lawful authority to continue any unconstitutional act and they may be held liable for monetary damages under 42 U.S.C. § 1983 for violations of constitutional rights.

These legal tests can be used to assess the likely outcomes of potential cases and as a guide in planning lawful future actions and policies. Whenever there is a question about whether a government action may violate the Establishment Clause, the relevant facts can be tested against the three-prongs of the *Lemon* test assessing: 1) Purpose; 2) Effect; and 3) Entanglement. To see how a legal test is applied in practice, try applying the *Lemon* test below by examining a "moment of silence" policy as measured against the three-prongs of the *Lemon* test.

Many states have adopted public school "moment of silence" statutes requiring students and teachers to observe a brief moment of silence during the school day. Moment of silence acts have been challenged as violations of the Establishment Clause. Are state "moment of silence" statutes constitutional under the *Lemon* test? Measuring these statutes against the three-prongs of the *Lemon* test, courts have generally upheld these statutes, finding:

> 1) *Purpose*: The state has an acceptable secular purpose in asking everyone to pause for a moment of quiet reflection (as long as prayer was not introduced or suggested by school officials, the state could have a legitimate secular purpose in encouraging quiet reflection on the events of the day, and state officials may legitimately find that this practice of reflection is educationally beneficial);

> 2) *Effect*: A moment of silent reflection is religiously neutral (anyone could choose to pray silently by private choice, but silent prayer is neither encouraged nor discouraged); and

> 3) *Entanglement*: Church representatives are not involved in these state actions so there is no entanglement.

If, however, the facts in a particular case proved that the primary purpose was religious, the effect was to advance (or inhibit) religion, or these policies significantly entangled church and state operations, the moment of silence act would be unconstitutional. Does your state have a moment of silence statute? Would it survive a facial challenge under the *Lemon* test (*i.e.*, measured against the *Lemon* test as the statute is written on the face of the document)? Would it pass the *Lemon* test as applied (*i.e.*, measured against the *Lemon* test as the practice is actually applied in the school)? A statute may be facially valid (constitutional as written) but unconstitutional as applied. For example, a facially valid moment of silence statute may be unconstitutionally applied if school officials conducted the moment of silence as a prayer.

Why didn't Justice Kennedy use the *Lemon* test in his majority opinion in *Lee v. Weisman*? Instead, Justice Kennedy used the "coercion test" one of the tests sometimes used as an alternative to the *Lemon* test. The coercion test holds that the Establishment Clause prohibits any coercive action by government officials concerning religion.

Justices Kennedy and Scalia agree that government officials may not coerce religious belief or practice. They disagree, however, concerning what state actions constitute unconstitutional coercion. Justice Kennedy argued that Debra Weisman was subjected to psychological coercion in this case, and that this type of social pressure has a powerful impact on children, sufficient to be prohibited by the Establishment Clause. Justice Scalia argued that legal coercion only exists when it is "by force of law and threat of penalty." Who is correct?

Justice Kennedy argued that the Establishment Clause was made binding on the states through the adoption of the Fourteenth Amendment, while Justice Scalia declared: "The Establishment Clause was adopted to prohibit such an establishment of religion at the federal level (and to protect state establishments of religion from federal interference)." Justice Kennedy's opinion is the well-established majority opinion (holding that that the Fourteenth Amendment made most provisions of the U.S. Bill of Rights, including the First Amendment, enforceable against state and local government officials). But what if Justice Scalia achieved a new majority on this question? *Lee* was a 5-4 opinion, with Kennedy in the Majority, but what would have happened if Justice Scalia had one more vote for his opinion in *Lee v. Weisman* and his parenthetical recognition of the legality of state establishments of religion became the law of the land?

If your state's General Assembly was given an opportunity to establish an official state religion, would they? Would this be a divisive issue in your state? What religious faith would most likely prevail in your state? How would members of minority faiths react to the adoption of an official state religion? Would they be willing to have their children in public schools that taught the majority faith to their children? Would they be willing to pay taxes to support a faith they did not believe in? Would an officially established state faith religiously balkanize the U.S., creating for example Baptist, Methodist, Catholic, Lutheran, Mormon, and Jewish states?

In his dissenting opinion Justice Scalia quoted inaugural addresses by Presidents Washington, Jefferson, and Madison in support of his argument that there is a long U.S. history of prayer at public ceremonies. Is this a persuasive argument? What facts legally distinguish a presidential address from a public school event?

In church-state litigation, cases at the extreme ends of the continuum between prohibited Establishment and protected Free Exercise/Free Speech are relatively easy. For example, in cases where the targeted audience is impressionable children subject to compulsory attendance and state officials are coercing religious belief or practice, courts will find these actions unconstitutional establishment of religion. At the other end of the continuum, in cases where private citizens are independently presenting prayers to members of the general public who freely choose to listen to these prayers, courts will find this to be protected Free Exercise of Religion/Free Speech. Cases closer to the middle of this continuum can be far more difficult. In these closer cases judges look for facts that bring the case under review closer to either prohibited Establishment or protected Free Exercise/Free Speech.

The Continuum between Prohibited Establishment and Protected Free Exercise

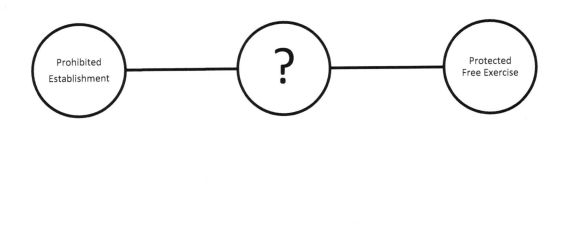

As noted above the Court's school prayer cases teach that the Establishment Clause prohibits school officials from composing prayers for students, asking students to pray or read Bible passages, or inviting members of the clergy to give prayers at public school graduation ceremonies. In each of these cases the facts established that government actions were close enough to prohibited Establishment of religion to merit judicial intervention. In *Santa Fe v. Doe* the Court had another opportunity to further clarify the boundaries between prohibited Establishment and protected Free Exercise/Free Speech in public schools, this time addressing the legality of prayers at athletic events.

Santa Fe Independent School District v. Doe
530 U.S. 290 (2000)
Supreme Court of the United States

Justice STEVENS delivered the opinion of the Court.

Prior to 1995, the Santa Fe High School student who occupied the school's elective office of student council chaplain delivered a prayer over the public address system before each varsity football game for the entire season. This practice, along with others, was challenged in District

Court as a violation of the Establishment Clause of the First Amendment. While these proceedings were pending in the District Court, the school district adopted a different policy that permits, but does not require, prayer initiated and led by a student at all home games. The District Court entered an order modifying that policy to permit only nonsectarian, nonproselytizing prayer. The Court of Appeals held that, even as modified by the District Court, the football prayer policy was invalid. We granted the school district's petition for certiorari to review that holding.

The Santa Fe Independent School District (District) is a political subdivision of the State of Texas, responsible for the education of more than 4,000 students in a small community in the southern part of the State. The District includes the Santa Fe High School, two primary schools, an intermediate school and the junior high school. Respondents are two sets of current or former students and their respective mothers. One family is Mormon and the other is Catholic. The District Court permitted respondents (Does) to litigate anonymously to protect them from intimidation or harassment.

Respondents commenced this action in April 1995 and moved for a temporary restraining order to prevent the District from violating the Establishment Clause at the imminent graduation exercises. In their complaint the Does alleged that the District had engaged in several proselytizing practices, such as promoting attendance at a Baptist revival meeting, encouraging membership in religious clubs, chastising children who held minority religious beliefs, and distributing Gideon Bibles on school premises. They also alleged that the District allowed students to read Christian invocations and benedictions from the stage at graduation ceremonies, and to deliver overtly Christian prayers over the public address system at home football games . . .

The policies enacted in May and July for graduation ceremonies provided the format for the August and October policies for football games. The May policy provided: "The board has chosen to permit the graduating senior class, with the advice and counsel of the senior class principal or designee, to elect by secret ballot to choose whether an invocation and benediction shall be part of the graduation exercise. If so chosen the class shall elect by secret ballot, from a list of student volunteers, students to deliver nonsectarian, nonproselytizing invocations and benedictions for the purpose of solemnizing their graduation ceremonies."

The parties stipulated that after this policy was adopted, "the senior class held an election to determine whether to have an invocation and benediction at the commencement [and that the] class voted, by secret ballot, to include prayer at the high school graduation." In a second vote the class elected two seniors to deliver the invocation and benediction.

In July, the District enacted another policy eliminating the requirement that invocations and benedictions be "nonsectarian and nonproselytising," but also providing that if the District were to be enjoined from enforcing that policy, the May policy would automatically become effective. The August policy, which was titled "Prayer at Football Games," was similar to the July policy for graduations. It also authorized two student elections, the first to determine whether "invocations" should be delivered, and the second to select the spokesperson to deliver them. Like the July policy, it contained two parts, an initial statement that omitted any requirement that the content of the invocation be "nonsectarian and nonproselytising," and a fallback provision that automatically added that limitation if the preferred policy should be enjoined. On August 31, 1995, according to the parties' stipulation: "The district's high school students voted to determine whether a student would deliver prayer at varsity football games . . . The students chose to allow a student to say a prayer at football games." A week later, in a separate election, they selected a student "to deliver the prayer at varsity football games." The final policy (October policy) is essentially the same as the August policy, though it omits the word "prayer" from its title, and refers to "messages" and "statements" as well as "invocations." It is the validity of that policy that is before us.

The District Court did enter an order precluding enforcement of the first, open-ended policy. Relying on our decision in *Lee v. Weisman*, 505 U.S. 577 (1992), it held that the school's "action must not 'coerce anyone to support or participate in' a religious exercise." Applying that test, it concluded that the graduation prayers appealed "to distinctively Christian beliefs," and that delivering a prayer "over the school's public address system prior to each football and baseball game coerces student participation in religious events" . . . We granted the District's petition for certiorari, limited to the following question: "Whether petitioner's policy permitting student-led, student-initiated prayer at football games violates the Establishment Clause." We conclude, as did the Court of Appeals, that it does.

The first Clause in the First Amendment to the Federal Constitution provides that "Congress shall make no law respecting an establishment of religion, or prohibiting the free exercise thereof." The Fourteenth Amendment imposes those substantive limitations on the legislative power of the States and their political subdivisions. In *Lee v. Weisman*, we held that a prayer delivered by a rabbi at a middle school graduation ceremony violated that Clause. Although this case involves student prayer at a different type of school function, our analysis is properly guided by the principles that we endorsed in *Lee*. As we held in that case:

> The principle that government may accommodate the free exercise of religion does not supersede the fundamental limitations imposed by the Establishment Clause. It is beyond dispute that, at a minimum, the Constitution guarantees that government may not coerce anyone to support or participate in religion or its exercise, or otherwise act in a way which "establishes a [state] religion or religious faith, or tends to do so."

In this case the District first argues that this principle is inapplicable to its October policy because the messages are private student speech, not public speech. It reminds us that "there is a crucial difference between government speech endorsing religion, which the Establishment Clause forbids, and private speech endorsing religion, which the Free Speech and Free Exercise Clauses protect." *Westside Community Schools v. Mergens*, 496 U.S. 226 (1990). We certainly agree with that distinction, but we are not persuaded that the pregame invocations should be regarded as "private speech."

These invocations are authorized by a government policy and take place on government property at government-sponsored school-related events. Of course, not every message delivered under such circumstances is the government's own. We have held, for example, that an individual's contribution to a government-created forum was not government speech. *Rosenberger v. Rector*, 515 U.S. 819 (1995). Although the District relies heavily on *Rosenberger* and similar cases involving such forums, it is clear that the pregame ceremony is not the type of forum discussed in those cases. The Santa Fe school officials simply do not "evince either by policy or by practice, any intent to open the [pregame ceremony] to indiscriminate use . . . by the student body generally." *Hazelwood v. Kuhlmeier*, 484 U.S. 260 (1983). Rather, the school allows only one student, the same student for the entire season, to give the invocation. The statement or invocation, moreover, is subject to particular regulations that confine the content and topic of the student's message . . . Although the District relies on these public forum cases, it does not actually argue that the pregame ceremony constitutes such a forum.

Granting only one student access to the stage at a time does not, of course, necessarily preclude a finding that a school has created a limited public forum. Here, however, Santa Fe's student election system ensures that only those messages deemed "appropriate" under the District's policy may be delivered. That is, the majoritarian process implemented by the District guarantees, by definition, that minority candidates will never prevail and that their views will be effectively silenced.

Recently, in *Board of Regents v. Southworth*, 529 U.S. 217 (2000), we explained why student elections that determine, by majority vote, which expressive activities shall receive or not receive school benefits are constitutionally problematic:

> To the extent the referendum substitutes majority determinations for viewpoint neutrality it would undermine the constitutional protection the program requires. The whole theory of viewpoint neutrality is that minority views are treated with the same respect as are majority views. Access to a public forum, for instance, does not depend upon majoritarian consent. That principle is controlling here.

Like the student referendum for funding in *Southworth*, this student election does nothing to protect minority views but rather places the students who hold such views at the mercy of the majority. Because "fundamental rights may not be submitted to vote; they depend on the outcome of no elections," *West Virginia v. Barnette*, 319 U.S. 624 (1943), the District's elections are insufficient safeguards of diverse student speech. The fact that the District's policy provides for the election of the speaker only after the majority has voted on her message identifies an obvious distinction between this case and the typical election of a "student body president, or even a newly elected prom king or queen."

In *Lee*, the school district made the related argument that its policy of endorsing only "civic or nonsectarian" prayer was acceptable because it minimized the intrusion on the audience as a whole. We rejected that claim by explaining that such a majoritarian policy "does not lessen the offense or isolation to the objectors. At best it narrows their number, at worst increases their sense of isolation and affront." Similarly, while Santa Fe's majoritarian election might ensure that most of the students are represented, it does nothing to protect the minority; indeed, it likely serves to intensify their offense.

Moreover, the District has failed to divorce itself from the religious content in the invocations. It has not succeeded in doing so, either by claiming that its policy is "one of neutrality rather than endorsement" or by characterizing the individual student as the "circuit-breaker" in the process. Contrary to the District's repeated assertions that it has adopted a "hands-off" approach to the pregame invocation, the realities of the situation plainly reveal that its policy involves both perceived and actual endorsement of religion. In this case, as we found in *Lee*, the "degree of school involvement" makes it clear that the pregame prayers bear "the imprint of the State and thus put school-age children who objected in an untenable position" . . .

In addition to involving the school in the selection of the speaker, the policy, by its terms, invites and encourages religious messages. The policy itself states that the purpose of the message is "to solemnize the event." A religious message is the most obvious method of solemnizing an event . . . We recognize the important role that public worship plays in many communities, as well as the sincere desire to include public prayer as a part of various occasions so as to mark those occasions' significance. But such religious activity in public schools, as elsewhere, must comport with the First Amendment . . .

The actual or perceived endorsement of the message, moreover, is established by factors beyond just the text of the policy. Once the student speaker is selected and the message composed, the invocation is then delivered to a large audience assembled as part of a regularly scheduled, school-sponsored function conducted on school property. The message is broadcast over the school's public address system, which remains subject to the control of school officials. It is fair to assume that the pregame ceremony is clothed in the traditional indicia of school sporting events, which generally include not just the team, but also cheerleaders and band members dressed in uniforms sporting the school name and mascot. The school's name is likely written in large print across the field and on banners and flags. The crowd will certainly include many who display the school colors and insignia on their school T-shirts, jackets, or hats and who may also be waving signs displaying the school name. It is in a setting such as this that "the board has chosen to permit" the elected student to rise and give the "statement or invocation."

In this context the members of the listening audience must perceive the pregame message as a public expression of the views of the majority of the student body delivered with the approval of the school administration. In cases involving state participation in a religious activity, one of the relevant questions is "whether an objective observer, acquainted with the text, legislative history, and implementation of the statute, would perceive it as a state endorsement of prayer in public schools" . . . Regardless of the listener's support for, or objection to, the message, an objective Santa Fe High School student will unquestionably perceive the inevitable pregame prayer as stamped with her school's seal of approval . . . According to the District, the secular purposes of the policy are to "foster free expression of private persons . . . as well [as to] solemnize sporting events, promote good sportsmanship and student safety, and establish an appropriate environment for competition." We note, however, that the District's approval of only one specific kind of message, an "invocation," is not necessary to further any of these purposes. Additionally, the fact that only one student is permitted to give a content-limited message suggests that this policy does little to "foster free expression." Furthermore, regardless of whether one considers a sporting event an appropriate occasion for solemnity, the use of an invocation to foster such solemnity is impermissible when, in actuality, it constitutes prayer sponsored by the school. And it is unclear what type of message would be both appropriately "solemnizing" under the District's policy and yet nonreligious.

Most striking to us is the evolution of the current policy from the long-sanctioned office of "Student Chaplain" to the candidly titled "Prayer at Football Games" regulation. This history indicates that the District intended to preserve the practice of prayer before football games. The conclusion that the District viewed the October policy simply as a continuation of the previous policies is dramatically illustrated by the fact that the school did not conduct a new election, pursuant to the current policy, to replace the results of the previous election, which occurred under the former policy. Given these observations, and in light of the school's history of regular delivery of a student-led prayer at athletic events, it is reasonable to infer that the specific purpose of the policy was to preserve a popular "state-sponsored religious practice."

School sponsorship of a religious message is impermissible because it sends the ancillary message to members of the audience who are non-adherents "that they are outsiders, not full members of the political community, and an accompanying message to adherents that they are insiders, favored members of the political community." The delivery of such a message--over the school's public address system, by a speaker representing the student body, under the supervision of school faculty, and pursuant to a school policy that explicitly and implicitly encourages public prayer--is not properly characterized as "private" speech.

The District next argues that its football policy is distinguishable from the graduation prayer in *Lee* because it does not coerce students to participate in religious observances. Its argument has two parts: first, that there is no impermissible government coercion because the pregame messages are the product of student choices; and second, that there is really no coercion at all because attendance at an extracurricular event, unlike a graduation ceremony, is voluntary.

The reasons just discussed explaining why the alleged "circuit-breaker" mechanism of the dual elections and student speaker do not turn public speech into private speech also demonstrate why these mechanisms do not insulate the school from the coercive element of the final message. In fact, this aspect of the District's argument exposes anew the concerns that are created by the majoritarian election system. The parties' stipulation clearly states that the issue resolved in the first election was "whether a student would deliver prayer at varsity football games," and the controversy in this case demonstrates that the views of the students are not unanimous on that issue.

One of the purposes served by the Establishment Clause is to remove debate over this kind of issue from governmental supervision or control. We explained in *Lee* that the "preservation and transmission of religious beliefs and worship is a responsibility and a choice committed to the private sphere." The two student elections authorized by the policy, coupled with the debates that presumably must precede each, impermissibly invade that private sphere. The election mechanism, when considered in light of the history in which the policy in question evolved, reflects a device the District put in place that determines whether religious messages will be delivered at home football games. The mechanism encourages divisiveness along religious lines in a public school setting, a result at odds with the Establishment Clause . . .

The District further argues that attendance at the commencement ceremonies at issue in *Lee* "differs dramatically" from attendance at high school football games, which it contends "are of no more than passing interest to many students" and are "decidedly extracurricular," thus dissipating any coercion. Attendance at a high school football game, unlike showing up for class, is certainly not required in order to receive a diploma. Moreover, we may assume that the District is correct in arguing that the informal pressure to attend an athletic event is not as strong as a senior's desire to attend her own graduation ceremony.

There are some students, however, such as cheerleaders, members of the band, and, of course, the team members themselves, for whom seasonal commitments mandate their attendance, sometimes for class credit . . . The Constitution, moreover, demands that the school may not force this difficult choice upon these students for "it is a tenet of the First Amendment that the State cannot require one of its citizens to forfeit his or her rights and benefits as the price of resisting conformance to state-sponsored religious practice."

Even if we regard every high school student's decision to attend a home football game as purely voluntary, we are nevertheless persuaded that the delivery of a pregame prayer has the improper effect of coercing those present to participate in an act of religious worship. For "the government may no more use social pressure to enforce orthodoxy than it may use more direct means." As in *Lee*, "what to most believers may seem nothing more than a reasonable request that the nonbeliever respect their religious practices, in a school context may appear to the nonbeliever or dissenter to be an attempt to employ the machinery of the State to enforce a religious orthodoxy." The constitutional command will not permit the District "to exact religious conformity from a student as the price" of joining her classmates at a varsity football game.

The Religion Clauses of the First Amendment prevent the government from making any law respecting the establishment of religion or prohibiting the free exercise thereof. By no means do these commands impose a prohibition on all religious activity in our public schools. Indeed, the common purpose of the Religion Clauses "is to secure religious liberty." Thus, nothing in the Constitution as interpreted by this Court prohibits any public school student from voluntarily praying at any time before, during, or after the school day. But the religious liberty protected by the Constitution is abridged when the State affirmatively sponsors the particular religious practice of prayer . . .

We have concluded that the resulting religious message under this policy would be attributable to the school, not just the student. For this reason, we now hold only that the District's decision to allow the student majority to control whether students of minority views are subjected to a school-sponsored prayer violates the Establishment Clause.

The judgment of the Court of Appeals is, accordingly, affirmed.

It is so ordered.

* * * * * *

Comments and Questions

Since *Engel v. Vitale*, 370 U.S. 421 (1962), the Court has consistently rejected arguments for public school sponsored prayer, whether the sponsorship was direct or indirect, noting that the First Amendment "tried to put an end to governmental control of religion and prayer." The majority of the Court continues to firmly hold that private religious choices belong to parents and children, and not to public officials. Essential to understanding the First Amendment is an understanding of the two distinct spheres of life under the constitutional system, a private sphere and a public sphere:

Private and Public Spheres of Life under the Constitution

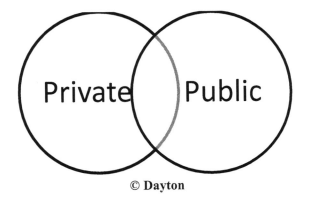

© Dayton

The constitutional system assumes the existence of a private sphere of life free from unnecessary governmental interference, and a public sphere of life dedicated to the pursuit of the common good. The Constitution and the Bill of Rights mediate between and protect both the private and public spheres of life. For example, concerning the First Amendment's

Establishment Clause the "wall of separation" mediates between the church in the private sphere and the state in the public sphere protecting both from the destructive results of co-mingling church and state powers.

The private sphere is the realm of protected individual belief, while the public sphere is the common domain dedicated to the common good. The common government should not interfere with individual rights of belief in the private sphere. And in the public sphere the focus must be on the common needs for public roads, utilities, police and fire protection, parks, schools, etc., without unnecessary and divisive sectarian disputes. In this way the Establishment Clause protects both the individual by guarding free will in the private sphere, and the common good by minimizing the disruptions and divisiveness of sectarian religious conflict in the public sphere.

When acting in the private sphere of life, all private citizens, including students, and even school officials (when they are clearly acting in their private capacity only) are protected by the Free Exercise and Free Speech Clauses of the First Amendment in praying or not praying as they choose. When acting in the public sphere in their public capacities, however, government officials are prohibited by the Establishment Clause from conducting and controlling prayers in public schools.

Students are private citizens, even when they are in public schools. The Constitution only limits the actions of government officials. As private citizens students have a right to pray as they wish subject only to reasonable time, place, and manner limitations in school to avoid unnecessary disruptions. Students may pray at football games or other events to the same extent that they may engage in any other similar activities. They cannot disrupt school activities. But if they can cheer for the team, they can pray for the team if they independently choose to pray.

Based on the Court's decision in *Santa Fe v. Doe*, if school officials conduct a student vote on whether to have a prayer at a school event, do you believe this process would adequately shift the religious activity and control from the public sphere into the private sphere? Does limiting public school controlled invocations to prayers that are "non-sectarian and non-proselytizing" transform these prayers into constitutional permissible civic invocations in the public sphere? Or does it compound the constitutional violations: 1) By establishing religion in the common public sphere; and 2) By intruding on Free Exercise/Free Speech rights of private citizens through excluding constitutionally protected sectarian and proselytizing prayers by private citizens?

Few question whether public school officials have good intentions in leading students in prayer. Good intentions alone, however, will not shield anyone from the potential harms of government sponsored religion, nor transform unconstitutional public sponsored prayer into a lawful power held by public school officials. Is public school sponsored prayer permissible in any context? Would it be legally permissible to have the public school principal lead students in prayer in response to a tragic event in the school community? Could a teacher or school counselor pray individually with a student in need of comfort and guidance? May coaches lead their players in prayers for safety before games?

The controversy over prayer at football games in *Santa Fe v. Doe* captured the attention of millions of Americans, including members of Congress. A resolution concerning this issue was presented in the U.S. Congress:

SENSE OF CONGRESS SUPPORTING PRAYER AT PUBLIC SCHOOL SPORTING EVENTS -- 145 Congressional Record 11325 (House of Representatives -- November 02, 1999)

Mr. GREEN of Texas:

Mr. Speaker, I am a cosponsor of the resolution. Coming from Texas, I noticed a lot of the cosponsors of the resolution are from Texas. There are a lot of things we hold sacred in Texas and one of them is high school football. One can go to any Friday night game or Saturday night game and it is important to the community, and growing up in Texas and having an opportunity to play high school football I know how important that event is for the community.

Since then, I have attended football games both as a State legislator and Member of Congress and participating in the pre-game ceremonies, including giving the prayer as a Member of Congress at some of our high schools. This last February, the Fifth Circuit Court of Appeals in *Doe v. Santa Fe Independent School District* caused a great deal of concern and ultimately with this coming school year I talked with some of our superintendents in my own district to see how they were dealing with it . . . If we in Congress can start our business day as we do [with a prayer], then why would it not be constitutional to pray for the safety of our young men and women before they participate in some sporting event?

I am a firm believer in the First Amendment and I oppose actions that would violate the establishment clause. I ask, though, where is this violation? How does a prayer before a football game act to establish a religion? We cannot go back to the 1950s because it was wrong where children all recited the Lord's Prayer and we know that as a Methodist and Presbyterians, even Catholics, we have a different Lord's Prayer but I do think we can invoke the wish and the hope and the prayer for the safety of the participants.

Ms. JACKSON-LEE of Texas:

Mr. Speaker, I think this is a debate that bears much more attention than we are able to give it, primarily because it involves children, because it involves guiding children. But it also involves the Constitution.

Mr. Speaker, I am the mother of an eighth grade football player. Football is an intrinsic part of the culture of Texas, as it is in many, many places, as sports are an intrinsic part of America.

I would simply say to my colleagues that we set, I think, not the right tone if we would suggest to those students that they do not have the freedom to exercise their beliefs and pray. But I do think it is equally important for us to protect the isolated or the single person of a different faith.

That is why I bring some concern to this resolution, not because there is not good intention, but because there are the opportunities to have a story, such as Plaintiff Jane Doe, II, who was attending the seventh grade Texas history class, and her teacher handed out advertising regarding a Baptist religious revival, some of which I have attended. In fact, tomorrow I will be hosting a number of religious liberty activists from the 7th Day Adventist Church.

But Jane Doe was not a Baptist, and she was inquired about her religious affiliation. It was noted that she was from the Church of Jesus Christ of the Latter Day Saints, Mormons. Her teacher launched into a diatribe about the non-Christian cult-like nature of Mormonism and its general evils. In fact . . . the plaintiff's history teacher referred to her as a little atheist.

I would simply say, Mr. Speaker, that this resolution emphasizes too much that we are separated rather than we are welcoming the diversity of religion. It establishes one faith over another. It establishes a religion.

What we are trying to do, Mr. Speaker, is to make sure that this country is free for all religions. I want the football team to pray. I want the Capitol to pray. I want those in the stadium to pray, and they have every right to pray. The idea, of course, is that they cannot force upon others a prayer that others would not want to have.

I applaud those young people who are praying, and I think we, as adults, should create the atmosphere for them to pray. But I do not think we should instruct the Supreme Court to rule against the Constitution where it says there is a separation of Church and State.

In *Santa Fe* the Court noted that students holding minority religious beliefs had been insulted, intimidated, and harassed, even by school officials, and that therefore: "The District Court permitted respondents (Does) to litigate anonymously to protect them from intimidation or harassment." The Court also noted "that many District officials apparently neither agreed with nor particularly respected" that decision, and engaged in efforts to discover the identities of the children involved as plaintiffs, requiring the Federal District Court to issue this order:

Any further attempt on the part of District or school administration, officials, counselors, teachers, employees or servants of the School District, parents, students or anyone else, overtly or covertly to ferret out the identities of the Plaintiffs in this cause, by means of bogus petitions, questionnaires, individual interrogation, or downright 'snooping', will cease immediately. ANYONE TAKING ANY ACTION ON SCHOOL PROPERTY, DURING SCHOOL HOURS, OR WITH SCHOOL RESOURCES OR APPROVAL FOR PURPOSES OF ATTEMPTING TO ELICIT THE NAMES OR IDENTITIES OF THE PLAINTIFFS IN THIS CAUSE OF ACTION, BY OR ON BEHALF OF ANY OF THESE INDIVIDUALS, WILL FACE THE HARSHEST POSSIBLE CONTEMPT SANCTIONS FROM THIS COURT, AND MAY ADDITIONALLY FACE CRIMINAL LIABILITY. The Court wants these proceedings addressed on their merits, and not on the basis of intimidation or harassment of the participants on either side.

Despite well-established law prohibiting public school sponsored prayers, prayers by state officials continue in many public schools, from coaches praying with their student athletes, to principals praying with their teachers. The limitations of the Establishment Clause only apply in relationships involving state power. But public school coaches have great authority over student athletes, generally deciding who is a member of the team; what positions they may play; how much and when they play; etc. Public school principals have great authority over teachers, especially untenured teachers, controlling assignments; annual evaluations; continued employment; etc. Under these circumstances, are those who choose not to participate in prayers conducted by their public school supervisors truly free to decline without fear of any related stigma or consequences?

Even if there were no intentional consequences related to refusing to join in these prayers, isn't a coach or principal who leads these prayers far more vulnerable to claims of religious discrimination from a disgruntled athlete or employee? How would school officials defend against these claims when the defense included an admission that the school official had been violating well-established law by leading prayers in their official capacity?

While acting in their official capacities, public employees must respect the limits of the Establishment Clause. As private citizens, however, public employees retain their full rights to free exercise of religion including prayer and the right to use free speech to advocate for their faith. For example, a public school educator could serve as a minister on Sunday and a public school official on Monday, as long as the private role of clergy and the public role of state official were appropriately separated. The First Amendment requires official neutrality concerning religion by state officials only when they are acting in their official capacities.

State sponsored public school prayer still has many advocates who see public school prayer as a long recognized and important activity perfectly compatible with the First Amendment. But what if the Court were to allow state sponsored public school prayer? What prayer should be selected?

Although the options in selecting a prayer are infinite, all are potentially problematic in a religiously diverse nation. At one end of the spectrum of potential prayers are prayers that are narrowly sectarian in nature. For example, invoking "Allah"; "Hashem"; "Jesus Christ our Lord and Savior"; or "Holy Mary, Mother of God", may be offensive to all persons who do not share that particular sectarian faith. At the other end of the spectrum of potential prayers are prayers that omit any specific religious references. These generic prayers, however, may be offensive to all sincere believers because a diluted, religiously neutral prayer is no real prayer at all, tending to trivialize sincere, sacred prayer consistent with religious faith.

The more specific the prayer, the more likely it is to be divisive; the less specific the prayer, the less likely it is to satisfy the religious intentions of those that wanted the prayer adopted in the first place. The U.S. is the most religiously diverse nation on Earth, and that diversity is increasing. Is it possible to find a common creed in such a religiously diverse nation? Is the "Ten Commandments" an appropriate common creed?

Challenges to the display of the Ten Commandments on public property have become a perennial issue in federal courts. The U.S. Supreme Court decided two cases on this issue in 2005, resulting in two different 5-4 splits among the Justices. In *McCreary County v. ACLU*, 545 U.S. 844 (2005), the Court affirmed lower court decisions that the display of the Ten Commandments in two Kentucky courthouses violated the Establishment Clause. In *Van Orden v. Perry*, 545 U.S. 677 (2005), a different 5-4 alignment of Justices held that a six-foot tall stone monolith inscribed with the Ten Commandments did not violate the Establishment Clause. The Court noted that the monolith had stood for over 40 years in an open area on the Texas State Capital grounds, generating no controversy other than the litigation in this case.

While neither of these opinions directly addressed the display of the Ten Commandments in public schools, the Court referred to an earlier public school case, *Stone v. Graham*, 449 U.S. 39 (1980), as an important guide in deciding these types of controversies. In *Stone*, the Court ruled that a state statute requiring the display of the Ten Commandments on the wall of every public school classroom was unconstitutional.

Read together these cases may indicate that although the Court will continue to review these types of disputes on a case-by-case basis, a prominent, official display of the Ten Commandments in a public school is likely to be held unconstitutional, particularly if there was evidence of a religious motivation; a reasonable person would perceive that the state was not remaining neutral in a religious controversy; or the display was not a legitimate part of a broader secular message related to the law, history, or other parts of the curriculum.

In *Van Orden*, one of the plaintiff's chief complaints was that: "Even among religions that accept the Ten Commandments, there are significant differences in content of each religion's version of the Ten Commandments . . . The Texas Ten Commandments is virtually identical to the Protestant version." Can school officials adopt one version over the others without appearing to endorse one religious interpretation over the others?

Many have come to see the Ten Commandments as a universal statement of moral and religious principles. With visions of Charlton Heston as Moses in Cecil B. DeMille's "The Ten Commandments" they see a universal iconic religious figure carrying two stone tablets down from the mountain to serve as a common moral and religious foundation.

But on closer examination rather than a uniform creed and interpretation there are highly divergent opinions concerning even the most fundamental elements of the Ten Commandments. Even among Christians, the Protestant and Catholic versions of the Ten Commandments vary significantly. For example, the Second Commandment in the King James Bible states: "Thou shalt not make unto thee any graven image" while the Catholic version of the Ten Commandments makes no express mention of this prohibition against a "graven image."

Reference to the original Hebrew reveals even more divergence concerning interpretations of the Ten Commandments. The versions of the Ten Commandments that appear in the books of Exodus and Deuteronomy are slightly different (the latter is a restatement by Moses). The Hebrew version of the "Ten Commandments" is actually the "Aseres haDibros" (the "Ten Utterances"), the first of which declares: "I am the Lord your God who brought you out of the land of Egypt" and is a statement of Divine Sovereignty and not a commandment.

Further, under the Jewish interpretation of the Bible there are 613 commandments; the "Aseres haDibros" are only binding religious law for Jews; and it is the Seven Laws of Noah (prohibiting: 1) Idolatry; 2) Blaspheme; 3) Murder; 4) Immoral acts; 5) Theft; 6) Cruelty to animals; and 7) Recognizing a mandate to pursue justice) that establishes the common code of morality for all of humanity, not the Ten Commandments.

Similarly, in selecting a version of "The Bible" do you select the Catholic Bible or one of the many Protestant translations, none of which would be acceptable to non-Christians. Even the terms "New Testament" and "Old Testament" are objectionable to members of the Jewish faith as both terms imply that the "New Testament" has superseded the Torah, the Jewish Holy Book.

The Court held that requiring Bible readings by public school students was unconstitutional in *Abington v. Schempp*, 374 U.S. 203 (1963). The Court noted, however:

> It might well be said that one's education is not complete without a study of comparative religion or the history of religion and its relationship to the advancement of civilization. It certainly may be said that the Bible is worthy of study for its literary and historic qualities. Nothing we have said here indicates that such study of the Bible or of religion, when presented objectively as part of a secular program of education, may not be effected consistently with the First Amendment.

If public school officials are in fact genuinely offering academic studies of religion or the Bible, and not merely using these as a pretext for inculcating their preferred religion to students, studies of religion, the Bible, and other holy books are an important part of a complete education. Because religion plays such a central role in human history, one cannot truly understand the human experience without understanding the religious beliefs that have motivated people throughout human history.

Most Americans identify themselves as religious and indicate that religion is an important part of their lives. Yet in study after study it has been demonstrated that most Americans know shockingly little about the history and theology of even their own faith, and even less about the beliefs of others. Is it possible that religious bigotry, hatred, and conflict may be driven more by ignorance about the religious beliefs of others than substantive differences?

Often, much of what people "know" about the religious beliefs of others turns out to be untrue. Studies of religion may be a very useful addition to everyone's education. But how can you help to assure that these studies are as the Court suggested "presented objectively as part of a secular program of education" and do not become the slippery slope on which the local majority faith becomes the "official" faith of the school, causing all others to become religious outsiders in their own school and community?

Use of Public School Facilities by Religious Groups

Public officials are required to remain neutral concerning religion. This does not, however, make public school facilities religion free zones. When public facilities are made available to students or members of the public, government officials can neither favor nor disfavor religious groups and religious speech. Facilities must be made available to all on an equal basis.

Lamb's Chapel v. Center Moriches Union Free School District
508 U.S. 384 (1993)
Supreme Court of the United States

\
Justice WHITE delivered the opinion of the Court.

New York Educ. Law § 414 authorizes local school boards to adopt reasonable regulations for the use of school property for 10 specified purposes when the property is not in use for school purposes. Among the permitted uses is the holding of "social, civic and recreational meetings and entertainments, and other uses pertaining to the welfare of the community; but such meetings, entertainment and uses shall be non-exclusive and shall be open to the general public." The list of permitted uses does not include meetings for religious purposes, and a New York appellate court in *Trietley v. Board*, ruled that local boards could not allow student bible clubs to meet on school property because "religious purposes are not included in the enumerated purposes for which a school may be used under section 414." In *Deeper Life Christian Fellowship v. Sobol*, the Court of Appeals for the Second Circuit accepted *Trietley* as an authoritative interpretation of state law. Furthermore, the Attorney General of New York supports *Trietley* as an appropriate approach to deciding this case.

Pursuant to § 414's empowerment of local school districts, the Board of Center Moriches Union Free School District (District) has issued rules and regulations with respect to the use of school property when not in use for school purposes. The rules allow only 2 of the 10 purposes authorized by § 414: social, civic, or recreational uses (Rule 10) and use by political organizations if secured in compliance with § 414 (Rule 8). Rule 7, however, consistent with the judicial interpretation of state law, provides that "the school premises shall not be used by any group for religious purposes."

The issue in this case is whether, against this background of state law, it violates the Free Speech Clause of the First Amendment, made applicable to the States by the Fourteenth Amendment, to deny a church access to school premises to exhibit for public viewing and for assertedly religious purposes, a film series dealing with family and child-rearing issues faced by parents today. Petitioners (Church) are Lamb's Chapel, an evangelical church in the community of Center Moriches, and its pastor John Steigerwald. Twice the Church applied to the District for permission to use school facilities to show a six-part film series containing lectures by Doctor James Dobson. A brochure provided on request of the District identified Dr. Dobson as a licensed psychologist, former associate clinical professor of pediatrics at the University of Southern California, best-selling author, and radio commentator. The brochure stated that the film series would discuss Dr. Dobson's views on the undermining influences of the media that could only be counterbalanced by returning to traditional, Christian family values instilled at an early stage. The brochure went on to describe the contents of each of the six parts of the series. The District denied the first application, saying that "this film does appear to be church related and therefore your request must be refused." The second application for permission to use school premises for showing the film series, which described it as a "Family oriented movie-from a Christian perspective," was denied using identical language.

The Church brought suit in the District Court, challenging the denial as a violation of the Freedom of Speech and Assembly Clauses, the Free Exercise Clause, and the Establishment Clause of the First Amendment, as well as the Equal Protection Clause of the Fourteenth Amendment. As to each cause of action, the Church alleged that the actions were undertaken under color of state law, in violation of 42 U.S.C. § 1983. The District Court granted summary judgment for respondents, rejecting all the Church's claims. . . The Court of Appeals affirmed the judgment of the District Court "in all respects" . . . Because the holding below was questionable under our decisions, we granted the petition for certiorari, which in principal part challenged the holding below as contrary to the Free Speech Clause of the First Amendment.

There is no question that the District, like the private owner of property, may legally preserve the property under its control for the use to which it is dedicated. It is also common ground that the District need not have permitted after-hours use of its property for any of the uses permitted by N.Y. Educ. Law § 414. The District, however, did open its property for 2 of the 10 uses permitted by § 414. The Church argued below that because under Rule 10 of the rules issued by the District, school property could be used for "social, civic, and recreational" purposes, the District had opened its property for such a wide variety of communicative purposes that restrictions on communicative uses of the property were subject to the same constitutional limitations as restrictions in traditional public forums such as parks and sidewalks. Hence, its view was that subject matter or speaker exclusions on District property were required to be justified by a compelling state interest and to be narrowly drawn to achieve that end. Both the District Court and the Court of Appeals rejected this submission, which is also presented to this Court. The argument has considerable force, for the District's property is heavily used by a wide variety of private organizations, including some that presented a "close question," which the Court of Appeals resolved in the District's favor, as to whether the District had in fact already opened its property for religious uses. We need not rule on this issue, however, for even if the courts below were correct in this respect--and we shall assume for present purposes that they were--the judgment below must be reversed.

With respect to public property that is not a designated public forum open for indiscriminate public use for communicative purposes, we have said that "control over access to a non-public forum can be based on subject matter and speaker identity so long as the distinctions drawn are reasonable in light of the purpose served by the forum and are viewpoint neutral." The Court of Appeals appeared to recognize that the total ban on using District property for religious purposes could survive First Amendment challenge only if excluding this category of speech was reasonable and viewpoint neutral. The court's conclusion in this case was that Rule 7 met this test. We cannot agree with this holding, for Rule 7 was unconstitutionally applied in this case.

The Court of Appeals thought that the application of Rule 7 in this case was viewpoint neutral because it had been, and would be, applied in the same way to all uses of school property for religious purposes. That all religions and all uses for religious purposes are treated alike under Rule 7, however, does not answer the critical question whether it discriminates on the basis of viewpoint to permit school property to be used for the presentation of all views about family issues and child rearing except those dealing with the subject matter from a religious standpoint.

There is no suggestion from the courts below or from the District or the State that a lecture or film about child rearing and family values would not be a use for social or civic purposes otherwise permitted by Rule 10. That subject matter is not one that the District has placed off limits to any and all speakers. Nor is there any indication in the record before us that the application to exhibit the particular film series involved here was, or would have been, denied for any reason other than the fact that the presentation would have been from a religious perspective. In our view, denial on that basis was plainly invalid under our holding in *Cornelius v. NAACP*, 473 U.S. 788 (1985) that "although a speaker may be excluded from a non-public forum if he wishes to address a topic not encompassed within the purpose of the forum . . . or if he is not a member of the class of speakers for whose especial benefit the forum was created . . . the government violates the First Amendment when it denies access to a speaker solely to suppress the point of view he espouses on an otherwise includible subject."

The film series involved here no doubt dealt with a subject otherwise permissible under Rule 10, and its exhibition was denied solely because the series dealt with the subject from a religious standpoint. The principle that has emerged from our cases "is that the First Amendment forbids the government to regulate speech in ways that favor some viewpoints or ideas at the expense of others." That principle applies in the circumstances of this case; as Judge Posner said for the Court of Appeals for the Seventh Circuit, to discriminate "against a particular point of view . . . would . . . flunk the test . . . [of] *Cornelius*, provided that the defendants have no defense based on the establishment clause."

The District, as a respondent, would save its judgment below on the ground that to permit its property to be used for religious purposes would be an establishment of religion forbidden by the First Amendment. This Court suggested in *Widmar v. Vincent*, 454 U.S. 263 (1981) that the interest of the State in avoiding an Establishment Clause violation "may be [a] compelling" one justifying an abridgment of free speech otherwise protected by the First Amendment; but the Court went on to hold that permitting use of university property for religious purposes under the open access policy involved there would not be incompatible with the Court's Establishment Clause cases.

We have no more trouble than did the *Widmar* Court in disposing of the claimed defense on the ground that the posited fears of an Establishment Clause violation are unfounded. The showing of this film series would not have been during school hours, would not have been sponsored by the school, and would have been open to the public, not just to church members. The District property had repeatedly been used by a wide variety of private organizations. Under these circumstances, as in *Widmar*, there would have been no realistic danger that the community would think that the District was endorsing religion or any particular creed, and any benefit to religion or to the Church would have been no more than incidental. As in *Widmar*, permitting District property to be used to exhibit the film series involved in this case would not have been an establishment of religion under the three-part test articulated in *Lemon v. Kurtzman*: The challenged governmental action has a secular purpose, does not have the principal or primary effect of advancing or inhibiting religion, and does not foster an excessive entanglement with religion.

The District also submits that it justifiably denied use of its property to a "radical" church for the purpose of proselytizing, since to do so would lead to threats of public unrest and even violence. There is nothing in the record to support such a justification, which in any event would be difficult to defend as a reason to deny the presentation of a religious point of view about a subject the District otherwise opens to discussion on District property . . .

For the reasons stated in this opinion, the judgment of the Court of Appeals is

Reversed.

Justice SCALIA, with whom Justice THOMAS joins, concurring in the judgment.

I join the Court's conclusion that the District's refusal to allow use of school facilities for petitioners' film viewing, while generally opening the schools for community activities, violates petitioners' First Amendment free-speech rights . . . I also agree with the Court that allowing Lamb's Chapel to use school facilities poses "no realistic danger" of a violation of the Establishment Clause, but I cannot accept most of its reasoning in this regard. The Court explains that the showing of petitioners' film on school property after school hours would not cause the community to "think that the District was endorsing religion or any particular creed," and further notes that access to school property would not violate the three-part test articulated in *Lemon v. Kurtzman*.

As to the Court's invocation of the *Lemon* test: Like some ghoul in a late-night horror movie that repeatedly sits up in its grave and shuffles abroad, after being repeatedly killed and buried, *Lemon* stalks our Establishment Clause jurisprudence once again, frightening the little children and school attorneys of Center Moriches Union Free School District. Its most recent burial, only last Term, was, to be sure, not fully six feet under: Our decision in *Lee v. Weisman*, conspicuously avoided using the supposed "test" but also declined the invitation to repudiate it. Over the years, however, no fewer than five of the currently sitting Justices have, in their own opinions, personally driven pencils through the creature's heart (the author of today's opinion repeatedly), and a sixth has joined an opinion doing so.

The secret of the *Lemon* test's survival, I think, is that it is so easy to kill. It is there to scare us (and our audience) when we wish it to do so, but we can command it to return to the tomb at will. When we wish to strike down a practice it forbids, we invoke it, when we wish to uphold a practice it forbids, we ignore it entirely. Such a docile and useful monster is worth keeping around, at least in a somnolent state; one never knows when one might need him. For my part, I agree with the long list of constitutional scholars who have criticized *Lemon* and bemoaned the strange Establishment Clause geometry of crooked lines and wavering shapes its intermittent use has produced.

* * * * * * *

105

In *Lamb's Chapel* the Court found that when government officials choose to open public facilities for public use, those facilities must be available to all eligible persons on an equal basis. Government officials do not have to open facilities to use by any outside groups. But when they do, government officials violate the Free Speech provisions of the First Amendment if they deny access to speakers solely to suppress a point of view, in this case, a religious point of view.

The prohibition against Establishment of religion applies to school officials and not to groups of private citizens lawfully meeting in public school facilities. And in this case concerns about possible perceptions of Establishment were outweighed by Free Speech rights. But what if the outside group wanted to lead prayers, Bible readings, and other religious activities after school in the public school owned facilities for children ages 6 to 12? Would the Establishment Clause concerns of public school officials in this case outweigh the Free Speech rights of the outside group? The Court addressed these questions in *Good News Club v. Milford*.

Good News Club v. Milford Central School
533 U.S. 98 (2001)
Supreme Court of the United States

Justice THOMAS delivered the opinion of the Court.

This case presents two questions. The first question is whether Milford Central School violated the free speech rights of the Good News Club when it excluded the Club from meeting after hours at the school. The second question is whether any such violation is justified by Milford's concern that permitting the Club's activities would violate the Establishment Clause. We conclude that Milford's restriction violates the Club's free speech rights and that no Establishment Clause concern justifies that violation.

The State of New York authorizes local school boards to adopt regulations governing the use of their school facilities. In particular, N.Y. Educ. Law § 414 enumerates several purposes for which local boards may open their schools to public use. In 1992, respondent Milford Central School (Milford) enacted a community use policy adopting seven of § 414's purposes for which its building could be used after school. Two of the stated purposes are relevant here. First, district residents may use the school for "instruction in any branch of education, learning or the arts." Second, the school is available for "social, civic and recreational meetings and entertainment events, and other uses pertaining to the welfare of the community, provided that such uses shall be nonexclusive and shall be opened to the general public."

Stephen and Darleen Fournier reside within Milford's district and therefore are eligible to use the school's facilities as long as their proposed use is approved by the school. Together they are sponsors of the local Good News Club, a private Christian organization for children ages 6 to 12. Pursuant to Milford's policy, in September 1996 the Fourniers submitted a request to Dr. Robert McGruder, interim superintendent of the district, in which they sought permission to hold the Club's weekly afterschool meetings in the school cafeteria. The next month, McGruder formally denied the Fourniers' request on the ground that the proposed use--to have "a fun time of singing songs, hearing a Bible lesson and memorizing scripture,"--was "the equivalent of religious worship." According to McGruder, the community use policy, which prohibits use "by any individual or organization for religious purposes," foreclosed the Club's activities.

In response to a letter submitted by the Club's counsel, Milford's attorney requested information to clarify the nature of the Club's activities. The Club sent a set of materials used or distributed at the meetings and the following description of its meeting:

> The Club opens its session with Ms. Fournier taking attendance. As she calls a child's name, if the child recites a Bible verse the child receives a treat. After attendance, the Club sings songs. Next Club members engage in games that involve, *inter alia*, learning Bible verses. Ms. Fournier then relates a Bible story and explains how it applies to Club members' lives. The Club closes with prayer. Finally, Ms. Fournier distributes treats and the Bible verses for memorization.

McGruder and Milford's attorney reviewed the materials and concluded that "the kinds of activities proposed to be engaged in by the Good News Club were not a discussion of secular subjects such as child rearing, development of character and development of morals from a religious perspective, but were in fact the equivalent of religious instruction itself." In February 1997, the Milford Board of Education adopted a resolution rejecting the Club's request to use Milford's facilities "for the purpose of conducting religious instruction and Bible study."

In March 1997, petitioners, the Good News Club, Ms. Fournier, and her daughter Andrea Fournier (collectively, the Club), filed an action under 42 U.S.C. § 1983, against Milford in the United States District Court for the Northern District of New York. The Club alleged that Milford's denial of its application violated its free speech rights under the First and Fourteenth Amendments . . .

When the State establishes a limited public forum, the State is not required to and does not allow persons to engage in every type of speech. The State may be justified "in reserving [its forum] for certain groups or for the discussion of certain topics." *Rosenberger v. Rector and Visitors of University of Virginia*, 515 U.S. 819 (1995); *see also, Lamb's Chapel v. Center Moriches Union Free School District*, 508 U.S. 364 (1993). The State's power to restrict speech, however, is not without limits. The restriction must not discriminate against speech on the basis of viewpoint, and the restriction must be "reasonable in light of the purpose served by the forum."

Applying this test, we first address whether the exclusion constituted viewpoint discrimination. We are guided in our analysis by two of our prior opinions, *Lamb's Chapel* and *Rosenberger*. In *Lamb's Chapel*, we held that a school district violated the Free Speech Clause of the First Amendment when it excluded a private group from presenting films at the school based solely on the films' discussions of family values from a religious perspective. Likewise, in *Rosenberger*, we held that a university's refusal to fund a student publication because the publication addressed issues from a religious perspective violated the Free Speech Clause. Concluding that Milford's exclusion of the Good News Club based on its religious nature is indistinguishable from the exclusions in these cases, we hold that the exclusion constitutes viewpoint discrimination. Because the restriction is viewpoint discriminatory, we need not decide whether it is unreasonable in light of the purposes served by the forum.

Milford has opened its limited public forum to activities that serve a variety of purposes, including events "pertaining to the welfare of the community." Milford interprets its policy to permit discussions of subjects such as child rearing, and of "the development of character and morals from a religious perspective." For example, this policy would allow someone to use Aesop's Fables to teach children moral values. Additionally, a group could sponsor a debate on whether there should be a constitutional amendment to permit prayer in public schools, and the Boy Scouts could meet "to influence a boy's character, development and spiritual growth." In short, any group that "promotes the moral and character development of children" is eligible to use the school building.

Just as there is no question that teaching morals and character development to children is a permissible purpose under Milford's policy, it is clear that the Club teaches morals and character development to children. For example, no one disputes that the Club instructs children to overcome feelings of jealousy, to treat others well regardless of how they treat the children, and to be obedient, even if it does so in a non-secular way. Nonetheless, because Milford found the Club's activities to be religious in nature--"the equivalent of religious instruction itself,"--it excluded the Club from use of its facilities.

Applying *Lamb's Chapel*, we find it quite clear that Milford engaged in viewpoint discrimination when it excluded the Club from the afterschool forum. In *Lamb's Chapel*, the local New York school district similarly had adopted § 414's "social, civic or recreational use" category as a permitted use in its limited public forum. The district also prohibited use "by any group for religious purposes." Citing this prohibition, the school district excluded a church that wanted to present films teaching family values from a Christian perspective. We held that, because the films "no doubt dealt with a subject otherwise permissible" under the rule, the teaching of family values, the district's exclusion of the church was unconstitutional viewpoint discrimination.

Like the church in *Lamb's Chapel*, the Club seeks to address a subject otherwise permitted under the rule, the teaching of morals and character, from a religious standpoint. Certainly, one could have characterized the film presentations in *Lamb's Chapel* as a religious use . . . And one easily could conclude that the films' purpose to instruct that "society's slide toward humanism . . . can only be counterbalanced by a loving home where Christian values are instilled from an early age" was "quintessentially religious." The only apparent difference between the activity of *Lamb's Chapel* and the activities of the Good News Club is that the Club chooses to teach moral lessons from a Christian perspective through live storytelling and prayer, whereas *Lamb's Chapel* taught lessons through films. This distinction is inconsequential. Both modes of speech use a religious viewpoint. Thus, the exclusion of the Good News Club's activities, like the exclusion of Lamb's Chapel's films, constitutes unconstitutional viewpoint discrimination.

Our opinion in *Rosenberger* also is dispositive. In *Rosenberger*, a student organization at the University of Virginia was denied funding for printing expenses because its publication, Wide Awake, offered a Christian viewpoint. Just as the Club emphasizes the role of Christianity in students' morals and character, Wide Awake "challenged Christians to live, in word and deed, according to the faith they proclaim and . . . encouraged students to consider what a personal relationship with Jesus Christ means." Because the university "selected for disfavored treatment those student journalistic efforts with religious editorial viewpoints," we held that the denial of funding was unconstitutional. Although in *Rosenberger* there was no prohibition on religion as a subject matter, our holding did not rely on this factor. Instead, we concluded simply that the university's denial of funding to print Wide Awake was viewpoint discrimination, just as the school district's refusal to allow *Lamb's Chapel* to show its films was viewpoint discrimination. Given the obvious religious content of Wide Awake, we cannot say that the Club's activities are any more "religious" or deserve any less First Amendment protection than did the publication of Wide Awake in *Rosenberger* . . .

Milford argues that, even if its restriction constitutes viewpoint discrimination, its interest in not violating the Establishment Clause outweighs the Club's interest in gaining equal access to the school's facilities. In other words, according to Milford, its restriction was required to avoid violating the Establishment Clause. We disagree . . . the Club's meetings were held after school hours, not sponsored by the school, and open to any student who obtained parental consent, not just to Club members . . . Milford made its forum available to other organizations. The Club's activities are materially indistinguishable from those in *Lamb's Chapel* . . . Thus, Milford's reliance on the Establishment Clause is unavailing . . . None of the cases discussed by Milford persuades us that our Establishment Clause jurisprudence has gone this far. For example, Milford cites *Lee v. Weisman,* for the proposition that "there are heightened concerns with protecting freedom of conscience from subtle coercive pressure in the elementary and secondary public schools." In *Lee,* however, we concluded that attendance at the graduation exercise was obligatory. See also *Santa Fe Independent School Dist. v. Doe,* 530 U.S. 290 (2000) (holding the school's policy of permitting prayer at football games unconstitutional where the activity took place during a school-sponsored event and not in a public forum). We did not place independent significance on the fact that the graduation exercise might take place on school premises. Here, where the school facilities are being used for a non-school function and there is no government sponsorship of the Club's activities, *Lee* is inapposite.

Equally unsupportive is *Edwards v. Aguillard,* 482 U.S. 578 (1987), in which we held that a Louisiana law that proscribed the teaching of evolution as part of the public school curriculum, unless accompanied by a lesson on creationism, violated the Establishment Clause. In *Edwards,* we mentioned that students are susceptible to pressure in the classroom, particularly given their possible reliance on teachers as role models . . . Moreover, we did note that mandatory attendance requirements meant that state advancement of religion in a school would be particularly harshly felt by impressionable students. But we did not suggest that, when the school was not actually advancing religion, the impressionability of students would be relevant to the Establishment Clause issue. Even if *Edwards* had articulated the principle Milford believes it did, the facts in *Edwards* are simply too remote from those here to give the principle any weight. *Edwards* involved the content of the curriculum taught by state teachers during the schoolday to children required to attend. Obviously, when individuals who are not schoolteachers are giving lessons after school to children permitted to attend only with parental consent, the concerns expressed in *Edwards* are not present.

In further support of the argument that the impressionability of elementary school children even after school is significant, Milford points to several cases in which we have found Establishment Clause violations in public schools. For example, Milford relies heavily on *School District of Abington Township v. Schempp,* 374 U.S. 203 (1963), in which we found unconstitutional Pennsylvania's practice of permitting public schools to read Bible verses at the opening of each schoolday. *Schempp,* however, is inapposite because this case does not involve activity by the school during the schoolday . . .

Finally, even if we were to inquire into the minds of schoolchildren in this case, we cannot say the danger that children would misperceive the endorsement of religion is any greater than the danger that they would perceive a hostility toward the religious viewpoint if the Club were excluded from the public forum . . . We cannot operate, as Milford would have us do, under the assumption that any risk that small children would perceive endorsement should counsel in favor of excluding the Club's religious activity. We decline to employ Establishment Clause jurisprudence using a modified heckler's veto, in which a group's religious activity can be

109

proscribed on the basis of what the youngest members of the audience might misperceive. There are countervailing constitutional concerns related to rights of other individuals in the community. In this case, those countervailing concerns are the free speech rights of the Club and its members. And, we have already found that those rights have been violated . . . When Milford denied the Good News Club access to the school's limited public forum on the ground that the Club was religious in nature, it discriminated against the Club because of its religious viewpoint in violation of the Free Speech Clause of the First Amendment. Because Milford has not raised a valid Establishment Clause claim, we do not address the question whether such a claim could excuse Milford's viewpoint discrimination.

The judgment of the Court of Appeals is reversed, and the case is remanded for further proceedings consistent with this opinion.

It is so ordered.

* * * * * * *

Lamb's Chapel and *Good News Club* involved the use of school facilities only by community groups not officially sanctioned by the school. School sanctioned meetings of student groups during non-instructional time, such as student meetings immediately before or after school, during lunch-time, etc., are governed by the Equal Access Act, 20 U.S.C. § 4071, passed by the U.S. Congress in 1984. Believing that student religious groups had been unfairly marginalized and excluded from these activities in some schools, advocates for these groups lobbied for passage of the Equal Access Act to assure non-discrimination when schools established a limited open forum by allowing non-curriculum related student groups to meet during non-instructional time.

Some school officials believed the Equal Access Act violated the Establishment Clause by mandating the opening of public school sanctioned meetings to student religious groups. In *Westside School District v. Mergens*, 496 U.S. 226 (1990), school officials challenged the Equal Access Act as unconstitutional under the Establishment Clause. The U.S. Supreme Court ruled 8-1 that the Equal Access Act did not violate the Establishment Clause, but was a neutral recognition of student Free Speech rights in a public limited open forum.

When a limited open forum has been created by school officials, the Equal Access Act prohibits discrimination based on the "religious, political, philosophical, or other content" of speech at student initiated meetings. School officials create a limited open forum by opening school sanctioned student initiated meetings to any non-curriculum related student group. When the Equal Access Act applies, school officials must open the door to all student groups, regardless of their religious, political, philosophical, or other perspectives:

Equal Access Act, 20 U.S.C. § 4071: Denial of equal access prohibited

(a) *Restriction of limited open forum on basis of religious, political, philosophical, or other speech content prohibited*
It shall be unlawful for any public secondary school which receives Federal financial assistance and which has a limited open forum to deny equal access or a fair opportunity to, or discriminate against, any

students who wish to conduct a meeting within that limited open forum on the basis of the religious, political, philosophical, or other content of the speech at such meetings.

(b) ``*Limited open forum*'' *defined*

A public secondary school has a limited open forum whenever such school grants an offering to or opportunity for one or more non-curriculum related student groups to meet on school premises during non-instructional time.

(c) *Fair opportunity criteria*

Schools shall be deemed to offer a fair opportunity to students who wish to conduct a meeting within its limited open forum if such school uniformly provides that--

(1) The meeting is voluntary and student-initiated;
(2) There is no sponsorship of the meeting by the school, the government, or its agents or employees;
(3) Employees or agents of the school or government are present at religious meetings only in a non-participatory capacity;
(4) The meeting does not materially and substantially interfere with the orderly conduct of educational activities within the school; and
(5) Non-school persons may not direct, conduct, control, or regularly attend activities of student groups.

(d) *Construction of subchapter with respect to certain rights*

Nothing in this subchapter shall be construed to authorize the United States or any State or political subdivision thereof--

(1) To influence the form or content of any prayer or other religious activity;
(2) To require any person to participate in prayer or other religious activity;
(3) To expend public funds beyond the incidental cost of providing the space for student-initiated meetings;
(4) To compel any school agent or employee to attend a school meeting if the content of the speech at the meeting is contrary to the beliefs of the agent or employee;
(5) To sanction meetings that are otherwise unlawful;
(6) To limit the rights of groups of students which are not of a specified numerical size; or
(7) To abridge the constitutional rights of any person.

(e) *Federal financial assistance to schools unaffected*

Notwithstanding the availability of any other remedy under the Constitution or the laws of the United States, nothing in this subchapter shall be construed to authorize the United States to deny or

111

withhold Federal financial assistance to any school.

(f) *Authority of schools with respect to order, discipline, well-being, and attendance concerns*
Nothing in this subchapter shall be construed to limit the authority of the school, its agents or employees, to maintain order and discipline on school premises, to protect the well-being of students and faculty, and to assure that attendance of students at meetings is voluntary.

In *Mergens* the Court strictly interpreted "non-curriculum related" to mean that there must be a direct relationship between student groups and courses in the curriculum or the Equal Access Act is triggered and the door is opened to non-curriculum related groups. For example, a Math Club is curriculum related because there is a math class in the curriculum. But unless there is chess class, a Chess Club is not directly attached to the curriculum even though chess involves mathematical principles. School officials do not have to allow non-curriculum related groups to meet. But when they do, the provisions of the Equal Access Act govern student meetings.

Under the Equal Access Act can an outside adult lead these groups? Can teachers participate in religious activities? Can school officials ban controversial groups? If you are assigned to supervise a student group where the content of the speech is contrary to your beliefs can you be compelled to attend? What authority do school officials retain to assure safety, order, and discipline at these meetings?

Although the Equal Access Act and decisions by the Court require school officials to respect Free Speech rights of students and outside groups using school facilities, Free Speech rights do not excuse students from compliance with the student code of conduct or applicable laws. Further, school officials can apply reasonable usage rules and reasonable time, place, and manner regulations to all students and non-school organizations, prohibiting, for example, any use of dangerous animals, illegal substances, chemicals, explosives, fire, or other objects or conduct that violates reasonable school rules or public health and safety regulations.

Teaching Evolution and Creationism

Every culture and religious faith teaches their beliefs concerning the origins of humanity to their children. The Judeo-Christian tradition includes the Book of Genesis which says that God created humans on the sixth day of Creation. But is this biblical account intended to be literal or religiously symbolic?

When the King James Version of the Book of Genesis stated: "God created man in His own image . . . male and female created He them . . . And the evening and the morning were the sixth day" many of those who champion a literal interpretation of the Bible believe that Creation was completed in six 24 hour days. They believe humans and all species were created in their current form. Fossils of now extinct animals are believed to be relics of the Great Flood. And based on counting backwards through biblical events, they calculate that the Earth and the rest of Creation are about 6,000 years old.

Many of those who see these events as religiously symbolic, however, view the Bible as a tool for exploring the spiritual realm with some historical and some allegorical meanings. They view science as a tool for exploring the physical world, and find no conflict between the Bible and science concerning the origins of humanity: The Bible describes humanity's spiritual origins and science describes physical origins. Based on observations of the Universe and fossil records current science estimates that the Universe is 14 billion years old. Earth's Sun is a 5 billion year old second-generation star made from the remains of first-generation stars. And life on Earth began about 3 billion years ago, setting in motion an evolutionary process that resulted in the emergence of modern humans 250 million years ago.

A great strength of American Law and Democracy is that everyone has the right to decide for themselves what to believe, and to share their beliefs with their children. But what should the common public schools teach children concerning these issues? In 1925 the State of Tennessee passed House Bill 185 (the "monkey law") which declared:

> *Section 1*: Be it enacted by the General Assembly of the State of Tennessee, That it shall be unlawful for any teacher in any of the Universities, Normals and all other public schools of the State which are supported in whole or in part by the public school funds of the State, to teach any theory that denies the story of the Divine Creation of man as taught in the Bible, and to teach instead that man has descended from a lower order of animals.
> *Section 2*: Be it further enacted, That any teacher found guilty of the violation of this Act, Shall be guilty of a misdemeanor and upon conviction, shall be fined not less than One Hundred $ (100.00) Dollars nor more than Five Hundred ($ 500.00) Dollars for each offense.
> *Section 3*: Be it further enacted, That this Act take effect from and after its passage, the public welfare requiring it.

The clash between religious fundamentalists who believed in a literal interpretation of the Bible and modernists who saw the biblical account and science as compatible was further fueled by rapid technological and social changes in the 1920s. Many fundamentalists saw these changes as threatening ideals they held as sacred, while the modernists saw these changes as inevitable and essential to progress. These tensions resulted in a dramatic confrontation in 1925 in *Tennessee v. Scopes*, 278 S.W. 57 (Tenn. 1925).

High school teacher John Scopes violated the Tennessee "monkey law" by teaching theories based on Charles Darwin's On the Origin of Species in his science class. Scopes was charged with violating the anti-evolution Act. Scopes' trial became a national obsession--a court-room drama pitting fundamentalists against modernists. The trial featured three-time presidential candidate and Creationism advocate William Jennings Bryan for the prosecution, and the famous American Civil Liberties Union (ACLU) defense lawyer Clarence Darrow for the defense.

As tension mounted in the trial, Darrow called Bryan as a witness. When asked the purpose of this unusual move by Darrow (calling opposing council Bryan as a witness), Bryan declared: "The purpose is to cast ridicule on everybody who believes in the Bible, and I am perfectly willing that the world shall know that these gentlemen have no other purpose than ridiculing every Christian who believes in the Bible." Darrow responded: "We have the purpose of preventing bigots and ignoramuses from controlling the education of the United States and you know it, and that is all." At the conclusion of the trial the judge stated:

> Mr. Scopes, the jury has found you guilty under this indictment, charging you with having taught in the schools of Rhea county, in violation of what is commonly known as the anti-evolution statute, which makes it unlawful for any teacher to teach in any of the public schools of the state, supported in whole or in part by the public school funds of the state, any theory that denies the story of the divine creation of man, and teach instead

thereof that man has descended from a lower order of animals. The jury has found you guilty. The statute makes this an offense punishable by fine of not less than $100 nor more than $500. The court now fixes your fine at $100, and imposes that fine upon you . . . Oh--Have you anything to say, Mr. Scopes, as to why the court should not impose punishment upon you?

Mr. Scopes responded:

Your honor, I feel that I have been convicted of violating an unjust statute. I will continue in the future, as I have in the past, to oppose this law in any way I can. Any other action would be in violation of my ideal of academic freedom--that is, to teach the truth as guaranteed in our constitution of personal and religious freedom. I think the fine is unjust.

On appeal to the Supreme Court of Tennessee, Mr. Scopes challenged the constitutionality of the anti-evolution statute and his conviction and fine under this Act. The court upheld the statute, but reversed the judgment against Mr. Scopes on a technicality of state law concerning the process for assessing fines, a diplomatically convenient result that neither angered politically powerful fundamentalists nor allowed Mr. Scopes any legal basis to appeal the court's decision. Fundamentalist were, however, emboldened by this result and they pushed for the adoption of anti-evolution statutes in other states.

Cold War competition and the Sputnik scare in the 1950s resulted in a national push in science education, which included biological sciences and the teaching of evolution. By the 1960s evolution was commonly included in science textbooks and taught in science classes. State statutes that prohibited the teaching of evolution were challenged as unconstitutional. In *Epperson v. Arkansas*, 393 U.S. 97 (1968), the U.S. Supreme Court addressed a constitutional challenge to the Arkansas anti-evolution statute. The Court wrote:

This appeal challenges the constitutionality of the "anti-evolution" statute which the State of Arkansas adopted in 1928 to prohibit the teaching in its public schools and universities of the theory that man evolved from other species of life. The statute was a product of the upsurge of "fundamentalist" religious fervor of the twenties. The Arkansas statute was an adaption of the famous Tennessee "monkey law" which that State adopted in 1925. The constitutionality of the Tennessee law was upheld by the Tennessee Supreme Court in the celebrated *Scopes* case . . . The overriding fact is that Arkansas' law selects from the body of knowledge a particular segment which it proscribes for the sole reason that it is deemed to conflict with a particular religious doctrine; that is, with a particular interpretation of the Book of Genesis by a particular religious group . . . There is and can be no doubt that the First Amendment does not permit the State to require that teaching and learning must be tailored to the principles or prohibitions of any religious sect or dogma . . . In the present case, there can be no doubt that Arkansas has sought to prevent its teachers from discussing the theory of evolution because it is contrary to the belief of some that the Book of Genesis must be the exclusive source of doctrine as to the origin of man. No suggestion has been made that Arkansas' law may be justified by considerations of state policy other than the religious views of some of its citizens. It is clear that fundamentalist sectarian conviction was and is the law's reason for existence. Its

114

antecedent, Tennessee's "monkey law," candidly stated its purpose: to make it unlawful "to teach any theory that denies the story of the Divine Creation of man as taught in the Bible, and to teach instead that man has descended from a lower order of animals." Perhaps the sensational publicity attendant upon the *Scopes* trial induced Arkansas to adopt less explicit language. It eliminated Tennessee's reference to "the story of the Divine Creation of man" as taught in the Bible, but there is no doubt that the motivation for the law was the same: to suppress the teaching of a theory which, it was thought, "denied" the divine creation of man. Arkansas' law cannot be defended as an act of religious neutrality. Arkansas did not seek to excise from the curricula of its schools and universities all discussion of the origin of man. The law's effort was confined to an attempt to blot out a particular theory because of its supposed conflict with the Biblical account, literally read. Plainly, the law is contrary to the mandate of the First, and in violation of the Fourteenth, Amendment to the Constitution. The judgment of the Supreme Court of Arkansas is reversed.

In the 1980s, however, there was a legislative push in many states to enact statutes allowing or requiring the teaching of "Creation-Science" which were lessons for science classes consistent with Creationist beliefs. In *Edwards v. Aguillard* the U.S. Supreme Court ruled on a challenge to a Creation-Science Act.

Edwards v. Aguillard
482 U.S. 578 (1987)
Supreme Court of the United States

Justice BRENNAN delivered the opinion of the Court.

The question for decision is whether Louisiana's "Balanced Treatment for Creation-Science and Evolution-Science in Public School Instruction" Act (Creationism Act), is facially invalid as violative of the Establishment Clause of the First Amendment. The Creationism Act forbids the teaching of the theory of evolution in public schools unless accompanied by instruction in "creation science." No school is required to teach evolution or creation science. If either is taught, however, the other must also be taught. The theories of evolution and creation science are statutorily defined as "the scientific evidences for [creation or evolution] and inferences from those scientific evidences."

Appellees, who include parents of children attending Louisiana public schools, Louisiana teachers, and religious leaders, challenged the constitutionality of the Act in District Court, seeking an injunction and declaratory relief. Appellants, Louisiana officials charged with implementing the Act, defended on the ground that the purpose of the Act is to protect a legitimate secular interest, namely, academic freedom. Appellees attacked the Act as facially invalid because it violated the Establishment Clause and made a motion for summary judgment. The District Court granted the motion. The court held that there can be no valid secular reason for prohibiting the teaching of evolution, a theory historically opposed by some religious denominations. The court further concluded that "the teaching of 'creation-science' and 'creationism,' as contemplated by the statute, involves teaching 'tailored to the principles' of a particular religious sect or group of sects." The District Court therefore held that the Creationism Act violated the Establishment Clause either because it prohibited the teaching of evolution or because it required the teaching of creation science with the purpose of advancing a particular religious doctrine.

The Court of Appeals affirmed. The court observed that the statute's avowed purpose of protecting academic freedom was inconsistent with requiring, upon risk of sanction, the teaching of creation science whenever evolution is taught. The court found that the Louisiana Legislature's actual intent was "to discredit evolution by counterbalancing its teaching at every turn with the teaching of creationism, a religious belief." Because the Creationism Act was thus a law furthering a particular religious belief, the Court of Appeals held that the Act violated the Establishment Clause. A suggestion for rehearing *en banc* was denied over a dissent. We noted probable jurisdiction, and now affirm.

The Establishment Clause forbids the enactment of any law "respecting an establishment of religion." The Court has applied a three-pronged test to determine whether legislation comports with the Establishment Clause. First, the legislature must have adopted the law with a secular purpose. Second, the statute's principal or primary effect must be one that neither advances nor inhibits religion. Third, the statute must not result in an excessive entanglement of government with religion. *Lemon v. Kurtzman*, 403 U.S. 602 (1971). State action violates the Establishment Clause if it fails to satisfy any of these prongs.

In this case, the Court must determine whether the Establishment Clause was violated in the special context of the public elementary and secondary school system. States and local school boards are generally afforded considerable discretion in operating public schools. *See Bethel School Dist. No. 403 v. Fraser*, 478 U.S. 675 (1986); *Tinker v. Des Moines Independent Community School Dist.*, 393 U.S. 503 (1969). "At the same time . . . we have necessarily recognized that the discretion of the States and local school boards in matters of education must be exercised in a manner that comports with the transcendent imperatives of the First Amendment." *Board of Education, Island Trees Union Free School Dist. No. 26 v. Pico*, 457 U.S. 853 (1982).

The Court has been particularly vigilant in monitoring compliance with the Establishment Clause in elementary and secondary schools. Families entrust public schools with the education of their children, but condition their trust on the understanding that the classroom will not purposely be used to advance religious views that may conflict with the private beliefs of the student and his or her family. Students in such institutions are impressionable and their attendance is involuntary. The State exerts great authority and coercive power through mandatory attendance requirements, and because of the students' emulation of teachers as role models and the children's susceptibility to peer pressure. Furthermore, "the public school is at once the symbol of our democracy and the most pervasive means for promoting our common destiny. In no activity of the State is it more vital to keep out divisive forces than in its schools." *Illinois ex rel. McCollum v. Board of Education*, 333 U.S. 203 (1948).

Consequently, the Court has been required often to invalidate statutes which advance religion in public elementary and secondary schools. *See, e.g., Grand Rapids School Dist. v. Ball*, 473 U.S. 373 (1985) (school district's use of religious school teachers in public schools); *Wallace v. Jaffree*, 472 U.S. 38 (1985) (Alabama statute authorizing moment of silence for school prayer); *Stone v. Graham*, 449 U.S. 39 (1980) (posting copy of Ten Commandments on public classroom wall); *Epperson v. Arkansas*, 393 U.S. 97 (1968) (statute forbidding teaching of evolution); *Abington School Dist. v. Schempp*, 374 U.S. 203 (1963) (daily reading of Bible); *Engel v. Vitale*, 370 U.S. 421 (1962) (recitation of "denominationally neutral" prayer).

Therefore, in employing the three-pronged *Lemon* test, we must do so mindful of the particular concerns that arise in the context of public elementary and secondary schools. We now turn to the evaluation of the Act under the *Lemon* test.

Lemon's first prong focuses on the purpose that animated adoption of the Act. "The purpose prong of the *Lemon* test asks whether government's actual purpose is to endorse or disapprove of religion." *Lynch v. Donnelly*, 465 U.S. 668 (1984) (O'Connor, J., concurring). A governmental intention to promote religion is clear when the State enacts a law to serve a religious purpose. This intention may be evidenced by promotion of religion in general, *see Wallace v. Jaffree*, (Establishment Clause protects individual freedom of conscience "to select any religious faith or none at all"), or by advancement of a particular religious belief, *e.g., Stone v. Graham* (invalidating requirement to post Ten Commandments, which are "undeniably a sacred text in the Jewish and Christian faiths"); *Epperson v. Arkansas* (holding that banning the teaching of evolution in public schools violates the First Amendment since "teaching and learning" must not "be tailored to the principles or prohibitions of any religious sect or dogma"). If the law was enacted for the purpose of endorsing religion, "no consideration of the second or third criteria [of *Lemon*] is necessary." *Wallace v. Jaffree*. In this case, appellants have identified no clear secular purpose for the Louisiana Act.

True, the Act's stated purpose is to protect academic freedom. This phrase might, in common parlance, be understood as referring to enhancing the freedom of teachers to teach what they will. The Court of Appeals, however, correctly concluded that the Act was not designed to further that goal. We find no merit in the State's argument that the "legislature may not have used the terms 'academic freedom' in the correct legal sense. They might have had in mind, instead, a basic concept of fairness; teaching all of the evidence." Even if "academic freedom" is read to mean "teaching all of the evidence" with respect to the origin of human beings, the Act does not further this purpose. The goal of providing a more comprehensive science curriculum is not furthered either by outlawing the teaching of evolution or by requiring the teaching of creation science.

While the Court is normally deferential to a State's articulation of a secular purpose, it is required that the statement of such purpose be sincere and not a sham. As Justice O'Connor stated in *Wallace*: "It is not a trivial matter, however, to require that the legislature manifest a secular purpose and omit all sectarian endorsements from its laws. That requirement is precisely tailored to the Establishment Clause's purpose of assuring that Government not intentionally endorse religion or a religious practice."

It is clear from the legislative history that the purpose of the legislative sponsor, Senator Bill Keith, was to narrow the science curriculum. During the legislative hearings, Senator Keith stated: "My preference would be that neither [creationism nor evolution] be taught." Such a ban on teaching does not promote--indeed, it undermines--the provision of a comprehensive scientific education.

It is equally clear that requiring schools to teach creation science with evolution does not advance academic freedom. The Act does not grant teachers a flexibility that they did not already possess to supplant the present science curriculum with the presentation of theories, besides evolution, about the origin of life. Indeed, the Court of Appeals found that no law prohibited Louisiana public school teachers from teaching any scientific theory. As the president of the Louisiana Science Teachers Association testified, "any scientific concept that's based on established fact can be included in our curriculum already, and no legislation allowing this is necessary." The Act provides Louisiana school teachers with no new authority. Thus the stated purpose is not furthered by it.

The Alabama statute held unconstitutional in *Wallace v. Jaffree*, is analogous. In *Wallace*, the State characterized its new law as one designed to provide a 1-minute period for meditation. We rejected that stated purpose as insufficient, because a previously adopted Alabama law already provided for such a 1-minute period. Thus, in this case, as in *Wallace*, "appellants have not identified any secular purpose that was not fully served by [existing state law] before the enactment of [the statute in question]."

Furthermore, the goal of basic "fairness" is hardly furthered by the Act's discriminatory preference for the teaching of creation science and against the teaching of evolution. While requiring that curriculum guides be developed for creation science, the Act says nothing of comparable guides for evolution. Similarly, resource services are supplied for creation science but not for evolution. Only "creation scientists" can serve on the panel that supplies the resource services. The Act forbids school boards to discriminate against anyone who "chooses to be a creation-scientist" or to teach "creationism," but fails to protect those who choose to teach evolution or any other non-creation science theory, or who refuse to teach creation science.

If the Louisiana Legislature's purpose was solely to maximize the comprehensiveness and effectiveness of science instruction, it would have encouraged the teaching of all scientific theories about the origins of humankind. But under the Act's requirements, teachers who were once free to teach any and all facets of this subject are now unable to do so. Moreover, the Act fails even to ensure that creation science will be taught, but instead requires the teaching of this theory only when the theory of evolution is taught. Thus we agree with the Court of Appeals' conclusion that the Act does not serve to protect academic freedom, but has the distinctly different purpose of discrediting "evolution by counterbalancing its teaching at every turn with the teaching of creationism" . . .

Stone v. Graham invalidated the State's requirement that the Ten Commandments be posted in public classrooms. "The Ten Commandments are undeniably a sacred text in the Jewish and Christian faiths, and no legislative recitation of a supposed secular purpose can blind us to that fact." As a result, the contention that the law was designed to provide instruction on a "fundamental legal code" was "not sufficient to avoid conflict with the First Amendment." Similarly *Abington School Dist. v. Schempp* held unconstitutional a statute "requiring the selection and reading at the opening of the school day of verses from the Holy Bible and the recitation of the Lord's Prayer by the students in unison," despite the proffer of such secular purposes as the "promotion of moral values, the contradiction to the materialistic trends of our times, the perpetuation of our institutions and the teaching of literature."

As in *Stone* and *Abington*, we need not be blind in this case to the legislature's preeminent religious purpose in enacting this statute. There is a historic and contemporaneous link between the teachings of certain religious denominations and the teaching of evolution. It was this link that concerned the Court in *Epperson v. Arkansas*, 393 U.S. 97 (1968), which also involved a facial challenge to a statute regulating the teaching of evolution. In that case, the Court reviewed an Arkansas statute that made it unlawful for an instructor to teach evolution or to use a textbook that referred to this scientific theory. Although the Arkansas antievolution law did not explicitly state its predominant religious purpose, the Court could not ignore that "the statute was a product of the upsurge of 'fundamentalist' religious fervor" that has long viewed this particular scientific theory as contradicting the literal interpretation of the Bible. After reviewing the history of antievolution statutes, the Court determined that "there can be no doubt that the motivation for the [Arkansas] law was the same [as other anti-evolution statutes]: to suppress the teaching of a theory which, it was thought, 'denied' the divine creation of man." The Court found that there can be no legitimate state interest in protecting particular religions from scientific views "distasteful to them," and concluded "that the First Amendment does not permit the State to require that teaching and learning must be tailored to the principles or prohibitions of any religious sect or dogma."

These same historic and contemporaneous antagonisms between the teachings of certain religious denominations and the teaching of evolution are present in this case. The preeminent purpose of the Louisiana Legislature was clearly to advance the religious viewpoint that a supernatural being created humankind. The term "creation science" was defined as embracing this particular religious doctrine by those responsible for the passage of the Creationism Act. Senator Keith's leading expert on creation science, Edward Boudreaux, testified at the legislative hearings that the theory of creation science included belief in the existence of a supernatural creator (noting that "creation scientists" point to high probability that life was "created by an intelligent mind"). Senator Keith also cited testimony from other experts to support the creation-science view that "a creator [was] responsible for the universe and everything in it." The legislative history therefore reveals that the term "creation science," as contemplated by the legislature that adopted this Act, embodies the religious belief that a supernatural creator was responsible for the creation of humankind.

Furthermore, it is not happenstance that the legislature required the teaching of a theory that coincided with this religious view. The legislative history documents that the Act's primary purpose was to change the science curriculum of public schools in order to provide persuasive advantage to a particular religious doctrine that rejects the factual basis of evolution in its entirety. The sponsor of the Creationism Act, Senator Keith, explained during the legislative hearings that his disdain for the theory of evolution resulted from the support that evolution supplied to views contrary to his own religious beliefs. According to Senator Keith, the theory of evolution was consonant with the "cardinal principles of religious humanism, secular humanism, theological liberalism, aetheistism [sic]." The state senator repeatedly stated that scientific evidence supporting his religious views should be included in the public school curriculum to redress the fact that the theory of evolution incidentally coincided with what he characterized as religious beliefs antithetical to his own. The legislation therefore sought to alter the science curriculum to reflect endorsement of a religious view that is antagonistic to the theory of evolution.

In this case, the purpose of the Creationism Act was to restructure the science curriculum to conform with a particular religious viewpoint. Out of many possible science subjects taught in the public schools, the legislature chose to affect the teaching of the one scientific theory that historically has been opposed by certain religious sects. As in *Epperson*, the legislature passed the Act to give preference to those religious groups which have as one of their tenets the creation of humankind by a divine creator. The "overriding fact" that confronted the Court in *Epperson* was "that Arkansas' law selects from the body of knowledge a particular segment which it proscribes for the sole reason that it is deemed to conflict with . . . a particular interpretation of the Book of Genesis by a particular religious group." Similarly, the Creationism Act is designed either to promote the theory of creation science which embodies a particular religious tenet by requiring that creation science be taught whenever evolution is taught or to prohibit the teaching of a scientific theory disfavored by certain religious sects by forbidding the teaching of evolution when creation science is not also taught. The Establishment Clause, however, "forbids alike the

119

preference of a religious doctrine or the prohibition of theory which is deemed antagonistic to a particular dogma." Because the primary purpose of the Creationism Act is to advance a particular religious belief, the Act endorses religion in violation of the First Amendment.

We do not imply that a legislature could never require that scientific critiques of prevailing scientific theories be taught. Indeed, the Court acknowledged in *Stone* that its decision forbidding the posting of the Ten Commandments did not mean that no use could ever be made of the Ten Commandments, or that the Ten Commandments played an exclusively religious role in the history of Western Civilization. In a similar way, teaching a variety of scientific theories about the origins of humankind to schoolchildren might be validly done with the clear secular intent of enhancing the effectiveness of science instruction. But because the primary purpose of the Creationism Act is to endorse a particular religious doctrine, the Act furthers religion in violation of the Establishment Clause . . .

The Louisiana Creationism Act advances a religious doctrine by requiring either the banishment of the theory of evolution from public school classrooms or the presentation of a religious viewpoint that rejects evolution in its entirety. The Act violates the Establishment Clause of the First Amendment because it seeks to employ the symbolic and financial support of government to achieve a religious purpose. The judgment of the Court of Appeals therefore is

Affirmed.

* * * * * * *

Comments and Questions

Is there any common ground between a literal interpretation of the Bible and science? Is it possible to harmonize a Creationist view of a human-centered Universe literally created in only six days and less than 6,000 years ago, with scientific evidence that humans are just one species in an ongoing process of evolution; on just one small planet; orbiting one small star; among roughly 100 billion stars in our single galaxy; among an estimated 125 billion galaxies based on data from the Hubble Telescope?

Is it a satisfactory resolution to conclude that the Bible and science have two distinct and separate purposes: The Bible being a tool for studying spiritual questions in the metaphysical religious realm, while science is a tool for studying questions in the physical world? And that spiritual questions concerning the Bible are appropriately addressed to parents and clergy, while science classes do not attempt to answer questions of spiritual meaning, but instead attempt only to present objective evidence about the physical world?

Amid this ongoing controversy, scientists continue to explore the biological origins of humans. Research in human genetics is a rapidly developing branch of science with the potential to produce medical breakthroughs and shed further light on the history and origins of humanity. Genetic research has traced human origins back to Africa, with a small tribe first leaving Africa only 50,000 years ago. This means that despite superficial differences in physical appearances resulting from rapid human adaption to dramatically different climates, scientific evidence suggests that all humans are much more closely related than previously believed. Genetic research has established, for example, that all humans had brown eyes until about 10,000 years ago when one human was born with a mutation in the OCA2 gene controlling eye color. That individual is the direct ancestor of all persons carrying a gene for blue eyes today.

How closely are humans related? Consider this: Every human has 2 parents; 4 grandparents; 8 great-grandparents; and the numbers double every generation in geometric progression to 16; 32; 64; 128; 256; 512; 1,024; 2,048; 4,096; 8,192; 16,384; 32,768; 65,536; 131,072; 262,144; 524,288; 1,048,576; 2,097,152; 4,194,304; 8,388,608; 16,777,216; 33,554,432; 67,108,864; 134,217,728; 268,435,456; 536,870,912; 1,073,741,824; etc. This means that every individual human has over a million direct ancestors after only 20 generations and over a billion ancestors in 30 generations. Assuming an average generation of 20 years, every individual human theoretically had over a million ancestors just 400 years ago and over a billion ancestors 600 years ago.

But the human population did not exceed 1 billion until just over 200 years ago, around the year 1800. The numbers of necessary ancestors for each individual quickly exceeds total historical human populations, meaning that humans are necessarily related and interrelated to the same relatively small number of people, and most humans are direct descendants of the small tribe that left Africa only 50,000 years ago. The human race is much more closely related than previously known. For every person you know, and every person that ever lived on Earth, it is not a question of whether you are related, but how closely you are related. And it is likely that you are related much more closely than you might think. Studies in human genetics confirm the close relationship of all humans.

How closely are humans related to their nearest non-human relatives? Humans and chimpanzees share at least 96% of the same DNA. Bonobo Chimpanzees have an even closer genetic match with humans than do the other two varieties of chimpanzees. The *Scopes* "monkey trial" was in 1925, but how would members of your community react to this information today? Would they react with interest or with outrage? How would they react to teaching this to their children? Does the close genetic relationship of all humans, and even all humans and animals, inspire them to greater closeness and common empathy, or provoke them to reject these connections as irrelevant or untrue?

Biogenetics is among the most promising new frontiers medically, scientifically, and economically. Nations that lead in this area will likely be among the future economic leaders. Should the science curriculum in your school be influenced directly or indirectly by majority religious beliefs in the community? Does the First Amendment allow this?

Religious Displays on Public School Property

Generally, the Court has allowed limited religious displays as part of a secular celebration of the holidays on public owned and controlled property. In *Lynch v. Donnelly*, 465 U.S. 668 (1984), in a 5-4 decision the Court upheld a challenged display in a public park near a shopping area. Although the display included a creche ("nativity scene") with the baby Jesus, it also included Santa, reindeers, candy canes, and a banner declaring "Seasons Greetings." Measuring these facts against the *Lemon* test the Court found that the display: 1) Had the secular purpose of celebrating the holiday season generally; 2) Did not advance religion; and 3) Did not entangle church and state. In contrast, in *Allegheny v. ACLU*, 492 U.S. 573 (1989), the Court declared a creche owned by a private church and erected in front of a courthouse with only religious symbols and a banner reading "Gloria in Excelsis Deo" unconstitutional in a 5-4 decision.

The display of religious symbols on public school property presents special concerns under the Establishment Clause because of the presence of impressionable children subject to compulsory attendance. It is unlikely that challenged religious displays on public school property would survive judicial review under the Establishment Clause unless it was clear to reasonable observers that any religious element was only an incidental part of a broader secular celebration of the holiday season, or was the free speech of a student in a school sponsored forum (*e.g.*, part of a student art display, etc.). Consistent with the *Lemon* test the school's true purpose cannot be to promote religion; the school's actions may neither advance nor inhibit religion; and there can be no improper entanglement between church and state.

State Aid to Religious Schools

Among the practices the Establishment Clause sought to end was public funding of government preferred religious institutions. Many citizens found it highly offensive to be taxed to support religious institutions they did not wish to support voluntarily, but were forced to support by government officials. The Establishment Clause prohibits government officials from taking tax dollars and directly transferring these dollars to religious institutions. Nonetheless, just as the wall of separation between church and state is not an absolute bar, neither is the prohibition against government aid to religious schools. Government officials cannot directly transfer tax dollars to religious institutions. But they can support education for all children, including children in private religious schools.

States are not required to use state money to support instruction in religious schools. But in some cases state support is constitutionally permissible. State financial support under the "child benefit" doctrine may be lawful if the primary beneficiary of the state aid is the child and not the religious institution. To support the education of all children in the state (including children in private religious schools), state funding can be used, for example, to subsidize student transportation and the purchase of textbooks on secular subjects such as math, science, etc.

The Court has also upheld state funding for tuition vouchers, where the decision to use these vouchers at religious schools was attributable to private choices by parents and students, and the voucher program was not a direct transfer of public aid to religious schools by the state. In *Zelman v. Simmons-Harris*, 536 U.S. 639 (2002), the Court upheld an Ohio school voucher program even though the vast majority of funding was going to private religious schools.

The Court seems to have adopted a policy of allowing public funding for students in religious schools when the primary beneficiary is the student and religious choices are attributable to private citizens and not state officials. In *Zobrest v. Catalina Foothills School District*, 509 U.S. 1 (1993), the Court allowed public funding for a sign-language interpreter, noting that the interpreter merely translated messages for the benefit of the student and did not alter any religious message. In *Rosenberger v. Rector*, 515 U.S. 819 (1995), the Court held that the University of Virginia could not exclude a religious student group from public funding intended to support student speech. In *Agostini v. Felton*, 521 U.S. 203 (1997), the Court allowed public funding for remedial instruction for students in private religious schools under Title I. And in *Mitchell v. Helms*, 530 U.S. 793 (2000), the Court allowed public funding for computers, library books, and other instructional materials for religious schools.

Limits on religious accommodation were recognized in *Board of Education of Kiryas Joel v. Grumet*, 512 U.S. 687 (1994), in which the Court struck down a legislatively created special school district for Satmar Hasidic Jews which used religious gerrymandering to functionally exclude other religious groups. Further, even when public support for private religious schools may be permissible under the U.S. Constitution, some state constitutions have much more restrictive language concerning state aid to religious institutions. Over two-thirds of U.S. states have adopted "Blaine Amendments" to their constitutions that generally prohibit the transfer of public funds to religious institutions. Georgia's Constitution, for example, states: "No money shall ever be taken from the public treasury, directly or indirectly, in aid of any church, sect, cult, or religious denomination or of any sectarian institution." Some state courts have held that these more restrictive state constitutional provisions prohibit state aid to religious schools that would otherwise be permissible under the U.S. Constitution.

Free Exercise of Religion in Public Schools

The Establishment Clause created a negative prohibition against official Establishment of religion. In contrast, the Free Exercise Clause created a positive duty for government officials to respect the individual Free Exercise of religion, and to provide an exemption or other reasonable accommodation for the Free Exercise of religion in appropriate cases.

Otherwise valid governmental actions may sometimes conflict with individual Free Exercise of religion. For example, deciding to serve pork products in the public school cafeteria because of favorable costs and demand is a valid governmental decision. But some students and faculty may be religiously prohibited from eating pork. While no one can be required to eat the pork products of course, the reasonable accommodation may be offering an alternative menu item or an opportunity to bring lunch from home.

In many cases, respecting the Free Exercise of religion is as simple as granting an exemption to the individual, or providing a reasonable accommodation such as an opportunity for an alternative assignment, etc. If a reasonable accommodation can be provided without undue costs, administrative burdens, disruptions, or health and safety risks to others, a simple exemption or other reasonable accommodation is generally in everyone's best interests.

The more difficult cases are those in which school officials believe they must refuse to grant an exemption or that the requested accommodation is unreasonable. In these cases, plaintiffs may attempt to force official recognition of the Free Exercise right and obtain a requested accommodation through litigation. To prevail in these cases plaintiffs must establish:

1) *The belief is religious*: Only religious beliefs are entitled to Free Exercise protection. Political or philosophical beliefs may be advanced through Free Speech, but they are not protected under the Free Exercise Clause;

2) *The belief is sincerely held by the plaintiff*: The plaintiff must prove by a preponderance of the evidence that the religious belief is sincerely held and not a sham belief only for purposes of obtaining the exemption or reasonable accommodation;

3) *The belief is central to the plaintiff's faith*: The belief impacted by the government action must be a core element of the plaintiff's faith, and not merely tangential.

4) *The government action is a direct burden on Free Exercise*: The government action must impose a direct burden on the Free Exercise of religion, and not merely an incidental burden.

If a plaintiff meets this burden of proof, the plaintiff has established a prima facie case for a protected Free Exercise right unless the government can establish:

5) *There is a compelling governmental interest*: Government officials can prove a compelling governmental interest (*e.g.*, protecting public security, health, safety, or respecting the Establishment Clause) for denying the exemption or other reasonable accommodation; and

6) *Government actions are narrowly tailored to achieving that interest*: The government's means of achieving the compelling interest must not be over-broad in limiting individual rights beyond what is necessary.

If the plaintiff ultimately prevails, the plaintiff is entitled to an exemption or other reasonable accommodation, but the government action remains valid for everyone else. This Free Exercise test can provide useful guidance for school officials in helping sort out which requests are valid and which ones are not entitled to protection. For example, if a Native American student presented credible evidence that his Tribe prohibited the use of vaccinations based on religious convictions, and that he also sincerely held this religious view, the objection to the state immunization policy is a religious belief under the Free Exercise Clause and sincerely held. In contrast, if parents request an exemption because they are concerned about a possible link between vaccinations and autism (an understandable parental health concern, but not a religious belief), this is not a religious belief protected under the Free Exercise Clause. And what if after the parents' request is denied, they then claim that their belief is instead religious? Obviously, this would raise serious doubts about whether the belief was sincerely held. State law or local policy may provide a process for exemption for these parents. But non-religious beliefs are not protected by the Free Exercise Clause.

While the U.S. Supreme Court's Free Exercise cases do provide some guidance, the law in this area is complex, controversial, and in some respects unsettled. The Court's 5-4 decision in *Employment Division of Oregon v. Smith*, 494 U.S. 872 (1990), further complicated the law in this area. In *Smith*, the Court redefined the fourth-prong of the Free Exercise test, holding that "direct burden" did not refer to the impact of the government's actions in obstructing the individual's Free Exercise of religion, but to the intent of government officials. Under this new interpretation, government actions only burdened Free Exercise within the protections of the First Amendment if the plaintiff could prove that the religious practice in question had been intentionally targeted by government officials. Rules of general application that did not target religious practices did not violate the Free Exercise Clause.

In *Smith*, a Native American employed by the State had been dismissed based on a positive test for the use of peyote, a traditional sacrament commonly used by his Tribe for religious purposes. Under the prior Free Exercise test his use of peyote was based on a religious belief, it was sincerely held, the practice was central to his faith, and the State's actions directly burdened his religious practice. Nonetheless, under this new interpretation of the Free Exercise test, Smith lost the case, making it very difficult for future plaintiffs to prevail in other Free Exercise cases.

Unless Free Exercise plaintiffs can prove that government officials directly targeted their religious practice, as in *Church of Lukumi Babalu Aye v. Hialeah*, 508 U.S. 520 (1993), their free exercise is not protected under the U.S. Constitution. In *Hialeah* the Court found that city officials had directly targeted and punished religious animal sacrifices by members of the Santeria religion, and that this targeted discrimination was an unconstitutional direct burden on free exercise of religion. But after the Court's decisions in *Smith* and *Hialeah*, couldn't government officials who intended to target a religious practice simply offer a plausible pretext for the general applicability of the rule and leave no evidence of the real intent to discriminate? Critics of the Court's decision in *Smith* suggested that after *Smith*, everyone's right to Free Exercise of religion ultimately depended on the political standing of their faith and how good government officials were at offering a pretext and covering up their real intention to discriminate against a politically unpopular religious practice.

This dramatic reversal of law by the Court was seen as so shocking and damaging to Free Exercise rights that the U.S. Congress intervened to reverse the Court's decision. Congress overwhelming passed the Religious Freedom Restoration Act (RFRA), 42 U.S.C. § 2000bb (1993), which attempted to overrule the Court's decision in *Smith*, and restore the Court's former interpretation of the Free Exercise Clause. However, while Congress has the power to enact statutes, since *Marbury v. Madison*, 1 Cranch 137 (1803), it is well established law that the Court that has the power to interpret the Constitution. In *Boerne v. Flores*, 521 U.S. 507 (1997), the Court declared the RFRA unconstitutional, reinstating *Smith* as the legal standard under the U.S. Constitution. Nonetheless, even if a Free Exercise right is not protected under the U.S. Constitution, it may still be protected under the State Constitution, requiring exemptions or reasonable accommodations by state officials in appropriate cases.

Exemptions from School Attendance Laws

In *Yoder v. Wisconsin*, 406 U.S. 205 (1972), the U.S. Supreme Court allowed Amish children a limited exemption from otherwise valid public school attendance laws. State law required school attendance until age 16. Amish parents asserted that their religious adherence to a traditional agrarian lifestyle did not allow their children to attend school beyond the Eighth Grade or age 14. Further academic instruction was contrary to their sincerely held religious beliefs in a life of agrarian simplicity.

In balancing the burdens on Free Exercise and the significance of the legitimate State interests under these facts, the Court ruled in favor of the Amish families. Amish children were receiving an appropriate education through Eighth Grade or age 14, which sufficiently prepared them for work and citizenship in their community. Further, they were unlikely to become a financial burden to anyone or otherwise infringe on the rights of others simply because they had been exempted from two years of the otherwise mandated educational experience.

This exemption has not been repeated for other faiths, however, and seems to be limited to the unique facts in this case. The principle that may survive from *Yoder* is that while the State may pursue legitimate objectives like universal education, the State must also show some reasonable flexibility in achieving this purpose, appropriately pursuing legitimate state interests while still respecting Free Exercise of religion.

Exemptions from School Vaccinations and other Health Requirements

In *Cruzan v. Missouri*, 497 U.S. 261 (1990), the U.S. Supreme Court held that legally competent adults have a liberty interest, protected by the Due Process Clause of the Fourteenth Amendment, to refuse medical treatment. This right is further strengthened when the individual's refusal of medical treatment is required by sincerely held religious beliefs. The limits of this right occur when the individual poses a serious health risk to others; the individual is not legally competent; or parental decisions could seriously endanger the health of a minor child.

Although there may be a liberty right under the Due Process Clause to refuse medical treatment that does not necessarily prevent the state from conditioning a state benefit, such as public school attendance, on compliance with legitimate health regulations. State school attendance laws could be satisfied through home school, etc. A reasonable accommodation for Free Exercise of religion (*i.e.*, admission to school without vaccination) would require administrative permission or the establishment of a legal right to admission.

The Court's decision in *Employment Division of Oregon v. Smith*, 494 U.S. 872 (1990) casts serious doubt on any federal constitutional right to Free Exercise exemptions related to vaccinations or other health requirements. State health requirements are likely rules of general applicability aimed at legitimate health concerns. Under current federal law plaintiffs are unlikely to be able to prove that state health requirements were targeted at their religious practices.

There may, however, be a right to a Free Exercise exemption under the State's religious freedom provisions. Further, some states have enacted statutes expressly granting exemptions from school vaccination policies when these exemptions are religiously required. In most cases these exemptions have posed no significant health risks to the vast majority of vaccinated persons and only limited health risks to the few persons exempted from vaccinations. In individual cases state administrators or courts may determine that liberty or Free Exercise interests outweigh these limited risks.

Accommodations for Religious Holidays

School districts are commonly closed during religious holidays observed by the majority of students and faculty. These school closing policies recognize that the majority of students and faculty would not be present at these times and continued operation of the school would be inefficient. For students and teachers who practice minority faiths, however, school officials must provide reasonable accommodations for their Free Exercise of religion to avoid charges of religious discrimination.

What accommodations are reasonable depends on the circumstances in each case. But a policy that clearly treated members of minority faiths unfairly in comparison to the treatment of the religious majority would constitute religious discrimination. At the other end of the continuum, a requested accommodation that involved preferential treatment or excessive accommodations, such as excessive absences (*e.g.*, a request to be excused every Friday), or that required excessive administrative burdens, costs, or unreasonable health and safety risks, is not a reasonable accommodation. While students are responsible for work missed during religious holidays, they should be given a fair opportunity to complete missed assignments and tests, and they should not be unfairly disadvantaged or punished for absences related to religious holidays.

Concerning reasonable accommodations for state employees' observances of religious holidays, in *Sherbert v. Verner*, 374 U.S. 398 (1963), the U.S. Supreme Court held that the State could not apply employment laws that discriminated on the basis of religious observance of the Sabbath. In *Sherbert* a Seventh Day Adventist who was religiously mandated to observe a Saturday Sabbath was denied employment benefits that were available to persons who observed a Sunday Sabbath. The Court declared the state policy unconstitutional, finding that there was no compelling interest for denying a Free Exercise exemption to those who observed a Saturday Sabbath.

In *Sherbert*, state officials could have easily granted a Free Exercise exemption to the policy while still achieving the policy's legitimate objectives and without changing the fundamental nature of the state program. In contrast if a plaintiff who observed a Saturday Sabbath would have applied for a position as the principal of a Saturday School Program, for example, no reasonable accommodation would be possible. Government officials have a legal duty under the Free Exercise Clause, applicable state religious freedom provisions, and Title VII in employment to provide for reasonable accommodations for the Free Exercise of religion. But where religious mandates are not compatible with any reasonable accommodation by the State, attendance or employment in a private religious school may be a more appropriate option. Excessive religious accommodations by the State may become religious preferences that violate the Establishment Clause.

Exemptions from School Activities

Otherwise legitimate public school activities may sometimes conflict with students and parents sincerely held religious beliefs, leading them to request a Free Exercise exemption. These may include, for example, requests to be exempted from sex education; co-ed physical education; dancing; dissecting a pig or other animal; objections to certain music or reading assignments; etc. Most of these disputes can be resolved locally and informally simply by an administrative allowance of a case-by-case exemption or a reasonable accommodation.

If the dispute cannot be resolved informally, however, courts generally attempt to balance the State's legitimate interests in requiring the activity against the magnitude of the burdens on the religious believer. For example, courts would likely grant a request to be exempted from a particular reading assignment, but would reject a request to be exempted from all reading. School officials may be able to require that the student learn essential principles of anatomy in order to pass a course. But dissecting a pig is not the only legitimate way to achieve that goal. In general, when students and parents request relatively minor exemptions or reasonable accommodations school officials usually honor these requests, and judges also tend to support these requests.

Although teachers and other school employees may also successfully claim Free Exercise exemptions from school activities that are otherwise valid duties, generally courts have not been quite as accommodating to these requests as they have been to students subject to compulsory attendance. Nonetheless, accommodations for Free Exercise of religion by employees are required under Title VII when those accommodations are reasonable. Free Exercise accommodations for school employees are reasonable if they do not cause undue costs, administrative burdens, or health or safety risks; diminish general job performance; excessively burden other employees; or intrude on the education or rights of students.

Release Time for Religious Instruction

The U.S. Supreme Court has upheld the practice of "release time" in which as a reasonable accommodation for Free Exercise of religion public school students are allowed to attend periodic religious instruction during regular school attendance hours at an off-campus location. In *McCollum v. Board of Education*, 333 U.S. 203 (1948), the U.S. Supreme Court struck down the practice of allowing clergymen to use public school classrooms for religious instruction of students during the school day. But in *Zorach v. Clauson*, 343 U.S. 306 (1952), the Court upheld a program that provided religious instruction to public school students during the school day in locations off of school property. The off-campus location may be, for example, a separate building not on school property or a van or other vehicle parked just off-campus.

The Court's decisions in *McCollum* and *Zorach* established a bright-line constitutional test in the physical world: Religious instruction on public school property during school hours was prohibited, but permitted off school property. What if the religious instruction is provided through the cyber-world? In *McCollum* the Court prohibited religious instruction by members of the clergy in public school classrooms during the school day. If the religious teacher is physically off-campus, consistent with *Zorach*, but the students are accessing the religious instruction through an on-campus computer, is this in violation of the Court's decision in *McCollum*? Future courts will have to answer this and other church-state questions by deciding whether the facts in a particular case bring it closer to the negative prohibitions of the Establishment Clause or the positive mandates of the Free Exercise Clause.

General Guidance on Constitutionally Protected Prayer in Public Schools

Church-state law and its application in schools can be a complex and sometimes confusing area of study. To help educators and others in better understanding the application of these principles the U.S. Department of Education's Guidance on Constitutionally Protected Prayer in Public Elementary and Secondary Schools provides useful guidance on applying the First Amendment's religion clauses in public schools:

Prayer During Non-instructional Time
Students may pray when not engaged in school activities or instruction, subject to the same rules designed to prevent material disruption of the educational program that are applied to other privately initiated expressive activities. Among other things, students may read their Bibles or other scriptures, say grace before meals, and pray or study religious materials with fellow students during recess, the lunch hour, or other non-instructional time to the same extent that they may engage in non-religious activities. While school authorities may impose rules of order and pedagogical restrictions on student activities, they may not discriminate against student prayer or religious speech in applying such rules and restrictions.

Organized Prayer Groups and Activities
Students may organize prayer groups, religious clubs, and "see you at the pole" gatherings before school to the same extent that students are permitted to organize other non-curricular student activities groups. Such groups must be given the same access to school facilities for assembling as is given to other non-curricular groups, without discrimination because of the religious content of their expression. School authorities possess substantial discretion concerning whether to permit the use of school media for student advertising or announcements regarding non-curricular activities. However, where student groups that meet for non-religious activities are permitted to advertise or announce their meeting--for example, by advertising in a student newspaper, making announcements on a

student activities bulletin board or public address system, or handing out leaflets-- school authorities may not discriminate against groups who meet to pray. School authorities may disclaim sponsorship of non-curricular groups and events, provided they administer such disclaimers in a manner that neither favors nor disfavors groups that meet to engage in prayer or religious speech.

Teachers, Administrators, and other School Employees

When acting in their official capacities as representatives of the state, teachers, school administrators, and other school employees are prohibited by the Establishment Clause from encouraging or discouraging prayer, and from actively participating in such activity with students. Teachers may, however, take part in religious activities where the overall context makes clear that they are not participating in their official capacities. Before school or during lunch, for example, teachers may meet with other teachers for prayer or Bible study to the same extent that they may engage in other conversation or non-religious activities. Similarly, teachers may participate in their personal capacities in privately sponsored baccalaureate ceremonies.

Moments of Silence

If a school has a "minute of silence" or other quiet periods during the school day, students are free to pray silently, or not to pray, during these periods of time. Teachers and other school employees may neither encourage nor discourage students from praying during such time periods.

Accommodation of Prayer During Instructional Time

It has long been established that schools have the discretion to dismiss students to off-premises religious instruction, provided that schools do not encourage or discourage participation in such instruction or penalize students for attending or not attending. Similarly, schools may excuse students from class to remove a significant burden on their religious exercise, where doing so would not impose material burdens on other students. For example, it would be lawful for schools to excuse Muslim students briefly from class to enable them to fulfill their religious obligations to pray during Ramadan. Where school officials have a practice of excusing students from class on the basis of parents' requests for accommodation of non-religious needs, religiously motivated requests for excusal may not be accorded less favorable treatment. In addition, in some circumstances, based on federal or state constitutional law or pursuant to state statutes, schools may be required to make accommodations that relieve substantial burdens on students' religious exercise. Schools officials are therefore encouraged to consult with their attorneys regarding such obligations.

Religious Expression and Prayer in Class Assignments

Students may express their beliefs about religion in homework, artwork, and other written and oral assignments free from discrimination based on the religious content of their submissions. Such home and classroom work should be judged by ordinary academic standards of substance and relevance and against other legitimate pedagogical concerns identified by the school. Thus, if a teacher's assignment involves writing a poem, the work of a student who submits a poem in the form of a prayer (for example, a psalm) should be judged on the basis of academic standards (such as literary quality) and neither penalized nor rewarded on account of its religious content.

Student Assemblies and Extracurricular Events

Student speakers at student assemblies and extracurricular activities such as sporting events may not be selected on a basis that either favors or disfavors religious speech. Where student speakers are selected on the basis of genuinely neutral, evenhanded criteria and retain primary control over the content of their expression, that expression is not attributable to the school and therefore may not be restricted because of its religious (or anti-religious) content. By contrast, where school officials determine or substantially control the content of what is expressed, such speech is attributable to the school and may not include prayer or other specifically religious (or anti-religious) content. To avoid any mistaken perception that a school endorses student speech that is not in fact attributable to the school, school officials may make appropriate, neutral disclaimers to clarify that such speech (whether religious or non-religious) is the speaker's and not the school's.

Prayer at Graduation

School officials may not mandate or organize prayer at graduation or select speakers for such events in a manner that favors religious speech such as prayer. Where students or other private graduation speakers are selected on the basis of genuinely neutral, evenhanded criteria and retain primary control over the content of their expression, however, that expression is not attributable to the school and therefore may not be restricted because of its religious (or anti-religious) content. To avoid any mistaken perception that a school endorses student or other private speech that is not in fact attributable to the school, school officials may make appropriate, neutral disclaimers to clarify that such speech (whether religious or non-religious) is the speaker's and not the school's.

Baccalaureate Ceremonies

School officials may not mandate or organize religious ceremonies. However, if a school makes its facilities and related services available to other private groups, it must make its facilities and services available on the same terms to organizers of privately sponsored religious baccalaureate ceremonies. In addition, a school may disclaim official endorsement of events sponsored by private groups, provided it does so in a manner that neither favors nor disfavors groups that meet to engage in prayer or religious speech.

Free Exercise Rights in Employment

Concerning private religious school employment, § 702 of Title VII allows private religious schools to discriminate in employment on the basis of religion if the employee's religious faith is "a bona fide occupational qualification reasonably necessary to the normal operation of that particular business or enterprise." The U.S. Supreme Court upheld this provision in *Corporation of the Presiding Bishop v. Amos*, 483 U.S. 327 (1987). If religious faith is an essential part of the institutional mission, and a bona fide part of the job description, a private religious school may legitimately choose to hire only employees that meet the institution's religious requirements.

Concerning public schools, the U.S. Constitution's First Amendment prohibits the establishment of religion by a government institution. Therefore, in a public school an employee's religion can never be "a bona fide occupational qualification reasonably necessary to the normal operation of that particular business or enterprise" as it could be in a private religious school under Title VII. A public employees' religion cannot be a factor in employment either negatively or positively. The Establishment Clause mandates that public employers must remain neutral concerning religion.

As noted above, the Free Exercise Clause and Title VII, however, do require public institutions to provide reasonable accommodations for individual Free Exercise of religion. This may include, for example, reasonable adjustments to the work schedule for observances of religious holidays, and other reasonable accommodations in working assignments and conditions.

An accommodation is not reasonable if it causes an unreasonable financial or administrative burden or creates health or safety risks for others. Further, while employers are required to attempt to provide reasonable accommodations for employees' sincerely held religious exercises, in *Ansonia Board of Education v. Philbrook*, 479 U.S. 60 (1986), the Court held that where a reasonable accommodation has been provided, it is not necessary that the employer provide the accommodation preferred by the employee.

Chapter Summary

This chapter reviewed First Amendment rights generally, and focused on the application of church-state law in public schools. After reading this chapter, please consider the following points in review and for further thought and discussion:

I. *Review Points*:

1) The abilities to think, choose, and communicate define humanity and drive human progress.

2) New ideas change people; and people with new ideas change the world.

3) New ideas can threaten the status quo. Institutional powers have too often been used not for institutional progress but to censor ideas that challenged the status quo.

4) Censorship efforts ultimately fail. The pen is mightier than the sword; the printing press is mightier than the pen; and the Internet is the most powerful communications tool ever invented making it possible to communicate to a global audience instantly, allowing new ideas and information to spread globally with the speed of light. In view of how dramatically the invention of the written word and the printing press changed the world, the Internet and other individual mass communication technologies will change the world in ways that can only be imagined now.

5) Individual freedom of belief is protected absolutely. All other individual rights must be balanced against their impact on the rights of others.

6) In a system of laws dedicated to the advancement of liberty, the most vigorous constitutional protections are given to those rights closest to the core of individual free-will belief.

7) The height and strength of the symbolic wall of separation between church and state increases or diminishes in each case depending on the degree of danger presented by the co-mingling of church and state power. This wall protects the free exercise of religion from governmental interference, and protects the state against dangerous conflicts over religious control.

8) In Establishment cases the Court uses the *Lemon* test or related alternative tests:

> Under the *Lemon* test, a government action challenged as violating the Establishment Clause will be constitutionally valid only if it satisfies each of the following conditions:
>
>> 1) *Purpose*: There must a legitimate secular purpose for the challenged government action. The primary purpose underlying the government action cannot be religious in nature.
>> 2) *Effect*: The primary effect of the government action must be religiously neutral. It must neither advance nor inhibit religion.
>> 3) *Entanglement*: The government action must not foster excessive entanglement between church and state.

If a government action is found to have violated any of the three-prongs of the *Lemon* test, the challenged action is declared unconstitutional. Government officials have no lawful authority to continue any unconstitutional act and they may be held liable for monetary damages under 42 U.S.C. § 1983 for violations of constitutional rights.

9) Alternatives to the *Lemon* test include:

The Endorsement Test: The endorsement test asks whether based on the totality of the circumstances a reasonable observer would conclude that government officials had taken sides in a religious controversy. Government officials are either lending official endorsement or disapproval to a religious debate in a way that sends a message to reasonable observers that those who disagree with government officials are now institutional outsiders because of their religious opinions. Consistent with the *Lemon* test, the endorsement test requires governmental neutrality towards religion.

The Coercion Test: The coercion test asks whether government officials are using the power or prestige of the state to coerce belief or practice concerning religion. Government officials may not use the force of law or the threat of penalty to coerce belief or practice concerning religion. But more subtle forms of coercion are also prohibited. Concerning children, for example, the use of psychological coercion or social pressure concerning religion are prohibited. Consistent with the *Lemon* test, governmental neutrality toward religion is required.

10) The key to navigating the murky and precarious waters of the Establishment Clause is for government officials to maintain neutrality concerning religion while acting in their official capacities as agents of the state, neither advancing nor inhibiting private expression of religion.

11) In Free Exercise cases the Court uses this legal test:

The plaintiff must establish:

> 1) *The belief is religious*: Only religious beliefs are entitled to Free Exercise protection. Political or philosophical beliefs may be advanced through Free Speech, but they are not protected under the Free Exercise Clause;
> 2) *The belief is sincerely held by the plaintiff*: The plaintiff must prove by a preponderance of the evidence that the religious belief is sincerely held and not a sham belief only for purposes of obtaining the exemption or reasonable accommodation;
> 3) *The belief is central to the plaintiff's faith*: The belief impacted by the government action must be a core element of the plaintiff's faith, and not merely tangential.
> 4) *The government action is a direct burden on Free Exercise*: The government action must impose a direct burden on the Free Exercise of religion, and not merely an incidental burden.

If the plaintiff meets this burden of proof, the plaintiff has established a prima facie case for a protected Free Exercise right, and is entitled to an exemption from the policy or other reasonable accommodations unless the government can establish:

5) *There is a compelling governmental interest*: Government officials can prove a compelling governmental interest (*i.e.*, protecting public security, health, safety, or respecting the Establishment Clause) for denying the exemption or other reasonable accommodation; and

6) *Government actions are narrowly tailored to achieving that interest*: The government's means of achieving the compelling interest must not be over-broad in limiting individual rights beyond what is necessary.

If the plaintiff prevails, the plaintiff is entitled to a free exercise exemption or other reasonable accommodation, but the government action remains valid for everyone else.

12) The limitations of the Constitution, including the Establishment and Free Exercise Clauses, only apply to agents of the government while they are acting in their official capacities. For example, as long as the public and private roles are appropriately separated, it is perfectly lawful for a public school educator to serve as a public official during working hours (taking care to maintain neutrality while acting in an official capacity) and as a member of the clergy in a private capacity while off-duty as a state official.

13) When public facilities are made available to students or members of the public, government officials may neither favor nor disfavor religious groups and religious speech. Facilities must be made available to all eligible persons and groups on an equal basis.

14) The Equal Access Act prohibits discrimination based on the "religious, political, philosophical, or other content" of speech at school sanctioned student initiated meetings. The Act applies when school officials subject to the Act create a limited open forum by allowing non-curriculum related student groups to meet.

15) Under the U.S. system of federalism, the U.S. and state constitutions are compatible but not identical. No state may act to abridge rights of federal citizenship, establishing a legal baseline for the protection of individual rights. States must respect religious freedoms protected by the U.S. Constitution. But under state constitutions, states may apply greater restrictions (than those required by the U.S. Constitution) concerning the Establishment of religion by the state. And the state may require greater protections (than those required by the U.S. Constitution) for the Free Exercise of religion by its citizens.

16) To help educators and others in better understanding the application of church-state principles the U.S. Department of Education's Guidance on Constitutionally Protected Prayer in Public Elementary and Secondary Schools provides useful guidance on applying the First Amendment's religion clauses in public schools

II. *Principles to Practice Tips*:

1) *Religious Neutrality*: Practice religious neutrality in your professional duties, neither advancing nor inhibiting religion. In your private capacity religious faith and practice are your choice and right. But as a government official always be certain that no reasonable person could perceive you as using your official power to reward or punish on the basis of religious belief. This is especially important when there is a power relationship between you and the other person. For example, peers may ask other peers if they would like to visit their church, etc. But if there is a positional power relationship (*e.g.*, administrator/teacher; teacher/student) this may be seen as misusing positional authority to coerce religious compliance.

2) *Separation of Church and State*: Respect the rights of individuals to make their own decisions concerning matters of faith free from state interference. And remember that the state belongs equally to all persons, and not just to those in the religious majority. All private citizens, whether they are in the majority or a minority of one, have rights to pray or not pray as they choose, and state officials must respect the appropriate bounds of church and state within the respective private and public spheres of life.

3) *Free Exercise*: State officials should avoid placing persons in circumstance where they have to choose between what their religious faith requires and what the state requires. Whenever possible, seek to provide a reasonable accommodation for the free exercise of religion. A requested accommodation is not reasonable if it would result in health or safety dangers to others; unreasonable costs; unreasonable administrative burdens; or require a fundamental alteration of the legitimate state program. But in most instances religious believers are merely asking to be exempted or allowed an alternative assignment, costing the state little or nothing. Even when you do not share or understand the individual's religious belief, try to see the situation through their eyes and treat that person as you would like to be treated under the circumstances. This is both the right thing to do, and the legally safe thing to do. If a reasonable accommodation has been provided there is no legitimate basis for a complaint or law suit.

4) *Respect for Religious Diversity*: Practice genuine respect for the sincerely held beliefs of all persons. Learn about the religious beliefs and practices of others, and teach children about the World's many faiths, their cultural differences, their common purposes, and how all persons of good faith can live together in peace.

III. *Questions for Discussion*: Please consider these questions and be prepared to discuss:

1) *Prohibited Endorsement v. Protected Free Exercise/Free Speech*: State endorsement of religion is prohibited. But private free speech and free exercise of religion are protected. In the continuum between prohibited state endorsement of religion and protected individual religious expression/free speech, where is the legal line? Under what circumstances is prayer at a football game prohibited as state establishment or protected as individual free speech and free exercise? Who can and cannot pray at a state school sponsored football game?

2) *Official State Religion*: Imagine that the U.S. Supreme Court reversed its decisions prohibiting compulsory participation in flag salutes, oaths, and public school sponsored prayers.

Your local school plans to require participation in daily prayers. But whose prayer will you pray? Will you take a vote and pray the prayers of the majority? How will those in the religious minority react to having their prayers excluded and their children compelled to say the majority's prayer? Can you compose a generic prayer that would offend no one? Would a generic prayer satisfy anyone? What about non-believers and atheists? Do your perspectives on these questions depend on whether you are in the religious majority or the minority?

3) *Shock the Monkey*: Two very different world-views form the foundations for the ongoing debate over the teaching of evolution in schools. And like most "culture war" issues, nearly everyone has already taken a side and they have no intention of changing their minds, making these discussions often less of a debate and more of an argument. Generally the only persons who haven't chosen a side (yet) are young children, which is why schools are the battle ground of choice for these issues. Although you may not agree with those holding opposing views on these issues: Do you fully understand what they believe? Do you understand why they believe this? Can we find a way to respectfully disagree and to peacefully co-exist? Can we teach these principles of respectful disagreement and tolerance to our children, regardless of which side we may be on concerning these issues?

4) *Open Forum*: What other related issues or current events would you like to discuss?

IV. *Suggested Activities*:

1) Regardless of any of our individual opinions concerning religion, the reality is that religious beliefs are a driving force for billions of people, shaping their world views. And the choices they make based on religious beliefs shape our common world. But how much do religious believers actually know about the histories and religious doctrines of their own faiths? How much do they know about the religious histories and beliefs of others? Whatever are your beliefs, learn more about the history and ideas that form the foundations of your belief system. Learn more about the different religious beliefs of colleagues and friends and talk with them about what you have learned. Useful resources for exploring religious beliefs can be found at www.beliefnet.com

2) Read a book about religious beliefs, such as Stephen Prothero's "Religious Literacy: What Every American Needs to Know--And Doesn't." Discuss what you learned with colleagues and if appropriate look for ways to incorporate this knowledge into lessons for your students.

Chapter 4: First Amendment Freedoms and Speech

Freedom is never free. Frederick Douglas said: "Those who profess to favor freedom, and yet depreciate agitation, are men who want crops without plowing up the ground. They want rain without thunder and lightning." While it may seem more expedient at the time to raise children to be seen and not heard, using authoritarian means to stop children from questioning and expressing themselves will not produce adult citizens prepared to actively participate in a strong democracy. And as Frederick Douglas also forewarned: "It is easier to build strong children than to repair broken men." If public schools are to serve as the functional nurseries of a strong and enduring democracy students' free speech rights must be respected, protected, and encouraged so they may mature into citizens well prepared to actively discuss ideas, ask essential questions, speak out on important public matters, vote wisely, and participate fully in a free and democratic society.

> ### *Education, Free Speech, Civility, and Civic Courage are the Necessary Foundations of Democracy*

Education, free speech, civility, and civic courage are essential elements in sustaining democracy. Totalitarian regimes are only possible when the people are kept ignorant, silenced, divided, and fearful of speaking up and making their own decisions. Children spend much of their formative years in schools where they can either learn the skills of democratic citizens or learn to become passive subordinates vulnerable to totalitarian control. In *Tinker v. Des Moines Independent School District*, 393 U.S. 503 (1969), the Court firmly declared: "In our system, state-operated schools may not be enclaves of totalitarianism."

A free society is not, however, a chaotic society. Democracy is incompatible with both chaos and oppression. Democratic lessons are best learned in an environment that is both free and orderly; both candid and civil. Maintaining proper order and discipline in schools is a paramount concern and an essential duty for school officials. The Court has consistently recognized the authority and obligation of school officials to protect order and discipline in schools, while appropriately respecting legitimate free speech rights of both students and educators. Students are learning to become democratic citizens, and educators are in a unique position to observe school operations and inform the public of legitimate matters of public concern in their schools. For these reasons, the Court has vigorously protected free speech rights of both students and teachers, and declared in *Tinker*: "It can hardly be argued that either students or teachers shed their constitutional rights to freedom of speech or expression at the schoolhouse gate."

Freedom of speech is the necessary protector of all other rights and therefore of universal human importance. The United Nations Universal Declaration of Human Rights states: "Everyone has the right to freedom of opinion and expression; this right includes freedom to hold opinions without interference and to seek, receive and impart information and ideas through any media and regardless of frontiers." To protect rights of free speech in the U.S. the First Amendment states:

Congress shall make no law . . . abridging the freedom of speech, or of the press; or the right of the people peaceably to assemble, and to petition the government for a redress of grievances.

These protections were made applicable to state and local governments through the Fourteenth Amendment.

At of the core of the First Amendment's free speech protections are strong safeguards for individual political or religious speech. Political or religious speech is most vigorously protected because these types of speech have historically been the primary targets of government censorship. Government officials have always been tempted to use their powers to silence criticism of them and their government, and to stifle political or religious ideas that could threaten the existing status quo.

Political or religious speech is protected regardless of whether the speaker can prove the expressed ideas are true (although untrue personal accusations in the form of defamation are not protected speech). All speakers have the right to express their beliefs, and it is up to listeners, not government officials, to decide what is true. But historically, government censorship was most zealous in those cases in which the criticisms of the government were true, or religious ideas were unorthodox but potentially popular. False claims and unpopular ideas are easily disproven and defeated. But an ugly truth about those in power or a new and powerful religious idea provides a potent threat to the status quo, and therefore often provokes the strongest censorship efforts from those whose power is threatened.

To guard against these abuses of government power, the First Amendment provides broad protections for free speech. But these protections cannot be absolute when the free speech of one person threatens the rights or safety of others. As Justice Holmes said: "The most stringent protection of free speech would not protect a man falsely shouting fire in a theater and causing a panic." Within an evolving hierarchy of First Amendment protections the Court generally prohibits content-based censorship, with political and religious speech receiving the greatest protections, commercial speech receiving less rigorous protection, and obscenity falling outside of the scope of constitutional protection.

The Court recognizes freedom of speech as a fundamental right under the U.S. Constitution. Government officials may only limit fundamental rights, including constitutionally protected speech, by establishing that limitations are necessary to a compelling interest and narrowly tailored to achieving that interest. The Court has also recognized, however, that government officials may apply reasonable time, place, and manner regulations to speech where these regulations are content-neutral, serve an important public interest, and leave open adequate alternative routes of communication.

Further, the Court has recognized the necessity of different standards for different mediums of communication. For example, the Court has allowed greater restrictions on general broadcast communications than on print media. The Court has also recognized different protections in different contexts, vigorously protecting free speech in traditional open public forums such as public streets and parks, and allowing stronger regulations in forums dedicated to limited purposes, such as public business meetings, when these restrictions are warranted under the circumstances and are not a mere pretext for limiting protected speech.

Public forums range from open forums such as public parks and streets, to limited open forums including public schools, and closed forums such as meetings on national security or other matters legitimately requiring exclusion of direct public participation. In some circumstances reasonable time, place, and manner restrictions on speech are necessary to preserve the public forum for its intended purposes. These restrictions do not violate the First Amendment when they serve important public interests, do not discriminate based on the political or religious viewpoint of the speaker, and leave open adequate alternative routes for free speech.

Freedom of speech is protected not only for the benefit of individuals, but also to assure the free flow of information that leads to the political, intellectual, and cultural advancement of the community through the free market of ideas. Innovative and productive ideas flourish in a free environment where the only limits these ideas are subjected to are the tests of public debate and the reason of an educated and free people. Similarly, ideas that are potentially dangerous to the community are also best refuted in open debate.

> *"The Ultimate Good . . . is Better Reached by Free Trade in Ideas . . . the Best Test of Truth is the Power of the Thought to get itself Accepted in the Competition of the Market"* **Justice Oliver Wendell Holmes**

American Founders believed in a free market of ideas, with individuals free to accept those ideas that they believed were best, and self-interested government officials prevented from interfering with the operation of this free process. Open public debate and the reasoning power of an educated and free people are the best guarantees that good ideas will prevail, and also the best protections against ideas that are flawed or threats to the common good. As Thomas Jefferson declared after prevailing in one of the nation's most bitter political battles "if there be any among us who would wish to dissolve this Union or to change its republican form, let them stand undisturbed as monuments of the safety with which error of opinion may be tolerated where reason is left free to combat it."

A public school is not, however, a public street or a public park. To maintain the order necessary for effective instruction and educational success school officials must exercise substantial control over the classroom and keep order in the hallways and on the campus. But public schools are also not military units in which free speech exists only in theory, absolute conformity is required, and subordinates are expected to follow all orders immediately and without question. In *Tinker* the Court addressed the scope of students' free speech rights in schools.

Individual Student Speech

Tinker v. Des Moines Independent Community School District
393 U.S. 503 (1969)
Supreme Court of the United States

Mr. Justice FORTAS delivered the opinion of the Court.

Petitioner John F. Tinker, 15 years old, and petitioner Christopher Eckhardt, 16 years old, attended high schools in Des Moines, Iowa. Petitioner Mary Beth Tinker, John's sister, was a 13-year-old student in junior high school.

In December 1965, a group of adults and students in Des Moines held a meeting at the Eckhardt home. The group determined to publicize their objections to the hostilities in Vietnam and their support for a truce by wearing black armbands during the holiday season and by fasting on December 16 and New Year's Eve. Petitioners and their parents had previously engaged in similar activities, and they decided to participate in the program.

The principals of the Des Moines schools became aware of the plan to wear armbands. On December 14, 1965, they met and adopted a policy that any student wearing an armband to school would be asked to remove it, and if he refused he would be suspended until he returned without the armband. Petitioners were aware of the regulation that the school authorities adopted.

On December 16, Mary Beth and Christopher wore black armbands to their schools. John Tinker wore his armband the next day. They were all sent home and suspended from school until they would come back without their armbands. They did not return to school until after the planned period for wearing armbands had expired--that is, until after New Year's Day.

This complaint was filed in the United States District Court by petitioners, through their fathers, under § 1983 of Title 42 of the United States Code. It prayed for an injunction restraining the respondent school officials and the respondent members of the board of directors of the school district from disciplining the petitioners, and it sought nominal damages. After an evidentiary hearing the District Court dismissed the complaint. It upheld the constitutionality of the school authorities' action on the ground that it was reasonable in order to prevent disturbance of school discipline. The court referred to but expressly declined to follow the Fifth Circuit's holding in a similar case that the wearing of symbols like the armbands cannot be prohibited unless it "materially and substantially interferes with the requirements of appropriate discipline in the operation of the school."

On appeal, the Court of Appeals for the Eighth Circuit considered the case *en banc*. The court was equally divided, and the District Court's decision was accordingly affirmed, without opinion. We granted *certiorari*.

The District Court recognized that the wearing of an armband for the purpose of expressing certain views is the type of symbolic act that is within the Free Speech Clause of the First Amendment. As we shall discuss, the wearing of armbands in the circumstances of this case was entirely divorced from actually or potentially disruptive conduct by those participating in it. It was closely akin to "pure speech" which, we have repeatedly held, is entitled to comprehensive protection under the First Amendment.

First Amendment rights, applied in light of the special characteristics of the school environment, are available to teachers and students. It can hardly be argued that either students or teachers shed their constitutional rights to freedom of speech or expression at the schoolhouse gate. This has been the unmistakable holding of this Court for almost 50 years. In *Meyer v. Nebraska*, 262 U.S. 390 (1923), and *Bartels v. Iowa*, 262 U.S. 404 (1923), this Court, in opinions by Mr. Justice McReynolds, held that the Due Process Clause of the Fourteenth Amendment prevents States from forbidding the teaching of a foreign language to young students. Statutes to this effect, the Court held, unconstitutionally interfere with the liberty of teacher, student, and parent.

In *West Virginia State Board of Education v. Barnette*, this Court held that under the First Amendment, the student in public school may not be compelled to salute the flag. Speaking through Mr. Justice Jackson, the Court said:

> The Fourteenth Amendment, as now applied to the States, protects the citizen against the State itself and all of its creatures--Boards of Education not excepted. These have, of

course, important, delicate, and highly discretionary functions, but none that they may not perform within the limits of the Bill of Rights. That they are educating the young for citizenship is reason for scrupulous protection of Constitutional freedoms of the individual, if we are not to strangle the free mind at its source and teach youth to discount important principles of our government as mere platitudes.

On the other hand, the Court has repeatedly emphasized the need for affirming the comprehensive authority of the States and of school officials, consistent with fundamental constitutional safeguards, to prescribe and control conduct in the schools. Our problem lies in the area where students in the exercise of First Amendment rights collide with the rules of the school authorities.

The problem posed by the present case does not relate to regulation of the length of skirts or the type of clothing, to hair style, or deportment. It does not concern aggressive, disruptive action or even group demonstrations. Our problem involves direct, primary First Amendment rights akin to "pure speech."

The school officials banned and sought to punish petitioners for a silent, passive expression of opinion, unaccompanied by any disorder or disturbance on the part of petitioners. There is here no evidence whatever of petitioners' interference, actual or nascent, with the schools' work or of collision with the rights of other students to be secure and to be let alone. Accordingly, this case does not concern speech or action that intrudes upon the work of the schools or the rights of other students.

Only a few of the 18,000 students in the school system wore the black armbands. Only five students were suspended for wearing them. There is no indication that the work of the schools or any class was disrupted. Outside the classrooms, a few students made hostile remarks to the children wearing armbands, but there were no threats or acts of violence on school premises.

The District Court concluded that the action of the school authorities was reasonable because it was based upon their fear of a disturbance from the wearing of the armbands. But, in our system, undifferentiated fear or apprehension of disturbance is not enough to overcome the right to freedom of expression. Any departure from absolute regimentation may cause trouble. Any variation from the majority's opinion may inspire fear. Any word spoken, in class, in the lunchroom, or on the campus, that deviates from the views of another person may start an argument or cause a disturbance. But our Constitution says we must take this risk, and our history says that it is this sort of hazardous freedom--this kind of openness--that is the basis of our national strength and of the independence and vigor of Americans who grow up and live in this relatively permissive, often disputatious, society.

In order for the State in the person of school officials to justify prohibition of a particular expression of opinion, it must be able to show that its action was caused by something more than a mere desire to avoid the discomfort and unpleasantness that always accompany an unpopular viewpoint. Certainly where there is no finding and no showing that engaging in the forbidden conduct would "materially and substantially interfere with the requirements of appropriate discipline in the operation of the school," the prohibition cannot be sustained.

In the present case, the District Court made no such finding, and our independent examination of the record fails to yield evidence that the school authorities had reason to anticipate that the wearing of the armbands would substantially interfere with the work of the school or impinge upon the rights of other students. Even an official memorandum prepared after the suspension that listed the reasons for the ban on wearing the armbands made no reference to the anticipation of such disruption.

On the contrary, the action of the school authorities appears to have been based upon an urgent wish to avoid the controversy which might result from the expression, even by the silent symbol of armbands, of opposition to this Nation's part in the conflagration in Vietnam. It is revealing, in this respect, that the meeting at which the school principals decided to issue the contested regulation was called in response to a student's statement to the journalism teacher in one of the schools that he wanted to write an article on Vietnam and have it published in the school paper. (The student was dissuaded).

It is also relevant that the school authorities did not purport to prohibit the wearing of all symbols of political or controversial significance. The record shows that students in some of the schools wore buttons relating to national political campaigns, and some even wore the Iron Cross, traditionally a symbol of Nazism. The order prohibiting the wearing of armbands did not extend to these. Instead, a particular symbol--black armbands worn to exhibit opposition to this Nation's involvement in Vietnam--was singled out for prohibition. Clearly, the prohibition of expression of one particular opinion, at least without evidence that it is necessary to avoid material and substantial interference with schoolwork or discipline, is not constitutionally permissible.

In our system, state-operated schools may not be enclaves of totalitarianism. School officials do not possess absolute authority over their students. Students in school as well as out of school are "persons" under our Constitution. They are possessed of fundamental rights which the State must respect, just as they themselves must respect their obligations to the State. In our system, students may not be regarded as closed-circuit recipients of only that which the State chooses to communicate. They may not be confined to the expression of those sentiments that are officially approved. In the absence of a specific showing of constitutionally valid reasons to regulate their speech, students are entitled to freedom of expression of their views. As Judge Gewin, speaking for the Fifth Circuit, said, school officials cannot suppress "expressions of feelings with which they do not wish to contend."

In *Meyer v. Nebraska*, 262 U.S. 390 (1923), Mr. Justice McReynolds expressed this Nation's repudiation of the principle that a State might so conduct its schools as to "foster a homogeneous people." He said:

> In order to submerge the individual and develop ideal citizens, Sparta assembled the males at seven into barracks and intrusted their subsequent education and training to official guardians. Although such measures have been deliberately approved by men of great genius, their ideas touching the relation between individual and State were wholly different from those upon which our institutions rest; and it hardly will be affirmed that any Legislature could impose such restrictions upon the people of a state without doing violence to both letter and spirit of the Constitution.

This principle has been repeated by this Court of numerous occasions during the intervening years. Mr. Justice Brennan, speaking for the Court, said: "The vigilant protection of constitutional freedoms is nowhere more vital than in the community of American schools." The classroom is peculiarly the "marketplace of ideas." The Nation's future depends upon leaders trained through wide exposure to that robust exchange of ideas which discovers truth "out of a multitude of tongues, (rather) than through any kind of authoritative selection."

142

The principle of these cases is not confined to the supervised and ordained discussion which takes place in the classroom. The principal use to which the schools are dedicated is to accommodate students during prescribed hours for the purpose of certain types of activities. Among those activities is personal intercommunication among the students. This is not only an inevitable part of the process of attending school; it is also an important part of the educational process. A student's rights, therefore, do not embrace merely the classroom hours. When he is in the cafeteria, or on the playing field, or on the campus during the authorized hours, he may express his opinions, even on controversial subjects like the conflict in Vietnam, if he does so without "materially and substantially interfer(ing) with the requirements of appropriate discipline in the operation of the school" and without colliding with the rights of others. But conduct by the student, in class or out of it, which for any reason--whether it stems from time, place, or type of behavior--materially disrupts classwork or involves substantial disorder or invasion of the rights of others is, of course, not immunized by the constitutional guarantee of freedom of speech.

Under our Constitution, free speech is not a right that is given only to be so circumscribed that it exists in principle but not in fact. Freedom of expression would not truly exist if the right could be exercised only in an area that a benevolent government has provided as a safe haven for crackpots. The Constitution says that Congress (and the States) may not abridge the right to free speech. This provision means what it says. We properly read it to permit reasonable regulation of speech-connected activities in carefully restricted circumstances. But we do not confine the permissible exercise of First Amendment rights to a telephone booth or the four corners of a pamphlet, or to supervised and ordained discussion in a school classroom.

If a regulation were adopted by school officials forbidding discussion of the Vietnam conflict, or the expression by any student of opposition to it anywhere on school property except as part of a prescribed classroom exercise, it would be obvious that the regulation would violate the constitutional rights of students, at least if it could not be justified by a showing that the students' activities would materially and substantially disrupt the work and discipline of the school. In the circumstances of the present case, the prohibition of the silent, passive "witness of the armbands," as one of the children called it, is no less offensive to the constitution's guarantees.

As we have discussed, the record does not demonstrate any facts which might reasonably have led school authorities to forecast substantial disruption of or material interference with school activities, and no disturbances or disorders on the school premises in fact occurred. These petitioners merely went about their ordained rounds in school. Their deviation consisted only in wearing on their sleeve a band of black cloth, not more than two inches wide. They wore it to exhibit their disapproval of the Vietnam hostilities and their advocacy of a truce, to make their views known, and, by their example, to influence others to adopt them. They neither interrupted school activities nor sought to intrude in the school affairs or the lives of others. They caused discussion outside of the classrooms, but no interference with work and no disorder. In the circumstances, our Constitution does not permit officials of the State to deny their form of expression.

We express no opinion as to the form of relief which should be granted, this being a matter for the lower courts to determine.

We reverse and remand for further proceedings consistent with this opinion.

* * * * * * *

According to the Court in *Tinker*, in cases involving student political speech school officials may only limit this speech if they can establish it would "materially and substantially interfere with the requirements of appropriate discipline in the operation of the school." And "where there is no finding and no showing that engaging in the forbidden conduct" meets this standard "the prohibition cannot be sustained." This required threshold of showing a "material and substantial" interference is the Court's "*Tinker* test" used to distinguish between student speech that is protected under the First Amendment and student speech that is subject to prohibition and punishment by public school officials.

In articulating this standard, the Court provided a benchmark for school officials in deciding whether the lawful response to the student speech in question was simply to allow the speech or to attempt to intervene to avoid a "material and substantial" interference with school discipline and operations. Intervention by school officials is lawful when school officials can meet the standard established in *Tinker*. But where exactly is the line between protected and unprotected student speech and what must school officials do to comply with the *Tinker* test? Consider this continuum of student speech:

The Continuum of Student Speech

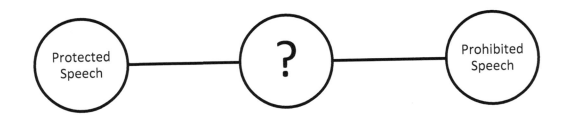

© **Dayton**

At one end of the continuum is speech that is clearly protected by the First Amendment, including legitimate political and religious speech that causes no interference with discipline or the operations of the school. At the other end of the spectrum is speech that is clearly unprotected including obscenity, slander, terroristic threats, and other obviously unprotected student speech that directly threatens safety, discipline, or school operations. It is easy for school officials to make decisions concerning student speech that clearly falls toward either end of this continuum. It is the cases closer to the middle of this continuum that present the greatest challenges to school officials in deciding whether to allow the speech or to intervene.

The *Tinker* standard is the Court's attempt to provide guidance for school officials and courts in making decisions in these closer cases. But while the *Tinker* standard is a useful general test against which to measure whether the speech is protected, the *Tinker* standard is not a "bright line" test. Bright line tests establish a definite, clear line between protected and prohibited conduct. A speed limit sign, for example, provides a bright line test where going over 55 mph is prohibited while 55 mph and under is lawful. Instead of providing a bright line test, the *Tinker* test acts as a standard in the continuum that must be interpreted in the unique context in which the speech occurs. This makes the *Tinker* test more like a speed limit sign that requires a speed that is "reasonable and prudent under the conditions" rather than providing a definite and absolute limit such as 55 mph.

For administrative convenience it might seem preferable to have a bright line test for what speech is permissible and prohibited, for example, a definite list of permissible and prohibited expressive conduct. The problem of course, is that in human communications context and tone are critically important. The exact same words and conduct may be acceptable in some circumstances and clearly unacceptable in others. Further, the human mind is far too creative to be corralled within the bounds of a finite list, and students would quickly find creative ways around the listed prohibitions. Bright line tests are very helpful where simple measures are possible, such as measuring the speed of a car, applying rules based on the property boundaries of the school, etc. But a bright line test is unworkable in governing more complex human interactions.

A bright line test for speech would be too simplistic and inflexible to govern the complexities of human interactions. And such a rigid test would be likely to produce results inconsistent with justice and common sense, punishing some speech that should not be punished, and allowing some speech that clearly should not be allowed. Instead, the *Tinker* test requires a common sense consideration of the facts and circumstances in each case to determine whether these facts and circumstances move the speech in question closer to either protected or prohibited speech.

A careful reading of *Tinker* and subsequent cases, however, does provide some useful guidance in applying the *Tinker* test. To justify limiting individual student speech, school officials must show more than a desire to avoid the unpleasantness, discomfort, or minor arguments and disturbances that normally occur with the expression of unpopular views. Further, mere speculation or an abstract, undifferentiated fear of disruption will not suffice. When challenged, school officials must be able to articulate facts and circumstances that would convince a reasonable person that a material and substantial interference was likely.

The *Tinker* test does not require school officials to prove there was an actual disruption, nor are school officials required to allow the disruption to occur before intervening. In order to justify limiting otherwise protected student speech the *Tinker* test requires school officials to show through evidence of facts and circumstances that they reasonably anticipated a material and substantial interference with appropriate discipline in the operation of the school.

So while the Court noted that the mere "discomfort and unpleasantness that always accompany an unpopular viewpoint" are not sufficiently disruptive to establish a material and substantial interference, evidence of violence associated with such conduct; threats of violence; acts of intimidation; significant property destruction or vandalism; substantial disorder; invasion of the rights of others; or sufficient disruption of the educational process, work, order, or discipline of the school would constitute a material and substantial interference under the *Tinker* test.

In summary *Tinker* and subsequent cases teach that the unique context and the totality of the circumstances must be considered in each case. Student behavior that might constitute a material and substantial interference under one set of circumstances may not in another. The *Tinker* test is a useful guide, but it still requires school officials to exercise common sense in dealing with the inevitable and endlessly varied disputes over student speech. The *Tinker* test is both a benchmark for lawfully establishing school authority over student speech, and a check and balance against the potential abuse of that authority. Try to recall a dispute over student speech in your school. How would the *Tinker* test apply in that case? What is the lawful response for school officials under those circumstances?

Mary Beth Tinker was engaged in non-disruptive expression of her own personal political opinions. She was in school because of compulsory attendance laws, and did not otherwise use school resources or a school sponsored forum to express her political opinions. Further, it was clear from the context that this was Mary Beth's individual speech, and not school sponsored speech. In *Bethel School District v. Fraser,* and *Hazelwood School District v. Kuhlmeier,* the Court addressed the scope of lawful student speech in a school sponsored forum.

School Sponsored Speech

Bethel School District v. Fraser
478 U.S. 675 (1986)
Supreme Court of the United States

Chief Justice BURGER delivered the opinion of the Court.

We granted certiorari to decide whether the First Amendment prevents a school district from disciplining a high school student for giving a lewd speech at a school assembly.

On April 26, 1983, respondent Matthew N. Fraser, a student at Bethel High School in Pierce County, Washington, delivered a speech nominating a fellow student for student elective office. Approximately 600 high school students, many of whom were 14-year-olds, attended the assembly. Students were required to attend the assembly or to report to the study hall. The assembly was part of a school-sponsored educational program in self-government . . . During the entire speech, Fraser referred to his candidate in terms of an elaborate, graphic, and explicit sexual metaphor.

Two of Fraser's teachers, with whom he discussed the contents of his speech in advance, informed him that the speech was "inappropriate and that he probably should not deliver it," and that his delivery of the speech might have "severe consequences." During Fraser's delivery of the speech, a school counselor observed the reaction of students to the speech. Some students hooted and yelled; some by gestures graphically simulated the sexual activities pointedly alluded to in respondent's speech. Other students appeared to be bewildered and embarrassed by the speech. One teacher reported that on the day following the speech, she found it necessary to forgo a portion of the scheduled class lesson in order to discuss the speech with the class.

A Bethel High School disciplinary rule prohibiting the use of obscene language in the school provides: "Conduct which materially and substantially interferes with the educational process is prohibited, including the use of obscene, profane language or gestures." The morning after the assembly, the Assistant Principal called Fraser into her office and notified him that the school considered his speech to have been a violation of this rule. Fraser was presented with copies of five letters submitted by teachers, describing his conduct at the assembly; he was given a chance to explain his conduct, and he admitted to having given the speech described and that he deliberately used sexual innuendo in the speech. Fraser was then informed that he would be suspended for three days, and that his name would be removed from the list of candidates for graduation speaker at the school's commencement exercises.

Fraser sought review of this disciplinary action through the School District's grievance procedures. The hearing officer determined that the speech given by respondent was "indecent, lewd, and offensive to the modesty and decency of many of the students and faculty in attendance at the assembly." The examiner determined that the speech fell within the ordinary meaning of "obscene," as used in the disruptive-conduct rule, and affirmed the discipline in its entirety. Fraser served two days of his suspension, and was allowed to return to school on the third day.

Respondent, by his father as guardian ad litem, then brought this action in the United States District Court for the Western District of Washington. Respondent alleged a violation of his First Amendment right to freedom of speech and sought both injunctive relief and monetary damages under 42 U.S.C. § 1983. The District Court held that the school's sanctions violated respondent's right to freedom of speech under the First Amendment to the United States Constitution, that the school's disruptive-conduct rule is unconstitutionally vague and overbroad, and that the removal of respondent's name from the graduation speaker's list violated the Due Process Clause of the Fourteenth Amendment because the disciplinary rule makes no mention of such removal as a possible sanction. The District Court awarded respondent $278 in damages, $12,750 in litigation costs and attorney's fees, and enjoined the School District from preventing respondent from speaking at the commencement ceremonies. Respondent, who had been elected graduation speaker by a write-in vote of his classmates, delivered a speech at the commencement ceremonies on June 8, 1983.

The Court of Appeals for the Ninth Circuit affirmed the judgment of the District Court, holding that respondent's speech was indistinguishable from the protest armband in *Tinker v. Des Moines* (1969). The court explicitly rejected the School District's argument that the speech, unlike the passive conduct of wearing a black armband, had a disruptive effect on the educational process. The Court of Appeals also rejected the School District's argument that it had an interest in protecting an essentially captive audience of minors from lewd and indecent language in a setting sponsored by the school, reasoning that the School District's "unbridled discretion" to determine what discourse is "decent" would "increase the risk of cementing white, middle-class standards for determining what is acceptable and proper speech and behavior in our public schools." Finally, the Court of Appeals rejected the School District's argument that, incident to its responsibility for the school curriculum, it had the power to control the language used to express ideas during a school-sponsored activity. We granted *certiorari*. We reverse.

This Court acknowledged in *Tinker*, that students do not "shed their constitutional rights to freedom of speech or expression at the schoolhouse gate." The Court of Appeals read that case as precluding any discipline of Fraser for indecent speech and lewd conduct in the school assembly. That court appears to have proceeded on the theory that the use of lewd and obscene speech in order to make what the speaker considered to be a point in a nominating speech for a fellow student was essentially the same as the wearing of an armband in *Tinker* as a form of protest or the expression of a political position.

The marked distinction between the political "message" of the armbands in *Tinker* and the sexual content of respondent's speech in this case seems to have been given little weight by the Court of Appeals. In upholding the students' right to engage in a non-disruptive, passive expression of a political viewpoint in *Tinker*, this Court was careful to note that the case did "not concern speech or action that intrudes upon the work of the schools or the rights of other students." It is against this background that we turn to consider the level of First Amendment protection accorded to Fraser's utterances and actions before an official high school assembly attended by 600 students.

The role and purpose of the American public school system were well described by two historians, who stated: "Public education must prepare pupils for citizenship in the Republic . . . It must inculcate the habits and manners of civility as values in themselves conducive to happiness and as indispensable to the practice of self-government in the community and the nation." C. Beard & M. Beard, *New Basic History of the United States* 228 (1968). In *Ambach v. Norwick*, 441 U.S. 68 (1979), we echoed the essence of this statement of the objectives of public education as the "inculcation of fundamental values necessary to the maintenance of a democratic political system."

These fundamental values of "habits and manners of civility" essential to a democratic society must, of course, include tolerance of divergent political and religious views, even when the views expressed may be unpopular. But these "fundamental values" must also take into account consideration of the sensibilities of others, and, in the case of a school, the sensibilities of fellow students. The undoubted freedom to advocate unpopular and controversial views in schools and classrooms must be balanced against the society's countervailing interest in teaching students the boundaries of socially appropriate behavior. Even the most heated political discourse in a democratic society requires consideration for the personal sensibilities of the other participants and audiences.

In our Nation's legislative halls, where some of the most vigorous political debates in our society are carried on, there are rules prohibiting the use of expressions offensive to other participants in the debate. The *Manual of Parliamentary Practice*, drafted by Thomas Jefferson and adopted by the House of Representatives to govern the proceedings in that body, prohibits the use of "impertinent" speech during debate and likewise provides that "no person is to use indecent language against the proceedings of the House." The Rules of Debate applicable in the Senate likewise provide that a Senator may be called to order for imputing improper motives to another Senator or for referring offensively to any state. Senators have been censured for abusive language directed at other Senators. Can it be that what is proscribed in the halls of Congress is beyond the reach of school officials to regulate?

The First Amendment guarantees wide freedom in matters of adult public discourse. A sharply divided Court upheld the right to express an anti-draft viewpoint in a public place, albeit in terms highly offensive to most citizens. *See Cohen v. California*, 403 U.S. 15 (1971) [arrested for wearing a jacket reading "Fuck the Draft" inside a courthouse]. It does not follow, however, that simply because the use of an offensive form of expression may not be prohibited to adults making what the speaker considers a political point, the same latitude must be permitted to children in a public school. In *New Jersey v. T.L.O.*, 469 U.S. 325 (1985), we reaffirmed that the constitutional rights of students in public school are not automatically coextensive with the rights of adults in other settings. As cogently expressed by Judge Newman, "the First Amendment gives a high school student the classroom right to wear Tinker's armband, but not Cohen's jacket."

Surely it is a highly appropriate function of public school education to prohibit the use of vulgar and offensive terms in public discourse. Indeed, the "fundamental values necessary to the maintenance of a democratic political system" disfavor the use of terms of debate highly offensive or highly threatening to others. Nothing in the Constitution prohibits the states from insisting that certain modes of expression are inappropriate and subject to sanctions. The inculcation of these values is truly the "work of the schools." The determination of what manner of speech in the classroom or in school assembly is inappropriate properly rests with the school board.

The process of educating our youth for citizenship in public schools is not confined to books, the curriculum, and the civics class; schools must teach by example the shared values of a civilized social order. Consciously or otherwise, teachers--and indeed the older students-- demonstrate the appropriate form of civil discourse and political expression by their conduct and deportment in and out of class. Inescapably, like parents, they are role models. The schools, as instruments of the state, may determine that the essential lessons of civil, mature conduct cannot be conveyed in a school that tolerates lewd, indecent, or offensive speech and conduct such as that indulged in by this confused boy.

The pervasive sexual innuendo in Fraser's speech was plainly offensive to both teachers and students--indeed to any mature person. By glorifying male sexuality, and in its verbal content, the speech was acutely insulting to teenage girl students. The speech could well be seriously damaging to its less mature audience, many of whom were only 14 years old and on the threshold of awareness of human sexuality. Some students were reported as bewildered by the speech and the reaction of mimicry it provoked.

This Court's First Amendment jurisprudence has acknowledged limitations on the otherwise absolute interest of the speaker in reaching an unlimited audience where the speech is sexually explicit and the audience may include children. In *Ginsberg v. New York*, 390 U.S. 629 (1968), this Court upheld a New York statute banning the sale of sexually oriented material to minors, even though the material in question was entitled to First Amendment protection with respect to adults. And in addressing the question whether the First Amendment places any limit on the authority of public schools to remove books from a public school library, all Members of the Court, otherwise sharply divided, acknowledged that the school board has the authority to remove books that are vulgar. *Board of Education v. Pico*, 457 U.S. 853 (1982). These cases recognize the obvious concern on the part of parents, and school authorities acting in loco parentis, to protect children--especially in a captive audience--from exposure to sexually explicit, indecent, or lewd speech.

We have also recognized an interest in protecting minors from exposure to vulgar and offensive spoken language . . . We hold that petitioner School District acted entirely within its permissible authority in imposing sanctions upon Fraser in response to his offensively lewd and indecent speech. Unlike the sanctions imposed on the students wearing armbands in *Tinker*, the penalties imposed in this case were unrelated to any political viewpoint. The First Amendment does not prevent the school officials from determining that to permit a vulgar and lewd speech such as respondent's would undermine the school's basic educational mission. A high school assembly or classroom is no place for a sexually explicit monologue directed towards an unsuspecting audience of teenage students. Accordingly, it was perfectly appropriate for the school to disassociate itself to make the point to the pupils that vulgar speech and lewd conduct is wholly inconsistent with the "fundamental values" of public school education.

Respondent contends that the circumstances of his suspension violated due process because he had no way of knowing that the delivery of the speech in question would subject him to disciplinary sanctions. This argument is wholly without merit. We have recognized that "maintaining security and order in the schools requires a certain degree of flexibility in school disciplinary procedures, and we have respected the value of preserving the informality of the student-teacher relationship." *New Jersey v. T.L.O.* Given the school's need to be able to impose disciplinary sanctions for a wide range of unanticipated conduct disruptive of the educational process, the school disciplinary rules need not be as detailed as a criminal code which imposes criminal sanctions. Two days' suspension from school does not rise to the level of a penal sanction calling for the full panoply of procedural due process protections applicable to a criminal prosecution. *Goss v. Lopez*, 419 U.S. 565 (1975). The school disciplinary rule proscribing "obscene" language and the pre-speech admonitions of teachers gave adequate warning to Fraser that his lewd speech could subject him to sanctions. The judgment of the Court of Appeals for the Ninth Circuit is

Reversed.

Justice BRENNAN, concurring in the judgment:

Respondent gave the following speech at a high school assembly in support of a candidate for student government office:

> I know a man who is firm--he's firm in his pants, he's firm in his shirt, his character is firm--but most . . . . of all, his belief in you, the students of Bethel, is firm. Jeff Kuhlman is a man who takes his point and pounds it in. If necessary, he'll take an issue and nail it to the wall. He doesn't attack things in spurts--he drives hard, pushing and pushing until finally--he succeeds. Jeff is a man who will go to the very end--even the climax, for each and every one of you. So vote for Jeff for A.S.B. vice-president--he'll never come between you and the best our high school can be.

The Court, referring to these remarks as "obscene," "vulgar," "lewd," and "offensively lewd," concludes that school officials properly punished respondent for uttering the speech. Having read the full text of respondent's remarks, I find it difficult to believe that it is the same speech the Court describes. To my mind, the most that can be said about respondent's speech--and all that need be said--is that in light of the discretion school officials have to teach high school students how to conduct civil and effective public discourse, and to prevent disruption of school educational activities, it was not unconstitutional for school officials to conclude, under the circumstances of this case, that respondent's remarks exceeded permissible limits.

* * * * * * *

Comments and Questions

In *Tinker* the Court ruled on a student's expression of a controversial political opinion, finding her speech protected under the First Amendment. Was the student's speech in *Fraser* genuinely political speech, or was the student merely hiding behind *Tinker* as a thin veil to cover adolescent comedy and bad student conduct? If the latter, wouldn't protecting this mockery of the political process denigrate rather than teach respect for civility and the very serious business of democracy and self-governance?

Why would the Court of Appeals for the Ninth Circuit have ruled in favor of the student? Who was right, the Court of Appeals or the U.S. Supreme Court? What exactly distinguishes Mary Beth Tinker's expressive conduct and Matthew N. Fraser's expressive conduct in these cases? Does clarifying these distinctions help school officials and courts to decide what constitutes protected speech and what is not protected? Did the Court of Appeals understand these distinctions?

Fraser was allowed to speak in a school sponsored forum. When parents learned about Fraser's speech, who were they likely to call with their complaints? School officials have a responsibility to exercise reasonable control over school sponsored forums, they are granted legal authority to achieve this mission, and they will be held accountable for failing to do so. In *Hazelwood v. Kuhlmeier* the Court addressed the scope of lawful authority school officials may exercise over school sponsored publications.

Hazelwood School District v. Kuhlmeier
484 U.S. 260 (1988)
Supreme Court of the United States

Justice WHITE delivered the opinion of the Court.

This case concerns the extent to which educators may exercise editorial control over the contents of a high school newspaper produced as part of the school's journalism curriculum. Petitioners are the Hazelwood School District in St. Louis County, Missouri; various school officials; Robert Eugene Reynolds, the principal of Hazelwood East High School; and Howard Emerson, a teacher in the school district. Respondents are three former Hazelwood East students who were staff members of Spectrum, the school newspaper. They contend that school officials violated their First Amendment rights by deleting two pages of articles from the May 13, 1983, issue of Spectrum.

Spectrum was written and edited by the Journalism II class at Hazelwood East. The newspaper was published every three weeks or so during the 1982-1983 school year. More than 4,500 copies of the newspaper were distributed during that year to students, school personnel, and members of the community.

The Board of Education allocated funds from its annual budget for the printing of Spectrum. These funds were supplemented by proceeds from sales of the newspaper. The printing expenses during the 1982-1983 school year totaled $4,668.50; revenue from sales was $1,166.84. The other costs associated with the newspaper--such as supplies, textbooks, and a portion of the journalism teacher's salary--were borne entirely by the Board.

The Journalism II course was taught by Robert Stergos for most of the 1982-1983 academic year. Stergos left Hazelwood East to take a job in private industry on April 29, 1983, when the May 13 edition of Spectrum was nearing completion, and petitioner Emerson took his place as newspaper adviser for the remaining weeks of the term.

The practice at Hazelwood East during the spring 1983 semester was for the journalism teacher to submit page proofs of each Spectrum issue to Principal Reynolds for his review prior to publication. On May 10, Emerson delivered the proofs of the May 13 edition to Reynolds, who objected to two of the articles scheduled to appear in that edition. One of the stories described three Hazelwood East students' experiences with pregnancy; the other discussed the impact of divorce on students at the school.

Reynolds was concerned that, although the pregnancy story used false names "to keep the identity of these girls a secret," the pregnant students still might be identifiable from the text. He also believed that the article's references to sexual activity and birth control were inappropriate for some of the younger students at the school. In addition, Reynolds was concerned that a student identified by name in the divorce story had complained that her father "wasn't spending enough time with my mom, my sister and I" prior to the divorce, "was always out of town on business or out late playing cards with the guys," and "always argued about everything" with her mother. Reynolds believed that the student's parents should have been given an opportunity to respond to these remarks or to consent to their publication. He was unaware that Emerson had deleted the student's name from the final version of the article.

Reynolds believed that there was no time to make the necessary changes in the stories before the scheduled press run and that the newspaper would not appear before the end of the school year if printing were delayed to any significant extent. He concluded that his only options under the circumstances were to publish a four-page newspaper instead of the planned six-page newspaper, eliminating the two pages on which the offending stories appeared, or to publish no newspaper at all. Accordingly, he directed Emerson to withhold from publication the two pages containing the stories on pregnancy and divorce. He informed his superiors of the decision, and they concurred.

Respondents subsequently commenced this action in the United States District Court for the Eastern District of Missouri seeking a declaration that their First Amendment rights had been violated, injunctive relief, and monetary damages. After a bench trial, the District Court denied an injunction, holding that no First Amendment violation had occurred.

The District Court concluded that school officials may impose restraints on students' speech in activities that are "an integral part of the school's educational function" including the publication of a school-sponsored newspaper by a journalism class--so long as their decision has "a substantial and reasonable basis." The court found that Principal Reynolds' concern that the pregnant students' anonymity would be lost and their privacy invaded was "legitimate and reasonable," given "the small number of pregnant students at Hazelwood East and several identifying characteristics that were disclosed in the article." The court held that Reynolds' action was also justified "to avoid the impression that [the school] endorses the sexual norms of the subjects" and to shield younger students from exposure to unsuitable material. The deletion of the article on divorce was seen by the court as a reasonable response to the invasion of privacy concerns raised by the named student's remarks. Because the article did not indicate that the student's parents had been offered an opportunity to respond to her allegations, said the court, there was cause for "serious doubt that the article complied with the rules of fairness which are standard in the field of journalism and which were covered in the textbook used in the Journalism II class." Furthermore, the court concluded that Reynolds was justified in deleting two full pages of the newspaper, instead of deleting only the pregnancy and divorce stories or requiring that those stories be modified to address his concerns, based on his "reasonable belief that he had to make an immediate decision and that there was no time to make modifications to the articles in question."

The Court of Appeals for the Eighth Circuit reversed. The court held at the outset that Spectrum was not only "a part of the school adopted curriculum," but also a public forum, because the newspaper was "intended to be and operated as a conduit for student viewpoint." The court then concluded that Spectrum's status as a public forum precluded school officials from censoring its contents except when "necessary to avoid material and substantial interference with school work or discipline . . . or the rights of others."

The Court of Appeals found "no evidence in the record that the principal could have reasonably forecast that the censored articles or any materials in the censored articles would have materially disrupted classwork or given rise to substantial disorder in the school." School officials were entitled to censor the articles on the ground that they invaded the rights of others, according to the court, only if publication of the articles could have resulted in tort liability to the school. The court concluded that no tort action for libel or invasion of privacy could have been maintained against the school by the subjects of the two articles or by their families. Accordingly, the court held that school officials had violated respondents' First Amendment rights by deleting the two pages of the newspaper. We granted *certiorari*, and we now reverse.

Students in the public schools do not "shed their constitutional rights to freedom of speech or expression at the schoolhouse gate." *Tinker v. Des Moines*. They cannot be punished merely for expressing their personal views on the school premises--whether "in the cafeteria, or on the playing field, or on the campus during the authorized hours,"--unless school authorities have reason to believe that such expression will "substantially interfere with the work of the school or impinge upon the rights of other students."

We have nonetheless recognized that the First Amendment rights of students in the public schools "are not automatically coextensive with the rights of adults in other settings," *Bethel v. Fraser*, and must be "applied in light of the special characteristics of the school environment." A school need not tolerate student speech that is inconsistent with its "basic educational mission," *Fraser*, even though the government could not censor similar speech outside the school. Accordingly, we held in *Fraser* that a student could be disciplined for having delivered a speech that was "sexually explicit" but not legally obscene at an official school assembly, because the school was entitled to "disassociate itself" from the speech in a manner that would demonstrate to others that such vulgarity is "wholly inconsistent with the 'fundamental values' of public school education." We thus recognized that "the determination of what manner of speech in the classroom or in school assembly is inappropriate properly rests with the school board," rather than with the federal courts. It is in this context that respondents' First Amendment claims must be considered.

We deal first with the question whether Spectrum may appropriately be characterized as a forum for public expression. The public schools do not possess all of the attributes of streets, parks, and other traditional public forums that "time out of mind, have been used for purposes of assembly, communicating thoughts between citizens, and discussing public questions." Hence, school facilities may be deemed to be public forums only if school authorities have "by policy or by practice" opened those facilities "for indiscriminate use by the general public," or by some segment of the public, such as student organizations. If the facilities have instead been reserved for other intended purposes, "communicative or otherwise," then no public forum has been created, and school officials may impose reasonable restrictions on the speech of students, teachers, and other members of the school community. "The government does not create a public forum by inaction or by permitting limited discourse, but only by intentionally opening a nontraditional forum for public discourse" . . .

The policy of school officials toward Spectrum was reflected in Hazelwood School Board Policy 348.51 and the Hazelwood East Curriculum Guide. Board Policy 348.51 provided that

153

"school sponsored publications are developed within the adopted curriculum and its educational implications in regular classroom activities." The Hazelwood East Curriculum Guide described the Journalism II course as a "laboratory situation in which the students publish the school newspaper applying skills they have learned in Journalism I." The lessons that were to be learned from the Journalism II course, according to the Curriculum Guide, included development of journalistic skills under deadline pressure, "the legal, moral, and ethical restrictions imposed upon journalists within the school community," and "responsibility and acceptance of criticism for articles of opinion." Journalism II was taught by a faculty member during regular class hours. Students received grades and academic credit for their performance in the course.

School officials did not deviate in practice from their policy that production of Spectrum was to be part of the educational curriculum and a "regular classroom activity." The District Court found that Robert Stergos, the journalism teacher during most of the 1982-1983 school year, "both had the authority to exercise and in fact exercised a great deal of control over Spectrum." For example, Stergos selected the editors of the newspaper, scheduled publication dates, decided the number of pages for each issue, assigned story ideas to class members, advised students on the development of their stories, reviewed the use of quotations, edited stories, selected and edited the letters to the editor, and dealt with the printing company. Many of these decisions were made without consultation with the Journalism II students. The District Court thus found it "clear that Mr. Stergos was the final authority with respect to almost every aspect of the production and publication of Spectrum, including its content." Moreover, after each Spectrum issue had been finally approved by Stergos or his successor, the issue still had to be reviewed by Principal Reynolds prior to publication. Respondents' assertion that they had believed that they could publish "practically anything" in Spectrum was therefore dismissed by the District Court as simply "not credible." These factual findings are amply supported by the record, and were not rejected as clearly erroneous by the Court of Appeals . . . In sum, the evidence relied upon by the Court of Appeals fails to demonstrate the "clear intent to create a public forum. Accordingly, school officials were entitled to regulate the contents of Spectrum in any reasonable manner. It is this standard, rather than our decision in *Tinker*, that governs this case.

The question whether the First Amendment requires a school to tolerate particular student speech--the question that we addressed in *Tinker*--is different from the question whether the First Amendment requires a school affirmatively to promote particular student speech. The former question addresses educators' ability to silence a student's personal expression that happens to occur on the school premises. The latter question concerns educators' authority over school-sponsored publications, theatrical productions, and other expressive activities that students, parents, and members of the public might reasonably perceive to bear the imprimatur of the school. These activities may fairly be characterized as part of the school curriculum, whether or not they occur in a traditional classroom setting, so long as they are supervised by faculty members and designed to impart particular knowledge or skills to student participants and audiences.

Educators are entitled to exercise greater control over this second form of student expression to assure that participants learn whatever lessons the activity is designed to teach, that readers or listeners are not exposed to material that may be inappropriate for their level of maturity, and that the views of the individual speaker are not erroneously attributed to the school. Hence, a school may in its capacity as publisher of a school newspaper or producer of a school play "disassociate itself," *Fraser*, not only from speech that would "substantially interfere with [its] work ... or impinge upon the rights of other students," but also from speech that is, for example, ungrammatical, poorly written, inadequately researched, biased or prejudiced, vulgar or profane, or unsuitable for immature audiences. A school must be able to set high standards for the student speech that is disseminated under its auspices--standards that may be higher than those demanded by some newspaper publishers or theatrical producers in the "real" world--and may refuse to disseminate student speech that does not meet those standards. In addition, a school must be able to take into account the emotional maturity of the intended audience in determining whether to disseminate student speech on potentially sensitive topics, which might range from the existence of Santa Claus in an elementary school setting to the particulars of teenage sexual activity in a high school setting. A school must also retain the authority to refuse to sponsor student speech that might reasonably be perceived to advocate drug or alcohol use, irresponsible sex, or conduct otherwise inconsistent with "the shared values of a civilized social order," or to associate the school with any position other than neutrality on matters of political controversy. Otherwise, the schools would be unduly constrained from fulfilling their role as "a principal instrument in awakening the child to cultural values, in preparing him for later professional training, and in helping him to adjust normally to his environment." *Brown v. Board of Education*, 347 U.S. 483 (1954).

Accordingly, we conclude that the standard articulated in *Tinker* for determining when a school may punish student expression need not also be the standard for determining when a school may refuse to lend its name and resources to the dissemination of student expression. Instead, we hold that educators do not offend the First Amendment by exercising editorial control over the style and content of student speech in school-sponsored expressive activities so long as their actions are reasonably related to legitimate pedagogical concerns.

This standard is consistent with our oft-expressed view that the education of the Nation's youth is primarily the responsibility of parents, teachers, and state and local school officials, and not of federal judges. It is only when the decision to censor a school-sponsored publication, theatrical production, or other vehicle of student expression has no valid educational purpose that the First Amendment is so "directly and sharply implicated," as to require judicial intervention to protect students' constitutional rights . . . The judgment of the Court of Appeals for the Eighth Circuit is therefore:

Reversed.

* * * * * * *

Comments and Questions

Viewed together, the Court's decisions indicate that public school student speech cases generally fall into two categories: 1) Individual student expression as in *Tinker*; or 2) Student speech in public school sponsored forums as in *Fraser* and *Hazelwood*. In *Tinker* the Court declared that to lawfully limit individual student speech, school officials must establish that the speech would "materially and substantially interfere with the requirements of appropriate discipline in the operation of the school." Although school officials may apply reasonable Time, Place, and Manner (TPM) restrictions (these restrictions are general regulations that are: a) Content neutral; b) Narrowly tailored to serve a significant governmental interest; and c) Leave open an adequate alternative channel of communication) to all student expressive activities, if they cannot establish that the speech materially and substantially interferes with appropriate discipline in the operation of the school, the speech generally cannot be prohibited or punished consistent with the First Amendment.

Concerning student speech in public school sponsored forums, under the *Fraser/Hazelwood* test school officials need only establish "legitimate pedagogical concerns", *i.e.*, there was a "legitimate educational rationale" for limiting student speech. School sponsored forums include school convocations, performances, athletic events, school newspapers, and other expressive activities that students, parents, and other members of the public would reasonably perceive as bearing the "imprimatur of the school" even if they are not in fact school sponsored.

For example a publication titled "The James Madison Public High School Gazette" would clearly fall under the legitimate authority of school officials if James Madison Public High School paid for and supervised the production of the student paper. School officials need only establish a legitimate educational rationale to limit student speech in this school sponsored forum. But what if students produced an Internet based or home published paper they called "The James Madison Public High School Gazette" without any school funding or supervision? Because the publication bears the name of the public school, members of the public would reasonably perceive this publication as bearing the imprimatur of the school. For this reason, students would be subject to the authority of school officials as if the publication were in fact a school sponsored forum. If students did not wish to be subject to school authority, they must change the name of the publication or otherwise adequately clarify that this is a strictly private publication, with no school sponsorship, and the publication includes only their own individual speech for which the students, and not school officials, are fully responsibility.

Fraser and *Hazelwood* teach that where the forum for expression is sponsored by the school, or reasonably perceived as bearing the imprimatur of the school, student expression in a school sponsored forum can be limited based on establishing a legitimate educational rationale for limiting the speech. These legitimate educational rationales could include, for example, limiting the speech because it is not age-appropriate for students; contrary to important lessons the school is teaching students (*e.g.*, the dangers of drugs; the importance of civility, responsible citizenship, etc.); or the speech is otherwise inconsistent with the legitimate educational mission. The *Fraser/Hazelwood* test establishes a much lower threshold of proof than the *Tinker* test, making it much easier for school officials to exercise control over student speech in school sponsored forums.

Tinker, *Fraser*, and *Hazelwood* are now well-established law. In *Morse v. Frederick*, 551 U.S. 393 (2007), the U.S. Supreme Court issued its first major student speech case in nearly 20 years. *Morse* involved a dispute over student speech at a public school sanctioned and supervised event at which Frederick, a student at the public high school, unexpectedly unfurled a 14 foot long banner stating "BONG HiTS 4 JESUS." Holding up the large banner required the assistance of several other students. It was clearly visible to all persons in the area, including other students, community members, and television cameras covering the Olympic Torch Relay as it passed in front of the school.

The public high school's principal, Morse, saw the students holding the banner, and determined that Frederick's message was intended to promote illegal drug use. Consistent with school policy prohibiting such messages by students at school sponsored events Morse demanded that Frederick take down the banner. When he refused, she confiscated the banner and punished Frederick with a suspension from school. The school superintendent and school board upheld the suspension, and Frederick filed suit under 42 U.S.C. § 1983, alleging that his First Amendment rights had been violated by the actions of Morse and other school officials.

Frederick argued that because he arrived late to school the day of the event and joined the other students on the street rather than formally reporting to school, that he was therefore acting as a private citizen, not as a public school student, and he was not subject to school authority in this case.

Concerning whether Frederick was subject to school authority in this case, Chief Justice Roberts, writing for the Majority, stated: "At the outset, we reject Frederick's argument that this is not a school speech case--as has every other authority to address the question . . . we agree with the superintendent that Frederick cannot 'stand in the midst of his fellow students, during school hours, at a school-sanctioned activity and claim he is not at school.'" Chief Justice Roberts continued: "Our cases make clear that students do not 'shed their constitutional rights to freedom of speech or expression at the schoolhouse gate.'" "At the same time, we have held that 'the constitutional rights of students in public school are not automatically coextensive with the rights of adults in other settings'" and "the rights of students 'must be applied in light of the special characteristics of the school environment.'"

Justice Roberts noted the dangers that illegal drugs present for children, that existing school policies expressly prohibited messages promoting illegal drug use, and that Frederick's message included a prohibited reference to drug use. Justice Roberts relied on the school superintendent's findings to conclude that the message of Frederick's banner was a drug related message. The superintendent had stated:

> The common-sense understanding of the phrase "bong hits" is that it is a reference to a means of smoking marijuana. Given [Frederick's] inability or unwillingness to express any other credible meaning for the phrase, I can only agree with the principal and countless others who saw the banner as advocating the use of illegal drugs. [Frederick's] speech was not political. He was not advocating the legalization of marijuana or promoting a religious belief. He was displaying a fairly silly message promoting illegal drug usage in the midst of a school activity, for the benefit of television cameras covering the Torch Relay. [Frederick's] speech was potentially disruptive to the event and clearly disruptive of and inconsistent with the school's educational mission to educate students about the dangers of illegal drugs and to discourage their use.

Justice Roberts concluded:

> School principals have a difficult job, and a vitally important one. When Frederick suddenly and unexpectedly unfurled his banner, Morse had to decide to act--or not act-- on the spot. It was reasonable for her to conclude that the banner promoted illegal drug use--in violation of established school policy--and that failing to act would send a powerful message to the students in her charge, including Frederick, about how serious the school was about the dangers of illegal drug use. The First Amendment does not require schools to tolerate at school events student expression that contributes to those dangers.

The decision in *Morse* was a 6-3 opinion in favor of the school principal, Morse. But beyond their agreement that Morse should prevail, there was considerable divergence in the views of the six Justices ruling in favor of Principal Morse, with the case producing a total of five separate opinions. The decision in *Morse* does not appear to be an opinion shedding much new and useful light on the boundaries of free speech in public schools. In their opinions, several justices expressed concerns that ultimately the Court's opinion in *Morse* provided little useful guidance. Justice Thomas stated: "I am afraid that our jurisprudence now says that students have a right to speak in schools except when they don't--a standard continuously developed through litigation against local schools and their administrators." Similarly, Justice Breyer declared: "I cannot find much guidance in today's decision."

While it is too soon to draw definitive conclusions about the long-term impact of *Morse*, some initial patterns emerged in the early cases citing *Morse*, with these cases falling into two general categories: 1) Courts that viewed the U.S. Supreme Court's decision in *Morse* as very limited; and 2) Courts that interpreted *Morse* as recognizing some broader extension of school authority. Those that viewed the Court's decision in *Morse* as limited need only point to Justice Thomas' and Justice Breyer's opinions in *Morse* for support. Nonetheless, other courts reasoned that the Court's decision in *Morse* logically opened the door to an expansion of school authority concerning student speech when that speech promoted the dangers of drugs or other dangers to those in the school community more generally.

Was it necessary for school officials in *Morse* to argue this case based on the content of the speech in Frederick's banner? In doing so, school officials actually lost this case in the Court of Appeals, where the court ruled that school officials had failed to meet the standard articulated in *Tinker*, requiring school officials to establish that restrictions on student speech are supported by a showing that the speech in question threatened a material and substantial disruption in the education process. Concluding that Morse had failed to comply with the well-established standard of law in *Tinker*, the Court of Appeals also determined that Principal Morse was not entitled to qualified immunity and that she could therefore be held personally liable for monetary damages resulting from her violation of Frederick's free speech rights. If the U.S. Supreme Court would have denied *certiorari*, or failed to reverse, Morse would have been personally liable for monetary damages.

Why didn't school officials just apply reasonable time, place, and manner (TPM) restrictions to the surprise unveiling of a 14 foot long banner so large that it required the assistance of several other students to support? The application of reasonable TPM restrictions could make the content of the banner irrelevant, avoiding the free speech dispute in this case. All school officials would have been required to show was that the TPM restrictions were reasonable under the circumstances, *i.e.*, that the TPM restrictions were: 1) Content neutral; 2) Narrowly tailored to serve a significant governmental interest; and 3) Left open an adequate alternative channel of communication. Could school officials have avoided becoming the test case in this situation simply by arguing that the large banner obstructed the views of others and/or presented a potential danger in the crowd (*e.g.*, risks of tripping, falling, etc.)? And that the entire rest of the world was open for Frederick to express his opinion, but doing so with the surprise unveiling of a 14 foot long banner in the middle of the crowd at a school sponsored rally was unreasonable under the circumstances regardless of what the banner said?

Student Groups and Meetings

Student groups and meetings offer beneficial social and leadership opportunities for students, and provide a forum for discussing special interests and issues beyond the boundaries of the regular school curriculum. Consistent with *Tinker*, students may exercise their rights of free speech in these groups and meetings, but they remain otherwise subject to the same general rules of discipline and conduct that apply throughout the school.

These meetings may also be governed by the Equal Access Act, 20 U.S.C. § 4071 (see Chapter 3). The text of the Equal Access Act expressly limits the Act's application to "any public secondary school which receives Federal financial assistance and which has a limited open forum." But because the Act is essentially a Congressional codification of principles of free speech, even when the Act itself does not expressly apply, similar principles of free speech law apply to any public institution that has created a forum for free speech.

The Equal Access Act prohibits discrimination by school officials on the "basis of the religious, political, philosophical, or other content of the speech at such meetings." After the passage of this Act, many school officials feared that highly controversial student groups (*e.g.*, racist groups; hate groups, etc.) would attempt to meet in their schools. Most of these concerns, however, turned out to be overblown or unfounded.

Controversial groups that did seek a presence in these forums often cared more about the controversy their application might provoke and resulting publicity for their cause than they cared about holding any regular meetings. When they were allowed to meet with little or no controversy under the Equal Access Act, their interest in holding regular meetings often diminished. Attempts to suppress controversial speech often fuel the controversy and allow those who seek controversy to argue that their "truth" is being suppressed. When those who seek controversy are simply allowed to speak, they are revealed to all for what they are, reasonable people reject messages of hate, and absent the emotional heat of the controversy there is often little left of substance.

Nonetheless, free speech will always result in some controversy, and the Equal Access Act broadly protects free speech. Under the democratic rule of law, however, controversy need not be feared. To the contrary, controversy can create learning experiences and provoke positive change. And school officials retain sufficient authority to protect safety and order in their schools when needed. The Equal Access Act incorporated the *Tinker* standard, stating "the meeting [must] not materially and substantially interfere with the orderly conduct of educational activities within the school." The Act further states: "Nothing in this subchapter shall be construed to limit the authority of the school, its agents or employees, to maintain order and discipline on school premises [and] to protect the well-being of students and faculty."

In creating a limited open forum school officials can restrict the forum to certain groups (*e.g.*, students) and certain broad areas (*e.g.*, age appropriate student issues; non-commercial speech; etc.). But school officials must remain careful not to discriminate based on the ideology, opinions, or the perspectives of the speakers. For example, in *Rosenberger v. Rector*, 515 U.S. 819 (1995), the University of Virginia had adopted a policy of distributing funds from student activity fees to student organizations to help support expressive activities of these organizations. Funding was denied, however, to "Wide Awake" because of its religious message. Wide Awake intended to publish a student magazine with a religious perspective. In *Rosenberger* the Court ruled in favor of Wide Awake, holding that when the State creates a limited public forum, the State cannot discriminate based on the perspective of the speakers.

This is consistent with the general principles of the Equal Access Act, even though the coverage of the Act itself is limited to public secondary schools. The First Amendment's free speech provisions apply to all government institutions, and the Equal Access Act incorporated principles of free speech.

Since the passage of the Equal Access Act in 1984, school officials have feared that it would force them to either allow controversial groups to meet in their schools or to close down the forum to all non-curriculum related groups. This is in fact the choice the Equal Access Act presents to school officials when faced with the prospect of allowing especially controversial groups to meet. As noted above, however, these fears have generally been larger than the actual controversies in most cases.

Curriculum and Library Censorship

The curriculum is the educational infrastructure of the school, setting the foundational parameters for what will be taught and learned. In a democracy the public school curriculum is controlled through a democratic process. Elected federal, state, and local officials all exercise influence over the public school curriculum. The federal government issues conditional grants linked to national education programs and goals. State officials exercise broad control over public schools through state education statutes, regulations, and control of state funding. Traditionally, however, local officials have been allowed significant discretion concerning the local school curriculum and the daily operations of the school, including the administration of the local school library. Community members' objections to the policies of all elected officials and their professional appointees (*i.e.*, superintendents, administrators, and teachers) can be expressed through free speech, assembly with others to advocate for or against policies, and voting against elected officials who are insufficiently responsive to expressed concerns.

While still in their elected offices, however, local school officials generally have broad authority over the school curriculum and the contents of the school library. Nonetheless, this authority must be exercised within the limits of the Constitution and applicable federal and state laws. In *Meyer v. Nebraska*, 262 U.S. 390 (1923), the U.S. Supreme Court declared a state-wide ban on teaching modern foreign languages to elementary students in public and private schools an unconstitutional intrusion on the liberty of teachers to teach and students to learn. State limitations on teaching evolution were also declared unconstitutional in *Epperson v. Arkansas*, 393 U.S. 97 (1968) and *Edwards v. Aguillard*, 482 U.S. 578 (1987). Unless curriculum decisions directly conflict with the Constitution or other applicable laws, however, courts are generally very deferential to the decisions of state and local school officials on curriculum matters.

For example, some schools have adopted mandatory community service as part of the local school curriculum. Students have challenged these requirements alleging that mandated community service violated both the First Amendment (by requiring students to profess a belief in altruism) and the Thirteenth Amendment's prohibition against involuntary servitude. Courts have dismissed both of these claims, deferring to the curricular judgments of local school officials, and holding that absent a clear violation of the law decisions on the curriculum were outside of judicial competence and grievances should be addressed through the political process. School officials may decide to teach lessons of altruism through the school curriculum. And even when required for course credit, students' service to their own communities hardly constitutes the serious evils of involuntary servitude prohibited by the Thirteenth Amendment.

Local school officials exercise similar broad discretion over the operation of the school library. These decisions are, however, subject to public accountability through the political process, and judicial scrutiny in those instances where the decisions of local school officials intrude on First Amendment rights or other applicable laws. In *Board of Education v. Pico*, the U.S. Supreme Court reviewed a challenge to the removal of books from the school library.

Board of Education v. Pico
Supreme Court of the United States
457 U.S. 853 (1982)

Justice BRENNAN announced the judgment of the Court.

The principal question presented is whether the First Amendment imposes limitations upon the exercise by a local school board of its discretion to remove library books from high school and junior high school libraries . . . When this suit was brought, Ahrens was the President of the Board, Martin was the Vice President, and the remaining petitioners were Board members . . . In September, 1975, petitioners Ahrens, Martin, and Hughes attended a conference sponsored by Parents of New York United (PONYU), a politically conservative organization of parents concerned about education legislation in the State of New York. At the conference, these petitioners obtained lists of books described by Ahrens as "objectionable," and by Martin as "improper fare for school students." It was later determined that the High School library contained nine of the listed books, and that another listed book was in the Junior High School library. In February, 1976, at a meeting with the Superintendent of Schools and the Principals of the High School and Junior High School, the Board gave an "unofficial direction" that the listed books be removed from the library shelves and delivered to the Board's offices so that Board members could read them. When this directive was carried out, it became publicized, and the Board issued a press release justifying its action. It characterized the removed books as "anti-American, anti-Christian, anti-Semitic, and just plain filthy," and concluded that "it is our duty, our moral obligation, to protect the children in our schools from this moral danger as surely as from physical and medical dangers."

A short time later, the Board appointed a "Book Review Committee," consisting of four Island Trees parents and four members of the Island Trees schools staff, to read the listed books and to recommend to the Board whether the books should be retained, taking into account the books' "educational suitability," "good taste," "relevance," and "appropriateness to age and grade level." In July, the Committee made its final report to the Board, recommending that five of the listed books be retained and that two others be removed from the school libraries . . . The Board substantially rejected the Committee's report later that month, deciding that only one book should be returned to the High School library without restriction, that another should be made available subject to parental approval but that the remaining nine books should "be removed from elementary and secondary libraries and from use in the curriculum." The Board gave no reasons for rejecting the recommendations of the Committee that it had appointed.

Respondents reacted to the Board's decision by bringing the present action . . . They alleged that petitioners had ordered the removal of the books from school libraries and proscribed their use in the curriculum because particular passages in the books offended their social, political and moral tastes, and not because the books, taken as a whole, were lacking in educational value. Respondents claimed that the Board's actions denied them their rights under the First Amendment. They asked the court for a declaration that the Board's actions were unconstitutional, and for preliminary and permanent injunctive relief ordering the Board to return the nine books to the school libraries and to refrain from interfering with the use of those books in the schools' curricula . . .

We emphasize at the outset the limited nature of the substantive question presented by the case before us. Our precedents have long recognized certain constitutional limits upon the power of the State to control even the curriculum and classroom. For example, *Meyer v. Nebraska*, 262 U.S. 390 (1923), struck down a state law that forbade the teaching of modern foreign languages in public and private schools, and *Epperson v. Arkansas*, 393 U.S. 97 (1968), declared unconstitutional a state law that prohibited the teaching of the Darwinian theory of evolution in any state-supported school. But the current action does not require us to reenter this difficult terrain . . . For as this case is presented to us, it does not involve textbooks, or indeed any books that Island Trees students would be required to read. Respondents do not seek in this Court to impose limitations upon their school Board's discretion to prescribe the curricula of the Island Trees schools. On the contrary, the only books at issue in this case are library books, books that, by their nature, are optional, rather than required, reading. Our adjudication of the present case thus does not intrude into the classroom, or into the compulsory courses taught there. Furthermore, even as to library books, the action before us does not involve the acquisition of books. Respondents have not sought to compel their school Board to add to the school library shelves any books that students desire to read. Rather, the only action challenged in this case is the removal from school libraries of books originally placed there by the school authorities, or without objection from them . . .

The Court has long recognized that local school boards have broad discretion in the management of school affairs . . . We are therefore in full agreement with petitioners that local school boards must be permitted "to establish and apply their curriculum in such a way as to transmit community values," and that "there is a legitimate and substantial community interest in promoting respect for authority and traditional values be they social, moral, or political."

At the same time, however, we have necessarily recognized that the discretion of the States and local school boards in matters of education must be exercised in a manner that comports with the transcendent imperatives of the First Amendment . . . courts should not "intervene in the resolution of conflicts which arise in the daily operation of school systems" unless "basic constitutional values" are "directly and sharply implicated" in those conflicts. But we think that the First Amendment rights of students may be directly and sharply implicated by the removal of books from the shelves of a school library. Our precedents have focused not only on the role of the First Amendment in fostering individual self-expression, but also on its role in affording the public access to discussion, debate, and the dissemination of information and ideas. And we have recognized that "the State may not, consistently with the spirit of the First Amendment, contract the spectrum of available knowledge." In keeping with this principle, we have held that, in a variety of contexts, "the Constitution protects the right to receive information and ideas." This right is an inherent corollary of the rights of free speech and press that are explicitly guaranteed by the Constitution, in two senses. First, the right to receive ideas follows ineluctably from the sender's First Amendment right to send them: "The right of freedom of speech and press . . . embraces the right to distribute literature, and necessarily protects the right to receive it." The dissemination of ideas can accomplish nothing if otherwise willing addressees are not free to receive and consider them. It would be a barren marketplace of ideas that had only sellers, and no buyers.

More importantly, the right to receive ideas is a necessary predicate to the recipient's meaningful exercise of his own rights of speech, press, and political freedom. Madison admonished us:

A popular Government, without popular information, or the means of acquiring it, is but a Prologue to a Farce or a Tragedy, or perhaps both. Knowledge will forever govern ignorance, and a people who mean to be their own Governors must arm themselves with the power which knowledge gives.

As we recognized in *Tinker*, students too are beneficiaries of this principle:

In our system, students may not be regarded as closed-circuit recipients of only that which the State chooses to communicate . . . School officials cannot suppress "expressions of feeling with which they do not wish to contend."

In sum, just as access to ideas makes it possible for citizens generally to exercise their rights of free speech and press in a meaningful manner, such access prepares students for active and effective participation in the pluralistic, often contentious society in which they will soon be adult members. Of course all First Amendment rights accorded to students must be construed "in light of the special characteristics of the school environment." But the special characteristics of the school library make that environment especially appropriate for the recognition of the First Amendment rights of students.

A school library, no less than any other public library, is "a place dedicated to quiet, to knowledge, and to beauty." *Keyishian v. Board of Regents*, 385 U.S. 589 (1967), observed that "students must always remain free to inquire, to study and to evaluate, to gain new maturity and understanding." The school library is the principal locus of such freedom. As one District Court has well put it, in the school library, a student can literally explore the unknown, and discover areas of interest and thought not covered by the prescribed curriculum . . . The student learns that a library is a place to test or expand upon ideas presented to him, in or out of the classroom.

Petitioners emphasize the inculcative function of secondary education, and argue that they must be allowed unfettered discretion to "transmit community values" through the Island Trees schools. But that sweeping claim overlooks the unique role of the school library. It appears from the record that use of the Island Trees school libraries is completely voluntary on the part of students. Their selection of books from these libraries is entirely a matter of free choice; the libraries afford them an opportunity at self-education and individual enrichment that is wholly optional. Petitioners might well defend their claim of absolute discretion in matters of curriculum by reliance upon their duty to inculcate community values. But we think that petitioners' reliance upon that duty is misplaced where, as here, they attempt to extend their claim of absolute discretion beyond the compulsory environment of the classroom, into the school library and the regime of voluntary inquiry that there holds sway.

In rejecting petitioners' claim of absolute discretion to remove books from their school libraries, we do not deny that local school boards have a substantial legitimate role to play in the determination of school library content. We thus must turn to the question of the extent to which the First Amendment places limitations upon the discretion of petitioners to remove books from their libraries. In this inquiry, we enjoy the guidance of several precedents. *West Virginia v. Barnette* stated:

If there is any fixed star in our constitutional constellation, it is that no official, high or petty, can prescribe what shall be orthodox in politics, nationalism, religion, or other matters of opinion . . . If there are any circumstances which permit an exception, they do not now occur to us . . .

Petitioners rightly possess significant discretion to determine the content of their school libraries. But that discretion may not be exercised in a narrowly partisan or political manner. If a Democratic school board, motivated by party affiliation, ordered the removal of all books written by or in favor of Republicans, few would doubt that the order violated the constitutional rights of the students denied access to those books. The same conclusion would surely apply if an all-white school board, motivated by racial animus, decided to remove all books authored by blacks or advocating racial equality and integration. Our Constitution does not permit the official suppression of ideas. Thus, whether petitioners' removal of books from their school libraries denied respondents their First Amendment rights depends upon the motivation behind petitioners' actions. If petitioners intended by their removal decision to deny respondents access to ideas with which petitioners disagreed, and if this intent was the decisive factor in petitioners' decision, then petitioners have exercised their discretion in violation of the Constitution. To permit such intentions to control official actions would be to encourage the precise sort of officially prescribed orthodoxy unequivocally condemned in *Barnette*. On the other hand, respondents implicitly concede that an unconstitutional motivation would not be demonstrated if it were shown that petitioners had decided to remove the books at issue because those books were pervasively vulgar. And again, respondents concede that, if it were demonstrated that the removal decision was based solely upon the "educational suitability" of the books in question, then their removal would be "perfectly permissible." In other words, in respondents' view, such motivations, if decisive of petitioners' actions, would not carry the danger of an official suppression of ideas, and thus would not violate respondents' First Amendment rights.

As noted earlier, nothing in our decision today affects in any way the discretion of a local school board to choose books to add to the libraries of their schools. Because we are concerned in this case with the suppression of ideas, our holding today affects only the discretion to remove books. In brief, we hold that local school boards may not remove books from school library shelves simply because they dislike the ideas contained in those books and seek by their removal to "prescribe what shall be orthodox in politics, nationalism, religion, or other matters of opinion." *West Virginia v. Barnette*. Such purposes stand inescapably condemned by our precedents . . . The mandate shall issue forthwith.

Affirmed.

* * * * * * *

Comments and Questions

Pico is the only U.S. Supreme Court case on book removals in public schools. *Pico* was a 5-4 decision that produced seven separate and divergent opinions from the Justices. Despite these differences of opinion, many of the general principles in *Pico* are rooted in well-established law following *Barnette* and other enduring precedents. Based on the plurality opinion's articulated principles in *Pico*, it seems that the following general lessons can be extracted from *Pico*: School officials have very broad discretion in decisions concerning the acquisition of library materials. It is only the removal of materials already officially placed in the library that raises the serious

First Amendment concerns addressed in *Pico*. The Constitution prohibits the suppression of ideas by government officials. Government officials cannot deny access to ideas, using their official powers to impose their personal opinions on others. Whether a removal of library materials is lawful depends on the motivation for the removal. Decisions cannot be motivated by narrow partisan politics, religion, or other improper personal bias. Books and other materials can be removed, however, for legitimate educational reasons, *e.g.*, a subsequent discovery that the library media contained vulgar materials, was not age appropriate, or other legitimate findings concerning the library material's educational value. The books in question in *Pico* included:

Slaughter House Five, by Kurt Vonnegut, Jr.
The Naked Ape, by Desmond Morris
Down These Mean Streets, by Piri Thomas
Best Short Stories of Negro Writers, edited by Langston Hughes
Go Ask Alice, of anonymous authorship
Laughing Boy, by Oliver LaFarge
Black Boy, by Richard Wright
A Hero Ain't Nothin' But A Sandwich, by Alice Childress
Soul On Ice, by Eldridge Cleaver.
A Reader for Writers, edited by Jerome Archer
The Fixer, by Bernard Malamud

A press release issued by the School Board in *Pico* characterized these books as "anti-American, anti-Christian, anti-Semitic, and just plain filthy." The Court noted that when asked to "give an example of 'anti-Americanism' in the removed books" Board members identified *A Hero Ain't Nothin' But A Sandwich*, which "notes at one point that George Washington was a slaveholder." A Board member stated: "I believe it is anti-American to present one of the nation's heroes, the first President . . . in such a negative and obviously one-sided light. That is one example of what I would consider anti-American." Should High School students be protected from books like these?

Books mentioning witches or witchcraft, including J.K. Rowling's *Harry Potter* series, are frequently targeted for removal, as are books discussing sexual themes, racial themes, political or environmental themes, and books with content seen by some as anti-religious or unpatriotic. Other commonly targeted books have included:

The Adventures of Huckleberry Finn, by Mark Twain
Fahrenheit 451, by Ray Bradbury
1984, by George Orwell
The Grapes of Wrath, by John Steinbeck
Lord of the Flies, by William Golding
The Lorax, by Dr. Seuss

Pressure to remove books often comes from very vocal political and religious groups outside of the school. While it may seem expedient to appease politically powerful groups and simply remove challenged books, what are the future consequences of unilaterally surrendering to these requests? If books are readily removed simply to appease objectors, isn't this likely to provoke more objectors, each seeking to remove materials inconsistent with their personal views? Isn't

165

nearly everything potentially objectionable to someone? And on what basis do you refuse the next removal request to avoid this slippery slope of book removals?

In negotiations over challenged books, objectors' views are represented, and the interests of school officials are represented, but who is advocating for the interests of students and the broader community? If the curriculum and library are to be truly democratically controlled, shouldn't the interests of teachers, students, and the broader community be represented also? Why should just the loudest voices get a unilateral veto over what is in the school curriculum and library?

To address these challenges, most schools have established review committees, representing the diversity of views in the community, to consider objections to the curriculum, books, and other media in the school. There was an established policy for committee reviews in *Pico*, but the Board circumvented the process. The Superintendent in *Pico* objected to the Board's unilateral actions which were contrary to the established process and stated: "We already have a policy . . . designed expressly to handle such problems. It calls for the Superintendent, upon receiving an objection to a book or books, to appoint a committee to study them and make recommendations. I feel it is a good policy--and it is Board policy--and that it should be followed in this instance." Failure to follow your own official policies is a common "red flag" to courts, often resulting in closer judicial scrutiny. Why didn't the Board follow its own policy in *Pico*?

In addressing objections to library books and other media, what policy is best for students: Protecting them from controversial issues; or preparing them to make informed decisions concerning controversial issues? Curriculum and library materials should be age-appropriate, but to what degree can you protect students from the realities of the world in which they live? Older students will soon be faced with real-world decisions concerning sexuality, politics, religion, voting, military service, etc., and challenged with making life-changing decisions based on their own personal beliefs. Where should students obtain information to help them in developing their own personal beliefs and in making informed decisions about these important issues?

For most students the Internet has become a far more common source of information than library books. Many students do, however, use the school library for Internet access while in school. The Internet offers a wealth of resources on virtually every subject. Clearly, however, the Internet also contains many materials that are inappropriate for children and should not be accessed through the school library. Children should not be exposed to obscene, harmful, or otherwise inappropriate materials through the school's Internet service. Congress addressed this problem in the Children's Internet Protection Act (CIPA), P.L. 106-554 (2000). Under CIPA schools that receive conditional federal technology grants or e-rate discounts are required to install Internet filters on all computers used by minor children and to implement other appropriate Internet usage protections for children. The U.S. Supreme Court upheld the CIPA in *U.S. v. American Library Association*, 539 U.S. 194 (2003).

Free Speech in the Cyber-World

Free speech in the cyber-world is governed by the same general legal principles that apply to the physical-world. The standard for regulating individual student speech is the *Tinker* standard requiring school officials to show that the student's speech threatened a material and substantial interference with the requirements of appropriate discipline in the operation of the school.

Fraser and *Hazelwood* govern student speech in school sponsored forums, including school sponsored electronic forums. School officials need only establish a legitimate educational rationale for limiting student speech in school sponsored electronic media.

School officials may also establish fair-use policies for school technology including reasonable time, place, and manner (TPM) restrictions in using school computers and other school controlled electronic media. These policies may include prohibitions against accessing indecent, harmful, or inappropriate materials, careless or destructive use of equipment, engaging in online harassment, violating copyright laws, etc. Students who violate reasonable fair-use policies may be denied access to school controlled technology and appropriately disciplined.

Although most free speech principles can be readily applied to the realm of electronic communications, the problem of jurisdiction in the cyber-world presents some unique challenges. The physical-world provides clear and tangible property boundaries defining on-campus and off-campus events. School officials generally have jurisdiction over events that physically occur on-campus, or at school-related events. Although these lines are less clear in the cyber-world, and the law and technology continue to evolve, in the cyber-world "on-campus" general means school controlled media (or use of any media while physically at school), and "off-campus" is the use of purely private media while not under the physical jurisdiction of the school.

Students can be appropriately sanctioned for on-campus misconduct. In order to exercise disciplinary authority over the "off-campus" misbehavior of students in the physical or cyber-world, school officials must be able to establish a clear logical nexus between the off-campus misconduct and a legitimate need for school officials to have jurisdiction over this misconduct. The jurisdiction of school officials in both the physical and cyber-world is not unlimited. In the cyber-world, unless school officials can establish the necessary logical nexus between "off-campus" misuse of electronic media and sufficient negative impacts on the school, the issue may be more appropriately dealt with by parents or law enforcement officials.

Speech that is not protected in the physical-world isn't protected in the cyber-world either. The First Amendment broadly protects speech, and especially political and religious speech. But obscenity, defamation, criminal conduct, and harassment are not within the bounds of protected speech. From a home computer, for example, a student has a free speech right to question and criticize the actions and policies of public school officials. They do not, however, have a right to post edited, false, and obscene images of teachers; to make threats or defame teachers or other students; or to engage in online harassment and bullying.

Cyber-Bullying

Cyber-bullying is the use of high-tech electronic media to engage in bullying. This type of bullying appears to be increasing as the use of electronic communications technologies increases. Cyber-bullying may include, for example, sending intentionally rude, cruel, or hurtful comments; online rumor spreading; or posting humiliating or threatening images or comments. This misconduct may occur through social media, e-mail, chat rooms, websites, text messages, etc. Bullying messages are most likely to come from persons the victim knows from in-person interactions. Cyber-bullying is becoming increasingly common, but face-to-face bullying remains the most common form of bullying.

For perpetrators seeking to inflict maximum suffering on their victims, cyber-bullying is often an extension of face-to-face bullying. Traditional school bullying ended when school ended and

167

the victim had some relief away from school. But cyber-bullying allows bullies to expand the harassment beyond school grounds and the regular school day, to a 24 hour boundless threat of harassment, thereby maximizing control, intimidation, and harm to the victim. For this reason, cyber-bullying can be far more psychologically damaging to the victim than in-school bullying alone.

School officials may appropriately punish children for misconduct occurring in school, including bullying and harassment, and they generally have a legal responsibility to do so. But when cyber-bullying among students is occurring off-campus it may sometimes be unclear whether the conduct falls within the lawful scope of school discipline; is instead off-campus free speech beyond the legitimate authority of school officials; or is misconduct more appropriately within the realm of parental discipline or police action.

Courts have long recognized that punishments for off-campus misconduct were appropriate when the off-campus misconduct involved non-protected speech aimed at students or faculty that reasonably threatened safety or a substantial disruption to the educational process. For example, in *Donavan* v. *Ritchie*, 68 F.3d 14 (1st Cir. 1995), the First Circuit Court of Appeals upheld the punishment of a student involved in the off-campus production of a document titled "The Shit List" which included the names of 140 students with crude comments about their appearances, social skills, and sexuality, comments which defamed students and resulted in school disruptions.

However, in *Layshock* v. *Hermitage School District*, 496 F. Supp. 2d. 587 (W.D. Pa. 2007), when school officials punished a student for creating an offensive "MySpace" parody of his principal on his grandmother's home computer, with comedic alcohol, drug, and sexual promiscuity related responses presented as the principal's answers to standard user profile questions, a federal district court overturned the punishment imposed on the student. The federal district court found that the school failed to establish a sufficient nexus between the student's off-campus speech and any substantial disruption of the school. The court noted that the "mere fact that the internet may be accessed at school does not authorize school officials to become censors of the world-wide web. Public schools are vital institutions, but their reach is not unlimited."

Ambiguity in this area of law seems to put school officials in a difficult position: If they act to address online misconduct their disciplinary actions may be overturned by a judge and they may be subject to liability for intruding on free speech; but if they don't act to protect the victims of harassment they may be found negligent and subject to liability.

A closer look at the cases, however, reveals that courts have generally been reluctant to impose liability on school officials for failing to address relatively minor acts of misconduct by students, especially when these acts were unknown to school officials despite reasonable efforts to establish protections for students against bullying and harassment. However, in more extreme, persistent, and harmful cases of bullying and harassment, when school officials knew of should have known about the abuse, courts have recognized a duty for school officials to take reasonable actions to protect the safety of children in their care.

Further, as states increasingly enact statutes prohibiting bullying (including cyber-bullying); more clearly define jurisdiction for school officials; and affirmatively require school officials to act to protect children under the defined jurisdiction of the statute, it will become increasingly difficult for school officials not to take action, and far easier for courts to hold them accountable if they do not. State anti-bullying laws are increasingly clarifying the responsibilities of school officials to address bullying, but also making it easier for potential plaintiffs to hold negligent school officials accountable for failing to act under the statute when necessary.

School Dress and Grooming Policies

The U.S. Supreme Court has not directly ruled on a student dress and grooming case. In *Tinker* the Court noted that the "problem posed by the present case does not relate to regulation of the length of skirts or the type of clothing, to hair style, or deportment." These issues were not before the Court in *Tinker*. But in view of the Court's decision in *Tinker*, concerning individual symbolic expression in schools, what would the Court have likely said about legal limits on dress and grooming policies in public schools?

There have been two distinct schools of thought on this issue among the U.S. Courts of Appeals: 1) Student dress and grooming is individual symbolic expression protected under the Constitution; or 2) Student dress and grooming rules are general regulations within the lawful province of school board members and not federal judges, and objections to local policies should be addressed to local school officials and resolved through the political process.

The U.S. Courts of Appeals for the First, Fourth, Seventh, and Eighth Circuits generally follow the first approach, balancing student interests in self-expression through dress and grooming against the interests of school officials in maintaining appropriate student discipline and avoiding disruptions of the educational process. The U.S. Courts of Appeals for the Third, Fifth, Sixth, Ninth, and Tenth Circuits, however, follow the second approach. These Circuits treat student dress and grooming issues as disputes over local school policies, giving great deference to the decisions of local school officials. Policies that are clearly discriminatory; arbitrary and capricious; violate due process; or directly intrude on protected religious or political speech are likely to receive judicial attention. But otherwise courts in the Circuits that follow this second approach tend to hold that dress and grooming disputes should be resolved through appeals to local school officials and the political process, and these disputes are not appropriate issues for federal judicial intervention.

Many of the student dress and grooming decisions from U.S. Courts of Appeals date back to the late 1960s and early 1970s, when the length of a student's hair or a skirt above the knee seemed to provoke much more zealous social and political debate among students, school officials, parents, and community members. In this time period, long hair was seen by many students as a political rejection of discredited establishment values, and by many school officials as a rebellion against legitimate authority and respectable social norms. In this political culture, dress and grooming may very well have been political speech for some students.

More recently, however, were saggy pants a political statement or a fashion trend? Are the real issues individual and cultural expressions; or health, safety, and discipline problems? The current trend in dress and grooming cases appears to be greater judicial deference to school dress and grooming regulations, especially when these regulations are based on legitimate health, safety, or educational concerns.

Dress and grooming policies that are still likely to provoke judicial intervention are those that unnecessarily intrude on sincere religious beliefs; take sides in a political dispute; or fail to provide sufficient notice and due process. For example, a rule that requires a Native American child to cut his hair, when doing so violates a sincerely held tribal belief, is likely to be declared unconstitutional as applied to the Native American child. A practice that allows campaign t-shirts for one candidate but prohibits t-shirts representing opposing candidates is unlawful. And all government regulations are subject to the requirements of the Due Process Clause.

169

Among the requirements of the Due Process Clause is a mandate that government officials provide adequate notice of what is required and what is prohibited by the government regulation. In the context of school dress and grooming policies, this means that students and parents must have adequate notice of what the school dress and grooming policy requires or prohibits in school. Further, this notice must be reasonably clear so that persons of ordinary intelligence can understand what is required and prohibited.

Overly vague policies are unconstitutional because they give both too little notice to students and too much discretion to school officials, in violation of the Due Process Clause. For example, a dress and grooming policy that only stated "all students must dress in good taste" tells students and parents almost nothing about what is actually required or prohibited. Further, this vague policy leaves enforcement open to the arbitrary whims of school administrators who could punish anyone arbitrarily based on their own subjective determination of what constituted "good taste." The key to drafting lawful and effective dress and grooming policies is to strike a proper balance between specificity (to satisfy the notice requirement of the Due Process Clause) and breadth of coverage (to assure that the policy will cover the intended prohibited conduct) in the language of the policy. Policies must be clear enough not to be unconstitutional vague, but broad enough to achieve the intended policy goals.

School officials enjoy even greater latitude in establishing dress and grooming policies for employees, as while most students are in public schools because of compulsory attendance laws, public school employees are in schools because of a voluntary contractual relationship. Further, school employees are free to express themselves through personal attire while not on duty. School officials could, for example, adopt a policy that would require all male teachers to wear a tie while on duty. Exceptions must be made based on legitimate health or safety concerns. For example, a male teacher with a health condition that prohibited wearing a tie must be exempted, and ties could not be required when there was a legitimate safety risk (*e.g.*, in shop or physical education classes). As long as female teachers were required to wear similar professional attire, the policy does not discriminate based on gender. Dress and grooming policies for employees need only be based on a legitimate health, safety, or educational rationale to satisfy the highly deferential standard of judicial review applied in these cases.

Gang Symbols in Schools

The First Amendment protects many types of speech, with special protections for political or religious speech. The First Amendment also protects freedom of assembly, guaranteeing citizens' rights to meet together in public places and to collectively engage in free speech and political action. The First Amendment does not, however, protect gang-related gatherings in schools for purposes of planning or engaging in criminal conduct or any actions that threaten a material and substantial interference with the educational process. Gang symbols cloaked as free speech in schools are not protected under the First Amendment.

The criminal history, violence, and disruptions associated with gang activity give school officials good cause to proactively address gang problems in their schools. Especially when these symbols have been linked to acts of violence and disruptions triggered by these symbols, gang symbols receive no First Amendment protection in schools. Although the Court recognized in *Tinker*: "It can hardly be argued that either students or teachers shed their constitutional rights to freedom of speech or expression at the schoolhouse gate" it cannot be credible argued that the gang member is the legal equal of Mary Beth Tinker. If the display of a particular symbol, color, etc., has become clearly identified with gang activities in the school, school officials can prohibit this symbol and punish its intentional display for gang-related purposes.

Care should be taken, however, to provide adequate notice of what is prohibited, and to give students an adequate opportunity to respond to allegations of gang-related conduct prior to punishment. School officials must also distinguish between gang-related uses of symbols and sincere religious expression. For example, while wearing a Cross or a Star of David is not protected speech when the purpose of the symbol is clearly gang-related, genuinely wearing a Cross or a Star of David in observance of sincerely held religious beliefs is protected speech. In most cases, however, it is not difficult for school officials to distinguish between who is wearing the symbol because of gang-related activity and who is engaged in sincere religious observance.

Comments and Questions

Disputes over free speech have frequently involved public schools, with the Court addressing the proper balance between individuals' rights of free speech and legitimate public and institutional needs. Although recognizing a constitutional right to free speech by students, the Court has also emphasized the importance of teaching children civility and tolerance. The Court stated in *Bethel School District v. Fraser* that public schools "must inculcate the habits and manners of civility" and that this must "include tolerance of divergent political and religious views, even when the views expressed may be unpopular."

While recognizing students' rights to free speech, the Court has emphasized the accompanying responsibility of exercising civility in expressing their opinions. The Court noted: "Indeed the fundamental values necessary to the maintenance of a democratic political system disfavor the use of terms of debate highly offensive or highly threatening to others . . . The inculcation of these values is truly the work of the schools." Courts have recognized that divergent views are tolerated in a democratic society, and that civil discourse is the appropriate way to express individual views and opposition to the views of others.

The Court has also distinguished between individual student speech, as in *Tinker v. Des Moines*, and student speech in public school sponsored forums, as in *Bethel v. Fraser*, and *Hazelwood v. Kuhlmeier*. In *Hazelwood* the Court held "educators do not offend the First Amendment by exercising editorial control over the style and content of student speech in school sponsored expressive activities so long as their actions are reasonably related to legitimate pedagogical concerns." Further, the Court suggested that student speech in public school sponsored forums can be distinguished from individual student speech because school sponsored speech involves "expressive activities that students, parents, and members of the public might reasonably perceive to bear the imprimatur of the school."

Viewed together, the Court's cases indicate that student speech in public schools generally falls into one of two categories: 1) Student speech involving individual student expression, as in *Tinker v. Des Moines*; or 2) Student speech in public school sponsored forums, as in *Bethel v. Fraser*, and *Hazelwood v. Kuhlmeier*. In *Tinker* the Court declared that to lawfully limit individual student speech, school officials must establish that the speech would "materially and substantially interfere with the requirements of appropriate discipline in the operation of the school." Although school officials may apply reasonable time, place, and manner restrictions to all expressive activities, if they cannot establish that the speech "materially and substantially" interferes with "appropriate discipline in the operation of the school" the speech generally cannot be prohibited or punished consistent with the First Amendment.

Tinker was a 7-2 decision in which the majority of the Court solidly endorsed the vigorous protection of free speech rights for students and teachers. In *Tinker*, it is clear that the Court expected school officials to take the First Amendment seriously in public schools. The Court declared in *Tinker*: "The Constitution says that Congress (and the States) may not abridge the right to free speech. This provision means what it says." The Court established a high burden of proof in *Tinker*, because school officials are being asked to justify silencing what would otherwise be protected free speech. But the Court also wanted to make clear that school officials had legitimate authority to limit student speech when necessary. The Court's "material and substantial interference" standard in *Tinker* attempts to strike a reasonable balance in these competing concerns, and to provide some guidance to school officials and judges in fairly resolving disputes over these issues.

Concerning student speech in public school sponsored forums, such as school convocations, performances, athletic events, school newspapers, and other expressive activities that students, parents, and members of the public might reasonably perceive as bearing the "imprimatur of the school" school officials generally have much broader discretion to limit student speech in a school-sponsored forum. Where the forum for expression is sponsored by the school or reasonably perceived as bearing the imprimatur of the school, as in *Fraser*, and *Hazelwood*, student expression in a school sponsored forum can be limited based on establishing a legitimate educational rationale for limiting the speech. Legitimate educational rationales for limiting speech in a school sponsored forum may include, for example, the need to teach civility, limit messages inconsistent with legitimate educational goals, or prohibit age-inappropriate speech.

The Court's tests in *Tinker* and *Fraser/Hazelwood* provide useful guidance for school officials, lawyers, and judges in sorting out what student speech is protected, what student speech may be prohibited, and in proactively establishing lawful school policies and practices concerning student speech. In recalling a student speech controversy in your school, how would the tests in *Tinker* or *Fraser/Hazelwood* have applied in that case? Was the speech individual speech or student speech in a school sponsored forum? Under the facts and circumstances in that case could school officials satisfy the appropriate legal test in order to exercise lawful control over the speech, or should school officials have allowed the speech? Would the application of reasonable time, place, and manner (TPM) restrictions have helped to both protect student speech rights and prevent unnecessary disruptions in the school? To qualify as reasonable TPM restrictions the limitations must be: 1) Content neutral; 2) Narrowly tailored to serving a significant governmental interest; and 3) Leave open an adequate alternative channel of communication. What would have constituted appropriate TPM restrictions in this case?

Free Speech Rights of Public School Educators

As the U.S. Supreme Court declared in *Tinker*: "It can hardly be argued that either students or teachers shed their constitutional rights to freedom of speech or expression at the schoolhouse gate." Public school educators retain their rights as citizens to freedom of speech. They do not, however, have an unconditional right to serve as public employees. Free speech is broadly protected in public schools, for students and teachers. Nonetheless, school officials have a duty to maintain proper order and discipline in school operations. When necessary, school officials may appropriately sanction or remove persons who disrupt the work of the school, including members of the faculty.

Allowing school officials to fire educators simply for expressing their opinions, however, would make a mockery of free speech in schools. Further, if retaliatory firings for speech were allowed, educators would become hesitant to speak out on important matters of legitimate public concern. When schools are operated ineffectively or inefficiently educators have a professional duty to reveal problems so they may be remedied for the common good. Further, if there is corruption or other misconduct in the school, educators are in the best positions to see these problems and to disclose any malfeasance to proper authorities and the public. A closed culture of retaliation, fear, and silence is a breeding ground for corruption. The broad protection of free speech is the best means of shining the light of truth into every corner of the institution to assure honesty and accountability. As Justice Brandeis said: "Sunlight is the best disinfectant."

In *Pickering v. Board of Education*, the Court attempted to strike a proper balance between public educators' rights to free speech, and the legitimate interests of school officials in effectively and efficiently operating the school. The dispute in the *Pickering* case began when Marvin Pickering, a public school teacher, sent the following letter to the local newspaper:

LETTERS TO THE EDITOR
Graphic Newspapers, Inc. Thursday, September 24, 1964, Page 4

Dear Editor:

I enjoyed reading the back issues of your paper which you loaned to me. Perhaps others would enjoy reading them in order to see just how far the two new high schools have deviated from the original promises by the Board of Education. First, let me state that I am referring to the February thru November, 1961 issues of your paper, so that it can be checked.

One statement in your paper declared that swimming pools, athletic fields, and auditoriums had been left out of the program. They may have been left out but they got put back in very quickly because Lockport West has both an auditorium and athletic field. In fact, Lockport West has a better athletic field than Lockport Central. It has a track that isn't quite regulation distance even though the board spent a few thousand dollars on it. Whose fault is that? Oh, I forgot, it wasn't supposed to be there in the first place. It must have fallen out of the sky. Such responsibility has been touched on in other letters but it seems one just can't help noticing it. I am not saying the school shouldn't have these facilities, because I think they should, but promises are promises, or are they?

Since there seems to be a problem getting all the facts to the voter on the twice defeated bond issue, many letters have been written to this paper and probably more will follow, I feel I must say something about the letters and their writers. Many of these letters did not give the whole story. Letters by your Board and Administration have stated that teachers' salaries total $1,297,746 for one year. Now that must have been the total payroll, otherwise the teachers would be getting $10,000 a year. I teach at the high school and I know this just isn't the case. However, this shows their 'stop at nothing' attitude. To illustrate further, do you know that the superintendent told the teachers, and I quote, "Any teacher that opposes the referendum should be prepared for the consequences." I think this gets at the reason we have problems passing bond issues. Threats take something away; these are insults to voters in a free society. We should try to sell a program on its merits, if it has any.

Remember those letters entitled "District 205 Teachers Speak," I think the voters should know that those letters have been written and agreed to by only five or six teachers, not 98% of the teachers in the high school. In fact, many teachers didn't even know who was writing them. Did you know that those letters had to have the approval of the superintendent before they could be put in the paper? That's the kind of totalitarianism teachers live in at the high school, and your children go to school in.

In last week's paper, the letter written by a few uninformed teachers threatened to close the school cafeteria and fire its personnel. This is ridiculous and insults the intelligence of the voter because properly managed school cafeterias do not cost the school district any money. If the cafeteria is losing money, then the board should not be packing free lunches for athletes on days of athletic contests. Whatever the case, the taxpayer's child should only have to pay about 30¢ for his lunch instead of 35¢ to pay for free lunches for the athletes.

In a reply to this letter your Board of Administration will probably state that these lunches are paid for from receipts from the games. But $20,000 in receipts doesn't pay for the $200,000 a year they have been spending on varsity sports while neglecting the wants of teachers.

You see we don't need an increase in the transportation tax unless the voters want to keep paying $50,000 or more a year to transport athletes home after practice and to away games, etc. Rest of the $200,000 is made up in coaches' salaries, athletic directors' salaries, baseball pitching machines, sodded football fields, and thousands of dollars for other sports equipment.

These things are all right, provided we have enough money for them. To sod football fields on borrowed money and then not be able to pay teachers' salaries is getting the cart before the horse. If these things aren't enough for you, look at East High. No doors on many of the classrooms, a plant room without any sunlight, no water in a first aid treatment room, are just a few of many things. The taxpayers were really taken to the cleaners. A part of the sidewalk in front of the building has already collapsed. Maybe Mr. Hess would be interested to know that we need blinds on the windows in that building also.

Once again, the board must have forgotten they were going to spend $3,200,000 on the West building and $2,300,000 on the East building. As I see it, the bond issue is a fight between the Board of Education that is trying to push tax-supported athletics down our throats with education, and a public that has mixed emotions about both of these items because they feel they are already paying enough taxes, and simply don't know whom to trust with any more tax money.

I must sign this letter as a citizen, taxpayer and voter, not as a teacher, since that freedom has been taken from the teachers by the administration. Do you really know what goes on behind those stone walls at the high school?

Respectfully,

Marvin L. Pickering

Mr. Pickering's letter contained some statements that turned out to be false, although the Court stated in a footnote: "We shall not bother to enumerate some of the statements which the Board found to be false because their triviality is so readily apparent that the Board could not rationally have considered them as detrimental to the interests of the schools regardless of their truth or falsity." In *Pickering* the Court addressed whether a public school educator can be fired for making false public statements about the school or school officials.

Pickering v. Board of Education
391 U.S. 563 (1968)
Supreme Court of the United States

Mr. Justice MARSHALL delivered the opinion of the Court.

Appellant Marvin L. Pickering, a teacher in Township High School District 205, Will County, Illinois, was dismissed from his position by the appellee Board of Education for sending a letter to a local newspaper in connection with a recently proposed tax increase that was critical of the way in which the Board and the district superintendent of schools had handled past proposals to raise new revenue for the schools. Appellant's dismissal resulted from a determination by the Board, after a full hearing, that the publication of the letter was "detrimental to the efficient operation and administration of the schools of the district" and hence, under the relevant Illinois statute . . . that "interests of the schools required (his dismissal)."

Appellant's claim that his writing of the letter was protected by the First and Fourteenth Amendments was rejected. Appellant then sought review of the Board's action in the Circuit Court of Will County, which affirmed his dismissal on the ground that the determination that appellant's letter was detrimental to the interests of the school system was supported by substantial evidence and that the interests of the schools overruled appellant's First Amendment rights. On appeal, the Supreme Court of Illinois, two Justices dissenting, affirmed the judgment of the Circuit Court. We noted probable jurisdiction of appellant's claim that the Illinois statute permitting his dismissal on the facts of this case was unconstitutional as applied under the First and Fourteenth Amendments. For the reasons detailed below we agree that appellant's rights to freedom of speech were violated and we reverse.

In February of 1961 the appellee Board of Education asked the voters of the school district to approve a bond issue to raise $4,875,000 to erect two new schools. The proposal was defeated. Then, in December of 1961, the Board submitted another bond proposal to the voters which called for the raising of $5,500,000 to build two new schools. This second proposal passed and the schools were built with the money raised by the bond sales. In May of 1964 a proposed increase in the tax rate to be used for educational purposes was submitted to the voters by the Board and was defeated. Finally, on September 19, 1964, a second proposal to increase the tax rate was submitted by the Board and was likewise defeated. It was in connection with this last proposal of the School Board that appellant wrote the letter to the editor . . . that resulted in his dismissal.

Prior to the vote on the second tax increase proposal a variety of articles attributed to the District 205 Teachers' Organization appeared in the local paper. These articles urged passage of the tax increase and stated that failure to pass the increase would result in a decline in the quality of education afforded children in the district's schools. A letter from the superintendent of schools making the same point was published in the paper two days before the election and submitted to the voters in mimeographed form the following day. It was in response to the foregoing material, together with the failure of the tax increase to pass, that appellant submitted the letter in question to the editor of the local paper.

The letter constituted, basically, an attack on the School Board's handling of the 1961 bond issue proposals and its subsequent allocation of financial resources between the schools' educational and athletic programs. It also charged the superintendent of schools with attempting to prevent teachers in the district from opposing or criticizing the proposed bond issue.

The Board dismissed Pickering for writing and publishing the letter. Pursuant to Illinois law, the Board was then required to hold a hearing on the dismissal. At the hearing the Board charged that numerous statements in the letter were false and that the publication of the statements unjustifiably impugned the "motives, honesty, integrity, truthfulness, responsibility and competence" of both the Board and the school administration. The Board also charged that the false statements damaged the professional reputations of its members and of the school administrators, would be disruptive of faculty discipline, and would tend to foment "controversy, conflict and dissension" among teachers, administrators, the Board of Education, and the residents of the district. Testimony was introduced from a variety of witnesses on the truth or falsity of the particular statements in the letter with which the Board took issue. The Board found the statements to be false as charged. No evidence was introduced at any point in the proceedings as to the effect of the publication of the letter on the community as a whole or on the administration of the school system in particular, and no specific findings along these lines were made.

The Illinois courts reviewed the proceedings solely to determine whether the Board's findings were supported by substantial evidence and whether, on the facts as found, the Board could reasonably conclude that appellant's publication of the letter was "detrimental to the best interests of the schools." Pickering's claim that his letter was protected by the First Amendment was rejected on the ground that his acceptance of a teaching position in the public schools obliged him to refrain from making statements about the operation of the schools "which in the absence of such position he would have an undoubted right to engage in." It is not altogether clear whether the Illinois Supreme Court held that the First Amendment had no applicability to appellant's dismissal for writing the letter in question or whether it determined that the particular statements made in the letter were not entitled to First Amendment protection. In any event, it clearly rejected Pickering's claim that, on the facts of this case, he could not constitutionally be dismissed from his teaching position.

To the extent that the Illinois Supreme Court's opinion may be read to suggest that teachers may constitutionally be compelled to relinquish the First Amendment rights they would otherwise enjoy as citizens to comment on matters of public interest in connection with the operation of the public schools in which they work, it proceeds on a premise that has been unequivocally rejected in numerous prior decisions of this Court. "The theory that public employment which may be denied altogether may be subjected to any conditions, regardless of how unreasonable, has been uniformly rejected." At the same time it cannot be gainsaid that the State has interests as an employer in regulating the speech of its employees that differ significantly from those it possesses in connection with regulation of the speech of the citizenry in general. The problem in any case is to arrive at a balance between the interests of the teacher, as a citizen, in commenting upon matters of public concern and the interest of the State, as an employer, in promoting the efficiency of the public services it performs through its employees.

The Board contends that "the teacher by virtue of his public employment has a duty of loyalty to support his superiors in attaining the generally accepted goals of education and that, if he must speak out publicly, he should do so factually and accurately, commensurate with his education and experience." Appellant, on the other hand, argues that the test applicable to defamatory statements directed against public officials by persons having no occupational relationship with them, namely, that statements to be legally actionable must be made "with knowledge that (they were) . . . false or with reckless disregard of whether (they were) . . . false or not," should also be applied to public statements made by teachers. Because of the enormous variety of fact situations in which critical statements by teachers and other public employees may be thought by their superiors, against whom the statements are directed to furnish grounds for dismissal, we do not deem it either appropriate or feasible to attempt to lay down a general standard against which all such statements may be judged. However, in the course of evaluating the conflicting claims of First Amendment protection and the need for orderly school administration in the context of this case, we shall indicate some of the general lines along which an analysis of the controlling interests should run.

An examination of the statements in appellant's letter objected to by the Board reveals that they, like the letter as a whole, consist essentially of criticism of the Board's allocation of school funds between educational and athletic programs, and of both the Board's and the superintendent's methods of informing, or preventing the informing of, the district's taxpayers of the real reasons why additional tax revenues were being sought for the schools. The statements are in no way directed towards any person with whom appellant would normally be in contact in the course of his daily work as a teacher. Thus no question of maintaining either discipline by immediate superiors or harmony among coworkers is presented here. Appellant's employment relationships with the Board and, to a somewhat lesser extent, with the superintendent are not the kind of close working relationships for which it can persuasively be claimed that personal loyalty and confidence are necessary to their proper functioning. Accordingly, to the extent that the Board's position here can be taken to suggest that even comments on matters of public concern that are substantially correct, such as statements (1)-(4) of appellant's letter, may furnish grounds for dismissal if they are sufficiently critical in tone, we unequivocally reject it.

We next consider the statements in appellant's letter which we agree to be false. The Board's original charges included allegations that the publication of the letter damaged the professional reputations of the Board and the superintendent and would foment controversy and conflict among the Board, teachers, administrators, and the residents of the district. However, no evidence to support these allegations was introduced at the hearing. So far as the record reveals, Pickering's letter was greeted by everyone but its main target, the Board, with massive apathy and total disbelief. The Board must, therefore, have decided, perhaps by analogy with the law of libel, that the statements were per se harmful to the operation of the schools.

However, the only way in which the Board could conclude, absent any evidence of the actual effect of the letter, that the statements contained therein were per se detrimental to the interest of the schools was to equate the Board members' own interests with that of the schools. Certainly an accusation that too much money is being spent on athletics by the administrators of the school system (which is precisely the import of that portion of appellant's letter containing the statements that we have found to be false) cannot reasonably be regarded as per se detrimental to the district's schools. Such an accusation reflects rather a difference of opinion between Pickering and the Board as to the preferable manner of operating the school system, a difference of opinion that clearly concerns an issue of general public interest.

In addition, the fact that particular illustrations of the Board's claimed undesirable emphasis on athletic programs are false would not normally have any necessary impact on the actual operation of the schools, beyond its tendency to anger the Board. For example, Pickering's letter was written after the defeat at the polls of the second proposed tax increase. It could, therefore, have had no effect on the ability of the school district to raise necessary revenue, since there was no showing that there was any proposal to increase taxes pending when the letter was written.

More importantly, the question whether a school system requires additional funds is a matter of legitimate public concern on which the judgment of the school administration, including the School Board, cannot, in a society that leaves such questions to popular vote, be taken as conclusive. On such a question free and open debate is vital to informed decision-making by the electorate. Teachers are, as a class, the members of a community most likely to have informed and definite opinions as to how funds allotted to the operations of the schools should be spent. Accordingly, it is essential that they be able to speak out freely on such questions without fear of retaliatory dismissal.

In addition, the amounts expended on athletics which Pickering reported erroneously were matters of public record on which his position as a teacher in the district did not qualify him to speak with any greater authority than any other taxpayer. The Board could easily have rebutted appellant's errors by publishing the accurate figures itself, either via a letter to the same newspaper or otherwise. We are thus not presented with a situation in which a teacher has carelessly made false statements about matters so closely related to the day-to-day operations of the schools that any harmful impact on the public would be difficult to counter because of the teacher's presumed greater access to the real facts. Accordingly, we have no occasion to consider at this time whether under such circumstances a school board could reasonably require that a teacher make substantial efforts to verify the accuracy of his charges before publishing them.

What we do have before us is a case in which a teacher has made erroneous public statements upon issues then currently the subject of public attention, which are critical of his ultimate employer but which are neither shown nor can be presumed to have in any way either impeded the teacher's proper performance of his daily duties in the classroom or to have interfered with the regular operation of the schools generally. In these circumstances we conclude that the interest of the school administration in limiting teachers' opportunities to contribute to public debate is not significantly greater than its interest in limiting a similar contribution by any member of the general public.

The public interest in having free and unhindered debate on matters of public importance--the core value of the Free Speech Clause of the First Amendment--is so great that it has been held that a State cannot authorize the recovery of damages by a public official for defamatory statements directed at him except when such statements are shown to have been made either with knowledge of their falsity or with reckless disregard for their truth or falsity. *New York Times Co. v. Sullivan*, 376 U.S. 254 (1964). The same test has been applied to suits for invasion of privacy based on false statements where a "matter of public interest" is involved. It is therefore perfectly clear that, were appellant a member of the general public, the State's power to afford the appellee Board of Education or its members any legal right to sue him for writing the letter at issue here would be limited by the requirement that the letter be judged by the standard laid down in *New York Times*.

This Court has also indicated, in more general terms, that statements by public officials on matters of public concern must be accorded First Amendment protection despite the fact that the statements are directed at their nominal superiors. *Garrison v. State of Louisiana*, 379 U.S. 64 (1964). In *Garrison*, the *New York Times* test was specifically applied to a case involving a criminal defamation conviction stemming from statements made by a district attorney about the judges before whom he regularly appeared.

While criminal sanctions and damage awards have a somewhat different impact on the exercise of the right to freedom of speech from dismissal from employment, it is apparent that the threat of dismissal from public employment is nonetheless a potent means of inhibiting speech. We have already noted our disinclination to make an across-the-board equation of dismissal from public employment for remarks critical of superiors with awarding damages in a libel suit by a public official for similar criticism. However, in a case such as the present one, in which the fact of employment is only tangentially and insubstantially involved in the subject matter of the public communication made by a teacher, we conclude that it is necessary to regard the teacher as the member of the general public he seeks to be.

In sum, we hold that, in a case such as this, absent proof of false statements knowingly or recklessly made by him, a teacher's exercise of his right to speak on issues of public importance may not furnish the basis for his dismissal from public employment. Since no such showing has been made in this case regarding appellant's letter, his dismissal for writing it cannot be upheld and the judgment of the Illinois Supreme Court must, accordingly, be reversed and the case remanded for further proceedings not inconsistent with this opinion. It is so ordered.

Judgment reversed and case remanded with directions.

* * * * * * *

Comments and Questions

Concerning the free speech rights of public educators, in *Pickering* the Court ruled that teachers have a First Amendment right to comment on legitimate matters of public concern and "absent proof of false statements knowingly or recklessly made by him, a teacher's exercise of his right to speak on issues of public importance may not furnish the basis for his dismissal from public employment."

Generally, public employees have the same free speech rights as all citizens. If public school officials wish to sanction speech by school employees, including dismissal or other employment sanctions, school officials must be prepared to show that the speech negatively impacted the employment relationship, and that the speech was unprotected in the context. The *Pickering* test is used to distinguish between protected and unprotected speech by public employees:

> The *Pickering* Test: To determine whether speech is protected, courts generally balance the employee's speech rights against the employer's legitimate interests in efficient operation of the public institution. Questions considered in this balance include:
>
> 1) *Was the speech related to a legitimate matter of public concern?* Speech regarding legitimate public concerns generally receives First Amendment protection.
>
> 2) *Was the speech true?* True statements receive more protection than false statements.
>
> > Note: Even if the speech is true, courts will also consider public officials' legitimate needs for: 1) Regular close contact and a working relationship of loyalty and trust with the speaker; 2) Appropriate office discipline; and 3) Harmony among co-workers.
>
> 3) *If false, was the false statement merely negligently made by the public employee?* False statements made only negligently may still receive First Amendment protection.

PURPOSELY
KNOWINGLY
RECKLESSLY
-----Pickering Line-----
NEGLIGENTLY

> Note: Courts will also consider whether the false statements interfere with the performance of duties or the regular operations of the institution.

In *Pickering* the Court drew the constitutional line for protection of false statements as free speech at mere negligence. False statements made recklessly, knowingly, or purposely by public employees are not protected. The Court determined that culpability greater than negligence was generally required before public officials could lawfully sanction false statements by employees on matters of legitimate public concern. To be subject to sanctions, the false statement must be made, in increasing order of culpability: Recklessly; Knowingly; or Purposely.

To make a false statement "negligently" means that the speaker merely failed to use ordinary care in determining whether the statement was true. To make a false statement "recklessly" means that the speaker engaged in reckless disregard for the truth. To make a false statement "knowingly" means that the speaker knew the statement was false but made it anyway. To make a false statement "purposely" is to make a statement known to be false for the purpose of inflicting harm.

Pickering continues to serve as the foundation for the law governing free speech rights of public employees. The Court heavily relied on the principles of *Pickering* to resolve disputes in its subsequent public employee speech cases in *Connick v. Myers*, 461 U.S. 138 (1983), *Rankin v. McPherson*, 483 U.S. 378 (1987), and *Garcetti v. Ceballos*, 547 U.S. 410 (2006), with each case further clarifying and developing public employee free speech law.

In *Connick v. Myers* the Court clarified: 1) The legal consequences of failing to establish the matter at issue was speech as a citizen on a legitimate public concern; and 2) What constitutes a matter of public concern:

> We hold only that, when a public employee speaks not as a citizen upon matters of public concern, but instead as an employee upon matters only of personal interest, absent the most unusual circumstances, a federal court is not the appropriate forum in which to review the wisdom of a personnel decision taken by a public agency allegedly in reaction to the employee's behavior. Our responsibility is to ensure that citizens are not deprived of fundamental rights by virtue of working for the government; this does not require a grant of immunity for employee grievances not afforded by the First Amendment to those who do not work for the State. Whether an employee's speech addresses a matter of public concern must be determined by the content, form, and context of a given statement, as revealed by the whole record . . . To presume that all matters which transpire within a government office are of public concern would mean that virtually every remark--and certainly every criticism directed at a public official--would plant the seed of a constitutional case.

In *Rankin v. McPherson*, the Court addressed the appropriate balance between the interests of employers and employees:

> On the one hand, public employers are employers, concerned with the efficient function of their operations; review of every personnel decision made by a public employer could, in the long run, hamper the performance of public functions. On the other hand, "the threat of dismissal from public employment is . . . a potent means of inhibiting speech." Vigilance is necessary to ensure that public employers do not use authority over employees to silence discourse, not because it hampers public functions but simply because superiors disagree with the content of employees' speech.

And in *Garcetti v. Ceballos*, the U.S. Supreme Court recognized a significant limitation to the *Pickering* line of cases, holding that when public employees' speech is part of their official duties, this speech is not protected under the First Amendment:

> Speech pursuant to official duties is not protected speech under the First Amendment. When public supervisors reasonably believe that public employees official comments are

181

inappropriate, inflammatory, or otherwise detrimental to legitimate institutional goals the First Amendment does not shield public employees from employment consequences in these cases. It is well settled that "a State cannot condition public employment on a basis that infringes the employee's constitutionally protected interest in freedom of expression" . . . *Pickering* provides a useful starting point in explaining the Court's doctrine . . . "The problem in any case . . . is to arrive at a balance between the interests of the teacher, as a citizen, in commenting upon matters of public concern and the interest of the State, as an employer, in promoting the efficiency of the public services it performs through its employees." The Court found the teacher's speech "neither [was] shown nor can be presumed to have in any way either impeded the teacher's proper performance of his daily duties in the classroom or to have interfered with the regular operation of the schools generally." Thus, the Court concluded that "the interest of the school administration in limiting teachers' opportunities to contribute to public debate is not significantly greater than its interest in limiting a similar contribution by any member of the general public." *Pickering* and the cases decided in its wake identify two inquiries to guide interpretation of the constitutional protections accorded to public employee speech. The first requires determining whether the employee spoke as a citizen on a matter of public concern. If the answer is no, the employee has no First Amendment cause of action based on his or her employer's reaction to the speech. If the answer is yes, then the possibility of a First Amendment claim arises. The question becomes whether the relevant government entity had an adequate justification for treating the employee differently from any other member of the general public. This consideration reflects the importance of the relationship between the speaker's expressions and employment. A government entity has broader discretion to restrict speech when it acts in its role as employer, but the restrictions it imposes must be directed at speech that has some potential to affect the entity's operations. To be sure, conducting these inquiries sometimes has proved difficult. This is the necessary product of "the enormous variety of fact situations in which critical statements by teachers and other public employees may be thought by their superiors . . . to furnish grounds for dismissal." The Court's overarching objectives, though, are evident. When a citizen enters government service, the citizen by necessity must accept certain limitations on his or her freedom. Government employers, like private employers, need a significant degree of control over their employees' words and actions; without it, there would be little chance for the efficient provision of public services . . . "Government offices could not function if every employment decision became a constitutional matter" . . . Public employees, moreover, often occupy trusted positions in society. When they speak out, they can express views that contravene governmental policies or impair the proper performance of governmental functions. At the same time, the Court has recognized that a citizen who works for the government is nonetheless a citizen. The First Amendment limits the ability of a public employer to leverage the employment relationship to restrict, incidentally or intentionally, the liberties employees enjoy in their capacities as private citizens. So long as employees are speaking as citizens about matters of public concern, they must face only those speech restrictions that are necessary for their employers to operate efficiently and effectively. The Court's employee-speech jurisprudence protects, of course, the constitutional rights of public employees. Yet the First Amendment interests at stake extend beyond the individual speaker. The Court has acknowledged the importance of promoting the public's interest in receiving the well-informed views of government employees engaging in civic discussion. *Pickering* again provides an instructive example. The Court characterized its holding as rejecting the attempt of school administrators to "limit teachers' opportunities to contribute to public debate." It also noted that teachers are "the members of a community most likely to have informed and definite opinions" about school expenditures. The Court's approach acknowledged the necessity for informed, vibrant dialogue in a democratic society. It suggested, in addition, that widespread costs may arise when dialogue is repressed . . . The Court's decisions, then, have sought both to promote the individual and societal interests that are served when employees speak as citizens on matters of public concern and to respect the needs of government employers attempting to perform their important public functions. Underlying our cases has been the premise that while the First Amendment invests public employees with certain rights, it does not empower them to "constitutionalize the employee grievance" . . . We hold that when public employees make statements pursuant to their official duties, the employees are not speaking as citizens for First Amendment purposes, and the Constitution does not insulate their communications from employer discipline . . . Restricting speech that owes its existence to a public employee's professional responsibilities does not infringe any liberties the employee might have enjoyed as a private citizen. It simply reflects the exercise of employer control over what the employer itself has commissioned or created. Contrast, for example, the expressions made by the speaker in *Pickering*, whose letter to the newspaper had no official significance and bore similarities to letters submitted by numerous citizens every day . . . This result is consistent with our precedents' attention to the potential societal value of employee speech. Refusing to recognize First Amendment claims based on government employees' work product does not prevent them from participating in public debate. The employees retain the prospect of constitutional protection for their contributions to the civic discourse. This prospect of protection, however, does not invest them with a right to perform their jobs however they see fit. Our holding likewise is supported by the emphasis of our precedents on affording government employers sufficient discretion to manage their operations. Employers have heightened interests in controlling speech made by an employee in his or her professional capacity. Official communications have official consequences, creating a need for substantive consistency and clarity. Supervisors must ensure that their employees' official communications are accurate, demonstrate sound judgment, and promote the employer's mission . . . When an employee speaks as a citizen addressing a matter of public concern, the First Amendment requires a delicate balancing of the competing interests surrounding the speech and its consequences. When, however, the employee is simply performing his or her job duties, there is no warrant for a similar degree of scrutiny. To hold otherwise would be to demand permanent judicial intervention in the conduct of governmental operations to a degree inconsistent with sound principles of federalism and the separation of powers . . . Employees who make public statements outside the course of performing their official duties retain some possibility of First Amendment protection because that is the kind of activity engaged in by citizens who do not work for the government. The same goes for writing a letter to a local newspaper, or discussing politics with a co-worker. When a public employee speaks pursuant to employment responsibilities, however, there is no relevant analogue to speech by citizens who are not government employees . . . Justice

Souter suggests today's decision may have important ramifications for academic freedom, at least as a constitutional value. There is some argument that expression related to academic scholarship or classroom instruction implicates additional constitutional interests that are not fully accounted for by this Court's customary employee-speech jurisprudence. We need not, and for that reason do not, decide whether the analysis we conduct today would apply in the same manner to a case involving speech related to scholarship or teaching. Exposing governmental inefficiency and misconduct is a matter of considerable significance . . . public employers should, "as a matter of good judgment," be "receptive to constructive criticism offered by their employees." The dictates of sound judgment are reinforced by the powerful network of legislative enactments--such as whistle-blower protection laws and labor codes--available to those who seek to expose wrongdoing . . . We reject, however, the notion that the First Amendment shields from discipline the expressions employees make pursuant to their professional duties. Our precedents do not support the existence of a constitutional cause of action behind every statement a public employee makes in the course of doing his or her job.

In *Pickering* the Court protected the free speech rights of public employees as citizens. For many decades prior to *Pickering*, however, the U.S. Supreme Court had followed Justice Holmes' view in *McAuliffe v. New Bedford*, 155 Mass. 216 (1892), holding that: "A policeman may have a constitutional right to talk politics, but he has no right to be a policeman." By the 1960s, however, the Court had firmly rejected this view, holding instead that public employment cannot be conditioned on surrendering fundamental rights. But what if the Court returned to its prior doctrine and public employees had to waive their rights to free speech as a condition of employment? What would be the consequences of this judicial policy change?

If there were no legal protections for the free speech of public employees, would teachers be willing to publicly question the decisions of school officials on matters of public concern if it meant being fired? Would they be willing to publicly disclose corruption or other misconduct by their supervisors if termination was the price? Do these concerns justify rigorous protection of teachers' free speech rights, given that the price is allowing public dissent and some disruption in the institution and community? Or was Justice Holmes' view correct, and those who wish to serve in public employment should understand that the price is holding your tongue?

If you were a member of the Court in the *Pickering* case, would you have supported Justice Marshall's view in *Pickering* that "a teacher's exercise of his right to speak on issues of public importance may not furnish the basis for his dismissal from public employment" or Justice Holmes' view that accepting limits on free speech is the price of public employment?

What if a teacher can prove that school officials wanted to fire him because of his exercise of protected free speech; but school officials can also prove that they wanted to fire him because he was an unfit teacher? The Court addressed these "mixed motive" cases (where there is both an illegitimate and a legitimate reason for termination) in *Mt. Healthy City School District v. Doyle*, 429 U.S. 274 (1977). The Court noted that Mr. Doyle, an untenured teacher, had been involved in multiple incidents including an argument with another teacher that resulted in the teacher slapping him; Mr. Doyle refusing any apology and demanding punishment; punishment for both teachers; and a teacher walk-out in support of the teacher who slapped Doyle. Mr. Doyle also got in an argument with cafeteria workers "over the amount of spaghetti which had been served him"; he referred to students as "sons of bitches" in a disciplinary complaint; and he "made an obscene gesture to two girls."

The Court noted that: "Chronologically the last in the series of incidents" involving Mr. Doyle was his call to a local radio station concerning school policy. If school officials already intended to end a teacher's employment based on prior misconduct, can the teacher raise the First Amendment as a shield to being fired at the eleventh hour? No. In *Doyle* the Court determined:

> Initially, in this case, the burden was properly placed upon [the employee] to show that his conduct [contacting the radio station regarding school policy] was constitutionally protected, and that his conduct was . . . a "motivating factor" in the Board's decision not to rehire him . . . having carried that burden, however, the District Court should have gone on to determine whether the Board had shown by a preponderance of the evidence that it would have reached the same decision as to . . . reemployment even in the absence of the protected conduct.

As the Court declared in *Tinker*: "It can hardly be argued that either students or teachers shed their constitutional rights to freedom of speech or expression at the schoolhouse gate." Nonetheless, if a teacher merits termination independent of a subsequent free speech controversy, school officials do not have to continue the employment of an unfit teacher. The teacher is free to proceed in pressing a free speech claim under 42 U.S.C. § 1983. But the question of employment was resolved based on teacher conduct independent of the free speech claim.

Academic Freedom

Academic freedom is a form of free speech unique to the practices of teaching, learning, and the scholarly search for truth. Claims of academic freedom go back at least to the tradition of Plato's Academy. Historically, educational institutions have been controlled either internally by scholars engaged in the academic search for truth, or externally through political power. Ideally educational institutions would be governed by scholars zealously engaged in the search for truth, the advancement of knowledge, and committed to student learning and the common good. Nonetheless, external political controls of education have been common historically. The realities of this external control have ranged from relatively benign and permissive to virulently intrusive controls by dangerous political forces using their power to substitute political propaganda for the truth.

The Dark Ages were in part a result of prolonged external political control of knowledge. When education is politically controlled, the truth is whatever those with power say it is, and any truth that challenges the status quo and the perpetuation of the established regime may be prohibited, punished, and purged, regardless of its truth or utility. The re-emergence of academic freedom helped to end the Dark Ages and usher in the Age of Enlightenment.

European universities that increasingly championed academic freedom also increasingly enjoyed the successes of discovery in the arts and sciences. These discoveries helped to fuel an explosion of learning and progress. American universities adopted European principles of academic freedom. American practices of these general principles were codified in the American Association of University Professors (AAUP) *Statement of Principles on Academic Freedom and Tenure* (1940):

185

Institutions of higher education are conducted for the common good and not to further the interest of either the individual teacher or the institution as a whole.

1) The common good depends upon the free search for truth and its free exposition. Academic freedom is essential to these purposes and applies to both teaching and research. Freedom in research is fundamental to the advancement of truth. Academic freedom in its teaching aspect is fundamental for the protection of the rights of the teacher in teaching and of the student to freedom in learning. It carries with it duties correlative with rights.

2) Teachers are entitled to freedom in the classroom in discussing their subject, but they should be careful not to introduce into their teaching controversial matter which has no relation to their subject.

3) College and university teachers are citizens, members of a learned profession, and officers of an educational institution. When they speak or write as citizens, they should be free from institutional censorship or discipline, but their special position in the community imposes special obligations. As scholars and educational officers, they should remember that the public may judge their profession and their institution by their utterances. Hence they should at all times be accurate, should exercise appropriate restraint, should show respect for the opinions of others, and should make every effort to indicate that they are not speaking for the institution.

These principles of academic freedom would soon be challenged by political powers external to academia. During the Cold War era, in an atmosphere of "Red Scare" and "McCarthyism" state officials began questioning faculty members about any "subversive" speech, their lectures, beliefs, and membership in political organizations. They also required faculty members to divulge the names of others in disfavored political organizations. In *Sweezy v. New Hampshire*, 354 U.S. 234 (1957), for example, the State General Assembly had authorized the State Attorney General to investigate whether there were any "subversive persons" in the State. A predictable witch hunt ensued. Professor Sweezy was questioned about the contents of his academic lectures, his knowledge of the "Progressive Party" and ordered to disclose the identities of its other members. Sweezy refused and he was found guilty of contempt, a judgment reversed by the U.S. Supreme Court in *Sweezy v. New Hampshire*.

In *Keyishian v. Board of Regents*, 385 U.S. 589 (1967), faculty members were terminated if they refused to comply with a vaguely drafted New York "treason and sedition act." But the U.S. Supreme Court found that "no teacher can know just where the line is drawn between 'seditious' and non-seditious utterances and acts" giving the State boundless discretion to prohibit virtually any speech state officials deem "seditious" and creating an ominous chilling effect on academic freedom. Concerning the challenges these Acts presented to academic freedom the Court declared:

Our Nation is deeply committed to safeguarding academic freedom, which is of transcendent value to all of us and not merely to the teachers concerned. That freedom is therefore a special concern of the First Amendment, which does not tolerate laws that cast a pall of orthodoxy over the classroom. "The vigilant protection of constitutional freedoms is nowhere more vital than in the community of American schools." The classroom is peculiarly the "marketplace of ideas." The Nation's future depends upon leaders trained through wide exposure to that robust exchange of ideas which discovers truth "out of a multitude of tongues, [rather] than through any kind of authoritative selection." In *Sweezy v. New Hampshire*, 354 U.S. 234 (1957) we said: "The essentiality of freedom in the community of American universities is almost self-evident. No one should underestimate the vital role in a democracy that is played by those who guide and train our youth. To impose any strait jacket upon the intellectual leaders in our colleges and universities would imperil the future of our Nation. No field of education is so thoroughly comprehended by man that new discoveries cannot yet be made. Particularly is that true in the social sciences, where few, if any, principles are accepted as absolutes. Scholarship cannot flourish in an atmosphere of suspicion and distrust. Teachers and students must always remain free to inquire, to study and to evaluate, to gain new maturity and understanding; otherwise our civilization will stagnate and die."

Comments and Questions

Those who doubt the importance of academic freedom should consider the saga of warning involving the Soviet Union's Trofim Lysenko. Lysenko may have been the uneducated son of peasants, but what he lacked in education he more than made up for in zealous commitment to political dogma, ambition, and an attitude of absolute certainty. Based on his interpretation of Marxist theory, Lysenko rejected Western "bourgeois" scientific methods in general, and specifically rejected the work of Mendel, the founder of modern genetics, whose field-based scientific observations established that inherited variations in organisms resulted from combinations of genes from parent organisms.

Lysenko rejected Mendelism in favor of Lamarckism (the belief that organisms could inherit the acquired traits of progenitors). Under the theory of Lamarckism, for example, dogs with cropped ears and tails would in time produce pups with cropped ears and tails, and human body builders could pass the massive muscle development acquired through exercise on to their children. Lamarckism has been proven false: Genetic traits are inherited; acquired traits are not. Nonetheless, Lamarckism fit much better with Soviet ideology, which taught that through Communism's acquired life experiences of ideal collectivism, future generations of humans could be purged of human tendencies toward Capitalism and individual greed.

Lysenko also fit the model of the "peasant genius" the Soviets wished to promote over academics trained in Western science. And importantly, while scientific theories, debate, and testing take time; produce only degrees of certainty; and may raise unwanted questions about the status quo and political dogma; Lysenko offered regime supporting immediate answers with absolute certainty.

Based on his untested but politically useful theories, Lysenko quickly gained favor with Stalin and became the Director of Biology in the Soviet Union. Lysenko combined his political ideology and his theories into a political/agricultural movement known as Lysenkoism. Using the power of his position he implemented his theories nation-wide in Soviet controlled agriculture with disastrous results.

In his failed "cluster planting" theory, for example, Lysenko insisted that seeds, trees, etc., should be planted very closely together, to increase the yield per acre. Lysenko reasoned that in uncorrupted nature it must surely be true that plants of the same type would never compete with others of their kind (as do the corrupted Capitalists) but would instead coexist and thrive collectively. Simple field tests would have proven his theories false. Plants that are growing too closely together compete for space, light, water, and nutrients, reducing yields and wasting expensive seeds and seedlings. But field testing and the scientific method were discredited by Lysenko as tools of Western sedition.

Rather than allowing the truth to interfere with useful propaganda, Soviet controlled media touted Lysenko's genius and ignored the consequences of his theories. Lysenko was even given his own "scientific" journal to provide an additional facade of credibility to his work. And before the failures of his last theory could be confronted, his prior failed mandate would be superseded by his next theory as the essential missing step in his great plan. For example, cluster planting would work, it was argued, if only the seed had been properly prepared, or the soil had been tilled deeper, and yet deeper the next year. In practice, however, the seed treatments failed to produce greater yields, and tilling too deeply was crushingly labor intensive; energy inefficient; turned under fertile top soil; and brought poor quality sub-soils and rocks to the surface.

Any scientists who dared to exercise academic freedom and question Lysenko's theories were attacked as Western sympathizers and purged from government controlled science and academia. The fact that the Nazis had so thoroughly embraced Mendelian genetics and Western scientific methods (albeit with the darkest of motives) made these attacks very easy for Lysenko and his supporters. The final blow to Soviet academic freedom came when the government made it illegal to challenge Lysenko's theories. Scientists and academics practicing or advocating orthodox genetics, science, or agriculture were imprisoned and killed. Lysenko's chief academic rival was starved to death in prison.

In 1964 the famous Soviet physicist and human rights advocate Andrei Sakharov wrote that Lysenko was "responsible for the shameful backwardness of Soviet biology and of genetics in particular, for the dissemination of pseudo-scientific views, for adventurism, for the degradation of learning, and for the defamation, firing, arrest, even death, of many genuine scientists." Lysenko's pseudo-science theories are also blamed for contributing to millions of deaths from famine when China adopted Lysenko's failed theories; theories which had been disproven in practice, but were politically protected from any academic challenge.

Without academic freedom, science, research, and learning are vulnerable to political control, often with disastrous consequences. As the tragic tale of Lysenko demonstrates, academic freedom is of vital importance. The search for the truth is essential to progress, and lies can prove deadly, especially when they are protected from the truth by coercive government power.

Both history and popular fiction are replete with similar tales. In J.K. Rowling's "Harry Potter" series how does the "Ministry of Magic" seize control of Hogwarts? What happens to academic freedom under the rule of "Professor Umbridge"? What was the quality of education like under this politically controlled regime? Umbridge is a fictional character, while Lysenko was a real person, but the lessons they teach us are the same: Political control of knowledge and learning presents a grave danger. Academic freedom is the best protection against this danger.

Although the full-scope of academic freedom has been reserved for research and teaching in higher education, public school teachers also enjoy some aspects of academic freedom. Teachers must teach the Board adopted curriculum, for example, but in the absence of express prohibitions on teaching methods, educators may generally select among effective, relevant, professionally recognized methods of instruction.

For all educators, the scope of academic freedom is not unlimited and these rights are not absolute. The scope of academic freedom in the classroom is related to the subject taught and the maturity of the students. For example, advanced social sciences classes allow for more academic freedom than instruction in basic math; and graduate students well prepared to challenge faculty opinions allow for more academic freedom than the instruction of elementary school students unable to distinguish between truth and error on their own. Rights of academic freedom are also linked to duties of academic integrity and professional conduct. Academic freedom is essential to the health and progress of educational institutions and democracy. But it will not shield educators from the consequences of academic dishonesty, unprofessional conduct, or other misconduct inconsistent with professional responsibilities.

Freedom of Association

Freedom of association is a fundamental human right. The United Nations Universal Declaration of Human Rights, Article 20, recognized: "Everyone has the right to freedom of peaceful assembly and association . . . No one may be compelled to belong to an association." The Canadian Charter of Rights and Freedoms (2011) declares:

Everyone has the following fundamental freedoms:

(a) Freedom of conscience and religion;
(b) Freedom of thought, belief, opinion and expression, including freedom of the press and other media of communication;
(c) Freedom of peaceful assembly; and
(d) Freedom of association.

The U.S. Constitution does not expressly include freedom of association. But rights of association have been recognized as essential to the rights of free speech, assembly, liberty and privacy. As citizens, educators also have rights of freedom of association. There is no right, of course, to belong to criminal gangs or organizations that advocate or practice violence. But educators enjoy the same freedoms as all other citizens to participate in political parties, professional associations, etc. Educators commonly belong to unions or professional education associations, and the State must respect these rights of freedom of association.

Nonetheless, unions, professional associations, and political action groups have sometimes become the targets of political ire, resulting in efforts to discourage membership in these groups. In *NAACP v. Patterson*, 357 U.S. 449 (1958), the State of Alabama attempted to force the National Association for the Advancement of Colored People (NAACP) to reveal its membership under the force of civil contempt and a $100,000 fine. The U.S. Supreme Court held:

It is beyond debate that freedom to engage in association for the advancement of beliefs and ideas is an inseparable aspect of the "liberty" assured by the Due Process Clause of the Fourteenth Amendment, which embraces freedom of speech. Of course, it is immaterial whether the beliefs sought to be advanced by association pertain to political, economic, religious or cultural matters, and state action which may have the effect of curtailing the freedom to associate is subject to the closest scrutiny . . . It is hardly a novel perception that compelled disclosure of affiliation with groups engaged in advocacy may constitute . . . a restraint on freedom of association . . . This Court has recognized the vital relationship between freedom to associate and privacy in one's associations. When referring to the varied forms of governmental action which might interfere with freedom of assembly, it said in *American Communications Association v. Douds*, 339 U.S. 382 (1950): "A requirement that adherents of particular religious faiths or political parties wear identifying armbands, for example, is obviously of this nature." Compelled disclosure of membership in an organization engaged in advocacy of particular beliefs is of the same order. Inviolability of privacy in group association may in many circumstances be indispensable to preservation of freedom of association, particularly where a group espouses dissident beliefs . . . We hold that the immunity from state scrutiny of membership lists which the Association claims on behalf of its members is here so related to the right of the members to pursue their lawful private interests privately and to associate freely with others in so doing as to come within the protection of the Fourteenth Amendment. And we conclude that Alabama has fallen short of showing a controlling justification for the deterrent effect on the free enjoyment of the right to associate which disclosure of membership lists is likely to have. Accordingly, the judgment of civil contempt and the $100,000 fine which resulted from petitioner's refusal to comply with the production order in this respect must fall.

Teachers generally cannot be required to disclose their private associations to state officials. These activities are outside of the jurisdiction of school officials unless it can be shown that they negatively affect job performance or fitness for duties. For example, membership in controversial but lawful, non-violent political groups are protected associations. But membership in a group that practices or advocates pedophilia or other serious dangers to children or the school community could be subject to employment action.

Political Participation by Public Educators

Public school educators are often among the most capable and respected leaders in their communities, making them good candidates for elected offices. Participation in the political process as a voter or as a candidate is a fundamental right rooted in constitutional protections of free speech and freedom of association. There is, however, no unqualified right to a position as a public educator, and in some cases the roles of elected official and public school employee may be incompatible.

Federal and state legislators and courts have attempted to strike a proper balance between the political rights of government employees and legitimate governmental concerns. Among the dangers associated with politicizing civil service positions are: The misuse of public resources for partisan political purposes; public employment based on political loyalty rather than professional competence; increased partisan conflict in the public work place; and a loss of public confidence in the fair and non-partisan operation of civil services.

Congress sought to address these concerns in the Hatch Act, 5 U.S.C. § 7324(a). The Hatch Act declared that a federal employee may not: "(1) use his official authority or influence for the purpose of interfering with or affecting the result of an election; or (2) take an active part in political management or in political campaigns." In *U.S. Civil Service Commission v. National Association of Letter Carriers*, 413 U.S. 548 (1973), the U.S. Supreme Court found that:

190

Congress . . . has, the power to prevent [federal employees] from holding a party office, working at the polls, and acting as party paymaster for other party workers. An Act of Congress going no farther would in our view unquestionably be valid. So would it be if, in plain and understandable language, the statute forbade activities such as organizing a political party or club; actively participating in fund-raising activities for a partisan candidate or political party; becoming a partisan candidate for, or campaigning for, an elective public office; actively managing the campaign of a partisan candidate for public office; initiating or circulating a partisan nominating petition or soliciting votes for a partisan candidate for public office; or serving as a delegate, alternate or proxy to a political party convention. Our judgment is that neither the First Amendment nor any other provision of the Constitution invalidates a law barring this kind of partisan political conduct by federal employees. Such decision on our part would no more than confirm the judgment of history, a judgment made by this country over the last century that it is in the best interest of the country, indeed essential, that federal service should depend upon meritorious performance rather than political service, and that the political influence of federal employees on others and on the electoral process should be limited . . . The restrictions so far imposed on federal employees are not aimed at particular parties, groups, or points of view, but apply equally to all partisan activities of the type described. They discriminate against no racial, ethnic, or religious minorities. Nor do they seek to control political opinions or beliefs, or to interfere with or influence anyone's vote at the polls . . . employees in the Executive Branch of the Government, or those working for any of its agencies, should administer the law in accordance with the will of Congress, rather than in accordance with their own or the will of a political party. They are expected to enforce the law and execute the programs of the Government without bias or favoritism for or against any political party or group or the members thereof. A major thesis of the Hatch Act is that to serve this great end of Government--the impartial execution of the laws--it is essential that federal employees, for example, not take formal positions in political parties, not undertake to play substantial roles in partisan political campaigns, and not run for office on partisan political tickets. Forbidding activities like these will reduce the hazards to fair and effective government . . . it is not only important that the Government and its employees in fact avoid practicing political justice, but it is also critical that they appear to the public to be avoiding it, if confidence in the system of representative Government is not to be eroded to a disastrous extent.

No citizen can lawfully be prevented from holding a party office or from direct and active participation in partisan political activities. But under the Hatch Act, there is no right to do so while serving as a federal employee. In *Broadrick v. Oklahoma*, 413 U.S. 601 (1973), a companion case decided the same day as *U.S. Civil Service Commission v. National Association of Letter Carriers,* the U.S. Supreme Court upheld a state statute similar to the federal Hatch Act and limiting the partisan political activities of state employees. Although the Court has ruled that these limitations on partisan political activities by federal or state employees are constitutionally permissible, it is up to federal or state lawmakers to decide whether or not to exercise these limits.

Some states allow public employees, including public school educators, to run for and serve in partisan elected offices, *e.g.*, as members of the State General Assembly, without resigning

191

their state positions. If there is a substantial conflict between the positions, however, a public educator may be required to take a leave of absence while serving in the General Assembly if the duties of the elected office conflict with school work duties. State laws vary, but in summary, reasonable limits may be set on the partisan political activities of government employees to protect the resources and integrity of civil service divisions, and to maintain public confidence in non-partisan civil service and the equal administration of the laws.

Courts have also upheld reasonable limits on the political activities of school employees while on campus and while on duty. Public educators may not, for example, use their official positions or classrooms to make political speeches or to solicit votes; use the school copier to print campaign flyers; use the school public address system or official e-mail to communicate partisan political messages, etc. However, restrictions that unreasonably limit off campus and off duty political activities have not been sustained. As private citizens public educators have a right to express their political views and to participate in the political process.

Educators are also generally well qualified to serve in non-partisan elected offices, such as service as an elected member of a school board. State statutes prohibiting conflicts of interests in dual roles and prohibiting nepotism have been upheld by courts. A public school educator cannot, for example, be a member of his or her own employing school board, as doing so would constitute a clear conflict of interests. The educator could, however, serve as a member of another school district's school board. Some states also set limits on nepotism, prohibiting spouses or other close family members from supervising their relatives in the same school district where there is a legitimate risk of a conflict of interests.

In summary, reasonable restrictions can be imposed to protect the school from misuse of public resources for partisan political purposes; public employment based on political loyalty rather than professional competence; increased partisan conflict in the work place; conflicts of interests, nepotism, and a loss of public confidence in the fair and non-partisan operation of the school. School resources and employee time paid for by all tax payers cannot lawfully be used for partisan political purposes. Overbroad restrictions on political participation by school employees, however, violate the First Amendment and state free speech protections.

Chapter Summary

This chapter reviewed First Amendment freedoms focusing on freedom of speech in schools. After reading this chapter, please consider the following points in review and for further thought and discussion:

I. *Review Points*:

1) If public schools are to serve as the functional nurseries of an enduring democracy students' free speech rights must be protected, respected, and encouraged so they can mature into citizens well prepared to actively discuss ideas, ask necessary questions, speak out on important public matters, vote wisely, and participate fully in a democratic society.

2) Education, free speech, civility, and civic courage are the necessary foundations of democracy. Totalitarian regimes are only possible when the people are kept ignorant, silenced, divided, and fearful of speaking up and making their own decisions.

3) A closed culture of retaliation, fear, and silence is a breeding ground for corruption. The broad protection of free speech is the best means of shining the light of truth into every corner of the institution to assure honesty and accountability. As Justice Brandeis said: "Sunlight is the best disinfectant."

4) The general rule under the free speech provisions of the First Amendment is that government cannot limit individual speech and expression of ideas.

5) Broad protections for free speech in the U.S. are founded on beliefs in:

   a) *A free market place of ideas* free from the distortions of government officials' selfish interests, partialities, and control;
   b) *Individual rights to freely express beliefs* in the market place of ideas and to have the merit of ideas judged by other individuals and not government censors; and
   c) *The tests of reason and experience* by an educated people, and an experience based trust that good ideas will ultimately prevail, and bad ideas will ultimately fail when subjected to the tests of reason and experience.

6) Political and religious speech are granted special protection under the First Amendment, as these are historically the most common targets of government censorship.

7) The First Amendment generally prohibits content-based censorship, with political and religious viewpoints receiving the greatest protections, commercial speech receiving less rigorous protection, and obscenity falling outside of the scope of constitutional protection.

8) The Court recognizes some universal exceptions to First Amendment protection, and these limitations are always available to government officials:

a) Government officials can always apply reasonable time, place, and manner (TPM) restrictions on speech. TPM restrictions are held reasonable if they are:

    i) Content neutral;

    ii) Narrowly tailored to serve a significant governmental interest; and

    iii) Leave open an adequate alternative channel of communication.

b) Government officials can always limit free speech by establishing a compelling governmental interest for the intrusion on freedom of expression, and that no less restrictive alternative exists.

9) The Court recognizes some special exceptions to general First Amendment protections for free speech. Government officials can limit speech if it is:

    a) Illegal or subversive speech, which can be controlled if it is:

        i) Directed towards inciting illegal or subversive action; and is

        ii) Likely to incite imminent lawless action (includes "fighting words" and "yelling fire in crowded theatre").

    b) Obscenity.

    c) Defamatory speech.

    d) Commercial speech.

    e) Speech in a non-public forum: Regulations must be reasonable in light of the purposes of the forum.

10) Democracy is incompatible with both chaos and oppression. The school culture must be both free and orderly; both candid and civil. The Court has consistently recognized the authority and obligation of school officials to protect order and discipline in schools, while appropriately respecting free speech rights.

11) Concerning free speech in public schools the Court has distinguished between two different types of student expression: a) Individual student expression; and b) Public school sponsored student expression:

    a) *Individual student expression* is speech not sponsored, controlled, or reasonably perceived as attributable to the school. The *Tinker* standard governs individual student speech. School officials must show through evidence of facts and circumstances that student expression would "materially and substantially interfere with the requirements of appropriate discipline in the operation of the school." Avoiding minor disruptions, discomforts, and unpleasantness are not sufficient justifications to limit individual expression.

    b) *School sponsored expression* (*e.g.*, school newspapers, forums, performances, etc.) that are sponsored, controlled, or reasonably perceived as attributable to the school. The *Fraser* and *Hazelwood* decisions govern school sponsored speech. School officials have wide discretion to control content where the expression is sponsored by the school. Limitations can be based on any legitimate educational rationale (*e.g.*, age appropriateness; fit with the educational mission, etc.).

12) If school officials open the door to any non-curriculum related student group, then meetings during non-instructional time are governed by the Equal Access Act which prohibits discrimination on the "basis of the religious, political, philosophical, or other content of the speech at such meetings."

13) Mandatory compliance with the Equal Access Act is limited to public secondary schools receiving federal funds. But because the Act incorporated principles of free speech that apply to all public institutions the general principles of the Act are a useful guide in all public schools.

14) The curriculum should reflect a reasonable balance of sound professional educational judgment and democratic community input. School officials must have a legitimate educational rationale for limiting access to information (*e.g.*, age appropriateness; inconsistent with the educational mission; etc.).

15) School officials generally have broad discretion in decisions concerning the acquisition of library materials. It is only the improper removal of materials already placed in the library by school officials that may raise direct First Amendment concerns. Removals cannot be motivated by narrow partisan politics, religion, or other improper personal biases by school officials. Books and other materials can be removed, however, for legitimate educational reasons such as age appropriateness, educational suitability, pervasive vulgarity, etc. Outdated or damaged library materials may also be discarded in the normal course of library maintenance.

16) Free speech in the school related cyber-world is governed by the same general legal principles that apply to the physical-world, with *Tinker* regulating individual student speech and *Fraser* and *Hazelwood* governing student speech in school sponsored electronic forums.

17) The problem of jurisdiction in the cyber-world presents some unique challenges. In the cyber-world "on-campus" general means school controlled media (or use of any media while physically at school), and "off-campus" is the use of purely private media while not under the physical jurisdiction of the school.

18) School officials may establish fair-use policies for the use of school technology including reasonable time, place, and manner (TPM) restrictions. Students who violate reasonable fair-use policies may be denied access to school controlled technology and appropriately disciplined.

19) The current trend in dress and grooming cases appears to be greater judicial deference to school dress and grooming regulations, especially when these regulations are based on legitimate health, safety, or educational concerns.

20) Dress and grooming policies most likely to provoke judicial intervention are those that unnecessarily intrude on sincere religious beliefs; take sides in a political dispute; or fail to provide adequate notice and due process.

21) The key to drafting lawful and effective dress and grooming policies is to strike a proper balance between specificity and breadth of coverage in the language of the policy. Policies must

be clear enough not to be unconstitutional vague, but broad enough to achieve the intended policy goals.

22) Gang symbols are not protected speech in schools. School officials can prohibit the display of gang symbols that are likely to disrupt the school, and there is a compelling interest in preventing gang related speech that is likely to provoke gang related violence.

23) Generally, public employees have the same free speech rights as all citizens. If public school officials wish to sanction speech by school employees, including dismissal or other employment sanctions, school officials must be prepared to show that the speech negatively impacted the employment relationship, and that the speech was unprotected in the context. The *Pickering* test is used to distinguish between protected and unprotected speech by public employees:

> The *Pickering* Test: To determine whether speech is protected, courts generally balance the employee's speech rights against the employer's legitimate interests in efficient operation of the public institution. Questions considered in this balance include:
>
> 1) *Was the speech related to a legitimate matter of public concern?* Speech regarding legitimate public concerns generally receives First Amendment protection.
>
> 2) *Was the speech true?* True statements receive more protection than false statements.
>
>> Note: Even if the speech is true, courts will also consider public officials' legitimate needs for: 1) Regular close contact and a working relationship of loyalty and trust with the speaker; 2) Appropriate office discipline; and 3) Harmony among co-workers.
>
> 3) *If false, was the false statement merely negligently made by the public employee?* False statements made only negligently may still receive First Amendment protection.

PURPOSELY
KNOWINGLY
RECKLESSLY
-----*Pickering Line*-----
NEGLIGENTLY

> Note: Courts will also consider whether the false statements interfere with the performance of duties or the regular operations of the institution.

24) In "mixed motive" cases if a teacher merits termination independent of a subsequent free speech controversy, school officials do not have to continue the employment of an unfit teacher.

25) For all educators, the scope of academic freedom is not unlimited and these rights are not absolute. The scope of academic freedom in the classroom is related to the subject taught and the maturity of the students. Rights of academic freedom are also linked to duties of academic integrity and professional conduct. Academic freedom will not shield educators from the

consequences of academic dishonesty, unprofessional conduct, or other misconduct inconsistent with professional responsibilities.

26) Educators have rights to freedom of association and generally cannot be required to disclose their private associations to state officials. These activities are outside of the jurisdiction of school officials unless it can be shown that they negatively affect job performance or fitness for duties.

27) Reasonable restrictions can be imposed to protect the school from misuse of public resources for partisan political purposes. Overbroad restrictions on political participation by school employees, however, violate First Amendment and state free speech protections.

II. *Principles to Practice Tips*:

1) *Expressive Speech*: Individual expression is an essential part of being human. Trying to stop people from expressing themselves is like squeezing a handful of sand: The harder you squeeze, the faster it flows through your fingers. Don't squeeze any harder than you have to. Maintain proper order and discipline, but do so in a fair, respectful, and balanced way. Welcome the honest expression of opinions. But build shared cultural expectations that require everyone to express their opinions in an appropriate and respectful time, place, and manner.

2) *Controversy and Conflict:* Controversy is inevitable, but it can be destructive or constructive. Learn to steer controversy in healthier directions as creative tension that moves people toward positive change. Steer conversations toward a focus on the real core problems and not just the personalities; towards shared problem solving and not just blaming others. Rarely is a serious institutional problem solely attributable to the actions of a single person or group. More commonly we all bear some responsibility for the problem, either through action or inaction. And while blaming one person or group is easy, actually solving problems takes everyone's cooperation. When someone comes to you with a controversy, conflict, or other problem, it is fair to ask them what they can do to help in implementing a positive solution.

3) *Civility*: Cultural norms are generally learned through role models in the community. Be the role model for civility in your institution. Learn to stay above the fray; to keep your perspective and not "take the bait" when provoked. No matter what the other person says, respond calmly, professionally, and respectfully. Take a deep breath before responding when necessary. You can speak firmly and resolutely in making your point while still modeling civility. Dishing back the same abusive treatment you received may feel good at the time. But it also makes you look no better than the other person. In the longer run you will never regret taking the moral and professional high road in your interactions with others. You can become the model of civility in your institution, positively changing the culture in your school and teaching students (and colleagues) invaluable lessons about the real power of civility. The wise individual understands that you are not just trying to win an argument with the other person: You are trying to win the respect and support of everyone.

4) *Redress of Grievances*: Learn to listen to others. What most people really want is to be heard. They can often accept not getting what they wanted, if they feel they have been respectfully

heard and treated fairly. Try to really hear what the other person is telling you, and attempt to demonstrate to them that you see their perspective, even if you don't agree.

5) *TPM Restrictions*: Effectively use reasonable time, place, and manner (TPM) restrictions to assure appropriate discipline and avoid disruptions in the operation of the educational mission while not discriminating based on the perspective of the speakers and leaving open other appropriate channels for them to communicate without disrupting the school.

III. *Questions for Discussion*: Please consider these questions and be prepared to discuss:

1) *Free Speech and Democracy*: How important are rights of free speech in a democracy? How important is democracy? When the free speech rights of individuals conflict with public order, how should these conflicts be resolved?

2) *Free Speech Rights of Students*: In *Tinker* the Court recognized that as students, children did not "shed their constitutional rights to freedom of speech or expression at the schoolhouse gate." But the Court has also long recognized that children's rights are not necessarily coequal with the rights of adults. In balancing students' rights to free speech and the interests of school officials in maintaining order did the Court strike the correct balance in *Tinker*?

3) *Free Speech Rights of Teachers*: How important are teachers' free speech rights in schools? How important is academic freedom? How should these rights be balanced with the competing interests of school officials, students, and the community?

4) *Open Forum*: What other related issues or current events would you like to discuss?

IV. *Suggested Activities*:

1) Words have the power to change people and change the world. The simple act of speaking the truth can become a great and enduring act of courage that inspires listeners and countless readers in future generations. Select a speech you find inspiring and share with your colleagues what you have learned from this speech, for example: Plato: The Apology (400 B.C.E.); Jesus: The Sermon on the Mount (33 C.E.); Patrick Henry: Give me Liberty or Give Me Death (1775); Sojourner Truth: Ain't I a Woman? (1851); Frederick Douglass: What to the Slave is the Fourth of July? (1852); Abraham Lincoln: Gettysburg Address (1863); Ghandi: Quit India Speech (1942); Nelson Mandela: I am Prepared to Die (1964); Dwight D. Eisenhower: Farewell Address (1961); John F. Kennedy: The Decision to Go to the Moon (1961); Martin Luther King, Jr.: I Have a Dream (1963); John Perry Barlow: A Declaration of the Independence of Cyberspace (1996).

2) Review your school's policies related to free speech, including student and faculty speech, use of school technology, dress codes, academic freedom, etc.

Chapter 5: Search and Seizure

A reasonable expectation of privacy is a fundamental human right respected by any just government. Humans have a fundamental right to feel safe and secure in their homes; to not have unwarranted intrusions on their bodies or personal belongings; and to enjoy personal, family, and associational privacy in their lives. Government officials should not use the official resources and power they acquire from the People to spy on their own citizens; search them arbitrarily; or seize their property without sufficient cause. In order to maintain lawful order and public safety, however, government officials sometimes do have a legitimate need to search a particular individual or seize something in the individual's possession.

Students and teachers in schools do not "shed their constitutional rights . . . at the schoolhouse gate." Among the rights protected by the Constitution is the right to be free from unreasonable searches by public officials. Given the limitations of the Fourth Amendment, how do public school officials continue to respect individual rights of privacy while also protecting the public school community from serious disruptions, drugs, weapons and other unreasonable disturbances and dangers in schools?

The legal principles defining this balance between individual rights and legitimate community needs have roots that can be traced back thousands of years through Roman law and Biblical principles. The Fourth Amendment's more direct historical antecedents, however, were the predictably abusive results of the general warrants for searches allowed under English rule in the American Colonies. Laws enacted during the American Colonial Period allowed for general warrantless searches of the poor, searches of any other "suspicious" persons, and for other vaguely defined purposes. In practice these policies set virtually no limits on official powers to search and seize arbitrarily.

The abuse of these general warrants also included government officials breaking into private homes at will allegedly to enforce religious prohibitions. Government agents could kick in the door of a family home to be certain that no one was profaning the Sabbath with their loom or butter churn; they weren't lying idle the other days of the week; or otherwise engaging in any act of "debauchery" such as drinking, gluttony, or any lustful or lewd behavior in their homes.

If a government agent kicked in a family's door and found nothing unlawful, citizens still had no legal rights to object to unwarranted and unreasonable searches. It was irrelevant that the searches were based on nothing more than "suspicion in the air" and the government agent's vague belief that "someone somewhere must be doing something wrong." As an agent of the government it was his official duty to find any "wrong doers" wherever they may be, even those harming no one in the privacy of their own homes.

Such broad and unlimited grants of power were inevitably abused by overzealous government officials; by those seeking to instill public fear of their official powers in order to gain obedient deference from citizens; and by those motivated to harass particular individuals for personal reasons. Not surprisingly, these intrusive and oppressive practices helped to fuel the general rebellion against English rule that resulted in the American Revolution and the creation of a new Constitution with a strong Bill of Rights limiting the power of government and protecting citizens' rights.

The Fourth Amendment was intended to protect against abuses of government power and unreasonable searches and seizure. The Fourth Amendment states:

> The right of the people to be secure in their persons, houses, papers, and effects, against unreasonable searches and seizures, shall not be violated, and no Warrants shall issue, but upon probable cause, supported by Oath or affirmation, and particularly describing the place to be searched, and the persons or things to be seized.

The Core Right of Privacy and other Associated Fourth Amendment Rights

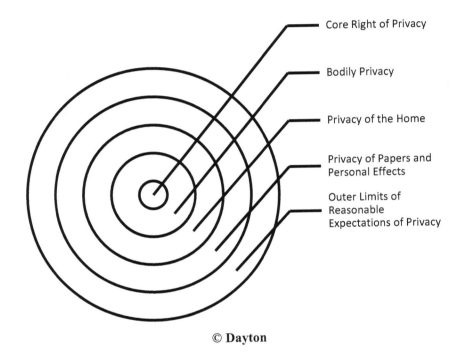

© Dayton

As noted above individual freedom of belief is at the core of the First Amendment and the core of human liberty. Similarly, there is a core right to privacy in the human mind protected by the Fourth Amendment. Your personal thoughts and beliefs belong to you alone, and are beyond the legitimate reach of government powers. Humans should enjoy complete freedom of individual thought and belief, free from governmental intrusions and interference. And in the physical world, beyond the realm of pure thought, the right to bodily privacy must be vigorously protected by the Fourth Amendment. To have government agents exposing, touching, probing, or removing anything from a person's body without consent is obviously a severe intrusion on individual privacy requiring a compelling justification. Although an intrusion on the home is not as directly personal as an intrusion on the body, it is nonetheless a very serious intrusion on individual privacy. Individual's personal papers and effects are also protected under the Fourth Amendment. Today these rights extend not just to paper letters and leather purses, but also to private electronic versions of these papers and effects.

Whenever there is a reasonable expectation of privacy, the Fourth Amendment protects against unreasonable intrusions by government agents. Outside of that reasonable expectation of privacy, however, there is no Fourth Amendment protection. Individuals do not, for example, have any reasonable expectation of privacy in things they place in plain view, leave unsupervised in public areas, or otherwise fail to maintain reasonable privacy or control over.

The Fourth Amendment protects individuals' reasonable expectations of privacy in their "persons, houses, papers, and effects" and requires government officials to establish that a challenged search was reasonable in its inception and scope. To conduct a permissible search, the government is generally required to establish "probable cause" to obtain a valid search warrant prior to any search under the Fourth Amendment.

Probable cause is established by showing that the government agents seeking the warrant have knowledge of facts and circumstances based on reasonably trustworthy information in a quantum sufficient to warrant a reasonably prudent person to believe that a crime has been committed or property subject to seizure is present. There are exceptions to these general requirements, however, including searches incident to arrest; emergency situations; search by consent; international border searches; and seizure of items in plain view.

Penalties for failing to respect the Fourth Amendment rights of citizens include the exclusionary rule and monetary damages under federal or state law. The exclusionary rule bars government officials from using evidence that was obtained in violation of the Fourth Amendment, which is prohibited as the "fruit of a poison tree." And under 42 U.S.C. § 1983, monetary damages may be assessed against both the institution and individual government officials. Damages against individual government officials, however, are allowed only when these officials have violated well established law.

While these Fourth Amendment limitations clearly apply to police and other law enforcement officers, prior to the Court's decision in *New Jersey v. T.L.O.*, it was unclear how the Fourth Amendment applied to school officials in searches of children in public schools. The Fourth Amendment established strong limitations on government officials engaged in the exercise of police powers, requiring that searches generally must be based on probable cause and a warrant. Parents, however, are private citizens not bound by the Constitution in any way. A parent can search their own child anytime they choose to in the exercise of legitimate parental authority. In *New Jersey v. T.L.O.*, the Court was asked to decide what rules apply to searches by public school officials. Should searches of students by school officials be subject to the rules that apply to police officers; should they be allowed to search as "parents" under the *in loco parentis* doctrine; or should some intermediate standard of law apply?

Searches by School Officials

New Jersey v. T.L.O.
469 U.S. 325 (1985)
Supreme Court of the United States

Justice WHITE delivered the opinion of the Court.

We granted certiorari in this case to examine the appropriateness of the exclusionary rule as a remedy for searches carried out in violation of the Fourth Amendment by public school authorities. Our consideration of the proper application of the Fourth Amendment to the public schools, however, has led us to conclude that the search that gave rise to the case now before us did not violate the Fourth Amendment. Accordingly, we here address only the questions of the proper standard for assessing the legality of searches conducted by public school officials and the application of that standard to the facts of this case.

On March 7, 1980, a teacher at Piscataway High School in Middlesex County, N.J., discovered two girls smoking in a lavatory. One of the two girls was the respondent T.L.O., who at that time was a 14-year-old high school freshman. Because smoking in the lavatory was a violation of a school rule, the teacher took the two girls to the Principal's office, where they met with Assistant Vice Principal Theodore Choplick. In response to questioning by Mr. Choplick, T.L.O.'s companion admitted that she had violated the rule. T.L.O., however, denied that she had been smoking in the lavatory and claimed that she did not smoke at all.

Mr. Choplick asked T.L.O. to come into his private office and demanded to see her purse. Opening the purse, he found a pack of cigarettes, which he removed from the purse and held before T.L.O. as he accused her of having lied to him. As he reached into the purse for the cigarettes, Mr. Choplick also noticed a package of cigarette rolling papers. In his experience, possession of rolling papers by high school students was closely associated with the use of marihuana. Suspecting that a closer examination of the purse might yield further evidence of drug use, Mr. Choplick proceeded to search the purse thoroughly. The search revealed a small amount of marihuana, a pipe, a number of empty plastic bags, a substantial quantity of money in one-dollar bills, an index card that appeared to be a list of students who owed T.L.O. money, and two letters that implicated T.L.O. in marihuana dealing.

Mr. Choplick notified T.L.O.'s mother and the police, and turned the evidence of drug dealing over to the police. At the request of the police, T.L.O.'s mother took her daughter to police headquarters, where T.L.O. confessed that she had been selling marihuana at the high school. On the basis of the confession and the evidence seized by Mr. Choplick, the State brought delinquency charges against T.L.O. in the Juvenile and Domestic Relations Court of Middlesex County. Contending that Mr. Choplick's search of her purse violated the Fourth Amendment, T.L.O. moved to suppress the evidence found in her purse as well as her confession, which, she argued, was tainted by the allegedly unlawful search . . .

In determining whether the search at issue in this case violated the Fourth Amendment, we are faced initially with the question whether that Amendment's prohibition on unreasonable searches and seizures applies to searches conducted by public school officials. We hold that it does. It is now beyond dispute that "the Federal Constitution, by virtue of the Fourteenth Amendment, prohibits unreasonable searches and seizures by state officers" . . . Equally indisputable is the proposition that the Fourteenth Amendment protects the rights of students against encroachment by public school officials:

> The Fourteenth Amendment, as now applied to the States, protects the citizen against the State itself and all of its creatures--Boards of Education not excepted. These have, of course, important, delicate, and highly discretionary functions, but none that they may not perform within the limits of the Bill of Rights. That they are educating the young for citizenship is reason for scrupulous protection of Constitutional freedoms of the individual, if we are not to strangle the free mind at its source and teach youth to discount important principles of our government as mere platitudes. *West Virginia v. Barnette*, 319 U.S. 624 (1943) . . .

It may well be true that the evil toward which the Fourth Amendment was primarily directed was the resurrection of the pre-Revolutionary practice of using general warrants or "writs of

202

assistance" to authorize searches for contraband by officers of the Crown. But this Court has never limited the Amendment's prohibition on unreasonable searches and seizures to operations conducted by the police. Rather, the Court has long spoken of the Fourth Amendment's strictures as restraints imposed upon "governmental action"--that is, "upon the activities of sovereign authority" . . . Accordingly, we have held the Fourth Amendment applicable to the activities of civil as well as criminal authorities . . . Because the individual's interest in privacy and personal security "suffers whether the government's motivation is to investigate violations of criminal laws or breaches of other statutory or regulatory standards," . . . it would be "anomalous to say that the individual and his private property are fully protected by the Fourth Amendment only when the individual is suspected of criminal behavior" . . .

Notwithstanding the general applicability of the Fourth Amendment to the activities of civil authorities, a few courts have concluded that school officials are exempt from the dictates of the Fourth Amendment by virtue of the special nature of their authority over schoolchildren. Teachers and school administrators, it is said, act *in loco parentis* in their dealings with students: their authority is that of the parent, not the State, and is therefore not subject to the limits of the Fourth Amendment.

Such reasoning is in tension with contemporary reality and the teachings of this Court. We have held school officials subject to the commands of the First Amendment, *see, Tinker v. Des Moines*, 393 U.S. 503 (1969), and the Due Process Clause of the Fourteenth Amendment, *see, Goss v. Lopez*, 419 U.S. 565 (1975). If school authorities are state actors for purposes of the constitutional guarantees of freedom of expression and due process, it is difficult to understand why they should be deemed to be exercising parental rather than public authority when conducting searches of their students. More generally, the Court has recognized that "the concept of parental delegation" as a source of school authority is not entirely "consonant with compulsory education laws." *Ingraham v. Wright*, 430 U.S. 651 (1977). Today's public school officials do not merely exercise authority voluntarily conferred on them by individual parents; rather, they act in furtherance of publicly mandated educational and disciplinary policies . . . In carrying out searches and other disciplinary functions pursuant to such policies, school officials act as representatives of the State, not merely as surrogates for the parents, and they cannot claim the parents' immunity from the strictures of the Fourth Amendment.

To hold that the Fourth Amendment applies to searches conducted by school authorities is only to begin the inquiry into the standards governing such searches. Although the underlying command of the Fourth Amendment is always that searches and seizures be reasonable, what is reasonable depends on the context within which a search takes place. The determination of the standard of reasonableness governing any specific class of searches requires "balancing the need to search against the invasion which the search entails" . . . On one side of the balance are arrayed the individual's legitimate expectations of privacy and personal security; on the other, the government's need for effective methods to deal with breaches of public order.

We have recognized that even a limited search of the person is a substantial invasion of privacy. We have also recognized that searches of closed items of personal luggage are intrusions on protected privacy interests, for "the Fourth Amendment provides protection to the owner of every container that conceals its contents from plain view" . . . A search of a child's person or of a closed purse or other bag carried on her person, no less than a similar search carried out on an adult, is undoubtedly a severe violation of subjective expectations of privacy.

Of course, the Fourth Amendment does not protect subjective expectations of privacy that are unreasonable or otherwise "illegitimate" . . . To receive the protection of the Fourth Amendment, an expectation of privacy must be one that society is "prepared to recognize as legitimate" . . . The State of New Jersey has argued that because of the pervasive supervision to which children in the schools are necessarily subject, a child has virtually no legitimate expectation of privacy in articles of personal property "unnecessarily" carried into a school. This argument has two factual premises: (1) the fundamental incompatibility of expectations of privacy with the maintenance of a sound educational environment; and (2) the minimal interest of the child in bringing any items of personal property into the school. Both premises are severely flawed.

Although this Court may take notice of the difficulty of maintaining discipline in the public schools today, the situation is not so dire that students in the schools may claim no legitimate expectations of privacy. We have recently recognized that the need to maintain order in a prison is such that prisoners retain no legitimate expectations of privacy in their cells, but it goes almost without saying that "the prisoner and the schoolchild stand in wholly different circumstances, separated by the harsh facts of criminal conviction and incarceration." *Ingraham v. Wright*, 430 U.S. 651 (1977). We are not yet ready to hold that the schools and the prisons need be equated for purposes of the Fourth Amendment.

Nor does the State's suggestion that children have no legitimate need to bring personal property into the schools seem well anchored in reality. Students at a minimum must bring to school not only the supplies needed for their studies, but also keys, money, and the necessaries of personal hygiene and grooming. In addition, students may carry on their persons or in purses or wallets such non-disruptive yet highly personal items as photographs, letters, and diaries. Finally, students may have perfectly legitimate reasons to carry with them articles of property needed in connection with extracurricular or recreational activities. In short, schoolchildren may find it necessary to carry with them a variety of legitimate, non-contraband items, and there is no reason to conclude that they have necessarily waived all rights to privacy in such items merely by bringing them onto school grounds.

Against the child's interest in privacy must be set the substantial interest of teachers and administrators in maintaining discipline in the classroom and on school grounds. Maintaining order in the classroom has never been easy, but in recent years, school disorder has often taken particularly ugly forms: drug use and violent crime in the schools have become major social problems. Even in schools that have been spared the most severe disciplinary problems, the preservation of order and a proper educational environment requires close supervision of schoolchildren, as well as the enforcement of rules against conduct that would be perfectly permissible if undertaken by an adult. "Events calling for discipline are frequent occurrences and sometimes require immediate, effective action." *Goss v. Lopez*, 419 U.S. 565 (1975). Accordingly, we have recognized that maintaining security and order in the schools requires a certain degree of flexibility in school disciplinary procedures, and we have respected the value of preserving the informality of the student-teacher relationship.

How, then, should we strike the balance between the schoolchild's legitimate expectations of privacy and the school's equally legitimate need to maintain an environment in which learning can take place? It is evident that the school setting requires some easing of the restrictions to which searches by public authorities are ordinarily subject. The warrant requirement, in particular, is unsuited to the school environment: requiring a teacher to obtain a warrant before searching a child suspected of an infraction of school rules (or of the criminal law) would unduly interfere with the maintenance of the swift and informal disciplinary procedures needed in the schools. Just as we have in other cases dispensed with the warrant requirement when "the burden of obtaining a warrant is likely to frustrate the governmental purpose behind the search" .

. . we hold today that school officials need not obtain a warrant before searching a student who is under their authority.

The school setting also requires some modification of the level of suspicion of illicit activity needed to justify a search. Ordinarily, a search--even one that may permissibly be carried out without a warrant--must be based upon "probable cause" to believe that a violation of the law has occurred. However, "probable cause" is not an irreducible requirement of a valid search. The fundamental command of the Fourth Amendment is that searches and seizures be reasonable, and although "both the concept of probable cause and the requirement of a warrant bear on the reasonableness of a search, . . . in certain limited circumstances neither is required" . . . Thus, we have in a number of cases recognized the legality of searches and seizures based on suspicions that, although "reasonable," do not rise to the level of probable cause. Where a careful balancing of governmental and private interests suggests that the public interest is best served by a Fourth Amendment standard of reasonableness that stops short of probable cause, we have not hesitated to adopt such a standard.

We join the majority of courts that have examined this issue in concluding that the accommodation of the privacy interests of schoolchildren with the substantial need of teachers and administrators for freedom to maintain order in the schools does not require strict adherence to the requirement that searches be based on probable cause to believe that the subject of the search has violated or is violating the law. Rather, the legality of a search of a student should depend simply on the reasonableness, under all the circumstances, of the search. Determining the reasonableness of any search involves a twofold inquiry: first, one must consider whether the action was justified at its inception; second, one must determine whether the search as actually conducted was reasonably related in scope to the circumstances which justified the interference in the first place. Under ordinary circumstances, a search of a student by a teacher or other school official will be "justified at its inception" when there are reasonable grounds for suspecting that the search will turn up evidence that the student has violated or is violating either the law or the rules of the school. Such a search will be permissible in its scope when the measures adopted are reasonably related to the objectives of the search and not excessively intrusive in light of the age and sex of the student and the nature of the infraction.

This standard will, we trust, neither unduly burden the efforts of school authorities to maintain order in their schools nor authorize unrestrained intrusions upon the privacy of schoolchildren. By focusing attention on the question of reasonableness, the standard will spare teachers and school administrators the necessity of schooling themselves in the niceties of probable cause and permit them to regulate their conduct according to the dictates of reason and common sense. At the same time, the reasonableness standard should ensure that the interests of students will be invaded no more than is necessary to achieve the legitimate end of preserving order in the schools.

There remains the question of the legality of the search in this case. We recognize that the "reasonable grounds" standard applied by the New Jersey Supreme Court in its consideration of this question is not substantially different from the standard that we have adopted today. Nonetheless, we believe that the New Jersey court's application of that standard to strike down the search of T.L.O.'s purse reflects a somewhat crabbed notion of reasonableness. Our review of the facts surrounding the search leads us to conclude that the search was in no sense unreasonable for Fourth Amendment purposes . . . the New Jersey Supreme Court . . . held that Mr. Choplick had no reasonable suspicion that the purse would contain cigarettes. This conclusion is puzzling. A teacher had reported that T.L.O. was smoking in the lavatory.

Certainly this report gave Mr. Choplick reason to suspect that T.L.O. was carrying cigarettes with her; and if she did have cigarettes, her purse was the obvious place in which to find them. Mr. Choplick's suspicion that there were cigarettes in the purse was not an "inchoate and unparticularized suspicion or 'hunch'" . . . rather, it was the sort of "common-sense conclusion about human behavior" upon which "practical people"--including government officials--are entitled to rely. Of course, even if the teacher's report were true, T.L.O. might not have had a pack of cigarettes with her; she might have borrowed a cigarette from someone else or have been sharing a cigarette with another student. But the requirement of reasonable suspicion is not a requirement of absolute certainty: "sufficient probability, not certainty, is the touchstone of reasonableness under the Fourth Amendment" . . .

Our conclusion that Mr. Choplick's decision to open T.L.O.'s purse was reasonable brings us to the question of the further search for marihuana once the pack of cigarettes was located. The suspicion upon which the search for marihuana was founded was provided when Mr. Choplick observed a package of rolling papers in the purse as he removed the pack of cigarettes. Although T.L.O. does not dispute the reasonableness of Mr. Choplick's belief that the rolling papers indicated the presence of marihuana, she does contend that the scope of the search Mr. Choplick conducted exceeded permissible bounds when he seized and read certain letters that implicated T.L.O. in drug dealing. This argument, too, is unpersuasive. The discovery of the rolling papers concededly gave rise to a reasonable suspicion that T.L.O. was carrying marihuana as well as cigarettes in her purse. This suspicion justified further exploration of T.L.O.'s purse, which turned up more evidence of drug-related activities: a pipe, a number of plastic bags of the type commonly used to store marihuana, a small quantity of marihuana, and a fairly substantial amount of money. Under these circumstances, it was not unreasonable to extend the search to a separate zippered compartment of the purse; and when a search of that compartment revealed an index card containing a list of "people who owe me money" as well as two letters, the inference that T.L.O. was involved in marihuana trafficking was substantial enough to justify Mr. Choplick in examining the letters to determine whether they contained any further evidence. In short, we cannot conclude that the search for marihuana was unreasonable in any respect.

Because the search resulting in the discovery of the evidence of marihuana dealing by T.L.O. was reasonable, the New Jersey Supreme Court's decision to exclude that evidence from T.L.O.'s juvenile delinquency proceedings on Fourth Amendment grounds was erroneous. Accordingly, the judgment of the Supreme Court of New Jersey is

Reversed.

* * * * * *

In *New Jersey v. T.L.O.* the Court held that because of the special context of public schools only "reasonable suspicion" of a violation of the law or school rules was required to conduct a reasonable search in schools, not the higher standard of probable cause. The Fourth Amendment prohibits unreasonable searches. To be reasonable under the *T.L.O.* test the search must be:

1) *Justified in its inception*: The school agent had reasonable grounds to believe that a search would produce evidence of wrong doing (*i.e.*, illegal activity or a breach of school rules).

2) *Reasonably related in scope to the objectives of the search and not excessively intrusive in light of the*:

    a) Age of the student
    b) Sex of the student
    c) Nature of the infraction

In summary, the Fourth Amendment protects reasonable expectations of individual privacy from governmental intrusion, and prohibits unreasonable searches and seizures by government officials. To justify a challenged search, government officials must establish sufficient reason for the search. Courts evaluate these claims by weighing the individual's reasonable expectation of privacy under the circumstances against the government's legitimate need to search. Police searches are subject to the higher standard of "probable cause" but public school officials generally need only show that their searches of students were based on the lower standard of "reasonable suspicion." This was the standard of law the Court applied in the search of a student's "papers and effects" in *T.L.O.* But for a far more intrusive search of the student's "person" including a strip search revealing the student's private areas, should school officials be subject to a more rigorous standard of law?

Strip Searches of Students

Safford v. Redding
557 U.S. ___ (2009)
Supreme Court of the United States

Justice SOUTER delivered the opinion of the Court.

The issue here is whether a 13-year-old student's Fourth Amendment right was violated when she was subjected to a search of her bra and underpants by school officials acting on reasonable suspicion that she had brought forbidden prescription and over-the-counter drugs to school. Because there were no reasons to suspect the drugs presented a danger or were concealed in her underwear, we hold that the search did violate the Constitution, but because there is reason to question the clarity with which the right was established, the official who ordered the unconstitutional search is entitled to qualified immunity from liability.

The events immediately prior to the search in question began in 13-year-old Savana Redding's math class at Safford Middle School one October day in 2003. The assistant principal of the school, Kerry Wilson, came into the room and asked Savana to go to his office. There, he showed her a day planner, unzipped and open flat on his desk, in which there were several knives, lighters, a permanent marker, and a cigarette. Wilson asked Savana whether the planner was hers; she said it was, but that a few days before she had lent it to her friend, Marissa Glines. Savana stated that none of the items in the planner belonged to her.

Wilson then showed Savana four white prescription-strength ibuprofen 400-mg pills, and one over-the-counter blue naproxen 200-mg pill, all used for pain and inflammation but banned under school rules without advance permission. He asked Savana if she knew anything about the pills. Savana answered that she did not. Wilson then told Savana that he had received a report that she was giving these pills to fellow students; Savana denied it and agreed to let Wilson search her belongings. Helen Romero, an administrative assistant, came into the office, and together with Wilson they searched Savana's backpack, finding nothing.

At that point, Wilson instructed Romero to take Savana to the school nurse's office to search her clothes for pills. Romero and the nurse, Peggy Schwallier, asked Savana to remove her jacket, socks, and shoes, leaving her in stretch pants and a T-shirt (both without pockets), which she was then asked to remove. Finally, Savana was told to pull her bra out and to the side and shake it, and to pull out the elastic on her underpants, thus exposing her breasts and pelvic area to some degree. No pills were found.

Savana's mother filed suit against Safford Unified School District # 1, Wilson, Romero, and Schwallier for conducting a strip search in violation of Savana's Fourth Amendment rights. The individuals (hereinafter petitioners) moved for summary judgment, raising a defense of qualified immunity. The District Court for the District of Arizona granted the motion on the ground that there was no Fourth Amendment violation, and a panel of the Ninth Circuit affirmed. A closely divided Circuit sitting *en banc*, however, reversed . . . the Ninth Circuit held that the strip search was unjustified under the Fourth Amendment test for searches of children by school officials set out in *New Jersey v. T.L.O.* The Circuit then applied the test for qualified immunity, and found that Savana's right was clearly established at the time of the search: "these notions of personal privacy are 'clearly established' in that they inhere in all of us, particularly middle school teenagers, and are inherent in the privacy component of the Fourth Amendment's proscription against unreasonable searches." The upshot was reversal of summary judgment as to Wilson, while affirming the judgments in favor of Schwallier, the school nurse, and Romero, the administrative assistant, since they had not acted as independent decision-makers . . .

In this case, the school's policies strictly prohibit the nonmedical use, possession, or sale of any drug on school grounds, including "any prescription or over-the-counter drug, except those for which permission to use in school has been granted pursuant to Board policy." A week before Savana was searched, another student, Jordan Romero (no relation of the school's administrative assistant), told the principal and Assistant Principal Wilson that "certain students were bringing drugs and weapons on campus," and that he had been sick after taking some pills that "he got from a classmate." On the morning of October 8, the same boy handed Wilson a white pill that he said Marissa Glines had given him. He told Wilson that students were planning to take the pills at lunch . . . There is no need here either to explain the imperative of keeping drugs out of schools, or to explain the reasons for the school's rule banning all drugs, no matter how benign, without advance permission. Teachers are not pharmacologists trained to identify pills and powders, and an effective drug ban has to be enforceable fast . . . Wilson learned from Peggy Schwallier, the school nurse, that the pill was Ibuprofen 400 mg, available only by prescription. Wilson then called Marissa out of class. Outside the classroom, Marissa's teacher handed Wilson the day planner, found within Marissa's reach, containing various contraband items. Wilson escorted Marissa back to his office.

208

In the presence of Helen Romero, Wilson requested Marissa to turn out her pockets and open her wallet. Marissa produced a blue pill, several white ones, and a razor blade. Wilson asked where the blue pill came from, and Marissa answered, "I guess it slipped in when she gave me the IBU 400s." When Wilson asked whom she meant, Marissa replied, "Savana Redding." Wilson then enquired about the day planner and its contents; Marissa denied knowing anything about them. Wilson did not ask Marissa any follow-up questions to determine whether there was any likelihood that Savana presently had pills: neither asking when Marissa received the pills from Savana nor where Savana might be hiding them.

Schwallier did not immediately recognize the blue pill, but information provided through a poison control hotline indicated that the pill was a 200-mg dose of an anti-inflammatory drug, generically called naproxen, available over the counter. At Wilson's direction, Marissa was then subjected to a search of her bra and underpants by Romero and Schwallier, as Savana was later on. The search revealed no additional pills.

It was at this juncture that Wilson called Savana into his office and showed her the day planner. Their conversation established that Savana and Marissa were on friendly terms: while she denied knowledge of the contraband, Savana admitted that the day planner was hers and that she had lent it to Marissa. Wilson had other reports of their friendship from staff members, who had identified Savana and Marissa as part of an unusually rowdy group at the school's opening dance in August, during which alcohol and cigarettes were found in the girls' bathroom. Wilson had reason to connect the girls with this contraband, for Wilson knew that Jordan Romero had told the principal that before the dance, he had been at a party at Savana's house where alcohol was served. Marissa's statement that the pills came from Savana was thus sufficiently plausible to warrant suspicion that Savana was involved in pill distribution.

This suspicion of Wilson's was enough to justify a search of Savana's backpack and outer clothing. If a student is reasonably suspected of giving out contraband pills, she is reasonably suspected of carrying them on her person and in the carryall that has become an item of student uniform in most places today. If Wilson's reasonable suspicion of pill distribution were not understood to support searches of outer clothes and backpack, it would not justify any search worth making. And the look into Savana's bag, in her presence and in the relative privacy of Wilson's office, was not excessively intrusive, any more than Romero's subsequent search of her outer clothing.

Here it is that the parties part company, with Savana's claim that extending the search at Wilson's behest to the point of making her pull out her underwear was constitutionally unreasonable. The exact label for this final step in the intrusion is not important, though strip search is a fair way to speak of it. Romero and Schwallier directed Savana to remove her clothes down to her underwear, and then "pull out" her bra and the elastic band on her underpants. Although Romero and Schwallier stated that they did not see anything when Savana followed their instructions, we would not define strip search and its Fourth Amendment consequences in a way that would guarantee litigation about who was looking and how much was seen. The very fact of Savana's pulling her underwear away from her body in the presence of the two officials who were able to see her necessarily exposed her breasts and pelvic area to some degree, and both subjective and reasonable societal expectations of personal privacy support the treatment of such a search as categorically distinct, requiring distinct elements of justification on the part of school authorities for going beyond a search of outer clothing and belongings.

Savana's subjective expectation of privacy against such a search is inherent in her account of it as embarrassing, frightening, and humiliating. The reasonableness of her expectation (required by the Fourth Amendment standard) is indicated by the consistent experiences of other young people similarly searched, whose adolescent vulnerability intensifies the patent intrusiveness of the exposure. The common reaction of these adolescents simply registers the obviously different meaning of a search exposing the body from the experience of nakedness or near undress in other school circumstances. Changing for gym is getting ready for play; exposing for a search is responding to an accusation reserved for suspected wrongdoers and fairly understood as so degrading that a number of communities have decided that strip searches in schools are never reasonable and have banned them no matter what the facts may be.

The indignity of the search does not, of course, outlaw it, but it does implicate the rule of reasonableness as stated in *T.L.O.*, that "the search as actually conducted [be] reasonably related in scope to the circumstances which justified the interference in the first place." The scope will be permissible, that is, when it is "not excessively intrusive in light of the age and sex of the student and the nature of the infraction."

Here, the content of the suspicion failed to match the degree of intrusion. Wilson knew beforehand that the pills were prescription-strength ibuprofen and over-the-counter naproxen, common pain relievers equivalent to two Advil, or one Aleve. He must have been aware of the nature and limited threat of the specific drugs he was searching for, and while just about anything can be taken in quantities that will do real harm, Wilson had no reason to suspect that large amounts of the drugs were being passed around, or that individual students were receiving great numbers of pills.

Nor could Wilson have suspected that Savana was hiding common painkillers in her underwear. Petitioners suggest, as a truth universally acknowledged, that "students . . . hide contraband in or under their clothing," and cite a smattering of cases of students with contraband in their underwear. But when the categorically extreme intrusiveness of a search down to the body of an adolescent requires some justification in suspected facts, general background possibilities fall short; a reasonable search that extensive calls for suspicion that it will pay off. But non-dangerous school contraband does not raise the specter of stashes in intimate places, and there is no evidence in the record of any general practice among Safford Middle School students of hiding that sort of thing in underwear; neither Jordan nor Marissa suggested to Wilson that Savana was doing that, and the preceding search of Marissa that Wilson ordered yielded nothing. Wilson never even determined when Marissa had received the pills from Savana; if it had been a few days before, that would weigh heavily against any reasonable conclusion that Savana presently had the pills on her person, much less in her underwear.

In sum, what was missing from the suspected facts that pointed to Savana was any indication of danger to the students from the power of the drugs or their quantity, and any reason to suppose that Savana was carrying pills in her underwear. We think that the combination of these deficiencies was fatal to finding the search reasonable.

In so holding, we mean to cast no ill reflection on the assistant principal, for the record raises no doubt that his motive throughout was to eliminate drugs from his school and protect students from what Jordan Romero had gone through. Parents are known to overreact to protect their children from danger, and a school official with responsibility for safety may tend to do the same. The difference is that the Fourth Amendment places limits on the official, even with the high degree of deference that courts must pay to the educator's professional judgment.

We do mean, though, to make it clear that the *T.L.O.* concern to limit a school search to reasonable scope requires the support of reasonable suspicion of danger or of resort to underwear for hiding evidence of wrongdoing before a search can reasonably make the quantum leap from outer clothes and backpacks to exposure of intimate parts. The meaning of such a search, and the degradation its subject may reasonably feel, place a search that intrusive in a category of its own demanding its own specific suspicions.

A school official searching a student is "entitled to qualified immunity where clearly established law does not show that the search violated the Fourth Amendment." To be established clearly, however, there is no need that "the very action in question [have] previously been held unlawful." The unconstitutionality of outrageous conduct obviously will be unconstitutional, this being the reason, as Judge Posner has said, that "the easiest cases don't even arise." But even as to action less than an outrage, "officials can still be on notice that their conduct violates established law . . . in novel factual circumstances."

T.L.O. directed school officials to limit the intrusiveness of a search, "in light of the age and sex of the student and the nature of the infraction," and as we have just said at some length, the intrusiveness of the strip search here cannot be seen as justifiably related to the circumstances. But we realize that the lower courts have reached divergent conclusions regarding how the *T.L.O.* standard applies to such searches.

A number of judges have read *T.L.O.* as the *en banc* minority of the Ninth Circuit did here . . . We think these differences of opinion from our own are substantial enough to require immunity for the school officials in this case . . . The strip search of Savana Redding was unreasonable and a violation of the Fourth Amendment, but petitioners Wilson, Romero, and Schwallier are nevertheless protected from liability through qualified immunity. Our conclusions here do not resolve, however, the question of the liability of petitioner Safford Unified School District . . . The judgment of the Ninth Circuit is therefore affirmed in part and reversed in part, and this case is remanded . . .

It is so ordered.

* * * * * * *

Comments and Questions

Strip searches of children are recognized as a distinct category of searches generally disfavored by courts. These highly intrusive searches require additional elements of proof beyond the *T.L.O.* test. For a strip search to satisfy the requirements of the second prong of the *T.L.O.* test (that the search be reasonably related in scope to the objectives of the search) the *Redding* test further requires that strip searches must be based on: 1) A reasonable suspicion of danger and; 2) A reasonable basis for believing that the danger is hidden in an intimate area. A genuine need for urgency in preventing the danger (*e.g.*, seizing a dangerous weapon; explosive; etc.) would also bolster the case for an intrusive search by school officials. Strip searches falling short of these standards may result not only in institutional liability, but also individual liability for public school officials conducting strip searches contrary to well established law after *Redding*. In all searches, school officials should carefully weigh the intrusiveness of the search against the reason for the search. If the intrusiveness of the search outweighs the reason for the search, the search is unreasonable and therefore unlawful.

Strip searches are those searches that go beyond a search of personal belongings and outer clothing to reveal intimate garments and private areas. In *Redding* the Court noted that if a strip search by school officials is ever lawful it would have to satisfy the *T.L.O.* test that "the search as actually conducted be reasonably related in scope to the circumstances which justified the interference in the first place" and "not excessively intrusive in light of the age and sex of the student and the nature of the infraction." Theoretically then, a strip search of a very young student may be less intrusive than the search of a post-pubescent student; a search by a same-sex school official may be less intrusive than an opposite sex search; and a search for dangerous weapons, explosives, or hazardous drugs may provide greater license to search than searches for more trivial items. That said, the Court was very clear that strip searches are highly disfavored, noting that strip searches are "so degrading that a number of communities have decided that strip searches in schools are never reasonable and have banned them no matter what the facts may be." In *Redding* the Court declared:

> We do mean . . . to make it clear that the *T.L.O.* concern to limit a school search to reasonable scope requires the support of reasonable suspicion of danger or of resort to underwear for hiding evidence of wrongdoing before a search can reasonably make the quantum leap from outer clothes and backpacks to exposure of intimate parts. The meaning of such a search, and the degradation its subject may reasonably feel, place a search that intrusive in a category of its own demanding its own specific suspicions.

What type of evidence would Assistant Principal Wilson have been required to produce to justify the strip search in the *Redding* case? Was Wilson's search justified in its inception? Was it reasonably related in scope to the objectives of the search? How serious was the danger posed by the pills in this case? What evidence did Wilson have that Savana was hiding the suspected drugs in her underwear? How credible is it to argue that it was reasonably believed that drugs would still be in her underwear several days after the events in question?

School officials have conducted strip searches of entire classes looking for relatively small amounts of missing money or even candy. Could these searches ever survive a Fourth Amendment challenge? Consider the necessary balance between the governmental justification for the search and the intrusiveness of the search. What have school officials proven if they find a student in possession of a $5 bill? Is it less discriminatory to search every student, or do you only multiply the number of potential plaintiffs?

Even if school officials believe they can survive the court of law, would school officials survive the court of public opinion in your community if they engaged in a mass strip search of children, or a highly intrusive strip search of any child? If you were ordered to assist with a strip search, what would you do? If you follow an unlawful order, it is no defense to claim you were only following orders. There is a legal duty to refuse to follow an unlawful order. On the other hand, it is insubordination to refuse to follow a lawful order. The *T.L.O.* and *Redding* standards help to clarify when a search is lawful. In general, however, strip searches are disfavored and should only be resorted to in situations where there is a reasonable suspicion of danger; and a reason to believe the danger is hidden in an intimate area. In summary, if a strip search of a public school student is ever lawful, it must satisfy both the *T.L.O.* test and the *Redding* test:

> The *Redding* Test: A strip search of a public school student is only lawful if it satisfies the *T.L.O.* test, and there is:
>
> 1) A reasonable suspicion of danger; and
> 2) A reasonable basis for believing that the danger is hidden in an intimate area.

Random Student Drug Testing

Vernonia School District v. Acton
515 U.S. 646 (1995)
Supreme Court of the United States

Justice SCALIA delivered the opinion of the Court.

The Student Athlete Drug Policy adopted by School District 47J in the town of Vernonia, Oregon, authorizes random urinalysis drug testing of students who participate in the District's school athletics programs. We granted certiorari to decide whether this violates the Fourth and Fourteenth Amendments to the United States Constitution.

Petitioner Vernonia School District 47J (District) operates one high school and three grade schools in the logging community of Vernonia, Oregon. As elsewhere in small-town America, school sports play a prominent role in the town's life, and student athletes are admired in their schools and in the community.

Drugs had not been a major problem in Vernonia schools. In the mid-to-late 1980's, however, teachers and administrators observed a sharp increase in drug use. Students began to speak out about their attraction to the drug culture, and to boast that there was nothing the school could do about it. Along with more drugs came more disciplinary problems. Between 1988 and 1989 the number of disciplinary referrals in Vernonia schools rose to more than twice the number reported in the early 1980's, and several students were suspended. Students became increasingly rude during class; outbursts of profane language became common.

Not only were student athletes included among the drug users but, as the District Court found, athletes were the leaders of the drug culture. This caused the District's administrators particular concern, since drug use increases the risk of sports-related injury. Expert testimony at the trial confirmed the deleterious effects of drugs on motivation, memory, judgment, reaction, coordination, and performance. The high school football and wrestling coach witnessed a severe sternum injury suffered by a wrestler, and various omissions of safety procedures and mis-executions by football players, all attributable in his belief to the effects of drug use.

Initially, the District responded to the drug problem by offering special classes, speakers, and presentations designed to deter drug use. It even brought in a specially trained dog to detect drugs, but the drug problem persisted. According to the District Court:

> The administration was at its wits end and . . . a large segment of the student body, particularly those involved in interscholastic athletics, was in a state of rebellion. Disciplinary actions had reached "epidemic proportions." The coincidence of an almost three-fold increase in classroom disruptions and disciplinary reports along with the staff's direct observations of students using drugs or glamorizing drug and alcohol use led the administration to the inescapable conclusion that the rebellion was being fueled by alcohol and drug abuse as well as the student's misperceptions about the drug culture.

At that point, District officials began considering a drug-testing program. They held a parent "input night" to discuss the proposed Student Athlete Drug Policy (Policy), and the parents in attendance gave their unanimous approval. The school board approved the Policy for

213

implementation in the fall of 1989. Its expressed purpose is to prevent student athletes from using drugs, to protect their health and safety, and to provide drug users with assistance programs.

The Policy applies to all students participating in interscholastic athletics. Students wishing to play sports must sign a form consenting to the testing and must obtain the written consent of their parents. Athletes are tested at the beginning of the season for their sport. In addition, once each week of the season the names of the athletes are placed in a "pool" from which a student, with the supervision of two adults, blindly draws the names of 10% of the athletes for random testing. Those selected are notified and tested that same day, if possible.

The student to be tested completes a specimen control form which bears an assigned number. Prescription medications that the student is taking must be identified by providing a copy of the prescription or a doctor's authorization. The student then enters an empty locker room accompanied by an adult monitor of the same sex. Each boy selected produces a sample at a urinal, remaining fully clothed with his back to the monitor, who stands approximately 12 to 15 feet behind the student. Monitors may (though do not always) watch the student while he produces the sample, and they listen for normal sounds of urination. Girls produce samples in an enclosed bathroom stall, so that they can be heard but not observed. After the sample is produced, it is given to the monitor, who checks it for temperature and tampering and then transfers it to a vial.

The samples are sent to an independent laboratory, which routinely tests them for amphetamines, cocaine, and marijuana. Other drugs, such as LSD, may be screened at the request of the District, but the identity of a particular student does not determine which drugs will be tested. The laboratory's procedures are 99.94% accurate. The District follows strict procedures regarding the chain of custody and access to test results. The laboratory does not know the identity of the students whose samples it tests. It is authorized to mail written test reports only to the superintendent and to provide test results to District personnel by telephone only after the requesting official recites a code confirming his authority. Only the superintendent, principals, vice-principals, and athletic directors have access to test results, and the results are not kept for more than one year.

If a sample tests positive, a second test is administered as soon as possible to confirm the result. If the second test is negative, no further action is taken. If the second test is positive, the athlete's parents are notified, and the school principal convenes a meeting with the student and his parents, at which the student is given the option of (1) participating for six weeks in an assistance program that includes weekly urinalysis, or (2) suffering suspension from athletics for the remainder of the current season and the next athletic season. The student is then retested prior to the start of the next athletic season for which he or she is eligible. The Policy states that a second offense results in automatic imposition of option (2); a third offense in suspension for the remainder of the current season and the next two athletic seasons.

In the fall of 1991, respondent James Acton, then a seventh grader, signed up to play football at one of the District's grade schools. He was denied participation, however, because he and his parents refused to sign the testing consent forms. The Actons filed suit, seeking declaratory and injunctive relief from enforcement of the Policy on the grounds that it violated the Fourth and Fourteenth Amendments to the United States Constitution and Article I, § 9, of the Oregon Constitution. After a bench trial, the District Court entered an order denying the claims on the merits and dismissing the action. The United States Court of Appeals for the Ninth Circuit reversed, holding that the Policy violated both the Fourth and Fourteenth Amendments and Article I, § 9, of the Oregon Constitution. We granted certiorari.

The Fourth Amendment to the United States Constitution provides that the Federal Government shall not violate "the right of the people to be secure in their persons, houses, papers, and effects, against unreasonable searches and seizures." We have held that the Fourteenth Amendment extends this constitutional guarantee to searches and seizures by state officers, including public school officials. In *Skinner v. Railway Labor Executives' Assn.,* 489 U.S. 602 (1989), we held that state-compelled collection and testing of urine, such as that required by the Policy, constitutes a "search" subject to the demands of the Fourth Amendment.

As the text of the Fourth Amendment indicates, the ultimate measure of the constitutionality of a governmental search is "reasonableness." At least in a case such as this, where there was no clear practice, either approving or disapproving the type of search at issue, at the time the constitutional provision was enacted, whether a particular search meets the reasonableness standard "is judged by balancing its intrusion on the individual's Fourth Amendment interests against its promotion of legitimate governmental interests."

Where a search is undertaken by law enforcement officials to discover evidence of criminal wrongdoing, this Court has said that reasonableness generally requires the obtaining of a judicial warrant. Warrants cannot be issued, of course, without the showing of probable cause required by the Warrant Clause. But a warrant is not required to establish the reasonableness of all government searches; and when a warrant is not required (and the Warrant Clause therefore not applicable), probable cause is not invariably required either. A search unsupported by probable cause can be constitutional, we have said, "when special needs, beyond the normal need for law enforcement, make the warrant and probable-cause requirement impracticable."

We have found such "special needs" to exist in the public school context. There, the warrant requirement "would unduly interfere with the maintenance of the swift and informal disciplinary procedures [that are] needed," and "strict adherence to the requirement that searches be based upon probable cause" would undercut "the substantial need of teachers and administrators for freedom to maintain order in the schools." *New Jersey v. T.L.O.* The school search we approved in *T.L.O.,* while not based on probable cause, was based on individualized suspicion of wrongdoing. As we explicitly acknowledged, however, "the Fourth Amendment imposes no irreducible requirement of such suspicion." We have upheld suspicionless searches and seizures to conduct drug testing of railroad personnel involved in train accidents; to conduct random drug testing of federal customs officers who carry arms or are involved in drug interdiction; and to maintain automobile checkpoints looking for illegal immigrants and contraband, and drunk drivers.

The first factor to be considered is the nature of the privacy interest upon which the search here at issue intrudes. The Fourth Amendment does not protect all subjective expectations of privacy, but only those that society recognizes as "legitimate." What expectations are legitimate varies, of course, with context, depending, for example, upon whether the individual asserting the privacy interest is at home, at work, in a car, or in a public park. In addition, the legitimacy of certain privacy expectations vis-à-vis the State may depend upon the individual's legal relationship with the State. For example . . . although a "probationer's home, like anyone else's, is protected by the Fourth Amendment," the supervisory relationship between probationer and State justifies "a degree of impingement upon [a probationer's] privacy that would not be constitutional if applied to the public at large." Central, in our view, to the present case is the

215

fact that the subjects of the Policy are (1) children, who (2) have been committed to the temporary custody of the State as schoolmaster.

Traditionally at common law, and still today, unemancipated minors lack some of the most fundamental rights of self-determination including even the right of liberty in its narrow sense, *i.e.*, the right to come and go at will. They are subject, even as to their physical freedom, to the control of their parents or guardians. When parents place minor children in private schools for their education, the teachers and administrators of those schools stand *in loco parentis* over the children entrusted to them. In fact, the tutor or schoolmaster is the very prototype of that status. As Blackstone describes it, a parent "may . . . delegate part of his parental authority, during his life, to the tutor or schoolmaster of his child; who is then *in loco parentis*, and has such a portion of the power of the parent committed to his charge, *viz.* that of restraint and correction, as may be necessary to answer the purposes for which he is employed." 1 W. Blackstone, COMMENTARIES ON THE LAWS OF ENGLAND 441 (1769).

In *T.L.O.* we rejected the notion that public schools, like private schools, exercise only parental power over their students, which of course is not subject to constitutional constraints. Such a view of things, we said, "is not entirely consonant with compulsory education laws," and is inconsistent with our prior decisions treating school officials as state actors for purposes of the Due Process and Free Speech Clauses. But while denying that the State's power over schoolchildren is formally no more than the delegated power of their parents, *T.L.O.* did not deny, but indeed emphasized, that the nature of that power is custodial and tutelary, permitting a degree of supervision and control that could not be exercised over free adults. "A proper educational environment requires close supervision of schoolchildren, as well as the enforcement of rules against conduct that would be perfectly permissible if undertaken by an adult." While we do not, of course, suggest that public schools as a general matter have such a degree of control over children as to give rise to a constitutional "duty to protect," we have acknowledged that for many purposes "school authorities act *in loco parentis*," with the power and indeed the duty to "inculcate the habits and manners of civility." Thus, while children assuredly do not "shed their constitutional rights . . . at the schoolhouse gate," the nature of those rights is what is appropriate for children in school.

Fourth Amendment rights, no less than First and Fourteenth Amendment rights, are different in public schools than elsewhere; the "reasonableness" inquiry cannot disregard the schools' custodial and tutelary responsibility for children. For their own good and that of their classmates, public school children are routinely required to submit to various physical examinations, and to be vaccinated against various diseases. According to the American Academy of Pediatrics, most public schools "provide vision and hearing screening and dental and dermatological checks . . . Others also mandate scoliosis screening at appropriate grade levels". . . Particularly with regard to medical examinations and procedures, therefore, "students within the school environment have a lesser expectation of privacy than members of the population generally."

Legitimate privacy expectations are even less with regard to student athletes. School sports are not for the bashful. They require "suiting up" before each practice or event, and showering and changing afterwards. Public school locker rooms, the usual sites for these activities, are not notable for the privacy they afford. The locker rooms in Vernonia are typical: No individual dressing rooms are provided; shower heads are lined up along a wall, unseparated by any sort of partition or curtain; not even all the toilet stalls have doors. As the United States Court of

Appeals for the Seventh Circuit has noted, there is "an element of 'communal undress' inherent in athletic participation."

There is an additional respect in which school athletes have a reduced expectation of privacy. By choosing to "go out for the team," they voluntarily subject themselves to a degree of regulation even higher than that imposed on students generally. In Vernonia's public schools, they must submit to a preseason physical exam (James testified that his included the giving of a urine sample), they must acquire adequate insurance coverage or sign an insurance waiver, maintain a minimum grade point average, and comply with any "rules of conduct, dress, training hours and related matters as may be established for each sport by the head coach and athletic director with the principal's approval." Somewhat like adults who choose to participate in a "closely regulated industry," students who voluntarily participate in school athletics have reason to expect intrusions upon normal rights and privileges, including privacy.

Having considered the scope of the legitimate expectation of privacy at issue here, we turn next to the character of the intrusion that is complained of. We recognized in *Skinner* that collecting the samples for urinalysis intrudes upon "an excretory function traditionally shielded by great privacy." We noted, however, that the degree of intrusion depends upon the manner in which production of the urine sample is monitored. Under the District's Policy, male students produce samples at a urinal along a wall. They remain fully clothed and are only observed from behind, if at all. Female students produce samples in an enclosed stall, with a female monitor standing outside listening only for sounds of tampering. These conditions are nearly identical to those typically encountered in public restrooms, which men, women, and especially schoolchildren use daily. Under such conditions, the privacy interests compromised by the process of obtaining the urine sample are in our view negligible.

The other privacy-invasive aspect of urinalysis is, of course, the information it discloses concerning the state of the subject's body, and the materials he has ingested. In this regard it is significant that the tests at issue here look only for drugs, and not for whether the student is, for example, epileptic, pregnant, or diabetic. Moreover, the drugs for which the samples are screened are standard, and do not vary according to the identity of the student. And finally, the results of the tests are disclosed only to a limited class of school personnel who have a need to know; and they are not turned over to law enforcement authorities or used for any internal disciplinary function.

Respondents argue, however, that the District's Policy is in fact more intrusive than this suggests, because it requires the students, if they are to avoid sanctions for a falsely positive test, to identify in advance prescription medications they are taking. We agree that this raises some cause for concern . . . On the other hand, we have never indicated that requiring advance disclosure of medications is *per se* unreasonable . . . The General Authorization Form that respondents refused to sign, which refusal was the basis for James's exclusion from the sports program, said only (in relevant part): "I . . . authorize the Vernonia School District to conduct a test on a urine specimen which I provide to test for drugs and/or alcohol use. I also authorize the release of information concerning the results of such a test to the Vernonia School District and to the parents and/or guardians of the student." While the practice of the District seems to have been to have a school official take medication information from the student at the time of the test, that practice is not set forth in, or required by, the Policy, which says simply: "Student athletes who . . . are or have been taking prescription medication must provide verification (either by a copy of the prescription or by doctor's authorization) prior to being tested." It may well be that, if and when James was selected for random testing at a time that he was taking medication, the School District would have permitted him to provide the requested information in a confidential manner--for example, in a sealed envelope delivered to the testing lab. Nothing in the Policy contradicts that, and when respondents choose, in effect, to challenge the Policy on its face, we will not assume the worst. Accordingly, we reach the same conclusion as in *Skinner*: that the invasion of privacy was not significant.

Finally, we turn to consider the nature and immediacy of the governmental concern at issue here, and the efficacy of this means for meeting it . . . the District Court held that because the District's program also called for drug testing in the absence of individualized suspicion, the District "must demonstrate a 'compelling need' for the program." The Court of Appeals appears to have agreed with this view . . . It is a mistake, however, to think that the phrase "compelling state interest," in the Fourth Amendment context, describes a fixed, minimum quantum of governmental concern, so that one can dispose of a case by answering in isolation the question: Is there a compelling state interest here? Rather, the phrase describes an interest that appears important enough to justify the particular search at hand, in light of other factors that show the search to be relatively intrusive upon a genuine expectation of privacy. Whether that relatively high degree of government concern is necessary in this case or not, we think it is met.

That the nature of the concern is important--indeed, perhaps compelling--can hardly be doubted . . . School years are the time when the physical, psychological, and addictive effects of drugs are most severe. "Maturing nervous systems are more critically impaired by intoxicants than mature ones are; childhood losses in learning are lifelong and profound"; "children grow chemically dependent more quickly than adults, and their record of recovery is depressingly poor" . . . And of course the effects of a drug-infested school are visited not just upon the users, but upon the entire student body and faculty, as the educational process is disrupted. In the present case, moreover, the necessity for the State to act is magnified by the fact that this evil is being visited not just upon individuals at large, but upon children for whom it has undertaken a special responsibility of care and direction. Finally, it must not be lost sight of that this program is directed more narrowly to drug use by school athletes, where the risk of immediate physical harm to the drug user or those with whom he is playing his sport is particularly high. Apart from psychological effects, which include impairment of judgment, slow reaction time, and a lessening of the perception of pain, the particular drugs screened by the District's Policy have been demonstrated to pose substantial physical risks to athletes. Amphetamines produce an "artificially induced heart rate increase, peripheral vasoconstriction, blood pressure increase, and masking of the normal fatigue response," making them a "very dangerous drug when used during exercise of any type." Marijuana causes "irregular blood pressure responses during changes in body position . . . reduction in the oxygen-carrying capacity of the blood," and "inhibition of the normal sweating responses resulting in increased body temperature." Cocaine produces "vasoconstriction, elevated blood pressure," and "possible coronary artery spasms and myocardial infarction."

As for the immediacy of the District's concerns: We are not inclined to question--indeed, we could not possibly find clearly erroneous--the District Court's conclusion that "a large segment of the student body, particularly those involved in interscholastic athletics, was in a state of rebellion," that "disciplinary actions had reached 'epidemic proportions,'" and that "the rebellion was being fueled by alcohol and drug abuse as well as by the student's misperceptions about the drug culture" . . . As to the efficacy of this means for addressing the problem: It seems to us self-evident that a drug problem largely fueled by the "role model" effect of athletes' drug use, and of particular danger to athletes, is effectively addressed by making sure that athletes do not use drugs.

Respondents argue that a "less intrusive means to the same end" was available, namely, "drug testing on suspicion of drug use." We have repeatedly refused to declare that only the "least intrusive" search practicable can be reasonable under the Fourth Amendment. Respondents' alternative entails substantial difficulties--if it is indeed practicable at all. It may be impracticable, for one thing, simply because the parents who are willing to accept random drug testing for athletes are not willing to accept accusatory drug testing for all students, which transforms the process into a badge of shame. Respondents' proposal brings the risk that teachers will impose testing arbitrarily upon troublesome but not drug-likely students. It generates the expense of defending lawsuits that charge such arbitrary imposition, or that simply demand greater process before accusatory drug testing is imposed. And not least of all, it adds to the ever-expanding diversionary duties of schoolteachers the new function of spotting and bringing to account drug abuse, a task for which they are ill prepared, and which is not readily compatible with their vocation . . . In many respects, we think, testing based on "suspicion" of drug use would not be better, but worse.

Taking into account all the factors we have considered above--the decreased expectation of privacy, the relative unobtrusiveness of the search, and the severity of the need met by the search--we conclude Vernonia's Policy is reasonable and hence constitutional.

We caution against the assumption that suspicionless drug testing will readily pass constitutional muster in other contexts. The most significant element in this case is the first we discussed: that the Policy was undertaken in furtherance of the government's responsibilities, under a public school system, as guardian and tutor of children entrusted to its care . . . when the government acts as guardian and tutor the relevant question is whether the search is one that a reasonable guardian and tutor might undertake. Given the findings of need made by the District Court, we conclude that in the present case it is.

We may note that the primary guardians of Vernonia's schoolchildren appear to agree. The record shows no objection to this districtwide program by any parents other than the couple before us here--even though, as we have described, a public meeting was held to obtain parents' views. We find insufficient basis to contradict the judgment of Vernonia's parents, its school board, and the District Court, as to what was reasonably in the interest of these children under the circumstances.

The Ninth Circuit held that Vernonia's Policy not only violated the Fourth Amendment, but also, by reason of that violation, contravened Article I, § 9, of the Oregon Constitution. Our conclusion that the former holding was in error means that the latter holding rested on a flawed premise. We therefore vacate the judgment, and remand the case to the Court of Appeals for further proceedings consistent with this opinion.

It is so ordered.

Justice O'CONNOR, with whom Justice STEVENS and Justice SOUTER join, dissenting.

The population of our Nation's public schools, grades 7 through 12, numbers around 18 million. By the reasoning of today's decision, the millions of these students who participate in interscholastic sports, an overwhelming majority of whom have given school officials no reason whatsoever to suspect they use drugs at school, are open to an intrusive bodily search.

219

In justifying this result, the Court dispenses with a requirement of individualized suspicion on considered policy grounds. First, it explains that precisely because every student athlete is being tested, there is no concern that school officials might act arbitrarily in choosing whom to test. Second, a broad-based search regime, the Court reasons, dilutes the accusatory nature of the search. In making these policy arguments, of course, the Court sidesteps powerful, countervailing privacy concerns. Blanket searches, because they can involve "thousands or millions" of searches, "pose a greater threat to liberty" than do suspicion-based ones, which "affect one person at a time." Searches based on individualized suspicion also afford potential targets considerable control over whether they will, in fact, be searched because a person can avoid such a search by not acting in an objectively suspicious way. And given that the surest way to avoid acting suspiciously is to avoid the underlying wrongdoing, the costs of such a regime, one would think, are minimal.

But whether a blanket search is "better," than a regime based on individualized suspicion is not a debate in which we should engage. In my view, it is not open to judges or government officials to decide on policy grounds which is better and which is worse. For most of our constitutional history, mass, suspicionless searches have been generally considered *per se* unreasonable within the meaning of the Fourth Amendment. And we have allowed exceptions in recent years only where it has been clear that a suspicion-based regime would be ineffectual. Because that is not the case here, I dissent . . .

In addition to overstating its concerns with a suspicion-based program, the District seems to have understated the extent to which such a program is less intrusive of students' privacy. By invading the privacy of a few students rather than many (nationwide, of thousands rather than millions), and by giving potential search targets substantial control over whether they will, in fact, be searched, a suspicion-based scheme is significantly less intrusive . . . The great irony of this case is that most (though not all) of the evidence the District introduced to justify its suspicionless drug testing program consisted of first or second-hand stories of particular, identifiable students acting in ways that plainly gave rise to reasonable suspicion of in-school drug use--and thus that would have justified a drug-related search under our *T.L.O.* decision. Small groups of students, for example, were observed by a teacher "passing joints back and forth" across the street at a restaurant before school and during school hours. Another group was caught skipping school and using drugs at one of the students' houses. Several students actually admitted their drug use to school officials (some of them being caught with marijuana pipes). One student presented himself to his teacher as "clearly obviously inebriated" and had to be sent home. Still another was observed dancing and singing at the top of his voice in the back of the classroom; when the teacher asked what was going on, he replied, "Well, I'm just high on life." To take a final example, on a certain road trip, the school wrestling coach smelled marijuana smoke in a motel room occupied by four wrestlers, an observation that (after some questioning) would probably have given him reasonable suspicion to test one or all of them . . . ("in most instances the evidence of wrongdoing prompting teachers or principals to conduct searches is sufficiently detailed and specific to meet the traditional probable cause test").

In light of all this evidence of drug use by particular students, there is a substantial basis for concluding that a vigorous regime of suspicion-based testing (for which the District appears already to have rules in place) would have gone a long way toward solving Vernonia's school drug problem while preserving the Fourth Amendment rights of James Acton and others like him. And were there any doubt about such a conclusion, it is removed by indications in the record that suspicion-based testing could have been supplemented by an equally vigorous campaign to have Vernonia's parents encourage their children to submit to the District's voluntary drug testing program . . . (noting widespread parental support for drug testing). In these circumstances, the Fourth Amendment dictates that a mass, suspicionless search regime is categorically unreasonable.

I recognize that a suspicion-based scheme, even where reasonably effective in controlling in-school drug use, may not be as effective as a mass, suspicionless testing regime. In one sense, that is obviously true--just as it is obviously true that suspicion-based law enforcement is not as effective as mass, suspicionless enforcement might be. "But there is nothing new in the realization" that Fourth Amendment protections come with a price. Indeed, the price we pay is higher in the criminal context, given that police do not closely observe the entire class of potential search targets (all citizens in the area) and must ordinarily adhere to the rigid requirements of a warrant and probable cause.

The principal counterargument to all this, central to the Court's opinion, is that the Fourth Amendment is more lenient with respect to school searches. That is no doubt correct, for, as the Court explains, schools have traditionally had special guardian-like responsibilities for children that necessitate a degree of constitutional leeway. This principle explains the considerable Fourth Amendment leeway we gave school officials in *T.L.O.* In that case, we held that children at school do not enjoy two of the Fourth Amendment's traditional categorical protections against unreasonable searches and seizures: the warrant requirement and the probable cause requirement. And this was true even though the same children enjoy such protections "in a non-school setting."

The instant case, however, asks whether the Fourth Amendment is even more lenient than that, *i.e.*, whether it is so lenient that students may be deprived of the Fourth Amendment's only remaining, and most basic, categorical protection: its strong preference for an individualized suspicion requirement, with its accompanying antipathy toward personally intrusive, blanket searches of mostly innocent people. It is not at all clear that people in prison lack this categorical protection, and we have said "we are not yet ready to hold that the schools and the prisons need be equated for purposes of the Fourth Amendment." Thus, if we are to mean what we often proclaim--that students do not "shed their constitutional rights . . . at the schoolhouse gate," the answer must plainly be no.

By contrast, intrusive, blanket searches of schoolchildren, most of whom are innocent, for evidence of serious wrongdoing are not part of any traditional school function of which I am aware. Indeed, many schools, like many parents, prefer to trust their children unless given reason to do otherwise. As James Acton's father said on the witness stand, "[suspicionless testing] sends a message to children that are trying to be responsible citizens . . . that they have to prove that they're innocent . . . and I think that kind of sets a bad tone for citizenship" . . .

It might also be noted that physical exams (and of course vaccinations) are not searches for conditions that reflect wrongdoing on the part of the student, and so are wholly non-accusatory and have no consequences that can be regarded as punitive . . . The best proof that the District's testing program is to some extent accusatory can be found in James Acton's own explanation on the witness stand as to why he did not want to submit to drug testing: "Because I feel that they have no reason to think I was taking drugs." It is hard to think of a manner of explanation that resonates more intensely in our Fourth Amendment tradition than this.

I do not believe that suspicionless drug testing is justified on these facts. But even if I agreed that some such testing were reasonable here, I see two other Fourth Amendment flaws in the District's program. First, and most serious, there is virtually no evidence in the record of a drug problem at the Washington Grade School, which includes the seventh and eighth grades, and which Acton attended when this litigation began . . . Second, even as to the high school, I find unreasonable the school's choice of student athletes as the class to subject to suspicionless testing--a choice that appears to have been driven more by a belief in what would pass constitutional muster . . . than by a belief in what was required to meet the District's principal disciplinary concern. Reading the full record in this case, as well as the District Court's authoritative summary of it, it seems quite obvious that the true driving force behind the District's adoption of its drug testing program was the need to combat the rise in drug-related disorder and disruption in its classrooms and around campus. I mean no criticism of the strength of that interest. On the contrary, where the record demonstrates the existence of such a problem, that interest seems self-evidently compelling. "Without first establishing discipline and maintaining order, teachers cannot begin to educate their students." And the record in this case surely demonstrates there was a drug-related discipline problem in Vernonia of "epidemic proportions." The evidence of a drug-related sports injury problem at Vernonia, by contrast, was considerably weaker.

On this record, then, it seems to me that the far more reasonable choice would have been to focus on the class of students found to have violated published school rules against severe disruption in class and around campus, disruption that had a strong nexus to drug use, as the District established at trial. Such a choice would share two of the virtues of a suspicion-based regime: testing dramatically fewer students, tens as against hundreds, and giving students control, through their behavior, over the likelihood that they would be tested. Moreover, there would be a reduced concern for the accusatory nature of the search, because the Court's feared "badge of shame," would already exist, due to the antecedent accusation and finding of severe disruption . . .

It cannot be too often stated that the greatest threats to our constitutional freedoms come in times of crisis. But we must also stay mindful that not all government responses to such times are hysterical overreactions; some crises are quite real, and when they are, they serve precisely as the compelling state interest that we have said may justify a measured intrusion on constitutional rights. The only way for judges to mediate these conflicting impulses is to do what they should do anyway: stay close to the record in each case that appears before them, and make their judgments based on that alone. Having reviewed the record here, I cannot avoid the conclusion that the District's suspicionless policy of testing all student athletes sweeps too broadly, and too imprecisely, to be reasonable under the Fourth Amendment.

Comments and Questions

Among the objections to the Court's opinion in *Vernonia* was the concern that this decision created a "slippery slope" that would further erode Fourth Amendment rights. Specifically, advocates for civil liberties were concerned that the Fourth Amendment exception recognized for intrusive suspicionless searches of student athletes in *Vernonia* would become the tool used for expanding this "limited" exception to other student groups and beyond, further eroding Fourth Amendment protections for everyone in the future. If no warrant, probable cause, or individualized suspicion is required to justify these searches of student athletes, what if anything remained of the Fourth Amendment's protections? Couldn't this same reasoning be used to extend suspicionless blanket searches to all students in extra-curricular activities; to all students;

to all educators; to all state employees; to all citizens? At what point do these boundless random searches become a greater danger to the People than the evil they were intended to prevent?

Americans need only look to their own Colonial history to confirm that the Fourth Amendment serves as an essential check and balance protecting individual privacy from unwarranted intrusions by government agents, and helping to prevent the establishment of a dangerous police state culture. Exceptions to the Fourth Amendment are sometimes warranted and necessary, but when there is no clear limit on the exception, the exception can eventually swallow the rule.

Where the critics of *Vernonia* proven correct in *Earls* or is *Earls* simply another common sense exception to the Fourth Amendment? If no warrant, probable cause, or individualized suspicion is required to justify these searches, what is the legal limit under the Fourth Amendment? In *Earls* the Court noted that the "drug abuse problem among our Nation's youth . . . has only grown worse" since *Vernonia* was decided in 1995. Is this evidence that random drug testing of students has failed to achieve its stated goals, or that further exceptions to the Fourth Amendment are warranted?

Board of Education v. Earls
536 U.S. 822 (2002)
Supreme Court of the United States

Justice THOMAS delivered the opinion of the Court.

The Student Activities Drug Testing Policy implemented by the Board of Education of Independent School District No. 92 of Pottawatomie County (School District) requires all students who participate in competitive extracurricular activities to submit to drug testing. Because this Policy reasonably serves the School District's important interest in detecting and preventing drug use among its students, we hold that it is constitutional.

The city of Tecumseh, Oklahoma, is a rural community located approximately 40 miles southeast of Oklahoma City . . . In the fall of 1998, the School District adopted the Student Activities Drug Testing Policy (Policy), which requires all middle and high school students to consent to drug testing in order to participate in any extracurricular activity. In practice, the Policy has been applied only to competitive extracurricular activities sanctioned by the Oklahoma Secondary Schools Activities Association, such as the Academic Team, Future Farmers of America, Future Homemakers of America, band, choir, pom-pom, cheerleading, and athletics. Under the Policy, students are required to take a drug test before participating in an extracurricular activity, must submit to random drug testing while participating in that activity, and must agree to be tested at any time upon reasonable suspicion. The urinalysis tests are designed to detect only the use of illegal drugs, including amphetamines, marijuana, cocaine, opiates, and barbituates, not medical conditions or the presence of authorized prescription medications.

At the time of their suit, both respondents attended Tecumseh High School. Respondent Lindsay Earls was a member of the show choir, the marching band, the Academic Team, and the National Honor Society. Respondent Daniel James sought to participate in the Academic Team. Together with their parents, Earls and James brought a 42 U.S.C. § 1983, action against the School District, challenging the Policy both on its face and as applied to their participation in extracurricular activities. They alleged that the Policy violates the Fourth Amendment as incorporated by the Fourteenth Amendment and requested injunctive and declarative relief. They also argued that the School District failed to identify a special need for testing students who participate in extracurricular activities, and that the "Drug Testing Policy neither addresses a proven problem nor promises to bring any benefit to students or the school."

Applying the principles articulated in *Vernonia*, in which we upheld the suspicionless drug testing of school athletes, the United States District Court for the Western District of Oklahoma rejected respondents' claim that the Policy was unconstitutional and granted summary judgment to the School District. The court noted that "special needs" exist in the public school context and that, although the School District did "not show a drug problem of epidemic proportions," there was a history of drug abuse starting in 1970 that presented "legitimate cause for concern." The District Court also held that the Policy was effective because "it can scarcely be disputed that the drug problem among the student body is effectively addressed by making sure that the large number of students participating in competitive, extracurricular activities do not use drugs."

The United States Court of Appeals for the Tenth Circuit reversed, holding that the Policy violated the Fourth Amendment. The Court of Appeals agreed with the District Court that the Policy must be evaluated in the "unique environment of the school setting," but reached a different conclusion as to the Policy's constitutionality. Before imposing a suspicionless drug testing program, the Court of Appeals concluded that a school "must demonstrate that there is some identifiable drug abuse problem among a sufficient number of those subject to the testing, such that testing that group of students will actually redress its drug problem." The Court of Appeals then held that because the School District failed to demonstrate such a problem existed among Tecumseh students participating in competitive extracurricular activities, the Policy was unconstitutional. We granted certiorari, and now reverse.

The Fourth Amendment to the United States Constitution protects "the right of the people to be secure in their persons, houses, papers, and effects, against unreasonable searches and seizures." Searches by public school officials, such as the collection of urine samples, implicate Fourth Amendment interests. We must therefore review the School District's Policy for "reasonableness," which is the touchstone of the constitutionality of a governmental search.

In the criminal context, reasonableness usually requires a showing of probable cause. The probable cause standard, however, "is peculiarly related to criminal investigations" and may be unsuited to determining the reasonableness of administrative searches where the "Government seeks to prevent the development of hazardous conditions." The Court has also held that a warrant and finding of probable cause are unnecessary in the public school context because such requirements "would unduly interfere with the maintenance of the swift and informal disciplinary procedures [that are] needed."

Given that the School District's Policy is not in any way related to the conduct of criminal investigations, respondents do not contend that the School District requires probable cause before testing students for drug use. Respondents instead argue that drug testing must be based at least on some level of individualized suspicion. It is true that we generally determine the reasonableness of a search by balancing the nature of the intrusion on the individual's privacy against the promotion of legitimate governmental interests. But we have long held that "the Fourth Amendment imposes no irreducible requirement of [individualized] suspicion." "In certain limited circumstances, the Government's need to discover such latent or hidden conditions, or to prevent their development, is sufficiently compelling to justify the intrusion on privacy entailed by conducting such searches without any measure of individualized suspicion." Therefore, in the context of safety and administrative regulations, a search unsupported by probable cause may be reasonable "when special needs, beyond the normal need for law enforcement, make the warrant and probable cause requirement impracticable."

Significantly, this Court has previously held that "special needs" inhere in the public school context. While schoolchildren do not shed their constitutional rights when they enter the schoolhouse, "Fourth Amendment rights . . . are different in public schools than elsewhere; the 'reasonableness' inquiry cannot disregard the schools' custodial and tutelary responsibility for children." In particular, a finding of individualized suspicion may not be necessary when a school conducts drug testing.

In *Vernonia*, this Court held that the suspicionless drug testing of athletes was constitutional. The Court, however, did not simply authorize all school drug testing, but rather conducted a fact-specific balancing of the intrusion on the children's Fourth Amendment rights against the promotion of legitimate governmental interests. Applying the principles of *Vernonia* to the somewhat different facts of this case, we conclude that Tecumseh's Policy is also constitutional.

We first consider the nature of the privacy interest allegedly compromised by the drug testing. As in *Vernonia*, the context of the public school environment serves as the backdrop for the analysis of the privacy interest at stake and the reasonableness of the drug testing policy in general ("Central . . . is the fact that the subjects of the Policy are (1) children, who (2) have been committed to the temporary custody of the State as schoolmaster"); ("The most significant element in this case is the first we discussed: that the Policy was undertaken in furtherance of the government's responsibilities, under a public school system, as guardian and tutor of children entrusted to its care"); ("When the government acts as guardian and tutor the relevant question is whether the search is one that a reasonable guardian and tutor might undertake").

A student's privacy interest is limited in a public school environment where the State is responsible for maintaining discipline, health, and safety . . . Respondents argue that because children participating in nonathletic extracurricular activities are not subject to regular physicals and communal undress, they have a stronger expectation of privacy than the athletes tested in *Vernonia*. This distinction, however, was not essential to our decision in *Vernonia*, which depended primarily upon the school's custodial responsibility and authority.

In any event, students who participate in competitive extracurricular activities voluntarily subject themselves to many of the same intrusions on their privacy as do athletes. Some of these clubs and activities require occasional off-campus travel and communal undress. All of them have their own rules and requirements for participating students that do not apply to the student body as a whole . . . Given the minimally intrusive nature of the sample collection and the limited uses to which the test results are put, we conclude that the invasion of students' privacy is not significant.

Finally, this Court must consider the nature and immediacy of the government's concerns and the efficacy of the Policy in meeting them. This Court has already articulated in detail the importance of the governmental concern in preventing drug use by schoolchildren. The drug abuse problem among our Nation's youth has hardly abated since *Vernonia* was decided in 1995. In fact, evidence suggests that it has only grown worse. As in *Vernonia*, "the necessity for the State to act is magnified by the fact that this evil is being visited not just upon individuals at large, but upon children for whom it has undertaken a special responsibility of care and direction." The health and safety risks identified in *Vernonia* apply with equal force to Tecumseh's children. Indeed, the nationwide drug epidemic makes the war against drugs a pressing concern in every school.

Additionally, the School District in this case has presented specific evidence of drug use at Tecumseh schools. Teachers testified that they had seen students who appeared to be under the influence of drugs and that they had heard students speaking openly about using drugs. A drug dog found marijuana cigarettes near the school parking lot. Police officers once found drugs or drug paraphernalia in a car driven by a Future Farmers of America member. And the school board president reported that people in the community were calling the board to discuss the "drug situation." We decline to second-guess the finding of the District Court that "viewing the evidence as a whole, it cannot be reasonably disputed that the [School District] was faced with a 'drug problem' when it adopted the Policy."

Respondents consider the proffered evidence insufficient and argue that there is no "real and immediate interest" to justify a policy of drug testing nonathletes. We have recognized, however, that "a demonstrated problem of drug abuse . . . is not in all cases necessary to the validity of a testing regime," but that some showing does "shore up an assertion of special need for a suspicionless general search program." The School District has provided sufficient evidence to shore up the need for its drug testing program . . . the need to prevent and deter the substantial harm of childhood drug use provides the necessary immediacy for a school testing policy. Indeed, it would make little sense to require a school district to wait for a substantial portion of its students to begin using drugs before it was allowed to institute a drug testing program designed to deter drug use.

Given the nationwide epidemic of drug use, and the evidence of increased drug use in Tecumseh schools, it was entirely reasonable for the School District to enact this particular drug testing policy. We reject the Court of Appeals' novel test that "any district seeking to impose a random suspicionless drug testing policy as a condition to participation in a school activity must demonstrate that there is some identifiable drug abuse problem among a sufficient number of those subject to the testing, such that testing that group of students will actually redress its drug problem." Among other problems, it would be difficult to administer such a test. As we cannot articulate a threshold level of drug use that would suffice to justify a drug testing program for schoolchildren, we refuse to fashion what would in effect be a constitutional quantum of drug use necessary to show a "drug problem" . . .

Finally, we find that testing students who participate in extracurricular activities is a reasonably effective means of addressing the School District's legitimate concerns in preventing, deterring, and detecting drug use. While in *Vernonia* there might have been a closer fit between the testing of athletes and the trial court's finding that the drug problem was "fueled by the 'role model' effect of athletes' drug use," such a finding was not essential to the holding. *Vernonia* did not require the school to test the group of students most likely to use drugs, but rather considered the constitutionality of the program in the context of the public school's custodial responsibilities. Evaluating the Policy in this context, we conclude that the drug testing of Tecumseh students who participate in extracurricular activities effectively serves the School District's interest in protecting the safety and health of its students.

Within the limits of the Fourth Amendment, local school boards must assess the desirability of drug testing schoolchildren. In upholding the constitutionality of the Policy, we express no opinion as to its wisdom. Rather, we hold only that Tecumseh's Policy is a reasonable means of furthering the School District's important interest in preventing and deterring drug use among its schoolchildren. Accordingly, we reverse the judgment of the Court of Appeals.

It is so ordered.

Justice O'CONNOR, with whom Justice SOUTER joins, dissenting.

I dissented in *Vernonia*, and continue to believe that case was wrongly decided. Because *Vernonia* is now this Court's precedent, and because I agree that petitioners' program fails even under the balancing approach adopted in that case, I join Justice Ginsburg's dissent.

Justice GINSBURG, with whom Justice STEVENS, Justice O'CONNOR, and Justice SOUTER join, dissenting.

Seven years ago, in *Vernonia*, this Court determined that a school district's policy of randomly testing the urine of its student athletes for illicit drugs did not violate the Fourth Amendment. In so ruling, the Court emphasized that drug use "increased the risk of sports-related injury" and that Vernonia's athletes were the "leaders" of an aggressive local "drug culture" that had reached "epidemic proportions." Today, the Court relies upon *Vernonia* to permit a school district with a drug problem its superintendent repeatedly described as "not . . . major," to test the urine of an academic team member solely by reason of her participation in a nonathletic, competitive extracurricular activity--participation associated with neither special dangers from, nor particular predilections for, drug use.

"The legality of a search of a student," this Court has instructed, "should depend simply on the reasonableness, under all the circumstances, of the search." Although "special needs inhere in the public school context," those needs are not so expansive or malleable as to render reasonable any program of student drug testing a school district elects to install. The particular testing program upheld today is not reasonable; it is capricious, even perverse: Petitioners' policy targets for testing a student population least likely to be at risk from illicit drugs and their damaging effects. I therefore dissent . . .

The *Vernonia* Court concluded that a public school district facing a disruptive and explosive drug abuse problem sparked by members of its athletic teams had "special needs" that justified suspicionless testing of district athletes as a condition of their athletic participation. This case presents circumstances dispositively different from those of *Vernonia* . . . *Vernonia* cannot be read to endorse invasive and suspicionless drug testing of all students upon any evidence of drug use, solely because drugs jeopardize the life and health of those who use them. Many children, like many adults, engage in dangerous activities on their own time; that the children are enrolled in school scarcely allows government to monitor all such activities. If a student has a reasonable subjective expectation of privacy in the personal items she brings to school, surely she has a similar expectation regarding the chemical composition of her urine . . .

Nationwide, students who participate in extracurricular activities are significantly less likely to develop substance abuse problems than are their less-involved peers. Even if students might be deterred from drug use in order to preserve their extracurricular eligibility, it is at least as likely that other students might forgo their extracurricular involvement in order to avoid detection of their drug use. Tecumseh's policy thus falls short doubly if deterrence is its aim: It invades the privacy of students who need deterrence least, and risks steering students at greatest risk for substance abuse away from extracurricular involvement that potentially may palliate drug problems . . .

In *Chandler*, this Court inspected "Georgia's requirement that candidates for state office pass a drug test"; we held that the requirement "did not fit within the closely guarded category of constitutionally permissible suspicionless searches." Georgia's testing prescription, the record showed, responded to no "concrete danger," was supported by no evidence of a particular problem, and targeted a group not involved in "high-risk, safety-sensitive tasks." We concluded:

> What is left, after close review of Georgia's scheme, is the image the State seeks to project. By requiring candidates for public office to submit to drug testing, Georgia displays its commitment to the struggle against drug abuse . . . The need revealed, in short, is symbolic, not "special," as that term draws meaning from our case law.

Close review of Tecumseh's policy compels a similar conclusion . . . What is left is the School District's undoubted purpose to heighten awareness of its abhorrence of, and strong stand against, drug abuse. But the desire to augment communication of this message does not trump the right of persons--even of children within the schoolhouse gate--to be "secure in their persons . . . against unreasonable searches and seizures."

In *Chandler*, the Court referred to a pathmarking dissenting opinion in which "Justice Brandeis recognized the importance of teaching by example: 'Our Government is the potent, the omnipresent teacher. For good or for ill, it teaches the whole people by its example.'" That wisdom should guide decisionmakers in the instant case: The government is nowhere more a teacher than when it runs a public school.

It is a sad irony that the petitioning School District seeks to justify its edict here by trumpeting "the schools' custodial and tutelary responsibility for children" . . . schools' tutelary obligations to their students require them to "teach by example" by avoiding symbolic measures that diminish constitutional protections. "That [schools] are educating the young for citizenship is reason for scrupulous protection of Constitutional freedoms of the individual, if we are not to strangle the free mind at its source and teach youth to discount important principles of our government as mere platitudes." *West Virginia v. Barnette* (1943). For the reasons stated, I would affirm the judgment of the Tenth Circuit declaring the testing policy at issue unconstitutional.

Comments and Questions

Concerning the expanded student drug testing policy in *Earls* the Court's majority opinion stated: "In upholding the constitutionality of the Policy, we express no opinion as to its wisdom." Is a policy of drug testing students in all extra-curricular activities including purely academic and occupational groups a wise policy? Mass suspicionless drug testing is an expensive undertaking, including lab costs, administrative costs, legal costs, etc. Is this a wise use of limited educational time and money? Rather than using mass testing, why not simply require a test when there is reasonable suspicion a particular student may be using drugs? Will the policy in *Earls* be effective in deterring drug use, or just effective in deterring those who use drugs from engaging in any extra-curricular activities?

Dissenting Justices in *Earls* argued: "The particular testing program upheld today is not reasonable; it is capricious, even perverse: Petitioners' policy targets for testing a student population least likely to be at risk from illicit drugs and their damaging effects . . . Tecumseh's policy thus falls short doubly if deterrence is its aim: It invades the privacy of students who need deterrence least, and risks steering students at greatest risk for substance abuse away from extracurricular involvement that potentially may palliate drug problems."

Further, the dissenting Justices suggested that the real motivation did not appear to be deterrence of drug use as much as it was the desire of school officials (including elected Board members) to make a symbolic public statement about their own strong "zero tolerance" anti-drug message. Should constitutional rights and public dollars be sacrificed if the real motivation is a political message? The use of dangerous drugs by students is most certainly a serious concern. But what is the best policy for addressing these concerns? How far can the Fourth Amendment bend to accommodate policy concerns before it breaks and ceases to provide any real protections against unreasonable searches? Is diminishing the legal protections of the Constitution's Fourth Amendment acceptable to support policies aimed at winning the "war on drugs"? Are we winning? What is wrong with testing based on individual suspicion and the *T.L.O.* standard?

The Fourth Amendment requires a delicate balance between granting government officials the authority they legitimately need to protect the life, liberty, and property of the People, while also carefully guarding against the police power excesses that are the essential instruments of the police state: Constant and unbounded government surveillance; spying on their own citizens; and generating the self-censorship of fear that arises when there are no meaningful limits between the individual's privacy and government authority.

One way this balance is achieved under the Fourth Amendment is through recognition of the inherent differences between the private and public spheres of life. The Fourth Amendment broadly protects reasonable expectations of privacy in the private sphere. But the scope of privacy may be appropriately reduced when individuals enter the common public sphere where the judicious balancing of private rights with public needs is essential to safety and order.

Under the Court's "plain view" doctrine, for example, when government officials are merely observing things that are in plain view to the public, there is no search involved and the Fourth Amendment does not apply. Anyone wishing to claim a reasonable expectation of privacy must keep objects and conduct they wish to remain private out of public view, and under their private control. Failing this, they may waive reasonable expectations of privacy, at least to the extent that government officials can detect prohibited objects or conduct through the use of the common senses including sight, hearing, smell, feeling of vibrations, etc. The following sections address other common Fourth Amendment concerns in schools, and how courts have balanced private individual rights with public government needs in these cases.

School Locker Searches

School lockers are school property owned by the school and controlled by school officials. Unless a right of privacy is established by state law, policy, or local practice, there is generally no reasonable expectation of privacy in property owned and controlled by the school. Providing formal notice concerning the status of the locker further reduces any argument for an individual reasonable expectation of privacy in the locker. School officials commonly provide students with official notice through student handbooks or signed consent forms that school lockers are the property of the school, and that there is therefore no reasonable expectation of privacy in items that students choose to place in school lockers.

Students may have privacy rights in their lockers relative to other students. But there is generally no reasonable expectation of privacy under the Fourth Amendment that would prevent school officials from examining the contents of school lockers for custodial, safety, or other legitimate purposes. Even where a reasonable expectation of privacy in the locker is recognized, under *T.L.O.*, a search by school officials would only require reasonable suspicion of a violation

229

of the law or a school rule. Contraband items found in the process of a lawful inspection of the locker may be seized and used as evidence in school disciplinary and law enforcement proceedings.

Metal Detectors and Administrative Searches

Government searches of individuals generally require individualized suspicion and sufficient cause to justify the search under the circumstances. Courts have, however, recognized "administrative searches" as an exception to these general rules. To qualify as an administrative search, the search must be:

1) Aimed at a general danger (*e.g.*, keeping weapons out of public gathering areas); and
2) Unintrusive.

Metal detectors may be used for administrative searches, and when properly administered, they can help prevent general dangers and do so unintrusively.

For example, a door-frame style metal detector may be placed at entrances to areas school officials need to secure. All persons must pass through this metal detector to enter the area, and they are notified to remove metal objects prior to passing through. Otherwise, there is no further intrusion on the individual, unless the detector "alerts" indicating the likely presence of a substantial metal object. The individual may be asked to pass through again to confirm the alert, at which point a hand-held detector may be used to pin-point the metal object, all with no bodily contact or other unnecessary intrusions or delays on the individual.

A school official properly trained in administrative search procedures may ask appropriate questions concerning any possible concealed metal objects, and based on the results of this brief, informal questioning decide whether a more thorough search is warranted. Administrative searches are limited to what is reasonably necessary to guard against an immediate general danger (*e.g.*, in a proper case a lawful pat down search may be warranted to assure safety in the area; but a urinalysis is not related to any general and immediate danger). All follow-up individual searches must comply with the *T.L.O.* and *Redding* tests for students and the standard of probable cause for adults. Evidence supporting individualized suspicion and cause for searches may be based on the metal detector alerts (both frame and hand-held); responses to questions; the demeanor of the individual; and other relevant facts and circumstances.

Administrative searches cannot be a pretext for unlawful blanket searches or "fishing expeditions" aimed at finding general individual violations of the law or school rules. The focus must remain on deterring the presence of serious common dangers such as weapons. Further, metal detectors should not be used arbitrarily. The use of metal detectors should be in response to a demonstrable legitimate need. School officials may wish to make factual findings documenting a need to protect a common area (*e.g.*, prior instances of weapons in the area); adopt a lawful policy for the use of metal detectors; and assure that assigned personnel are adequately trained in the lawful, non-discriminatory application of the policy.

In summary, to qualify as an administrative search the purpose cannot be to find non-dangerous individual misconduct, but must be an unintrusive means of preventing a serious common danger, *e.g.*, preventing anyone from bringing a dangerous weapon into the area. However, contraband found in the process of a lawful administrative search may be seized and used as evidence in subsequent school disciplinary and law enforcement proceedings.

Security Cameras

Conduct in plain view of the public is not within any reasonable expectation of privacy under the Fourth Amendment. Government officials, including school officials, can place security cameras in public areas to promote public safety, security, and to record evidence of misconduct. Cameras should not, however, be placed in areas in which there may be a legitimate expectation of privacy such as restrooms, showering and changing areas, etc. Other more private and appropriate means of supervision and security may be used in these areas.

In addition to the use of security cameras in school entrances, hallways, cafeterias, and other common areas, security cameras are increasingly being used on school buses. Uses on buses include supervision and discipline of students on the bus, and also cameras aimed at vehicles near the bus. Bus cameras aimed at surrounding traffic are used to document evidence of dangerous illegal passing of the school bus while stopped and children are crossing the road, and to generally deter unsafe driving that endangers students. Public streets are public areas, and there is generally no reasonable expectation of privacy concerning conduct in public areas.

Electronic Privacy

Personal electronic devices have become commonplace tools in daily life for adults and children, often replacing traditional paper versions of written letters, notes, pictures, calendars, etc. Although unknown to the Founders, it is fair to say that the contents stored in individuals' personal electronic devices are the modern electronic equivalents of the "papers, and effects" they envisioned as protected under the Fourth Amendment. Therefore these electronic files receive the same constitutional protections accorded to hard copies of private documents. There is generally a legitimate expectation of privacy in the contents of personal electronic devices.

While the contents of electronic devices may be protected, consistent with state law and local policy school officials may lawfully prohibit students from having or using cell phones or other electronic devises in school. If a cell phone or other device is lawfully confiscate during school hours, however, that does not grant school officials a legal license to go on a "fishing expedition" through the student's private electronic device.

School officials may only search the contents of students' personal electronic devices if there is sufficient justification to do so under the guidelines established in *T.L.O.* The scope of the search cannot exceed the parameters of the justification for the search. If there is only reasonable suspicion for searching recent text messages, for example, older saved messages or stored photos should not be searched. If there is no valid cause to search the electronic device, the device should be secured and returned to the student or parent consistent with school policy.

Materials that students or teachers post on-line, however, are not protected by the Fourth Amendment. To legitimately claim any reasonable expectation of privacy, the individual's actions must be consistent with the maintenance of privacy. By posting materials on-line and available to the general public, any reasonable expectation of privacy is waived, and school officials may search these materials without violating the Fourth Amendment. Further, any reasonable expectation of privacy is limited to private electronic devices. There is no reasonable expectation of privacy when using public school computers, school e-mail, or other school owned and controlled electronic devices.

Dog Searches

The U.S. Supreme Court has not yet directly addressed the legality of dog searches in public schools, and lower courts have issued conflicting opinions. The Court has, however, addressed dog searches in other contexts. By viewing these cases in conjunction with the Court's articulated Fourth Amendment standards in public schools, some general principles can be reasonably deduced in this still evolving area of the law.

As noted above, under the "plain view" doctrine, to the extent that government officials can detect any prohibited contraband or conduct simply through the use of the common senses in public areas, there is no "search" under the Fourth Amendment and no reasonable expectation of privacy. Dogs are highly sensitive to smells, and police canines can be trained to detect the scent of drugs, explosives, etc. When government controlled search dogs smell the air in open public areas such as school parking lots, hallways, locker areas, etc., the Fourth Amendment is unlikely to be applicable as no "search" is involved.

There are, however, Fourth Amendment limits to the use of search dogs in public schools. Fourth Amendment limits may be breached if the dogs are allowed to poke and jab their noses into the students; come too close to students; students are asked to individually submit to very close smelling of their person by dogs; students are detained for an unreasonable time; or the dog search is otherwise administered in a way that is unreasonable, frightening, or embarrassing.

If the dog "alerts" to an individual this action by a trained canine may serve as the basis for the individual suspicion and cause necessary for a further lawful search. The reasonableness of the subsequent search is determined by balancing the intrusiveness of the search against the government's legitimate justification for the search.

To help assure that any searches involving dogs are lawful under the Fourth Amendment, school officials should plan appropriately prior to initiating dog searches. School officials should take steps to minimize the intrusiveness of the searches as much as is practicable under the circumstances. Based on evidence of facts and circumstances in the school, they should be prepared to explain why search dogs were necessary. The search should be conducted by well trained and tested dogs and professional handlers to assure that if the dogs alert that evidence is reasonably reliable. School officials should also assure in advance of the search that handlers will not allow dogs to touch students, come too close to the students, or otherwise act in ways likely to frighten or embarrass children.

Police Involvement in Student Searches

The U.S. Supreme Court allowed a lower standard governing searches conducted by public school officials in *T.L.O.* For police officers, however, the higher standard of probable cause still generally applies, even when police are acting with school officials. But what about a School Resource Officer (SRO), who arguably blends some of the duties of an educator with regular law enforcement responsibilities?

Although there are contrary decisions among lower courts, and the U.S. Supreme Court has not definitively resolved this issue, the more conservative approach has been for school officials to assume that the Fourth Amendment standard for SROs is probable cause, the same as the standard for regular police officers involved in searches. This approach is based on the theory that where the law is uncertain, applying the higher standard of law is safer than assuming the lower standard is valid, and this makes school officials less likely to become the test case for this

232

issue. SROs are in fact police officers, with badges, weapons, and arrest powers. Until the Court definitely resolves the status of SROs under the Fourth Amendment it is safer to assume that the legal standard for SROs is probable cause when SROs are involved in school searches.

In a situation where school officials believe a search is necessary for purposes of school discipline or safety, but they only believe they have reasonable suspicion and not probable cause, school officials may choose to conduct the search themselves, without any police assistance. If school officials find evidence of a crime, however, this evidence can be presented to the SRO or other law enforcement officers and the evidence may serve as a basis for probable cause if additional searches are required. Further, school officials may be mandated by state law to report criminal activity occurring at the school to law enforcement officials. In contrast, a search initiated by police for purposes of criminal prosecution, and instructing school officials to search under the lower standard of *T.L.O.* simply to avoid the Fourth Amendment's probable cause and warrant requirements, is likely to be found unlawful.

Searches of School Employees

Like many other issues under the Fourth Amendment, the law governing searches of school employees remains unsettled. Some argue that the *T.L.O.* standard should apply to all school searches, even those of adult school employees. Others argue that the rules concerning private employers should apply when the government is merely acting as an employer and not with police powers. And yet others argue that government searches of adults with adult consequences should be subject to the general standard of probable cause under the Fourth Amendment. The Court addressed this issue in *O'Connor v. Ortega*, 480 U.S. 709 (1987), but in a 5-4 decision that produced no majority opinion, the standard of law remained unsettled. The Court again failed to settle this issue in *City of Ontario v. Quon*, 560 U.S. ___ (2010).

Nonetheless, many lower courts have applied Justice O'Connor's plurality opinion standard in *Ortega,* holding that when the government conducts a search in its capacity as employer the relevant standard is whether that intrusion on the privacy of the employee is one that a reasonable employer might follow in the ordinary conduct of business, or whether it is unreasonable in the context. Others suggest that until the law is more clearly settled in this area, following the higher standard of probable cause is a safer practice.

What is currently clear is that a search of a government employee (including their private papers and effects) by a government supervisor or other government agent is in fact a search within the protections of the Fourth Amendment. It is the standard of proof required to justify these searches that remains unsettled. When the law remains uncertain, complying with the higher standard of law is the safest option, as you cannot lose a lawsuit by providing more constitutional protection than was required. For this reason, school officials may choose to assume that the standard of law for searches of adult employees is probable cause until this issue is finally resolved by the U.S. Supreme Court. It is also clear that there is no reasonable expectation of privacy in items left in plain view in the work place, or in communications sent through the school district's publicly controlled e-mail system or other school controlled media.

In *O'Connor v. Ortega*, 480 U.S. 209 (1987), public hospital officials searched Dr. Ortega's office while he was on administrative leave. Based on the record before the Court it was unclear whether the search was done for non-investigatory work-related purposes, or as an investigation to obtain evidence of work-related misconduct. The case was remanded to clarify this issue, and Dr. Ortega ultimately prevailed.

Nonetheless, on the record before the Court prior to remand the Court held that public employees generally have a reasonable expectation of privacy in their office, desk, files, personal belongings, etc. They are protected from unreasonable searches by both law enforcement agents and supervisors. However, "operational realities" may reduce or remove any reasonable expectation of privacy in certain circumstances. For example, there is a lower reasonable expectation of privacy in an office or desk that is shared, open, and commonly used by other employees, than in an office or desk that is assigned solely to the employee, locked, or otherwise objectively regarded as privately used. The scope of the expectation of privacy must be determined on a case-by-case basis, considering the unique circumstances and balancing the individual's legitimate privacy interests against the employer's legitimate interests in work-place supervision, safety, and efficiency.

Concerning drug testing for teachers, there is currently no clear, binding legal authority for requiring suspicionless urinalysis for public school teachers. The Supreme Court has allowed suspicionless testing of public employees where government officials have established a special need. In *Skinner v. Railway Executives Association*, 489 U.S. 602 (1989), the Court allowed random testing of transportation employees. And in *National Treasury Employees Union v. Von Raab*, 489 U.S. 656 (1989), the Court allowed random testing of U.S. Customs Service employees. School officials may have great difficulty, however, arguing that the safety and security concerns recognized by the Court in these cases apply equally to classroom teachers. Further, because of significant factual distinctions, decisions involving the constitutional rights of students cannot be automatically extended to decisions on the constitutional rights of adult public school employees.

Until this issue is definitively resolved by the Court, a school district that adopts random drug testing programs for teachers, similar to those allowed for students, risks becoming the legal test case for these policies. The legal risks are high, and the outcome remains uncertain. It is very unlikely that illegal drug use is wide-spread among teachers. And if it is, there is likely sufficient evidence to justify testing based on individual probable cause. If school officials believe it is necessary to test particular teachers, it is much safer legally to establish individualized suspicion and test individual teachers, rather than to adopt a broad-based suspicionless search policy for all teachers.

Seizure and Bailment

The terms search and seizure are often blended together when discussing the Fourth Amendment. But there are clear distinctions between these terms: Searches involve individual's privacy rights; while seizures involve individual's property or liberty rights. Seizures may result from school officials taking a student's property, or seizing their person and detaining them in an office or other area of the school. Students have a right to be free from unreasonable seizures, just as they have a right to be free from unreasonable searches. They do not, however, have any right to be free from a reasonable seizure based on a lawful cause.

Although the U.S. Supreme Court ruled in *New Jersey v. T.L.O.* that the standard for school officials in student search cases is reasonable suspicion, the Court did not directly address seizures in *T.L.O.* Lower courts, however, have applied the *T.L.O.* reasonable suspicion standard to student seizures as well.

Seizure of students should only occur when doing so is necessary to protect health, safety, or order in the school. Seized students must be supervised in a safe area, treated appropriately, and only detained for the time necessary. Concerning seized property, school officials hold seized property in bailment. School officials must use ordinary care in protecting the seized property from damage, loss, or theft. And they must provide students and/or parents with a fair process for redeeming items of value.

Chapter Summary

This chapter reviewed Fourth Amendment search and seizure laws as they are applied in public schools. After reading this chapter, please consider the following points in review and for further thought and discussion:

I. *Review Points*:

1) When there is a reasonable expectation of privacy, the Fourth Amendment protects against unreasonable intrusions by government agents. Outside of that reasonable expectation of privacy, however, there is no Fourth Amendment protection.

2) The Fourth Amendment protects individuals' reasonable expectations of privacy in their "persons, houses, papers, and effects" and requires government officials to establish that a challenged search was reasonable in its inception and scope.

3) To conduct a lawful search, the government is generally required to establish "probable cause" to obtain a valid search warrant prior to any search under the Fourth Amendment. Probable cause is established by proving to a reviewing judge that the government agents seeking the warrant have:

> 1) Knowledge of facts and circumstances;
> 2) Based on reasonably trustworthy information; and
> 3) In a quantum sufficient to warrant a reasonably prudent person to believe that a crime has been committed or property subject to seizure is present.

Exceptions to these general requirements include:

> 1) Searches incident to arrest;
> 2) Emergency situations;
> 3) Searches by consent;
> 4) International border searches; and
> 5) Seizure of items in plain view.

4) Penalties for failing to respect the Fourth Amendment rights of citizens include the exclusionary rule and monetary damages under federal or state law. Evidence that was obtained in violation of the Fourth Amendment cannot be used against a defendant. Monetary damages may be assessed against the institution and the individual for violations of well-established law.

5) In *T.L.O.* the Court held that because of the special context of public schools, the legal standard for school officials under the Fourth Amendment is reasonable suspicion. To be reasonable under the *T.L.O.* test the search must be:

1) *Justified in its inception*: The school agent had reasonable grounds to believe that a search would produce evidence of wrong doing (*i.e.*, illegal activity or a breach of school rules).

2) *Reasonably related in scope to the objectives of the search and not excessively intrusive in light of the*:

   a) Age of the student
   b) Sex of the student
   c) Nature of the infraction

6) Strip searches are generally disfavored by courts and require additional elements of proof beyond the *T.L.O.* test. In *Redding* the Court required the following test:

The *Redding* Test: A strip search of a public school student is only lawful if it satisfies the *T.L.O.* test, and there is:

   1) A reasonable suspicion of danger; and
   2) A reasonable basis for believing that the danger is hidden in an intimate area.

7) Under the "plain view" doctrine there is no reasonable expectation of privacy in objects or conduct in plain public view. Contraband or misconduct government officials can detect with the use of the common senses in public areas including through sight, hearing, smell, feeling of vibrations, etc., are outside of the protections of the Fourth Amendment.

8) There is generally no reasonable expectation of privacy in property owned and controlled by the school including school lockers and school computers.

9) When government controlled search dogs smell the air in open public areas such as school parking lots, hallways, locker areas, etc., the Fourth Amendment is unlikely to be applicable as no "search" is involved (*i.e.*, smelling the air is permissible under the "plain view" doctrine). There are, however, Fourth Amendment limits to the use of search dogs in public schools. Fourth Amendment limits may be breached if the dogs are allowed to poke and jab their noses into the students; come too closely to students; students are asked to individually submit to very close smelling of their person by dogs; students are detained for an unreasonable time; or the dog search is otherwise administered in a way that is unreasonable, frightening, or embarrassing to children under the circumstances.

10) The U.S. Supreme Court allowed a lower standard governing searches conducted by public school officials in *T.L.O.* For police officers, however, the higher standard of probable cause still generally applies, even when police are acting with school officials.

11) Searches of individuals generally require individualized suspicion and sufficient cause. Administrative searches (*e.g.*, metal detectors) are an exception to this general rule. To qualify as an administrative search, the search must be:

1) Aimed at a general danger (*e.g.*, keeping weapons out of public gathering areas); and
2) Unintrusive.

12) The contents stored in students' personal electronic devices are electronic versions of their "papers, and effects" under the Fourth Amendment. School officials may only search students' personal electronic devices if there is sufficient justification to do so under the guidelines established in *T.L.O.*

13) Public employees generally have a reasonable expectation of privacy in their office, desk, files, personal belongings, etc. They are protected from unreasonable searches by both law enforcement agents and supervisors. However, "operational realities" may reduce or remove any reasonable expectation of privacy in certain circumstances.

14) Seizure of students should only occur when doing so is necessary to protect health, safety, or order in the school. Seized students must be supervised in a safe area, treated appropriately, and only detained for the time necessary.

15) School officials must use ordinary care in protecting seized property from damage, loss, or theft, and they must provide students and/or parents with a fair process for redeeming items of value.

II. *Principles to Practice Tips*:

1) *Student Searches*: Always seek the most efficient and least intrusive means of achieving necessary discipline and safety objectives. For example, a search can often be avoided by simply asking the student to voluntarily hand over the prohibited object. Whenever possible seek cooperation; not confrontation. If searches are necessary avoid body contact whenever possible, especially any contact with private areas. An adult witness should be present. If a coat or other exterior garment (not essential clothing) must be searched, ask the student to remove the coat before searching it. Only go beyond exterior garments in an emergency (see below). If the object sought is believed to be a dangerous weapon, make sure proper security precautions are in place before anyone approaches the student, or attempt to keep the student from endangering others by calmly steering the student toward a safer area until law enforcement officials can arrive.

2) *Strip Searches*: Generally, do not engage in strip searches. Strip searches are disfavored under the law, and should be avoided whenever possible. Strip searches of children are not only humiliating to the student searched, but they present grave professional dangers to school officials as well. If an intrusive search related to serious criminal conduct is warranted but there is no immediate danger, make a police report and allow law enforcement officials to assume responsibility for any necessary search after the suspect is taken into police custody and away from school. If necessary monitor the student until police arrive to prevent disposal of evidence, etc. If an intrusive search is necessary because of an immediate danger, assure compliance with the *Redding* test and search no further than necessary. Never engage in an intrusive search for trivial items (*e.g.*, candy, small amounts of money, etc.) unrelated to serious criminal conduct. Neither judges nor community members are likely to accept strip searches of children over such

trivial matters. Remember that your actions may be reviewed not only by a court of law, but also by the court of public opinion in your community.

3) *Employee Searches*: Retrieving files and other office necessities from a common work area in the absence of the employee because they are reasonable needed at the time generally does not constitute a "search." If, however, the true purpose is seeking evidence against the employee; the employee was available to retrieve what was needed; or there is a reasonable expectation of privacy in the office area of the employee, Fourth Amendment protections should be respected.

III. *Questions for Discussion*: Please consider these questions and be prepared to discuss:

1) *Janie's Got a Gun?*: There is a rumor that Janie has a gun. There is a noticeable bulge in the area of her left breast. What do you do?

2) *How Far is too Far?*: Should public school officials ever conduct strip searches of students? If yes, how far is too far? Down to underwear; removal of underwear; a search of a body cavity? If no, what are the alternatives if students are believed to be hiding contraband in intimate areas?

3) *Employee Privacy Rights*: What privacy rights should employees have while at work? If a principal is looking for a key, should the principal be allowed to search a teacher's desk? If the teacher's purse is in the desk, can the principal look in the purse for the key? What if the principal finds contraband in this process? What factors would tend to make this a lawful search; and what factors would tend to make this an unlawful search?

4) *Open Forum*: What other related issues or current events would you like to discuss?

IV. *Suggested Activities*:

1) Review your school's search related policies including rules concerning searches of individuals; lockers; work areas; use of metal detectors; dogs; etc.

2) Review your school's seizure policies including policies and processes for emergency detention; seizure and bailment of property; and return of seized items.

Chapter 6: Due Process of Law

Due process of law is a phrase that resounds through legal history. It is an ancient intuitive principle of common sense fairness forming the necessary foundation of any just legal system. The ideal that all fair legal proceedings require notice of the charges and evidence, and an opportunity to be heard, is a basic and universal premise of justice. Principles of due process can be traced back to ancient Chinese, Egyptian, and Hebrew laws. Further, the essential elements of due process were no doubt part of an even more ancient pre-history tradition of tribal laws.

Early legal writings confirm the deep historical roots of due process. The Mesopotamian Code of Hummurabi (circa 1780 BCE), for example, was an ancient legal writing that attempted to provide fair notice of the law and establish a common legal standard for citizens. The Code of Hummurabi declared it was written "to give the protection of right to the land . . . and in righteousness bring justice to the oppressed."

In the Anglo-American legal tradition requirements of due process were codified in the Magna Carta (1215). The Magna Carta prohibited the use of government powers to punish anyone "but by lawful judgment of his peers, or by the law of the land. We will sell to no man, we will not deny or defer to any man either justice or right." Similarly, the English Petition of Rights (1628) stated "no man of what estate or condition that he be, should be put out of his lands or tenements, nor taken, nor imprisoned, nor disherited, nor put to death, without being brought to answer by due process of law."

These concepts were incorporated into U.S. law through the Fifth Amendment to the U.S. Constitution which stated: "No person shall . . . be deprived of life, liberty, or property, without due process of law." Similarly, the Fourteenth Amendment declared that no State shall "deprive any person of life, liberty, or property, without due process of law."

> ### Due Process Requires Adequate Notice, an Opportunity to be Heard, and Fundamental Fairness

In its most basic form due process requires that government agents must treat individuals fairly in actions that significantly affect their life, liberty, or property rights. They must provide adequate notice; an opportunity to be heard; and fundamental fairness. When government actions may significantly impinge on protected rights due process guards against two significant dangers: 1) Abuse of power; and 2) Erroneous decisions.

Concerning due process protections against abuse of power, history demonstrates that absent a firm requirement of due process of law, government officials acting in bad faith can too easily exercise their official powers arbitrarily and abuse governmental power to punish their personal enemies or dissenters. Concerning due process protections against erroneous decisions, even when government officials are acting in good faith, due process of law helps to guard against erroneous decisions and preventable mistakes by introducing procedural and substantive checks and balances into the process, *i.e.*, procedural (fairness in procedures) and substantive (fairness in substance) due process.

Procedural due process refers to how the proceedings are conducted, while substantive due process concerns what is done. Procedural due process requires fair and adequate processes, including adequate general notice of the law to all persons in the jurisdiction; specific notice of charges and evidence to individuals accused of breaching the law; and an opportunity to be heard in response to the charges and evidence.

Substantive due process requires that government actions must be fundamentally fair; supported by an adequate justification; and must not unjustly intrude on protected liberties. Among practices prohibited by substantive due process requirements are: Rules beyond the scope of legitimate government regulation; arbitrary or grossly disproportionate sanctions; evident conflicts of interests by adjudicators; and other government actions so inconsistent with basic fairness as to deny fundamental liberties.

Government may impinge on a protected life interest through capital punishment, and liberty through imprisonment. Impingements on life through capital punishment or liberty in the form of imprisonment are limited to criminal proceedings and do not directly involve school officials. The constitutional concept of liberty, however, extends far beyond the scope of liberty under criminal law. As the U.S. Supreme Court recognized in *Board of Regents v. Roth*, 408 U.S. 564 (1972): "In a Constitution for a free people, there can be no doubt that the meaning of 'liberty' must be broad indeed."

The Court has recognized that official civil sanctions far short of criminal punishments may significantly impinge on protected liberty interests. Civil sanctions that require due process for protected liberty interests include employment actions that suggest individual moral turpitude, dishonesty, professional incompetence, or otherwise impose a personal stigma on individuals, potentially limiting future opportunities. In *Roth* the Court stated: "Where a person's good name, reputation, honor, or integrity is at stake because of what the government is doing to him, notice and an opportunity to be heard are essential." Similarly, student disciplinary sanctions may impinge on protected liberty interests.

Protected property interests in public schools include employees' contractual rights and students' rights to a free public education. Educators' property rights to payment consistent with their state contracts are protected by the Due Process Clause. The U.S. Constitution grants no educational rights, but the Constitution's Due Process Clause protects the educational property rights granted to all age-eligible students by their state constitutions. These rights can only be denied through adequate notice and hearing under due process of law.

To provide adequate notice, all government rules must be at a minimum publicly enacted, published, and available for review. In a democracy, government officials may not enact or enforce secret rules. Further, to avoid being unconstitutional vague and therefore void, government rules must be defined clearly enough so that persons of ordinary intelligence can reasonable know what is required or prohibited.

> *The Vagueness Doctrine Requires that All Rules must be Reasonable Clear so that Persons of Ordinary Intelligence can know what is Required or Prohibited*

School officials may, for example, establish a lawful dress code for students and teachers, and they may enforce that dress code with appropriate sanctions. But everyone subject to the rules must have a fair opportunity to know the rules, and the rules must clearly define what constitutes a violation of the dress code. Rules are constitutionally inadequate if they are not publicly available or the rules are so vague that they give too much discretion in enforcement to government officials, or give too little notice to citizens concerning what is required or prohibited.

Individuals accused of violating government rules must be provided with specific information about the charges against them, and any witnesses or other evidence the government plans to use to prove its case so that the individual has a fair opportunity prepare a response to the charges and evidence. Government officials must not hide exculpatory evidence or use hidden evidence to ambush the accused. Hearings must be conducted as good faith efforts to get to the truth and fairly enforce the common rules.

A determination of how much process is due is based on balancing the magnitude of the potential loss of rights by the individual against the magnitude of the burden on the government in providing due process. The smaller the individual interest at stake, the less due process is required; the larger the interest at stake, the more due process is required.

Determining How Much Process is Due

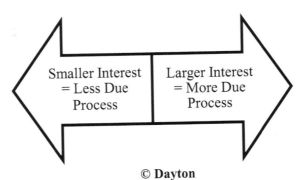

© Dayton

For example, a permanent expulsion of a student, or the dismissal of a tenured teacher, involves a significant impingement on individual property and liberty interests. Formal and comparatively extensive due process procedures are required in these situations. School officials must provide thorough written notice of the charges and evidence, and notify the individual of applicable procedural rights including the right to obtain copies of relevant documents, to call and confront witnesses, to be represented by legal counsel, etc.

In contrast a short suspension from school may only require an informal notice and hearing. For example: "Johnny, your teacher Ms. Smith reported to me that she saw you push and hit Jimmy. The student handbook says that the punishment for this violation of the code of conduct is a 3 day suspension from school. What do you have to say for yourself Johnny?" Informal due process proceedings can be quick, simple, and inexpensive. In this example, Johnny has been given notice of the evidence and witness against him, informed of the charges and the proposed consequences, and he has been given an opportunity to be heard.

Courts view some disciplinary actions as *de minimis* in nature, for example the seizing of inexpensive prohibited items such as candy, balloons, etc., or minor punishments such as an informal reprimand, a brief removal from a class, etc. These frequent disciplinary actions are so minor as to require no due process protections under the Due Process Clause. They do not sufficiently impinge on any protected life, liberty, or property rights, and requiring due process for such trivial matters would unreasonably interfere with daily classroom discipline and waste limited resources.

How Much Process is Due in Student Discipline and Removals?

> *More than 10 Days = Formal Due Process*
> *10 Days or Less = Informal Due Process*
> *De Minimis in Nature = No Due Process*

© Dayton

Due process rights have been solidly established as constitutionally required checks and balances in criminal proceedings. In criminal trials defendants must stand against the full power of the State, facing serious punishments including fines, imprisonment, or capital punishment. Disciplinary proceedings in public schools are not criminal proceedings. These are civil hearings where students have been accused of non-compliance with school rules. Nonetheless, the charges against the student may be serious events in their lives. These proceedings may impinge on protected liberty rights by harming the student's public reputation, or take away property rights by removing the student from access to educational opportunities through a suspension or expulsion. These actions could seriously limit the student's future education and employment opportunities. In *Goss v. Lopez* the Court addressed due process requirements for students in public school disciplinary proceedings.

Goss v. Lopez
419 U.S. 565 (1975)
Supreme Court of the United States

Mr. Justice WHITE delivered the opinion of the Court.

This appeal by various administrators of the Columbus, Ohio, Public School System (CPSS) challenges the judgment of a three-judge federal court, declaring that appellees--various high school students in the CPSS--were denied due process of law contrary to the command of the Fourteenth Amendment in that they were temporarily suspended from their high schools without a hearing either prior to suspension or within a reasonable time thereafter, and enjoining the administrators to remove all references to such suspensions from the students' records.

Ohio law, § 3313.64 (1972), provides for free education to all children between the ages of six and 21. Section 3313.66 of the Code empowers the principal of an Ohio public school to suspend a pupil for misconduct for up to 10 days or to expel him. In either case, he must notify the student's parents within 24 hours and state the reasons for his action. A pupil who is expelled, or his parents, may appeal the decision to the Board of Education and in connection therewith shall be permitted to be heard at the board meeting. The Board may reinstate the pupil following the hearing. No similar procedure is provided in § 3313.66 or any other provision of state law for a suspended student. Aside from a regulation tracking the statute, at the time of the imposition of the suspensions in this case the CPSS itself had not issued any written procedure applicable to suspensions. Nor, so far as the record reflects, had any of the individual high schools involved in this case. Each, however, had formally or informally described the conduct for which suspension could be imposed.

The nine named appellees, each of whom alleged that he or she had been suspended from public high school in Columbus for up to 10 days without a hearing pursuant to § 3313.66, filed an action under 42 U.S.C. § 1983 against the Columbus Board of Education and various administrators of the CPSS. The complaint sought a declaration that § 3313.66 was unconstitutional in that it permitted public school administrators to deprive plaintiffs of their rights to an education without a hearing of any kind, in violation of the procedural due process component of the Fourteenth Amendment . . .

Lopez . . . was suspended in connection with a disturbance in the lunchroom which involved some physical damage to school property. Lopez testified that at least 75 other students were suspended from his school on the same day. He also testified below that he was not a party to the destructive conduct but was instead an innocent bystander. Because no one from the school testified with regard to this incident, there is no evidence in the record indicating the official basis for concluding otherwise. Lopez never had a hearing . . .

At the outset, appellants contend that because there is no constitutional right to an education at public expense, the Due Process Clause does not protect against expulsions from the public school system. This position misconceives the nature of the issue and is refuted by prior decisions. The Fourteenth Amendment forbids the State to deprive any person of life, liberty, or property without due process of law. Protected interests in property are normally "not created by the Constitution. Rather, they are created and their dimensions are defined" by an independent source such as state statutes or rules entitling the citizen to certain benefits. *Board of Regents v. Roth*, 408 U.S. 564 (1972) . . .

Here, on the basis of state law, appellees plainly had legitimate claims of entitlement to a public education. Ohio Rev. Code Ann. §§ 3313.48 and 3313.64 direct local authorities to provide a free education to all residents between five and 21 years of age, and a compulsory-attendance law requires attendance for a school year of not less than 32 weeks. It is true that § 3313.66 of the Code permits school principals to suspend students for up to 10 days; but suspensions may not be imposed without any grounds whatsoever. All of the schools had their own rules specifying the grounds for expulsion or suspension. Having chosen to extend the right to an education to people of appellees' class generally, Ohio may not withdraw that right on grounds of misconduct absent, fundamentally fair procedures to determine whether the misconduct has occurred.

Although Ohio may not be constitutionally obligated to establish and maintain a public school system, it has nevertheless done so and has required its children to attend. Those young people do not shed their constitutional rights at the schoolhouse door. *Tinker v. Des Moines*, 393 U.S. 503 (1969). "The Fourteenth Amendment, as now applied to the States, protects the citizen against the State itself and all of its creatures--Boards of Education not excepted." *West Virginia v. Barnette*, 319 U.S. 624 (1943). The authority possessed by the State to prescribe and enforce standards of conduct in its schools, although concededly very broad, must be exercised consistently with constitutional safeguards. Among other things, the State is constrained to recognize a student's legitimate entitlement to a public education as a property interest which is protected by the Due Process Clause and which may not be taken away for misconduct without adherence to the minimum procedures required by that Clause.

The Due Process Clause also forbids arbitrary deprivations of liberty. "Where a person's good name, reputation, honor, or integrity is at stake because of what the government is doing to him," the minimal requirements of the Clause must be satisfied. *Board of Regents v. Roth*, 408 U.S. 564 (1972). School authorities here suspended appellees from school for periods of up to 10 days based on charges of misconduct. If sustained and recorded, those charges could seriously damage the students' standing with their fellow pupils and their teachers as well as

244

interfere with later opportunities for higher education and employment. It is apparent that the claimed right of the State to determine unilaterally and without process whether that misconduct has occurred immediately collides with the requirements of the Constitution . . .

Appellants proceed to argue that even if there is a right to a public education protected by the Due Process Clause generally, the Clause comes into play only when the State subjects a student to a "severe detriment or grievous loss." The loss of 10 days, it is said, is neither severe nor grievous and the Due Process Clause is therefore of no relevance. Appellants' argument is again refuted by our prior decisions; for in determining "whether due process requirements apply in the first place, we must look not to the 'weight' but to the nature of the interest at stake." *Board of Regents v. Roth*, 408 U.S. 564 (1972). Appellees were excluded from school only temporarily, it is true, but the length and consequent severity of a deprivation, while another factor to weigh in determining the appropriate form of hearing, "is not decisive of the basic right" to a hearing of some kind. The Court's view has been that as long as a property deprivation is not *de minimis*, its gravity is irrelevant to the question whether account must be taken of the Due Process Clause. A 10-day suspension from school is not *de minimis* in our view and may not be imposed in complete disregard of the Due Process Clause.

A short suspension is, of course, a far milder deprivation than expulsion. But, "education is perhaps the most important function of state and local governments," *Brown v. Board of Education*, 347 U.S. 483 (1954), and the total exclusion from the educational process for more than a trivial period, and certainly if the suspension is for 10 days, is a serious event in the life of the suspended child. Neither the property interest in educational benefits temporarily denied nor the liberty interest in reputation, which is also implicated, is so insubstantial that suspensions may constitutionally be imposed by any procedure the school chooses, no matter how arbitrary.

"Once it is determined that due process applies, the question remains what process is due." We turn to that question, fully realizing as our cases regularly do that the interpretation and application of the Due Process Clause are intensely practical matters and that "the very nature of due process negates any concept of inflexible procedures universally applicable to every imaginable situation." We are also mindful of our own admonition: "Judicial interposition in the operation of the public school system of the Nation raises problems requiring care and restraint . . . By and large, public education in our Nation is committed to the control of state and local authorities." *Epperson v. Arkansas*, 393 U.S. 97 (1968).

There are certain bench marks to guide us, however. *Mullane v. Central Hanover Trust Co.*, 339 U.S. 306 (1950), a case often invoked by later opinions, said that "many controversies have raged about the cryptic and abstract words of the Due Process Clause but there can be no doubt that at a minimum they require that deprivation of life, liberty or property by adjudication be preceded by notice and opportunity for hearing appropriate to the nature of the case." "The fundamental requisite of due process of law is the opportunity to be heard," a right that "has little reality or worth unless one is informed that the matter is pending and can choose for himself whether to . . . contest." At the very minimum, therefore, students facing suspension and the consequent interference with a protected property interest must be given some kind of notice and afforded some kind of hearing. "Parties whose rights are to be affected are entitled to be heard; and in order that they may enjoy that right they must first be notified."

It also appears from our cases that the timing and content of the notice and the nature of the hearing will depend on appropriate accommodation of the competing interests involved. The student's interest is to avoid unfair or mistaken exclusion from the educational process, with all of its unfortunate consequences. The Due Process Clause will not shield him from suspensions properly imposed, but it disserves both his interest and the interest of the State if his suspension is in fact unwarranted. The concern would be mostly academic if the disciplinary process were a totally accurate, unerring process, never mistaken and never unfair. Unfortunately, that is not the case, and no one suggests that it is. Disciplinarians, although proceeding in utmost good faith, frequently act on the reports and advice of others; and the controlling facts and the nature of the conduct under challenge are often disputed. The risk of error is not at all trivial, and it should be guarded against if that may be done without prohibitive cost or interference with the educational process.

The difficulty is that our schools are vast and complex. Some modicum of discipline and order is essential if the educational function is to be performed. Events calling for discipline are frequent occurrences and sometimes require immediate, effective action. Suspension is considered not only to be a necessary tool to maintain order but a valuable educational device. The prospect of imposing elaborate hearing requirements in every suspension case is viewed with great concern, and many school authorities may well prefer the untrammeled power to act unilaterally, unhampered by rules about notice and hearing. But it would be a strange disciplinary system in an educational institution if no communication was sought by the disciplinarian with the student in an effort to inform him of his dereliction and to let him tell his side of the story in order to make sure that an injustice is not done. "Fairness can rarely be obtained by secret, one-sided determination of facts decisive of rights . . . Secrecy is not congenial to truth-seeking and self-righteousness gives too slender an assurance of rightness. No better instrument has been devised for arriving at truth than to give a person in jeopardy of serious loss notice of the case against him and opportunity to meet it" . . .

At least in Lopez' case there may have been an immediate need to send home everyone in the lunchroom in order to preserve school order and property; and the administrative burden of providing "hearings" of any kind is considerable. However, neither factor justifies a disciplinary suspension without at any time gathering facts relating to Lopez specifically, confronting him with them, and giving him an opportunity to explain.

We do not believe that school authorities must be totally free from notice and hearing requirements if their schools are to operate with acceptable efficiency. Students facing temporary suspension have interests qualifying for protection of the Due Process Clause, and due process requires, in connection with a suspension of 10 days or less, that the student be given oral or written notice of the charges against him and, if he denies them, an explanation of the evidence the authorities have and an opportunity to present his side of the story. The Clause requires at least these rudimentary precautions against unfair or mistaken findings of misconduct and arbitrary exclusion from school.

There need be no delay between the time "notice" is given and the time of the hearing. In the great majority of cases the disciplinarian may informally discuss the alleged misconduct with the student minutes after it has occurred. We hold only that, in being given an opportunity to explain his version of the facts at this discussion, the student first be told what he is accused of doing and what the basis of the accusation is . . . Since the hearing may occur almost immediately following the misconduct, it follows that as a general rule notice and hearing should precede removal of the student from school . . . there are recurring situations in which prior notice and hearing cannot be insisted upon. Students whose presence poses a continuing danger to persons or property or an ongoing threat of disrupting the academic process may be immediately removed from school. In such cases, the necessary notice and rudimentary hearing should follow as soon as practicable . . .

In holding as we do, we do not believe that we have imposed procedures on school disciplinarians which are inappropriate in a classroom setting. Instead we have imposed requirements which are, if anything, less than a fair-minded school principal would impose upon himself in order to avoid unfair suspensions. Indeed, according to the testimony of the principal of Marion-Franklin High School, that school had an informal procedure, remarkably similar to that which we now require, applicable to suspensions generally but which was not followed in this case. Similarly, according to the most recent memorandum applicable to the entire CPSS, school principals in the CPSS are now required by local rule to provide at least as much as the constitutional minimum which we have described.

We stop short of construing the Due Process Clause to require, countrywide, that hearings in connection with short suspensions must afford the student the opportunity to secure counsel, to confront and cross-examine witnesses supporting the charge, or to call his own witnesses to verify his version of the incident. Brief disciplinary suspensions are almost countless. To impose in each such case even truncated trial-type procedures might well overwhelm administrative facilities in many places and, by diverting resources, cost more than it would save in educational effectiveness. Moreover, further formalizing the suspension process and escalating its formality and adversary nature may not only make it too costly as a regular disciplinary tool but also destroy its effectiveness as part of the teaching process.

On the other hand, requiring effective notice and informal hearing permitting the student to give his version of the events will provide a meaningful hedge against erroneous action. At least the disciplinarian will be alerted to the existence of disputes about facts and arguments about cause and effect. He may then determine himself to summon the accuser, permit cross-examination, and allow the student to present his own witnesses. In more difficult cases, he may permit counsel. In any event, his discretion will be more informed and we think the risk of error substantially reduced.

Requiring that there be at least an informal give-and-take between student and disciplinarian, preferably prior to the suspension, will add little to the fact finding function where the disciplinarian himself has witnessed the conduct forming the basis for the charge. But things are not always as they seem to be, and the student will at least have the opportunity to characterize his conduct and put it in what he deems the proper context.

We should also make it clear that we have addressed ourselves solely to the short suspension, not exceeding 10 days. Longer suspensions or expulsions for the remainder of the school term, or permanently, may require more formal procedures. Nor do we put aside the possibility that in unusual situations, although involving only a short suspension, something more than the rudimentary procedures will be required.

The District Court found each of the suspensions involved here to have occurred without a hearing, either before or after the suspension, and that each suspension was therefore invalid and the statute unconstitutional insofar as it permits such suspensions without notice or hearing. Accordingly, the judgment is:

Affirmed.

* * * * * * *

247

Comments and Questions

In *Goss* the U.S. Supreme Court held that punishments that could result in a suspension or expulsion from school (impinging on a property right to education), or significantly stigmatize the student's public reputation (impinging on a liberty interest), require due process of law prior to the imposition of these punishments. The Court stated due process requires "in connection with a suspension of 10 days or less, that the student be given oral or written notice of the charges against him, and if he denies them, an explanation of the evidence the authorities have and an opportunity to present his side of the story. The [Due Process] Clause requires at least these rudimentary precautions against unfair or mistaken findings of misconduct and arbitrary exclusion from school." In *Goss*, did the Court strike a proper balance between the rights of the student and the burdens on school officials in dealing with student discipline?

It should also be noted that although the Court generally requires notice and a hearing prior to the removal of students, in *Goss*, the Court recognized: "Students whose presence poses a continuing danger to persons or property or an ongoing threat of disrupting the academic process may be immediately removed from school. In such cases, the necessary notice and rudimentary hearing should follow as soon as practicable." Generally, this hearing can be offered at a "practicable" time such as the next regular school day or later by agreement with the student and parents. For potentially dangerous students school officials should arrange for appropriate security precautions prior to the hearing. If the student disrupts the hearing, engages in violence, etc., the hearing can be discontinued, rescheduled, and any serious misconduct in the hearing could constitute a separate punishable offense.

In summary, short-term suspensions of 10 days or less require at least informal: 1) Notice (oral or written notice of the charges and the evidence); and 2) Hearing (prior to removal, unless the student's behavior continues to be disruptive or dangerous, in which case the student may be removed pending an appropriate hearing). Also note that disciplinary removals of special education students must also comply with the provisions of the Individuals with Disabilities Education Act (IDEA), which are thoroughly addressed in Chapter 8. Summaries of other due process and discipline issues commonly arising in public schools are addressed below.

Student Expulsions

Disciplinary removals exceeding 10 consecutive days, including long-term suspensions, expulsions, or permanent expulsions, require more formal due process proceedings because the impingement on the student's right to education is greater, as is the stigma associated with these more serious punishments. In *Goss*, the Court only ruled on short-term suspensions of 10 days or less, but the Court noted: "Longer suspensions or expulsions for the remainder of the school term, or permanently, may require more formal procedures."

Although the U.S. Supreme Court has not provided direct guidance on this issue, other than to indicate that more serious punishments may require more extensive due process, concerning long-term suspensions, expulsions, and permanent expulsions (if permanent expulsions are permissible in your state), state statutes generally define in detail the specific due process requirements for your state. For removals beyond 10 consecutive days consult your state statute. State statutory provisions must be strictly followed, and failure to do so may be a per se violation of due process. Generally, however, student removals beyond 10 consecutive days require formal disciplinary notices and hearings.

Formal Disciplinary Notices and Hearings

Consistent with minimum federal constitutional standards of due process, state statutes generally require more formal notice and hearing procedures for disciplinary removals beyond 10 consecutive days, including formal written notice sent to the student and the parent. This notice must be specific enough to allow the student, parents, or other legal representatives to fairly prepare a defense to the charges. The formal notice must include a list of the charges; evidence to be introduced and witnesses to be called; information concerning the time, place, and nature of the hearing; the student's rights; the general rules of the hearing; the process for appeal; and the process must allow sufficient time and access to necessary information to adequately prepare for the hearing.

During the hearing, students and legal representatives will have the right to present evidence and witnesses on their behalf. They will also have the right to examine and contest all evidence and witnesses presented against the student. Students have the right to be represented by legal counsel if desired. But because this is a civil proceeding and not a criminal trial, students and their families are responsible for obtaining and paying for their own legal representative (under *Gideon v. Wainwright*, 372 U.S. 335 (1963), only indigent defendants in criminal cases are constitutionally guaranteed the right to legal counsel at public expense).

When possible, however, school officials should notify students and their families of the availability of free or reduced cost legal counsel, so that all students' rights are equitably protected regardless of family income. As much as possible, the hearing process should be fair and equitable to all, and the outcomes of disciplinary hearings should be a function of student conduct and not the financial status of the student's family. Many students and their families will nonetheless decline to retain legal counsel or be unable to afford an attorney in their community. As much as possible the hearing should be conducted without unnecessary legalize or technical formalities, and in a manner so that persons of ordinary intelligence can understand and meaningfully participate even if they do not have the benefit of legal counsel.

It should also be noted, however, that school officials are only required to provide students with an opportunity for a hearing. Students may choose to waive the hearing process. Many students, when presented with the charges and the evidence against them, will acknowledge fault and accept an appropriate punishment. If a student does choose to go forward with the hearing and contest the charges, the student must be provided with a fair hearing before an impartial trier of fact.

Some schools use a hearing officer for these proceedings, while others may use an impartial panel, or a tribunal. All decisions from the hearing officer or tribunal should be in writing, and should be rendered and delivered to all parties in a timely manner. The decision must be based solely on the evidence presented in the hearing. This insures that the student had an opportunity to contest all evidence supporting the charges. Further, unless the evidence is actually presented in the hearing, it cannot be entered in the record for possible appeals.

To allow for the possibility of an appeal and otherwise document the proceedings an official record of the hearing must be made. The record may consist of an audio/video recording or a typed transcript. It should be remembered that student disciplinary proceedings are generally confidential, and school officials should not disclose information about a student's disciplinary record to third parties unless this is otherwise required by law. Parties in the case, however, including the student charged, the student's parents, and legal counsel, have a right to a copy of the record.

If there is an appeal of the initial decision, the appeal will be based on a review of the record of the original hearing, and generally no new evidence or witnesses are allowed. The appeal process usually includes the possibility of appealing the hearing officer or tribunal's decision to the local school board; then to the State Board of Education; and subsequently to a state court, or a federal court if a federal issue is involved.

In-School Suspensions

A limited disciplinary in-school suspension that allows the student to experience reasonable consequences for misbehavior, while continuing educational progress, generally does not significantly impinge on a property right when used as an occasional disciplinary tool. However, extended or frequent in-school suspensions; a denial of access to the required curriculum; or a significant public stigma associated with the removal does raise greater concerns about whether these weightier in-school suspensions may impinge on protected property or liberty rights.

To guard against these concerns school officials can assure that students under in-school suspensions are provided with minimal informal due process procedures prior to the temporary removal from their regular educational placement; provided with access to required curriculum materials; and given an equal opportunity to continue their progress toward graduation. Even if informal due process procedures for in-school suspensions are not constitutionally required, judicial concerns over due process are never triggered by providing too much due process, only too little.

This informal due process can be provided quickly and inexpensively by simply explaining the charges and evidence to the student, and giving the student a moment to explain his or her conduct. Further, this process can be educational and a useful part of a behavior improvement plan. Students are more likely to improve their behavior if problem behaviors are directly addressed and the student is expected to take personal responsibility for the misconduct. Having the student respond to the charges provides an opportunity for the student to actively accept personal responsibility; to accept the consequences of their own behavior; and to agree to improve future behavior. When appropriately administered, in-school suspension can provide a useful disciplinary tool without removing the student from educational opportunities.

Corporal Punishment

In *Ingraham v. Wright*, 430 U.S. 651 (1977), the U.S. Supreme Court rejected arguments that the use of corporal punishment in public schools violated the Eight Amendment's prohibition against cruel and unusual punishment. The Court held that the use of reasonable corporal punishment in public schools generally did not violate the U.S. Constitution, and pointed to state criminal and tort laws for legal remedies in cases involving excessive punishments.

Nonetheless, the use of corporal punishment has declined dramatically since the Court's decision in *Ingraham*. Corporal punishment is now commonly prohibited in most metro-area schools. Concerns over racially disproportionate punishments and tort suits caused many local school boards to end the practice. Further, many educators, parents, and child advocates challenged both the efficacy and appropriateness of corporal punishment. Lawmakers in many states have prohibited corporal punishment state-wide by statute. Corporal punishment is still common in some of the more rural areas of the Nation, and especially in the Southern U.S. Where corporal punishment is still used, legal challenges to the use of corporal punishment continue, as do concerns about the racially disproportionate use of corporal punishment.

If corporal punishment is used, school officials should take care to assure that it is used only in full compliance with federal and state laws. Corporal punishment should never be administered in anger or as a form of retaliation. Any use of corporal punishment should be part of a fair disciplinary policy; students should know in advance what misconduct may result in corporal punishment; the punishment should be applied professionally and observed by an impartial witness; the punishment must not be excessive or unduly severe; nor should it ever be administered in a discriminatory manner.

Transfers, Disciplinary Transfers, and Alternative Schools

Generally, neither students nor teachers have a right to a specific assignment in the school system. As long as they are not deprived of any significant property or liberty rights, they may be assigned to alternative assignments any time school officials decide that an alternative assignment is in the best interests of the school or the students.

Nonetheless, it is good practice to provide basic due process including notice and an informal opportunity to express any concerns about the proposed transfer. This helps to assure that the transfer is fair and appropriate. Further, when properly handled, giving the person being reassigned a respectful opportunity to be heard concerning proposed changes may help in achieving a more amicable reassignment.

Appropriate due process is especially important, however, if the primary reason for the reassignment is disciplinary in nature rather than simply administrative. A transfer from one assignment to another for educational or work force needs does not significantly stigmatize the person being transferred. But where it is clear that the transfer is punitive in nature, the associated public stigma may require adequate notice and an opportunity to be heard.

State law may recommend or require an alternative school placement in some situations. When an alternative school assignment is being offered as an alternative to a lawful school removal, however, students and parents cannot legitimately complain about a placement they voluntarily agreed to in order to avoid a valid suspension or expulsion.

In these circumstances school officials may also require that alternative school students with recent and serious violations submit to reasonable additional discipline and safety rules. For example, an alternative school serving students suspended or expelled for carrying dangerous weapons or drugs to school may require agreement to reasonable searches for weapons and drugs as a condition of attendance in order to protect the safety of students and faculty in this higher risk context.

These conditions could not be lawfully imposed on the general population of students. However, those students choosing to attend the alternative school and having a recent history of possession of weapons or drugs are in a different legal status. There is good reason to suspect that they may carry weapons or drugs to school, because there is evidence that they recently did so. Further, they may also choose not to attend the alternative school, and parents will be responsible for private or home schooling for students still subject to compulsory school attendance. Under these circumstances, students and parents are likely to agree to reasonable conditions of attendance, and courts are likely to allow additional discipline and safety rules as a condition of attendance at the alternative school.

251

Investigations

Investigations are an important tool in promoting school safety and discipline. Investigative procedures must, however, appropriately respect privacy and due process rights. Investigations play an essential role in uncovering the truth in order to resolve school safety and discipline problems. Once a problem comes to the attention of school officials, the keys to conducting successful investigations are to start with an open mind; identify available evidence; and follow the trail of evidence to the truth through the use of logical deductions and common sense. Throughout this process the investigator must always maintain the highest fidelity to finding the truth; acting with fairness; treating all persons with respect; and acting only in full compliance with the law and professional ethics.

It should be remembered, however, that the best way to deal with safety and discipline problems is to proactively prevent them. In discouraging crime and misconduct, an ounce of prevention is worth many pounds of cure. Establishing a positive school culture is essential to both avoiding serious problems and addressing problems effectively. In contrast, a negative school culture of disrespect and personal irresponsibility is an invitation to crime and misconduct, and can make investigations unnecessarily difficult.

School officials should strive to promote a culture in which everyone understands the personal and collective importance of focusing on the educational mission, and understands that current success in school means future success in life. To accomplish this, everyone must take responsibility for maintaining a safe, positive, culture of success, and work together to discourage behaviors that interfere with a healthy school culture and everyone's future success. In a positive culture investigations can be conducted quickly and effectively, with students fully cooperating with school officials to protect their school from crime and misconduct.

Some problems, however, are inevitable. When an individual comes to school officials to report a problem involving serious misconduct, unless the situation presents an emergency, sound investigative techniques suggest that school officials should respectfully allow the person to talk; keep an open mind while listening; and resist impulses to prejudge or jump to conclusions that exceed the evidence. Avoid leading questions that only tend to confirm prejudgments (e.g., "do you think Johnny did it?"). Instead, ask open-ended questions about what the individual actually saw, heard, etc., (e.g., "What did you see? Where did this happen? When did it occur? How was it done? Who was there?"). By focusing on eye witness accounts of factual events, and not subjective personal conclusions, school officials can gather facts and not just unsubstantiated opinions. Through asking what; where; when; how; and who school officials can put together a more accurate assessment of events and gain greater clarity concerning other individuals they may need to talk with and where else they might find the necessary evidence.

In further investigating, school officials should attempt to use the least intrusive methods first, including gathering available documents and other evidence; visiting the physical site to look for further evidence or to confirm/refute claims about what allegedly happened by testing claims against the physical realities of the site; or to engage in appropriate surveillance of an area in which the conduct regularly occurs. After gathering available relevant evidence, they should thoughtfully review the evidence to determine whether further action is warranted. The concern may have proven unwarranted; further investigation may be needed; or the evidence may clearly identify a particular suspect for a disciplinary interview, search, or referral to law enforcement.

Disciplinary Interviews

Honesty and building a relationship of trust are generally the best means of getting cooperation from everyone. When presented with incriminating evidence and respectfully asked to explain, many people will simply tell the truth, especially when they believe that they will be treated fairly under the circumstances. But what do you do if a student refuses to cooperate?

In seeking the truth from someone suspected of wrong doing the use of deception by government officials is generally not unlawful. Depending on the circumstances, however, techniques involving deception may raise serious ethical concerns about whether the ends of finding the truth can be justified by these means.

For example, a school principal who has reason to suspect that a student has stolen missing property might say: "I called you here to give you a fair opportunity to tell me the truth and return the missing property. A security video shows you taking the property. Given that, don't you think it would be better for you to do the right thing now and return the property? Don't you have something you want to tell me now?" If the student did not steal the property, the student knows there cannot be a security tape of him or her stealing it. But if the student did steal the property, the student cannot be sure whether there is a video of the crime or not. If the student confesses and offers to return the property, proof of possession of the property is further evidence that the confession was valid. Do the ends of getting to the truth and possibly having the property returned justify the means here?

In a disciplinary interview a principal could also ask a leading question that assumes guilt has already been established and asks the student not to admit guilt directly, but jumps to inviting the student to justify the guilty action, thereby implicitly confessing to the charge. For example, if the principal believes the student hit another student in the back of the head, rather than asking whether the student hit the other student, the principal could ask: "What did he do that caused you to hit him?"

"Good cop/bad cop," the "Reid Technique," and other methods are commonly employed by police conducting interrogations in the U.S. But these are ethically and potentially legally problematic when used against children, because they are generally not age appropriate and may very likely induce false confessions. This is a special problem with younger children, very sensitive children, or children with disabilities who seek to please authority figures and do what they believe the adult wants even if it means giving a false confession.

As noted above, better and more acceptable techniques for dealing with children include building relationships of honesty and trust with students, so that even when they are facing potential discipline, students are more likely to be honest with school officials who they believe want the truth but will be fair in disciplining them.

If the truth is not forthcoming, however, school officials can use techniques that respect the legal rights and unique vulnerabilities of children, but also help to uncover the truth. These include separation of witnesses to cross-check statements; checking students' accounts against physical realities (*i.e.*, reality is complex; lies almost always have flaws that won't fit when tested against actual time and space limitations); the appropriate use of reliable informants; and carefully watching and assessing the demeanors and reactions of students to questioning, with follow up questions and investigations were deception is indicated by the individual being interviewed.

Questioning Faculty and other Employees

It is not only students that engage in misconduct requiring investigation and possible disciplinary action. It may sometimes be necessary for school officials to investigate allegations of employment related misconduct by faculty members or other school employees. Special care must be taken in these cases as employment disputes are among the most frequent and contentious areas of litigation. Further, while children's rights in school may not be co-equal with adults in many circumstances, adult employees hold all the legal protections available to adults.

In questioning faculty and employees, the conditions of the interview should always be such that the person being questioned is treated professionally and with appropriate respect. Angry accusations, threatening behavior, or disrespectful treatment are inappropriate in the professional setting and are generally counter-productive in questioning and investigation. Treating people with respect is not only a superior approach ethically and morally, but it is also more likely to result in cooperation and a faster, better resolution of the problem. The person being questioned should not reasonably feel harassed, intimidated, or coerced. They should feel free to remain silent or leave the room if they choose, and any confession is then a product of their free-will and they cannot legitimately claim coercion by school officials.

All questioning should be professional and focused on resolving only the school-related problem. Even though these conversations may disclose evidence of a crime or a serious personal problem, school administrators should treat the person with respect and address only the school related issues. School administrators are not police officers or counselors. The circumstances may require a report to police, or a referral to a counselor. But the administrator should observe the professional limits of being a school administrator and focus on the school-related problem, respecting the law, professional ethics, and the best interests of the school.

Evidence and Chain of Custody

In the process of investigating alleged misconduct, school officials may discover stolen property, drugs, alcohol, weapons, or other contraband and evidence of crimes. When appropriate school officials and law enforcement agents should cooperate in documenting a chain of custody from seizure through prosecution. The chain of custody documents the identity of the person found in possession of the seized property; the identity of the person seizing the evidence; and the time, place, and circumstances of the seizure.

Seized evidence should generally be bagged and tagged to preserve and identify the evidence. Seized property must be described in sufficient detail to allow positive identification in future proceedings. A record should be made of when evidence is placed in a secured location, transferred, or accessed by anyone and for what purposes. The chain of custody must be secure and well documented to assure that evidence is not stolen or tampered with, and to guard against allegations that school officials or law enforcement agents planted false evidence or otherwise tampered with evidence to make the person charged appear guilty.

For example, if a bag of suspicious pills believed to be illegal drugs is seized from a student, the school administrator documents this event and transfers the pills to a law enforcement officer along with a copy of the administrator's documentation of events related to the seizure. If a search was involved, this is also an opportunity to officially document compliance with *T.L.O.* or *Redding*. The law enforcement officer then takes custody of the evidence and transports it to the evidence clerk who documents its receipt and holds the evidence secured in a locked area. The clerk documents anyone who had access to this evidence (*e.g.*, for a lab test). And when needed, the clerk transfers custody of the evidence and all documentation to the prosecutor for use as evidence in any subsequent legal proceedings.

In general the fewer transfers and the fewer people who have access to the evidence or the secured area the better. If at any time the secure chain of custody is broken, for example, the evidence is lost or misplaced, documentation is inadequate, or security is otherwise compromised, the defendant can challenge the authenticity of the evidence and claim that the evidence presented was never in his possession; that it was planted; tampered with; or accidentally mixed up with other evidence in transfer, storage, or the lab, compromising the value of the evidence and jeopardizing any prosecution.

Conducting Hearings

Hearing officers or members of a tribunal should be clear concerning their duties in the hearing, the rules of the hearing, and the essential requirements of federal and state laws in these proceedings. These include adequate procedural and substantive due process, non-discrimination, and compliance with FERPA and other federal laws concerning student records, privacy, and confidentiality. Otherwise, these proceedings are mostly governed by state law and local policies. School officials responsible for these hearings should be certain they know and understand applicable state laws and local policies prior to conducting a hearing. When state laws or local policies mandate clear hearing procedures, it is difficult to defend against charges that school officials representing the state and the local school district failed to follow their own rules in these proceedings.

As the accusing party school officials bear the initial burden of proof and generally must prove their charges by a preponderance of the evidence. All parties are provided with an opportunity to call witnesses, cross-examine witnesses, and to present and respond to evidence. State and local rules vary as to how closely these hearings must comply with formal rules of evidence. Allowing more flexibility in the rules of evidence has the benefit of not turning a school disciplinary action into a formal trial, making it far easier for those without legal counsel to meaningfully participate in the hearing. But it should also be remembered that in the event of an appeal, state and federal judges are likely to disfavor gross breaches of the basic rules of evidence, especially when failing to follow these basic rules functionally denied a fair hearing to the student.

Generally, it is not necessary that school officials have extensive expertise in the rules of evidence. But great care should be taken to assure that the hearing process is fundamentally fair. For example, there should be no surprise evidence or unannounced ambush witnesses allowed. This drama may make television trials more spectacular, but it makes real hearings unfair and unlawful. These surprise revelations unfairly advantage one party and deny the other party a fair opportunity to prepare a response, which is of course the real purpose of the "surprise" evidence or witness, to catch the other party unprepared to respond. All evidence supporting the charges must be revealed in advance, and a list of witnesses and a summary of the issues they will testify on must be disclosed.

Irrelevant evidence or testimony should not be allowed. Evidence is irrelevant if it does not prove or disprove any unresolved issue in the proceedings, or only tends to prove that the charged student is a "bad person" generally. To determine whether evidence should be admitted the hearing officer should weigh the probative value of the evidence (the degree to which it proves or disproves an unresolved issue) against the prejudicial effect (the degree to which it simply prejudices the trier of fact or superfluously attacks the character of the accused). At all times, it should be remembered that the hearing is about whether the student actually committed the alleged violation of the code of conduct in this instance, and irrelevant prior history, personal beliefs, or the fundamental character of the accused are not on trial.

Although most student disciplinary proceedings are not rigidly bound by the legal rules of evidence, "hearsay" evidence (out-of-hearing statements offered in evidence as proof of the matter asserted, including repeating rumors, second-hand statements, etc.) may be problematic if the admission of an out-of-hearing statement denies the tribunal an opportunity to assess the demeanor and honesty of the person making the statement, or denies the accused party any meaningful opportunity to cross-examine and contest the out-of-hearing statement.

Because hearings can be emotionally charged and confrontational, it is important to have a security plan in place to assure everyone's safety. This may include the use of metal detectors at the entrance of the facility; setting up the room with appropriate physical distance and symbolic boundary markers between parties; a safe distance for hearing officers or tribunal members (close enough to hear and observe demeanor; but far enough to protect safety); and a plan of action in an emergency. Depending on the circumstances, school officials may have a School Resource Officer or other law enforcement officer present or nearby if needed.

Weapons

What constitutes a weapon? Firearms, explosives, knives, clubs, etc., that are clearly designed and carried with the intention of assault are weapons. But most of these objects also have legitimate, lawful purposes, or may be in the possession of a student who has no malicious intent or is unaware that the object is in his or her possession.

The term "weapon" often has different definitions in different code sections under federal, state, or local rules. For example, under some sections of state school disciplinary codes the term "weapon" means a "firearm" as it is defined under federal law, 18 U.S.C. § 921(3) (2011):

> The term "firearm" means (A) any weapon (including a starter gun) which will or is designed to or may readily be converted to expel a projectile by the action of an explosive; (B) the frame or receiver of any such weapon; (C) any firearm muffler or firearm silencer; or (D) any destructive device. Such term does not include an antique firearm.
> (4) The term "destructive device" means -
> (A) Any explosive, incendiary, or poison gas -
> (i) Bomb,
> (ii) Grenade,
> (iii) Rocket having a propellant charge of more than four ounces,
> (iv) Missile having an explosive or incendiary charge of more than one-quarter ounce,
> (v) Mine, or
> (vi) Device similar to any of the devices described in the preceding clauses.

This federal definition of "weapon" is relatively narrow. State definitions may be significantly broader and local definitions even broader. For example, under the above federal definition, when used in a state statute related to expulsions for bringing a "weapon" to school, only a "firearm" or a "destructive device" qualifies as a prohibited weapon under this statute. A knife, for example, is not a "weapon" within the meaning of this statute. It is very likely, however, that other state laws include a "knife" as a prohibited weapon in a school safety zone, but may for example define "knife" as having a blade of two or more inches. A knife with a blade of 1.75 inches would not be a prohibited weapon under this state statute.

Does this mean that local school officials would have to allow these shorter knives in their schools? No. Local policy could prohibit a knife with any length blade. The difference would be, for example, that only "firearms" and "destructive devices" would be violations of specific federal or state statutes incorporating the federal definition; only knives with blades of two inches or more would be felonies under the state statute; and the shorter blades may be violations of the local student code of conduct. It is important that school officials know the specific weapons statutes in their State, and be certain that when a student is found in possession of a weapon, that the proper statute or rule is cited in disciplinary proceedings. School officials are required to prove that the student violated the statute or rule cited in the notice of the charges.

Zero Tolerance Policies

Some schools have adopted "zero tolerance" policies when students are found in possession of an object deemed to be a weapon, resulting in a mandatory uniform punishment of these students, often an expulsion for a calendar year. Expulsion is appropriate when violent students willfully possess dangerous prohibited weapons at school with evident intent to intimidate or harm others. Controversy has centered on the application of zero tolerance policies to instances involving nail-files, cake-knives, and other similar objects with legitimate non-violent uses, and where credible evidence of violent intent or even knowledge of the presence of the object is lacking. Worse yet, these overbroad policies have sometimes been applied in cases where no reasonable person would have deemed the object a "weapon" including a "Tweety Bird" keychain; a pointed finger; a toy soldier; and a chicken nugget; all deemed "weapons" by a school official under zero tolerance policies.

It is likely that overbroad use of zero tolerance policies in marginal cases could create both legal and public relations problems for school officials. Regarding legal concerns, students cannot be suspended or expelled without sufficient procedural due process: Specifically, adequate notice and a fair hearing. In addition to being informed about the specific charges against the student, notice also means that students must be adequately informed in advance regarding what constitutes a prohibited "weapon." Vague definitions and overbroad interpretations of what constitutes a weapon could be declared constitutionally deficient. Students may also challenge the constitutional sufficiency of a "zero tolerance" hearing process when no real discretion is allowed and guilt and the punishment were functionally decided prior to the hearing.

To survive constitutional scrutiny, school policies must also satisfy substantive due process standards. Fundamental fairness requires that punishment should be proportional to culpability. Minor infractions should be less severely punished than more serious violations. Further, there should be a logical nexus between the harm the school seeks to avoid, and the means the school chooses to accomplish that end. If not carefully tailored towards legitimate dangers and judiciously administered, weapons policies could be applied in a manner that is both over inclusive and under inclusive in nature. There may be relatively harmless objects that are subject to punishment and legitimate dangers that fall outside the scope of the policy. Regulations as both written and applied must at a minimum be rationally related to a legitimate governmental purpose to withstand judicial scrutiny.

When students knowingly bring dangerous prohibited weapons to school with the intent to use them for malicious purposes, punishment should be swift and certain. But applying the same punishment to a child for innocently bringing a cake-knife to cut birthday cake for her classmates obviously causes reasonable persons to question the fairness and rationality of the policy. A set of nail clippers is inherently less dangerous than a loaded handgun, just as a ceremonial African artifact brought with only the intention of presentation during show-and-tell is fundamentally different than a knife brought for purposes of intimidating or harming others. In some cases zero tolerance makes zero sense. The true nature of the object and the evident intentions of the child are essential factors that should be submitted to the judgment of objective school officials who are then charged with making a just decision based on the totality of the circumstances.

Complex problems can rarely be resolved by simplistic one-size-fits-all solutions such as a "zero tolerance" policy. There is broad agreement that schools must be safe havens from violence. It is not possible for children to concentrate on learning when they feel unsafe because of threats of violence in the school. To protect everyone's safety violent individuals must be removed from the school, with or without weapons. All cases are not the same, and cannot fairly be treated the same. The strongest weapons cases are built on evidence that the person charged with the weapons violation: 1) Possessed a weapon that was clearly dangerous; 2) Had knowledge of possession of the weapon; and 3) Had malicious intent.

Gangs in Schools

Gang activities present serious discipline and safety problems in many communities and schools. Gangs are distinguished from legitimate associations by their involvement in illegal activities and violent conflicts with other gangs over turf, power, and control. While there is a constitutional right for individuals to freely associate with others, there is no right to associate for purposes of planning or engaging in crime, violence, and school disruptions. Gang activity and the display of gang symbols threaten order and safety in schools, constituting a material and substantial interference with essential school order, discipline, and safety. Further, unless schools remain neutral areas free from outside gang activities and symbols, there will likely be escalating disruptions and violent conflicts over which gang controls the school.

The display of gang symbols in schools is not protected under the First Amendment. School officials can establish dress codes and student codes of conduct to prohibit gang activities likely to cause a material and substantial interference in the school, including the display of gang symbols. Further, there is a compelling governmental interest in preventing the display of gang symbols in schools. The display of these symbols has been associated with extreme violence sometimes motivated by nothing more than seeing another student wearing a rival gang color or symbol. Younger students may imitate older students without even knowing what the symbols mean, putting these students in serious danger. Protecting the safety of children in school is a compelling governmental interest.

Although school officials do not have to tolerate gang symbols in schools, one area of caution is warranted. Gangs have sometimes adopted religious symbols as gang symbols. For example, gangs have used the Star of David or a Crucifix as a symbol associated with their gang. While these symbols may be prohibited where it can be shown that the intended meaning is as a gang symbol, for students who are wearing these symbols only as part of their sincerely held religious beliefs, there is a free exercise right for these students to wear the religious symbol. Nonetheless, with carefully crafted student codes of conduct and dress codes judiciously applied by school officials, school officials should be able to distinguish between any protected First Amendment activities and prohibited gang activities.

Police Involvement in Schools

It is in everyone's best interests to establish a positive and cooperative working relationship between school systems and law enforcement agencies. Working together appropriately, school administrators and police officers can better protect safety and order in schools and the community. School administrators and police officers both perform essential but separate functions. For this reason appropriate boundaries must be maintained between the educational institution and law enforcement agencies.

School officials should avoid unnecessary interference with police officers engaged in the conduct of their official duties. And police officers should respect the school as a sanctuary for learning administered by school officials acting *in loco parentis* and responsible for protecting the children in their care. Everyone should recognize that a school is a civil educational institution and that the school should never become a *de facto* branch of the criminal justice system.

State laws generally require school officials to notify law enforcement agents of violations of designated federal or state criminal laws occurring under the jurisdiction of the school. These generally include felony level offenses and possession of weapons or illegal drugs in the school. But ordinary student misbehavior should not be over-criminalized, misusing police tactics to address common non-dangerous student discipline issues.

It is inappropriate and likely unlawful to respond to minor non-violent student disciplinary problems with police force. Student discipline issues that do not involve criminal conduct should be handled by school officials and not law enforcement agents. Criminal acts by students, however, should not be minimized as ordinary discipline problems. An assault or other serious crime is not a minor disciplinary event.

> *School Officials are Responsible for Student Discipline;*
> *Police Officers are Responsible for Law Enforcement*

Anything that is a crime outside of the school is also a crime inside the school. Ordinary discipline problems should not be criminalized; and crimes should not be minimized. A student should not be hand-cuffed by police for talking in class. But a student who sexually assaults a student or teacher is not just misbehaving. Sexual assault is a serious crime. Consistent with federal and state laws, school officials should establish negotiated protocols with local police that safeguard students' rights and safety; minimize educational disruptions; and maintain the civil integrity of the educational setting without unnecessarily interfering with the ability of law enforcement agents to perform their official duties.

259

Off-Campus Misconduct

School officials generally have jurisdiction over conduct occurring on school property or at school related events. They do not, however, have general jurisdiction over off-campus conduct. To acquire valid jurisdiction over off-campus misconduct, school officials must establish that there is a clear logical nexus between the off-campus misconduct and a sufficient negative impact on discipline or safety in the school.

Acquiring Jurisdiction over Off-Campus Misconduct

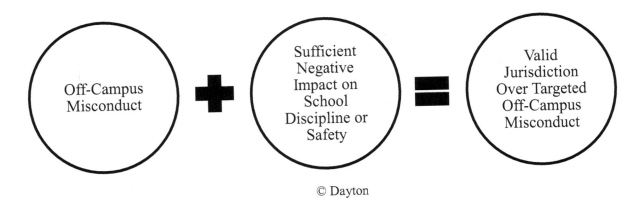

© Dayton

Serious off-campus bullying of another student, for example, may negatively impact school discipline or safety. School officials can strengthen their case for jurisdiction over off-campus misconduct by documenting evidence of on-campus harms and disruptions resulting from the off-campus misconduct. By establishing a clear logical nexus between the off-campus misconduct and legitimate school discipline or safety interests, school officials may lawfully punish students for off-campus misconduct. If school officials cannot establish the necessary logical nexus between off-campus misconduct and sufficient negative impacts on legitimate school interests, the off-campus misconduct may be more appropriately dealt with by parents or law enforcement officials.

Due Process and Grading Policies

Grades may either expand or limit future options for students. Students' grades are a critical factor, for example, in the admissions process in higher education, either opening or closing doors to future educational and employment opportunities. One of the ironies associated with grades, however, is that although there is broad agreement that grades are important and that they may dramatically affect students' futures, there is much less agreement on what grades should actually represent.

Should grades be based exclusively on academic achievement, or should other non-academic factors be weighed into the calculation of grades? If factors other than academic achievement are permissible, what other factors should be considered, and how closely must these factors be related to academic achievement? For example, should the level of participation in class discussions be a significant factor? What about the level of sincere student effort regardless of achievement? Should student grades be affected by class absences? Does it matter why the student was absent? Should discipline related issues, such as a negative attitude, disrupting class, or off-campus use of alcohol or drugs be considered in assigning grades to students?

Because good grades are the keys to future opportunities for students, it is not surprising that students and parents who believe the student has been cheated with a poor grade may file a lawsuit challenging a grade or the school grading policy. Published judicial opinions on grade challenges go back at least a century in the U.S. Historically, judges granted great deference to the decisions of educators and were reluctant to interfere with the internal operations of schools absent clear proof of abuse of discretion, discrimination, or wholly arbitrary and capricious conduct by school officials.

However, the U.S. Supreme Court's decision in *Goss v. Lopez* (1975) opened the door for students to challenge decisions by school officials that may affect their protected liberty or property rights, including decisions on grades and academic credit. In *Board of Curators of the University of Missouri v. Horowitz*, 435 U.S. 78 (1978), the U.S. Supreme Court adopted principles governing challenges to grades and guiding lower courts in ruling on these disputes, including: 1) Distinguishing between purely academic decisions and cases involving allegations of student misconduct; 2) Granting broad deference to purely academic decisions; and 3) Requiring less due process for academic decisions than would be required for disciplinary decisions. The Court noted "the significant difference between the failure of a student to meet academic standards and the violation by a student of valid rules of conduct" and that a purely academic decision "calls for far less stringent procedural requirements." The U.S. Supreme Court affirmed these principles of law again in *Regents of the University of Michigan v. Ewing*, 474 U.S. 214 (1985). In upholding an academic dismissal, that Court stated:

> When judges are asked to review the substance of a genuinely academic decision, such as this one, they should show great respect for the faculty's professional judgment. Plainly, they may not override it unless it is such a substantial departure from accepted academic norms as to demonstrate that the person or committee responsible did not actually exercise professional judgment.

Students are unlikely to prevail in challenges against purely academic decisions by school officials absent evidence that school officials abused their discretion by acting in bad faith; rendered decisions that were arbitrary and capricious; or issued decisions in violation of applicable laws and policies. Judges will not re-grade an essay or exam, as doing so is the province of educators and clearly not within the realm of judicial competence. Unless plaintiffs can provide proof of misconduct by educators, grades will stand when based solely on the academic judgment of the teacher regarding the quality of the student's work. Teachers make academic judgments; judges do not.

When grading policies factor in non-academic factors, however, such as grades based on student conduct, judges have not shown the same degree of judicial deference. Grades based on student misconduct raise the same concerns the Court addressed in *Goss*, potentially intruding on protected property and liberty interests, and therefore requiring adequate due process. Judges have no legitimate business re-grading exams. But judges must assure that the mandates of the Due Process Clause are respected by public school officials.

Plaintiffs have used a variety of legal theories in challenging grades and grading policies involving non-academic factors, including suits based on procedural due process, substantive due

261

process, breach of contract, and alleged conflicts with state statutes. In challenges based on procedural due process, plaintiffs claim the assigned grade resulted in a deprivation of a protected property or liberty interest, and that school officials failed to provide required procedural protections, such as adequate notice and a fair opportunity to be heard. In cases based on substantive due process claims, plaintiffs allege that there was too great a disparity between the offense and the grade penalty, and that the sanction was unduly harsh. Allegations based on breach of contract involve a claim by the plaintiff that the grading policy or its application was contrary to the contractual obligations of school officials. And cases based on state statutes generally claim that the grading policy exceeded school board authority under state statutes, or that the actions of school officials were in conflict with applicable state statutes.

The results of these cases have been mixed because of the significant factual differences in these disputes; the varied willingness of judges to intervene in these matters; and significant differences in states' statutes on local authority, grading, discipline, and school attendance policies. Further, there is a deep and persistent philosophical divide among both educators and judges about what grades should represent.

Some argue that grades should reflect more than just a student's performance on an examination. They argue that attendance and positive participation are important elements in the learning process. And because the education process is aimed at least in part at preparing students to be responsible citizens and employees, they argue educators may legitimately use grades to encourage positive behavior and character in students, and to discourage the use of alcohol, drugs, etc.

In contrast, others insist that grades must reflect academic achievement only. They argue that allowing non-academic factors to affect academic grades distorts the truth about students' real academic achievement. An earned "A" should be an "A" regardless of the teacher's views about the student's personal conduct or character. Advocates for purely academic grades argue that using non-academic factors results in a misrepresentation of academic achievement, falsely lowering or raising academic grades based on non-academic factors, and opens the door to arbitrariness and abuse of discretion by the teacher and school officials.

Some educators suggest a middle ground between these views. Regardless of which view is preferred, however, school officials would be wise to take potential legal challenges to their grading policies seriously, especially if they are using non-academic factors in assigning grades. Despite general judicial deference in challenges to grades and grading policies, judges do overturn grading policies and award damages in appropriate cases.

School officials can take precautionary measures to help assure that their grading policies are legally sound. Reasonable and proportional school grading policies that focus primarily on academic evaluations; respect students' due process rights; and comply with applicable laws are likely to survive challenges. Policies that drift too far from these safe harbors may not survive a legal challenge.

Individual teachers have historically been granted broad discretion in grading their students. Ultimately, however, the grade comes from the educational institution, not the individual instructor. School administrators should not change a grade secretly or for improper reasons (*e.g.*, as a personal favor, for athletic eligibility, etc.). But if a teacher has failed to follow lawful school policies in grading, or engaged in discriminatory, unprofessional, or other improper conduct in grading, school administrators may change the grade to assure institutional fair treatment of the student.

Chapter Summary

This chapter reviewed due process of law and its application in public schools. After reading this chapter, please consider the following points in review and for further thought and discussion:

I. *Review Points*:

1) Due process requires adequate notice, an opportunity to be heard, and fundamental fairness.

2) Due process is required when government actions may significantly impinge on a protected life, liberty, or property interest.

3) Protected liberty interests in public schools include persons' interests in their good name, reputation, honor, or integrity.

4) Protected property interests in public schools include students' rights to a free public education and employees' contractual rights.

5) Concerning adequate notice of rules, the vagueness doctrine requires that to avoid being unconstitutional vague and therefore void, government rules must be defined clearly enough so that persons of ordinary intelligence can reasonable know what is required or prohibited.

6) How much process is due is based on balancing the magnitude of the potential loss of rights by the individual against the magnitude of the burden on the government in providing due process.

7) More serious punishments and longer disciplinary removals require more due process:

Removals of more than 10 days = Formal due process is required (see state statute)
Removals of 10 days or less = Informal due process is required (oral or written)
Punishments that are *De minimis* in nature = No due process required (but may be given)

8) Informal due process requires basic oral or written notice of the charges, a brief summary of the evidence, and an informal opportunity to be heard.

9) Formal due process procedures are defined by state statute and must be strictly followed.

10) A limited in-school suspension generally does not significantly impinge on due process rights. However, extended or frequent in-school suspensions; a denial of access to the required curriculum; or a significant public stigma associated with the removal may require adequate due process.

11) Generally, neither students nor teachers have a right to a specific assignment in the school system. As long as they are not deprived of any significant property or liberty rights, they may

be assigned to alternative assignments any time school officials decide that an alternative assignment is in the best interests of the school or the students.

12) In *Ingraham* the Court held that the use of reasonable corporal punishment in public schools generally did not violate the U.S. Constitution, and pointed to state criminal and tort laws for legal remedies. However, many states and school districts now prohibit corporal punishment by state statute or local policy.

13) All questioning should be professional, non-coercive, and focused on resolving only the school-related problem.

14) Hearing officers or members of a tribunal should be clear concerning their duties in the hearing, the rules of the hearing, and the essential requirements of federal and state laws in these proceedings.

15) Irrelevant evidence should not be allowed. Evidence is irrelevant if it does not prove or disprove any unresolved issue in the proceedings, or only tends to prove that the accused is a "bad person" generally. To determine whether evidence should be admitted the hearing officer should weigh the probative value against the prejudicial effect.

16) To acquire valid jurisdiction over off-campus misconduct, school officials must establish that there is a clear logical nexus between the off-campus misconduct and a sufficient negative impact on discipline or safety in the school.

17) Reasonable and proportional school grading policies that focus primarily on academic evaluations; respect students' due process rights; and comply with applicable laws are likely to survive legal challenges.

II. *Principles to Practice Tips*:

1) *Uncertainty about How Much Process is Due*: When in doubt, provide more due process rather than less. Judicial concerns over due process are never triggered by providing too much due process, only too little.

2) *School Culture, Safety, and Discipline*: Establishing a positive school culture is essential to both avoiding serious problems and addressing problems effectively. The best way to deal with safety and discipline problems is to proactively prevent them. In discouraging crime and misconduct, an ounce of prevention is worth many pounds of cure.

3) *Investigations*: The keys to conducting successful investigations are to start with an open mind; identify relevant evidence; and follow the trial of evidence to the truth through the use of logical deductions and common sense. Throughout this process the investigator must always maintain the highest fidelity to finding the truth; acting with fairness; treating all persons with respect; and acting only in full compliance with the law and professional ethics.

4) *Teaching Moments and Turning Points*: When students are facing serious consequences for misconduct, this may also be a powerful teaching moment and potential turning point for the student. In Dickens' A Christmas Carol, when Ebenezer Scrooge asked the Ghost of what is yet to come: "Before I draw nearer to that stone to which you point . . . answer me one question. Are these the shadows of the things that will be, or are they shadows of things that may be, only?" In this classic story the shocking realization of the consequences of the path he was on changed Scrooge's life forever. Similarly, in the wake of an emotionally significant event, if you can help the student to understand the very real consequences of his or her current path, this teaching moment could become a turning point for the student towards a more positive future.

5) *The Suspended Sentence*: In schools even punishments should be educational. Rather than approaching school discipline as a punitive tool only, look for ways to use the discipline process to educate and encourage personal growth. One powerful tool is the suspended punishment. In appropriate cases consider a suspended punishment in exchange for clear, good faith proof of positive change and personal growth. For example, a punishment may be temporarily suspended pending sincere apologies, appropriate restitution, community service, proof of positive behavioral change, etc. If the agreed change is not forthcoming within the designated time the punishment is executed. Having the punishment hanging over one's head can, however, be a powerful incentive for positive change and personal growth.

III. *Questions for Discussion*: Please consider these questions and be prepared to discuss:

1) *Preventive Discipline*: Concerning school discipline, an ounce of prevention can be worth many pounds of cure. What are the most effective means of preventing discipline problems in schools? How can you build a positive culture of trust and cooperation with students and faculty in your school? What methods of student discipline are most effective in improving student behavior? What are the laws and local rules concerning suspensions, expulsions, and corporal punishment in your state and your school? Is corporal punishment an effective disciplinary technique?

2) *"Double Secret Probation"*: A formal letter of reprimand was placed in a teacher's personnel file by a supervisor without prior notice or any opportunity to respond. Was this a lawful procedure? Why or why not?

3) *The Hunter Becomes the Hunted*: A student athlete fell asleep in class. Based on this behavior, the teacher reduced the student's grade. This grade reduction caused the student to fail the class, making the student ineligible to participate in team competition. School policy prohibited the use of non-academic factors in grading. School officials asked the teacher to change the grade. The teacher refused. The teacher was fired for insubordination, and the student's grade was changed by school officials to reflect only his academic achievement, and not his conduct in class. With the grade changed he passed the class and was eligible to participate in team competition again. The dismissal of the teacher for insubordination was upheld by the State Board of Education. Was this a correct decision by the State Board of Education? Should the teacher have changed the grade? Do school administrators have the legal authority to change students' grades over the objections of the teachers who issued the grades?

4) *Open Forum*: What other related issues or current events would you like to discuss?

IV. *Suggested Activities*:

1) Review the laws governing formal due process proceedings for long-term suspensions and expulsions in your state.

2) Review your school's student code of conduct.

3) Volunteer to serve on a student disciplinary tribunal.

4) Shadow a school administrator to observe the daily administration of student discipline in your school.

5) Talk with a juvenile court judge about the judge's work with children and how school officials and court officials can work together to help at risk children.

Chapter 7: Equal Protection of the Laws

Fundamental fairness requires equal treatment of all persons in equal circumstances. If persons are in circumstances that are different in relevant ways, however, fundamental fairness may allow or even require differential treatment. For example, a child's race or gender is irrelevant to the child's right to educational opportunity. All children have the same legal right to educational opportunity regardless of their race or gender. There is no relevant or permissible connection between these factors and the right to educational opportunity.

A child's disability, however, may legitimately affect the scope of the child's right to educational opportunity. Children with disabilities may have special needs requiring educational opportunities and support beyond those generally available to non-disabled children. Or a student's criminal acts or a significant breach of the school code of conduct may also allow or require differential treatment, resulting in a loss of educational opportunities through lawful suspension or expulsion. Equal protection of the laws prohibits differential treatment based on factors that are legally irrelevant, and are instead the products of irrational prejudice or discrimination, but may allow or even require differential treatment when there are legally relevant differences among individuals.

> ***The Purpose of the Equal Protection Clause is to Eliminate Discriminatory Classifications by Government and Assure a Sufficient Justification for Differential Treatment of Persons***

The ideals of fundamental human equality and equal treatment are essential to just and rational governance. Irrational discrimination in governance, however, has historically been driven by ignorance, fear, and hatred. Ignorance is the foundation of fear, and fear is the fuel of hatred. When rational thought collides with such powerful negative emotions, too often irrational emotionalism prevails. For these reasons, realizing the ideals of equal protection under the laws has been a painfully protracted process.

The U.S. Declaration of Independence (1776) declared "all men are created equal" but the achievement of that ideal remains an ongoing challenge under the laws. The legacy of race-based slavery that divided the U.S. since its founding is a stark example of the vast distance that too often exists between the ideals of equality and the actual circumstances of citizens denied equal protection under the laws because of irrational discrimination.

Bitter disputes over slavery, rights of citizenship, and the balance between federal and state powers exploded in the U.S. Civil War in 1861. After the Civil War, the Fourteenth Amendment was proposed by Congress in 1866 and ratified by the states in 1868. As ratified, the Equal Protection Clause of the Fourteenth Amendment declared: "No State shall . . . deny to any person within its jurisdiction the equal protection of the laws." The Fourteenth Amendment created a legal basis for challenging unequal treatment by government officials in a court of law. To withstand equal protection scrutiny, government officials must prove that there is a sufficient link between the basis for the differential treatment by government and an appropriate governmental objective.

In interpreting the Equal Protection Clause of the Fourteenth Amendment, the U.S. Supreme Court developed a multi-tiered approach for adjudicating allegations of governmental denial of equal protection of the laws. Where differential treatment by government is established by plaintiffs, the purpose of the Court's inquiry is to determine whether the differential treatment is justified by a sufficient governmental interest. The graduated levels of scrutiny reflect the Court's determination that certain categories of government action (*i.e.*, discrimination based on race, national origin, or a fundamental right) are inherently more suspect than others (*i.e.*, general social and economic regulations), and therefore merit heightened levels of judicial scrutiny and require greater levels of proof by government officials seeking to defend the differential treatment.

Basic Framework for Judicial Review of Equal Protection Challenges

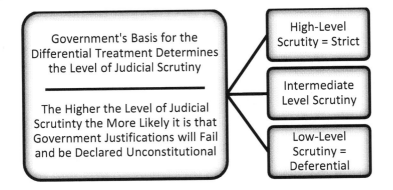

© Dayton

The Court has recognized three basic levels of judicial scrutiny based on how suspect the government's differential treatment is: Low-level; intermediate; and high-level judicial scrutiny. Concerning when low-level scrutiny is appropriate, members of the legislative and administrative braches are elected to make decisions about general social and economic issues. The judicial branch is not a general overseer of all government decisions. Courts should defer to the political branches concerning general social and economic issues, and only intervene where warranted because of irrational governmental discrimination. Therefore, differential treatments based on general social and economic regulations (*e.g.*, tax rates, zoning regulations, etc.) are only subjected to the low-level scrutiny of the rational basis test. Under the rational basis test government officials need only establish that their actions are rationally related to a legitimate governmental interest. Whether legislative and administrative decisions on general social and economic issues are unwise is for voters to decide in subsequent elections. It is only when these actions discriminate without any rational basis that judicial intervention is warranted.

Government actions that discriminate based on gender, age, or legitimacy have been considered quasi-suspect by the Court and subjected to an intermediate-level of scrutiny. Differential treatment based on these quasi-suspect criteria is deemed unconstitutional under the equal protection clause unless government officials can prove that the differential treatment was substantially related to an important government interest. More recently, however, the Court has applied a further elevated scrutiny to differential treatment based on gender, requiring that differential treatment based on gender be justified by an exceedingly persuasive justification,

Differential treatment based on fundamental rights or suspect classifications such as race and national origin, are subjected to the strictest judicial scrutiny. To qualify as a suspect classification, the Court has held that the government action must be aimed at a "discrete and insular minority" that is: 1) Politically powerless; and 2) Historically discriminated against. To be politically powerless doesn't mean the group has no political power, but instead they have no realistic opportunity to defend their rights against majoritarian power in the common legislative realm. Women, for example, have not been deemed a suspect class because adult women outnumber adult men, making it politically possible for women to defend their rights in the legislative realm or to even dominate the political process. Men are not a suspect class, however, because there is no substantial legislative history of discrimination against men. The Court treats gender discrimination as a quasi-suspect class, subject to an elevated standard of review.

Racial discrimination has been so pervasive, however, that the Court subjects any governmental use of race or ethnicity to strict scrutiny. All suspect classifications are subject to strict judicial scrutiny and must be justified by establishing that the differential treatment is necessary to a compelling governmental interest and narrowly tailored to achieving that interest. In practice, governmental actions subjected to strict judicial scrutiny rarely survive this rigorous judicial test. Justice Marshall recognized that strict scrutiny is generally "strict in theory, but fatal in fact." Until the Court's sharply divided 5-4 decision in *Grutter v. Bollinger*, 539 U.S. 306 (2003), the last time a governmental racial classification survived strict scrutiny by the Court was in *Korematsu v. U.S.*, 323 U.S. 214 (1944), the now universally condemned case in which the Court upheld forced relocations and internments of Japanese-Americans in "war relocation camps."

Summary of Judicial Standards of Review under the Equal Protection Clause

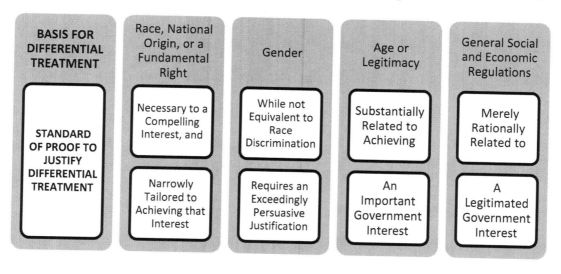

BASIS FOR DIFFERENTIAL TREATMENT	Race, National Origin, or a Fundamental Right	Gender	Age or Legitimacy	General Social and Economic Regulations
STANDARD OF PROOF TO JUSTIFY DIFFERENTIAL TREATMENT	Necessary to a Compelling Interest, and	While not Equivalent to Race Discrimination	Substantially Related to Achieving	Merely Rationally Related to
	Narrowly Tailored to Achieving that Interest	Requires an Exceedingly Persuasive Justification	An Important Government Interest	A Legitimated Government Interest

© Dayton

The core teaching of the Court's cases on equal protection is that government officials cannot legally treat individuals differently for irrelevant, discriminatory reasons, such as the person's race, color, religion, sex, national origin, disability, etc., when those factors bear no appropriate relationship to a sufficient governmental justification. Absent a legitimate and sufficient reason for differential treatment, federal, state, and local governments must treat all persons equally under the laws. The Fourteenth Amendment also grants Congress the power to enforce the Fourteenth Amendment through appropriate legislation, legislation which includes, for example, the Civil Rights Act of 1964 and subsequent legislation prohibiting discrimination based on race, color, religion, sex, national origin, and disability.

Among the first major challenges to reach the Court under the Equal Protection Clause was the case of *Plessy v. Ferguson*, in which the Court was asked to define the requirements of "equal" under the Fourteenth Amendment.

Plessy v. Ferguson
163 U.S. 537 (1896)
Supreme Court of the United States

Mr. Justice BROWN . . . delivered the opinion of the court:

This case turns upon the constitutionality of an act of the general assembly of the state of Louisiana, passed in 1890, providing for separate railway carriages for the white and colored races. The first section of the statute enacts "that all railway companies carrying passengers in their coaches in this state, shall provide equal but separate accommodations for the white, and colored races, by providing two or more passenger coaches for each passenger train, or by dividing the passenger coaches by a partition so as to secure separate accommodations: provided, that this section shall not be construed to apply to street railroads. No person or persons shall be permitted to occupy seats in coaches, other than the ones assigned to them, on account of the race they belong to."

By the second section it was enacted "that the officers of such passenger trains shall have power and are hereby required to assign each passenger to the coach or compartment used for the race to which such passenger belongs; any passenger insisting on going into a coach or compartment to which by race he does not belong, shall be liable to a fine of twenty-five dollars, or in lieu thereof to imprisonment for a period of not more than twenty days in the parish prison, and any officer of any railroad insisting on assigning a passenger to a coach or compartment other than the one set aside for the race to which said passenger belongs, shall be liable to a fine of twenty-five dollars, or in lieu thereof to imprisonment for a period of not more than twenty days in the parish prison; and should any passenger refuse to occupy the coach or compartment to which he or she is assigned by the officer of such railway, said officer shall have power to refuse to carry such passenger on his train, and for such refusal neither he nor the railway company which he represents shall be liable for damages in any of the courts of this state."

The third section provides penalties for the refusal or neglect of the officers, directors, conductors, and employees of railway companies to comply with the act, with a proviso that "nothing in this act shall be construed as applying to nurses attending children of the other race" .

. .

The information filed in the criminal district court charged, in substance, that Plessy, being a passenger between two stations within the state of Louisiana, was assigned by officers of the company to the coach used for the race to which he belonged, but he insisted upon going into a coach used by the race to which he did not belong. Neither in the information nor plea was his particular race or color averred.

The petition for the writ of prohibition averred that petitioner was seven-eighths Caucasian and one-eighth African blood; that the mixture of colored blood was not discernible in him; and

270

that he was entitled to every right, privilege, and immunity secured to citizens of the United States of the white race; and that, upon such theory, he took possession of a vacant seat in a coach where passengers of the white race were accommodated, and was ordered by the conductor to vacate said coach, and take a seat in another, assigned to persons of the colored race, and, having refused to comply with such demand, he was forcibly ejected, with the aid of a police officer, and imprisoned in the parish jail to answer a charge of having violated the above act.

The constitutionality of this act is attacked upon the ground that it conflicts both with the thirteenth amendment of the constitution, abolishing slavery, and the fourteenth amendment, which prohibits certain restrictive legislation on the part of the states.

That it does not conflict with the thirteenth amendment, which abolished slavery and involuntary servitude, except as a punishment for crime, is too clear for argument. Slavery implies involuntary servitude, a state of bondage . . . A statute which implies merely a legal distinction between the white and colored races--a distinction which is founded in the color of the two races, and which must always exist so long as white men are distinguished from the other race by color--has no tendency to destroy the legal equality of the two races, or re-establish a state of involuntary servitude. Indeed, we do not understand that the thirteenth amendment is strenuously relied upon by the plaintiff in error in this connection.

By the fourteenth amendment, all persons born or naturalized in the United States, and subject to the jurisdiction thereof, are made citizens of the United States and of the state wherein they reside; and the states are forbidden from making or enforcing any law which shall abridge the privileges or immunities of citizens of the United States, or shall deprive any person of life, liberty, or property without due process of law, or deny to any person within their jurisdiction the equal protection of the laws . . .

The object of the amendment was undoubtedly to enforce the absolute equality of the two races before the law, but, in the nature of things, it could not have been intended to abolish distinctions based upon color, or to enforce social, as distinguished from political, equality, or a commingling of the two races upon terms unsatisfactory to either. Laws permitting, and even requiring, their separation, in places where they are liable to be brought into contact, do not necessarily imply the inferiority of either race to the other, and have been generally, if not universally, recognized as within the competency of the state legislatures in the exercise of their police power. The most common instance of this is connected with the establishment of separate schools for white and colored children, which have been held to be a valid exercise of the legislative power even by courts of states where the political rights of the colored race have been longest and most earnestly enforced.

One of the earliest of these cases is that of *Roberts v. City of Boston*, in which the supreme judicial court of Massachusetts held that the general school committee of Boston had power to make provision for the instruction of colored children in separate schools established exclusively for them, and to prohibit their attendance upon the other schools. "The great principle," said Chief Justice Shaw, "advanced by the learned and eloquent advocate for the plaintiff [Mr. Charles Sumner] is that, by the constitution and laws of Massachusetts, all persons, without distinction of age or sex, birth or color, origin or condition, are equal before the law. But, when this great principle comes to be applied to the actual and various conditions of persons in society, it will not warrant the assertion that men and women are legally clothed with the same civil and political powers, and that children and adults are legally to have the same functions and be subject to the same treatment; but only that the rights of all, as they are settled and regulated by law, are equally entitled to the paternal consideration and protection of the law for their maintenance and security." It was held that the powers of the committee extended to the establishment of separate schools for children of different ages, sexes and colors, and that they might also establish special schools for poor and neglected children, who have become too old to attend the primary school, and yet have not acquired the rudiments of learning, to enable them to enter the ordinary schools. Similar laws have been enacted by congress under its general power of legislation over the District of Columbia, as well as by the legislatures of many of the states, and have been generally, if not uniformly, sustained by the courts . . .

It is claimed by the plaintiff in error that, in any mixed community, the reputation of belonging to the dominant race, in this instance the white race, is "property," in the same sense that a right of action or of inheritance is property. Conceding this to be so, for the purposes of this case, we are unable to see how this statute deprives him of, or in any way affects his right to, such property. If he be a white man, and assigned to a colored coach, he may have his action for damages against the company for being deprived of his so-called "property." Upon the other hand, if he be a colored man, and be so assigned, he has been deprived of no property, since he is not lawfully entitled to the reputation of being a white man.

In this connection, it is also suggested by the learned counsel for the plaintiff in error that the same argument that will justify the state legislature in requiring railways to provide separate accommodations for the two races will also authorize them to require separate cars to be provided for people whose hair is of a certain color, or who are aliens, or who belong to certain nationalities, or to enact laws requiring colored people to walk upon one side of the street, and white people upon the other, or requiring white men's houses to be painted white, and colored men's black, or their vehicles or business signs to be of different colors, upon the theory that one side of the street is as good as the other, or that a house or vehicle of one color is as good as one of another color. The reply to all this is that every exercise of the police power must be reasonable, and extend only to such laws as are enacted in good faith for the promotion of the public good, and not for the annoyance or oppression of a particular class . . .

So far, then, as a conflict with the fourteenth amendment is concerned, the case reduces itself to the question whether the statute of Louisiana is a reasonable regulation, and with respect to this there must necessarily be a large discretion on the part of the legislature. In determining the question of reasonableness, it is at liberty to act with reference to the established usages, customs, and traditions of the people, and with a view to the promotion of their comfort, and the preservation of the public peace and good order. Gauged by this standard, we cannot say that a law which authorizes or even requires the separation of the two races in public conveyances is unreasonable, or more obnoxious to the fourteenth amendment than the acts of congress requiring separate schools for colored children in the District of Columbia, the constitutionality of which does not seem to have been questioned, or the corresponding acts of state legislatures.

We consider the underlying fallacy of the plaintiff's argument to consist in the assumption that the enforced separation of the two races stamps the colored race with a badge of inferiority. If this be so, it is not by reason of anything found in the act, but solely because the colored race chooses to put that construction upon it. The argument necessarily assumes that if, as has been more than once the case, and is not unlikely to be so again, the colored race should become the dominant power in the state legislature, and should enact a law in precisely similar terms, it would thereby relegate the white race to an inferior position. We imagine that the white race, at least, would not acquiesce in this assumption. The argument also assumes that social prejudices may be overcome by legislation, and that equal rights cannot be secured to the negro except by an enforced commingling of the two races. We cannot accept this proposition. If the two races are to meet upon terms of social equality, it must be the result of natural affinities, a mutual appreciation of each other's merits, and a voluntary consent of individuals . . . Legislation is powerless to eradicate racial instincts, or to abolish distinctions based upon physical differences, and the attempt to do so can only result in accentuating the difficulties of the present situation. If the civil and political rights of both races be equal, one cannot be inferior to the other civilly or politically. If one race be inferior to the other socially, the constitution of the United States cannot put them upon the same plane.

It is true that the question of the proportion of colored blood necessary to constitute a colored person, as distinguished from a white person, is one upon which there is a difference of opinion in the different states; some holding that any visible admixture of black blood stamps the person as belonging to the colored race; others, that it depends upon the preponderance of blood; and still others, that the predominance of white blood must only be in the proportion of three-fourths. But these are questions to be determined under the laws of each state, and are not properly put in issue in this case. Under the allegations of his petition, it may undoubtedly become a question of importance whether, under the laws of Louisiana, the petitioner belongs to the white or colored race.

The judgment of the court below is therefore affirmed.

Mr. Justice HARLAN dissenting:

By the Louisiana statute the validity of which is here involved, all railway companies (other than street-railroad companies) carry passengers in that state are required to have separate but equal accommodations for white and colored persons . . . Thus, the state regulates the use of a public highway by citizens of the United States solely upon the basis of race. However apparent the injustice of such legislation may be, we have only to consider whether it is consistent with the constitution of the United States . . .

In respect of civil rights, common to all citizens, the constitution of the United States does not, I think, permit any public authority to know the race of those entitled to be protected in the enjoyment of such rights. Every true man has pride of race, and under appropriate circumstances, when the rights of others, his equals before the law, are not to be affected, it is his privilege to express such pride and to take such action based upon it as to him seems proper. But I deny that any legislative body or judicial tribunal may have regard to the race of citizens when the civil rights of those citizens are involved. Indeed, such legislation as that here in question is inconsistent not only with that equality of rights which pertains to citizenship, national and state, but with the personal liberty enjoyed by everyone within the United States.

The thirteenth amendment does not permit the withholding or the deprivation of any right necessarily inhering in freedom. It not only struck down the institution of slavery as previously existing in the United States, but it prevents the imposition of any burdens or disabilities that constitute badges of slavery or servitude. It decreed universal civil freedom in this country. This court has so adjudged. But, that amendment having been found inadequate to the protection of the rights of those who had been in slavery, it was followed by the fourteenth amendment, which added greatly to the dignity and glory of American citizenship, and to the security of personal liberty, by declaring that "all persons born or naturalized in the United States, and subject to the jurisdiction thereof, are citizens of the United States and of the state wherein they reside," and that "no state shall make or enforce any law which shall abridge the privileges or immunities of citizens of the United States; nor shall any state deprive any person of life, liberty or property without due process of law, nor deny to any person within its jurisdiction the equal protection of the laws." These two amendments, if enforced according to their true intent and meaning, will protect all the civil rights that pertain to freedom and citizenship. Finally, and to the end that no citizen should be denied, on account of his race, the privilege of participating in the political control of his country, it was declared by the fifteenth amendment that "the right of citizens of the United States to vote shall not be denied or abridged by the United States or by any state on account of race, color or previous condition of servitude." These notable additions to the fundamental law were welcomed by the friends of liberty throughout the world . . .

It was said in argument that the statute of Louisiana does not discriminate against either race, but prescribes a rule applicable alike to white and colored citizens. But this argument does not meet the difficulty. Everyone knows that the statute in question had its origin in the purpose, not so much to exclude white persons from railroad cars occupied by blacks, as to exclude colored people from coaches occupied by or assigned to white persons . . . If a white man and a black man choose to occupy the same public conveyance on a public highway, it is their right to do so; and no government, proceeding alone on grounds of race, can prevent it without infringing the personal liberty of each.

It is one thing for railroad carriers to furnish, or to be required by law to furnish, equal accommodations for all whom they are under a legal duty to carry. It is quite another thing for government to forbid citizens of the white and black races from traveling in the same public conveyance, and to punish officers of railroad companies for permitting persons of the two races to occupy the same passenger coach. If a state can prescribe, as a rule of civil conduct, that whites and blacks shall not travel as passengers in the same railroad coach, why may it not so regulate the use of the streets of its cities and towns as to compel white citizens to keep on one side of a street, and black citizens to keep on the other? Why may it not, upon like grounds, punish whites and blacks who ride together in street cars or in open vehicles on a public road or street? Why may it not require sheriffs to assign whites to one side of a court room, and blacks to the other? And why may it not also prohibit the commingling of the two races in the galleries of legislative halls or in public assemblages convened for the consideration of the political questions of the day? Further, if this statute of Louisiana is consistent with the personal liberty of citizens, why may not the state require the separation in railroad coaches of native and naturalized citizens of the United States, or of Protestants and Roman Catholics? The answer given at the argument to these questions was that regulations of the kind they suggest would be unreasonable, and could not, therefore, stand before the law . . .

The white race deems itself to be the dominant race in this country. And so it is, in prestige, in achievements, in education, in wealth, and in power. So, I doubt not, it will continue to be for all time, if it remains true to its great heritage, and holds fast to the principles of constitutional liberty. But in view of the constitution, in the eye of the law, there is in this country no superior, dominant, ruling class of citizens. There is no caste here. Our constitution is color-blind, and neither knows nor tolerates classes among citizens. In respect of civil rights, all citizens are equal before the law. The humblest is the peer of the most powerful. The law regards man as man, and takes no account of his surroundings or of his color when his civil rights as guaranteed by the supreme law of the land are involved. It is therefore to be regretted that this high tribunal, the final expositor of the fundamental law of the land, has reached the conclusion that it is competent for a state to regulate the enjoyment by citizens of their civil rights solely upon the basis of race.

In my opinion, the judgment this day rendered will, in time, prove to be quite as pernicious as the decision made by this tribunal in the *Dred Scott Case*. It was adjudged in that case that the descendants of Africans who were imported into this country, and sold as slaves, were not included nor intended to be included under the word "citizens" in the constitution, and could not claim any of the rights and privileges which that instrument provided for and secured to citizens of the United States; that, at the time of the adoption of the constitution, they were "considered as a subordinate and inferior class of beings, who had been subjugated by the dominant race, and, whether emancipated or not, yet remained subject to their authority, and had no rights or privileges but such as those who held the power and the government might choose to grant them."

The recent amendments of the constitution, it was supposed, had eradicated these principles from our institutions. But it seems that we have yet, in some of the states, a dominant race--a superior class of citizens--which assumes to regulate the enjoyment of civil rights, common to all citizens, upon the basis of race. The present decision, it may well be apprehended, will not only stimulate aggressions, more or less brutal and irritating, upon the admitted rights of colored citizens, but will encourage the belief that it is possible, by means of state enactments, to defeat the beneficent purposes which the people of the United States had in view when they adopted the recent amendments of the constitution, by one of which the blacks of this country were made citizens of the United States and of the states in which they respectively reside, and whose privileges and immunities, as citizens, the states are forbidden to abridge.

Sixty millions of whites are in no danger from the presence here of eight millions of blacks. The destinies of the two races, in this country, are indissolubly linked together, and the interests of both require that the common government of all shall not permit the seeds of race hate to be planted under the sanction of law. What can more certainly arouse race hate, what more certainly create and perpetuate a feeling of distrust between these races, than state enactments which, in fact, proceed on the ground that colored citizens are so inferior and degraded that they cannot be allowed to sit in public coaches occupied by white citizens? That, as all will admit, is the real meaning of such legislation as was enacted in Louisiana.

The sure guaranty of the peace and security of each race is the clear, distinct, unconditional recognition by our governments, national and state, of every right that inheres in civil freedom, and of the equality before the law of all citizens of the United States, without regard to race. State enactments regulating the enjoyment of civil rights upon the basis of race, and cunningly devised to defeat legitimate results of the war, under the pretense of recognizing equality of rights, can have no other result than to render permanent peace impossible, and to keep alive a conflict of races, the continuance of which must do harm to all concerned . . .

There is a race so different from our own that we do not permit those belonging to it to become citizens of the United States. Persons belonging to it are, with few exceptions, absolutely excluded from our country. I allude to the Chinese race. But, by the statute in question, a Chinaman can ride in the same passenger coach with white citizens of the United States, while citizens of the black race in Louisiana, many of whom, perhaps, risked their lives for the preservation of the Union, who are entitled, by law, to participate in the political control of the state and nation, who are not excluded, by law or by reason of their race, from public stations of any kind, and who have all the legal rights that belong to white citizens, are yet declared to be criminals, liable to imprisonment, if they ride in a public coach occupied by citizens of the white race. It is scarcely just to say that a colored citizen should not object to occupying a public coach assigned to his own race. He does not object, nor, perhaps, would he object to separate coaches for his race if his rights under the law were recognized. But he does object, and he ought never to cease objecting, that citizens of the white and black races can be adjudged criminals because they sit, or claim the right to sit, in the same public coach on a public highway.

The arbitrary separation of citizens, on the basis of race, while they are on a public highway, is a badge of servitude wholly inconsistent with the civil freedom and the equality before the law established by the constitution. It cannot be justified upon any legal grounds.

If evils will result from the commingling of the two races upon public highways established for the benefit of all, they will be infinitely less than those that will surely come from state legislation regulating the enjoyment of civil rights upon the basis of race. We boast of the freedom enjoyed by our people above all other peoples. But it is difficult to reconcile that boast with a state of the law which, practically, puts the brand of servitude and degradation upon a large class of our fellow citizens--our equals before the law. The thin disguise of "equal" accommodations for passengers in railroad coaches will not mislead anyone, nor atone for the wrong this day done . . . Such a system is inconsistent with the guaranty given by the constitution to each state of a republican form of government, and may be stricken down by congressional action, or by the courts in the discharge of their solemn duty to maintain the supreme law of the land, anything in the constitution or laws of any state to the contrary notwithstanding.

For the reason stated, I am constrained to withhold my assent from the opinion and judgment of the majority.

* * * * * * *

The majority opinion in *Plessy* provides a shocking look at normative racial attitudes in the post-Civil War U.S. Even the relatively more enlightened dissent by Justice Harlan casually endorses assumptions that are now recognized as patently offensive and unacceptable (*e.g.*, "The white race deems itself to be the dominant race in this country. And so it is, in prestige, in achievements, in education, in wealth, and in power. So, I doubt not, it will continue to be for all time, if it remains true to its great heritage, and holds fast to the principles of constitutional liberty"; "There is a race so different from our own that we do not permit those belonging to it to become citizens of the United States. Persons belonging to it are, with few exceptions, absolutely excluded from our country. I allude to the Chinese race").

A reading of *Plessy* illustrates the dramatic progress in racial attitudes in the U.S. between the Court's decision in *Plessy* and today. But after *Plessy* it would be over a half-century before the U.S. Supreme Court began a more aggressive effort to rectify the damage done by its endorsement of the "separate but equal" doctrine in *Plessy*. With the authority of the Court behind them in *Plessy*, segregationists used the separate but equal doctrine to justify and perpetuate racial segregation of public schools and other public accommodations in the U.S., effectively nullifying the fundamental purpose of the Equal Protection Clause: The abolition of any system of caste in the U.S. In the wake of *Plessy*, the National Association for the Advancement of Colored People (NAACP) was formed, to advance human equality through education, political action, and litigation.

The NAACP began a strategic attack on racial segregation. Initially the NAACP confronted separate accommodations on the basis that they were unequal. Given the gross disparities in public funding between black and white facilities this was an easy case to make. Accommodations for white citizens generally received significantly greater funding and were better constructed, supplied, and maintained. If a new public facility was constructed, for example, the new facility would commonly be assigned for use by white citizens only, and the old facility was designated for use by black citizens.

Leaders in the NAACP believed that the economic burden of funding two separate but genuinely equal accommodations would prove financially unsustainable for the states engaged in segregation, and racial segregation would then fall under its own burdensome weight. Racial segregation was clearly a massively inefficient policy, requiring segregated societies to fund separate and redundant facilities for black and white citizens from birth in segregated hospitals through burial in segregated graveyards. The economic drain of these discriminatory policies ultimately harmed everyone and impeded normal economic development in the region.

The list of potential targets for the NAACP was virtually endless, with everything from segregated water fountains to segregated transportation. But because black students were offered no accommodations at all for graduate level education in some states, and many law faculty and students understood and supported the legal and moral reasons segregation must be ended, segregated law schools were ideal targets. The Court ruled in favor of the NAACP plaintiffs in cases challenging unequal accommodations in graduate education, from *State of Missouri ex rel. Gaines v. Canada*, 305 U.S. 337 (1938), through *Sweatt v. Painter*, 339 U.S. 629 (1950), and *McLaurin v. Oklahoma*, 339 U.S. 637 (1950). But achieving greater equity in accommodations were limited victories that left *Plessy's* pernicious separate but equal doctrine intact.

In *Brown v. Board of Education*, the NAACP's lead attorney, Thurgood Marshall (later U.S. Supreme Court Justice Marshall), directly attacked *Plessy*, arguing that separate facilities are inherently unequal and caused severe harm to segregated children. Cases from several states with segregated schools were consolidated for review by the Court in *Brown*.

Brown v. Board of Education
347 U.S. 483 (1954)
Supreme Court of the United States

Mr. Chief Justice WARREN delivered the opinion of the Court.

These cases come to us from the States of Kansas, South Carolina, Virginia, and Delaware. They are premised on different facts and different local conditions, but a common legal question justifies their consideration together in this consolidated opinion . . . In each of the cases, minors of the Negro race, through their legal representatives, seek the aid of the courts in obtaining admission to the public schools of their community on a non-segregated basis. In each instance, they have been denied admission to schools attended by white children under laws requiring or permitting segregation according to race. This segregation was alleged to deprive the plaintiffs of the equal protection of the laws under the Fourteenth Amendment. In each of the cases other than the Delaware case, a three-judge federal district court denied relief to the plaintiffs on the so-called "separate but equal" doctrine announced by this Court in *Plessy v. Ferguson*. Under that doctrine, equality of treatment is accorded when the races are provided substantially equal facilities, even though these facilities be separate. In the Delaware case, the Supreme Court of Delaware adhered to that doctrine, but ordered that the plaintiffs be admitted to the white schools because of their superiority to the Negro schools.

The plaintiffs contend that segregated public schools are not "equal" and cannot be made "equal," and that hence they are deprived of the equal protection of the laws. Because of the obvious importance of the question presented, the Court took jurisdiction . . .

In the first cases in this Court construing the Fourteenth Amendment, decided shortly after its adoption, the Court interpreted it as proscribing all state-imposed discriminations against the Negro race. The doctrine of "separate but equal" did not make its appearance in this court until 1896 in the case of *Plessy v. Ferguson*, involving not education but transportation. American courts have since labored with the doctrine for over half a century. In this Court, there have been six cases involving the "separate but equal" doctrine in the field of public education. In *Cumming v. Board of Education*, 175 U.S. 528 (1899), and *Gong Lum v. Rice*, 275 U.S. 78 (1927), the validity of the doctrine itself was not challenged. In more recent cases, all on the graduate school level, inequality was found in that specific benefits enjoyed by white students were denied to Negro students of the same educational qualifications. *State of Missouri ex rel. Gaines v. Canada*, 305 U.S. 337 (1938); *Sipuel v. Board of Regents*, 332 U.S. 631 (1948); *Sweatt v. Painter*, 339 U.S. 629 (1950); *McLaurin v. Oklahoma*, 339 U.S. 637 (1950). In none of these cases was it necessary to re-examine the doctrine to grant relief to the Negro plaintiff. And in *Sweatt v. Painter*, the Court expressly reserved decision on the question whether *Plessy v. Ferguson* should be held inapplicable to public education.

In the instant cases, that question is directly presented. Here, unlike *Sweatt v. Painter*, there are findings below that the Negro and white schools involved have been equalized, or are being equalized, with respect to buildings, curricula, qualifications and salaries of teachers, and other "tangible" factors. Our decision, therefore, cannot turn on merely a comparison of these tangible factors in the Negro and white schools involved in each of the cases. We must look instead to the effect of segregation itself on public education.

In approaching this problem, we cannot turn the clock back to 1868 when the Amendment was adopted, or even to 1896 when *Plessy v. Ferguson* was written. We must consider public education in the light of its full development and its present place in American life throughout the Nation. Only in this way can it be determined if segregation in public schools deprives these plaintiffs of the equal protection of the laws.

Today, education is perhaps the most important function of state and local governments. Compulsory school attendance laws and the great expenditures for education both demonstrate our recognition of the importance of education to our democratic society. It is required in the performance of our most basic public responsibilities, even service in the armed forces. It is the very foundation of good citizenship. Today it is a principal instrument in awakening the child to cultural values, in preparing him for later professional training, and in helping him to adjust normally to his environment. In these days, it is doubtful that any child may reasonably be expected to succeed in life if he is denied the opportunity of an education. Such an opportunity, where the state has undertaken to provide it, is a right which must be made available to all on equal terms.

We come then to the question presented: Does segregation of children in public schools solely on the basis of race, even though the physical facilities and other "tangible" factors may be equal, deprive the children of the minority group of equal educational opportunities? We believe that it does.

In *Sweatt v. Painter*, in finding that a segregated law school for Negroes could not provide them equal educational opportunities, this Court relied in large part on "those qualities which are incapable of objective measurement but which make for greatness in a law school." In *McLaurin v. Oklahoma*, the Court, in requiring that a Negro admitted to a white graduate school be treated like all other students, again resorted to intangible considerations: "his ability to study, to engage in discussions and exchange views with other students, and, in general, to learn his profession." Such considerations apply with added force to children in grade and high schools. To separate them from others of similar age and qualifications solely because of their race generates a feeling of inferiority as to their status in the community that may affect their hearts and minds in a way unlikely ever to be undone. The effect of this separation on their educational opportunities was well stated by a finding in the Kansas case by a court which nevertheless felt compelled to rule against the Negro plaintiffs:

> Segregation of white and colored children in public schools has a detrimental effect upon the colored children. The impact is greater when it has the sanction of the law; for the policy of separating the races is usually interpreted as denoting the inferiority of the Negro group. A sense of inferiority affects the motivation of a child to learn. Segregation with the sanction of law, therefore, has a tendency to retard the educational and mental development of Negro children and to deprive them of some of the benefits they would receive in a racially integrated school system.

Whatever may have been the extent of psychological knowledge at the time of *Plessy v. Ferguson*, this finding is amply supported by modern authority. Any language in *Plessy v. Ferguson* contrary to this finding is rejected.

We conclude that in the field of public education the doctrine of "separate but equal" has no place. Separate educational facilities are inherently unequal. Therefore, we hold that the plaintiffs and others similarly situated for whom the actions have been brought are, by reason of the segregation complained of, deprived of the equal protection of the laws guaranteed by the Fourteenth Amendment. This disposition makes unnecessary any discussion whether such segregation also violates the Due Process Clause of the Fourteenth Amendment.

Because these are class actions, because of the wide applicability of this decision, and because of the great variety of local conditions, the formulation of decrees in these cases presents problems of considerable complexity. On reargument, the consideration of appropriate relief was necessarily subordinated to the primary question--the constitutionality of segregation in public education. We have now announced that such segregation is a denial of the equal protection of the laws . . .

It is so ordered.

* * * * * * *

Comments and Questions

Brown was a unanimous opinion by the Court. But while members of the Court were in the early stages of forming their opinions on the *Brown* cases, the constitutionality of the separate but equal doctrine, and whether *Plessy* should be affirmed or reversed, a law clerk for U.S. Supreme Court Justice Jackson wrote the following memo:

A Random Thought on the Segregation Cases

One-hundred fifty years ago this Court held that it was the ultimate judge of the restrictions which the Constitution imposed on the various branches of the national and state goverment. Marbury v. Madison. This was presumably on the basis that there are standards to be applied other than the personal predilections of the Justices.

As applied to questions of inter-state or state-federal relations, as well as to inter-departmental disputes within the federal goverment, this doctrine of judicial review has worked well. Where theoretically co-ordinate bodies of goverment are disputing, the Court is well suited to its role as arbiter. This is because these problems involve much less emotionally charged subject matter than do those discussed below. In effect, they determine the skeletal relations of the goverments to each other without influencing the substantive business of those goverments.

As applied to relations between the individual and the state, the system has worked much less well. The Constitution, of course, deals with individual rights, particularly in the first Ten and the fourteenth Amendments. But as I read the history of this Court, it has seldom been out of hot water when attempting to interpret these individual rights. Fletcher v. Peck, in 1810, represented an attempt by Chief Justice Marshall to extend the protection of the contract clause to infant business. Scott v. Sanford was the result of Taney's effort to protect slaveholders from legislative interference.

After the Civil War, business interest came to dominate the court, and they in turn ventured into the deep water of protecting certain types of individuals against legislative interference . . . Holmes replied that the fourteenth Amendment did not enact Herbert Spencer's Social Statics . . . But eventually the Court called a halt to this reading of its own economic views into the Constitution. Apparently it recognized that where a legislature was dealing with its own citizens, it was not part of the judicial function to thwart public opinion except in extreme cases. In these cases now before the Court, the Court is, as Davis suggested, being asked to read its own sociological views into the Constitution. Urging a view palpably at variance with precedent and probably with legislative history, appellants seek to convince the Court of the moral wrongness of the treatment they are receiving. I would suggest that this is a question the Court need never reach; for regardless of the Justice's individual views on the merits of segregation, it quite clearly is not one of those extreme cases which commands intervention from one of any conviction. If this Court, because its members individually are "liberal" and dislike segregation, now chooses to strike it down, it differs from the McReynolds court only in the kinds of litigants it favors and the kinds of special claims it protects. To those who would argue that "personal" rights are more sacrosanct than "property" rights, the short answer is that the Constitution makes no such distinction. To the argument made by Thurgood Marshall that a majority may not deprive a minority of its constitutional right, the answer must be made that while this is sound in theory, in the long run it is the majority who will determine what the constitutional rights of the minority are. One hundred and fifty years of attempts on the part of this Court to protect minority rights of any kind--whether those of business, slaveholders, or Jehovah's Witnesses--have been sloughed off, and crept silently to rest. If the present Court is unable to profit by this example it must be prepared to see its work fade in time, too, as embodying only the sentiments of a transient majority of nine men. I realize that it is an unpopular and unhumanitarian position, for which I have been excoriated by "liberal" colleagues, but I think <u>Plessy v. Ferguson</u> was right and should be re-affirmed. If the fourteenth Amendment did not enact Spencer's Social Statics, it just as surely did not enact Myrdal's American Dilemmna.

WHR

The "WHR" who wrote this memo was William Hubbs Rehnquist. When he wrote this memo Mr. Rehnquist was serving as a law clerk for Justice Jackson at the U.S. Supreme Court. Mr. Rehnquist later became Chief Justice of the U.S. Supreme Court. Rehnquist was questioned about this memo in his confirmation hearings before the U.S. Senate many years after it was written. By this time *Plessy* and the doctrine of separate but equal had been soundly rejected by a unanimous Court, Congress had enacted the Civil Rights Act of 1964, and the tide of public opinion had turned strongly against segregation. *Plessy*'s "separate but equal doctrine" and segregation by law had become a shameful memory and an embarrassing political albatross around the necks of former segregationists. Nonetheless, Mr. Rehnquist's memo clearly declared "I think <u>Plessy v. Ferguson</u> was right and should be re-affirmed."

In hearings before the U.S. Senate Mr. Rehnquist claimed that the opinions expressed in his memo were not his personal opinions, but instead reflected Justice Jackson's views. Justice Jackson died in October 1954 and was not around to confirm or refute Rehnquist's claims. Only Mr. Rehnquist knew the truth about whether these were his views about equal protection of the laws, segregation, and civil rights, or Justice Jackson's. What we do know is that Justice Jackson voted with the majority in *Brown*. And although very ill, Justice Jackson traveled from his hospital bed to the Court so he could be there the day the *Brown* decision was delivered.

After reviewing the "WHR" memo, if you were a member of the U.S. Senate voting on the nomination of William Hubbs Rehnquist to be Chief Justice of the U.S. Supreme Court, would you find Rehnquist's assertion that this memo represented Justice Jackson's views and not his own credible? Does this sentence written by WHR sound like Justice Jackson's view or the view of the author WHR?: "I realize that it is an unpopular and unhumanitarian position, for which I have been excoriated by 'liberal' colleagues, but I think <u>Plessy v. Ferguson</u> was right and should be re-affirmed."

The memo also raises important questions about the proper role of government, the Constitution, the Bill of Rights, the Fourteenth Amendment, and the role of the Court. Are Court opinions truly driven by legal principles or by the personal opinions of the Justices? Should the will of the political majority always prevail, or should the Court intervene to protect minority rights? Are personal rights (including the right to human equality) no different than property rights (which governments commonly regulate and limit) under the law? What role does the federal government have in protecting and promoting civil rights? What role should the Court play?

Rehnquist pointed out two clashing social views, those articulated in Herbert Spencer's Social Statics (1851), and Gunnar Myrdal's An American Dilemma: The Negro Problem and Modern Democracy (1944). In Social Statics and subsequent works, Spencer, a British economist, articulated principles of Social Darwinism, survival of the fittest, and Lamarckian molding of individuals through social conditions. Myrdal, the author of An American Dilemma, was a Swedish economist, who saw the "American Creed" (ideals of liberty, justice, and equality) as the essential common bond that kept together the great diversity of America, and allowed persons of all races, religions, and backgrounds to live and work together towards mutual progress. Myrdal saw government enforced segregation as a grave threat to the authenticity and survival of the American Creed. In his view, segregation was antithetical to the American Creed, denying liberty, justice, and equality on the basis of race. Segregation was the circular tool of racial oppression: Legally enforced segregation so limited opportunities for black citizens that it virtually assured inferior achievement, and then the resulting evidence of inferior achievement was used to justify continued segregation. The remedies were changes in social attitudes and improvements in the conditions of black citizens. Education was the essential key to both, making Brown a turning point in American history.

Over a half century after the Court's decision in Brown, what is the real legacy of Brown, positive and negative? What is the future of race relations in the U.S. as the U.S. transitions from a 1950s, Brown-era, largely black/white social structure in much of the Nation, to an infinitely more racially diverse, and ethnically and socially complex Nation? What groups will be fighting the struggles for greater equality in the future? Do courts still have a role in this process, or is the era of Brown-type judicial intervention over, and legal struggles replaced by social and economic struggles?

Summary of Desegregation Litigation

The Supreme Court's direct involvement in public school desegregation began in Brown v. Board of Education, 347 U.S. 483 (1954) (Brown I). In Brown I the Court overturned the separate but equal doctrine, but postponed consideration of the appropriate remedies for racially segregated public schools. One year later in Brown v. Board of Education, 349 U.S. 294 (1955) (Brown II), the Court ordered racially segregated schools to "make a prompt and reasonable start toward full compliance" with the Court's decision in Brown I, and to pursue desegregation of public schools with "all deliberate speed."

It soon became apparent, however, that public school desegregation would be a protracted process. In many heavily segregated areas opposition to public school desegregation was massive and intense. In the wake of the Court's 1954 decision in Brown, the Court addressed only a small number of the many cases of non-compliance with its desegregation mandate.

In the late 1960's, however, the Court became more assertive holding that schools must do more than merely refrain from additional constitutional violations. In Green v. County School Board, 391 U.S. 430 (1968), the Court held that segregated schools had an affirmative duty to move toward racially unitary schools and to eliminate the vestiges of past racial discrimination "root and branch." To define school officials' desegregation duties more specifically the Court in Green identified six factors: 1) Student assignments; 2) Faculty; 3) Staff; 4) Transportation; 5) Extracurricular activities; and 6) Facilities, (i.e., "the Green factors") as among the important factors courts must review to distinguish between racially unitary and racially segregated schools.

In the 1970's the Court addressed racial segregation in states without official segregation statutes. The Court distinguished between de jure segregation resulting from government actions (i.e., statutes mandating state-wide racial segregation or other government regulations, policies, or practices that intentionally caused racial segregation,) and *de facto* segregation resulting from private choices (*i.e.*, private family choices of residence or private sector economic factors). The Court held that since only *de jure* segregation involved intentional government action to segregate, and the Constitution only limits government action and not private choices within the private sphere, therefore only *de jure* segregation was constitutionally actionable. While *de facto* segregation was socially regrettably, it was not unconstitutional.

Milliken v. Bradley, 418 U.S. 717 (1974), involving Detroit area schools may have marked the beginning of the end of the Supreme Court's support for expansions of desegregation remedies. In *Milliken*, the Court overturned an inter-district remedy for segregation because of the failure of the plaintiffs to establish that intentional acts of the state, or *de jure* segregation, were a substantial cause of the inter-district segregation. The Court became increasingly hesitant to approve expansive remedies, and Court action on desegregation decreased substantially during the 1980's.

Desegregation regained prominence on the Court's docket in the 1990's in *Board of Education v. Dowell*, 498 U.S. 237 (1991). But now the focus turned to ending rather than advancing federal judicial involvement in desegregation. In *Dowell*, the Court signaled an end to aggressive federal involvement in school desegregation efforts, declaring: "From the very first, federal supervision of local school systems was intended as a temporary measure to remedy past discrimination." Following the Court's lead, as the proximity in time between *Brown*-era *de jure* segregation and current conditions in schools expanded, courts became increasing likely to find that racial segregation was *de facto* only, and not caused by lingering vestiges of legally actionable *de jure* segregation.

In *Dowell*, the Court addressed the proper standards for declaring a formerly segregated school system unitary and ending federal judicial supervision. A federal district court had declared the Oklahoma City school system unitary in 1977. In 1985, plaintiffs attempted to reopen the case based on alleged racial re-segregation in the school system. In response, the Oklahoma City Board of Education sought an end to federal judicial oversight of the district's schools. The district court ruled in favor of the school, finding that present residential segregation resulted from private choices and economic conditions, and that any alleged linkage to former segregation was too remote to justify a new constitutional remedy. The district court concluded that the 1977 declaration of unitary status was *res judicata* (*i.e.*, "a thing decided") and the school system remained unitary. A decision is deemed *res judicata* when a court with proper jurisdiction has issued a clear and final ruling on that issue. And thereafter that issue, because it has already been decided, cannot be re-litigated in that case.

However, the Supreme Court in *Dowell* ruled that the 1977 declaration of unitary status by the district court was too ambiguous at the time to be declared *res judicata*. The Court held that plaintiffs were entitled to an unambiguous statement by the district court before a declaration of unitary status could bar all future action on that issue. Regarding continued supervision by federal courts, the Court stated that federal supervision of local schools was never intended to operate in perpetuity. Ultimately, control must be returned to local school districts.

To achieve unitary status and end federal judicial supervision the Court held that the school district need only establish that it had been "operating in compliance with the commands of the Equal Protection Clause of the Fourteenth Amendment, and that it was unlikely that the school board would return to its former ways." Such a showing would demonstrate "that the purposes of the desegregation litigation had been fully achieved."

School officials could meet this burden of proof by demonstrating good faith compliance with the district court's order, and presenting evidence that vestiges of former segregation had been eliminated "to the extent practicable." In considering whether vestiges of segregation have been eliminated to the extent practicable, the Court explained that district courts should consider the *Green* factors to determine whether unitary status had been achieved. The Court did not clarify, however, whether the indicia of unitary status identified in *Green* may be satisfied incrementally, or whether these factors must all be satisfied concurrently, before a school district may be finally released from judicial supervision. The Court addressed this issue in *Freeman v. Pitts*, 503 U.S. 467 (1992).

In *Freeman* the Court held that school districts may be released from federal judicial supervision incrementally on each separate *Green* factor. Any subsequent re-segregation not proximately traceable to constitutional violations (*de jure*) and instead resulting from private choices (*de facto*) was not legally actionable under the Equal Protection Clause. The Court's decision in *Freeman* made it much easier for school districts to be released from judicial supervision.

The Court also approved a discretionary expansion of the *Green* factors in *Freeman*. According to the Court, the *Green* factors need not be a rigid framework and could include discretionary factors such as the quality of education. Presumably, if district courts included discretionary factors in addition to the *Green* factors, however, it became more difficult for school districts to establish full compliance with desegregation mandates.

Finally, the Court set out a mandatory checklist that district courts must follow prior to partial withdrawal, but kept the district court's decision to allow partial withdrawal discretionary even where a school system is in compliance with some but not all areas of the desegregation mandate. To exercise discretionary withdrawal the court must consider: 1) Whether there is full and satisfactory compliance in the area to be withdrawn; 2) The possibility of interconnectedness between the withdrawn area and areas not yet in compliance; and 3) Good faith commitment to the whole of the court's decree and the constitutional mandate.

Overall, the Court's decision in *Freeman* was a significant loss for public school desegregation advocates. The Court's decision was followed by a flood of school districts being declared unitary and no longer subject to federal judicial supervision or mandatory desegregation efforts. Further, after a school district was declared unitary, even voluntary desegregation efforts became constitutionally suspect if race remained a factor in official decisions. School districts under desegregation orders may have been required to consider race in student assignments, faculty assignments, etc., in order to remedy prior constitutional violations. But after school districts were no longer under desegregation orders, continued use of race in official decision making was likely unconstitutional.

As a remedy for *de jure* discrimination, government officials had been required to use race in structuring constitutional remedies. As courts increasingly found that racial disparities were the product of *de facto* and not *de jure* causes, however, the use of race by government officials became subject to strict judicial scrutiny.

Among the most contentious areas of equal protection litigation continues to be governmental use of race in employment, contracting, and school admissions and assignments. In *Adarand v. Pena*, 515 U.S. 200 (1995), the U.S. Supreme Court addressed whether the Equal Protection Clause prohibited race-based preferences in government contracting. Justice O'Connor's majority opinion in *Adarand* clarified several legal principles concerning equal protection of the laws and the judicial application of strict scrutiny. The Court declared that "any person, of whatever race, has the right to demand that any governmental actor subject to the Constitution justify any racial classification subjecting that person to unequal treatment under the strictest judicial scrutiny." The Court stated: "More than good motives should be required when government seeks to allocate its resources by way of an explicit racial classification system." The Court further noted:

> The Fifth and Fourteenth Amendments to the Constitution protect persons, not groups. It follows from that principle that all government action based on race--a group classification long recognized as "in most circumstances irrelevant and therefore prohibited" should be subjected to detailed judicial inquiry to ensure that the personal right to equal protection of the laws has not been infringed . . . "A free people whose institutions are founded upon the doctrine of equality" should tolerate no retreat from the principle that government may treat people differently because of their race only for the most compelling reasons. Accordingly, we hold today that all racial classifications, imposed by whatever federal, state, or local government actor, must be analyzed by a reviewing court under strict scrutiny. In other words, such classifications are constitutional only if they are narrowly tailored measures that further compelling governmental interests.

The Court rejected the argument that racial classifications intended to benefit historically disadvantaged racial groups are "benign" and should be reviewed under more lenient judicial scrutiny. According to the Court, "benign" racial classifications rest on an assumption "that those who are granted this special preference are less qualified in some respect that is identified purely by their race. Because that perception . . . can only exacerbate rather than reduce racial prejudice, it will delay the time when race will become a truly irrelevant, or at least insignificant, factor."

Although the Court struck down the government's use of racial preferences in *Adarand*, the Court did not declare that government decisions involving race could never meet constitutional standards. Instead, Justice O'Connor's majority opinion concluded:

> Finally, we wish to dispel the notion that strict scrutiny is "strict in theory, but fatal in fact." The unhappy persistence of both the practice and the lingering effects of racial discrimination against minority groups in this country is an unfortunate reality, and government is not disqualified from acting in response to it . . . When race-based action is necessary to further a compelling interest, such action is within constitutional constraints if it satisfies the "narrow tailoring" test this Court has set out in previous cases.

In *Adarand* the Court did not address what types of governmental interests could be sufficiently compelling to justify the use of race-based decisions by government. Could an educational interest in promoting student diversity qualify as a compelling governmental interest? In *Gratz v. Bollinger*, 539 U.S. 244 (2003), and *Grutter v. Bollinger*, 539 U.S. 306 (2003), rejected white applicants challenged race-based admissions criteria justified by the University of Michigan as necessary to a compelling governmental interest. *Gratz* involved an undergraduate admissions formula that gave significant weight to race. Under the system, 100 points total would guarantee admission, and any student identified as a member of an underrepresented racial minority was automatically awarded 20 points. The Court found that this use of race had the effect of making race a decisive factor in admissions, and declared this system unconstitutional in a 6-3 opinion. The Court stated:

> This example demonstrates the problematic nature of the . . . admissions system. Even if [a student's] "extraordinary artistic talent" rivaled that of Monet or Picasso, the applicant would receive, at most, five points under the [admissions] system. At the same time, every single underrepresented minority applicant . . . would automatically receive 20 points for submitting an application.

In the *Grutter* case, however, in a 5-4 decision, the Court upheld the University of Michigan Law School's voluntary race-conscious admissions plan. The plan considered race as only one of many factors, defined the school's interest in diversity broader than only race, and assured a holistic review of individual applicants without race becoming the decisive factor in admissions. In *Grutter* the Court recognized that student diversity may be "a compelling state interest that can justify the use of race in University admissions" but only the Law School's admissions plan was sufficiently narrowly tailored to survive strict scrutiny. Both of these cases, however, resulted in heavily fractured opinions from the Justices, leaving considerable uncertainty about whether and under what circumstances educational institutions could use voluntary race-conscious admissions or school assignment plans. Would the Court allow public schools to use race-conscious policies in student assignments to promote diversity in their schools?

Parents Involved in Community Schools v. Seattle School District No. 1
551 U.S. 701 (2007)
Supreme Court of the United States

Chief Justice ROBERTS announced the judgment of the Court:

The school districts in these cases voluntarily adopted student assignment plans that rely upon race to determine which public schools certain children may attend. The Seattle school district classifies children as white or nonwhite; the Jefferson County school district as black or "other." In Seattle, this racial classification is used to allocate slots in oversubscribed high schools. In Jefferson County, it is used to make certain elementary school assignments and to rule on transfer requests. In each case, the school district relies upon an individual student's race in assigning that student to a particular school, so that the racial balance at the school falls within a predetermined range based on the racial composition of the school district as a whole. Parents of students denied assignment to particular schools under these plans solely because of their race brought suit, contending that allocating children to different public schools on the basis of race violated the Fourteenth Amendment guarantee of equal protection. The Courts of Appeals below upheld the plans. We granted certiorari, and now reverse.

Both cases present the same underlying legal question--whether a public school that had not operated legally segregated schools or has been found to be unitary may choose to classify students by race and rely upon that classification in making school assignments . . .

It is well established that when the government distributes burdens or benefits on the basis of individual racial classifications, that action is reviewed under strict scrutiny. As the Court recently reaffirmed, "racial classifications are simply too pernicious to permit any but the most exact connection between justification and classification." *Gratz v. Bollinger*, 539 U.S. 244

(2003). In order to satisfy this searching standard of review, the school districts must demonstrate that the use of individual racial classifications in the assignment plans here under review is "narrowly tailored" to achieve a "compelling" government interest. *Adarand v. Pena*, 515 U.S. 200 (1995).

Without attempting in these cases to set forth all the interests a school district might assert, it suffices to note that our prior cases, in evaluating the use of racial classifications in the school context, have recognized two interests that qualify as compelling. The first is the compelling interest of remedying the effects of past intentional discrimination. *See, Freeman v. Pitts*, 503 U.S. 467 (1992). Yet the Seattle public schools have not shown that they were ever segregated by law, and were not subject to court-ordered desegregation decrees. The Jefferson County public schools were previously segregated by law and were subject to a desegregation decree entered in 1975. In 2000, the District Court that entered that decree dissolved it, finding that Jefferson County had "eliminated the vestiges associated with the former policy of segregation and its pernicious effects," and thus had achieved "unitary" status. Jefferson County accordingly does not rely upon an interest in remedying the effects of past intentional discrimination in defending its present use of race in assigning students.

Nor could it. We have emphasized that the harm being remedied by mandatory desegregation plans is the harm that is traceable to segregation, and that "the Constitution is not violated by racial imbalance in the schools, without more." *Milliken v. Bradley*, 433 U.S. 267 (1977). Once Jefferson County achieved unitary status, it had remedied the constitutional wrong that allowed race-based assignments. Any continued use of race must be justified on some other basis.

The second government interest we have recognized as compelling for purposes of strict scrutiny is the interest in diversity in higher education upheld in *Grutter*. The specific interest found compelling in *Grutter* was student body diversity "in the context of higher education." The diversity interest was not focused on race alone but encompassed "all factors that may contribute to student body diversity." We described the various types of diversity that the law school sought: "[The law school's] policy makes clear there are many possible bases for diversity admissions, and provides examples of admittees who have lived or traveled widely abroad, are fluent in several languages, have overcome personal adversity and family hardship, have exceptional records of extensive community service, and have had successful careers in other fields."

The Court quoted the articulation of diversity from Justice Powell's opinion in *Regents of the University of California v. Bakke*, 438 U.S. 265 (1978), noting that "it is not an interest in simple ethnic diversity, in which a specified percentage of the student body is in effect guaranteed to be members of selected ethnic groups, that can justify the use of race." Instead, what was upheld in *Grutter* was consideration of "a far broader array of qualifications and characteristics of which racial or ethnic origin is but a single though important element."

The entire gist of the analysis in *Grutter* was that the admissions program at issue there focused on each applicant as an individual, and not simply as a member of a particular racial group. The classification of applicants by race upheld in *Grutter* was only as part of a "highly individualized, holistic review." As the Court explained, "the importance of this individualized consideration in the context of a race-conscious admissions program is paramount." The point of the narrow tailoring analysis in which the *Grutter* Court engaged was to ensure that the use of racial classifications was indeed part of a broader assessment of diversity, and not simply an effort to achieve racial balance, which the Court explained would be "patently unconstitutional."

287

In the present cases, by contrast, race is not considered as part of a broader effort to achieve "exposure to widely diverse people, cultures, ideas, and viewpoints," race, for some students, is determinative standing alone. The districts argue that other factors, such as student preferences, affect assignment decisions under their plans, but under each plan when race comes into play, it is decisive by itself. It is not simply one factor weighed with others in reaching a decision, as in *Grutter*; it is *the* factor. Like the University of Michigan undergraduate plan struck down in *Gratz*, 539 U.S. 244 (2003), the plans here "do not provide for a meaningful individualized review of applicants" but instead rely on racial classifications in a "non-individualized, mechanical" way.

Even when it comes to race, the plans here employ only a limited notion of diversity, viewing race exclusively in white/nonwhite terms in Seattle and black/"other" terms in Jefferson County. *But see, Metro Broadcasting v. FCC*, 497 U.S. 547 (1990) (O'Connor, J., dissenting) ("We are a Nation not of black and white alone, but one teeming with divergent communities knitted together by various traditions and carried forth, above all, by individuals"). The Seattle "Board Statement Reaffirming Diversity Rationale" speaks of the "inherent educational value" in "providing students the opportunity to attend schools with diverse student enrollment." But under the Seattle plan, a school with 50 percent Asian-American students and 50 percent white students but no African-American, Native-American, or Latino students would qualify as balanced, while a school with 30 percent Asian-American, 25 percent African-American, 25 percent Latino, and 20 percent white students would not. It is hard to understand how a plan that could allow these results can be viewed as being concerned with achieving enrollment that is "broadly diverse."

Prior to *Grutter*, the courts of appeals rejected as unconstitutional attempts to implement race-based assignment plans--such as the plans at issue here--in primary and secondary schools. After *Grutter*, however, the two Courts of Appeals in these cases, and one other, found that race-based assignments were permissible at the elementary and secondary level, largely in reliance on that case.

In upholding the admissions plan in *Grutter*, though, this Court relied upon considerations unique to institutions of higher education, noting that in light of "the expansive freedoms of speech and thought associated with the university environment, universities occupy a special niche in our constitutional tradition." The Court explained that "context matters" in applying strict scrutiny, and repeatedly noted that it was addressing the use of race "in the context of higher education." The Court in *Grutter* expressly articulated key limitations on its holding--defining a specific type of broad-based diversity and noting the unique context of higher education--but these limitations were largely disregarded by the lower courts in extending *Grutter* to uphold race-based assignments in elementary and secondary schools. The present cases are not governed by *Grutter*.

Perhaps recognizing that reliance on *Grutter* cannot sustain their plans, both school districts assert additional interests, distinct from the interest upheld in *Grutter*, to justify their race-based assignments. In briefing and argument before this Court, Seattle contends that its use of race helps to reduce racial concentration in schools and to ensure that racially concentrated housing patterns do not prevent nonwhite students from having access to the most desirable schools. Jefferson County has articulated a similar goal, phrasing its interest in terms of educating its students "in a racially integrated environment." Each school district argues that educational and broader socialization benefits flow from a racially diverse learning environment, and each contends that because the diversity they seek is racial diversity--not the broader diversity at issue in *Grutter*--it makes sense to promote that interest directly by relying on race alone.

The parties and their *amici* dispute whether racial diversity in schools in fact has a marked impact on test scores and other objective yardsticks or achieves intangible socialization benefits. The debate is not one we need to resolve, however, because it is clear that the racial classifications employed by the districts are not narrowly tailored to the goal of achieving the educational and social benefits asserted to flow from racial diversity. In design and operation, the plans are directed only to racial balance, pure and simple, an objective this Court has repeatedly condemned as illegitimate . . .

In *Grutter*, the number of minority students the school sought to admit was an undefined "meaningful number" necessary to achieve a genuinely diverse student body. Although the matter was the subject of disagreement on the Court, the majority concluded that the law school did not count back from its applicant pool to arrive at the "meaningful number" it regarded as necessary to diversify its student body. Here the racial balance the districts seek is a defined range set solely by reference to the demographics of the respective school districts.

This working backward to achieve a particular type of racial balance, rather than working forward from some demonstration of the level of diversity that provides the purported benefits, is a fatal flaw under our existing precedent. We have many times over reaffirmed that "racial balance is not to be achieved for its own sake." *Freeman v. Pitts*, 503 U.S. 467 (1992). *Grutter* itself reiterated that "outright racial balancing" is "patently unconstitutional."

Accepting racial balancing as a compelling state interest would justify the imposition of racial proportionality throughout American society, contrary to our repeated recognition that "at the heart of the Constitution's guarantee of equal protection lies the simple command that the Government must treat citizens as individuals, not as simply components of a racial, religious, sexual or national class." Allowing racial balancing as a compelling end in itself would "effectively assure that race will always be relevant in American life, and that the ultimate goal of eliminating entirely from governmental decision-making such irrelevant factors as a human being's race will never be achieved." An interest "linked to nothing other than proportional representation of various races . . . would support indefinite use of racial classifications, employed first to obtain the appropriate mixture of racial views and then to ensure that the [program] continues to reflect that mixture."

The validity of our concern that racial balancing has "no logical stopping point," is demonstrated here by the degree to which the districts tie their racial guidelines to their demographics. As the districts' demographics shift, so too will their definition of racial diversity. The Ninth Circuit below stated that it "shared in the hope" expressed in *Grutter* that in 25 years racial preferences would no longer be necessary to further the interest identified in that case. But in Seattle the plans are defended as necessary to address the consequences of racially identifiable housing patterns. The sweep of the mandate claimed by the district is contrary to our rulings that remedying past societal discrimination does not justify race-conscious government action.

The principle that racial balancing is not permitted is one of substance, not semantics. Racial balancing is not transformed from "patently unconstitutional" to a compelling state interest simply by relabeling it "racial diversity." While the school districts use various verbal formulations to describe the interest they seek to promote-racial diversity, avoidance of racial isolation, racial integration--they offer no definition of the interest that suggests it differs from racial balance.

Jefferson County phrases its interest as "racial integration," but integration certainly does not require the sort of racial proportionality reflected in its plan. Even in the context of mandatory desegregation, we have stressed that racial proportionality is not required, and here Jefferson County has already been found to have eliminated the vestiges of its prior segregated school system . . .

The districts have also failed to show that they considered methods other than explicit racial classifications to achieve their stated goals. Narrow tailoring requires "serious, good faith consideration of workable race-neutral alternatives," and yet in Seattle several alternative assignment plans--many of which would not have used express racial classifications--were rejected with little or no consideration. Jefferson County has failed to present any evidence that it considered alternatives, even though the district already claims that its goals are achieved primarily through means other than the racial classifications.

Justice Breyer's dissent takes a different approach to these cases, one that fails to ground the result it would reach in law. Instead, it selectively relies on inapplicable precedent and even dicta while dismissing contrary holdings, alters and misapplies our well-established legal framework for assessing equal protection challenges to express racial classifications, and greatly exaggerates the consequences of today's decision . . .

Justice Breyer's position comes down to a familiar claim: The end justifies the means. He admits that "there is a cost in applying a state-mandated racial label," but he is confident that the cost is worth paying. Our established strict scrutiny test for racial classifications, however, insists on "detailed examination, both as to ends and as to means." Simply because the school districts may seek a worthy goal does not mean they are free to discriminate on the basis of race to achieve it, or that their racial classifications should be subject to less exacting scrutiny . . .

In *Brown v. Board of Education*, 347 U.S. 483 (1954) (*Brown I*), we held that segregation deprived black children of equal educational opportunities regardless of whether school facilities and other tangible factors were equal, because government classification and separation on grounds of race themselves denoted inferiority. It was not the inequality of the facilities but the fact of legally separating children on the basis of race on which the Court relied to find a constitutional violation in 1954. The next Term, we accordingly stated that "full compliance" with *Brown I* required school districts "to achieve a system of determining admission to the public schools on a nonracial basis" (*Brown II*).

The parties and their *amici* debate which side is more faithful to the heritage of *Brown*, but the position of the plaintiffs in *Brown* was spelled out in their brief and could not have been clearer: "The Fourteenth Amendment prevents states from according differential treatment to American children on the basis of their color or race." What do the racial classifications at issue here do, if not accord differential treatment on the basis of race? As counsel who appeared before this Court for the plaintiffs in *Brown* put it: "We have one fundamental contention which we will seek to develop in the course of this argument, and that contention is that no State has any authority under the equal-protection clause of the Fourteenth Amendment to use race as a factor in affording educational opportunities among its citizens." There is no ambiguity in that statement. And it was that position that prevailed in this Court, which emphasized in its remedial opinion that what was "at stake is the personal interest of the plaintiffs in admission to public schools as soon as practicable on a nondiscriminatory basis," and what was required was "determining admission to the public schools on a nonracial basis" (*Brown II*). What do the racial classifications do in these cases, if not determine admission to a public school on a racial basis?

Before *Brown*, schoolchildren were told where they could and could not go to school based on the color of their skin. The school districts in these cases have not carried the heavy burden of demonstrating that we should allow this once again--even for very different reasons. For schools that never segregated on the basis of race, such as Seattle, or that have removed the vestiges of past segregation, such as Jefferson County, the way "to achieve a system of determining admission to the public schools on a nonracial basis," is to stop assigning students on a racial basis. The way to stop discrimination on the basis of race is to stop discriminating on the basis of race.

The judgments of the Courts of Appeals for the Sixth and Ninth Circuits are reversed, and the cases are remanded for further proceedings.

It is so ordered.

Justice THOMAS, concurring:

Today, the Court holds that state entities may not experiment with race-based means to achieve ends they deem socially desirable. I wholly concur in the Chief Justice's opinion. I write separately to address several of the contentions in Justice Breyer's dissent (hereinafter the dissent). Contrary to the dissent's arguments, resegregation is not occurring in Seattle or Louisville; these school boards have no present interest in remedying past segregation; and these race-based student-assignment programs do not serve any compelling state interest. Accordingly, the plans are unconstitutional. Disfavoring a color-blind interpretation of the Constitution, the dissent would give school boards a free hand to make decisions on the basis of race--an approach reminiscent of that advocated by the segregationists in *Brown*. This approach is just as wrong today as it was a half-century ago. The Constitution and our cases require us to be much more demanding before permitting local school boards to make decisions based on race.

The dissent repeatedly claims that the school districts are threatened with resegregation and that they will succumb to that threat if these plans are declared unconstitutional. It also argues that these plans can be justified as part of the school boards' attempts to "eradicate earlier school segregation." Contrary to the dissent's rhetoric, neither of these school districts is threatened with resegregation, and neither is constitutionally compelled or permitted to undertake race-based remediation. Racial imbalance is not segregation, and the mere incantation of terms like resegregation and remediation cannot make up the difference.

Because this Court has authorized and required race-based remedial measures to address *de jure* segregation, it is important to define segregation clearly and to distinguish it from racial imbalance. In the context of public schooling, segregation is the deliberate operation of a school system to "carry out a governmental policy to separate pupils in schools solely on the basis of race." In *Brown*, this Court declared that segregation was unconstitutional under the Equal Protection Clause of the Fourteenth Amendment . . . Racial imbalance is the failure of a school district's individual schools to match or approximate the demographic makeup of the student population at large. Racial imbalance is not segregation. Although presently observed racial imbalance might result from past *de jure* segregation, racial imbalance can also result from any number of innocent private decisions, including voluntary housing choices. Because racial imbalance is not inevitably linked to unconstitutional segregation, it is not unconstitutional in and of itself.

Although there is arguably a danger of racial imbalance in schools in Seattle and Louisville, there is no danger of resegregation. No one contends that Seattle has established or that Louisville has reestablished a dual school system that separates students on the basis of race . . . racial imbalance without intentional state action to separate the races does not amount to segregation. To raise the specter of resegregation to defend these programs is to ignore the meaning of the word and the nature of the cases before us . . . To equate the achievement of a certain statistical mix in several schools with the elimination of the system of systematic *de jure* segregation trivializes the latter accomplishment. Nothing but an interest in classroom aesthetics and a hypersensitivity to elite sensibilities justifies the school districts' racial balancing programs . . . Assessed in any objective manner, there is no comparison between the two . . . The Constitution does not permit race-based government decision making simply because a school district claims a remedial purpose and proceeds in good faith with arguably pure motives . . . as a general rule, all race-based government decision making--regardless of context--is unconstitutional . . .

In place of the color-blind Constitution, the dissent would permit measures to keep the races together and proscribe measures to keep the races apart. Although no such distinction is apparent in the Fourteenth Amendment, the dissent would constitutionalize today's faddish social theories that embrace that distinction. The Constitution is not that malleable. Even if current social theories favor classroom racial engineering as necessary to "solve the problems at hand," the Constitution enshrines principles independent of social theories. Indeed, if our history has taught us anything, it has taught us to beware of elites bearing racial theories. Can we really be sure that the racial theories that motivated *Dred Scott* and *Plessy* are a relic of the past or that future theories will be nothing but beneficent and progressive? That is a gamble I am unwilling to take, and it is one the Constitution does not allow . . . The plans before us base school assignment decisions on students' race. Because "our Constitution is color-blind, and neither knows nor tolerates classes among citizens," such race-based decision making is unconstitutional. I concur in the Chief Justice's opinion so holding.

Justice KENNEDY, concurring in part and concurring in the judgment.

The Nation's schools strive to teach that our strength comes from people of different races, creeds, and cultures uniting in commitment to the freedom of all. In these cases two school districts in different parts of the country seek to teach that principle by having classrooms that reflect the racial makeup of the surrounding community. That the school districts consider these plans to be necessary should remind us our highest aspirations are yet unfulfilled. But the solutions mandated by these school districts must themselves be lawful. To make race matter now so that it might not matter later may entrench the very prejudices we seek to overcome. In my view the state-mandated racial classifications at issue, official labels proclaiming the race of all persons in a broad class of citizens--elementary school students in one case, high school students in another--are unconstitutional as the cases now come to us . . .

This Nation has a moral and ethical obligation to fulfill its historic commitment to creating an integrated society that ensures equal opportunity for all of its children. A compelling interest exists in avoiding racial isolation, an interest that a school district, in its discretion and expertise, may choose to pursue. Likewise, a district may consider it a compelling interest to achieve a diverse student population. Race may be one component of that diversity, but other demographic factors, plus special talents and needs, should also be considered. What the government is not

292

permitted to do, absent a showing of necessity not made here, is to classify every student on the basis of race and to assign each of them to schools based on that classification. Crude measures of this sort threaten to reduce children to racial chits valued and traded according to one school's supply and another's demand . . .

A sense of stigma may already become the fate of those separated out by circumstances beyond their immediate control. But to this the replication must be: Even so, measures other than differential treatment based on racial typing of individuals first must be exhausted.

The decision today should not prevent school districts from continuing the important work of bringing together students of different racial, ethnic, and economic backgrounds. Due to a variety of factors--some influenced by government, some not--neighborhoods in our communities do not reflect the diversity of our Nation as a whole. Those entrusted with directing our public schools can bring to bear the creativity of experts, parents, administrators, and other concerned citizens to find a way to achieve the compelling interests they face without resorting to widespread governmental allocation of benefits and burdens on the basis of racial classifications.

With this explanation I concur in the judgment of the Court.

Justice BREYER, with whom Justice STEVENS, Justice SOUTER, and Justice GINSBURG join, dissenting.

These cases consider the longstanding efforts of two local school boards to integrate their public schools. The school board plans before us resemble many others adopted in the last 50 years by primary and secondary schools throughout the Nation. All of those plans represent local efforts to bring about the kind of racially integrated education that *Brown v. Board of Education*, long ago promised--efforts that this Court has repeatedly required, permitted, and encouraged local authorities to undertake . . .

Until today, this Court understood the Constitution as affording the people, acting through their elected representatives, freedom to select the use of "race-conscious" criteria from among their available options. Today, however, the Court restricts (and some Members would eliminate) that leeway. I fear the consequences of doing so for the law, for the schools, for the democratic process, and for America's efforts to create, out of its diversity, one Nation . . . the Court's decision today slows down and sets back the work of local school boards to bring about racially diverse schools.

Indeed, the consequences of the approach the Court takes today are serious. Yesterday, the plans under review were lawful. Today, they are not. Yesterday, the citizens of this Nation could look for guidance to this Court's unanimous pronouncements concerning desegregation. Today, they cannot. Yesterday, school boards had available to them a full range of means to combat segregated schools. Today, they do not.

The Court's decision undermines other basic institutional principles as well. What has happened to *stare decisis*? The history of the plans before us, their educational importance, their highly limited use of race--all these and more--make clear that the compelling interest here is stronger than in *Grutter*. The plans here are more narrowly tailored than the law school admissions program there at issue. Hence, applying *Grutter's* strict test, their lawfulness follows *a fortiori* . . . And what of respect for democratic local decision-making by States and school boards? For several decades this Court has rested its public school decisions upon *Swann's* basic view that the Constitution grants local school districts a significant degree of leeway where the inclusive use of race-conscious criteria is at issue. Now localities will have to cope with the difficult problems they face (including resegregation) deprived of one means they may find necessary . . .

And what of the long history and moral vision that the Fourteenth Amendment itself embodies? The plurality cites in support those who argued in *Brown* against segregation, and Justice Thomas likens the approach that I have taken to that of segregation's defenders. But segregation policies did not simply tell schoolchildren "where they could and could not go to school based on the color of their skin," they perpetuated a caste system rooted in the institutions of slavery and 80 years of legalized subordination. The lesson of history, is not that efforts to continue racial segregation are constitutionally indistinguishable from efforts to achieve racial integration. Indeed, it is a cruel distortion of history to compare Topeka, Kansas, in the 1950's to Louisville and Seattle in the modern day--to equate the plight of Linda Brown (who was ordered to attend a Jim Crow school) to the circumstances of Joshua McDonald (whose request to transfer to a school closer to home was initially declined). This is not to deny that there is a cost in applying "a state-mandated racial label." But that cost does not approach, in degree or in kind, the terrible harms of slavery, the resulting caste system, and 80 years of legal racial segregation.

Finally, what of the hope and promise of *Brown*? For much of this Nation's history, the races remained divided. It was not long ago that people of different races drank from separate fountains, rode on separate buses, and studied in separate schools. In this Court's finest hour, *Brown v. Board of Education* challenged this history and helped to change it. For *Brown* held out a promise. It was a promise embodied in three Amendments designed to make citizens of slaves. It was the promise of true racial equality--not as a matter of fine words on paper, but as a matter of everyday life in the Nation's cities and schools. It was about the nature of a democracy that must work for all Americans. It sought one law, one Nation, one people, not simply as a matter of legal principle but in terms of how we actually live.

Not everyone welcomed this Court's decision in *Brown*. Three years after that decision was handed down, the Governor of Arkansas ordered state militia to block the doors of a white schoolhouse so that black children could not enter. The President of the United States dispatched the 101st Airborne Division to Little Rock, Arkansas, and federal troops were needed to enforce a desegregation decree. Today, almost 50 years later, attitudes toward race in this Nation have changed dramatically. Many parents, white and black alike, want their children to attend schools with children of different races. Indeed, the very school districts that once spurned integration now strive for it. The long history of their efforts reveals the complexities and difficulties they have faced. And in light of those challenges, they have asked us not to take from their hands the instruments they have used to rid their schools of racial segregation, instruments that they believe are needed to overcome the problems of cities divided by race and poverty. The plurality would decline their modest request.

The plurality is wrong to do so. The last half century has witnessed great strides toward racial equality, but we have not yet realized the promise of *Brown*. To invalidate the plans under review is to threaten the promise of *Brown*. The plurality's position, I fear, would break that promise. This is a decision that the Court and the Nation will come to regret.

I must dissent

* * * * * * *

In *Parents Involved in Community Schools* (*PICS*), Chief Justice Roberts flatly rejected *Grutter* as applicable precedent for K-12 schools, stating: "The Court in *Grutter* expressly articulated key limitations on its holding--defining a specific type of broad-based diversity and noting the unique context of higher education . . . The present [K-12] cases are not governed by *Grutter*." In his dissenting opinion, however, Justice Breyer argued that *Grutter* was binding precedent in these cases, stating:

> What has happened to *stare decisis*? The history of the plans before us, their educational importance, their highly limited use of race--all these and more--make clear that the compelling interest here is stronger than in *Grutter*. The plans here are more narrowly tailored than the law school admissions program there at issue. Hence, applying *Grutter's* strict test, their lawfulness follows *a fortiori*.

The reach of the Court's *Grutter* rationale has been hotly debated. At one extreme are those who argue that *Grutter* only applies to similar admissions programs in other highly selective public law schools. At the other extreme are those who argue that *Grutter* applies to all educational institutions and programs. The Court's decision in *PICS* seems to reject this latter argument, but on the continuum between these two extremes, where are the lawful limits of *Grutter*? Does *Grutter* apply to all highly selective graduate programs? All graduate programs? All highly selective higher education institutions? All higher education institutions? Trade schools and two-year colleges? Is Chief Justice Roberts' opinion declaring that *Grutter* does not apply to elementary and secondary schools dispositive of this issue? It is important to note that while four Justices signed on to this firm statement that *Grutter* does not apply to elementary and secondary schools, the fifth and deciding vote, Justice Kennedy, stated:

> This Nation has a moral and ethical obligation to fulfill its historic commitment to creating an integrated society that ensures equal opportunity for all of its children. A compelling interest exists in avoiding racial isolation, an interest that a school district, in its discretion and expertise, may choose to pursue. Likewise, a district may consider it a compelling interest to achieve a diverse student population. Race may be one component of that diversity, but other demographic factors, plus special talents and needs, should also be considered.

In his dissenting opinion, Justice Breyer noted: "Even apart from *Grutter*, five Members of this Court agree that 'avoiding racial isolation' and 'achieving a diverse student population' remain today compelling interests." Nonetheless, considerable uncertainty remains in this area of law making use of race-based programs for student admissions or assignments a legally risky undertaking for school officials. Further, note that state laws and state constitutions may further complicate, limit, or prohibit the use of race in student admissions or assignments by public educational institutions in your state.

Despite the division on the Court concerning these issues, Chief Justice Roberts intended to send a clear message: "The way to stop discrimination on the basis of race is to stop discriminating on the basis of race." In his opinion Chief Justice Roberts noted that on the basis of race some students were being denied the educational opportunities they would have otherwise received:

> The concerns of Parents Involved are illustrated by Jill Kurfirst, who sought to enroll her ninth-grade son, Andy Meeks, in Ballard High School's special Biotechnology Career Academy. Andy suffered from attention deficit hyperactivity disorder and dyslexia, but had made good progress with hands-on instruction, and his mother and middle school teachers thought that the smaller biotechnology program held the most promise for his continued success. Andy was accepted into this selective program but, because of the racial tiebreaker, was denied assignment to Ballard High School.

In his dissenting opinion Justice Breyer acknowledged that "there is a cost in applying a state-mandated racial label" for the persons negatively impacted by race-based programs. Is it fair to ask this high school student, Andy Meeks, to pay the price for segregation by prior generations? Why or why not? Does the asserted good of the many justify the costs to the few? Concerning this issue, Chief Justice Robert's argued:

> Justice Breyer's position comes down to a familiar claim: The end justifies the means. He admits that "there is a cost in applying a state-mandated racial label," but he is confident that the cost is worth paying. Our established strict scrutiny test for racial classifications, however, insists on "detailed examination, both as to ends and as to means." Simply because the school districts may seek a worthy goal does not mean they are free to discriminate on the basis of race to achieve it, or that their racial classifications should be subject to less exacting scrutiny.

Chief Justice Robert's opinion also declared: "The districts have also failed to show that they considered methods other than explicit racial classifications to achieve their stated goals. Narrow tailoring requires 'serious, good faith consideration of workable race-neutral alternatives.'" What other workable race-neutral alternatives exist?

Are social and economic disparities in the U.S. today still really about race, or are they more about income and social class? Could many of the same goals sought through racial integration also be achieved through economic integration? Economic integration policies are perfectly constitutional (subject only to the rational basis test), but are they politically viable? Do middle and upper income communities want poorer children attending schools in their communities, or will they vote, relocate, or choose private schools to avoid the economic integration of their children with poorer students?

When government plans are based on race, how is race defined? Is race a definitive reality or are racial classifications largely subjective social constructs? For a student that has one black parent and one white parent, should that student be classified by school officials as black or white? Why? Are parents and the child free to decide their own racial classification? Or is the subjective opinion of a school official based on viewing the child determinative? Children who look white have been born to two black parents and vice versa. On what basis could school officials deny anyone's claim to a particular racial classification? How would school officials disprove a claim of racial identity?

Are their significant generational differences in attitudes concerning the significance of race between younger and older Americans? If so, who sees race as more or less significant and why? Writing for the majority in *Grutter* (2003) (allowing race as a limited factor in a law school admissions program) Justice O'Connor declared: "We expect that 25 years from now, the use of racial preferences will no longer be necessary to further the interest approved today." Do you believe Justice O'Connor was correct? Does this statement by the Court constitute a "sunset" provision for any consideration of race by government after the 25 years has tolled in 2028? Why or why not?

Discrimination Based on National Origin and Immigration Status

The U.S. is a nation of immigrants. With each new wave of immigration, however, racial and ethnic ignorance, fear, and group competition for limited resources have resulted in conflict and prejudice against the new immigrants. If those opposed to the new immigrants attempt to use majoritarian politics and the force of law against the new immigrants, the Court has held that unequal treatment by government based on national origin, race, or ethnicity is subject to strict judicial scrutiny and is unconstitutional unless proven necessary to a compelling interest and narrowly tailored to achieving that interest. Government classifications that discriminate based on national origin, race, or ethnicity are routinely declared unconstitutional.

The more difficult cases involve differential treatment not because of national origin, race, or ethnicity, but because of non-citizenship status, commonly referred to as alienage. Differential governmental treatment of aliens has been subjected to less rigorous judicial scrutiny than discrimination based on national origin, race, or ethnicity because alienage is not an immutable characteristic. Individuals cannot change their national origin, race, or ethnicity, making these immutable characteristics. Alienage status, however, can be changed through acquiring lawful citizenship.

In a 5-4 opinion in *Ambach v. Norwick*, 441 U.S. 68 (1979), the Court upheld a New York State prohibition against aliens serving as public school teachers. While the Court has not allowed general discrimination against aliens, for example striking down exclusions of otherwise qualified lawful resident aliens from state welfare benefits and admission to the practice of law, the Court has allowed exclusion of aliens from elected offices or employment in core government functions, including service as state teachers and police officers, if prohibited under state law.

Because immigration is the province of the federal government, the Court has been even more deferential to disparate treatment of aliens by the federal government than by state governments. The Supremacy Clause in Article VI of the U.S. Constitution limits the ability of states to regulate in areas assigned to the federal government by the Constitution, including Congress' power to "establish an uniform Rule of Naturalization" under Article I, section 8.

The above decisions by the Court addressed the rights of adult aliens legally present in the U.S. What are the legal rights of undocumented minor children? In *Plyler v. Doe*, 457 U.S. 202 (1982), the Court ruled that undocumented children could not be excluded from public schools, concluding:

> It is difficult to understand precisely what the State hopes to achieve by promoting the creation and perpetuation of a subclass of illiterates within our boundaries, surely adding to the problems and costs of unemployment, welfare, and crime. It is thus clear that whatever savings might be achieved by denying these children an education, they are wholly insubstantial in light of the costs involved to these children, the State, and the

Nation. If the State is to deny a discrete group of innocent children the free public education that it offers to other children residing within its borders, that denial must be justified by a showing that it furthers some substantial state interest. No such showing was made here.

Discrimination Based on Language and Rights to English Instruction

Discrimination based on language has been treated as a form of national origin discrimination, and is unlawful under both the Equal Protection Clause and Title VI of the Civil Rights Act of 1964. In *Lau v. Nichols*, 414 U.S. 563 (1974) the U.S. Supreme Court held that failure to provide necessary English language instruction to non-English speaking students denied these students a meaningful opportunity to participate in public education programs in violation of Title VI of the Civil Rights Act of 1964. At a minimum, public schools must provide an adequate English language bridge for non-English speaking students, to give these students an opportunity to benefit from public education instruction in English.

The Equal Educational Opportunities Act (EEOA) of 1974, 20 U.S.C. § 1703, also mandates:

> No State shall deny equal educational opportunity to an individual on account of his or her race, color, sex, or national origin, by . . . the failure by an educational agency to take appropriate action to overcome language barriers that impede equal participation by its students in its instructional programs.

In *Horne v. Flores*, 557 U.S. ___ (2009), Arizona English Language-Learner (ELL) students and their parents alleged that ELL students were receiving inadequate instruction in violation of the "appropriate action" mandate of the EEOA. Lower courts found the State in violation of the EEOA based on inadequate funding. In reversing and remanding the case, the U.S. Supreme Court noted:

> By simply requiring a State "to take appropriate action to overcome language barriers" without specifying particular actions that a State must take, "Congress intended to leave state and local educational authorities a substantial amount of latitude in choosing the programs and techniques they would use to meet their obligations under the EEOA" . . . [State officials] argue that through compliance with NCLB, the State has established compliance with the EEOA. They note that when a State adopts a compliance plan under NCLB--as the State of Arizona has--it must provide adequate assurances that ELL students will receive assistance "to achieve at high levels in the core academic subjects so that those children can meet the same . . . standards as all children are expected to meet." They argue that when the Federal Department of Education approves a State's plan--as it has with respect to Arizona's--it offers definitive evidence that the State has taken "appropriate action to overcome language barriers" within the meaning of the EEOA . . . because of significant differences in the two statutory schemes, compliance with NCLB will not necessarily constitute "appropriate action" under the EEOA. Approval of a NCLB plan does not entail substantive review of a State's ELL programming or a determination that the programming results in equal educational opportunity for ELL students . . . The EEOA seeks to provide "equal educational opportunity" to "all children enrolled in public schools." Its ultimate focus is on the quality of educational

programming and services provided to students, not the amount of money spent on them. Accordingly, there is no statutory basis for precluding [State officials] from showing that [the school system] has achieved EEOA-compliant programming by means other than increased funding--for example, through . . . structural, curricular, and accountability-based reforms . . . In any event, the EEOA requires "appropriate action" to remove language barriers, not the equalization of results between native and nonnative speakers on tests administered in English--a worthy goal, to be sure, but one that may be exceedingly difficult to achieve, especially for older ELL students . . . The EEOA's "appropriate action" requirement grants States broad latitude to design, fund, and implement ELL programs that suit local needs and account for local conditions . . . the EEOA's "appropriate action" requirement does not necessarily require any particular level of funding, and to the extent that funding is relevant, the EEOA certainly does not require that the money come from any particular source. In addition, the EEOA plainly does not give the federal courts the authority to judge whether a State or a school district is providing "appropriate" instruction in other subjects. That remains the province of the States and the local schools. It is unfortunate if a school, in order to fund ELL programs, must divert money from other worthwhile programs, but such decisions fall outside the scope of the EEOA . . . There is no question that the goal of the EEOA--overcoming language barriers--is a vitally important one, and our decision will not in any way undermine efforts to achieve that goal.

The Court's decisions in both *Lau v. Nichols* and *Horne v. Flores* recognized a duty for state and local school officials to provide appropriate instruction for minority language students, but both decisions leave the details of these programs to state and local officials.

Discrimination Based on Gender

There is a long history of separate gender education. Many historically accepted practices, however, increasingly collided with progressing ideals of democratic and social equality, and ultimately fell in the wake of the Equal Protection Clause, the Civil Rights Act of 1964, Title IX (20 U.S.C. § 1681) of the Education Amendments of 1972, and other federal and state civil rights legislation. Title IX declares: "No person in the United States shall, on the basis of sex, be excluded from participation in, be denied the benefits of, or be subjected to discrimination under any education program or activity receiving Federal financial assistance."

In *Mississippi v. Hogan*, 458 U.S. 718 (1982), the U.S. Supreme Court struck down a nursing school's females only admissions policy, finding that the exclusion of otherwise qualified males was not substantially related to any important governmental objective. And in a 7-1 decision in *United States v. Virginia*, 518 U.S. 515 (1996), the U.S. Supreme Court struck down the exclusion of otherwise qualified females from a males only public military school, the Virginia Military Institute (VMI). The Court does not equate "gender classifications, for all purposes, to classifications based on race or national origin" but elevated the level of scrutiny for gender-based classifications in the VMI case. Writing for the majority, Justice Ginsberg stated:

The Court has repeatedly recognized that neither federal nor state government acts compatibly with the equal protection principle when a law or official policy denies to women, simply because they are women, full citizenship stature--equal opportunity to aspire, achieve, participate in and contribute to society based on their individual talents and capacities . . . To summarize the Court's current directions for cases of official classification based on gender: Focusing on the differential treatment or denial of opportunity for which relief is sought, the reviewing court must determine whether the proffered justification is "exceedingly persuasive." The burden of justification is demanding and it rests entirely on the State. The State must show "at least that the challenged classification serves `important governmental objectives and that the discriminatory means employed' are `substantially related to the achievement of those objectives.'" The justification must be genuine, not hypothesized or invented post hoc in response to litigation. And it must not rely on overbroad generalizations about the different talents, capacities, or preferences of males and females . . . The heightened review standard our precedent establishes does not make sex a proscribed classification. Supposed "inherent differences" are no longer accepted as a ground for race or national origin classifications. Physical differences between men and women, however, are enduring: "The two sexes are not fungible; a community made up exclusively of one sex is different from a community composed of both." "Inherent differences" between men and women, we have come to appreciate, remain cause for celebration, but not for denigration of the members of either sex or for artificial constraints on an individual's opportunity . . . such classifications may not be used, as they once were, to create or perpetuate the legal, social, and economic inferiority of women. Measuring the record in this case against the review standard just described, we conclude that Virginia has shown no "exceedingly persuasive justification" for excluding all women from the citizen-soldier training afforded by VMI . . . A prime part of the history of our Constitution . . . is the story of the extension of constitutional rights and protections to people once ignored or excluded. VMI's story continued as our comprehension of "We the People" expanded. There is no reason to believe that the admission of women capable of all the activities required of VMI cadets would destroy the Institute rather than enhance its capacity to serve the "more perfect Union."

* * * * * * *

VMI could not continue to take public tax dollars and exclude females or any otherwise qualified applicants without a showing of sufficient cause for the differential treatment. The Equal Protection Clause commands that the government and its agents must treat individuals as individuals, and not just as members of a group. For institutions operating in the public sphere, unless sufficient cause is shown, individuals are entitled to be considered based on their individual merits and not just their group status.

A purely private school could, however, discriminate in admissions based on gender with no requirement to justify its differential treatment to government officials. Unless schools operating in the private sphere become subject to government regulations through the conditional acceptance of government funding, private schools are not subject to the Equal Protection Clause or Title IX. Persons who object to the single gender policies of private schools can choose not to support those schools. Public schools, however, are funded by the common government for which everyone must pay taxes, and they are therefore bound by the limitations of the common Constitution, including the Equal Protection Clause.

The general rule of law under the Equal Protection Clause is that gender based actions in the public sphere are unconstitutional unless supported by an exceedingly persuasive justification. Are separate gender schools or programs in public educational institutions ever lawful? Title IX generally prohibits discrimination based on gender by any educational institution that receives federal funding, with some exceptions. As Justice Ginsberg noted in the VMI case, there are physical differences between females and males, and Title IX does not command that relevant differences be ignored. Consistent with the commands of the Equal Protection Clause, Title IX prohibits irrational discrimination based on gender, but allows for the recognition of important differences between females and males for which there is an exceedingly persuasive justification.

Separate Gender Education

Access to Classes and Schools: 34 C.F.R. § 106.34 (2011)

(a) *General standard*. Except as provided for in this section or otherwise in this part, a recipient shall not provide or otherwise carry out any of its education programs or activities separately on the basis of sex, or require or refuse participation therein by any of its students on the basis of sex.

(1) *Contact sports in physical education classes*. This section does not prohibit separation of students by sex within physical education classes or activities during participation in wrestling, boxing, rugby, ice hockey, football, basketball, and other sports the purpose or major activity of which involves bodily contact.

(2) *Ability grouping in physical education classes*. This section does not prohibit grouping of students in physical education classes and activities by ability as assessed by objective standards of individual performance developed and applied without regard to sex.

(3) *Human sexuality classes*. Classes or portions of classes in elementary and secondary schools that deal primarily with human sexuality may be conducted in separate sessions for boys and girls.

(4) *Choruses*. Recipients may make requirements based on vocal range or quality that may result in a chorus or choruses of one or predominantly one sex.

(b) *Classes and extracurricular activities*.

(1) *General standard*. Subject to the requirements in this paragraph, a recipient that operates a nonvocational coeducational elementary or secondary school may provide nonvocational single-sex classes or extracurricular activities, if--

(i) Each single-sex class or extracurricular activity is based on the recipient's important objective:

(A) To improve educational achievement of its students, through a recipient's overall established policy to provide diverse educational opportunities, provided that the single-sex nature of the class or extracurricular activity is substantially related to achieving that objective; or

(B) To meet the particular, identified educational needs of its students, provided that the single-sex nature of the class or extracurricular activity is substantially related to achieving that objective;

(ii) The recipient implements its objective in an evenhanded manner;

(iii) Student enrollment in a single-sex class or extracurricular activity is completely voluntary; and

(iv) The recipient provides to all other students, including students of the excluded sex, a substantially equal coeducational class or extracurricular activity in the same subject or activity.

(2) *Single-sex class or extracurricular activity for the excluded sex.* A recipient that provides a single-sex class or extracurricular activity, in order to comply with paragraph (b)(1)(ii) of this section, may be required to provide a substantially equal single-sex class or extracurricular activity for students of the excluded sex.

(3) *Substantially equal factors.* Factors the Department will consider, either individually or in the aggregate as appropriate, in determining whether classes or extracurricular activities are substantially equal include, but are not limited to, the following: the policies and criteria of admission, the educational benefits provided, including the quality, range, and content of curriculum and other services and the quality and availability of books, instructional materials, and technology, the qualifications of faculty and staff, geographic accessibility, the quality, accessibility, and availability of facilities and resources provided to the class, and intangible features, such as reputation of faculty.

(4) *Periodic evaluations.* (i) The recipient must conduct periodic evaluations to ensure that single-sex classes or extracurricular activities are based upon genuine justifications and do not rely on overly broad generalizations about the different talents, capacities, or preferences of either sex and that any single-sex classes or extracurricular activities are substantially related to the achievement of the important objective for the classes or extracurricular activities.

(ii) Evaluations for the purposes of paragraph (b)(4)(i) of this section must be conducted at least every two years.

(5) *Scope of coverage.* The provisions of paragraph (b)(1) through (4) of this section apply to classes and extracurricular activities provided by a recipient directly or through another entity, but the provisions of paragraph (b)(1) through (4) of this section do not apply to interscholastic, club, or intramural athletics, which are subject to the provisions of §§106.41 and 106.37(c) of this part.

(c) **Schools.**

(1) *General Standard.* Except as provided in paragraph (c)(2) of this section, a recipient that operates a public nonvocational elementary or secondary school that excludes from admission any students, on the basis of sex, must provide students of the excluded sex a substantially equal single-sex school or coeducational school.

(2) *Exception.* A nonvocational public charter school that is a single-school local educational agency under State law may be operated as a single-sex charter school without regard to the requirements in paragraph (c)(1) of this section.

(3) *Substantially equal factors.* Factors the Department will consider, either individually or in the aggregate as appropriate, in determining whether schools are substantially equal include, but are not limited to, the following: The policies and criteria of admission, the educational benefits provided, including the quality, range, and content of curriculum and other services and the quality and availability of books, instructional materials, and technology, the quality and range of extracurricular offerings, the qualifications of faculty and staff, geographic accessibility, the quality, accessibility, and availability of facilities and resources, and intangible features, such as reputation of faculty.

(4) *Definition.* For the purposes of paragraph (c)(1) through (3) of this section, the term "school" includes a "school within a school," which means an administratively separate school located within another school (Authority: 20 U.S.C. §1681).

* * * * * * *

Although the regulations for Title IX recognize certain instances in which separate gender educational assignments are deemed exempt from Title IX's general prohibition against differential treatment on the basis of gender, guidelines on Title IX from the U.S. Office of Civil Rights note school officials "also should be aware of constitutional requirements in this area" and "may be challenged in court litigation on constitutional grounds." Neither Congress nor any administrative agency has any authority to circumvent the mandates of the Constitution, and the Office of Civil Rights is serving notice to school officials that constitutional mandates overrule any contrary regulations issued for Title IX.

But if an administrative agency knew these regulations were constitutionally suspect enough to merit a formal legal disclaimer, why did the administrative agency issue these regulations? What types of single-sex schools or classes would survive a constitutional challenge? VMI argued that its males-only military preparation program was supportive of national security, and was consistent with the U.S. males-only military draft, yet VMI's justifications were found insufficient by the Court in a 7-1 decision. Given this judicial standard, what justifications and evidence would school officials be required to provide to defend challenged single-sex policies and programs in their schools? Is the social science data supporting separate gender education strong enough to overcome a constitutional principle of non-segregation?

34 C.F.R. § 106.34 appears to authorize some single-sex programs, but also contains extensive limitations and qualifications (*e.g.*, "Factors the Department will consider"). Most of these factors are highly subjective and leave considerable discretion to federal officials in deciding whether the challenged single-sex program is lawful. Given all of these factors, how much legal risk will local school officials be willing to accept to offer a single-sex program?

The real world is increasingly integrated and diverse. Schools are already geographically segregated and limited to classes of same-age peers. Does it help or harm children to further segregate them by gender and further limit their daily exposure to the real diversity of the world? When they leave school they will have to work in mixed gender settings and live in a mixed gender world. How are they helped by an educational setting that is isolated to same-sex peers only? Why are single-sex programs or schools wanted or needed? Do the benefits of single-sex programs outweigh the potential costs? There are relevant physical differences between males and females. But are there sufficient cultural, developmental, or other intellectual differences to justify gender segregation in academic instruction?

Among the most high profile impacts of Title IX have been regulations concerning athletic opportunities. Title IX has been very successful in opening the doors of athletic opportunities for female students, and female athletes have achieved remarkable successes since the passage of Title IX. Girls' and women's athletic teams are now among the most successful athletic programs at many schools and universities. Nonetheless, significant controversies over Title IX and athletic opportunities continue, including controversies over the participation of females in contact sports such as football or wrestling, and administrative efforts to achieve gender equity in athletic participation by cancelling low revenue producing male sports, effectively reducing opportunities for males rather than increasing opportunities for females.

Athletic Opportunities for Students

Athletic Opportunities: 45 C.F.R. § 86.41 (2011)

(a) *General*. No person shall, on the basis of sex, be excluded from participation in, be denied the benefits of, be treated differently from another person or otherwise be discriminated against in any interscholastic, intercollegiate, club or intramural athletics offered by a recipient, and no recipient shall provide any such athletics separately on such basis.

(b) *Separate teams*. Notwithstanding the requirements of paragraph (a) of this section, a recipient may operate or sponsor separate teams for members of each sex where selection for such teams is based upon competitive skill or the activity involved is a contact sport. However, where a recipient operates or sponsors a team in a particular sport for members of one sex but operates or sponsors no such team for members of the other sex, and athletic opportunities for members of that sex have previously been limited, members of the excluded sex must be allowed to try-out for the team offered unless the sport involved is a contact sport. For the purposes of this part, contact sports include boxing, wrestling, rugby, ice hockey, football, basketball and other sports the purpose of major activity of which involves bodily contact.

(c) *Equal opportunity*. A recipient which operates or sponsors interscholastic, intercollegiate, club or intramural athletics shall provide equal athletic opportunity for members of both sexes. In determining whether equal opportunities are available the Director will consider, among other factors:

(1) Whether the selection of sports and levels of competition effectively accommodate the interests and abilities of members of both sexes;
(2) The provision of equipment and supplies;
(3) Scheduling of games and practice time;
(4) Travel and per diem allowance;
(5) Opportunity to receive coaching and academic tutoring;
(6) Assignment and compensation of coaches and tutors;
(7) Provision of locker rooms, practice and competitive facilities;
(8) Provision of medical and training facilities and services;
(9) Provision of housing and dining facilities and services;
(10) Publicity.

Unequal aggregate expenditures for members of each sex or unequal expenditures for male and female teams if a recipient operates or sponsors separate teams will not constitute noncompliance with this section, but the Director may consider the failure to provide necessary funds for teams for one sex in assessing equality of opportunity for members of each sex.

* * * * * * *

Are unequal rates of athletic participation between females and males *de jure* or *de facto* in cause? Where females participate in sports at lesser rates than males, is this caused by the lingering effects of prior gender-based discrimination in school athletic programs, or are females just less interested in participating in school sports than males? Where are the boundaries between the duties of public officials to assure equity in the public sphere and what is beyond their authority in the private sphere? Even when school officials make appropriate efforts to achieve equity in athletic opportunities for females and males, how do school officials deal with local preferences of the public to attend male sports in greater numbers and the willingness pay more to see male football teams and other male sports? Are these lingering effects of prior societal discrimination? Without exceeding their lawful authority, what can school officials do to address private sector bias and discrimination related to school athletic programs?

Marital or Parental Status of Students

Historically, female teachers and students were expected to leave the school if they married or became pregnant. An even harsher social stigma was attached to unwed pregnancy. School officials generally did not know the full circumstances related to the pregnancy. Nor were these personal details any of their business. Nonetheless, unwed pregnancy carried with it a stigma of moral turpitude reinforced by moral judgments and sanctions from school officials. Victims of incest or rape might also be subjected to school sanctions and resulting public humiliation because of their unwed pregnancy.

In contrast, males who impregnated females were generally not subjected to such harsh school sanctions or social stigmas. Acting under the authority of the Equal Protection Clause, Congress sought to address this discrimination against females, prohibiting discrimination in public educational institutions based on marital or parental status.

Marital or Parental Status: 45 C.F.R. § 86.40 (2011)

(a) *Status generally*. A recipient shall not apply any rule concerning a student's actual or potential parental, family, or marital status which treats students differently on the basis of sex.

(b) *Pregnancy and related conditions*: (1) A recipient shall not discriminate against any student, or exclude any student from its education program or activity, including any class or extracurricular activity, on the basis of such student's pregnancy, childbirth, false pregnancy, termination of pregnancy or recovery therefrom, unless the student requests voluntarily to participate in a separate portion of the program or activity of the recipient.

(2) A recipient may require such a student to obtain the certification of a physician that the student is physically and emotionally able to continue participation so long as such a certification is required of all students for other physical or emotional conditions requiring the attention of a physician.

(3) A recipient which operates a portion of its education program or activity separately for pregnant students, admittance to which is completely voluntary on the part of the student as provided in paragraph (b)(1) of this section shall ensure that the separate portion is comparable to that offered to non-pregnant students.

(4) A recipient shall treat pregnancy, childbirth, false pregnancy, termination of pregnancy and recovery therefrom in the same manner and under the same policies as any other temporary disability with respect to any medical or hospital benefit, service, plan or

policy which such recipient administers, operates, offers, or participates in with respect to students admitted to the recipient's educational program or activity.

(5) In the case of a recipient which does not maintain a leave policy for its students, or in the case of a student who does not otherwise qualify for leave under such a policy, a recipient shall treat pregnancy, childbirth, false pregnancy, termination of pregnancy and recovery therefrom as a justification for a leave of absence for so long a period of time as is deemed medically necessary by the student's physician, at the conclusion of which the student shall be reinstated to the status which she held when the leave began.

* * * * * * *

Under 45 C.F.R. § 86.40 school officials must treat pregnancy as a medical condition. Pregnancy is not to be addressed punitively as a personal moral or social failing of the pregnant student, especially when such judgments have not been equally applied to males. It is virtually impossible, however, to apply gender neutral sanctions to disapproval of premarital sex for many reasons, including that premarital sex occurs without resulting pregnancy, and because only females show physical evidence of pregnancy. This necessarily makes pregnant females disproportionately subject to such sanctions.

While school officials may offer programs to help prevent and discourage premarital sex and teen pregnancy, pregnant students should not be subjected to official sanctions based on the personal moral judgments of school officials. Because pregnancy must be treated as a medical condition, the opinions of doctors, not school officials, determine what activities are safe and appropriate for the pregnant student. School officials may offer separate educational programs for pregnant students and new mothers to better accommodate their changing needs and schedules, to teach child-care skills, etc. But these separate programs must be completely voluntary and educational programs must be academically comparable to those offered to non-pregnant students.

Based on your reading of 45 C.F.R. § 86.40, could a pregnant student be asked to leave the cheerleading team because of her pregnancy? Could the pregnant student be asked to obtain certification from her doctor that her continued participation in cheerleading is safe? What reasonable accommodations might be required to allow her safe continued participation in this school program? How should school officials respond to complaints from community members that "allowing a pregnant girl to be a cheerleader will encourage teen pregnancy in our community"?

Sexual Harassment under Title IX

No one should have to tolerate sexual harassment in order to receive an education. Institutional tolerance of sexual harassment has been recognized as a form of sex discrimination. Accordingly, institutional tolerance of sexual harassment is prohibited by Title IX of the Education Amendments of 1972. In *Franklin v. Gwinnett*, 503 U.S. 60 (1992), the U.S. Supreme Court held that monetary damages are available to plaintiffs as a remedy in actions brought to enforce Title IX. The Court found that under Title IX there was an implied right of action for monetary damages. In *Franklin* the Court stated:

This case presents the question whether the implied right of action under Title IX of the Education Amendments of 1972 . . . supports a claim for monetary damages. Petitioner Christine Franklin was a student at North Gwinnett High School in Gwinnett County, Georgia, between September 1985 and August 1989. Respondent Gwinnett County School District operates the high school and receives federal funds. According to the complaint filed on December 29, 1988, in the United States District Court for the Northern District of Georgia, Franklin was subjected to continual sexual harassment beginning in the autumn of her tenth grade year (1986) from Andrew Hill, a sports coach and teacher employed by the district. Among other allegations, Franklin avers that Hill engaged her in sexually oriented conversations in which he asked about her sexual experiences with her boyfriend and whether she would consider having sexual intercourse with an older man; that Hill forcibly kissed her on the mouth in the school parking lot; that he telephoned her at her home and asked if she would meet him socially; and that, on three occasions in her junior year, Hill interrupted a class, requested that the teacher excuse Franklin, and took her to a private office where he subjected her to coercive intercourse. The complaint further alleges that though they became aware of and investigated Hill's sexual harassment of Franklin and other female students, teachers and administrators took no action to halt it and discouraged Franklin from pressing charges against Hill. On April 14, 1988, Hill resigned on the condition that all matters pending against him be dropped. The school thereupon closed its investigation.

In this action, the District Court dismissed the complaint on the ground that Title IX does not authorize an award of damages. The Court of Appeals affirmed . . . We reverse. Title IX placed on the Gwinnett County Public Schools the duty not to discriminate on the basis of sex, and "when a supervisor sexually harasses a subordinate because of the subordinate's sex, that supervisor 'discriminates' on the basis of sex." We believe the same rule should apply when a teacher sexually harasses and abuses a student . . . because Hill--the person she claims subjected her to sexual harassment--no longer teaches at the school and she herself no longer attends a school in the Gwinnett system, prospective relief accords her no remedy at all . . . In sum, we conclude that a damages remedy is available for an action brought to enforce Title IX. The judgment of the Court of Appeals, therefore, is reversed, and the case is remanded for further proceedings consistent with this opinion.

* * * * * * *

Why would school officials tolerate sexual harassment of students in their school? Why would they discourage the victim from pursuing legal remedies? If the perpetrator is allowed to resign, how likely is it that the perpetrator will simply go to another school and victimize other students? Professional ethics and personal morality should require school officials to protect students from sexual predators. But if these are lacking, there must be legal sanctions and remedies to compel school officials to take appropriate actions to protect students from abuse. The Court made it clear in *Franklin* that school districts could be held liable for monetary damages under Title IX. It was not clear, however, exactly when these damages were appropriate, and what legal standards were to be applied to the actions of school officials in these cases. These issues were addressed in *Gebser v. Lago*.

Gebser v. Lago Vista
524 U.S. 274 (1998)
Supreme Court of the United States

Justice O'CONNOR delivered the opinion of the Court.

The question in this case is when a school district may be held liable in damages in an implied right of action under Title IX of the Education Amendments of 1972, as amended, for the sexual harassment of a student by one of the district's teachers. We conclude that damages may not be recovered in those circumstances unless an official of the school district who at a minimum has authority to institute corrective measures on the district's behalf has actual notice of, and is deliberately indifferent to, the teacher's misconduct.

In the spring of 1991, when petitioner Alida Star Gebser was an eighth-grade student at a middle school in respondent Lago Vista Independent School District (Lago Vista), she joined a high school book discussion group led by Frank Waldrop, a teacher at Lago Vista's high school. Lago Vista received federal funds at all pertinent times. During the book discussion sessions, Waldrop often made sexually suggestive comments to the students. Gebser entered high school in the fall and was assigned to classes taught by Waldrop in both semesters. Waldrop continued to make inappropriate remarks to the students, and he began to direct more of his suggestive comments toward Gebser, including during the substantial amount of time that the two were alone in his classroom. He initiated sexual contact with Gebser in the spring, when, while visiting her home ostensibly to give her a book, he kissed and fondled her. The two had sexual intercourse on a number of occasions during the remainder of the school year. Their relationship continued through the summer and into the following school year, and they often had intercourse during class time, although never on school property.

Gebser did not report the relationship to school officials, testifying that while she realized Waldrop's conduct was improper, she was uncertain how to react and she wanted to continue having him as a teacher. In October 1992, the parents of two other students complained to the high school principal about Waldrop's comments in class. The principal arranged a meeting, at which, according to the principal, Waldrop indicated that he did not believe he had made offensive remarks but apologized to the parents and said it would not happen again. The principal also advised Waldrop to be careful about his classroom comments and told the school guidance counselor about the meeting, but he did not report the parents' complaint to Lago Vista's superintendent, who was the district's Title IX coordinator. A couple of months later, in January 1993, a police officer discovered Waldrop and Gebser engaging in sexual intercourse and arrested Waldrop. Lago Vista terminated his employment, and subsequently, the Texas Education Agency revoked his teaching license. During this time, the district had not promulgated or distributed an official grievance procedure for lodging sexual harassment complaints; nor had it issued a formal anti-harassment policy.

Gebser and her mother filed suit against Lago Vista and Waldrop in state court in November 1993, raising claims against the school district under Title IX, 42 U.S.C. § 1983, and state negligence law, and claims against Waldrop primarily under state law. They sought compensatory and punitive damages from both defendants. After the case was removed, the United States District Court for the Western District of Texas granted summary judgment in favor of Lago Vista on all claims, and remanded the allegations against Waldrop to state court. In rejecting the Title IX claim against the school district, the court reasoned that the statute "was enacted to counter policies of discrimination . . . in federally funded education programs," and that "only if school administrators have some type of notice of the gender discrimination and fail to respond in good faith can the discrimination be interpreted as a policy of the school district." Here, the court determined, the parents' complaint to the principal concerning Waldrop's comments in class was the only one Lago Vista had received about Waldrop, and that evidence was inadequate to raise a genuine issue on whether the school district had actual or constructive notice that Waldrop was involved in a sexual relationship with a student. Petitioners appealed only on the Title IX claim. The Court of Appeals for the Fifth Circuit affirmed . . . We granted certiorari to address the issue, and we now affirm.

Title IX provides in pertinent part: "No person . . . shall, on the basis of sex, be excluded from participation in, be denied the benefits of, or be subjected to discrimination under any education program or activity receiving Federal financial assistance." The express statutory means of enforcement is administrative: The statute directs federal agencies that distribute education funding to establish requirements to effectuate the nondiscrimination mandate, and permits the agencies to enforce those requirements through "any . . . means authorized by law," including ultimately the termination of federal funding . . . Title IX is also enforceable through an implied private right of action . . . We subsequently established in *Franklin v. Gwinnett*, that monetary damages are available in the implied private action.

In *Franklin*, a high school student alleged that a teacher had sexually abused her on repeated occasions and that teachers and school administrators knew about the harassment but took no action, even to the point of dissuading her from initiating charges . . . *Franklin* thereby establishes that a school district can be held liable in damages in cases involving a teacher's sexual harassment of a student; the decision, however, does not purport to define the contours of that liability.

We face that issue squarely in this case . . . we conclude that it would "frustrate the purposes" of Title IX to permit a damages recovery against a school district for a teacher's sexual harassment of a student based on principles of respondeat superior or constructive notice, *i.e.*, without actual notice to a school district official. Because Congress did not expressly create a private right of action under Title IX, the statutory text does not shed light on Congress' intent with respect to the scope of available remedies. Instead, "we attempt to infer how the 1972 Congress would have addressed the issue had the . . . action been included as an express provision in the" statute.

As a general matter, it does not appear that Congress contemplated unlimited recovery in damages against a funding recipient where the recipient is unaware of discrimination in its programs. When Title IX was enacted in 1972, the principal civil rights statutes containing an express right of action did not provide for recovery of monetary damages at all, instead allowing only injunctive and equitable relief. It was not until 1991 that Congress made damages available under Title VII, and even then, Congress carefully limited the amount recoverable in any individual case, calibrating the maximum recovery to the size of the employer. Adopting petitioners' position would amount, then, to allowing unlimited recovery of damages under Title IX where Congress has not spoken on the subject of either the right or the remedy, and in the face of evidence that when Congress expressly considered both in Title VII it restricted the amount of damages available.

Congress enacted Title IX in 1972 with two principal objectives in mind: "To avoid the use of federal resources to support discriminatory practices" and "to provide individual citizens effective protection against those practices." The statute was modeled after Title VI of the Civil

Rights Act of 1964, which is parallel to Title IX except that it prohibits race discrimination, not sex discrimination, and applies in all programs receiving federal funds, not only in education programs. The two statutes operate in the same manner, conditioning an offer of federal funding on a promise by the recipient not to discriminate, in what amounts essentially to a contract between the Government and the recipient of funds.

That contractual framework distinguishes Title IX from Title VII, which is framed in terms not of a condition but of an outright prohibition. Title VII applies to all employers without regard to federal funding and aims broadly to "eradicate discrimination throughout the economy." Title VII, moreover, seeks to "make persons whole for injuries suffered through past discrimination." Thus, whereas Title VII aims centrally to compensate victims of discrimination, Title IX focuses more on "protecting" individuals from discriminatory practices carried out by recipients of federal funds . . .

Title IX's contractual nature has implications for our construction of the scope of available remedies . . . If a school district's liability for a teacher's sexual harassment rests on principles of constructive notice or respondeat superior, it will likewise be the case that the recipient of funds was unaware of the discrimination. It is sensible to assume that Congress did not envision a recipient's liability in damages in that situation.

Most significantly, Title IX contains important clues that Congress did not intend to allow recovery in damages where liability rests solely on principles of vicarious liability or constructive notice. Title IX's express means of enforcement--by administrative agencies-- operates on an assumption of actual notice to officials of the funding recipient . . . Presumably, a central purpose of requiring notice of the violation "to the appropriate person" and an opportunity for voluntary compliance before administrative enforcement proceedings can commence is to avoid diverting education funding from beneficial uses where a recipient was unaware of discrimination in its programs and is willing to institute prompt corrective measures. The scope of private damages relief proposed by petitioners is at odds with that basic objective. When a teacher's sexual harassment is imputed to a school district or when a school district is deemed to have "constructively" known of the teacher's harassment, by assumption the district had no actual knowledge of the teacher's conduct. Nor, of course, did the district have an opportunity to take action to end the harassment or to limit further harassment.

It would be unsound, we think, for a statute's express system of enforcement to require notice to the recipient and an opportunity to come into voluntary compliance while a judicially implied system of enforcement permits substantial liability without regard to the recipient's knowledge or its corrective actions upon receiving notice. Moreover, an award of damages in a particular case might well exceed a recipient's level of federal funding. Where a statute's express enforcement scheme hinges its most severe sanction [withdrawal of federal funds] on notice and unsuccessful efforts to obtain compliance, we cannot attribute to Congress the intention to have implied an enforcement scheme that allows imposition of greater liability without comparable conditions.

Because the express remedial scheme under Title IX is predicated upon notice to an "appropriate person" and an opportunity to rectify any violation, we conclude, in the absence of further direction from Congress, that the implied damages remedy should be fashioned along the same lines. An "appropriate person" . . . is, at a minimum, an official of the recipient entity with authority to take corrective action to end the discrimination. Consequently, in cases like this one that do not involve official policy of the recipient entity, we hold that a damages remedy will not lie under Title IX unless an official who at a minimum has authority to address the alleged discrimination and to institute corrective measures on the recipient's behalf has actual knowledge of discrimination in the recipient's programs and fails adequately to respond.

We think, moreover, that the response must amount to deliberate indifference to discrimination. The administrative enforcement scheme presupposes that an official who is advised of a Title IX violation refuses to take action to bring the recipient into compliance. The premise, in other words, is an official decision by the recipient not to remedy the violation. That framework finds a rough parallel in the standard of deliberate indifference. Under a lower standard, there would be a risk that the recipient would be liable in damages not for its own official decision but instead for its employees' independent actions . . .

Applying the framework to this case is fairly straightforward, as petitioners do not contend they can prevail under an actual notice standard. The only official alleged to have had information about Waldrop's misconduct is the high school principal. That information, however, consisted of a complaint from parents of other students charging only that Waldrop had made inappropriate comments during class, which was plainly insufficient to alert the principal to the possibility that Waldrop was involved in a sexual relationship with a student. Lago Vista, moreover, terminated Waldrop's employment upon learning of his relationship with Gebser. Justice Stevens points out in his dissenting opinion that Waldrop of course had knowledge of his own actions. Where a school district's liability rests on actual notice principles, however, the knowledge of the wrongdoer himself is not pertinent to the analysis . . .

The number of reported cases involving sexual harassment of students in schools confirms that harassment unfortunately is an all too common aspect of the educational experience. No one questions that a student suffers extraordinary harm when subjected to sexual harassment and abuse by a teacher, and that the teacher's conduct is reprehensible and undermines the basic purposes of the educational system. The issue in this case, however, is whether the independent misconduct of a teacher is attributable to the school district that employs him under a specific federal statute designed primarily to prevent recipients of federal financial assistance from using the funds in a discriminatory manner. Our decision does not affect any right of recovery that an individual may have against a school district as a matter of state law or against the teacher in his individual capacity under state law or under 42 U.S.C. § 1983. Until Congress speaks directly on the subject, however, we will not hold a school district liable in damages under Title IX for a teacher's sexual harassment of a student absent actual notice and deliberate indifference. We therefore affirm the judgment of the Court of Appeals.

It is so ordered.

* * * * * * *

In *Gebser* the Court established that to prevail in a sexual harassment suit for monetary damages under Title IX, plaintiffs must establish that:

1) School officials had actual notice of the sexual harassment, and;
2) School officials reacted with deliberate indifference.

Both *Franklin* and *Gebser* involved sexual harassment of students by teachers. Could school officials be held liable under Title IX for student-on-student or peer sexual harassment? The Court addressed this issue in *Davis v. Monroe.*

311

Davis v. Monroe
526 U.S. 629 (1999)
Supreme Court of the United States

Justice O'CONNOR delivered the opinion of the Court.

Petitioner brought suit against the Monroe County Board of Education and other defendants, alleging that her fifth-grade daughter had been the victim of sexual harassment by another student in her class. Among petitioner's claims was a claim for monetary and injunctive relief under Title IX. The District Court dismissed petitioner's Title IX claim on the ground that "student-on-student," or peer, harassment provides no ground for a private cause of action under the statute. The Court of Appeals for the Eleventh Circuit, sitting *en banc*, affirmed. We consider here whether a private damages action may lie against the school board in cases of student-on-student harassment. We conclude that it may, but only where the funding recipient acts with deliberate indifference to known acts of harassment in its programs or activities. Moreover, we conclude that such an action will lie only for harassment that is so severe, pervasive, and objectively offensive that it effectively bars the victim's access to an educational opportunity or benefit . . .

Petitioner's minor daughter, LaShonda, was allegedly the victim of a prolonged pattern of sexual harassment by one of her fifth-grade classmates at Hubbard Elementary School, a public school in Monroe County, Georgia. According to petitioner's complaint, the harassment began in December 1992, when the classmate, G.F., attempted to touch LaShonda's breasts and genital area and made vulgar statements such as "I want to get in bed with you" and "I want to feel your boobs." Similar conduct allegedly occurred on or about January 4 and January 20, 1993. LaShonda reported each of these incidents to her mother and to her classroom teacher, Diane Fort. Petitioner, in turn, also contacted Fort, who allegedly assured petitioner that the school principal, Bill Querry, had been informed of the incidents. Petitioner contends that, notwithstanding these reports, no disciplinary action was taken against G.F.

G.F.'s conduct allegedly continued for many months. In early February, G.F. purportedly placed a door stop in his pants and proceeded to act in a sexually suggestive manner toward LaShonda during physical education class. LaShonda reported G.F.'s behavior to her physical education teacher, Whit Maples. Approximately one week later, G.F. again allegedly engaged in harassing behavior, this time while under the supervision of another classroom teacher, Joyce Pippin. Again, LaShonda allegedly reported the incident to the teacher, and again petitioner contacted the teacher to follow up.

Petitioner alleges that G.F. once more directed sexually harassing conduct toward LaShonda in physical education class in early March, and that LaShonda reported the incident to both Maples and Pippen. In mid-April 1993, G.F. allegedly rubbed his body against LaShonda in the school hallway in what LaShonda considered a sexually suggestive manner, and LaShonda again reported the matter to Fort.

The string of incidents finally ended in mid-May, when G.F. was charged with, and pleaded guilty to, sexual battery for his misconduct. The complaint alleges that LaShonda had suffered during the months of harassment, however; specifically, her previously high grades allegedly dropped as she became unable to concentrate on her studies, and, in April 1993, her father discovered that she had written a suicide note. The complaint further alleges that, at one point, LaShonda told petitioner that she "didn't know how much longer she could keep [G.F.] off her."

Nor was LaShonda G.F.'s only victim; it is alleged that other girls in the class fell prey to G.F.'s conduct. At one point, in fact, a group composed of LaShonda and other female students tried to speak with Principal Querry about G.F.'s behavior. According to the complaint, however, a teacher denied the students' request with the statement, "If [Querry] wants you, he'll call you."

Petitioner alleges that no disciplinary action was taken in response to G.F.'s behavior toward LaShonda. In addition to her conversations with Fort and Pippen, petitioner alleges that she spoke with Principal Querry in mid-May 1993. When petitioner inquired as to what action the school intended to take against G.F., Querry simply stated, "I guess I'll have to threaten him a little bit harder." Yet, petitioner alleges, at no point during the many months of his reported misconduct was G.F. disciplined for harassment. Indeed, Querry allegedly asked petitioner why LaShonda "was the only one complaining."

Nor, according to the complaint, was any effort made to separate G.F. and LaShonda. On the contrary, notwithstanding LaShonda's frequent complaints, only after more than three months of reported harassment was she even permitted to change her classroom seat so that she was no longer seated next to G.F. Moreover, petitioner alleges that, at the time of the events in question, the Monroe County Board of Education (Board) had not instructed its personnel on how to respond to peer sexual harassment and had not established a policy on the issue.

On May 4, 1994, petitioner filed suit in the United States District Court for the Middle District of Georgia against the Board, Charles Dumas, the school district's superintendent, and Principal Querry. The complaint alleged that the Board is a recipient of federal funding for purposes of Title IX, that "the persistent sexual advances and harassment by the student G.F. upon LaShonda interfered with her ability to attend school and perform her studies and activities," and that "the deliberate indifference by Defendants to the unwelcome sexual advances of a student upon LaShonda created an intimidating, hostile, offensive and abusive school environment in violation of Title IX." The complaint sought compensatory and punitive damages, attorney's fees, and injunctive relief . . .

We agree with respondents that a recipient of federal funds may be liable in damages under Title IX only for its own misconduct . . . We disagree with respondents' assertion, however, that petitioner seeks to hold the Board liable for G. F.'s actions instead of its own. Here, petitioner attempts to hold the Board liable for its own decision to remain idle in the face of known student-on-student harassment in its schools. In Gebser, we concluded that a recipient of federal education funds may be liable in damages under Title IX where it is deliberately indifferent to known acts of sexual harassment by a teacher . . . we concluded that the district could be liable for damages only where the district itself intentionally acted in clear violation of Title IX by remaining deliberately indifferent to acts of teacher-student harassment of which it had actual knowledge . . .

We consider here whether the misconduct identified in Gebser--deliberate indifference to known acts of harassment--amounts to an intentional violation of Title IX, capable of supporting a private damages action, when the harasser is a student rather than a teacher. We conclude that, in certain limited circumstances, it does . . .

Where, as here, the misconduct occurs during school hours and on school grounds--the bulk of G.F.'s misconduct, in fact, took place in the classroom--the misconduct is taking place "under" an "operation" of the funding recipient. In these circumstances, the recipient retains substantial

313

control over the context in which the harassment occurs. More importantly, however, in this setting the Board exercises significant control over the harasser . . . We thus conclude that recipients of federal funding may be liable for "subjecting" their students to discrimination where the recipient is deliberately indifferent to known acts of student-on-student sexual harassment and the harasser is under the school's disciplinary authority . . .

We stress that our conclusion here--that recipients may be liable for their deliberate indifference to known acts of peer sexual harassment--does not mean that recipients can avoid liability only by purging their schools of actionable peer harassment or that administrators must engage in particular disciplinary action. We thus disagree with respondents' contention that, if Title IX provides a cause of action for student-on-student harassment, "nothing short of expulsion of every student accused of misconduct involving sexual overtones would protect school systems from liability or damages." Likewise, the dissent erroneously imagines that victims of peer harassment now have a Title IX right to make particular remedial demands. In fact, as we have previously noted, courts should refrain from second-guessing the disciplinary decisions made by school administrators.

School administrators will continue to enjoy the flexibility they require so long as funding recipients are deemed "deliberately indifferent" to acts of student-on-student harassment only where the recipient's response to the harassment or lack thereof is clearly unreasonable in light of the known circumstances. The dissent consistently mischaracterizes this standard to require funding recipients to "remedy" peer harassment, and to "ensure that . . . students conform their conduct to" certain rules. Title IX imposes no such requirements. On the contrary, the recipient must merely respond to known peer harassment in a manner that is not clearly unreasonable. This is not a mere "reasonableness" standard, as the dissent assumes. In an appropriate case, there is no reason why courts, on a motion to dismiss, for summary judgment, or for a directed verdict, could not identify a response as not "clearly unreasonable" as a matter of law.

Like the dissent, we acknowledge that school administrators shoulder substantial burdens as a result of legal constraints on their disciplinary authority. To the extent that these restrictions arise from federal statutes, Congress can review these burdens with attention to the difficult position in which such legislation may place our Nation's schools. We believe, however, that the standard set out here is sufficiently flexible to account both for the level of disciplinary authority available to the school and for the potential liability arising from certain forms of disciplinary action. A university might not, for example, be expected to exercise the same degree of control over its students that a grade school would enjoy, and it would be entirely reasonable for a school to refrain from a form of disciplinary action that would expose it to constitutional or statutory claims.

While it remains to be seen whether petitioner can show that the Board's response to reports of G.F.'s misconduct was clearly unreasonable in light of the known circumstances, petitioner may be able to show that the Board "subjected" LaShonda to discrimination by failing to respond in any way over a period of five months to complaints of G.F.'s in-school misconduct from LaShonda and other female students . . .

Having previously determined that "sexual harassment" is "discrimination" in the school context under Title IX, we are constrained to conclude that student-on-student sexual harassment, if sufficiently severe, can likewise rise to the level of discrimination actionable under the statute. The statute's other prohibitions, moreover, help give content to the term "discrimination" in this context. Students are not only protected from discrimination, but also specifically shielded from being "excluded from participation in" or "denied the benefits of" any

314

"education program or activity receiving Federal financial assistance." The statute makes clear that, whatever else it prohibits, students must not be denied access to educational benefits and opportunities on the basis of gender. We thus conclude that funding recipients are properly held liable in damages only where they are deliberately indifferent to sexual harassment, of which they have actual knowledge, that is so severe, pervasive, and objectively offensive that it can be said to deprive the victims of access to the educational opportunities or benefits provided by the school.

The most obvious example of student-on-student sexual harassment capable of triggering a damages claim would thus involve the overt, physical deprivation of access to school resources. Consider, for example, a case in which male students physically threaten their female peers every day, successfully preventing the female students from using a particular school resource--an athletic field or a computer lab, for instance. District administrators are well aware of the daily ritual, yet they deliberately ignore requests for aid from the female students wishing to use the resource. The district's knowing refusal to take any action in response to such behavior would fly in the face of Title IX's core principles, and such deliberate indifference may appropriately be subject to claims for monetary damages. It is not necessary, however, to show physical exclusion to demonstrate that students have been deprived by the actions of another student or students of an educational opportunity on the basis of sex. Rather, a plaintiff must establish sexual harassment of students that is so severe, pervasive, and objectively offensive, and that so undermines and detracts from the victims' educational experience, that the victim-students are effectively denied equal access to an institution's resources and opportunities.

Whether gender-oriented conduct rises to the level of actionable "harassment" thus "depends on a constellation of surrounding circumstances, expectations, and relationships," including, but not limited to, the ages of the harasser and the victim and the number of individuals involved. Courts, moreover, must bear in mind that schools are unlike the adult workplace and that children may regularly interact in a manner that would be unacceptable among adults. Indeed, at least early on, students are still learning how to interact appropriately with their peers. It is thus understandable that, in the school setting, students often engage in insults, banter, teasing, shoving, pushing, and gender-specific conduct that is upsetting to the students subjected to it. Damages are not available for simple acts of teasing and name-calling among school children, however, even where these comments target differences in gender. Rather, in the context of student-on-student harassment, damages are available only where the behavior is so severe, pervasive, and objectively offensive that it denies its victims the equal access to education that Title IX is designed to protect.

The dissent fails to appreciate these very real limitations on a funding recipient's liability under Title IX. It is not enough to show, as the dissent would read this opinion to provide, that a student has been "teased," or "called . . . offensive names." Comparisons to an "overweight child who skips gym class because the other children tease her about her size," the student who "refuses to wear glasses to avoid the taunts of 'four-eyes'" and "the child who refuses to go to school because the school bully calls him a 'scaredy-cat' at recess," are inapposite and misleading. Nor do we contemplate, much less hold, that a mere "decline in grades is enough to survive" a motion to dismiss. The dropoff in LaShonda's grades provides necessary evidence of a potential link between her education and G.F.'s misconduct, but petitioner's ability to state a cognizable claim here depends equally on the alleged persistence and severity of G.F.'s actions, not to mention the Board's alleged knowledge and deliberate indifference. We trust that the

315

dissent's characterization of our opinion will not mislead courts to impose more sweeping liability than we read Title IX to require.

Moreover, the provision that the discrimination occur "under any education program or activity" suggests that the behavior be serious enough to have the systemic effect of denying the victim equal access to an educational program or activity. Although, in theory, a single instance of sufficiently severe one-on-one peer harassment could be said to have such an effect, we think it unlikely that Congress would have thought such behavior sufficient to rise to this level in light of the inevitability of student misconduct and the amount of litigation that would be invited by entertaining claims of official indifference to a single instance of one-on-one peer harassment. By limiting private damages actions to cases having a systemic effect on educational programs or activities, we reconcile the general principle that Title IX prohibits official indifference to known peer sexual harassment with the practical realities of responding to student behavior, realities that Congress could not have meant to be ignored. Even the dissent suggests that Title IX liability may arise when a funding recipient remains indifferent to severe, gender-based mistreatment played out on a "widespread level" among students.

The fact that it was a teacher who engaged in harassment in *Franklin* and *Gebser* is relevant. The relationship between the harasser and the victim necessarily affects the extent to which the misconduct can be said to breach Title IX's guarantee of equal access to educational benefits and to have a systemic effect on a program or activity. Peer harassment, in particular, is less likely to satisfy these requirements than is teacher-student harassment.

Applying this standard to the facts at issue here, we conclude that the Eleventh Circuit erred in dismissing petitioner's complaint. Petitioner alleges that her daughter was the victim of repeated acts of sexual harassment by G.F. over a 5–month period, and there are allegations in support of the conclusion that G.F.'s misconduct was severe, pervasive, and objectively offensive. The harassment was not only verbal; it included numerous acts of objectively offensive touching, and, indeed, G.F. ultimately pleaded guilty to criminal sexual misconduct. Moreover, the complaint alleges that there were multiple victims who were sufficiently disturbed by G.F.'s misconduct to seek an audience with the school principal. Further, petitioner contends that the harassment had a concrete, negative effect on her daughter's ability to receive an education. The complaint also suggests that petitioner may be able to show both actual knowledge and deliberate indifference on the part of the Board, which made no effort whatsoever either to investigate or to put an end to the harassment . . . the judgment of the United States Court of Appeals for the Eleventh Circuit is reversed, and the case is remanded for further proceedings consistent with this opinion.

It is so ordered.

* * * * * * *

In *Davis* the Court found that: "The fact that it was a teacher who engaged in harassment in *Franklin* and *Gebser* is relevant." It is the tolerance of sexual harassment in the school that is the basis for liability under Title IX, not the status of the perpetrator. Concerning plaintiffs' burden of proof in these cases, however, the Court did note that: "Peer harassment, in particular, is less likely to satisfy these requirements than is teacher-student harassment." Accordingly, in cases of peer harassment the Court added that the student-on-student harassment must be "so severe, pervasive, and objectively offensive that it can be said to deprive the victims of access to the educational opportunities or benefits provided by the school." The Court noted that this may include actual physical exclusion from school resources, such as harassment that keeps students away from an athletic field, lunch room, lab, etc., but also any sexual harassment that "so undermines and detracts from the victims' educational experience, that the victim-students are effectively denied equal access to an institution's resources and opportunities."

The Court also defined what would constitute "deliberate indifference" in violation of Title IX, stating that school officials will be "deemed 'deliberately indifferent' to acts of student-on-student harassment only where the recipient's response to the harassment or lack thereof is clearly unreasonable in light of the known circumstances." To avoid liability, school officials "must merely respond to known peer harassment in a manner that is not clearly unreasonable."

Together *Franklin*, *Gebser*, and *Davis* teach that school officials should: 1) Have a reasonable policy in place for the prevention and correction of sexual harassment; 2) Promptly and fairly investigate reports of alleged sexual harassment; and 3) Take reasonable remedial actions when appropriate to assure that no one is excluded from educational opportunities because of sexual harassment or other differential treatment based on gender.

Challenges to Inequities in School Funding

Inequities in public school funding have been challenged as violations of federal and state guarantees of equal protection of the laws, and as contrary to the commands of education clauses in state constitutions. Historically, public schools in the U.S. were supported by local funding. Wealthier communities could afford well-funded schools, while poorer communities could afford only less well-funded schools or no schools at all.

While this status quo of educational inequity may have been acceptable to many in a relatively isolated agrarian society, increased industrialization and international economic and military competition required higher levels of education throughout the population. Concerns over inadequate education led to the adoption of state constitutional mandates for state-level support of education. Education provisions in state constitutions shifted the legal duty to provide for public education to the State General Assembly, in order to help assure greater uniformity in educational opportunities throughout the state.

When states adopted constitutional language making support for public education a state-level duty, however, a collision between this constitutional ideal and political reality was inevitable. Commendably, many states adopted state constitutional language that required the legislature to support a high quality education for all children in the state. Generally, however, the more powerful the constitutional command to provide a well-funded, high quality education for all children in the state, the greater the gap between the constitutional ideal and the fiscal reality for the state's poorest schools.

Egalitarian support for providing high quality education for all children is an attractive ideal, but it becomes politically problematic when it requires higher taxes or the transfer of funds from wealthier districts to poorer districts.

Connected Questions with Disconnected Answers:
Who Wants All Children to Have a High Quality Education?
Who Wants to Pay Higher Taxes to Fund Other People's Schools?

Most everyone wants all children to be provided with a high quality education. In contrast, few want their property taxes raised, especially if the additional tax dollars are being sent to schools outside their home districts.

Although state constitutions in all fifty states recognized a state-level duty for funding public schools, nearly all state school funding formulas to some degree retained the historical practice of local taxation for local schools. Every local or state tax dollar collected for public education is lawfully a state controlled dollar. Under the U.S. system of federalism there are only two governmental sovereigns, the federal government and the state government. Local governments are simply branches of the state government and are not separate sovereigns. Nonetheless, state legislators have generally allowed local school districts to continue to exercise proprietary control over their locally generated funds.

Wealthier districts strongly resisted any "Robin Hood" legislation that would use locally generated revenue to equalize school funding throughout the state. There is a strong correlation between wealth and political power, so wealthier districts generally get their way in the General Assembly. State constitutions may have assigned the responsibility for funding public schools to the State. But because of the disproportionate influence of wealthier districts in the State General Assembly, state laws continued to allow local schools to keep local funding to supplement state funding. Further, in a zero-sum game for state money, wealthier districts generally did not support funding equalization legislation to bring poorer school districts up to the levels of funding available to wealthier school districts.

This delegation of school funding authority to local districts is at the root of school funding disparities. Local resources for school funding vary widely from district to district. Property wealthy districts have a large tax base to draw from, while property poor districts have relatively little to tax. Property wealthy districts can raise large amounts of money even with relatively lower tax rates, while property poor districts may fail to generate adequate funding for their schools even when levying the maximum legal tax rates.

Basic Formula for Local School Funding Resources

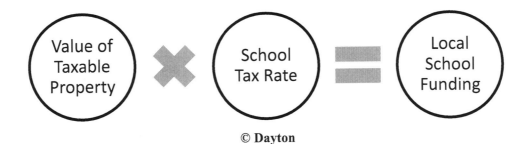

© Dayton

A school district with 3 times the property wealth of a poorer school district could generate 3 times as much local school funding with the same tax rate, or the same funding with a tax rate only one-third that of the poorer school district. This disparity in taxable wealth can create a dual inequity in which relatively wealthy school districts enjoy both generous funding for their schools and lower property tax rates, while poorer school districts may lack adequate school funding despite their relatively higher property tax rates. Further, poorer schools and higher tax rates are dual disincentives for the property development needed to improve the local tax base.

318

The use of local sales taxes to supplement local school funding only further aggravates these funding inequities. The most active areas of commerce tend to be in the more property wealthy suburban school districts. Not only does this leave many poorer rural and inner-city area residents without adequate property tax based funding for their schools, but they are functionally forced to supplement the sales tax funding of wealthier neighboring school districts because there are few places to shop for needed goods in their home districts.

Inspired by *Brown*, advocates for children in property poor districts began challenging state systems of funding based on local property wealth. Funding reform advocates argued that under these funding systems some wealthier districts were able to spend nearly 10 times what was available to the state's poorest school districts per student. Civil rights advocates nation-wide began attacking these fiscal disparities as an unconstitutional system resulting in the denial of equal educational opportunity to students in the poorer school districts. Civil rights advocates pressed for judicial mandates for school funding equity in both federal and state courts.

In *Serrano v. Priest*, 487 P. 2d 1241 (Cal. 1971), the Supreme Court of California issued its landmark decision on public school funding inequities. *Serrano* was the first successful challenge to a state system of public school finance. In addition, *Serrano* was the first case to establish a judicially manageable standard for courts to use when addressing inequities in school funding. The "Serrano principle" required that the quality of a child's education must not be a function of the wealth of the local community. Instead, public school funding must be a function of the wealth of the state as a whole.

In *San Antonio v. Rodriguez*, 411 U.S. 1 (1973), the U.S. Supreme Court was presented with an opportunity to establish a nation-wide mandate for greater school funding equity. Plaintiffs argued that education was a fundamental right under the U.S. Constitution; that poverty was a suspect classification; and inequities in funding denied fiscally disadvantaged students equal protection of the laws. But instead of using the *Rodriguez* case to establish a mandate for school funding equity in a 5-4 decision the Court delivered a significant defeat to school funding reform advocates. The Court held that education was not a fundamental right protected under the U.S. Constitution and that the Texas system of school finance did not disadvantage any suspect class.

The plaintiffs in *Rodriguez* were Mexican-American parents who sued on behalf of school children throughout the state that were members of minority groups or poor and resided in school districts having a low property tax base. In the plaintiffs' Edgewood School District, 90 percent of the student population was Mexican-American and over 6 percent was African-American. The Court noted that the average assessed property value per pupil in the Edgewood District was $5,960, and the median family income was $4,686. In contrast, the nearby Alamo Heights School District was predominately Anglo with only 18 percent Mexican-American children and less than 1 percent African-American children. The average assessed property value per pupil in the Alamo Heights District was over $49,000, and the median income was $8,001.

The state conceded that its system of funding public schools could not withstand the level of scrutiny the Court uses in reviewing legislation that interferes with fundamental rights, and the Court agreed that "the Texas financing system and its counterpart in virtually every other State would not pass muster" under strict judicial scrutiny. The Court then considered whether strict scrutiny was the appropriate standard of review.

First, the Court considered whether the Texas system disadvantaged any suspect class. Specifically, the Court considered the plaintiffs' allegations that poverty constituted a suspect classification. Concluding that it did not, the Court found no identifiable disfavored class in *Rodriguez*. The Court distinguished *Rodriguez* from prior cases protecting indigents by noting

319

that the plaintiffs had alleged only a relative rather than an absolute deprivation of education. Based on a study published in the Yale Law Journal, the Court criticized "the major factual assumption of *Serrano*--that the educational financing system discriminates against the 'poor.'" "There is no basis on the record in this case for assuming that the poorest people . . . are concentrated in the poorest districts." The Court was skeptical of the assumption that the amount of money available for education affects the quality of the education, stating "this is a matter of considerable dispute among educators and commentators." Since the Court refused to recognize any suspect class, the Court could not apply strict scrutiny unless it classified education as a fundamental right.

Justice Powell's majority opinion refused to hold that education was a fundamental right under the U.S. Constitution, observing: "It is not the province of this Court to create substantive constitutional rights in the name of guaranteeing equal protection of the laws." The Court criticized the *Serrano* court's method for determining whether education is a fundamental right (*i.e.*, weighing the importance of education in comparison to other fundamental rights recognized by the Court), noting that instead "the answer lies in assessing whether there is a right to education explicitly or implicitly guaranteed by the Constitution."

Finding no explicit or implicit guarantee regarding education in the U.S. Constitution, education was not a fundamental right under the U.S. Constitution. With no suspect class or fundamental right involved, the Court applied the rational basis test. Under this deferential standard of judicial review the Texas system need only bear some rational relationship to a legitimate state interest. The Court determined that the interest in promoting local control of public schools was sufficient to meet this low-level standard of review.

In conclusion, the majority recited a litany of concerns that virtually every opinion upholding an existing school funding system has echoed: 1) Criticism of the plaintiffs' statistical data and conclusions; 2) Fear of engaging in judicial activism; 3) Fear of opening the floodgates of litigation in other areas of social services; 4) Concerns related to judicial competence in an area where courts generally have limited expertise; 5) The importance of judicial deference to the legislature in this area; and 6) The need for the plaintiffs to address their grievances to the legislature instead of the courts.

Justice Marshall, in a dissenting opinion joined by Justice Douglas, asserted that the majority's opinion was "a retreat from our historical commitment to equality of educational opportunity" and an "unsupportable acquiescence in a system which deprives children in their earliest years of the chance to reach their full potential as citizens." Justice Marshall pointed out that the majority's solution--submitting the issue to the political process--was no solution at all, as the district court had delayed its decision in the case for two years hoping that the legislature would remedy the gross disparities in the Texas system.

Asserting the futility of depending on the Texas legislature, Justice Marshall stated, "The strong vested interest of property-rich districts in the existing property tax scheme poses a substantial barrier to self-initiated legislative reform in educational financing." Justice Marshall's objection referenced the Court's decision in *Brown*. Justice Marshall stated: "I, for one, am unsatisfied with the hope of an ultimate 'political' solution sometime in the indefinite future while, in the meantime, countless children unjustifiably receive inferior educations that 'may affect their hearts and minds in a way unlikely to be undone.'" Further, if money is unrelated to educational quality, as the majority suggested, Justice Marshall wondered why "a number of our country's wealthiest school districts, which have no legal obligation to argue in support of the constitutionality of the Texas legislation, have nevertheless zealously pursued its cause before this Court."

The Court's decision in *Rodriguez* effectively closed the door on plaintiffs who wished to use the federal Constitution and the federal courts as a vehicle for achieving greater equity in school funding. But Justice Marshall, in his dissenting opinion in *Rodriguez*, noted that "nothing in the Court's decision today should inhibit further review of state educational funding schemes under state constitutional provisions."

Battles over school funding have been waged on many fronts nation-wide including efforts to influence public opinion and attempts to pass federal and state legislation. When these efforts failed to provide adequate remedies, however, funding equity advocates turned to litigation. Following Justice Marshall's lead, plaintiffs appealed to state courts for school funding remedies with mixed results. Plaintiffs experienced both significant losses and victories in state courts. In some states, however, victory meant protracted serial litigation that extended for decades, with courts ordering costly remedies in some cases, and legislative non-compliance leading plaintiffs back to court again and again.

Following the financial collapse of 2008, however, massive state budget shortfalls put state constitutional mandates to fund education and mandates to balance annual budgets in increasing tension. The growing gap between stated constitutional ideals and current fiscal resources may prompt financially struggling schools to challenge funding disparities through litigation if their needs are left unmet by legislators focused on balancing budgets. Even successful litigation, however, is unlikely to lead to substantial new funding until state budgets recover. State funding resources and political will to raise taxes may be insufficient to meet the demands of plaintiffs, even if judges are bold enough to order additional funding in a negative fiscal climate.

Both funding advocates and judges now find themselves in a starkly changed fiscal landscape. Court opinions interpreting state constitutions as requiring expensive remedial mandates in school funding cases would be on a collision course with state constitutional mandates for balanced budgets. And unlike the federal government, state governments cannot simply ignore fiscal shortfalls by printing more money or pushing current fiscal obligations into the future. On the other hand, it can be argued that failure to adequately fund education in the present is just another form of borrowing for current expediency at far greater future costs. Cutting education funding may help to balance current budgets. But this could cost states far more in the future in wasted human capital, diminished quality of life for citizens, and a resulting diminished economic future for the State.

Legislators and judges have been the key players in post-*Serrano* school funding challenges. But ultimately it is the People themselves that must be persuaded that additional funding for education is needed, and that current sacrifices are necessary to secure a better future. Courts will likely remain an important forum for the ongoing debate over state constitutional rights to educational opportunity; what constitutes an adequate education; and the fair distribution of resources and tax burdens. But courts will face very difficult challenges in attempting to bridge the growing gap between constitutional ideals and fiscal realities if the General Assembly lacks public support and sufficient resources.

If education funding is inadequate, a resulting cycle of poverty can make it even more difficult for the state to generate adequate resources for education in the future. The paradox of cutting education to save money is that by viewing current educational expenditures only as a current cost and not a necessary long-term investment, short-term savings could cost the state its long-term economic future.

Challenges to School Fees

In the U.S. all 50 states offer a free system of public education, with a majority of states mandating "free" schools in their state constitutions. Although elementary and secondary school tuition is free, many states allow fees to be charged for services or supplies, including fees for textbooks, gym uniforms, or participation in athletics or other extracurricular activities. In *Kadrmas v. Dickinson*, the U.S. Supreme Court ruled on a challenge to fees for bus transportation to and from school.

Kadrmas v. Dickinson Public Schools
487 U.S. 450 (1988)
Supreme Court of the United States

Justice O'CONNOR delivered the opinion of the Court.

Appellants urge us to hold that the Equal Protection Clause forbids a State to allow some local school boards, but not others, to assess a fee for transporting pupils between their homes and the public schools. Applying well-established equal protection principles, we reject this claim and affirm the constitutionality of the challenged statute.

North Dakota is a sparsely populated State, with many people living on isolated farms and ranches . . . Since 1947, the legislature has authorized and encouraged thinly populated school districts to consolidate or "reorganize" themselves into larger districts so that education can be provided more efficiently. Reorganization proposals, which obviously must contemplate an increase in the distance that some children travel to school, are required by law to include provisions for transporting students back and forth from their homes . . . Appellee Dickinson Public Schools, which serves a relatively populous area, has chosen not to participate in such a reorganization. Until 1973, this school system provided free bus service to students in outlying areas, but the "pickup points" for this service were often at considerable distances from the students' homes. After a plebiscite of the bus users, Dickinson's School Board instituted door-to-door bus service and began charging a fee. During the period relevant to this case, about 13% of the students rode the bus; their parents were charged $97 per year for one child or $150 per year for two children. Such fees covered approximately 11% of the cost of providing the bus service, and the remainder was provided from state and local tax revenues.

In 1979, the State enacted the legislation at issue in this case. This statute expressly indicates that nonreorganized school districts, like Dickinson, may charge a fee for transporting students to school; such fees, however, may not exceed the estimated cost to the school district of providing the service . . .

Appellants are a Dickinson schoolchild, Sarita Kadrmas, and her mother, Paula. The Kadrmas family, which also includes Mrs. Kadrmas' husband and two preschool children, lives about 16 miles from Sarita's school. Mr. Kadrmas works sporadically in the North Dakota oil fields, and the family's annual income at the time of trial was at or near the officially defined poverty level. Until 1985, the Kadrmas family had agreed each year to pay the fee for busing Sarita to school. Having fallen behind on these and other bills, however, the family refused to sign a contract obligating them to pay $97 for the 1985 school year. Accordingly, the school bus no longer stopped for Sarita, and the family arranged to transport her to school privately. The costs they incurred that year for Sarita's transportation exceeded $1,000, or about 10 times the fee charged by the school district for bus service. This arrangement continued until the spring of 1987, when Paula Kadrmas signed a bus service contract for the remainder of the 1986 school year and paid part of the fee. Mrs. Kadrmas later signed another contract for the 1987 school year, and paid about half of the fee for that period.

In September 1985, appellants, along with others who have since withdrawn from the case, filed an action in state court seeking to enjoin appellees--the Dickinson Public Schools and various school district officials--from collecting any fee for the bus service . . .

Unless a statute provokes "strict judicial scrutiny" because it interferes with a "fundamental right" or discriminates against a "suspect class," it will ordinarily survive an equal protection attack so long as the challenged classification is rationally related to a legitimate governmental purpose. Appellants contend that Dickinson's user fee for bus service unconstitutionally deprives those who cannot afford to pay it of "minimum access to education." Sarita Kadrmas, however, continued to attend school during the time that she was denied access to the school bus. Appellants must therefore mean to argue that the busing fee unconstitutionally places a greater obstacle to education in the path of the poor than it does in the path of wealthier families. Alternatively, appellants may mean to suggest that the Equal Protection Clause affirmatively requires government to provide free transportation to school, at least for some class of students that would include Sarita Kadrmas. Under either interpretation of appellants' position, we are evidently being urged to apply a form of strict or "heightened" scrutiny to the North Dakota statute. Doing so would require us to extend the requirements of the Equal Protection Clause beyond the limits recognized in our cases, a step we decline to take.

We have previously rejected the suggestion that statutes having different effects on the wealthy and the poor should on that account alone be subjected to strict equal protection scrutiny. Nor have we accepted the proposition that education is a "fundamental right" . . . Relying primarily on *Plyler v. Doe*, however, appellants suggest that North Dakota's 1979 statute should be subjected to "heightened" scrutiny. This standard of review, which is less demanding than "strict scrutiny" but more demanding than the standard rational relation test, has generally been applied only in cases that involved discriminatory classifications based on sex or illegitimacy. In *Plyler*, which did not fit this pattern, the State of Texas had denied to the children of illegal aliens the free public education that it made available to other residents. Applying a heightened level of equal protection scrutiny, the Court concluded that the State had failed to show that its classification advanced a substantial state interest. We have not extended this holding beyond the "unique circumstances," that provoked its "unique confluence of theories and rationales." Nor do we think that the case before us today is governed by the holding in *Plyler*. Unlike the children in that case, Sarita Kadrmas has not been penalized by the government for illegal conduct by her parents. On the contrary, Sarita was denied access to the school bus only because her parents would not agree to pay the same user fee charged to all other families that took advantage of the service. Nor do we see any reason to suppose that this user fee will "promote the creation and perpetuation of a subclass of illiterates within our boundaries, surely adding to the problems and costs of unemployment, welfare, and crime." The case before us does not resemble *Plyler*, and we decline to extend the rationale of that decision to cover this case . . .

North Dakota does not maintain a legal or a practical monopoly on the means of transporting children to school . . . the Kadrmas family could and did find a private alternative to the public school bus service for which Dickinson charged a fee. That alternative was more expensive, to be sure, and we have no reason to doubt that genuine hardships were endured by the Kadrmas family when Sarita was denied access to the bus. Such facts, however, do not imply that the Equal Protection Clause has been violated . . .

Applying the appropriate test--under which a statute is upheld if it bears a rational relation to a legitimate government objective--we think it is quite clear that a State's decision to allow local school boards the option of charging patrons a user fee for bus service is constitutionally permissible. The Constitution does not require that such service be provided at all, and it is difficult to imagine why choosing to offer the service should entail a constitutional obligation to offer it for free. No one denies that encouraging local school districts to provide school bus service is a legitimate state purpose or that such encouragement would be undermined by a rule requiring that general revenues be used to subsidize an optional service that will benefit a minority of the district's families. It is manifestly rational for the State to refrain from undermining its legitimate objective with such a rule . . .

In sum, the statute challenged in this case discriminates against no suspect class and interferes with no fundamental right. Appellants have failed to carry the heavy burden of demonstrating that the statute is arbitrary and irrational. The Supreme Court of North Dakota correctly concluded that the statute does not violate the Equal Protection Clause of the Fourteenth Amendment, and its judgment is

Affirmed.

Justice MARSHALL, with whom Justice BRENNAN joins, dissenting.

In *San Antonio v. Rodriguez*, I wrote that the Court's holding was a "retreat from our historic commitment to equality of educational opportunity and an unsupportable acquiescence in a system which deprives children in their earliest years of the chance to reach their full potential." Today, the Court continues the retreat from the promise of equal educational opportunity by holding that a school district's refusal to allow an indigent child who lives 16 miles from the nearest school to use a school-bus service without paying a fee does not violate the Fourteenth Amendment's Equal Protection Clause. Because I do not believe that this Court should sanction discrimination against the poor with respect to "perhaps the most important function of state and local governments," *Brown v. Board of Education*, I dissent . . .

I believe the Court's approach forgets that the Constitution is concerned with "sophisticated as well as simple-minded modes of discrimination." This case involves state action that places a special burden on poor families in their pursuit of education. Children living far from school can receive a public education only if they have access to transportation; as the state court noted in this case, "a child must reach the schoolhouse door as a prerequisite to receiving the educational opportunity offered therein." Indeed, for children in Sarita's position, imposing a fee for transportation is no different in practical effect from imposing a fee directly for education. Moreover, the fee involved in this case discriminated against Sarita's family because it necessarily fell more heavily upon the poor than upon wealthier members of the community . . .

The intent of the Fourteenth Amendment was to abolish caste legislation. When state action has the predictable tendency to entrap the poor and create a permanent underclass, that intent is frustrated. Thus, to the extent that a law places discriminatory barriers between indigents and the basic tools and opportunities that might enable them to rise, exacting scrutiny should be applied. The statute at issue here burdens a poor person's interest in an education. The extraordinary nature of this interest cannot be denied. This Court's most famous statement on the subject is contained in *Brown v. Board of Education*:

> Education is perhaps the most important function of state and local governments. Compulsory school attendance laws and the great expenditures for education both demonstrate our recognition of the importance of education to our democratic society. It is required in the performance of our most basic public responsibilities, even service in the armed forces. It is the very foundation of good citizenship. Today it is a principal instrument in awakening the child to cultural values, in preparing him for later professional training, and in helping him to adjust normally to his environment. In these days, it is doubtful that any child may reasonably be expected to succeed in life if he is denied the opportunity of an education.

Since *Brown*, we frequently have called attention to the vital role of education in our society. We have noted that "education is necessary to prepare citizens to participate effectively and intelligently in our open political system." We also have recognized that education prepares individuals to become self-reliant participants in our economy. A statute that erects special obstacles to education in the path of the poor naturally tends to consign such persons to their current disadvantaged status. By denying equal opportunity to exactly those who need it most, the law not only militates against the ability of each poor child to advance herself or himself, but also increases the likelihood of the creation of a discrete and permanent underclass. Such a statute is difficult to reconcile with the framework of equality embodied in the Equal Protection Clause . . .

For the poor, education is often the only route by which to become full participants in our society. In allowing a State to burden the access of poor persons to an education, the Court denies equal opportunity and discourages hope. I do not believe the Equal Protection Clause countenances such a result. I therefore dissent.

* * * * * * *

After the Court's decision in *Kadrmas*, it appeared that absent a complete denial of educational opportunity as in *Plyler*, the legality of school fees was a question of state law, not federal law. State constitutions generally prohibit the charging of any tuition fee, at least to resident families. But what student fees may be allowed other than tuition varies among the states. State courts have struck down some student fees as unlawful under the state constitution. Where student fees are charged, however, they are more likely to be upheld if they are not related to the core required curriculum, and are instead only for genuinely optional activities for students. Further, it is easier to defend a fee system that provides appropriate waivers for students and families with financial hardships.

Chapter Summary

This chapter reviewed equal protection of the laws and its application in public schools. After reading this chapter, please consider the following points in review and for further thought and discussion:

I. *Review Points*:

1) The Equal Protection Clause was intended to abolish systems of social caste in the U.S.

2) Generally, government officials must provide equal treatment to individuals in equal circumstances.

3) Differential treatment must be justified by proving an appropriate relationship between the differential treatment and a sufficient governmental justification.

4) Equal protection of the laws prohibits differential treatment based on factors that are legally irrelevant (*e.g.*, race; color; national origin; etc.), and are instead the products of irrational prejudice or discrimination.

5) Differential treatment may be allowed or even required when there are legally relevant differences among individuals.

6) The U.S. Supreme Court has developed a multi-tiered test for reviewing equal protection claims. Where differential treatment by government is established by plaintiffs, the Court reviews whether the differential treatment is justified by a sufficient governmental interest:

> *High-level (strict) scrutiny*: Differential treatment must be necessary to a compelling interest and narrowly tailored to achieving that interest.

> *Intermediate-level scrutiny*: Differential treatment must be substantially related to achieving an important government interest.

> *Low-level (rational basis) scrutiny*: Government officials need only show that the differential treatment is rationally related to a legitimated government interest.

7) Strict scrutiny applies to differential treatment based on suspect classifications or fundamental rights, and the rational basis test applies to general social or economic regulations.

8) Government officials almost always lose under strict scrutiny, while plaintiffs nearly always lose under the rational basis test.

9) Since the VMI case, differential treatment based on gender has been subjected to elevated scrutiny, higher than intermediate-level scrutiny, but less than strict scrutiny. While not treated as equivalent to race discrimination, gender based discrimination requires an exceedingly persuasive justification.

10) In summary, the core teaching of the Court's cases on equal protection is that government officials cannot legally treat individuals differently for irrelevant, discriminatory reasons, such as the person's race, color, religion, sex, national origin, disability, etc., when those factors bear no appropriate relationship to a sufficient governmental justification.

11) In *Brown I* the Court overturned the *Plessy*-era separate but equal doctrine. In *Brown II* the Court ordered desegregation of public schools with "all deliberate speed."

12) In *Green* the Court identified the six *Green* factors: 1) Student assignments; 2) Faculty; 3) Staff; 4) Transportation; 5) Extracurricular activities; and 6) Facilities, for courts to review to distinguish between racially unitary and segregated schools.

13) In *Freeman* the Court held that school districts may be released from federal judicial supervision incrementally on each separate *Green* factor. Any subsequent re-segregation not proximately traceable to constitutional violations (*de jure*) and instead resulting from private choices (*de facto*) was not legally actionable under the Equal Protection Clause. The Court's decision in *Freeman* made it much easier for school districts to be released from judicial supervision.

14) The Constitution only limits *de jure* segregation (caused by government action); *de facto* segregation (caused by private choices) is beyond the legal reach of the Constitution.

15) In *Brown*-era desegregation efforts, as a remedy for *de jure* discrimination, government officials were permitted to use race in structuring constitutional remedies. But as courts increasingly found that racial disparities were the product of *de facto* and not *de jure* causes, the use of race by government officials increasingly became subject to strict judicial scrutiny.

16) In *Adarand* the Court held that "any person, of whatever race, has the right to demand that any governmental actor subject to the Constitution justify any racial classification subjecting that person to unequal treatment under the strictest judicial scrutiny . . . More than good motives should be required when government seeks to allocate its resources by way of an explicit racial classification system . . . all racial classifications, imposed by whatever federal, state, or local government actor, must be analyzed by a reviewing court under strict scrutiny. In other words, such classifications are constitutional only if they are narrowly tailored measures that further compelling governmental interests."

17) The Court views discrimination based on immutable characteristics with heightened suspicion. Immutable characteristics are those beyond the control of the individual and that cannot be changed. Government classifications that discriminate based on national origin, race, or ethnicity are subject to strict scrutiny in part because these are immutable characteristics. Differential governmental treatment of aliens has been subjected to less rigorous judicial scrutiny because alienage is not an immutable characteristic. Individuals may change their citizenship status.

18) Discrimination based on language has been treated as a form of national origin discrimination, and is unlawful under both the Equal Protection Clause and Title VI of the Civil Rights Act of 1964. The Court's decisions in both *Lau v. Nichols* and *Horne v. Flores* recognized a duty for state and local school officials to provide appropriate instruction for minority language students. But both decisions left the operational details of these programs to state and local officials.

19) Concerning differential treatment based on gender the Court has recognized: "Physical differences between men and women . . . are enduring: The two sexes are not fungible." Nonetheless, gender based classifications by government require an "exceedingly persuasive justification." Government officials must show "at least that the challenged classification serves important governmental objectives and that the discriminatory means employed are substantially related to the achievement of those objectives . . . The justification must be genuine, not hypothesized or invented post hoc in response to litigation. And it must not rely on overbroad generalizations about the different talents, capacities, or preferences of males and females."

20) To prevail in a sexual harassment suit for monetary damages under Title IX, plaintiffs must generally establish that:

1) School officials had actual notice of the sexual harassment, and;
2) School officials reacted with deliberate indifference.

21) The Court defined "actual notice" in *Gebser* finding that it required "notice to an 'appropriate person'" and that "an 'appropriate person' . . . is, at a minimum, an official of the recipient entity with authority to take corrective action to end the discrimination."

22) The Court defined "deliberate indifference" in *Davis* finding that "school officials will be "deemed 'deliberately indifferent' . . . where the recipient's response to the harassment or lack thereof is clearly unreasonable in light of the known circumstances."

23) Concerning peer sexual harassment among students under Title IX, in *Davis* the Court found that: "The fact that it was a teacher who engaged in harassment in *Franklin* and *Gebser* is relevant." School officials have greater responsibility for the conduct of employees, and students are more prone to engaging in some gender-based adolescent behavior. To hold school officials liable for peer sexual harassment under Title IX the plaintiff must prove:

1) School officials had actual notice of the sexual harassment;
2) School officials reacted with deliberate indifference; and
3) The harassment was so severe, pervasive, and objectively offensive; and so undermined and detracted from the educational experience; that the student was effectively denied equal access to an institution's resources and opportunities.

24) Under Title IX students are not only protected from discrimination, but they are also shielded from being "excluded from participation in" or "denied the benefits of" any "education program or activity receiving Federal financial assistance."

25) It is the tolerance of sexual harassment in the school that is the basis for liability under Title IX. To avoid liability, school officials "must merely respond to known peer harassment in a manner that is not clearly unreasonable." Together *Franklin*, *Gebser*, and *Davis* teach that school officials should: 1) Have a reasonable policy in place for the prevention and correction of sexual harassment; 2) Promptly and fairly investigate reports of alleged sexual harassment; and 3) Take reasonable remedial actions when appropriate to assure that no one is excluded from educational opportunities because of sexual harassment or other differential treatment based on gender.

26) In *Rodriguez* the Court found that education is not a fundamental right under the U.S. Constitution. School funding battles moved to state courts with mixed results.

27) Short of a complete denial of educational opportunity as in *Plyler*, the legality of school fees is a question of state law.

II. *Principles to Practice Tips*:

1) *Equal Protection of the Laws*: Treat everyone fairly and be diligent in assuring that prejudice, conscious or unconscious, plays no role in the treatment of individuals. Unless there is a sufficient justification for differential treatment, all persons in similar circumstances should be treated equally.

2) *Prevention of Sexual Harassment*: School officials should: 1) Have a reasonable policy in place for the prevention and correction of sexual harassment; 2) Promptly and fairly investigate reports of alleged sexual harassment; and 3) Take reasonable remedial actions when appropriate to assure that no one is excluded from educational opportunities because of sexual harassment or other differential treatment based on gender.

3) *Programs for Disadvantaged Students*: In allocating limited educational resources to provide special help for disadvantaged students, programs based on economic disadvantage are legally far safer than programs based on race. Any use of race is subject to strict judicial scrutiny, while the use of economic status is only subject to the rational basis test.

4) *School Related Fees*: Where student fees may be charged, these fees are more likely to be upheld if they are not related to the required core curriculum, and are instead only for genuinely optional activities for students. Further, it is easier to defend a fee system that provides appropriate waivers for students and families with financial hardships.

III. *Questions for Discussion*: Please consider these questions and be prepared to discuss:

1) *Ethnic Community Dynamics*: What is the ethnic and racial composition of your community? How has this changed, and what will your community look like in the future ethnically? How can ethnic and racial relationships in your community be improved? Where do significant social divisions exist in your community? Are these social divisions primarily related to race, ethnicity, or socio-economic status?

2) *Socio-economic Community Dynamics*: What is the socio-economic composition of your community? How has this changed, and what will your community look like in the future socially and economically? What can be done now to improve the economic future of your community?

3) *Gender Issues in the Community*: In the VMI case Justice Ginsberg, writing for the majority, noted relevant and enduring differences between the sexes, but also warned against overbroad generalizations. What are the relevant differences? What are the overbroad generalizations? Has gender equity been achieved in your community? Who faces the greatest educational challenges in your community, boys or girls? What could be done to improve educational opportunities for both boys and girls in your community?

4) *Open Forum*: What other related issues or current events would you like to discuss?

IV. *Suggested Activities*:

1) Read Dr. Martin Luther King Jr.'s *Letter from Birmingham Jail*. Discuss its lessons and continuing implications for the advancement of law and social justice locally, nationally, and globally.

2) Examine whether school related fees in your community may be limiting the participation of economically disadvantaged students in extra-curricular or other educational activities for which fees are charged. Could these activities be restructured to reduce costs and the need for additional fees? Could other sources of revenue (*e.g.*, donations from businesses or individuals) help to reduce or eliminate fees and help everyone to participate on an equal basis? Develop a proposal for improving access to school activities by reducing or eliminating student fees.

Chapter 8: Disability Law

Disability is a natural part of the human experience occurring world-wide throughout the human population. It is estimated that 10% of humans have a disability, making persons with disabilities the World's largest minority group. The treatment of persons with disabilities, however, has been among the darkest chapters in human history. Babies born with disabilities were commonly left to die. Those who survived were often locked away under deplorable circumstances, abused, forcibly sterilized, lobotomized, and treated as expendable. Persons with disabilities were among the earliest victims of the Holocaust. By 1941 more than 10,000 disabled persons had been killed by the Nazis through starvation, lethal injection, or gassing. Even in the U.S. there is a shocking history of using disabled persons for unconscionable medical experiments including, for example, intentionally injecting them with dangerous or fatal pathogens and carcinogens, and feeding mentally disabled children radioactive cereal. The rights of persons with disabilities were treated as nonexistent, including their rights to education.

Today there is common recognition of the evils of these practices, and expanding recognition that integrating persons with disabilities into the mainstream of society is both a moral imperative and a wise policy choice. Our common humanity requires that we recognize all persons' human rights as equal members of society, and respect their inalienable rights to life, liberty, and the pursuit of happiness. Impairment of an individual's physical or mental abilities in no way diminishes the individual's fundamental human rights.

> *There is a Fundamental Human Right for Every Person to have an Opportunity to Participate in and Contribute to Society*

With appropriate educational services children with disabilities, like all other children, can be prepared to lead productive, independent, adult lives to the maximum extent possible. Appropriate educational services help persons with disabilities to become more independent and develop their personal strengths and talents, reducing future costs and improving everyone's quality of life. As persons with disabilities are better integrated into mainstream society, including the work force, they are able to offer their unique skills and contribute to the economy and the common good.

Prior to the passage of laws protecting children with disabilities, however, these children were commonly excluded from public schools or did not receive appropriate educational services. Many believed that children who could not conform to standard physical and cognitive standards did not belong in regular public schools with their non-disabled peers. The burden of educating children with disabilities remained primarily with their families who often lacked sufficient resources to provide appropriate educational services.

Educational services that were available to these children were often provided in segregated facilities preventing them from interacting with their non-disabled peers. Following the Court's mandate to racially desegregate schools in *Brown v. Board of Education*, advocates for children with disabilities championed integrated education for children with disabilities also. Based on legal theories rooted in *Brown*, dozens of cases were filed nation-wide arguing that children with disabilities were being unconstitutionally excluded from public schools through a systemic denial of equal protection and due process rights.

Two of these cases, *Pennsylvania Association for Retarded Children (PARC) v. Pennsylvania*, 343 F. Supp. 279 (E.D. Pa. 1972), and *Mills v. Board of Education of the District of Columbia*, 348 F. Supp. 866 (D.D.C. 1972) resulted in landmark decisions recognizing educational rights for children with disabilities. In *PARC*, a federal district court held that mentally retarded students ages 6 through 21 should be provided with access to a free public education, and should be placed in regular classrooms when possible or in special classes when necessary. In *Mills*, a federal district court extended this doctrine to all school aged children with disabilities, holding that they must be provided with a free and adequate public education.

The U.S. Congress was also working to address these concerns through appropriate legislation, including the Elementary and Secondary Education Act (ESEA) of 1965, and Title VI, a 1966 amendment to the ESEA. In 1970, Title VI was repealed and replaced by the Education of the Handicapped Act (EHA). The EHA created a federal Bureau of Education for the Handicapped and brought increased national attention to the concerns of students with disabilities. This early legislation did not provide for "mainstreaming" or a "free appropriate public education" but it established the groundwork for future legislation concerning these issues. In 1973 Congress passed § 504 of the *Rehabilitation Act* (§ 504), prohibiting discrimination against handicapped persons in programs receiving federal funds.

In 1975 Congress passed Public Law 94-142, the Education for All Handicapped Children Act (EAHCA), enacting significant new substantive legal rights and procedural protections for handicapped children. Legislative history for P.L. 94-142 recorded that in 1975 the U.S. Congress found that:

1) There are more than eight million handicapped children in the United States today;
2) The special educational needs of such children are not being fully met;
3) More than half of the handicapped children in the United States do not receive appropriate educational services which would enable them to have full equality of opportunity;
4) One million of the handicapped children in the United States are excluded entirely from the public school system and will not go through the educational process with their peers;
5) There are many handicapped children throughout the United States participating in regular school programs whose handicaps prevent them from having a successful educational experience because their handicaps are undetected;
6) Because of the lack of adequate services within the public school system, families are often at great distance from their residence and at their own expense;
7) Developments in the training of teachers and in diagnostic and instructional procedures and methods have advanced to the point that, given appropriate funding, State and local educational agencies can and will provide effective special education and related services to meet the needs of handicapped children;
8) State and local educational agencies have a responsibility to provide education for all handicapped children, but present financial resources are inadequate to meet the special educational needs of handicapped children; and

9) It is in the national interest that the Federal Government assist State and local efforts to provide programs to meet the educational needs of handicapped children in order to assure equal protection of the law.

The EAHCA was renamed the Individuals with Disabilities Education Act (IDEA) in 1990, with the addition of some important substantive changes such as provisions for "transition services" and changes in terminology, including a change from "handicapped children" to "children with disabilities." In 1990 Congress also passed the Americans with Disabilities Act (ADA). The ADA extended antidiscrimination protections similar to those provided by § 504 for persons in public institutions to many private sector areas as well.

Although case law plays an important role in interpreting and clarifying disability laws, the law in this area is largely defined by federal statutes and regulations. These principally include the IDEA, § 504, and the ADA. The IDEA requires schools to provide a Free Appropriate Public Education (FAPE) and related services for all eligible students with disabilities. This is a critically important mission. But implementation of the IDEA is also a very complex and expensive undertaking. In contrast § 504 and the ADA generally only require non-discrimination and the provision of reasonable accommodations. Section 504 requires reasonable accommodations when they are necessary to allow persons with disabilities to participate in programs receiving federal funding. The ADA extends § 504 like protections to the private sector in employment, public accommodations, transportation, or telecommunications.

Contrasting the Scope of Who is Covered and What is Provided Under the IDEA, § 504, and the ADA

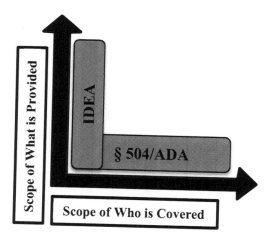

© Dayton

With §504 and the ADA Congress intended to cover large numbers of persons, children and adults, potentially including any person with a physical or mental disability that substantially limits a major life activity, including "caring for one's self, performing manual tasks, walking, seeing, hearing, speaking, breathing, learning, and working." Because the scope of who is potentially covered under § 504 and the ADA is so broad, the scope of what is provided is necessarily limited in recognition of finite resources. While § 504 and the ADA cover a broad range of the population, what is provided is fundamentally a right to non-discrimination and to the provision of a reasonable accommodation when necessary for the participation of the person with a disability.

In contrast, in the IDEA Congress recognized that some children would need vastly more resources to provide for their unmet educational needs due to the severity of their disabilities. For this reason, Congress limited who is covered under the IDEA to only those children who fit within 13 defined categories of eligibility, and who needed special education and related services under the IDEA because of an eligible disability. What is provided for IDEA eligible students may be extensive and expensive. IDEA eligible students are guaranteed the right to a FAPE, required related services, and extensive due process protections, all of which can prove to be very expensive and administratively burdensome in some cases.

Among these three laws, the IDEA has the most significant impact on public schools. Legislation, regulations, and judicial opinions concerning the IDEA form a complex system of legal rights and responsibilities. Schools are frequently involved in litigation concerning the IDEA. Accordingly, this chapter focuses greater attention on the IDEA, including significant provisions from the current legislative amendments and administrative regulations. Because the laws concerning individuals with disabilities continue to rapidly evolve, persons responsible for compliance with the IDEA, § 504, and the ADA should closely monitor new legislation, regulations, and judicial decisions concerning these laws to assure current compliance.

The Individuals with Disabilities Education Act

The purposes of the IDEA are to: 1) Assure that all children with disabilities are provided with a Free Appropriate Public Education (FAPE) that emphasizes special education and related services designed to meet their unique needs; 2) Prepare them for employment and independent living; 3) Assure that the rights of children with disabilities are protected; and 4) Assist states in providing appropriate services. These purposes are supported through a combination of federal, state, and local funding. The IDEA is a conditional funding statute that serves as a contract between the federal and state governments, with IDEA eligible students as the third-party beneficiaries of this contract. IDEA services are generally provided at the local school level, but in those instances where more extensive care is required state-level services may be provided.

Eligibility Requirements

To be eligible for services under the IDEA, a child must be declared a "child with a disability" under the statutory definition which requires consideration of a two-part test: 1) Whether the child has an eligible disability; and 2) Whether the child needs special education and related services because of that disability.

To satisfy the first prong of this test the child's disability must fit within one of the categories of eligibility under the IDEA. Under 20 U.S.C. § 1401 (2004) of the IDEA these categories include:

Mental retardation, hearing impairments (including deafness), speech or language impairments, visual impairments (including blindness), serious emotional disturbance . . ., orthopedic impairments, autism, traumatic brain injury, other health impairments, or specific learning disabilities.

334

To satisfy the second prong of the test, the child must need special education and related services because of the eligible disability. The IDEA defines special education as special instruction designed to meet the unique needs of a child with a disability. Related services are services required to assist a child with a disability to benefit from special education services. The IDEA also allows states to classify children ages 3 through 9 that are "experiencing developmental delays" and are in need of special education and related services as "children with disabilities" under the IDEA.

Not all children with physical or mental disabilities will satisfy the IDEA's two-part eligibility test. These children will not be eligible for IDEA services, although they may qualify for reasonable accommodations under § 504. Some children will not fit within an IDEA eligible category. For example, there is no specific category for children with Attention Deficit Disorder (ADD), diabetes, cancer, or many other chronic health problems. Further, these children would only be eligible as "other health impaired" (OHI) if their illnesses sufficiently limit their strength, vitality, or alertness and adversely affect their educational performance, requiring special education and related services.

Some children may fit in an IDEA eligible category, but not need special education and related services. For example, although "orthopedic impairment" is a proper category for IDEA eligibility, some orthopedically impaired children do not need special education and related services. These children may only require reasonable accommodations in facilities and transportation under § 504. They are not eligible for IDEA services, however, if they do not need special education and related services because of their disability.

Identification and Evaluation of Students

The IDEA's "child find" provision creates an affirmative duty for states to identify children with disabilities. IDEA 20 U.S.C. § 1412 (2004) mandates: "All children with disabilities residing in the State, including children with disabilities who are homeless children or are wards of the State and children with disabilities attending private schools, regardless of the severity of their disabilities, and who are in need of special education and related services, are identified." .

Some of these children are identified through mass screening tests including vision tests, hearing tests, and other basic tests administered to all school children. Parental consent is not required for mass screening tests administered to all children. Parents, school personnel, medical personnel, or other persons that suspect a child needs IDEA services may also refer the child for an individual evaluation to determine whether the child is eligible for these services.

Before any individual evaluations for IDEA eligibility may be conducted, however, school officials must obtain parental consent. If parents refuse consent, school officials may use counseling or mediation services to encourage parental cooperation. In more difficult cases, school officials may initiate due process proceedings to obtain permission for an evaluation from a hearing officer.

Refusal of consent by parents does not absolve the school district of its duty to provide a FAPE for children with disabilities. In cases where parents refuse consent and school officials have sufficient cause to believe the child may be a child with a disability, a hearing officer's determination concerning whether there is an adequate basis for suspecting a disability may help assure that children with disabilities receive needed services, and help to protect the school from future liability for failure to provide the student with a FAPE.

An evaluation for eligibility under the IDEA must include a variety of assessment tools and strategies, using technically sound instruments to assess the role of physical, cognitive, behavioral, and developmental factors in the child's disability. To avoid erroneous conclusions, no single procedure should determine whether a child has a disability. For example, children should not be improperly labeled as mentally impaired based on a single test result, or because of vision, hearing, or language problems in the testing process. Tests should be validated for the intended purpose; administered by qualified personnel; not racially or culturally discriminatory; and administered in the child's native language when possible. Based on evaluation data, including information from parents and classroom assessments, a determination is made concerning whether the child has an IDEA eligible disability, and whether the child needs special education and related services.

Substantive Educational Rights

Children eligible for IDEA services have a right to a "free appropriate public education" (FAPE). The right to a FAPE includes special education and related services that are free and without cost to parents or students; that are provided through an appropriate educational program under public supervision to assure IDEA compliance; and that are in conformity with the child's individualized education program (IEP). Although the meanings of the terms "free," "public," and "education" are relatively clear, "appropriate" is a highly subjective term. Further, the IDEA does not expressly define "appropriate."

Because the provision of a FAPE is essential to compliance with the IDEA, it is not surprising that the first United States Supreme Court case to address this law concerned defining the parameters of "appropriate" under the Act. In 1982, the United States Supreme Court delivered a 6-3 decision in *Rowley* concerning the scope of the Act's substantive guarantees.

Board of Education v. Rowley
458 U.S. 176 (1982)
United States Supreme Court

Justice REHNQUIST delivered the opinion of the Court.

This case presents a question of statutory interpretation. Petitioners contend that the Court of Appeals and the District Court misconstrued the requirements imposed by Congress upon States which receive federal funds under the Education of the Handicapped Act. We agree and reverse the judgment of the Court of Appeals.

The Education of the Handicapped Act (Act), as amended, 20 U.S.C. § 1401 (1976), provides federal money to assist state and local agencies in educating handicapped children, and conditions such funding upon a State's compliance with extensive goals and procedures. The Act represents an ambitious federal effort to promote the education of handicapped children, and was passed in response to Congress' perception that a majority of handicapped children in the United States "were either totally excluded from schools or were sitting idly in regular classrooms awaiting the time when they were old enough to 'drop out'" . . .

This case arose in connection with the education of Amy Rowley, a deaf student at the Furnace Woods School in the Hendrick Hudson Central School District, Peekskill, N.Y. Amy has minimal residual hearing and is an excellent lip-reader. During the year before she began attending Furnace Woods, a meeting between her parents and school administrators resulted in a decision to place her in a regular kindergarten class in order to determine what supplemental services would be necessary to her education. Several members of the school administration prepared for Amy's arrival by attending a course in sign-language interpretation, and a teletype machine was installed in the principal's office to facilitate communication with her parents who are also deaf. At the end of the trial period it was determined that Amy should remain in the kindergarten class, but that she should be provided with an FM hearing aid which would amplify words spoken into a wireless receiver by the teacher or fellow students during certain classroom activities. Amy successfully completed her kindergarten year.

As required by the Act, an IEP was prepared for Amy during the fall of her first-grade year. The IEP provided that Amy should be educated in a regular classroom at Furnace Woods, should continue to use the FM hearing aid, and should receive instruction from a tutor for the deaf for one hour each day and from a speech therapist for three hours each week. The Rowleys agreed with parts of the IEP, but insisted that Amy also be provided a qualified sign-language interpreter in all her academic classes in lieu of the assistance proposed in other parts of the IEP. Such an interpreter had been placed in Amy's kindergarten class for a 2-week experimental period, but the interpreter had reported that Amy did not need his services at that time. The school administrators likewise concluded that Amy did not need such an interpreter in her first-grade classroom. They reached this conclusion after consulting the school district's Committee on the Handicapped, which had received expert evidence from Amy's parents on the importance of a sign-language interpreter, received testimony from Amy's teacher and other persons familiar with her academic and social progress, and visited a class for the deaf.

When their request for an interpreter was denied, the Rowleys demanded and received a hearing before an independent examiner. After receiving evidence from both sides, the examiner agreed with the administrators' determination that an interpreter was not necessary because "Amy was achieving educationally, academically, and socially" without such assistance. The examiner's decision was affirmed on appeal by the New York Commissioner of Education on the basis of substantial evidence in the record. Pursuant to the Act's provision for judicial review, the Rowleys then brought an action in the United States District Court for the Southern District of New York, claiming that the administrators' denial of the sign-language interpreter constituted a denial of the "free appropriate public education" guaranteed by the Act.

The District Court found that Amy "is a remarkably well-adjusted child" who interacts and communicates well with her classmates and has "developed an extraordinary rapport" with her teachers. It also found that "she performs better than the average child in her class and is advancing easily from grade to grade," but "that she understands considerably less of what goes on in class than she could if she were not deaf" and thus "is not learning as much, or performing as well academically, as she would without her handicap." This disparity between Amy's achievement and her potential led the court to decide that she was not receiving a "free appropriate public education," which the court defined as "an opportunity to achieve [her] full potential commensurate with the opportunity provided to other children." According to the District Court, such a standard "requires that the potential of the handicapped child be measured and compared to his or her performance, and that the resulting differential or 'shortfall' be compared to the shortfall experienced by non-handicapped children." The District Court's definition arose from its assumption that the responsibility for "giving content to the requirement of an 'appropriate education'" had "been left entirely to the [federal] courts and the hearing officers."

A divided panel of the United States Court of Appeals for the Second Circuit affirmed. The Court of Appeals "agreed with the District Court's conclusions of law," and held that its "findings of fact were not clearly erroneous."

We granted certiorari to review the lower courts' interpretation of the Act. Such review requires us to consider two questions: What is meant by the Act's requirement of a "free appropriate public education"? And what is the role of state and federal courts in exercising the review granted by 20 U.S.C. § 1415? We consider these questions separately.

This is the first case in which this Court has been called upon to interpret any provision of the Act. As noted previously, the District Court and the Court of Appeals concluded that "the Act itself does not define 'appropriate education,'" but leaves "to the courts and the hearing officers" the responsibility of "giving content to the requirement of an 'appropriate education'" . . . It is beyond dispute that, contrary to the conclusions of the courts below, the Act does expressly define "free appropriate public education":

> The term "free appropriate public education" means special education and related services which (A) have been provided at public expense, under public supervision and direction, and without charge, (B) meet the standards of the State educational agency, (C) include an appropriate preschool, elementary, or secondary school education in the State involved, and (D) are provided in conformity with the individualized education program required under section 1414(a)(5) of this title." 20 U.S.C. § 1401(18).

"Special education," as referred to in this definition, means "specially designed instruction, at no cost to parents or guardians, to meet the unique needs of a handicapped child, including classroom instruction, instruction in physical education, home instruction, and instruction in hospitals and institutions." 20 U.S.C. § 1401(16). "Related services" are defined as "transportation, and such developmental, corrective, and other supportive services . . . as may be required to assist a handicapped child to benefit from special education." 20 U.S.C. § 1401(17).

Like many statutory definitions, this one tends toward the cryptic rather than the comprehensive, but that is scarcely a reason for abandoning the quest for legislative intent. Whether or not the definition is a "functional" one, as respondents contend it is not, it is the principal tool which Congress has given us for parsing the critical phrase of the Act. We think more must be made of it than either respondents or the United States seems willing to admit.

According to the definitions contained in the Act, a "free appropriate public education" consists of educational instruction specially designed to meet the unique needs of the handicapped child, supported by such services as are necessary to permit the child "to benefit" from the instruction. Almost as a checklist for adequacy under the Act, the definition also requires that such instruction and services be provided at public expense and under public supervision, meet the State's educational standards, approximate the grade levels used in the State's regular education, and comport with the child's IEP. Thus, if personalized instruction is being provided with sufficient supportive services to permit the child to benefit from the instruction, and the other items on the definitional checklist are satisfied, the child is receiving a "free appropriate public education" as defined by the Act . . .

By passing the Act, Congress sought primarily to make public education available to handicapped children. But in seeking to provide such access to public education, Congress did not impose upon the States any greater substantive educational standard than would be necessary to make such access meaningful. Indeed, Congress expressly "recognized that in many instances the process of providing special education and related services to handicapped children is not guaranteed to produce any particular outcome." Thus, the intent of the Act was more to open the door of public education to handicapped children on appropriate terms than to guarantee any particular level of education once inside.

Both the House and the Senate Reports attribute the impetus for the Act and its predecessors to two federal-court judgments rendered in 1971 and 1972. As the Senate Report states, passage of the Act "followed a series of landmark court cases establishing in law the right to education for all handicapped children." The first case, *Pennsylvania Association for Retarded Children v. Commonwealth* (1971) (PARC), was a suit on behalf of retarded children challenging the constitutionality of a Pennsylvania statute which acted to exclude them from public education and training. The case ended in a consent decree which enjoined the State from "denying to any mentally retarded child access to a free public program of education and training."

PARC was followed by *Mills v. Board of Education of District of Columbia* (1972), a case in which the plaintiff handicapped children had been excluded from the District of Columbia public schools. The court's judgment . . . provided that:

> No handicapped child eligible for a publicly supported education in the District of Columbia public schools shall be excluded from a regular school assignment by a Rule, policy, or practice of the Board of Education of the District of Columbia or its agents unless such child is provided (a) adequate alternative educational services suited to the child's needs, which may include special education or tuition grants, and (b) a constitutionally adequate prior hearing and periodic review of the child's status, progress, and the adequacy of any educational alternative.

Mills and *PARC* both held that handicapped children must be given access to an adequate, publicly supported education. Neither case purports to require any particular substantive level of education. Rather, like the language of the Act, the cases set forth extensive procedures to be followed in formulating personalized educational programs for handicapped children. The fact that both *PARC* and *Mills* are discussed at length in the legislative Reports suggests that the principles which they established are the principles which, to a significant extent, guided the drafters of the Act . . . That the Act imposes no clear obligation upon recipient States beyond the requirement that handicapped children receive some form of specialized education is perhaps best demonstrated by the fact that Congress, in explaining the need for the Act, equated an "appropriate education" to the receipt of some specialized educational services . . .

Respondents contend that "the goal of the Act is to provide each handicapped child with an equal educational opportunity." We think, however, that the requirement that a State provide specialized educational services to handicapped children generates no additional requirement that the services so provided be sufficient to maximize each child's potential "commensurate with the opportunity provided other children." Respondents and the United States correctly note that Congress sought "to provide assistance to the States in carrying out their responsibilities under . . . the Constitution of the United States to provide equal protection of the laws." But we do not think that such statements imply a congressional intent to achieve strict equality of opportunity or services.

The educational opportunities provided by our public school systems undoubtedly differ from student to student, depending upon a myriad of factors that might affect a particular student's ability to assimilate information presented in the classroom. The requirement that States provide "equal" educational opportunities would thus seem to present an entirely unworkable standard requiring impossible measurements and comparisons . . . The legislative conception of the requirements of equal protection was undoubtedly informed by the two District Court decisions referred to above. But cases such as *Mills* and *PARC* held simply that handicapped children may not be excluded entirely from public education. In *Mills*, the District Court said:

> If sufficient funds are not available to finance all of the services and programs that are needed and desirable in the system then the available funds must be expended equitably in such a manner that no child is entirely excluded from a publicly supported education consistent with his needs and ability to benefit therefrom.

The *PARC* court used similar language, saying "it is the commonwealth's obligation to place each mentally retarded child in a free, public program of education and training appropriate to the child's capacity." The right of access to free public education enunciated by these cases is significantly different from any notion of absolute equality of opportunity regardless of capacity. To the extent that Congress might have looked further than these cases which are mentioned in the legislative history, at the time of enactment of the Act this Court had held at least twice that the Equal Protection Clause of the Fourteenth Amendment does not require States to expend equal financial resources on the education of each child. *San Antonio Independent School Dist. v. Rodriguez*, 411 U.S. 1 (1973); *McInnis v. Ogilvie*, 394 U.S. 322 (1969).

In explaining the need for federal legislation, the House Report noted that "no congressional legislation has required a precise guarantee for handicapped children, *i.e.* a basic floor of opportunity that would bring into compliance all school districts with the constitutional right of equal protection with respect to handicapped children." Assuming that the Act was designed to fill the need identified in the House Report--that is, to provide a "basic floor of opportunity" consistent with equal protection--neither the Act nor its history persuasively demonstrates that Congress thought that equal protection required anything more than equal access. Therefore, Congress' desire to provide specialized educational services, even in furtherance of "equality," cannot be read as imposing any particular substantive educational standard upon the States.

The District Court and the Court of Appeals thus erred when they held that the Act requires New York to maximize the potential of each handicapped child commensurate with the opportunity provided non-handicapped children. Desirable though that goal might be, it is not the standard that Congress imposed upon States which receive funding under the Act. Rather, Congress sought primarily to identify and evaluate handicapped children, and to provide them with access to a free public education.

Implicit in the congressional purpose of providing access to a "free appropriate public education" is the requirement that the education to which access is provided be sufficient to confer some educational benefit upon the handicapped child. It would do little good for Congress to spend millions of dollars in providing access to a public education only to have the handicapped child receive no benefit from that education. The statutory definition of "free appropriate public education," in addition to requiring that States provide each child with "specially designed instruction," expressly requires the provision of "such . . . supportive services . . . as may be required to assist a handicapped child to benefit from special education." § 1401(17). We therefore conclude that the "basic floor of opportunity" provided by the Act consists of access to specialized instruction and related services which are individually designed to provide educational benefit to the handicapped child . . .

The Act requires participating States to educate handicapped children with non-handicapped children whenever possible. When that "mainstreaming" preference of the Act has been met and a child is being educated in the regular classrooms of a public school system, the system itself monitors the educational progress of the child. Regular examinations are administered, grades are awarded, and yearly advancement to higher grade levels is permitted for those children who attain an adequate knowledge of the course material. The grading and advancement system thus constitutes an important factor in determining educational benefit. Children who graduate from our public school systems are considered by our society to have been "educated" at least to the grade level they have completed, and access to an "education" for handicapped children is precisely what Congress sought to provide in the Act.

When the language of the Act and its legislative history are considered together, the requirements imposed by Congress become tolerably clear. Insofar as a State is required to provide a handicapped child with a "free appropriate public education," we hold that it satisfies this requirement by providing personalized instruction with sufficient support services to permit the child to benefit educationally from that instruction. Such instruction and services must be provided at public expense, must meet the State's educational standards, must approximate the grade levels used in the State's regular education, and must comport with the child's IEP. In addition, the IEP, and therefore the personalized instruction, should be formulated in accordance with the requirements of the Act and, if the child is being educated in the regular classrooms of the public education system, should be reasonably calculated to enable the child to achieve passing marks and advance from grade to grade . . .

In assuring that the requirements of the Act have been met, courts must be careful to avoid imposing their view of preferable educational methods upon the States. The primary responsibility for formulating the education to be accorded a handicapped child, and for choosing the educational method most suitable to the child's needs, was left by the Act to state and local educational agencies in cooperation with the parents or guardian of the child. The Act expressly charges States with the responsibility of "acquiring and disseminating to teachers and administrators of programs for handicapped children significant information derived from educational research, demonstration, and similar projects, and of adopting, where appropriate, promising educational practices and materials." § 1413(a)(3). In the face of such a clear statutory directive, it seems highly unlikely that Congress intended courts to overturn a State's choice of appropriate educational theories in a proceeding conducted pursuant to § 1415(e)(2).

We previously have cautioned that courts lack the "specialized knowledge and experience" necessary to resolve "persistent and difficult questions of educational policy." *San Antonio Independent School Dist. v. Rodriguez* (1973). We think that Congress shared that view when it passed the Act. As already demonstrated, Congress' intention was not that the Act displace the primacy of States in the field of education, but that States receive funds to assist them in extending their educational systems to the handicapped. Therefore, once a court determines that the requirements of the Act have been met, questions of methodology are for resolution by the States.

Entrusting a child's education to state and local agencies does not leave the child without protection. Congress sought to protect individual children by providing for parental involvement in the development of state plans and policies, and in the formulation of the child's individual educational program . . .

Applying these principles to the facts of this case, we conclude that the Court of Appeals erred in affirming the decision of the District Court. Neither the District Court nor the Court of

Appeals found that petitioners had failed to comply with the procedures of the Act, and the findings of neither court would support a conclusion that Amy's educational program failed to comply with the substantive requirements of the Act. On the contrary, the District Court found that the "evidence firmly establishes that Amy is receiving an 'adequate' education, since she performs better than the average child in her class and is advancing easily from grade to grade." In light of this finding, and of the fact that Amy was receiving personalized instruction and related services calculated by the Furnace Woods school administrators to meet her educational needs, the lower courts should not have concluded that the Act requires the provision of a sign-language interpreter. Accordingly, the decision of the Court of Appeals is reversed, and the case is remanded for further proceedings consistent with this opinion.

So ordered.

Justice WHITE, with whom Justice BRENNAN and Justice MARSHALL join, dissenting.

In order to reach its result in this case, the majority opinion contradicts itself, the language of the statute, and the legislative history. Both the majority's standard for a "free appropriate education" and its standard for judicial review disregard congressional intent . . . It would apparently satisfy the Court's standard of "access to specialized instruction and related services which are individually designed to provide educational benefit to the handicapped child," for a deaf child such as Amy to be given a teacher with a loud voice, for she would benefit from that service. The Act requires more. It defines "special education" to mean "specifically designed instruction, at no cost to parents or guardians, to meet the unique needs of a handicapped child." Providing a teacher with a loud voice would not meet Amy's needs and would not satisfy the Act. The basic floor of opportunity is instead, as the courts below recognized, intended to eliminate the effects of the handicap, at least to the extent that the child will be given an equal opportunity to learn if that is reasonably possible. Amy Rowley, without a sign-language interpreter, comprehends less than half of what is said in the classroom--less than half of what normal children comprehend. This is hardly an equal opportunity to learn, even if Amy makes passing grades . . . Because the standard of the courts below seems to me to reflect the congressional purpose and because their factual findings are not clearly erroneous, I respectfully dissent.

Comments and Questions

In *Rowley* the Court addressed the legal definition of "appropriate" in the EHA's (now the IDEA) guarantee of a FAPE. The Court held that an appropriate education is merely one that permits the child to benefit from special education and related services. School officials may select any option that meets the minimal standard of appropriate under the IDEA by providing the student with an opportunity to benefit educationally.

Because the term appropriate was not expressly defined in the statute, a broad range of interpretations were possible concerning the Act's substantive guarantees of a FAPE. The Court could have found that Congress intended schools to maximize the potential of each handicapped child, or to eliminate the effects of the handicap. In applying a less stringent standard, the Court held that schools need only provide sufficient services to permit the child to benefit educationally. Dissenting Justices in *Rowley* criticized the majority's decision by stating: "It would apparently satisfy the Court's standard of 'access to specialized instruction and related services which are individually designed to provide educational benefit to the handicapped child' for a deaf child such as Amy to be given a teacher with a loud voice, for she would benefit from that service."

Obvious judicial sarcasm aside, is this a fair criticism of the Court's decision in *Rowley*? What would have happened to special education costs if the Court had determined that the IDEA required schools to maximize the potential of every eligible child, or to eliminate the effects of their disabilities? While these higher standards are admirable educational goals that should be pursued when practicable, should these goals serve as the legal standard to which school officials can be held strictly accountable under the law? Could school officials ever really maximize the potential of the child, or would school officials always be subject to charges by parents that even more could be done to maximize their child's potential? Is it even possible to eliminate the effects of all disabilities on the learning process? What legal definition would you have found applicable as the substantive standard for providing a FAPE under the IDEA: 1) Maximizing the child's potential; 2) Eliminating the effects of the disability; or 3) Providing an opportunity to benefit? What would be the costs and benefits of each policy choice? What policy choice did Congress make in the IDEA? Do judges have any legitimate authority to select a particular policy choice without clear evidence that this was the intent of Congress?

Extended Year Services

Access to instruction during the regular school year may be sufficient to provide a FAPE for many children with disabilities. For some of these children, however, extended school year services may be required. Consistent with the Court's decision in *Rowley*, however, schools officials are not required to maximize the potential of IDEA eligible children. Extended school year services are not required merely because a child may benefit from these services. Nearly all children would benefit from extended school year services. Extended school year services are only required under the IDEA when a two-part test for eligibility is met. Extended school year services are only required if:

1) The IDEA eligible child would experience a significant regression in the absence of extended year services; and
2) Sufficient educational recoupment would not occur in a reasonable time when regular year services were resumed.

All children experience some regression in learning during breaks from instruction. Extended year services may always be offered as educational supplements for any child. But extended year services are only required under the IDEA when the above two-part test is met.

The Individualized Education Program (IEP)

The Individualized Education Program (IEP) is the basic plan for providing special education and related services under the IDEA. The IDEA describes an IEP as a written statement for each child with a disability that is developed, reviewed, and revised in accordance with IDEA requirements. The IEP is designed by an IEP Team. The IEP Team's membership varies, but must generally include the child's parents or legal guardians; a representative of the educational

343

agency; a special education teacher; a regular education teacher when the child is or may be participating in regular education; other appropriate persons having special knowledge about the child; and when appropriate the eligible child may participate in educational decisions concerning his or her future. There must also be someone on the IEP Team qualified to assess the instructional implications of evaluation results.

The IEP drafted by the IEP Team includes statements concerning the child's present levels of academic achievement and functional performance; measurable goals; what special education and related services are to be provided; and an explanation of the extent, if any, to which the child will not participate with non-disabled children in the regular classroom. The IEP is developed based on considerations of the strengths of the child, the parents' concerns, and the results of evaluations. An IEP should also address any serious behavioral problems. The IDEA 20 U.S.C. § 1414 (2004) states that the IEP Team must "in the case of a child whose behavior impedes the child's learning or that of others, consider the use of positive behavioral interventions and supports, and other strategies, to address that behavior." The child's IEP is reviewed periodically, but not less than annually, to determine whether annual goals are being achieved.

Appropriate Placements and the Least Restrictive Environment (LRE)

In developing an IEP, the IEP Team must decide on an appropriate placement for the child. According to 20 U.S.C. § 1412 (2004) of the IDEA, children with disabilities must be placed in the Least Restrictive Environment (LRE) appropriate for the child. To comply with LRE requirements, the IDEA mandates:

> To the maximum extent appropriate, children with disabilities, including children in public or private institutions or other care facilities, are educated with children who are not disabled, and special classes, separate schooling, or other removal of children with disabilities from the regular educational environment occurs only when the nature or severity of the disability of a child is such that education in regular classes with the use of supplementary aids and services cannot be achieved satisfactorily.

In accordance with the IDEA, placement decisions should be based on information from a variety of sources, these sources should be documented and carefully considered, and placement decisions should conform to LRE requirements. The IDEA mandates parental participation in placement decisions, but no single factor, including parental preferences, should be determinative in a placement decision. Children should be placed in the LRE, preferring regular classroom placements and education with non-handicapped students to the maximum extent appropriate. Further, unless the IEP requires other arrangements in order to provide a FAPE, children should be placed in the schools they would attend if non-disabled, or as close as practicable to their homes.

The IDEA does not, however, require "full inclusion" of all children in the regular classroom. The term "full inclusion" does not appear anywhere in the IDEA, and universal "full inclusion" of all children with disabilities would violate the mandates of the IDEA. The IDEA prohibits any one-size-fits-all approach to placements, and instead requires an individualized placement decision for each eligible child. Further, § 1401 of the IDEA defines "special education" as "instruction conducted in the classroom, in the home, in hospitals and institutions, and in other settings." If the regular classroom were the only lawful option under the IDEA, the IDEA would not have expressly included other placements as within the meaning of special education. To the contrary, the IDEA affirmatively requires schools to offer a "continuum of alternative placements" in recognition that some children cannot receive a FAPE in the regular classroom.

Although children with disabilities must be educated in the LRE and in regular classrooms with non-disabled children to the maximum extent appropriate, in order to provide a FAPE for some children, placement in more restrictive settings may be necessary. Placement in more restrictive settings is appropriate when education in regular classes cannot be achieved satisfactorily, even with the use of appropriate supplementary aids and services. Further, more restrictive placements are appropriate when a less restrictive placement threatens the safety of the disabled child or other students, or when a disabled child is so disruptive in a regular classroom that the education of other students is significantly impaired.

As the court recognized in *Clyde K. v. Puyallup School District*, 35 F.3d 1396 (9th Cir. 1994), "while school officials have a statutory duty to ensure that disabled students receive an appropriate education, they are not required to sit on their hands when a disabled student's behavioral problems prevent both him and those around him from learning." Further, the U.S. Department of Education's notice of interpretation, 34 C.F.R. § 300 app. A at 39 (1999), stated: "If the child's behavior in the regular classroom, even with the provision of appropriate behavioral supports, strategies or interventions, would significantly impair the learning of others, that placement would not meet his or her needs and would not be appropriate for that child." IDEA regulations, specifically 34 C.F.R. § 300.324 (2006), mandate that in making decisions about the child's education plan and placement, the IEP Team must consider cases where a child's "behavior impedes the child's learning or that of others" and "consider the use of positive behavioral interventions and supports, and other strategies, to address that behavior."

Placements in Private Schools

Children with disabilities are generally placed in public schools. To meet individual needs, however, some children may be placed in private schools by school officials or their parents. Through the IEP process, school officials may place a child with disabilities in a private school to provide special education and related services needed by the child. When public school officials decide a private school placement is necessary to provide the child with a FAPE, the private school placement must be paid for by the school district.

If public school officials reject a request for a private school placement, believing that it is not required by the IDEA, parents may still choose to place their child in a private school. Parents cannot receive financial reimbursement from the public school district for a unilateral placement in a private school, however, unless they can establish that the school district failed to make a FAPE available to the child in the public school. Section 1412 of the IDEA provides some additional limitations on reimbursement for private school placements, including requirements that parents notify school officials of their objections and their intent to enroll the child in private school; make the child available for evaluation; and otherwise act reasonably in the opinion of a reviewing judge. In *Forest Grove School District v. T.A.*, 557 U.S. ___ (2009), the U.S. Supreme Court held that these provisions do not bar parents from seeking reimbursement even if the child had not previously received special education and related services through the public school, if the public school had failed to provide a FAPE to a child later found to be eligible and the private school placement was appropriate.

Placements in Private Religious Schools

The provision of publicly funded IDEA services in private religious schools raises some potential legal concerns under the U.S. Constitution's Establishment Clause. However, 20 U.S.C. § 1412 (2004) states that IDEA services "may be provided to children with disabilities on the premises of private, including religious, schools, to the extent consistent with law." Courts have held that the provision of IDEA services in religious schools do not per se violate the Establishment Clause.

Zobrest v. Catalina Foothills School District, 509 U.S. 1 (1993), was a 5-4 decision by the U.S. Supreme Court addressing the refusal of a public school district to provide a sign-language interpreter to accompany a deaf child in classes at a Roman Catholic high school. The school district argued that the provision of these services would violate the Establishment Clause. However, the Court held that this service was not barred by the Establishment Clause. The Court found that such services were part of a general government program that distributed benefits neutrally to any child qualified as disabled under the IDEA without regard to the non-sectarian/sectarian, or public/non-public nature of the school the child attended.

Concerning the interpreter in this case, *Zobrest v. Catalina Foothills School District,* the Court determined that unlike a teacher or counselor the interpreter neither added to nor subtracted from the sectarian school's message. The interpreter merely translated whatever material was presented. The Establishment Clause presented no bar to placing a public employee in a sectarian school for such purposes.

State constitutional church-state provisions may raise additional concerns. However, providing a disabled student with publicly funded transportation from a public sidewalk in front of her parochial school to her special education classes at a public school was upheld as consistent with state constitutional church-state provisions under the Missouri Constitution in *Felter v. Cape Girardeau School District*, 810 F. Supp. 1062 (Mo. 1993).

In *Felter* a federal district court found that the transportation was a related service for her educational program under the IDEA and that the service benefitted the student, not the parochial school. It should be noted, however, that 20 U.S.C. § 1412 (2004) requires that: "Special education and related services provided to parentally placed private school children with disabilities, including materials and equipment, shall be secular, neutral, and non-ideological."

Related Services

Related services are those supportive services necessary for an IDEA eligible child to benefit from special education. Under 20 U.S.C. § 1401 (2004) related services may include the following:

> (A) IN GENERAL . . . Transportation, and such developmental, corrective, and other supportive services (including speech-language pathology and audiology services, interpreting services, psychological services, physical and occupational therapy, recreation, including therapeutic recreation, social work services, school nurse services designed to enable a child with a disability to receive a free appropriate public education as described in the individualized education program of the child, counseling services, including rehabilitation counseling, orientation and mobility services, and medical

services, except that such medical services shall be for diagnostic and evaluation purposes only) as may be required to assist a child with a disability to benefit from special education, and includes the early identification and assessment of disabling conditions in children.

(B) EXCEPTION - The term [related services] does not include a medical device that is surgically implanted, or the replacement of such device.

This list of related services is illustrative, not exhaustive, and other supportive, corrective, or developmental services may be required to assist a child with a disability to benefit from special education.

Because of the high costs associated with providing health related services for children with disabilities, there is often controversy over whether school districts must pay for particular health services as related services. The line between health services required as related services and medical services that are not required is not always clear.

The United States Supreme Court first addressed this issue in *Irving Independent School District v. Tatro*, 468 U.S. 883 (1984). In *Tatro* the parents of an 8 year-old girl born with spina bifida requested that clean intermittent catheterization (CIC) be performed by school personnel as a related service. The child needed CIC services every three to four hours, including during school, to prevent injury to her kidneys. Performing CIC takes only a few minutes, does not require medical expertise, and can be learned by a lay-person with less than an hour's training.

The Court held that CIC was not a medical service which school officials need only provide for purposes of diagnosis or evaluation, but was a required related service necessary for the child to benefit from special education under the IDEA. However, the Court did recognize that required related services included "only those services necessary to aid a handicapped child to benefit from special education . . . regardless how easily a school nurse or lay-person could furnish them. For example, if a particular medication or treatment may appropriately be administered to a handicapped child other than during the school day, a school is not required to provide nursing services to administer it." Further, the Court noted that "school nursing services must be provided only if they can be performed by a nurse or other qualified person, not if they must be performed by a physician."

The United States Supreme Court addressed the issue of school nursing services again in *Cedar Rapids v. Garret F.*, 526 U.S. 66 (1999). The Court applied the two-part test established in *Tatro* to determine whether a school district must provide health services as related services. Under the *Tatro* test, health services must be provided as related services if:

1) The supportive services are necessary for the child to benefit from special education; and

2) The services are not excluded as medical services that would require the services of a physician for other than diagnostic or evaluation purposes.

In *Garret F.*, parents requested one-on-one nursing care for a wheelchair bound and ventilator dependent student. In a 7-2 decision, the Court held that the school district must provide the requested services as related services under the IDEA. Under the *Tatro* test, the services were necessary for the student to benefit from special education, and although very expensive, need not be performed by a physician.

347

Due Process Protections

In order to protect the rights of children with disabilities, the IDEA provides significant procedural due process protections. Notice and hearing rights are provided throughout the special education process, from initial identification and consideration of eligibility through completion of the special education program or a determination of ineligibility. The procedural safeguards in the IDEA, 20 U.S.C. § 1415 (2004), include:

(1) An opportunity for the parents of a child with a disability to examine all records relating to such child and to participate in meetings with respect to the identification, evaluation, and educational placement of the child, and the provision of a free appropriate public education to such child, and to obtain an independent educational evaluation of the child;

(2) Procedures to protect the rights of the child whenever the parents of the child are not known;

(3) Written prior notice to the parents of the child whenever such agency--

    (A) Proposes to initiate or change; or

    (B) Refuses to initiate or change;

the identification, evaluation, or educational placement of the child . . . or the provision of a free appropriate public education to the child.

(4) Procedures designed to ensure that the notice required . . . is in the native language of the parents, unless it clearly is not feasible to do so;

(5) An opportunity for mediation;

(6) An opportunity to present complaints with respect to any matter relating to the identification, evaluation, or educational placement of the child, or the provision of a free appropriate public education to such child.

Under 20 U.S.C. § 1415 (2004) the written prior notice referred to in the above section must include:

(1) A description of the action proposed or refused by the agency;

(2) An explanation of why the agency proposes or refuses to take the action;

(3) A statement that the parents . . . have protection under the procedural safeguards . . . and . . . the means by which a copy of the description of the procedural safeguards can be obtained;

(4) Sources for the parents to contact to obtain assistance in understanding the provisions;

(5) A description of other options considered by the IEP Team and the reason why those options were rejected; and

(6) A description of the factors that are relevant to the agency's proposal or refusal.

A document describing these procedural safeguards must be given to parents upon initial referral of the child for evaluation, upon the first occurrence of filing a complaint, and upon request by a parent. The school must also have a model form available to assist parents in filing an IDEA complaint. The document describing these procedural safeguards must be written in the native language of the parents, unless it is not feasible to do so, and written in an easily understandable manner. The IDEA, 20 U.S.C. § 1415 (2004), requires that this document must contain a full explanation of rights related to:

(A) Independent educational evaluation;
(B) Prior written notice;
(C) Parental consent;
(D) Access to educational records;
(E) Opportunity to present complaints, including;
    (i) The time period in which to make a complaint;
    (ii) The opportunity for the agency to resolve the complaint; and
    (iii) The availability of mediation;
(F) The child's placement during the pendency of due process proceedings;
(G) Procedures for students who are subject to placement in an interim alternative educational setting;
(H) Requirements for unilateral placement by parents of children in private schools at public expense;
(I) Due process hearings, including requirements for disclosure of evaluation results and recommendations;
(J) State-level appeals (if applicable in that State);
(K) Civil actions; and
(L) Attorneys' fees.

One of the most important procedural protections in the IDEA is the right to an impartial due process hearing. Under the IDEA, 20 U.S.C. § 1415 (2004), any party to a hearing shall be accorded:

(1) The right to be accompanied and advised by counsel and by individuals with special knowledge or training with respect to the problems of children with disabilities;
(2) The right to present evidence and confront, cross-examine, and compel the attendance of witnesses;
(3) The right to a written, or, at the option of the parents, electronic verbatim record of such hearing; and
(4) The right to written, or, at the option of the parents, electronic findings of fact and decisions.

The IDEA, 20 U.S.C. § 1415 (2004), also includes a "stay-put" provision which states:

During the pendency of any proceedings conducted pursuant to this section, unless the State or local educational agency and the parents otherwise agree, the child shall remain in the then-current educational placement of such child, or, if applying for initial admission to a public school shall, with the consent of the parents, be placed in the public school program until all such proceedings have been completed.

However, there are exceptions to this "stay-put" provision, such as when the special education student poses a serious threat to safety or engages in certain other types of misconduct.

Discipline Procedures

Special legal concerns exist in disciplining children with disabilities. Consistent with *Goss v. Lopez*, 419 U.S. 565 (1975), all students are guaranteed due process of law including adequate notice and an opportunity for a hearing prior to removals from school or other significant disciplinary impingements on protected liberty or property rights. When school officials seek to suspend or expel children with disabilities, however, the IDEA imposes significant additional legal protections for these children. These protections include the "stay-put" provision to protect children with disabilities from unilateral removals from their current placements.

These special protections are rooted in concerns over historical prejudices against persons with disabilities; misunderstandings about physical and mental conditions that may cause problem behaviors; and historically justified fears that school officials may suspend or expel children with disabilities based on prejudice, misunderstanding, financial concerns, or other improper motives. The United States Supreme Court addressed the issue of disciplinary removals of children with disabilities and the effect of the "stay-put" provision in *Honig v. Doe*, 484 U.S. 305 (1988).

In *Honig*, school officials attempted to expel two children with serious emotional disturbance from school for violent and disruptive conduct related to their disabilities. In determining whether the "stay-put" provision prohibited unilateral removal of these students, the Court stated:

The language of the [stay-put provision] is unequivocal. It states plainly that during the pendency of any proceedings initiated under the Act, unless the state or local educational agency and the parents or guardian of a disabled child otherwise agree, "the child shall remain in the then current educational placement" . . . Faced with this clear directive, [school officials ask] us to read a "dangerousness" exception into the stay-put provision . . . [school officials'] arguments proceed . . . from a simple, common-sense proposition: Congress could not have intended the stay-put provision to be read literally, for such a construction leads to the clearly unintended, and untenable, result that school districts must return violent or dangerous students to school while the often lengthy [due process] proceedings run their course. We think it clear, however, that Congress very much meant to strip schools of the unilateral authority they had traditionally employed to exclude disabled students . . . from school. In so doing, Congress did not leave school administrators powerless to deal with dangerous students; it did, however, deny school officials their former right to "self-help," and directed that in the future the removal of disabled students could be accomplished only with the permission of the parents or, as a last resort, the courts . . . Congress passed the [Act] after finding that school systems across the country had excluded one out of every eight disabled students from classes. In drafting the law, Congress was largely guided by the recent decisions in [*PARC v. Pennsylvania* and *Mills v. Board of Education*], both of which involved the exclusion of hard-to-handle disabled students . . . Our conclusion that [the stay-put provision] means what it says does not leave educators hamstrung. The Department of Education has observed that, "while the [child's] placement may not be changed [during any complaint proceeding], this does not preclude the agency from using its normal procedures for dealing with children who are endangering themselves or others." Such procedures may include the use of study carrels, timeouts, detention, or the restriction of privileges. More drastically, where a student poses an immediate threat to the safety of others, officials may temporarily suspend him or her for up to 10 schooldays. This authority, which respondent in no way disputes, not only ensures that school administrators can protect the safety of others by promptly removing the most dangerous of students, it also provides a "cooling down" period during which officials can initiate IEP review and seek to persuade the child's parents to agree to an interim placement. And in those cases in which the parents of a truly dangerous child adamantly refuse to permit any change in placement, the 10-day respite gives school officials an opportunity to invoke the aid of the courts.

Since the passage of P.L. 94-142 (1975) Congress has wrestled with striking the proper balance between protecting the rights of students with disabilities, and protecting everyone else in the school from unreasonable disruptions or dangers. In response to heightened concerns over the dangers of weapons, violence, and drugs in schools, Congress amended the IDEA to provide school officials with additional authority to change the placement of special education students that carry weapons, are involved with drugs, or inflict serious bodily injury on others. 20 U.S.C. § 1415 (2004) states:

(G) SPECIAL CIRCUMSTANCES -- School personnel may remove a student to an interim alternative educational setting for not more than 45 school days without regard to whether the behavior is determined to be a manifestation of the child's disability, in cases where a child--

(i) Carries or possesses a weapon to or at school, on school premises, or to or at a school function under the jurisdiction of a State or local educational agency;
(ii) Knowingly possesses or uses illegal drugs, or sells or solicits the sale of a controlled substance, while at school, on school premises, or at a school function under the jurisdiction of a State or local educational agency; or
(iii) Has inflicted serious bodily injury upon another person while at school, on school premises, or at a school function under the jurisdiction of a State or local educational agency.

The term "weapon" in § 1415 is given the same meaning as "dangerous weapon" under 18 U.S.C. § 930 (2010), which defines a "dangerous weapon" as "a weapon, device, instrument, material, or substance, animate or inanimate, that is used for, or is readily capable of, causing death or serious bodily injury, except that such term does not include a pocket knife with a blade of less than 2 ½ inches in length." The term "illegal drugs" means a controlled substance (that is not legally possessed or used) as defined under the Controlled Substances Act, 21 U.S.C. § 812 (2010). Under 18 U.S.C. § 1365 (2010) the term "serious bodily injury" means "bodily injury which involves a substantial risk of death, extreme physical pain, protracted and obvious disfigurement, or protracted loss or impairment of the function of a bodily member, organ, or mental faculty."

The IDEA, 20 U.S.C. § 1415 (2004), also authorizes school officials to remove a child with a disability to an alternative educational setting if the child violates the school's code of student conduct. The child may be removed to the alternative placement for up to 10 school days regardless of whether the behavior was a manifestation of the child's disability. If the behavior is not a manifestation of the child's disability school officials may apply the same disciplinary

351

measures that apply to all children, except that a child with a disability must continue to receive a FAPE:

> PLACEMENT IN ALTERNATIVE EDUCATIONAL SETTING
> AUTHORITY OF SCHOOL PERSONNEL
> (A) CASE-BY-CASE DETERMINATION -- School personnel may consider any unique circumstances on a case-by-case basis when determining whether to order a change in placement for a child with a disability who violates a code of student conduct;
> (B) AUTHORITY-- School personnel under this subsection may remove a child with a disability who violates a code of student conduct from their current placement to an appropriate interim alternative educational setting, another setting, or suspension, for not more than 10 school days (to the extent such alternatives are applied to children without disabilities);
> (C) ADDITIONAL AUTHORITY-- If school personnel seek to order a change in placement that would exceed 10 school days and the behavior that gave rise to the violation of the school code is determined not to be a manifestation of the child's disability . . . the relevant disciplinary procedures applicable to children without disabilities may be applied to the child in the same manner and for the same duration in which the procedures would be applied to children without disabilities, except as provided in section 612(a)(1) [a FAPE must be available] although it may be provided in an interim alternative educational setting.
> (D) SERVICES -- A child with a disability who is removed from the child's current placement under subparagraph (G) [for weapons, drugs, or inflicting serious bodily injury] (irrespective of whether the behavior is determined to be a manifestation of the child's disability) or subparagraph (C) [behavior determined not to be a manifestation of disability] shall:

>> (i) Continue to receive educational services . . . so as to enable the child to continue to participate in the general education curriculum, although in another setting, and to progress toward meeting the goals set out in the child's IEP; and;
>> (ii) Receive, as appropriate, a functional behavioral assessment, behavioral intervention services and modifications that are designed to address the behavior violation so that it does not recur.

If school officials have sufficient cause to believe that a child with disabilities presents a serious danger to the child or others, school officials may present relevant evidence to a hearing officer and ask the hearing officer to place a dangerous child in a safer alternative setting. It should be noted that where a known danger exists, failure by school officials to take appropriate actions to protect against the known danger could result in potential tort liability if foreseeable injuries result from their negligence in addressing the known danger.

The 1999 IDEA regulations, 34 C.F.R. § 300.526(c)(4) (1999), stated that while this alternative placement for dangerousness may not exceed 45 days, additional 45 day extensions may be repeated as necessary to avoid a dangerous and inappropriate placement. The 2006 IDEA regulations, 34 C.F.R. § 300.532(b)(2)(ii) (2006), allowed a hearing officer to order a "change of placement of the child with a disability to an appropriate interim alternative educational setting for not more than 45 school days if the hearing officer determines that maintaining the current placement of the child is substantially likely to result in injury to the child or to others." The 2006 regulations, 34 C.F.R. § 300.532(b)(3) (2006), also provided that this 45 school day removal may be repeated as necessary if school officials can establish that "returning the child to the original placement is substantially likely to result in injury to the child or to others."

Manifestation Determinations

Another critical consideration in disciplining children with disabilities is determining whether the problem behavior is a manifestation of the student's disability. If a child's behavior is a manifestation of a disability, it would be unfair to punish that child for behavior that was caused by the disability and was not reasonably within the volitional control of the child. For example, children suffering from Tourette's syndrome may exhibit symptoms including involuntary movements or "tics", vocal sounds, and obscene or inappropriate language, resulting in behaviors that would likely merit punishment in most children, but may be uncontrollable manifestations for a child suffering from Tourette's syndrome. Accordingly, the IDEA, 20 U.S.C. § 1415 (2004), requires the IEP Team and other qualified personnel to conduct a review to determine whether an IDEA eligible child's problem behavior is a manifestation of a disability, when proposed disciplinary actions constitute a change in placement.

> (E) MANIFESTATION DETERMINATION --
>> (i) IN GENERAL -- Except as provided in subparagraph (B) [10 day or less removal for a violation of a code of student conduct], within 10 school days of any decision to change the placement of a child with a disability because of a violation of a code of student conduct, the local educational agency, the parent, and relevant members of the IEP Team (as determined by the parent and the local educational agency) shall review all relevant information in the student's file, including the child's IEP, any teacher observations, and any relevant information provided by the parents to determine--
>>> (I) If the conduct in question was caused by, or had a direct and substantial relationship to, the child's disability; or
>>> (II) If the conduct in question was the direct result of the local educational agency's failure to implement the IEP.
>> (ii) MANIFESTATION -- If the local educational agency, the parent, and relevant members of the IEP Team determine that either subclause (I) or (II) of clause (i) is applicable for the child, the conduct shall be determined to be a manifestation of the child's disability.

If the behavior is a manifestation of the child's disability, the IEP Team must implement a behavioral intervention plan, and except as provided for under the provisions of the IDEA, 20 U.S.C. § 1415 (2004), allowing for a removal for weapons, drugs, or serious bodily injury "return the child to the placement from which the child was removed, unless the parent and the local educational agency agree to a change of placement as part of the modification of the behavioral intervention plan."

Under 34 C.F.R. § 300.530(e) (2006) manifestation determinations are only required when a child is subjected to a disciplinary change of placement. A change in placement under 34 C.F.R. § 300.536(a) (2006) occurs when:

(1) The removal is for more than 10 consecutive school days; or
(2) The child has been subjected to a series of removals that constitute a pattern--
    (i) Because the series of removals total more than 10 school days in a school year;
    (ii) Because the child's behavior is substantially similar to the child's behavior in previous incidents that resulted in the series of removals; and
    (iii) Because of such additional factors as the length of each removal, the total amount of time the child has been removed, and the proximity of the removals to one another.

If the result of the review is a determination that the student's behavior was not a manifestation of the disability, school officials may discipline the student in the same manner that other student's would be disciplined, including suspension for up to 10 consecutive school days. No special services are required during this initial 10 school day suspension. Any removal for more than 10 consecutive school days, however, constitutes a change in placement and triggers the procedural protections of the IDEA.

When a student's behavior is not a manifestation of the student's disability school officials may lawfully long-term suspend for more than 10 consecutive school days or expel the student, subject to IDEA procedural protections. School officials cannot, however, terminate special education services for these students.

Continuation of IEP Services during Removals

Section 1412 of the IDEA requires the continuation of FAPE services for all eligible children with disabilities, even when they have been otherwise lawfully removed from school through suspension, expulsion, or incarceration. Eligible students are offered FAPE services at alternative settings. School officials cannot replicate all educational offerings in more limited or restrictive settings, and they are not required to do so under the IDEA. But under 34 C.F.R. § 300.530(d)(1)(i) (2006) school officials must provide services sufficient to permit the student to "continue to participate in the general education curriculum, although in another setting, and to progress toward meeting the goals set out in the child's IEP."

The 2006 IDEA regulations clarified that while school officials do not have to provide IDEA services during the first 10 school days a child is removed during the school year, for removals beyond 10 days in the same school year appropriate services must be provided. If there is no change in placement due to removals for the 11th cumulative day and beyond in the same school year, school officials determine what services are needed in consultation with at least one of the child's teachers. For any removal beyond 10 consecutive days, or any removal that constitutes a change in placement, the child's IEP Team determines what services are appropriate.

If the student's behavior is a manifestation of the student's disability, the student generally cannot be punished by school officials for that behavior. There are, nonetheless, many behavior management options still available to school officials. As the Court noted in *Honig*, school officials may use non-discriminatory in-school methods that are used with other students such as study carrels, time-outs, detention, or the restriction of privileges. Because these procedures are in-school, courts have held that they are not considered a change in placement and do not trigger the IDEA due process protections, unless they are used so extensively that they deny the student a FAPE.

As noted above, the 2004 amendments to the IDEA also allowed school officials to establish a 45 school day interim educational placement for students with violations related to weapons, drugs, causing serious bodily injury, or by convincing a hearing officer that the IDEA eligible child is dangerous to the child or others. Further, there is legal support for removing a student from the regular classroom when the student's disability related behavior results in excessive disruption of the regular classroom. School officials may also obtain a temporary court order for a removal or change of placement of any student that presents a serious potential danger to either the student or others. Permanent changes in the student's placement should be achieved through the IEP process by establishing that the current placement is not appropriate for the student.

It should be remembered that the IDEA limitations on disciplinary changes in placements only apply to situations in which schools have failed to obtain parental consent to proposed changes. The above limitations do not apply to situations in which school officials can successfully negotiate a mutually agreeable resolution with the student's parents concerning alternative settings for the provision of a FAPE.

It should also be noted that according to the Office for Civil Rights (OCR), exclusions from bus transportation are subject to the same procedural safeguards as other disciplinary exclusions, regardless of whether transportation is a required related service for that student. Nonetheless, if a student's behavior on the bus presents a serious problem, school officials may offer appropriate alternative transportation services to parents, or seek a change in the student's transportation services through a change in the IEP when appropriate.

Pre-Qualification Protections

The 2004 amendments to the IDEA established that students not currently eligible for IDEA services and facing disciplinary action are entitled to protections under the IDEA if school officials "had knowledge" that the student had a disability before the occurrence of the behavior that precipitated the disciplinary action. The IDEA, 20 U.S.C. § 1415 (2004), states that school officials shall be deemed to have knowledge that a student had a disability if:

> (i) The parent of the child has expressed concern in writing to supervisory or administrative personnel of the appropriate educational agency, or a teacher of the child, that the child is in need of special education and related services;
> (ii) The parent of the child has requested an evaluation of the child; or
> (iii) The teacher of the child, or other personnel of the local educational agency, has expressed specific concerns about a pattern of behavior demonstrated by the child, directly to the director of special education of such agency or to other supervisory personnel of the agency.

Amendments to the 2004 IDEA also stated: "A local educational agency shall not be deemed to have knowledge that the child is a child with a disability if the parent of the child has not allowed an evaluation of the child . . . or has refused services under this part or the child has been evaluated and it was determined that the child was not a child with a disability under this part." If there is no basis of knowledge prior to taking disciplinary actions "the child may be subjected to disciplinary measures applied to children without disabilities who engaged in comparable behaviors."

If, however, a request for an evaluation of the child is made during the time the child is subjected to disciplinary measures, under 20 U.S.C. § 1415 (2004) "the evaluation shall be conducted in an expedited manner." If it is determined that the child is a child with a disability, the child must be provided special education and related services "except that, pending the results of the evaluation, the child shall remain in the educational placement determined by school authorities."

Reporting Criminals Acts

School officials may report IDEA eligible students to law enforcement agents when students are suspected of committing criminal acts. The IDEA, 20 U.S.C. § 1415 (2004), states:

> Nothing in this part shall be construed to prohibit an agency from reporting a crime committed by a child with a disability to appropriate authorities or to prevent State law enforcement and judicial authorities from exercising their responsibilities with regard to the application of Federal and State law to crimes committed by a child with a disability.

Reports to law enforcement officials may be required by state law. School officials that report a crime must also transmit copies of the student's special education and disciplinary records to the appropriate authorities. However, law enforcement agents and judicial authorities have a duty to protect the public by enforcing criminal laws, and they are not bound by the mandates of the IDEA. Students with disabilities that are convicted of crimes may be subjected to the same penalties imposed on others convicted of those crimes, including incarceration. Eligible students retain their rights to a FAPE, however, even when incarcerated.

Transition Services

The transition from school to work, independent living, or further education is difficult for many young adults. Children with disabilities may face unique challenges in making this transition. In 1990 Congress amended the IDEA to require the provision of transition services for children with disabilities. The IDEA, 20 U.S.C. § 1401 (2004), defined transition services as "designed to be within a results-oriented process, that is focused on improving the academic and functional achievement of the child" to facilitate the child's transition from school to post-school activities.

Transition services may include instruction, related services, community experiences, and the development of employment and adult living skills. A 1997 amendment to the IDEA required that a "statement of the transition service needs" must be included in the IEP beginning at age fourteen, and updated annually. This amendment focused earlier attention on educational programming designed to transition the child from school to post-school activities. It was intended to augment, not replace, the transition services requirement that begins at age sixteen, or sooner if deemed appropriate by the IEP Team. A determination of what transition services are appropriate should be based on the individual student's needs, and should take into account the student's strengths, preferences and interests.

Termination of Special Education Services

Special education services terminate upon graduation with a regular high school diploma or age ineligibility. Under 34 C.F.R. § 300.102(a)(3) the term regular diploma does not include alternative degrees such as a GED, certificate of attendance, etc., unless the alternative degree is fully aligned with state academic standards. Students may be awarded alternative certificates but they retain a right to continued IDEA services. Under the 2006 regulations, 34 C.F.R. § 300.101(a), only graduation with a regular diploma or age ineligibility terminates that right.

Graduation is a change in placement, and parents must receive notification that the student is scheduled for graduation. The IDEA provides federal funds for special education services through age twenty-one. But if state law does not provide for public education for nondisabled children from ages eighteen through twenty-one, states are not required to provide special education for children with disabilities from ages eighteen in that age group. An exception to this rule occurs when students succeed in claims for compensatory education. If a student can prove that a FAPE was not provided and that no regular high school diploma was awarded, the student may be entitled to remedial services even if older than the maximum age under state law.

All students, including special education students, may be required to pass competency exams before obtaining a regular high school diploma. Because of the severity of their disabilities, some children will be unable to pass these exams and obtain a regular high school diploma. Courts have nonetheless upheld competency exam requirements, even for children with disabilities, provided that students with disabilities were given notice of the general contents of the exam, and an opportunity to learn the required academic content.

Cost-Based Objections to Requested IDEA Services

When facing parental requests for excessively expensive services, schools may find some potential relief in the United States Supreme Court's decision in *Board of Education v. Rowley*. In *Rowley*, the Court held that schools are not required to maximize a child's educational potential by providing superior special education and related services regardless of expense. Instead, the Court found that the requirements of the IDEA are satisfied when children with disabilities are provided with appropriate "personalized instruction with sufficient support services to permit the child to benefit educationally from that instruction."

Under *Rowley*, special education services need only be appropriate for the child and sufficient to provide educational benefits. The services offered do not have to be the best services available regardless of cost. As long as school officials' decisions concerning the provision of special education services are appropriate, the choice of which educational methodology and service to provide is left to school officials. Parents may express their preferences through the IEP process, but if school officials' choices are also appropriate, school officials may choose between appropriate options and need not choose the most expensive option.

For some children, however, the only appropriate option may still be very expensive. Before school officials may raise cost alone as a defense under the IDEA, they must establish that: 1) The school has provided a proper continuum of placements; 2) The child in question would not experience a total denial of educational opportunity because of the failure to provide the expensive service; and 3) Other special education students may be denied a FAPE because of excessive expenditures on one child.

Comments and Questions

Significant progress has occurred in providing educational services for children with disabilities. In 1973 testimony before the U.S. Senate, regarding the treatment of persons with disabilities and the need for remedial legislation, Professor Oliver L. Hurley of the University of Georgia recounted a scene all too typical of the circumstances of children with disabilities prior to the passage of P.L. 94-142:

> Some years ago, during the course of a visit to the State Institution for the mentally retarded, I encountered a little girl who was lying in a crib. Wondering why she was so confined while the other children were not, I began to play with her. I found that even though I could make eye contact with her, she was unable to follow me with her eyes for more than about 12 inches. I began to try to teach her. In about 15 minutes she could follow me about a quarter of the way around the bed. I was convinced then, and still am, that with a little work the child could have been taught some useful behavior and could have been gotten out of the crib. It seems safe to say that no one with any authority was concerned about the education of that little girl. For me, this child, who showed some ability to learn typified our reactions to these difficult cases--hide them away, exclude them, forget them . . . It seems antithetical to American philosophy, as I see it, that whether or not a handicapped child gets proper care and proper educational treatment depends on the fatness of that child's father's wallet.

Appropriate educational services can have remarkable benefits for children with disabilities, helping them to live more independent and productive lives. Although special education is expensive, what are the economic costs of failing to educate children with disabilities? In addition to the economic costs of failing to educate disabled children, how should the incalculable personal costs of denying education to disabled children be weighed, including the diminished quality of life for the girl discussed above, and the possibility that she might spend the rest of her natural life confined to a bed and staring at the ceiling if she does not receive appropriate educational assistance?

Since the passage of P.L. 94-142 in 1975, providing special education and related services for children with disabilities has required increasing allocations of resources to special education programs. How have escalating expenditures for special education programs affected regular education programs? How should Congress, the states, and schools balance the educational needs of children with disabilities and the fiscal realities of limited resources? Are the costs of current special education programs justified by the benefits? Are there more efficient ways of achieving equal or superior educational results?

Limitations on disciplining special education students and the placement of disruptive special education students in regular classrooms continue to generate controversy. Are different disciplinary policies for special education and regular education students justified? Do students, parents, and others in your community understand and accept this justification? Regular education students and their parents have no legal standing under the IDEA to challenge the placement of disruptive students in their classroom. Should they? If current provisions in the IDEA are problematic, what preferable alternatives and legislative amendments would you suggest to your members of Congress for the next reauthorization of the IDEA?

Like most laws, current special education laws are the product of a complex historical, legal, and political process. In examining the results of this process, have current special education laws achieved a fair and appropriate balancing of competing interests? Congress must, for example, strike an appropriate balance between the rights of children with disabilities and the needs of school officials to protect safety, order, and limited resources. In the 2004 amendments to the IDEA, Congress generally shifted the balance under the IDEA more in favor of school authority, and limited some student and parent rights. Congress reduced some due process protections, strengthened options for dealing with student discipline issues, and made it more difficult for parents to challenge school officials' decisions under the IDEA.

Two decisions from the U.S. Supreme Court contributed to this general trend toward greater school authority and diminished legal support for those challenging the decisions of school officials. In *Schaffer v. Weast*, 546 U.S. 45 (2005), the Court held that the party challenging an IEP bears the initial burden of proof. This effectively established a legal presumption that the IEP was valid. The end result is that those challenging the IEP, generally parents, are now less likely to prevail. The Court's decision in *Arlington Central School District v. Murphy*, 548 U.S. 291 (2006) further added to the difficulties of those challenging school officials' decisions under the IDEA by holding that even if parents were to prevail in their challenge, they still could not recover the costs of hiring the expert witnesses and consultants needed to prove their case. Together, the Court's decisions in these two cases make it much more difficult for parents, especially those with limited resources, to challenge school officials' decisions under the IDEA.

In *Winkelman v. Parma City School District*, 550 U.S. 516 (2007), the Court did, however, recognize that because the IDEA grants parents independent, enforceable rights, including an entitlement to a FAPE for their child, parents are entitled to prosecute those rights on their own behalf and to act *pro se* on behalf of their children. The balance of rights and powers under the IDEA continues to shift with Congress' perceptions of current needs and the Court's interpretations of Congressional intent and the commands of the Constitution.

The IDEA is driven by broad, constant principles, including the need to assure equal protection of the laws, to remedy discrimination, and to educate children with disabilities for better and more productive futures. How best to achieve these goals, however, is no simple task given the realities of competing interests and limited resources. The U.S. Congress and U.S. Administrative agencies continue to modify and adjust this system. The system is far from perfect, but to date, it is the best system we have for serving children with disabilities.

Because the system allows for continued amendments and corrections, there is hope that future systems of education for children with disabilities may be more efficient and effective in helping these children achieve happier and more productive lives. Whether these future improvements are realized depends on the knowledge and commitment of future legislators and educators. No one can fix something they don't understand, however, so understanding the current laws under the IDEA is an important part of improving future services for children from the local level to the national level.

Section 504 of the Rehabilitation Act

As recipients of federal funds, public schools must comply with the mandates of § 504 of the Rehabilitation Act of 1973, as codified in 29 U.S.C § 794 (2011). Section 504 protections may also apply to private schools and other institutions if they receive federal funds. The statutory text of § 504, 29 U.S.C § 794 (2011), mandates:

No otherwise qualified individual with a disability in the United States . . . shall, solely by reason of her or his disability, be excluded from the participation in, be denied the benefits of, or be subjected to discrimination under any program or activity receiving Federal financial assistance.

A person qualified for protections under § 504 is defined by 34 C.F.R. § 104.3 (2011) as:

Any person who (i) has a physical or mental impairment which substantially limits one or more major life activities; (ii) has a record of such an impairment; or (iii) is regarded as having such an impairment.

34 C.F.R. § 104.3 (2011) defines other significant terms as follows:

(i) "Physical or mental impairment" means (A) any physiological disorder or condition, cosmetic disfigurement, or anatomical loss affecting one or more of the following body systems: neurological; musculoskeletal; special sense organs; respiratory, including speech organs; cardiovascular; reproductive, digestive, genito-urinary; hemic and lymphatic; skin; and endocrine; or (B) any mental or psychological disorder, such as mental retardation, organic brain syndrome, emotional or mental illness, and specific learning disabilities.
(ii) "Major life activities" means functions such as caring for one's self, performing manual tasks, walking, seeing, hearing, speaking, breathing, learning, and working.
(iii) "Has a record of such an impairment" means has a history of, or has been misclassified as having, a mental or physical impairment that substantially limits one or more major life activities.
(iv) "Is regarded as having an impairment" means (A) has a physical or mental impairment that does not substantially limit major life activities but that is treated by a recipient as constituting such a limitation; (B) has a physical or mental impairment that substantially limits major life activities only as a result of the attitudes of others toward such impairment; or (C) has none of the impairments defined in . . . this section but is treated by a recipient as having such an impairment.

If otherwise qualified persons with disabilities fall within the protections of § 504, they may not be discriminated against because of their disabilities in programs receiving federal assistance. Further, they are entitled to "reasonable accommodations" to facilitate their participation. Reasonable accommodations often include making facilities accessible and usable by persons with disabilities, and making reasonable modifications in academic programs or working conditions.

An accommodation is not reasonable, and therefore not required, if it would result in unreasonable costs, administrative burdens, or health or safety risks. Institutions are not required to change the fundamental nature of their programs, nor can they provide a reasonable accommodation when no reasonable accommodation is possible under the circumstances. Further, an institution is not required to provide a specific accommodation requested by an individual. Instead, an institution is only required to provide a reasonable accommodation.

When more than one reasonable accommodation is being considered, institution officials may choose which reasonable accommodation to provide. The preference of the person requesting the accommodation should be fairly considered, but what is required under § 504 is a reasonable accommodation. Institution officials may consider legitimate factors such as costs, administrative burdens, health and safety, and minimizing unnecessary impacts on the rights of other persons in deciding which reasonable accommodations to provide.

Unlike the IDEA, which only covers children in limited categories of disabilities who need special education and related services, § 504 more broadly protects children and adults from discrimination based on disabilities in institutions receiving federal funds. Although the IDEA and § 504 are both intended to protect persons with disabilities, these are separate and distinct Acts covering different populations. The IDEA and § 504 protect different rights in different ways. To extend all IDEA substantive rights and procedural protections to the broader population covered by § 504 would be cost prohibitive, and would likely overwhelm available disabilities support systems, diverting limited resources away from children who most needed assistance. With the passage of § 504, the IDEA, and the ADA, Congress clearly intended to broadly prohibit discrimination based on disability. But Congress also appears to have established a triage system with these statutes, prioritizing children with the most severe disabilities and with the greatest needs for special education under the IDEA.

Section 504 rights may be enforced through either filing a complaint with the Office of Civil Rights (OCR), or through a private suit. Complaints must be filed with the OCR within 180 days from the alleged act of discrimination. Representatives from the OCR will initiate an investigation concerning alleged acts of discrimination and assure institutional compliance with § 504. In private suits, prevailing parties may be awarded attorneys' fees and damages. Where school officials have acted in good faith, however, compensatory and punitive damages are not available.

Protections for Students

As noted above, Congress prioritized children with the most severe disabilities under the IDEA. Students already served under the IDEA are generally not provided with a separate § 504 plan as they should be receiving a FAPE and other appropriate accommodations under the IDEA. Students that were eligible under the IDEA but were only offered a § 504 plan may, however, be entitled to compensation for services that should have been provided to them under the IDEA.

Section 504 protects qualified persons with disabilities who are not eligible under the IDEA. However, both the IDEA and the regulations for § 504 require school officials to provide a "FAPE" to eligible students. The provision of a "FAPE" is a clear affirmative duty under the IDEA (20 U.S.C. § 1400(d)(1)(A) which states that the purpose of the IDEA is "to ensure that all children with disabilities have available to them a free appropriate public education") identified by Congress as a core purpose of the IDEA. In contrast, the "FAPE" requirement under § 504 results from an administrative interpretation based on the negative prohibitions against exclusion, denial of benefits, or discrimination in § 504. The U.S. Department of Education (DOE) regulations for § 504, 34 C.F.R. § 104.33(a), state: "A recipient that operates a public elementary or secondary education program shall provide a free appropriate public education to each qualified handicapped person who is in the recipient's jurisdiction, regardless of the nature or severity of the person's handicap."

The statutory text of § 504 clearly prohibits exclusion, denial of benefits, or discrimination based on disability. But the statutory text of § 504 does not expressly mandate a FAPE for eligible students, raising questions about whether the DOE regulations exceeded the scope of statutory authority in requiring a FAPE for students under § 504. Until this issue is definitively resolved, however, school officials are likely to continue to comply with the current DOE regulations requiring a FAPE under § 504.

Nonetheless, because the scope of the statutory authority for a FAPE is not the same for both the IDEA and § 504, it is likely that what Congress intended to require is not the same either. Under § 504 a FAPE appears to mean that eligible students with disabilities cannot be provided with educational opportunities less than those provided to students without disabilities. The IDEA requires the provision of a FAPE through special education, while under § 504 a FAPE for eligible students may be provided through non-discriminatory regular education programs.

Section 504 protects students with disabilities from discrimination in all programs receiving federal funds. Students must, however, be otherwise qualified for participation in the school programs or activities they seek to participate in. School officials are not required to accommodate participation of a disabled student if the student is not otherwise qualified for participation in the program or activity, and no reasonable accommodation is possible.

For example, a student with a disability who failed to qualify for the school basketball team because of inadequate skills and preparation could not demand inclusion on the team simply because the student had a disability. Similarly, exclusion of a blind student whose disability made driving unsafe could lawfully be excluded from driving in a driver's education program, and this would not violate the mandates of § 504. The student could not be safely accommodated in this activity. Section 504 does not require preferential treatment or unreasonable accommodations for disabled students.

Instead, § 504 requires non-discrimination and reasonable accommodations to assure fair treatment and good faith efforts to facilitate participation of students with disabilities in programs receiving federal assistance. Protections for students apply from initial application for admission, through attendance, and to all post-attendance interactions between an eligible student and the institution.

Assessments of students with disabilities for purposes of admissions should be designed to measure factors relevant to admissions, and not the effects of a student's disability. If program assessments or requirements have a disproportionate impact on disabled students, and are not essential elements of the program, a waiver may be required to accommodate students with disabilities. This may include, for example, modifications of requirements or waivers in the admissions process or for courses and other requirements that cannot be shown to be essential to the academic program.

Section 504 does not require any fundamental alteration of programs. Elements of the program that have a disproportionate impact on students with disabilities, however, must be justified by showing that the requirement is essential to the program and that no reasonable accommodation can be provided without changing the essential nature of the program.

Tests that are essential to measuring academic achievement can be required of all students. Testing conditions may need to be modified, however, to accommodate students with disabilities. This may include alternative locations for exams, extended time limits, oral examinations, and other reasonable accommodations to assure that tests are measuring relevant knowledge and skills and not the effects of a student's disability.

Student codes of conduct apply to all students. School officials can discipline students with disabilities for misconduct. But students with disabilities may not be suspended, expelled, or otherwise punished for manifestations of their disabilities. The OCR generally applies the same standards to the suspension or expulsion of § 504 eligible students as are applied to IDEA eligible students.

School officials may sometimes want to exclude a student not for disciplinary reasons, but because the student carries a contagious disease. School officials may lawfully exclude students that pose a serious risk of infection to others. But absent evidence of a serious risk of infection, courts have required admissions and reasonable accommodations of excluded students.

To prevail, school officials must assure that decisions to exclude students because of a potentially communicable disease are based on valid medical evidence and medical doctors' opinions, and not the irrational fears and prejudices of school officials or others. Whether the exclusion is lawful is determined by weighing the legitimate interests of the student against the medically determined risk of infection to others.

School officials have a legal duty to protect all persons in the school from known dangers, including serious and preventable risks from infectious diseases. But a lawful decision to exclude a student because of risk of infection must be based on sound medical data and not irrational speculation or phobia.

School officials may also seek to exclude a disabled student from certain athletic activities to protect the student or to protect others. A decision on whether to exclude a disabled student from participation in an athletic program requires balancing the student's legitimate interests in participation against the legitimate concerns of school officials. A student may be excluded, however, if the student's participation creates serious health or safety dangers and no reasonable accommodation would effectively mitigate these dangers.

Protections for Employees

Section 504 prohibits employers in institutions receiving federal funds from discriminating in employment against any otherwise qualified persons because of disabilities. Employers must also provide reasonable accommodations for employees with disabilities. Providing reasonable accommodations may mean restructuring physical access to work areas; modifying work schedules; redistributing tasks among workers; eliminating unnecessary job qualifications; and other reasonable accommodations so that otherwise qualified employees with disabilities have a fair opportunity to function effectively in their positions. Section 504 does not, however, require employers to hire unqualified persons; to tolerate substandard job performance; or to refrain from addressing legitimate threats to health or safety.

Some positions may require adequate physical or cognitive abilities to perform essential duties or to prevent legitimate health or safety risks. For example, a teacher charged with the supervision of young children or students inclined to dangerous misconduct may need to visually supervise students for safety reasons. While there are many teaching positions that a visually impaired teacher could safety and successfully perform, § 504 does not require assigning a visually impaired teacher to a position for which that teacher is not otherwise qualified and the assignment presents legitimate safety risks.

Similarly, an employee that presents a legitimate health risk to others could be excluded. But as with students, to exclude an employee the health concern must be legitimate and not the product of unjustified fears or prejudices. The U.S. Supreme Court addressed the scope of protections for employees with contagious diseases under § 504 in *School Board of Nassau County v. Arline*, 480 U.S. 273 (1987). Arline was serving as a teacher, but was dismissed solely based on recurrences of tuberculosis. Arline challenged the dismissal as a violation of § 504. In a 7-2 decision, the Court held that contagious disease could be a disability under § 504, but remanded the case to determine whether Arline was otherwise qualified. The Court stated:

> Allowing discrimination based on the contagious effects of a physical impairment would be inconsistent with the basic purpose of § 504, which is to ensure that handicapped individuals are not denied jobs or other benefits because of the prejudiced attitudes or the ignorance of others. By amending the definition of "handicapped individual" to include not only those who are actually physically impaired, but also those who are regarded as impaired and who, as a result, are substantially limited in a major life activity, Congress acknowledged that society's accumulated myths and fears about disability and disease are as handicapping as are the physical limitations that flow from actual impairment. Few aspects of a handicap give rise to the same level of public fear and misapprehension as contagiousness. Even those who suffer or have recovered from such noninfectious diseases as epilepsy or cancer have faced discrimination based on the irrational fear that they might be contagious. The Act is carefully structured to replace such reflexive reactions to actual or perceived handicaps with actions based on reasoned and medically sound judgments: the definition of "handicapped individual" is broad, but only those individuals who are both handicapped and otherwise qualified are eligible for relief. The fact that some persons who have contagious diseases may pose a serious health threat to others under certain circumstances does not justify excluding from the coverage of the Act all persons with actual or perceived contagious diseases. Such exclusion would mean that those accused of being contagious would never have the opportunity to have their condition evaluated in light of medical evidence and a determination made as to whether they were "otherwise qualified." Rather, they would be vulnerable to discrimination on the basis of mythology--precisely the type of injury Congress sought to prevent.

If an employee presents a significant risk of transmitting a serious disease to others, and reasonable accommodations do not eliminate that risk, the employee is not "otherwise qualified." As the Court stated in *Arline*: "A person who poses a significant risk of communicating an infectious disease to others in the workplace will not be otherwise qualified for his or her job if reasonable accommodation will not eliminate that risk." The Court further noted that decisions on these matters must be grounded in findings of fact "based on reasonable medical judgments given the state of medical knowledge, about (a) the nature of the risk (how the disease is transmitted), (b) the duration of the risk (how long is the carrier infectious), (c) the severity of the risk (what is the potential harm to third parties) and (d) the probabilities the disease will be transmitted and will cause varying degrees of harm."

Employers may also lawfully decline to hire persons with disabilities that would make the work environment unreasonably dangerous to their own health. In *Chevron U.S.A., Inc. v. Echazabal*, 536 U.S. 73 (2002), the U.S. Supreme Court held that an EEOC regulation authorizing employers to refuse to hire an applicant because his performance on the job would endanger his own health, did not violate the Americans with Disabilities Act (ADA). In this case, Echazabal had a liver condition that doctors suggested would be further aggravated by exposure to the toxins he would encounter working in an oil refinery. The Court upheld the right of the employer to refuse to hire Echazabal for this position. Although this case involved a private employer and the ADA, the ADA and § 504 differ little in substance. The principle distinction between § 504 and the ADA is that the ADA extends § 504 type protections to the private sector.

The Americans with Disabilities Act

The Americans with Disabilities Act (ADA), 42 U.S.C. § 12101 (2011), extended § 504 type protections into the private sector and clarified obligations for public institutions. Title I of the ADA prohibits employment discrimination by employers with 15 or more employees and who are engaged in interstate commerce. Title II applies to public institutions including schools and other government institutions, and public transportation including school buses. Title III requires non-discrimination and access to public accommodations including hotels, restaurants, theaters, stores, recreation and education facilities, museums, etc. And Title IV requires telecommunications providers to offer access to persons with disabilities, *i.e.*, persons with hearing and speech impairments.

Although § 504 protects persons with disabilities from discrimination in institutions receiving federal funds, individuals with disabilities remained unprotected in many other vital aspects of life. The ADA extended these important protections to critical areas of the private sector including employment, transportation, commerce, and communications. The ADA is considered by many to be the most sweeping antidiscrimination law since the Civil Rights Act of 1964. Many provisions in the ADA are similar to § 504 provisions, but because passage of the ADA was based on Congress's power to enforce the Fourteenth Amendment and to regulate interstate commerce, the ADA prohibits discrimination against individuals with disabilities in both the public and private sectors, regardless of whether any federal funds are received. Under Title I, 42 U.S.C. § 12112 (2011):

> No covered entity shall discriminate against a qualified individual on the basis of disability in regard to job application procedures, the hiring, advancement, or discharge of employees, employee compensation, job training, and other terms, conditions, and privileges of employment.

Title II of the ADA prohibits discrimination against individuals with disabilities in all state and local government programs, including public schools. Similar to § 504, Title II of the ADA, 42 U.S.C. § 12132 (2011), declared:

> No qualified individual with a disability shall, by reason of such disability, be excluded from participation in or be denied the benefits of the services, programs, or activities of a public entity, or be subjected to discrimination by any such entity.

The ADA required modifications for accessibility and other reasonable accommodations for individuals with disabilities. Generally, public institutions were already in compliance with § 504 mandates. But in the private sector the ADA imposed sweeping new mandates, which while important, could prove prohibitively expensive in some cases. Smaller for-profit businesses could be bankrupted by excessively expensive modifications otherwise mandated by the ADA.

To guard against this problem Congress included an "undue hardship" clause under 42 U.S.C. § 121111(10) (2011):

(A) *In general*: The term "undue hardship" means an action requiring significant difficulty or expense, when considered in light of the factors set forth in subparagraph (B).

(B) *Factors to be considered*: In determining whether an accommodation would impose an undue hardship on a covered entity, factors to be considered include:

(i) The nature and cost of the accommodation needed under this chapter;

(ii) The overall financial resources of the facility or facilities involved in the provision of the reasonable accommodation; the number of persons employed at such facility; the effect on expenses and resources, or the impact otherwise of such accommodation upon the operation of the facility;

(iii) The overall financial resources of the covered entity; the overall size of the business of a covered entity with respect to the number of its employees; the number, type, and location of its facilities; and

(iv) The type of operation or operations of the covered entity, including the composition, structure, and functions of the workforce of such entity; the geographic separateness, administrative, or fiscal relationship of the facility or facilities in question to the covered entity.

Although the ADA provided significant new protections for individuals with disabilities, especially in the private sector, the impact of the ADA in public schools was less dramatic because discrimination against persons with disabilities in schools receiving federal funds was already prohibited by § 504.

Nonetheless, there are some situations in which the ADA significantly impacted the operation of schools receiving federal funds. For example, schools are required to make public accommodations such as athletic stadiums, auditoriums, and other facilities barrier-free for outside individuals with disabilities attending school events. Further, all new school construction must comply with barrier-free design requirements mandated by the ADA. The ADA, 42 U.S.C. § 12114 (2011), also helped to clarify the law concerning reasonable accommodations related to the use of illegal drugs and alcohol:

(a) *Qualified individual with a disability*: For purposes of this subchapter, qualified individual with a disability shall not include any employee or applicant who is currently engaging in the illegal use of drugs, when the covered entity acts on the basis of such use.

(b) *Rules of construction*: Nothing in subsection (a) of this section shall be construed to exclude as a qualified individual with a disability an individual who:

(1) Has successfully completed a supervised drug rehabilitation program and is no longer engaging in the illegal use of drugs, or has otherwise been rehabilitated successfully and is no longer engaging in such use;

(2) Is participating in a supervised rehabilitation program and is no longer engaging in such use; or

(3) Is erroneously regarded as engaging in such use, but is not engaging in such use; except that it shall not be a violation of this chapter for a covered entity to

adopt or administer reasonable policies or procedures, including but not limited to drug testing, designed to ensure that an individual described in paragraph (1) or (2) is no longer engaging in the illegal use of drugs.

(c) *Authority of covered entity*: A covered entity:

(1) May prohibit the illegal use of drugs and the use of alcohol at the workplace by all employees;

(2) May require that employees shall not be under the influence of alcohol or be engaging in the illegal use of drugs at the workplace;

(3) May require that employees behave in conformance with the requirements established under the Drug-Free Workplace Act of 1988 (41 U.S.C. 701 et seq.);

(4) May hold an employee who engages in the illegal use of drugs or who is an alcoholic to the same qualification standards for employment or job performance and behavior that such entity holds other employees, even if any unsatisfactory performance or behavior is related to the drug use or alcoholism of such employee.

Current illegal drug abusers are excluded from protection. In contrast, persons suffering from alcoholism are protected even if they are currently using alcohol. Alcohol and persons under the influence of alcohol may, however, be excluded from the workplace, and drug and alcohol abusers may be held to the same non-discriminatory performance and conduct standards as other employees.

In general, for both § 504 and the ADA, before any enforceable duty attaches institutional officials must have knowledge of the disability. And before a successful complaint can be filed, institutional officials must have engaged in discrimination or denied a request for a reasonable accommodation. Officials may require appropriate documentation of disabilities from persons claiming rights under either § 504 or the ADA.

Individuals with disabilities are entitled to a case-by-case decision based on the unique circumstances related to their disability. But there must otherwise be equity and non-discrimination across cases. Institutional policies for deciding on requests for reasonable accommodations must be rational and not arbitrary or discriminatory. Where professional judgment is required, the persons exercising that judgment must be qualified to exercise professional judgment in that area or seek an objective opinion from other qualified persons. Concerning academic decisions, courts tend to be very deferential to academic decisions, but only when school officials have followed fair procedures and exercised appropriate professional judgment.

Chapter Summary

This chapter reviewed disability law and its application in schools, including the IDEA, § 504, the ADA and the rights of students and employees under these Acts. After reading this chapter, please consider the following points in review and for further thought and discussion:

I. *Review Points*:

1) Based on legal theories rooted in *Brown*, advocates for children with disabilities successfully argued that these children were being unconstitutionally excluded from public schools through a systematic denial of equal protection and due process rights.

2) In the *PARC* and *Mills* cases in 1972 federal courts held that children with disabilities must have access to a free public education and that they should be placed in regular classrooms when possible or in special classes when necessary.

3) In 1975 Congress passed P.L. 94-142 creating a system of special education with significant new substantive rights and procedural protections for children with disabilities.

4) Although case law plays an important role in interpreting and clarifying disability laws, the law in this area is largely defined by federal statutes and regulations. These principally include the IDEA, § 504, and the ADA.

5) Eligibility under the IDEA is based on a two-part test:

  1) Whether the child has an IDEA eligible disability; and
  2) Whether the child needs special education and related services because of that IDEA eligible disability.

6) The IDEA's "child find" provision creates an affirmative duty for school officials to identify children with disabilities. Children may be identified for IDEA testing through mass screenings of all children, or through referrals from parents, school personnel, medical personnel, or other persons.

7) Parental consent is not required for mass screening tests administered to all children. Before individual evaluations for IDEA eligibility may be conducted, however, school officials generally must obtain parental consent.

8) Children eligible for IDEA services have a right to a "free appropriate public education" (FAPE), related services, and due process protections.

9) Concerning what constitutes an "appropriate" education under special education laws, in *Rowley* the Court conclude that "the 'basic floor of opportunity' provided by the Act consists of access to specialized instruction and related services which are individually designed to provide educational benefit to the handicapped child." The Court held that FAPE requirements are met by "providing personalized instruction with sufficient support services to permit the child to

benefit educationally from that instruction. Such instruction and services must be provided at public expense, must meet the State's educational standards, must approximate the grade levels used in the State's regular education, and must comport with the child's IEP. In addition, the IEP, and therefore the personalized instruction, should be formulated in accordance with the requirements of the Act and, if the child is being educated in the regular classrooms of the public education system, should be reasonably calculated to enable the child to achieve passing marks and advance from grade to grade."

10) The test for determining if extended school year services are required is an assessment of:

1) Whether the child would experience a significant regression in the absence of extended year services; and
2) Whether sufficient educational recoupment would occur in a reasonable time when regular year services were resumed.

11) The Individualized Education Program (IEP) is the basic plan for providing special education and related services under the IDEA.

12) Children with disabilities must be placed in the Least Restrictive Environment (LRE) appropriate for the child.

13) Related services are those supportive services necessary for an IDEA eligible child to benefit from special education. Under the *Tatro* test, health services must be provided as related services if:

1) The supportive services are necessary for the child to benefit from special education; and
2) The services are not excluded as medical services that would require the services of a physician for other than diagnostic or evaluation purposes.

14) Notice and hearing rights are provided throughout the special education process, from initial consideration of eligibility through completion of the special education program or a determination of ineligibility.

15) The "stay put" provision requires that during the pendency of any change in placement proceedings, unless school officials and parents otherwise agree, the child shall remain in the then-current educational placement.

16) A disciplinary removal that constitutes a change in placement triggers IDEA due process protections, requiring the IEP Team and other qualified personnel to conduct a review to determine whether the problem behavior is a manifestation of a disability.

17) If the behavior is not a manifestation of a disability, school officials may discipline the student in the same manner that other student's would be disciplined. Any removal for more than 10 consecutive school days, however, constitutes a change in placement and triggers the

procedural protections of the IDEA. If the behavior is a manifestation of the child's disability, the IEP Team must implement a behavioral intervention plan.

18) Discipline procedures under the IDEA may be among the most significant and the most confusing provisions for many educators and lawyers. Accordingly, the following summary of incrementally severe disciplinary options under the IDEA is provided:

Behavior Management Strategies: To attempt to modify problem behavior school officials may utilize a variety of behavior and conflict management strategies including student carrels, time-outs, detention, restrictions in privileges, etc. As long as IEP services are provided, and there is no change in placement, school officials may unilaterally implement these behavior management strategies.

Obtaining Parental Consent: If more serious measures are necessary school officials may first obtain parental consent for needed changes in placement or for other appropriate behavior management strategies. If parental consent is obtained, the IDEA limitations on disciplinary actions are generally not triggered.

Unilateral 10 School Day Removal: Provided their actions are not discriminatory school officials may unilaterally remove an IDEA eligible student for up to 10 consecutive school days for violating a code of student conduct. No services are required, and no manifestation determination is necessary.

Subsequent 10 School Day or Less Removals: The 1999 IDEA regulations clarified that there is no absolute limit on the total number of days per year that a student may be removed for separate incidents of misconduct, so long as no single removal exceeds 10 consecutive school days and there is no pattern of removals. Factors considered in determining whether there is a pattern of removals include the length of each removal; the total amount of time the child is removed; and the proximity of the removals to one another. However, school officials must provide services to the extent necessary to allow the child to make progress toward meeting IEP goals and participate in the general curriculum, although in a different setting. School officials determine which services are needed in consultation with at least one of the child's teachers. Manifestation determinations are only required when a child is subjected to a disciplinary change of placement.

Long-Term Suspensions and Expulsions: IDEA eligible students may be long-term suspended or expelled for a violation of a code of student conduct that is not a manifestation of the student's disability. Any removal beyond 10 consecutive school days, however, constitutes a change in placement, triggering IDEA due process protections. Further, school officials must continue to provide a FAPE to these students. For removals beyond 10 consecutive school days, the child's IEP team determines what services are necessary to provide a FAPE.

45 School Day Removals for Weapons, Drugs, or Inflicting Serious Bodily Injury: School officials may unilaterally remove a student to an alternative educational placement for up to 45 school days for possession of weapons, drugs, or inflicting serious bodily injury.

45 School Day Removals for Dangerousness: School officials may ask a hearing officer to remove a potentially dangerous student to an alternative educational placement for up to 45 school days by presenting evidence that "maintaining the current placement of such child is substantially likely to result in injury to the child or to others." Additional 45 school day extensions may be repeated as necessary to prevent a dangerous placement.

Court Ordered Remedies: In the event that the above options fail to provide appropriate remedies, school officials may obtain a court order for a removal or change of placement of a student that presents a serious danger to him or herself or others in the school.

Reporting Crimes: School officials may report students suspected of committing crimes to law enforcement agents, who have a duty to enforce criminal laws, and are not bound by IDEA limitations. Neither law enforcement agents nor judges are bound by the provisions of the IDEA. The State must continue to provide a FAPE to eligible incarcerated students.

19) Transition services facilitate the child's transition from school to post-school activities and may include instruction, related services, community experiences, and the development of employment and adult living skills.

20) Special education services terminate upon graduation with a regular high school diploma or age ineligibility.

21) A cost-based defense under the IDEA requires school officials to establish that:

> 1) The school has provided a proper continuum of placements;
> 2) The child in question would not experience a total denial of educational opportunity because of the failure to provide the expensive service; and
> 3) Other special education students may be denied a FAPE because of excessive expenditures on one child.

22) Section 504 prohibits discrimination against any person who has a physical or mental disability which substantially limits one or more major life activities; has a record of disability; or is regarded as having a disability.

23) Section 504 requires non-discrimination and reasonable accommodations.

24) Individuals must be otherwise qualified and fundamental alterations of programs are not required.

25) An accommodation is not reasonable, and therefore not required, if it would result in unreasonable costs, administrative burdens, or health or safety risks.

371

26) Persons may be excluded from activities if participation creates serious health or safety dangers and no reasonable accommodation would effectively mitigate these dangers.

27) Medical exclusions must be based on medical data and medical opinions, and not mere speculation or irrational phobias.

28) The ADA extended protections similar to § 504 protections to many areas of the private sector.

II. *Principles to Practice Tips*

1) *Close Calls between the IDEA and § 504*: To be eligible under the IDEA a student must meet minimum IDEA qualifications. In close cases, however, erring on the side of the IDEA may be prudent if it assures that the child will receive needed services, avoids contentious and expensive battles with parents, and forecloses future claims for compensatory damages.

2) *Developing Positive Parental Relationships and Cooperation*: The IDEA tends to be an advocacy driven, adversarial system. Parents that demand the most under the IDEA often get the most. Further, the system for resolving disputes under the IDEA is adversarial and litigation oriented, often aggravating rather than resolving tensions between parents and school officials. Litigation can make ongoing working relationships difficult and drain away resources that are needed to support education. It's easier to build strong relationships than to fix broken ones. Developing a relationship of mutual trust and cooperation with parents early in the IDEA process can be invaluable in effectively meeting the needs of the IDEA eligible children without undue conflict or expense. Not all relationships will be positive and functional. But with appropriate efforts at building positive working relationships less of them have to be negative and dysfunctional.

3) *Dealing with a Truly Dangerous Student*: In cases where parents refuse to cooperate with an appropriate change of placement and their child poses a genuine danger, safety must remain the first priority. School officials must take prompt, appropriate, and lawful action to assure safety. Allowing a known danger to persist could lead to consequences far more serious than a due process hearing with parents over the LRE for their child, including tragic injury, death, and resulting tort suits. A truly dangerous student cannot be allowed to cause self-injury or injury to others when the danger was known and the injuries could have been prevented. The IDEA does not require this result, and tort and criminal laws will not allow it.

4) *Promoting a Culture of Respect and Inclusion*: Children with disabilities are frequently misunderstood and dehumanized, becoming the targets of cruel bullying and abuse. Promoting a positive culture of respect, kindness, understanding, and inclusion in the school can help to reduce the frequency and severity of bullying and abuse of children with disabilities. Through leadership and educational efforts, school officials can help students to see special education students as friends and colleagues, and disabilities as a natural part of the human condition. With the development of mutual understanding and respect, special education students can become valued friends and not just the targets of misguided bullying and abuse.

III. *Questions for Discussion*: Please consider these questions and be prepared to discuss:

1) *Assessing the Personal Impacts of Special Education*: P.L. 94-142 was passed in 1975. How has special education changed the lives of children with disabilities, parents, educators, non-disabled students, and the community?

2) *Costs, Benefits, and Greater Efficacy*: What are the benefits of the IDEA, and what are the costs? What remains to be done to help children with disabilities and to improve the effectiveness and efficiency of special education?

3) *IDEA Discipline Policies*: Do IDEA discipline policies strike a fair balance between the rights of special education students and the rights of everyone else?

4) *Open Forum*: What other related issues or current events would you like to discuss?

IV. *Suggested Activities*:

1) Many very famous and successful persons have been challenged by disabilities. Nonetheless, they succeeded in spite of, or sometimes even because of their disability, when they were able to focus their special talents in a positive direction. Among those said to have been challenged by disabilities are: Moses, Sir Isaac Newton, and Thomas Jefferson (speech impairments); Leonardo Da Vinci, Albert Einstein, and Thomas Edison (dyslexia); Alexander the Great and Theodore Roosevelt (epilepsy); Michelangelo, General "Stonewall" Jackson, Sir Winston Churchill, and Howie Mandel (obsessive compulsive disorder); Stephen Hawking (cerebral palsy); Abraham Lincoln (mood disorder); Ludwig Van Beethoven (deafness); The Greek poet Homer and Stevie Wonder (blindness); Wolfgang Amadeus Mozart (hyperactivity, mood disorder, and possible Tourette's syndrome). Learn more about how throughout human history persons with disabilities have overcome personal challenges to achieve personal greatness and contribute to the progress of humanity. Share this knowledge to inspire children with disabilities to future success of their own.

2) Discuss ways to make your school more inclusive and welcoming to persons with disabilities. Identify positive ways of reaching out to persons with disabilities in your community to let them know that they are welcomed and valued members of the school community.

3) Learn more about how to prevent bullying of children with disabilities. Create a plan for what you could do to make your school culture more supportive for children with disabilities and to better protect these children from abuse.

Chapter 9: Contracts and Employment Law

Contract laws form the foundation for fair trade, and fair trade benefits everyone. Fair rules of commerce allow all persons to equitably exchange goods and services they have for goods and services they need. Commerce functions best in a stable, predictable business environment in which everyone is subject to the same fair rules designed for the common good. Good contract and employment laws help to promote stability, predictability, and economic fairness in hiring, conditions of employment, and the just resolution of disputes under the Rule of Law.

The just Rule of Law, universal education of the citizenry, and fair commerce systems form the necessary foundations for prosperity and democracy. Democracy can flourish where there is justice under the law, an educated citizenry, and a fair and prosperous economy. In contrast, injustice, ignorance, and economic disparity and poverty sow the seeds of social chaos and oppression. Just and efficacious legal, educational, and economic systems are the essential building blocks of a better future for all.

Necessary Foundations for Prosperity and Democracy

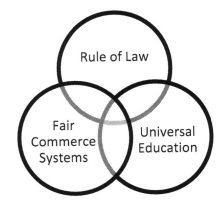

© Dayton

These foundational principles are interconnected and synergistic. Strengthening or weakening any of these will affect the others, thereby strengthening or weakening the foundations or our common democracy and prosperity. The quality of our lives and our children's futures depend on the strength of our democracy and prosperity. For these reasons, all citizens, and especially those responsible for educating other citizens, must understand the essential principles of a democratic economic system including fair contract laws, fair employment laws, and their roles in a functional, sustainable, and just economic system.

Educators who understand these essential principles and the critically important social foundations supported by the Rule of Law, education, and fair commerce will be better prepared to teach these lessons to their students for everyone's future benefit and security. The strongest democracy and prosperity are found in those nations with the strongest commitments to the Rule of Law, education, and fair commerce. Democracy supports sustainable prosperity, and prosperity supports sustainable democracy. President Franklin D. Roosevelt famously warned: "True individual freedom cannot exist without economic security and independence. People who are hungry and out of a job are the stuff of which dictatorships are made."

Contract Law

A contract is a legally enforceable bargain. A contract differs from an ordinary promise in that a contract can be enforced through a court of law. Everyone should strive to keep promises of course, but promises are not legally enforceable contracts. Promises carry ethical and moral obligations, but not legal obligations. To acquire the force of law as a contract a bargain must meet all the essential elements of a contract: Valid consideration, offer, and acceptance.

The essence of a contract is the agreement to exchange mutual benefits/detriments, or "legal consideration" (*i.e.*, *quid pro quo*) in which each party considers performing their part of the promised exchange (detriment) as the price of receiving the desired good or service (benefit) from the other party.

> ### To Form a Contract Both Parties must Give and Take Something of Value

The exchange of benefits/detriments must be mutual or there is no basis for a contract. A unilateral promise is not a contract. Something of value must be promised both ways or there is no valid legal consideration and no basis for a contract.

For example, a promise to give money to a school could only become a contract if legal consideration is exchanged both ways. The donor's promise to give money must be in exchange for something of value from the school. If a donor declared: "I will give the school $100,000" and nothing was promised in return, there is no enforceable contract because there is no valid consideration. But if the donor made a conditional promise, such as: "I will give the school $100,000 if the new athletic stadium is named after me" these bilateral benefits/detriments could serve as valid consideration and the foundation of a contract.

A valid contract requires not only mutual legal consideration as the foundation of the contract, but also a valid offer, and a valid acceptance of the offer to complete the contract.

Formation of a Contract

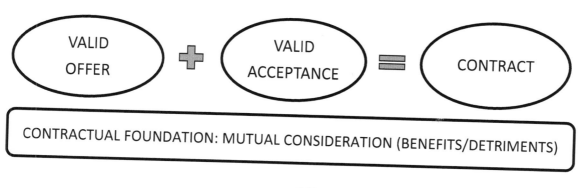

A valid offer is defined by:

1) Expression of present intent to contract; and
2) Definiteness of terms sufficient to describe the subject matter of the bargain.

Speculating about selling or buying in the future is not present intent to contract. A statement such as: "I have been thinking about selling my house" is not an expression of present intent to contract. Further, this statement does not sufficiently define the necessary terms of the contract, such as what house, how much property, the price and terms of sale, etc. Without a clear and present intent to contract and an adequate definition of the terms of the contract, there is no valid offer.

If there is an expression of present intent to contract and the terms of the bargain have been sufficiently defined, the offer remains open for the time stated. If the time is not stated, the offer remains open for a reasonable time based on the circumstances of the bargain and the common practice in the market. For example, where the timing of an offer is not expressly defined, an offer to sell a truck load of ripe bananas is necessarily a short-term offer that must be accepted quickly. The offer to sell a house, however, generally requires more extended time to reasonably secure necessary property inspections, a title search, financing, etc. In the absence of an express statement defining the timing of the offer (*e.g.*, "this offer is valid for 30 days"), in the common law system, common practices in the market govern the time window for the offer.

To form a contract the valid offer must be met with a valid acceptance. The acceptance must:

1) Mirror the terms of the offer evidencing a "meeting of the minds"; and
2) Be communicated while the offer is still open.

A "meeting of the minds" exists when both parties reasonably share a common understanding concerning the necessary elements of the bargain. If the party responding to the offer changes a necessary element of the bargain in the asserted "acceptance" of the offer, it is generally not a valid acceptance but is instead a counter-offer which may be accepted or not by the other party.

For example, if a distributor of playground equipment offered to sell a package of playground equipment to a school for $20,000 and the School Board President responded by saying: "We accept your offer provided that you throw in an extra slide" this conditional "acceptance" is not a valid acceptance at all. This is instead a counter-offer that the distributor may or may not accept. To constitute a valid acceptance the acceptance must mirror the terms of the offer, and there must be a sufficient meeting of the minds concerning the essential terms of the bargain.

Most people generally enter into contracts intending to fulfill the contract. Contracts tend to go bad not because of insincere intentions at the time the contract was formed, but because of misunderstandings or changed circumstances that make it difficult or impossible for a party to subsequently fulfill the contract. If a contract is breached, however, the aggrieved party may seek to have the contract enforced by a court of law. The aggrieved party becomes the plaintiff in the contract case, and the party charged with breaching the contract becomes the defendant. Possible defenses available to the defendant in a contract case may include:

Mutual mistake: The defendant argues that because of a mutual mistake, there was no "meeting of the minds" between the parties, and therefore no valid contract. The formation of a contract requires a sufficient meeting of the minds in which what is in the mind of each party sufficiently mirrors the understanding of the other concerning the essential elements of the bargain. Parties may have entered into the contract based on reasonable assumptions. But because of a mutual mistake unknown to either party at the time of the bargain, their understanding of the elements of the agreement were so different there was no meeting of the minds and no valid formation of a contract. When subsequent events reveal that mutual mistake existed at the time the contract was formed, rescission of the contract may be an appropriate remedy.

Unconscionable bargain: An unconscionable bargain is one in which there was extreme unfairness in the bargaining process, and one party acted in a predatory fashion to take advantage of the other party. For example, the use of a non-negotiable form contract with extremely one-sided terms known to the party presenting the contract but not reasonably known to the other party may constitute an unconscionable bargain. Courts are charged with enforcing justice. Courts should not help predatory merchants take advantage of vulnerable consumers. Simply making a bad deal, however, is not an unconscionable bargain, and a court will not save the defendant from the consequences of making a bad deal unless the bargain was genuinely unconscionable.

Misrepresentation or fraud: The formation of a contract requires knowing, voluntary consent to the genuine terms of the contract. Misrepresentation of a material fact may void a contract, where, for example, a merchant knows what the buyer is seeking but intentionally misrepresents the goods being sold as fit for the known intended purpose. Misrepresentation occurs when the seller knows the goods are not appropriate, but intentionally misleads the buyer into believing they are. Further, fraudulently obtaining "consent" to a contract, through deception or other trickery, is no real consent at all and voids the contract.

Duress or undue influence: Contracts must be entered into knowingly and through free will. The use of threats or intimidation to obtain consent to a contract constitutes unlawful duress. And the exercise of undue influence, for example the abuse of a relationship or position of power to obtain consent to a contract, would also void the contract.

Illegal subject matter: Courts will not enforce contracts involving illegal subject matter. If the terms of the contract do not conform to the applicable law, the contract cannot be enforced in a court of law. For example, where a state statute exclusively defines the terms of employment for a public educator, a contract that is contrary to the applicable statute is unlawful and unenforceable.

Legal incapacity: Both parties to a contract must be legally competent and able to understand the purposes and consequences of the contract. A person suffering from a mental incapacity due to a disability, obvious intoxication, etc., may not understand the purposes and consequences of the contract or be capable of the necessary "meeting of the minds" required for the formation of a contract. Further, courts will generally not enforce contracts against minor children.

Statute of frauds: This legal doctrine has its origins in the 1677 English Statute of Frauds intended to limit fraudulent testimony and perjury. Contracts falling within the Statute required a written contract signed by the defendant for goods that exceeded $500 in value or for personal services that could not be performed within a year of the making of the contract. The modern significance of the Statute of Frauds is that alleged "oral contracts" are generally disfavored. For contracts serious enough to seek judicial enforcement, a plaintiff should be prepared to produce a written memorandum of the agreement that identifies the parties; documents the exchange of legal consideration; adequately describes the complete subject matter of the bargain including necessary terms and conditions of the contract; and is signed by the defendant.

If the plaintiff has established the existence of a valid contract and a breach of contract by the defendant, and the defendant has failed to establish an adequate defense, the plaintiff is entitled to a legal remedy. Remedies available to the plaintiff may include the following:

Reasonable expectation damages: Generally the plaintiff is entitled to the "benefit of the bargain" and to be placed in the economic position the plaintiff would have achieved absent the breach of contract by the defendant. For example, if the plaintiff can prove that without the defendant's breach of contract the plaintiff would have profited $50,000 from the contract, $50,000 is the "benefit of the bargain" and the measure of damages awarded from the defendant to the plaintiff. Courts will not, however, award damages based on unsupported speculation concerning profits. The plaintiff must be able to adequately document and prove damages caused by the defendant's breach of contract.

Liquidated damages: To avoid uncertainty and prevent costly disputes over the amount of damages, parties may make an advance agreement in contract regarding the amount of damages to be paid by the defendant if the contract is breached. These liquidated damages clauses are common in transactions in which breaches are frequent occurrences, such as contracts for the rental of property (*e.g.*, "if the tenant breaches the 12 month lease, liquidated damages shall be equal to 2 monthly payments"). The limitation on liquidated damages clauses is that they must be reasonably related to the actual losses incurred because of the breach of contract. Liquidated damages should not be punitive to the defendant or provide an unfair windfall of profits for the plaintiff.

Specific performance: If the subject matter of the bargain was unique, like a specific property, work of art, etc., monetary damages may be inadequate as a remedy. The plaintiff may, for example, need a particular piece of land for building a business or a home, and no other piece of land offers the same location or other attributes. When appropriate, the court may order "specific performance" or the transfer of the unique property in exchange for the sale price as bargained for in the contract. Specific performance will not be awarded, however, when other damages provide an adequate remedy, or the contract was for personal services. Courts will not award specific performance for personal services, as doing so is unlawful, impractical, and inconsistent with public policy. Involuntary servitude is unlawful except as punishment for a crime, and even if forced work were lawful it would raise troubling enforcement problems and create unhealthy social conditions in the workplace.

Rescission of the contract: A voluntary rescission of the contract by mutual consent essentially calls off the bargain, thereby annulling the contract. A rescission can be requested by the plaintiff and judicially enforced, however, where the plaintiff can show wrongful conduct by the defendant in the contracting process.

Consequential and incidental damages: Consequential damages result from the foreseeable and provable negative consequences to the plaintiff because of the defendant's breach of contract. The claimed consequences of breach must have been reasonably known to the defendant, and therefore assumed as a potential cost of doing business. For example, a negligent failure by the defendant to deliver a critical good or service to the plaintiff at the agreed time, when that failure was reasonably known to be economically harmful to the plaintiff, especially if the contract stipulated that on time delivery was essential. Incidental damages are the costs incurred by the plaintiff in seeking substitute goods or services, or other transactional costs incurred because of the defendant's breach of contract.

Equitable relief: Courts have both legal and equitable powers. A court may issue a legal remedy, such as reasonable expectation damages, for a proven breach of contract. But if there is no legal contract, a legal remedy is unavailable. For example, where a plaintiff acting reasonably and in good faith has already performed all or a significant part of the bargain, but no legal remedy is available because the contract was technically deficient, this could result in the "unjust enrichment" of the defendant at the expense of the plaintiff. A plaintiff may have incurred the detriment, and the defendant the benefit, but no lawful contract existed. In such a case, a court may use its powers of equity to provide an equitable remedy sufficient to prevent unjust enrichment of the defendant at the plaintiff's expense: An order, for example, that the defendant compensate the plaintiff for the fair-market value of the services the plaintiff had already provided before learning of the defective contract.

It should be noted, however, that a plaintiff seeking relief for a breach of contract has a legal duty to reasonably attempt to "mitigate damages" and not unfairly run up the bill on the defendant. Allowing plaintiffs to unnecessarily run up the damages on defendants, through vindictiveness, waste, or other reasonably avoidable losses, ultimately hurts everyone by reducing economic efficiency, increasing legal costs, and thereby increasing costs of goods and services. In contracting for goods or services reasonable mitigation of damages includes an obligation for the plaintiff to reasonably attempt to find cover goods or services when the plaintiff learns of a pending breach of contract by the defendant.

For example, if the plaintiff contracted for the delivery of paper supplies and the defendant/vender notified the plaintiff/buyer of the pending breach of contract, the buyer must reasonably attempt to mitigate damages by finding another appropriate vender of paper supplies. If the price of cover goods from the new vender is lower there may be no damages as the buyer benefitted from the vender's breach. If the price of the cover goods is higher than the contracted price the plaintiff/buyer could sue for the difference in costs. If acceptable cover goods or services cannot be obtained, the plaintiff may sue for damages, having satisfied the plaintiff's duty to reasonably attempt to mitigate damages.

School officials regularly enter into contracts on behalf of the school for the purchase of necessary goods and services. From school facilities, buses, and supplies, to teaching and custodial services, every item used by the school, and every service necessary to keep the school operating, must be purchased through institutional procurement or personnel contracts.

Personnel costs consume the bulk of the school budget. Education is a labor intensive enterprise, and teachers and other school employees are essential to the successful operation of the school. School officials enter into contracts to secure needed personnel services. Salaries and benefits are offered in exchange for necessary professional services.

Hourly staff, non-certificated support personnel, and other at-will employees generally have no long-term contract or any reasonable expectation of continued employment. They can generally be dismissed at any time. Untenured teachers are offered year-to-year contracts until they acquire tenure. They can be let go simply by not renewing their contracts. Only tenured educators have a right to continued employment beyond the current contract term. They can only be dismissed based on a valid cause, and they are entitled to due process of law.

Academic tenure is a policy rooted in protecting academic freedom and limiting the influence of politics on the educational process. Teacher tenure also has an economic benefit for educational institutions. Tenure policies allow schools to offer the possibility of increased job security in lieu of higher salaries that may be available in the private sector to similarly qualified employees with bachelors, masters, or doctoral level degrees.

State teacher tenure statutes were originally enacted in the early 1900s as a means of reducing the influence of local politics, cronyism, and discrimination in teacher employment, and with the goal of long-term retention of teachers based on their professional qualifications and performance during a probationary period. If only high quality, productive teachers are tenured, tenure policies are a cost-free employment incentive for educational institutions, as good teachers would be retained anyway. Problems occur when tenure is granted to teachers that should not have been allowed tenure.

In higher education the promotion and tenure process is complex and varies significantly among educational institutions. Generally, however, the process tends to be very rigorous and focused on the individual faculty member's achievements in teaching, research, and service; reputation in the academic field; the likelihood of continued productivity; and the projected need for the faculty member's services in the future. The faculty member seeking tenure is required to make a strong case for tenure supported by extensive documentation, compelling evidence, and letters from external reviewers evaluating the faculty member's application for tenure.

While the tenure process in higher education is imperfect, and tenure is sometimes granted or denied in error, there is an opportunity to closely examine individual merit and make a decision on a case-by-case basis prior to the awarding of tenure. This process is, however, very time consuming and labor intensive, and it is therefore costly to the institution. Further, because the more senior faculty members are generally allowed broad discretion in voting on tenure applications from junior faculty, the process can sometimes become corrupted with personal and political bias, problems tenure policies were supposed to help guard against.

In contrast to the complex institutional policies governing tenure in higher education, in K-12 public education the tenure process is governed by state statute; it is uniform throughout the state; and tenure is generally granted automatically by statute after completing the designated years of continuous, successful service, usually two or three years. What is the tenure policy established by your state's statutes? When is tenure granted? For what reasons can tenured teachers be dismissed in your state?

Once a teacher has acquired tenure, the teacher is entitled to continued employment unless school officials can establish a lawful cause for dismissal. Any termination of a tenured teacher must provide adequate due process of law, including notice of the charges and evidence, and an opportunity to respond in a fair hearing. But what rights does an untenured teacher have if a contract is not renewed? Is the untenured teacher entitled to any due process? This was the issue the Court addressed in *Roth*.

Board of Regents v. Roth
408 U.S. 564 (1972)
Supreme Court of the United States

Mr. Justice STEWART delivered the opinion of the Court.

In 1968 the respondent, David Roth, was hired for his first teaching job as assistant professor of political science at Wisconsin State University-Oshkosh. He was hired for a fixed term of one academic year. The notice of his faculty appointment specified that his employment would begin on September 1, 1968, and would end on June 30, 1969. The respondent completed that term. But he was informed that he would not be rehired for the next academic year.

The respondent had no tenure rights to continued employment. Under Wisconsin statutory law a state university teacher can acquire tenure as a "permanent" employee only after four years of year-to-year employment. Having acquired tenure, a teacher is entitled to continued employment "during efficiency and good behavior." A relatively new teacher without tenure, however, is under Wisconsin law entitled to nothing beyond his one-year appointment . . . State law thus clearly leaves the decision whether to rehire a non-tenured teacher for another year to the unfettered discretion of university officials.

In conformance with these Rules, the President of Wisconsin State University-Oshkosh informed the respondent before February 1, 1969, that he would not be rehired for the 1969-1970 academic year. He gave the respondent no reason for the decision and no opportunity to challenge it at any sort of hearing.

The respondent then brought this action in Federal District Court alleging that the decision not to rehire him for the next year infringed his Fourteenth Amendment rights. He attacked the decision both in substance and procedure. First, he alleged that the true reason for the decision was to punish him for certain statements critical of the University administration, and that it therefore violated his right to freedom of speech. Second, he alleged that the failure of University officials to give him notice of any reason for non-retention and an opportunity for a hearing violated his right to procedural due process of law.

The District Court granted summary judgment for the respondent on the procedural issue, ordering the University officials to provide him with reasons and a hearing. The Court of Appeals, with one judge dissenting, affirmed this partial summary judgment. We granted certiorari. The only question presented to us at this stage in the case is whether the respondent had a constitutional right to a statement of reasons and a hearing on the University's decision not to rehire him for another year. We hold that he did not.

The requirements of procedural due process apply only to the deprivation of interests encompassed by the Fourteenth Amendment's protection of liberty and property. When protected interests are implicated, the right to some kind of prior hearing is paramount. But the range of interests protected by procedural due process is not infinite . . . We must look to see if the interest is within the Fourteenth Amendment's protection of liberty and property.

"Liberty" and "property" are broad and majestic terms. They are among the "great (constitutional) concepts . . . purposely left to gather meaning from experience . . . They relate to the whole domain of social and economic fact, and the statesmen who founded this Nation knew too well that only a stagnant society remains unchanged." For that reason, the Court has fully and finally rejected the wooden distinction between "rights" and "privileges" that once seemed to govern the applicability of procedural due process rights. The Court has also made clear that the property interests protected by procedural due process extend well beyond actual ownership of real estate, chattels, or money. By the same token, the Court has required due process protection for deprivations of liberty beyond the sort of formal constraints imposed by the criminal process . . . Yet, while the Court has eschewed rigid or formalistic limitations on the protection of procedural due process, it has at the same time observed certain boundaries. For the words "liberty" and "property" in the Due Process Clause of the Fourteenth Amendment must be given some meaning.

"While this court has not attempted to define with exactness the liberty . . . guaranteed (by the Fourteenth Amendment), the term has received much consideration and some of the included things have been definitely stated. Without doubt, it denotes not merely freedom from bodily restraint but also the right of the individual to contract, to engage in any of the common occupations of life, to acquire useful knowledge, to marry, establish a home and bring up children, to worship God according to the dictates of his own conscience, and generally to enjoy those privileges long recognized . . . as essential to the orderly pursuit of happiness by free men." In a Constitution for a free people, there can be no doubt that the meaning of "liberty" must be broad indeed.

There might be cases in which a State refused to re-employ a person under such circumstances that interests in liberty would be implicated. But this is not such a case. The State, in declining to rehire the respondent, did not make any charge against him that might seriously damage his standing and associations in his community. It did not base the nonrenewal of his contract on a charge, for example, that he had been guilty of dishonesty, or immorality. Had it done so, this would be a different case. For "where a person's good name, reputation, honor, or integrity is at stake because of what the government is doing to him, notice and an opportunity to be heard are essential." In such a case, due process would accord an opportunity to refute the charge before University officials. In the present case, however, there is no suggestion whatever that the respondent's "good name, reputation, honor, or integrity" is at stake.

Similarly, there is no suggestion that the State, in declining to re-employ the respondent, imposed on him a stigma or other disability that foreclosed his freedom to take advantage of other employment opportunities. The State, for example, did not invoke any regulations to bar the respondent from all other public employment in state universities. Had it done so, this, again, would be a different case . . . on the record before us, all that clearly appears is that the respondent was not rehired for one year at one university. It stretches the concept too far to suggest that a person is deprived of "liberty" when he simply is not rehired in one job but remains as free as before to seek another . . . To have a property interest in a benefit, a person clearly must have more than an abstract need or desire for it. He must have more than a

382

unilateral expectation of it. He must, instead, have a legitimate claim of entitlement to it . . . the terms of the respondent's appointment secured absolutely no interest in re-employment for the next year. They supported absolutely no possible claim of entitlement to re-employment. Nor, significantly, was there any state statute or University rule or policy that secured his interest in re-employment or that created any legitimate claim to it. In these circumstances, the respondent surely had an abstract concern in being rehired, but he did not have a property interest sufficient to require the University authorities to give him a hearing when they declined to renew his contract of employment.

Our analysis of the respondent's constitutional rights in this case in no way indicates a view that an opportunity for a hearing or a statement of reasons for non-retention would, or would not, be appropriate or wise in public colleges and universities. For it is a written Constitution that we apply. Our role is confined to interpretation of that Constitution.

We must conclude that the summary judgment for the respondent should not have been granted, since the respondent has not shown that he was deprived of liberty or property protected by the Fourteenth Amendment. The judgment of the Court of Appeals, accordingly, is reversed and the case is remanded for further proceedings consistent with this opinion. It is so ordered.

Reversed and remanded.

Teacher Tenure and Due Process

To claim a right to due process of law, a plaintiff must establish that there has been a sufficient impingement on a protected life, liberty, or property interest. Only liberty or property interests are relevant in the educational context. Untenured and tenured teachers hold very different types of property rights in employment. Untenured teachers are granted year-to-year contracts. The property right of an untenured teacher runs only from the start of the contract period to the end. In contrast, tenured teachers have a property right that extends indefinitely. The property right of a tenured teacher extends until the teacher leaves employment or school officials can show a valid cause for termination.

Untenured Teacher's Property Right to Employment

Tenured Teacher's Property Right to Employment

In *Roth*, the Court decided that when an untenured teacher has been paid the amount due under the contract, then no property right has been taken simply by not renewing the contract. The contract promised one year's pay, and once the teacher has received what was promised under the contract there were no further promises and no further property rights. Accordingly, there is no property right to due process based on not renewing the contract for another year.

Untenured teachers are also generally not entitled to any explanation for the non-renewal. Further, a knowledgeable school administrator is unlikely to voluntarily provide any explanation for the non-renewal, as providing an explanation for the non-renewal may arguably create a right to due process for the non-renewed teacher. In *Roth* the Court recognized that: "Where a person's good name, reputation, honor, or integrity is at stake because of what the government is doing to him, notice and an opportunity to be heard are essential." If the school administrator gives a negative reason for the non-renewal, the non-renewed teacher could argue that the administrator's statement concerning the non-renewal impinged on the teacher's "good name, reputation, honor, or integrity" and that "notice and an opportunity to be heard are essential."

Statements from school officials that call into question the good name, reputation, honor or integrity of the teacher related to the non-renewal could raise a liberty interest entitling the teacher to due process. But is non-renewal itself sufficiently stigmatizing? In *Roth*, the Court stated "there is no suggestion that the State, in declining to re-employ the respondent, imposed on him a stigma or other disability that foreclosed his freedom to take advantage of other employment opportunities." The lesson from *Roth* is that because untenured teachers are only promised a year-to-year contract, an untenured teacher can simply be non-renewed at the end of the contract term, without any notification of cause or other explanation. And arguably, no explanation should be given to avoid claims of infringement on a protected liberty interest.

The majority opinion in *Roth* remains the law. But not everyone agrees that a non-renewal is not a "stigma" foreclosing other employment opportunities. Many schools ask on employment forms whether the teacher has previously had a contract non-renewed, or news of the non-renewal may be well known in the educational community. In his dissenting opinion, Justice Douglas said: "Nonrenewal of a teacher's contract is tantamount in effect to a dismissal and the consequences may be enormous. Nonrenewal can be a blemish that turns into a permanent scar and effectively limits any chance the teacher has of being rehired as a teacher." Is Justice Douglas correct? Should non-renewed teachers be entitled to some due process? Or would these due process rights only increase legal costs for schools and make school officials less likely to non-renew ineffective teachers?

It should be noted that if a non-renewed teacher has evidence that the non-renewal was based on an improper motivation, such as discrimination related to race, gender, religion, national origin, age, disability, etc., the teacher has a right to contest the non-renewal. But the burden of proof is with the teacher challenging the non-renewal. Unless the teacher has credible evidence of unlawful actions by school officials the suit is likely to be dismissed. In contrast, in a termination of a tenured teacher the burden of proof lies with school officials. Unless school officials can meet their burden of proof the termination effort will fail. Tenure is clearly an advantageous employment status.

After acquiring tenure, tenured educators can only be terminated for a valid cause. The permissible reasons for termination are specified in state statutes, and may include, for example: incompetency; insubordination; willful neglect of duties; immorality; violation of school policy, state, or federal law; or any other good and sufficient cause. These statutes may also include non-punitive reasons for termination, including a reduction in force (RIF) due to loss of students or canceled programs. In general, any involuntary termination of a tenured educator requires extensive due process, as the right to continued employment is a substantial property interest.

Assuming that the charges are true, however, proving a charge of insubordination is a relatively simple two-step process: 1) The employee was given a lawful order; and 2) The employee refused to comply with the lawful order. Willful neglect of duties involves a similar pattern of proof. In contrast, incompetency and immorality are more subjective in nature, and while easy to prove in extreme cases, may be difficult to prove in closer cases. Conduct that some may view as immoral, others may see as an exercise of poor judgment but not immoral.

Employee Breach of Contract

When a teacher breaches a contract for personal services, the school district could sue the teacher for breach of contract. But what would be the value of such a suit and what remedies could be obtained? Specific performance cannot be awarded for a breach of contract related to personal services, leaving only the possibility of monetary damages.

Concerning monetary damages, plaintiffs in a contract suit have an obligation to reasonably attempt to mitigate damages by obtaining cover goods or services. In this instance, school officials as plaintiffs would have to try to mitigate damages by obtaining another suitable teacher. In most cases it is very likely that school officials could easily secure cover services simply by hiring another qualified teacher from the available applicants. The ability to so readily mitigate damages would mean that damages would be minimal.

The school district could be awarded nominal damages as the prevailing party (*i.e.*, $1 as a symbolic gesture). The school could also claim some incidental damages for the additional transaction costs of hiring another teacher. But even when the school prevails in a breach of contract suit for personal services, it is most likely a hollow victory, costing more in time and effort than it is worth to the school district.

The reality is that teachers will rarely be sued for a breach of an employment contract. The real risk for the teacher who willfully breaches a contract is in those states where a willful failure to honor a teaching contract is deemed unprofessional conduct under state teacher certification rules, and negative action could be taken against the teacher's professional certificate including suspension or revocation of the certificate. In states where there are no similar rules, however, the only real consequence may be a negative reputation in the area for willfully breaching a contract.

It should also be remembered, however, that sometimes teachers who entered into teaching contracts in good faith may end up breaching the contract because of an unforeseen change in circumstances, ranging from health and family reasons (including involuntary relocations of spouses), to an offer of a superior position in another school district. While the former reasons are very understandable, it may be better to simply accommodate even the latter reason with a mutual rescission of the contract.

Academic contracts are generally signed in the early spring. There is commonly a domino effect of positions opening from that time on, through the start of the school year in late summer. Educators often learn of a promising new opening after the initial contract was signed. Realistically, most teachers cannot assume the financial risk of not signing an offered teaching contract, especially when the circumstances that lead to the subsequent job offer are unknown to the teacher at the time. Should a teacher who has otherwise acted in good faith turn down a superior job offer that is a significant step up professionally and financially better for the teacher's family? Further, it is unlikely that an employee who really wants to be somewhere else is going to be an effective employee in the second choice position anyway and the employee will likely leave at the next opportunity. Under these circumstances, do school officials really need another disgruntled employee for one year?

Employees who will not be fulfilling their planned contract should, however, notify school officials as soon as possible to negotiate a mutual rescission of the contract, and so that a suitable replacement can be secured. Employees come and go, but students' interests and educational quality must still be protected. Teachers that do all they reasonably can to cooperate with school officials in assuring a smooth transition in instructional responsibilities are far more likely to get school officials to agree to a rescission of the contract and to retain good will with school officials.

Employment Discrimination

The U.S. Constitution's Establishment, Due Process, and Equal Protection Clauses broadly prohibit discrimination by government agencies based on religion, race, gender, or national origin. Through the Constitution's Commerce Clause and Congress' power to enact legislation necessary to enforce the 14th Amendment, Title VII of the Civil Rights Acts of 1964 expressly extended these prohibitions against discrimination to employment in both the public and private sectors.

Federal employment laws are enforced through the U.S. Equal Employment Opportunity Commission (EEOC). Plaintiffs must file their complaint with the EEOC within 180 days after the alleged unlawful employment practice. Generally, the 180 days tolls from the time the plaintiff received formal notice from institutional officials concerning the employment action. State constitutions and statutes may also prohibit employment discrimination, strengthening and expanding protections for employees. Under federal law private schools are prohibited from employment discrimination by Title VII, and public schools are prohibited from employment discrimination both by the Constitution and Title VII, 42 U.S.C. § 2000e-2 (2011):

Prohibited Employment Discrimination:
(a) *Employer practices*
It shall be an unlawful employment practice for an employer:

(1) To fail or refuse to hire or to discharge any individual, or otherwise to discriminate against any individual with respect to his compensation, terms, conditions, or privileges of employment, because of such individual's race, color, religion, sex, or national origin; or
(2) To limit, segregate, or classify his employees or applicants for employment in any way which would deprive or tend to deprive any individual of employment opportunities or otherwise adversely affect his status as an employee, because of such individual's race, color, religion, sex, or national origin . . .

(e) *Businesses or enterprises with personnel qualified on basis of religion, sex, or national origin; educational institutions with personnel of particular religion*
Notwithstanding any other provision of this subchapter:

(1) It shall not be an unlawful employment practice for an employer to hire and employ employees . . . on the basis of . . . religion, sex, or national origin in those certain instances where religion, sex, or national origin is a bona fide occupational qualification reasonably necessary to the normal operation of that particular business or enterprise . . .

(h) *Seniority or merit system; quantity or quality of production; ability tests*
Notwithstanding any other provision of this subchapter, it shall not be an unlawful employment practice for an employer to apply different standards of compensation, or different terms, conditions, or privileges of employment pursuant to a bona fide seniority or merit system, or a system which measures earnings by quantity or quality of production or to employees who work in different locations, provided that such differences are not the result of an intention to discriminate because of race, color, religion, sex, or national origin, nor shall it be an unlawful employment practice for an employer to give and to act upon the results of any professionally developed ability test provided that such test, its administration or action upon the results is not designed, intended or used to discriminate because of race, color, religion, sex or national origin . . .

(j) *Preferential treatment not to be granted on account of existing number or percentage imbalance*
Nothing contained in this subchapter shall be interpreted to require any employer . . . to grant preferential treatment to any individual or to any group because of the race, color, religion, sex, or national origin of such individual or group on account of an imbalance which may exist with respect to the total number or percentage of persons of any race, color, religion, sex, or national origin employed by any employer . . .

(m) *Impermissible consideration of race, color, religion, sex, or national origin in employment practices*
Except as otherwise provided in this subchapter, an unlawful employment practice is established when the complaining party demonstrates that race, color, religion, sex, or national origin was a motivating factor for any employment practice, even though other factors also motivated the practice.

Overview of Employment Discrimination Litigation

All institutions with more than 15 employees, public and private, fall under the mandates of Title VII. Government agencies, including public schools, are prohibited from discriminating in employment by both Title VII and the Constitution. Under the constitutional standard for alleged employment discrimination the level of judicial scrutiny depends on the established basis for the discrimination. Discrimination based on religion, race, or national origin is subject to strict scrutiny. Once the plaintiff has established a prima facie case of discrimination based on religion, race, or national origin government officials must show that the disparate treatment was necessary to a compelling interest and narrowly tailored to achieving that interest. Government officials rarely prevail under this strict judicial scrutiny. Further, discrimination based on gender requires an exceedingly persuasive justification by government officials. But discrimination based on general social or economic regulations, such as economic status, only requires a showing that the differential treatment was rationally related to a legitimate governmental interest.

A school could, for example, lawfully offer a summer employment program for economically disadvantaged students, to assist these students with educational costs and thereby support continued attendance and increase graduation rates, all legitimate interests. However, an employment program that used race or gender as the employment criteria is unlikely to survive a legal challenge.

Employment discrimination litigation under Title VII generally falls into two categories: Disparate treatment or disparate impact claims. Disparate treatment claims involve proving the intent to discriminate by the employer. Intent to discriminate could be proven through direct evidence, such as written documentation of intent to discriminate based on a prohibited criteria (*e.g.*, letters, memos, e-mail messages, etc., directly proving discriminatory animus and culpability).

Employers who intend to discriminate are rarely so careless, however, and more commonly plaintiffs must prove intent to discriminate through an accumulation of incriminating circumstantial evidence inferring intent to discriminate by a preponderance of the evidence. To establish a prima facie case of disparate treatment discrimination in employment the plaintiff must prove:

1) The plaintiff is a member of a protected class under Title VII;
2) The plaintiff suffered harm in employment;
3) The defendant illegally discriminated; and
4) The discrimination caused the harm in employment.

This is a general outline of a prima facie case of employment discrimination. As the Court noted in *McDonnell Douglas Corp. v. Green*, 411 U.S. 792 (1973): "The facts necessarily will vary in Title VII cases, and the specification above of the prima facie proof required from respondent is not necessarily applicable in every respect to differing factual situations." For example, in *McDonnell Douglas* the Court outlined a prima facie case of racial discrimination in employment under the unique facts of that case:

Establishing a prima facie case of racial discrimination . . . may be done by showing (i) that he belongs to a racial minority; (ii) that he applied and was qualified for a job for which the employer was seeking applicants; (iii) that, despite his qualifications, he was rejected; and (iv) that, after his rejection, the position remained open and the employer continued to seek applicants from persons of complainant's qualifications.

If the plaintiff fails to establish a prima facie case the suit is dismissed. If the plaintiff establishes a prima facie case the defendant may rebut the plaintiff's case with evidence of a non-discriminatory explanation for the employer's actions. The plaintiff may rebut the defendant's argument with evidence that the asserted non-discriminatory explanation is merely a pretext for discrimination. As the trier of fact, the judge or jury ultimately decides whether the plaintiff has proven the case by a preponderance of the evidence.

Shifting Burdens of Proof in Employment Discrimination Litigation

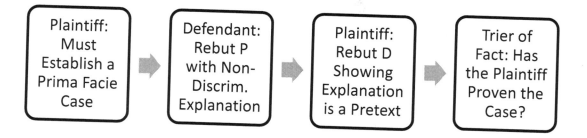

Disparate impact claims arise when the employment practice or policy is facially neutral, but has a significant negative impact based on race, color, religion, sex, or national origin. For example, a pre-employment test to see whether the applicant can lift 120 pounds is facially neutral, but it will have a disparate impact on female applicants or generally smaller ethnic groups. This employment practice would only be lawful under Title VII if lifting 120 pounds was "job related for the position in question and consistent with business necessity." Congress amended Title VII in 1991 to clarify the burden of proof under Title VII in disparate impact cases. As amended 42 U.S.C. § 2000e-2(k) (2011) states:

(k) Burden of proof in disparate impact cases
(1)(A) An unlawful employment practice based on disparate impact is established under this subchapter only if--
    (i) A complaining party demonstrates that a respondent uses a particular employment practice that causes a disparate impact on the basis of race, color, religion, sex, or national origin and the respondent fails to demonstrate that the challenged practice is job related for the position in question and consistent with business necessity; or
    (ii) The complaining party makes the demonstration described in subparagraph
    (C) with respect to an alternative employment practice and the respondent refuses to adopt such alternative employment practice.
(B)(i) With respect to demonstrating that a particular employment practice causes a disparate impact as described in subparagraph (A)(i), the complaining party shall demonstrate that each particular challenged employment practice causes a disparate impact, except that if the complaining party can demonstrate to the court that the elements of a respondent's decisionmaking process are not capable of separation for analysis, the decisionmaking process may be analyzed as one employment practice.
(ii) If the respondent demonstrates that a specific employment practice does not cause the disparate impact, the respondent shall not be required to demonstrate that such practice is required by business necessity.
(C) The demonstration referred to by subparagraph (A)(ii) shall be in accordance with the law as it existed on June 4, 1989, with respect to the concept of "alternative employment practice."

(2) A demonstration that an employment practice is required by business necessity may not be used as a defense against a claim of intentional discrimination under this subchapter.

In employment discrimination litigation required burdens of proof shifted over the years based on the U.S. Supreme Court's interpretations of Title VII and Congress' reactions to these judicial decisions. The amendment to Title VII in 42 U.S.C. § 2000e-2(k) was in response to the U.S. Supreme Court's decision in *Wards Cove Packing Co. v. Atonio*, 490 U.S. 642 (1989). This amendment represented a congressional rejection of the Court's interpretation of Title VII. The amendment restored the law to its status one day before the Court's *Wards Cove* decision. Congress cannot overturn the Court's interpretation of the Constitution by statute. But Congress can reject the Court's interpretation of a statute simply by amending the statute in question to clarify congressional intent. Similar litigation processes apply to disparate impact employment discrimination cases under the Americans with Disabilities Act (ADA) and the Age Discrimination in Employment Act (ADEA).

Religion, Sex, or National Origin as Bona Fide Occupational Qualifications

Title VII 42 U.S.C. § 2000e-2(e)(1) (2011), recognizes that under some limited circumstances employment discrimination based on religion, sex, or national origin may serve a legitimate employment purpose "in those certain instances where religion, sex, or national origin is a bona fide occupational qualification reasonably necessary to the normal operation of that particular business or enterprise." Employment discrimination based on religion, sex, or national origin remain unlawful, except in those circumstances where the employing institution can establish a legitimate employment purpose for considering an otherwise prohibited criteria in employment. Discrimination based on religion, sex, or national origin is presumed unlawful. But this presumption can be rebutted by a showing that the otherwise unlawful employment consideration is a Bona Fide Occupational Qualification (BFOQ) in a particular case.

For example, in religious institutions there are employment positions that require a particular religious faith as a core element of the job description. A religious institution may lawfully require that the minister, priest, rabbi, imam, etc., employed to lead the religious institution share the faith of the institution. Similarly, religious faith could be a BFOQ for all other employment positions in the religious institution for which religious faith is a central element in employment including teachers in religious schools. Although many religious schools choose to have a religiously diverse faculty, private religious schools may lawfully decide to employ only teachers who share the religious faith of the religious institution.

Sex may be a BFOQ when the gender of the employee is reasonably necessary to the normal operation of the institution. For example, it is not an unlawful employment practice for a school to hire a female P.E. teacher to supervise female students when necessary supervision duties extend to the shower and locker areas. Courts have also upheld the employment of an opposite sex counselor when a school added a second counselor, finding that providing students with an opportunity to talk with a same gender counselor was a BFOQ under that unique circumstance.

Discriminatory criteria are not a BFOQ if they are not reasonably necessary to the normal operation of that particular business or enterprise and serve only to appease or perpetuate discriminatory attitudes and practices. Religion is never a BFOQ for a public school or a secular private school. Sex and national origin are only BFOQs in those unique circumstances where these criteria are in fact reasonably necessary to the normal operation of the institution. National origin is listed in 42 U.S.C. § 2000e-2(e)(1) (2011) as a possible BFOQ but the institution bears the burden of proving the consideration of national origin is legitimate, a difficult burden to meet under most circumstances.

It is important to note that race and color are never BFOQs. Congress did not include race or color as exceptions under 42 U.S.C. § 2000e-2(e)(1) (2011). The race or color of the employee is irrelevant to the ability of an otherwise qualified employee to perform the necessary duties. Discrimination based on race or color is employment discrimination in violation of Title VII.

Employment Related Testing

Disparate impact challenges often involve pre-employment testing or testing used for certification, promotions, or raises. In many states educators are required to take tests for admission to teacher training programs, certification, and raises or promotions. From the perspective of the employer, standardized tests and other similar employment assessments may be useful and cost effective ways to measure abilities and knowledge believed necessary for employment success. Further, test scores can be useful as objective criteria in employment decisions. Employment decisions based only on subjective factors are generally more vulnerable to legal challenge than decisions made based on an appropriate balance of objective and subjective criteria.

Nonetheless, employment related tests sometimes have a disparate impact on the basis of race. In *Washington v. Davis*, 426 U.S. 229 (1976), African-American plaintiffs challenged the legality of a communications skills test used for admissions to a police training program. Plaintiffs demonstrated that the exam had a disproportionate adverse impact on African-America applicants. Nonetheless, the U.S. Supreme Court held that government actions are not unconstitutional merely because they happen to have a racially disproportionate impact. A test that is racially neutral on its face; administered without discriminatory intent; and reasonably related to a legitimate state interest is constitutional. Here, the asserted legitimate state interest was ensuring that police officers possessed the communications skills necessary for the successful completion of the police training program.

Title VII reflects an attempt to strike a balance between allowing the use of employment related tests for legitimate purposes, and prohibiting testing practices that do unlawfully discriminate based on race, color, religion, sex, or national origin. 42 U.S.C. § 2000e-2(h) states:

> Notwithstanding any other provision of this subchapter, it shall not be an unlawful employment practice for an employer to . . . give and to act upon the results of any professionally developed ability test provided that such test, its administration or action upon the results is not designed, intended or used to discriminate because of race, color, religion, sex or national origin.

In *Washington v. Davis* the Court held that the use of a facially neutral employment test with a disparate impact based on race was not an unlawful employment practice where there was no discriminatory intent and the test was related to a legitimate interest.

In *Ricci v. DeStefano*, 557 U.S. ___ (2009), the Court addressed whether government officials could choose to ignore the results of an otherwise legitimate employment test where there was a disparate impact based on race. In *Ricci* the City of New Haven used test results to determine which firefighters would qualify for promotion to lieutenant or captain. The Court noted: "Many firefighters studied for months, at considerable personal and financial costs." When test results among the 118 firefighters taking the test showed that white candidates had outperformed minority candidates "the mayor and other local politicians opened a public debate that turned rancorous." In response to political pressure and a threatened disparate impact suit City officials "threw out the examinations." Candidates that would likely have been promoted including 19 white and 1 Hispanic firefighter challenged this action as in violation of Title VII. The Court agreed, stating:

> The suit alleges that, by discarding the test results, the City and the named officials discriminated against the plaintiffs based on their race, in violation of Title VII . . . We conclude that race-based action like the City's in this case is impermissible under Title VII unless the employer can demonstrate a strong basis in evidence that, had it not taken action, it would have been liable under the disparate impact statute. The [City] . . . cannot meet that threshold standard. As a result, the City's action in discarding the tests was a violation of Title VII.

Whether used to advantage or disadvantage any group protected by Title VII, under 42 U.S.C. § 2000e-2(l):

> It shall be an unlawful employment practice for a respondent, in connection with the selection or referral of applicants or candidates for employment or promotion, to adjust the scores of, use different cutoff scores for, or otherwise alter the results of, employment related tests on the basis of race, color, religion, sex, or national origin.

Challenged tests that result in a disparate impact based on race, color, religion, sex, or national origin must be validated for the intended purpose; job related for the position in question; consistent with business necessity; and used without any intent to discriminate.

Affirmative Action in Employment

Affirmative action in government employment sought to address lingering vestiges of prior segregation and discrimination. As with desegregation efforts in the wake of *Brown*, a core question was to what degree and for how long were otherwise prohibited uses of race justified in remedial efforts to address past discrimination? In *Adarand Constructors v. Pena*, 515 U.S. 200 (1995), the U.S. Supreme Court dealt a serious blow to race-based affirmative action plans. In *Adarand* the Court addressed whether the Equal Protection Clause prohibited race-based preferences in government contracting. The Court declared that "any person, of whatever race, has the right to demand that any governmental actor subject to the Constitution justify any racial classification subjecting that person to unequal treatment under the strictest judicial scrutiny" and stated: "More than good motives should be required when government seeks to allocate its resources by way of an explicit racial classification system." The Court further noted:

> The Fifth and Fourteenth Amendments to the Constitution protect persons, not groups. It follows from that principle that all government action based on race--a group classification long recognized as in most circumstances irrelevant and therefore

392

prohibited should be subjected to detailed judicial inquiry to ensure that the personal right to equal protection of the laws has not been infringed . . . A free people whose institutions are founded upon the doctrine of equality should tolerate no retreat from the principle that government may treat people differently because of their race only for the most compelling reasons. Accordingly, we hold today that all racial classifications, imposed by whatever federal, state, or local government actor, must be analyzed by a reviewing court under strict scrutiny. In other words, such classifications are constitutional only if they are narrowly tailored measures that further compelling governmental interests.

Note that although Title VII provides for exceptions related to "religion, sex, or national origin" where there is "a bona fide occupational qualification reasonably necessary to the normal operation of that particular business or enterprise" there is no similar Title VII exception for race-based employment practices. Regardless of good motives, public institutions engaged in disparate treatment in employment based on race and challenged by a suit are likely in violation of both the Equal Protection Clause and Title VII.

Comments and Questions

It has been a long and difficult national journey from the ideals of "all men are created equal" in 1776 to legal protections for these ideals in Title VII and the Civil Rights Act of 1964. Nonetheless, Title VII and other federal civil rights legislation helped to transform the American workplace, helping to unleash the great diversity of American talent without regard to race, color, gender, national origin, or disability. Many would argue, however, that there is still a long way to go in realizing American ideals of equality.

Having laws protecting against employment discrimination and having real protections for people who need them are not the same thing. Realistically, how effective are employment discrimination laws in protecting persons who cannot afford legal counsel? Do protections against discrimination based on national origin help individuals with limited English speaking skills and no knowledge of these laws? What laws exist to protect persons from discrimination based on sexual orientation? Should Title VII be amended to protect against discrimination based on sexual orientation? Why or why not?

Sexual Harassment under Title VII

All invidious discrimination is offensive and unacceptable in the work place. Sexual harassment is a uniquely offensive type of discrimination, and certainly as harmful as other types of discrimination prohibited by Title VII. No one should be subjected to sexual harassment in the work place as a condition of making a living. Title VII, 42 U.S.C. § 2000e-2 (2011), however, does not expressly address sexual harassment. But in *Meritor Savings Bank v. Vinson,* 477 U.S. 57 (1986), the U.S. Supreme Court found that: "Without question, when a supervisor sexually harasses a subordinate because of the subordinate's sex, that supervisor 'discriminates' on the basis of sex."

The Court has also noted, however, that Title VII is not a "general civility code." Title VII does not extend to simple rudeness or other general inappropriate social conduct in the work place. Inappropriate social conduct may be addressed by supervisors in employment reviews, but Title VII prohibits more specific and serious work place misconduct. In *Clark County v.*

Breeden, 532 U.S. 268 (2001), the Court addressed the legal line for actionable misconduct under Title VII, stating "whether an environment is sufficiently hostile or abusive must be judged by looking at all the circumstances, including the frequency of the discriminatory conduct; its severity; whether it is physically threatening or humiliating, or a mere offensive utterance; and whether it unreasonably interferes with an employee's work performance."

The Court also noted that "a recurring point in our opinions is that simple teasing, offhand comments, and isolated incidents (unless extremely serious) will not amount to discriminatory changes in the terms and conditions of employment." The Court had noted in *Meritor* that: "For sexual harassment to be actionable, it must be sufficiently severe or pervasive to alter the conditions of the victim's employment and create an abusive working environment" and that the "gravamen of any sexual harassment claim is that the alleged sexual advances were unwelcome."

The Court has recognized two types of sexual harassment in the work place prohibited by Title VII: 1) Quid pro quo sexual harassment, and 2) Hostile environment sexual harassment. Quid pro quo sexual harassment is unwelcomed sexual requests or advances explicitly or implicitly linked to terms and conditions of employment. For example, a sexual request from a supervisor linked to continued employment, a promotion, etc. Hostile environment sexual harassment is unwelcomed sexual conduct in the work place that would be viewed as objectively creating a hostile work place on the basis of sex and that is so offensive that it interferes with work or conditions of employment. A hostile environment might be created, for example, if an employer tolerates or participates in sexually offensive comments or conduct in the work place, especially when there is a persistent pattern of this behavior or any especially egregious incidents. Federal Labor Regulations define sexual harassment in 29 C.F.R. § 1604.11 (2011) as follows:

> (a) Harassment on the basis of sex is a violation of section 703 of Title VII. Unwelcome sexual advances, requests for sexual favors, and other verbal or physical conduct of a sexual nature constitute sexual harassment when (1) submission to such conduct is made either explicitly or implicitly a term or condition of an individual's employment, (2) submission to or rejection of such conduct by an individual is used as the basis for employment decisions affecting such individual, or (3) such conduct has the purpose or effect of unreasonably interfering with an individual's work performance or creating an intimidating, hostile, or offensive working environment.
>
> (b) In determining whether alleged conduct constitutes sexual harassment, the Commission will look at the record as a whole and at the totality of the circumstances, such as the nature of the sexual advances and the context in which the alleged incidents occurred. The determination of the legality of a particular action will be made from the facts, on a case by case basis . . .
>
> (d) With respect to conduct between fellow employees, an employer is responsible for acts of sexual harassment in the workplace where the employer (or its agents or supervisory employees) knows or should have known of the conduct, unless it can show that it took immediate and appropriate corrective action.
>
> (e) An employer may also be responsible for the acts of non-employees, with respect to sexual harassment of employees in the workplace, where the employer (or its agents or supervisory employees) knows or should have known of the conduct and fails to take immediate and appropriate corrective action. In reviewing these cases the Commission

will consider the extent of the employer's control and any other legal responsibility which the employer may have with respect to the conduct of such non-employees.

(f) Prevention is the best tool for the elimination of sexual harassment. An employer should take all steps necessary to prevent sexual harassment from occurring, such as affirmatively raising the subject, expressing strong disapproval, developing appropriate sanctions, informing employees of their right to raise and how to raise the issue of harassment under Title VII, and developing methods to sensitize all concerned.

(g) Other related practices: Where employment opportunities or benefits are granted because of an individual's submission to the employer's sexual advances or requests for sexual favors, the employer may be held liable for unlawful sex discrimination against other persons who were qualified for but denied that employment opportunity or benefit.

In *Oncale v. Sundowner Offshore Services*, 523 U.S. 75 (1998), the Court found that the gender of the plaintiff or defendant is legally irrelevant. Sexual harassment has occurred when an employee is harassed on the basis of sex. This harassment may be opposite gender or same gender harassment. Concerning the parameters of liability under Title VII, in *Faragher v. City of Boca Raton*, 524 U.S. 775 (1998), the Court stated:

An employer is subject to vicarious liability to a victimized employee for an actionable hostile environment created by a supervisor with immediate (or successively higher) authority over the employee. When no tangible employment action is taken, a defending employer may raise an affirmative defense to liability or damages, subject to proof by a preponderance of the evidence. The defense comprises two necessary elements: (a) that the employer exercised reasonable care to prevent and correct promptly any sexually harassing behavior, and (b) that the plaintiff employee unreasonably failed to take advantage of any preventive or corrective opportunities provided by the employer or to avoid harm otherwise. While proof that an employer had promulgated an anti-harassment policy with complaint procedure is not necessary in every instance as a matter of law, the need for a stated policy suitable to the employment circumstances may appropriately be addressed in any case when litigating the first element of the defense. And while proof that an employee failed to fulfill the corresponding obligation of reasonable care to avoid harm is not limited to showing an unreasonable failure to use any complaint procedure provided by the employer, a demonstration of such failure will normally suffice to satisfy the employer's burden under the second element of the defense. No affirmative defense is available, however, when the supervisor's harassment culminates in a tangible employment action, such as discharge, demotion, or undesirable reassignment.

In summary, to prevail in a Title VII sexual harassment case the plaintiff must establish a prima facie case of sexual harassment, either:

1) Quid pro quo sexual harassment; or
2) Hostile environment sexual harassment.

If the plaintiff meets this initial burden of proof, it must be determined whether the plaintiff suffered any tangible injury (*e.g.*, discharge, demotion, undesirable reassignment, etc.) as a result of the sexual harassment. If there was tangible injury, liability is imputed to the employer. If there was no tangible injury, the employer may raise as an affirmative defense that:

1) The employer exercised reasonable care to prevent and correct any sexual harassment; and
2) The employee unreasonably failed to exercise an opportunity to report the sexual harassment.

Based on the Court's cases it may be prudent for employers to:

1) Have a reasonable policy in place for the prevention and correction of any sexual harassment;
2) Notify all employees of the policy; and
3) Act promptly and fairly to investigate and take reasonable remedial actions when appropriate.

Marriage and Pregnancy Discrimination

Historically females were asked to resign or were discharged from their teaching positions if they married or became pregnant. Dramatic changes in the law occurred in the wake of the U.S. Civil Rights movement. In *Loving v. Virginia*, 388 U.S. 1 (1967), the Court struck down a state law prohibiting inter-racial marriage, and the Court recognized liberty and privacy rights in marriage and family relations. Irrational discrimination based on pregnancy also fell to judicial decisions and legislative changes. Because only females become pregnant, employment sanctions based on pregnancy violate Title VII as gender based discrimination. Questions concerning marriage or pregnancy are inappropriate and unlawful in employment interviews and may be evidence of prohibited employment discrimination.

Concerning marriage discrimination, Federal Labor Regulations, 29 C.F.R. §1604.4 (2011), state:

(a) The Commission has determined that an employer's rule which forbids or restricts the employment of married women and which is not applicable to married men is a discrimination based on sex prohibited by Title VII of the Civil Rights Act. It does not seem to us relevant that the rule is not directed against all females, but only against married females, for so long as sex is a factor in the application of the rule, such application involves a discrimination based on sex . . .

Title VII generally makes it unlawful to discriminate in employment based on sex. The Pregnancy Discrimination Act (PDA) of 1978 defined "sex" to include discrimination on the basis of pregnancy or related medical conditions. 42 U.S.C. § 2000e(k) (2011) states:

The terms "because of sex" or "on the basis of sex" include, but are not limited to, because of or on the basis of pregnancy, childbirth, or related medical conditions; and women affected by pregnancy, childbirth, or related medical conditions shall be treated the same for all employment-related purposes, including receipt of benefits under fringe benefit programs, as other persons not so affected but similar in their ability or inability to work . . .

In 1993 Congress passed the Family and Medical Leave Act (FMLA) 29 U.S.C. § 2601 (2011). The FMLA allows eligible employees to take unpaid family or medical leave with continued group health insurance eligibility, and a right to return to the pre-leave job under the same terms and conditions that existed pre-leave. Up to 12 work weeks per year of unpaid leave may be taken for the birth of a child, newborn care, adoption, new foster care, care for a seriously ill child, spouse, or parent, or a serious illness of the employee. The FMLA also allows for up to 26 weeks of leave to care for a close family member who is an active duty member of the military service with a serious injury or illness.

Age Discrimination

The Age Discrimination in Employment Act (ADEA), 29 U.S.C. § 621 (2011), prohibits discrimination based on age against anyone 40 or over. The ADEA applies to all employers engaged in interstate commerce with 20 or more employees, including federal and state governments. Using age as a criteria in employment is not prohibited "where age is a bona fide occupational qualification reasonably necessary to the normal operation of the particular business." In practice, however, this is a very limited exception applicable to positions such as an acting role for a child or young adult, or legitimate public safety concerns for airline pilots, bus drivers, etc. Congress phased out and then eliminated lawful mandatory retirement for tenured faculty in 1993. All employees may be dismissed for legitimate cause, however, regardless of age, provided that poor performance or other good and sufficient cause was the motivating factor for the dismissal and not simply a pretext for age discrimination.

Title VII prohibits all employment discrimination based on the "individual's race, color, religion, sex, or national origin" requiring employer neutrality concerning these factors. Title VII generally allows neither negative discrimination nor preferential treatment. In *General Dynamics v. Cline*, 540 U.S. 581 (2004), however, the U.S. Supreme Court held that the ADEA only prohibited negative discrimination against older workers, and did not, for example, prohibit a policy that provided more favorable employment conditions for employees over 50 than for employees under 50.

A series of cases have questioned the legitimacy of federal limits on States as employers. In a complex opinion concerning the interaction of state sovereign immunity under the Eleventh Amendment and Congressional authority to prohibit discrimination under the Fourteenth Amendment, the Court held that although Congress clearly intended to abrogate States' immunity under the Eleventh Amendment in the ADEA, Congress lacked authority to do so under the Fourteenth Amendment. In *Kimel v. Florida Board of Regents*, 528 U.S. 62 (2000), university employees sued state officials for monetary damages, claiming age discrimination in violation of the ADEA. The State claimed immunity from suit based on state sovereign immunity under the U.S. Constitution's Eleventh Amendment. The result was that the Court's decision in *Kimel* barred suits for monetary damages under the ADEA against States, unless States voluntarily waived their sovereign immunity in these cases. State employees, however, could still sue for injunctive relief for violations of federal law under *Ex parte Young*, 209 U.S. 123 (1908). State employees may also be protected against age discrimination under state law, but state law protections may not be as comprehensive as protections under the ADEA.

National Origin Discrimination

Title VII generally prohibits discrimination based on national origin, except where "national origin is a bona fide occupational qualification reasonably necessary to the normal operation of that particular business or enterprise." In *Ambach v. Norwick*, 441 U.S. 68 (1979), the U.S. Supreme Court upheld a New York State statute prohibiting resident aliens from being hired as public school teachers. No state is required to adopt such a policy, but in *Ambach* the Court determined that where a resident alien had declined to obtain U.S. citizenship, the state could lawfully deny employment in certain public positions. Generally, the Court applies strict scrutiny to cases concerning differential treatment of individuals on the basis of alienage, making it very difficult for government officials to legally justify such policies. But the Court had established in prior cases that a different standard of review would apply when public positions are not merely functionary or custodial, but instead involved significant discretion and were more closely related to democratic governance.

In *Ambach* the Court determined that public school teachers exercise a significant degree of discretion and have sufficient responsibilities for the inculcation of democratic values to justify this otherwise discriminatory policy concerning public school teachers. Therefore the state need only establish a rational basis for differential treatment of aliens in employing public school teachers. Where the people through their elected representatives have concluded that U.S. citizens make better public school teachers than those that decline to become U.S. citizens, the Court will not disturb that decision.

However, it should be noted that *Ambach* was a 5-4 decision in 1979, and that it is unlikely that a unilateral decision to discriminate in the employment of aliens by an individual administrator or a local school board would receive the same deference the Court granted to a policy judgment by the state legislature in *Ambach*. Judicial deference to state legislative findings and policy judgments appear to be a significant element in the Court's decision in *Ambach*. Further, where there is evidence of invidious discrimination based on national origin, federal judicial intervention is certain.

Professional Ethics

Professionals hold themselves out to their communities as persons with special knowledge, skills, and experience worthy of public trust. Public trust in professionals is further reinforced by the awarding of professional degrees, the receipt of state licenses, and admission to membership in respected state and national professional organizations. The admission to professional practice also implies an acceptable record of honesty and good character in the conduct of duties. Based on these professional representations and credentials, persons needing special expertise rely on professionals for necessary services and guidance in health care, law, education, etc.

To help assure that the persons holding themselves out as professionals are worthy of this public trust, universities, state licensing boards, and professional organizations establish applicable codes of conduct and professional ethics. Professional codes of ethics help to clarify standards for professional conduct, codify professional responsibilities, provide guidance for ethical decision-making in practice, and serve as a basis for policing the profession and sanctioning unprofessional conduct when necessary.

Professional conduct is guided by a hierarchy of laws, ethics, and morality, with legal compliance forming the essential foundation, standards of professional ethics establishing higher professional norms, and moral ideals setting the highest aspirational goals in professional practice.

The Relationship between Law, Ethics, and Morality

Standard	Function	Applicability	Enforcement
Moral Ideals	Aspirational	Personal Choice	Conscience and Association
Professional Ethics	Normative	Condition of Membership	Sanction or Expulsion
Legal Compliance	Protective	Mandatory	Civil and Criminal Penalties

© Dayton

In order to protect the public from abuse, exploitation, and the dangers of malpractice, all professionals must comply with applicable laws or be subject to civil and criminal penalties. These penalties serve to deter and punish the worst types of professional misconduct. But they are insufficient to support the higher professional norms essential to good practice. Conduct that is legal may still be unethical or immoral.

Professional codes of ethics impose higher standards than general civil and criminal laws. Compliance with applicable ethical codes is a condition of holding a professional license, certificate, or membership in a professional association. Breach of the code makes the individual subject to professional sanctions including formal reprimand, probation, suspension, expulsion from the professional association, or revocation of the right to legally practice in the profession.

Moral ideals should impose even higher standards of care by professionals. But while moral ideals that exceed legal and professional standards may be desirable, unless moral conduct falls below established legal or ethical standards these higher ideals are based on voluntary personal decisions to pursue higher moral duties. Immoral conduct so extreme that it violates civil or criminal laws or breaches the ethical code is subject to appropriate sanctions. Otherwise, individual moral opinions are subject only to the individual's conscience, the personal judgments of peers and the community, and individual decisions concerning who to hire for professional services and who to associate with in practice. Professional codes of ethics should, however, be broad enough and strong enough to address immorality that exceeds mere differences of opinion and presents any credible risk of harm to clients or the community.

Each profession has a code of ethics uniquely appropriate to the profession, but these codes generally have common fundamental elements. An overview of general principles of professional ethics is provided below, but all professionals should also review the specific code of ethics applicable to their profession in their jurisdiction.

Essential Elements of Professional Ethics

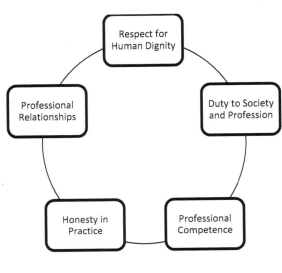

© Dayton

Respect for Human Dignity: Professionals respect the inalienable human dignity of all persons regardless of race, color, creed, gender, sexual orientation, national origin, social status, economic status or any other professionally irrelevant personal circumstances of the individual. All persons are treated with appropriate human dignity, equal respect, and non-discrimination in the provision of professional services. The professional further respects the individual human right to free-will and informed choice, protects individual and family dignity and privacy, and respects appropriate privacy and confidentiality in communications and records.

Professional Relationships: Professionals conduct all relationships with colleagues and clients/students in a professional manner. This includes good faith efforts to maintain a culture of mutual respect with colleagues, and refraining from any exploitation or abuse, especially where there is an imbalance in power or experience among colleagues. Because there is always an imbalance in power or experience among professionals and clients/students, there is a special duty to protect the interests of clients/students; to warn or protect them from known dangers; to exercise due diligence in advancing their best interests; and to refrain from any exploitation or abuse. This duty is especially strong when the clients/students are children or are otherwise diminished in their capacities to independently protect their own interests.

Honesty in Practice: Professionals have a fiduciary duty to manage finances, business relationships, and property in their care appropriately. Financial, personal, and other relevant conflicts of interests must be avoided or disclosed. To protect public trust the professional has a duty to recuse him or herself when an actual conflict or the appearance of a conflict of interests reasonable requires recusal. There should be appropriate transparency in all business operations; records must be honest and accurate; and all evaluations and advice must be honest, objective, and directed towards the best interests of the client/student.

Professional Competence: The professional owes nothing less than professional best efforts to clients/students and colleagues. The professional has an obligation to assure personal mental and physical fitness for duty, refraining from the use of alcohol or other substances that could impair judgment or performance while on duty. The professional should diligently perform duties in a timely and responsible manner; fairly assign and accept work-load burdens; maintain current and adequate knowledge and skills; and comply with all applicable requirements of the law.

Duty to Society and the Profession: Professionals have a right to fair payment for services provided, but the privilege of professional practice carries with it a corresponding duty to society and the profession. Professionals should actively work to protect and advance the public good, including regular engagement in appropriate pro bono service. Professionals should further strive to advance knowledge and practice in their profession. In order to protect society and the profession from the harms of misconduct, there is an affirmative duty to report any abuse, exploitation, corruption, or other unethical conduct to the appropriate governing board.

Professional codes of ethics can provide a fair and effective means of establishing and enforcing higher professional standards. Enforcement systems must provide adequate due process including public notice of the standards; sufficient clarity of requirements; fair hearings; adequate opportunity for appeals; and professional sanctions that are just and proportional to the offenses. Codes of ethics should also respect appropriate boundaries between the individual's professional responsibilities and their private life.

But where is the appropriate boundary between teachers' professional responsibilities and their private lives? Clearly, this boundary has changed over time.

Rules for Teachers: Sacramento, California (1915)

1. You will not marry during the term of your contract.
2. You are not to keep company with men.
3. You must be home between the hours of 8 PM and 6 AM unless at a school function.
4. You may not loiter downtown in any of the ice cream stores.
5. You may not travel beyond the city limits unless you have permission of the chairman of the school board.
6. You may not ride in carriages or automobiles with any man except your father or brother.
7. You may not smoke cigarettes.
8. You may not dress in bright colors.

9. *You may under no circumstances dye your hair.*
10. *You must wear at least 2 petticoats.*
11. *Your dresses may not be any shorter than 2 inches above the ankles.*
12. *To keep the classroom neat and clean you must sweep the floor once a day, scrub the floor with hot soapy water once a week, clean the blackboards once a day and start the fire at 7 AM to have the school warm by 8 AM when the scholars arrive.*

Many of the standards included in this 1915 code of conduct for teachers would be declared unconstitutional today. Free adult citizens, including teachers, have a right marry if they choose; to privately associate with other adults; they are subject to no home curfews or arbitrary limitations on travel; and they have a right to live their private lives as they choose, provided that their private lives do not interfere with the performance of their professional duties. To acquire valid jurisdiction over activities in teachers' private lives for purposes of employment sanctions, school officials must establish that there is a logical nexus between the challenged off-campus conduct and a resulting negative impact on the teacher's ability to perform professional duties.

Establishing a Logical Nexus between Private Conduct and Professional Responsibilities

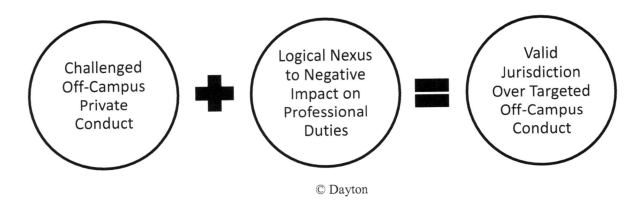

© Dayton

Comments and Questions

While many of the 1915 rules for teachers would not be sustained today, teachers remain role models for students, giving some continued validity to concerns about teacher's private conduct where the conduct can be shown to have a substantial negative impact on the teacher's ability to perform professional duties. An arrest and conviction for any serious crime could serve as a valid basis for the professional termination of a teacher, as could other conduct that established serious moral turpitude, dishonesty, or any credible danger to students or others in the school.

But what about private conduct that is simply disfavored by many community members? Sexual misconduct that constitutes a crime and official designation as a registered sex offender could clearly serve as a basis for dismissal. But what if the teacher is simply engaging in lawful, private sexual conduct that many in the community may disapprove of for personal or religious reasons, such as nude dancing; homosexuality; bi-sexuality; promiscuity; adultery; "swinging", cross-dressing; or other alternative life-styles? Should any of these otherwise lawful, private sexual behaviors be subject to investigation and employment action by school officials based on community disapproval?

Historically, homosexuality has gone from being designated a crime (sodomy) in some states to being a protected class in employment discrimination in some institutions, communities, and states. There are, however, many jurisdictions that provide no legal protections against employment discrimination based on sexual orientation. An increasing number of states are recognizing the validity of same-sex marriages. Can a teacher be legally married to a same-sex spouse in one state, but then be lawfully discriminated against in employment or fired for homosexuality in another state? What are the laws concerning these issues in your jurisdiction?

Is it ever acceptable for a teacher to "date" a student? What if the student is: 18 years old?; age 21?; not a student in the teacher's school?; the relationship is romantic but not physical?; the relationship is personally very close but not physical or romantic?; the teacher is 21 and the student is 21? While some circumstances seem less disturbing than others, many would argue that the core concerns in prohibiting these teacher-student relationships do not fundamentally change with the facts because they are based on the inherent status differentials between teachers and students; the risk of exploitation of students by teachers; the sexualizing and corrupting of the teacher-student relationship; the appearance of impropriety; and the risk of institutional liability for sexual harassment. Even if there is a legal right to engage in the relationship, that does not mean there is also a right to remain a teacher if the conduct results in a sufficient negative impact on the teacher's professional ability to serve as a teacher. And even if the conduct is not prohibited by law, an inappropriate relationship with a student violates professional ethics and moral ideals concerning the teacher-student relationship.

Drinking while on duty or alcohol associated crimes could serve as the basis for termination of employment, but if the local community disapproves of alcohol generally does this mean that off-duty local teachers can be prohibited by school officials from drinking beer or wine in their community? What is the proper balance between teachers' rights to live a private life free from governmental snooping and sanctions by school officials, and legitimate community concerns about the fitness of teachers as role models for their children?

Performance Evaluations of Employees

An effective system of performance evaluations is essential to any successful institution. The quality of work performance defines the institution. To support institutional success evaluations must effectively document work performance for reward, remediation, or dismissal of employees as appropriate. Work performance evaluations are very significant events for employees also. Evaluations affect retention, tenure, and promotion decisions, and may be used as the basis for performance pay, reassignments, or reduction in force decisions by the institution.

Most states have enacted statutes addressing teacher evaluations. But many of these statutes simply require an evaluation system; authorize local school officials to require evaluations; or otherwise leave considerable discretion to local school officials. Depending on state law, performance evaluations of school employees may be governed more or less by state law or local policy. Union agreements may also control aspects of the evaluation process. What is consistent, however, is that because an evaluation may significantly affect the individual's employment rights and professional reputation, evaluation policies must be in accordance with the requirements of due process. Evaluation systems must provide adequate notice, an opportunity to be heard, and policies and practices that are fundamentally fair.

403

Where state or local evaluation policies have been established, school officials must strictly comply with established policies or risk charges of arbitrariness and violations of due process in the evaluation process.

Due Process and Established State and Local Policies Must be Strictly Followed

---

Generally, judges tend to be highly deferential to professional judgments by school officials. But judges have been firm in enforcing requirements of established policy and due process in the evaluation process.

Evaluations should focus on criteria that are: 1) Related to essential job duties; and 2) Observable or measurable. Persons evaluated should have advance notice of the criteria for the evaluation, and a fair opportunity to demonstrate successful job performance under the established criteria. The employee should be notified of the results of the evaluation, including any noted deficiencies. The supervisor should explain what is necessary to correct any deficiencies; give the employee a fair opportunity to be heard in response; and allow a fair chance to make needed changes in preparation for the next evaluation. Failure to correct necessary deficiencies after notice and fair opportunity to do so may constitute insubordination and/or willful neglect of duties.

The evaluation process must be an open and honest process, with good faith efforts by the supervisor to help the employee improve performance. The evaluator is responsible for both coaching for success when possible and documenting failure when necessary. There should be no pretenses or duplicity about the evaluator's true role, and all aspects of the process should be fair and open. Honesty is essential to building real trust between the supervisor and the employee. Secrecy or duplicity in the process may unfairly blind-side the employee, and jeopardize employment actions based on any unfair evaluation processes.

When necessary, negative employment actions should be proportional and progressive. Consequences should be proportional to the employee's conduct and employment status. If necessary changes do not occur, however, the consequences should appropriately escalate in seriousness toward dismissal when necessary. For example, if employee conduct is serious enough to warrant sanctions but does not constituent an immediate peril, the employee may first be given a verbal warning; then a written notice and warning for a subsequent occurrence; followed by a suspension or other appropriate employment sanction as warned in the prior written notice; and then final dismissal if the problem is not remedied. Very serious misconduct or actions that pose a present danger may require immediate removal and the initiation of dismissal proceedings.

The employer should thoroughly document the process of proportional and progressive sanctions, proving that the employee had clear notice and an opportunity to conform conduct to acceptable standards but did not do so. This proportional and progressive approach, and the resulting paper trail, helps to document that any impacts on protected liberty or property rights are consistent with requirements of procedural and substantive due process, and that the process was fair even when the final result was dismissal.

Dismissal proceedings succeed or fail based on the fundamental fairness of the process and the quality of the documentation. No amount of documentation, however, could or should cover up an unfair dismissal rooted in retaliation, discrimination, or other improper motives. But a fair evaluation process and thorough documentation are the keys to success in necessary dismissals where the employee is being properly removed from the school for good and sufficient cause.

Personnel Files

Personnel files contain essential information concerning the employee, including, for example, copies of educational transcripts; professional certificates; employment contracts; evaluations; official employment related letters; and personal information such as home address, phone number, tax information, social security numbers, etc. Personnel files should only contain information that is necessary to document job qualifications and the relevant history and status of the employment relationship.

The most common controversies related to personnel files are: 1) Employee challenges to information in their own files; and 2) Requests for access to employee files by third parties. Concerning employee challenges to information in their own files, because the contents of these files may significantly affect the employee's liberty and property interests, adequate due process including notice and an opportunity to be heard are essential. It is unlawful to place "secret" reprimands or other negative information in the employee's file without prior notice to the employee and an opportunity to be heard concerning the matter at issue. Further, supervisors cannot use letters of reprimand as a means of retaliation or to chill protected speech rights. Employees must have a reasonable means to access to their own files, and a fair process for challenging and removing inaccurate or unlawful information.

Due process is the key to managing employee challenges to information in their own files. Requests for access to files by third parties, however, may pose more difficult legal questions. A delicate balance of the employee's rights; the employer's legitimate interests; and public rights to freedom of information may be involved. Differences in state Freedom of Information Acts (FOIA) may further complicate these cases. State laws vary significantly concerning what is subject to public disclosure and what is exempted.

Because state laws largely govern these decisions, school officials must know and comply with the FOIA in their state. Personal medical data and other clearly confidential information in personnel files must be kept private and should not be disclosed to third parties without the employee's permission. But depending on state law, much of the remaining information in employment files may be subject to disclosure through state FOIA or open records requests.

While some information may be confidential, and access to this confidential information may be lawfully limited under most circumstances, it should be remembered that ultimately nothing in public institutions is secret. In *University of Pennsylvania v. EEOC*, 493 U.S. 182 (1990), the U.S. Supreme Court rejected school officials claims of confidentiality concerning personnel information. This information was sought by the EEOC on behalf of a faculty member who had been denied tenure allegedly because of employment discrimination. The University sought to exclude what it called "confidential peer review information" which included: 1) Letters written by external evaluators; 2) The Department Chair's letter of evaluation; 3) Documents summarizing the internal deliberations of faculty committees considering applications for tenure; and (4) Tenure review files of other successful candidates. The Court stated:

> The University raises here essentially two claims. First, it urges us to recognize a qualified common-law privilege against disclosure of confidential peer review materials. Second, it asserts a First Amendment right of "academic freedom" against wholesale disclosure of the contested documents. With respect to each of the two claims, the remedy [the school] seeks is the same: a requirement of a judicial finding of

particularized necessity of access, beyond a showing of mere relevance, before peer review materials are disclosed to the Commission . . . confidentiality is important to the proper functioning of the peer review process under which many academic institutions operate. The costs that ensue from disclosure, however, constitute only one side of the balance. As Congress has recognized, the costs associated with racial and sexual discrimination in institutions of higher learning are very substantial. Few would deny that ferreting out this kind of invidious discrimination is a great, if not compelling, governmental interest. Often . . . disclosure of peer review materials will be necessary in order for the Commission to determine whether illegal discrimination has taken place. Indeed, if there is a "smoking gun" to be found that demonstrates discrimination in tenure decisions, it is likely to be tucked away in peer review files . . . the "chilling effect" [the school] fears is at most only incrementally worsened by the absence of a privilege. Finally, we are not so ready as petitioner seems to be to assume the worst about those in the academic community. Although it is possible that some evaluators may become less candid as the possibility of disclosure increases, others may simply ground their evaluations in specific examples and illustrations in order to deflect potential claims of bias or unfairness. Not all academics will hesitate to stand up and be counted when they evaluate their peers.

Personnel files must be kept in accordance with due process of law, and in compliance with applicable federal and state statutes, including the Health Insurance Portability and Accountability Act (HIPAA), 29 U.S.C. § 1181 (2011), and applicable state FOIA and open records acts.

Open Records and Open Meetings Laws

The U.S. Freedom of Information Act (FOIA), 5 U.S.C. § 552 (2011) applies to federal agencies. State schools are governed by state FOIAs or open records and meetings laws. All 50 states have some form of FOIAs concerning information held by state or local government agencies including public schools. State laws vary concerning what is expressly subject to disclosure; what is expressly exempted from disclosure; and the process for acquiring access to government records.

Generally, however, these statutes start with the assumption that all information held by government officials is public information subject to disclosure. Legislative decisions are then made in the statute concerning what specific categories of information should not be subject to disclosure. Records often excluded under these statutes include records that are: Confidential under federal law; medical records; personal information concerning employees; pending investigations; pending personnel issues; pending bids and appraisals; state owned intellectual property; records with information that would endanger persons, rare animals, plants, or other state property, etc. In all states, regardless of the specificity of the statute some ambiguity remains concerning what is subject to disclosure and what is not. This ambiguity may need to be resolved by a judge.

State statutes also vary concerning whether any cause must be shown for the request; the time state officials have to respond to the request; consequences for failure to comply with a lawful request; copying and other administrative charges that may be assessed to the requesting party; etc. Where only part of the document is excluded from disclosure (*e.g.* social security numbers), the excluded part must be redacted and the otherwise public record must be released consistent with state law.

All 50 states also have open meetings laws. The specifics of these laws vary concerning what meetings fall under the Act; public notice requirements; required records and minutes of the meetings; exceptions to the Act, and sanctions for violations of the Act. The purpose of these laws is to allow public access to the government decision making process, and allow openness to serve as a deterrent to corruption in government. Given these important purposes, when the law is unclear courts tend to err in favor of openness.

School officials must know and comply with the laws governing public records and meetings in their state. The applicable state law will define what remains confidential, what must be disclosed, and the process for compliance with the law. Failure to comply with these laws may result in civil liability or criminal penalties.

Labor Unions and Collective Bargaining

The National Labor Relations Act of 1935, as amended in 29 U.S.C. § 141 (2011), protects the rights of all private sector employees to form unions and engage in collective bargaining. Federal law governs collective bargaining rights for private school employees. State laws govern the right to collective bargaining for public school employees. Some states require school officials to bargain exclusively with union representatives, some states require school officials to meet with union representatives, and others proscribe collective bargaining in public schools. However, the First Amendment prohibits States from banning union membership. Even where there is no legal right to collective bargaining, public educators retain their right to freedom of association and may join professional and political organizations.

Where collective bargaining is required or allowed, union members designate a representative to bargain on their behalf. State law and union agreements govern what is subject to collective bargaining, ranging from salaries and conditions of employment to policies on personnel files and student discipline. Parties are required to bargain in good faith and either side may file an unfair labor practice complaint when warranted. For state schools labor disputes are reviewed by state labor relations boards. And for private schools claims are heard by the National Labor Relations Board (NLRB). Labor board decisions may be appealed to state or federal courts.

Alternative Dispute Resolution

Misunderstandings and interpersonal disputes are an inevitable part of human interactions. How workplace conflicts are resolved, however, can either enhance or diminish employee morale, loyalty, and productivity. Proactively clearing up misunderstandings and fairly resolving disputes can strengthen working relationships and build trust in the institution.

When disputes are allowed to fester and grow, however, the negative impacts can be devastating to the people involved and to the broader school culture. Simple disputes can escalate to unhealthy conflicts, and work place combatants may drag others into their battles, creating an increasingly toxic personnel climate. Toxic office cultures can drive off the most talented people, impede productivity, and eventually harm the mental and physical health of persons subjected to regular displays of anger, social dysfunction, and emotional abuse in the work place. For these reasons, school officials must do all they can reasonably do to promptly and fairly address interpersonal disputes and maintain a healthy school culture.

The first responsibility for dispute resolution, of course, lies with the parties themselves. Professionals take personal responsibility for maintaining a professional environment, which may require reasonable compromise, flexibility, and reaching out in good faith to attempt to resolve disputes and rebuild healthy working relationships. In some cases, however, good will and a handshake will be insufficient to resolve the dispute.

In these cases, Alternative Dispute Resolution (ADR) may be a useful alternative to litigation in resolving more serious disputes. Litigation can be extremely expensive; time consuming; stressful; adversarial; damaging to working relationships; publicly embarrassing; uncertain; and parties ultimately lose control of the process when judges and juries become involved. For all of these reasons, parties may wish to consider ADR before committing to litigation to resolve disputes.

Litigation is sometimes necessary. But in most cases ADR offers solutions that are far more cost effective, faster, less stressful and damaging to ongoing relationships, and generally better options for the parties. Options in ADR include informal resolutions; mediation; negotiations; and arbitration. Informal resolutions simply involve the parties engaging in good faith efforts to resolve their own disputes through informal means, *e.g.*, agreeing to talk things out, practice greater mutual consideration and respect in the future, work together to clear up misunderstandings, start over, move on, etc.

If the parties are unable to resolve their own disputes without assistance, mediation or negotiation may be helpful options. The process of mediation differs from negotiation in that mediators are neutral third parties present only to help facilitate problem resolution efforts and communications between the parties. The mediator is not a judge, and the parties are not there to resolve who is right or wrong. The mediation process is about reaching an informal resolution with the help and facilitation of a neutral party.

Negotiations are aimed at defining an agreeing on a settlement that will resolve the dispute between the parties. The parties may represent themselves or trained negotiators may represent the parties. An ideal resolution in a negotiation is a win-win result. In a true zero-sum scenario, however, win-win may not be possible. Mediation and negotiation both require cooperation, but negotiations can become more adversarial. It is important, however, that the final negotiated settlement be fair to all parties, as unfair bargains rarely last and subsequent negotiations are then tainted by the prior unfair bargain.

Skilled mediators or negotiators can help prevent disputes from escalating to broader conflicts in the school or community, or into adversarial litigation. Both mediations and negotiations involve parties working together to resolve a common problem, using open communication and common sense to find mutually satisfactory ways of resolving disputes.

If informal efforts, mediation, or negotiation fail to resolve the dispute, arbitration is a more formal ADR process short of litigation. In arbitration a qualified neutral third party acts like a judge, hearing the party's claims and issuing a decision. Arbitration is not litigation, however, and the arbitration process can be much less expensive, burdensome, and protracted. Depending on whether the arbitration process is voluntary, contractual, or required by statute, arbitration can be by consent or mandated, and the decisions can be non-binding or binding on the parties. ADR has advantages and disadvantages, but ADR may be worthy of consideration prior to initiating litigation.

Summary of ADR Options

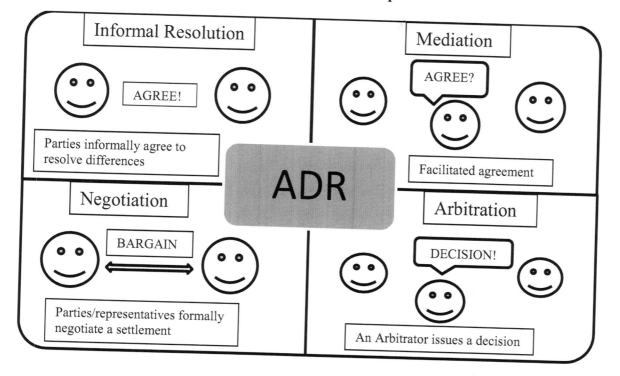

© Dayton

ADR works best when parties engage in bilateral good faith efforts. Not all disputes are bilateral, however, and when one party is clearly the aggressor and refuses to be reasonable or to relent in attacking other employees, more direct intervention by school officials is essential to protect parties and the institution from harm by the aggressor. Serious personnel action may be required.

Persons who perpetually disrupt the workplace and are commonly the clear aggressors in disputes must be professionally confronted and dealt with to protect the integrity of the institution and the safety of the people in it. School officials have a duty to not allow toxic personalities to destroy the school culture and the people necessary to the success of the institution. School officials must understand, however, that while taking appropriate personnel action against a disruptive employee who is toxic to the school culture is essential, personnel actions must be fair and lawful in order to assure that school officials will be successful in achieving the necessary personnel action.

Chapter Summary

This chapter reviewed contract law, employment discrimination, professional ethics, and alternative dispute resolution. After reading this chapter, please consider the following points in review and for further thought and discussion:

I. *Review Points*:

1) To acquire the force of law as a contract a bargain must satisfy all the essential elements of a contract: Valid consideration, offer, and acceptance.

2) Valid consideration (*i.e.*, *quid pro quo*) requires parties to exchange something of value, mutual detriments/benefits, and each party considers performing their part of the promised exchange (detriment) as the price of receiving the desired good or service (benefit) from the other party.

3) A valid offer is defined by:

      1) Expression of present intent to contract; and
      2) Definiteness of terms sufficient to describe the subject matter of the bargain.

4) A valid acceptance must:

      1) Mirror the terms of the offer evidencing a "meeting of the minds"; and
      2) Be communicated while the offer is still open.

5) Possible defenses to a suit for breach of contract include: mutual mistake; unconscionable bargain; misrepresentation or fraud; duress or undue influence; illegal subject matter; legal incapacity; and the statute of frauds.

6) If the plaintiff has established a valid contract, a breach by the defendant, and the defendant has failed to establish an adequate defense, the plaintiff may request an appropriate legal remedy.

7) Possible remedies include: reasonable expectation damages; liquidated damages; specific performance; rescission of the contract; consequential and incidental damages; and equitable relief.

8) The plaintiff also has a duty to reasonably attempt to mitigate damages. The defendant is not responsible for unnecessary costs resulting from the plaintiff's failure to reasonably attempt to mitigate damages.

9) Generally, non-certificated personnel are at-will employees with no reasonable expectation of continued employment and can be dismissed at any time. Untenured educators have property rights in their yearly contracts, but can be non-renewed at the end of the contract term. Only tenured educators have an ongoing property right to continued employment beyond the current contract term.

10) Untenured teachers are generally not entitled to any explanation for a non-renewal. Further, an explanation for the non-renewal may create a right to due process.

11) Tenured educators can only be dismissed for a valid cause specified in the applicable state statute, for example: incompetency; insubordination; willful neglect of duties; immorality; violation of school policy, state law, or federal law; reduction in force; or any other good and sufficient cause allowable under state law.

12) The Establishment, Due Process, and Equal Protection Clauses broadly prohibit discrimination by government agencies based on religion, race, gender, or national origin. Title VII extended these prohibitions to the private sector. Government agencies, including public schools, are prohibited from discriminating in employment by both Title VII and the Constitution.

13) Employment discrimination under Title VII generally falls into two categories: Disparate treatment or disparate impact claims. To establish a prima facie case of disparate treatment discrimination in employment the plaintiff must prove:

    1) The plaintiff is a member of a protected class under Title VII;
    2) The plaintiff suffered harm in employment;
    3) The defendant illegally discriminated; and
    4) The discrimination caused the harm in employment.

14) Disparate impact claims arise when the employment practice or policy is facially neutral, but has a significant negative impact based on race, color, religion, sex, or national origin. The plaintiff's burden of proof in disparate impact claims is defined by 42 U.S.C. § 2000e-2(k).

15) Employment discrimination based on age (40+) and discrimination based on pregnancy or related medical conditions are prohibited.

16) Under appropriate circumstances, religion, sex, or national origin may be BFOQs and permissible employment criteria under Title VII. Race and color are never BFOQs.

17) To prevail in a Title VII sexual harassment case the plaintiff must establish either:

    1) Quid pro quo sexual harassment; or
    2) Hostile environment sexual harassment.

18) If the plaintiff meets this initial burden of proof, it must be determined whether the plaintiff suffered any tangible injury (*e.g.*, discharge, demotion, undesirable reassignment, etc.) as a result of the sexual harassment. If there was tangible injury, liability is imputed to the employer. If there was no tangible injury, the employer may raise as an affirmative defense that:

    1) The employer exercised reasonable care to prevent and correct any sexual harassment; and

2) The employee unreasonably failed to exercise an opportunity to report the sexual harassment.

19) Professional conduct is guided by a hierarchy of laws, ethics, and morality, with legal compliance forming the essential foundation, standards of professional ethics establishing higher professional norms, and moral ideals setting the highest aspirational goals in professional practice.

20) Public educators have a right to privacy and liberty in their private lives, provided that their private lives do not interfere with the performance of their professional duties. To acquire valid jurisdiction over activities in teachers' private lives for purposes of employment sanctions, school officials must establish that there is a logical nexus between the challenged off-campus conduct and a resulting negative impact on the teacher's ability to perform professional duties.

21) In the performance evaluation process, established state and local policies and due process must be strictly followed.

22) Personnel files must be kept in accordance with due process of law, and in compliance with HIPAA, FOIA, and other applicable federal and state laws.

23) School officials must know and comply with the laws governing public records and meetings in their state. Failure to comply with these laws may result in civil liability or criminal penalties.

24) The National Labor Relations Act protects the rights of all private sector employees to form unions and engage in collective bargaining. State laws govern rights to collective bargaining for state employees. Even where there is no legal right to collective bargaining, public educators retain their right to freedom of association and may join professional and political organizations.

25) Alternative Dispute Resolution (ADR) may be a useful alternative to litigation. Options in ADR include informal resolutions; mediation; negotiations; and arbitration.

II. *Principles to Practice Tips*:

1) *Contracts and Tenure*: Take great care in who is offered a contract and even more care in who is granted tenure. Serious personnel problems are far easier to prevent than they are to fix. In addition to objective job qualifications, also legitimately assess the professional ethics and collegiality of potential employees. Even more important, do not grant tenure to employees who clearly failed tests of professional ethics and collegiality during the probationary period prior to tenure. Personnel problems rarely get better after tenure. A positive, professional culture is essential to everyone's success. One rotten apple can spoil the barrel for everyone. Do not tenure a rotten apple.

2) *Employment Discrimination*: Never be a party to employment discrimination in any form. Further, take care to assure that employment decisions are made fairly and on the basis of valid employment criteria, and that even unconscious bias is guarded against. Actively seek a diverse pool of applicants; make the employment decision based only on lawful criteria; and hire the

most qualified candidate regardless of race, color, religion, sex, national origin, disability, age, family status, or any other criteria unrelated to legitimate employment qualifications.

3) *Professional Ethics*: Compliance with the law is necessary, but it is not sufficient. Professionals hold themselves to the higher callings of professional ethics and personal morality. You will never regret doing the good and right thing, even when it is difficult at the time. There is no honor in prevailing dishonorably. Always do the right thing, and then win or lose you will have won personal honor and self-respect. And by having a reputation for personal integrity you will win the respect of your colleagues as well. In all cases, do what is right and treat others as you would wish to be treated. Do not allow the negative emotions of anger, fear, etc., to deter you from doing what you know is right, always choosing what is right over what is easy at the time.

4) *Alternative Dispute Resolution*: In most cases, neither party in a dispute wants to see the dispute escalate to litigation. As Sun Tzu said in *The Art of War* build your enemy a golden bridge to retreat on, as the greatest victory comes from achieving your goals without the costs of battle. With some careful thought and planning, you may be able to achieve your necessary goals in a win-win scenario, thereby building rather than harming working relationships. Negotiation and mediation skills can be invaluable assets. Nonetheless, throughout the process, document and prepare to prevail in litigation if necessary. The preparation of a solid legal case will also strengthen your hand in negotiations.

III. *Questions for Discussion*: Please consider these questions and be prepared to discuss:

1) *The Bad Apple*: Why are bad teachers allowed to receive tenure? Why are truly incompetent teachers allowed to remain in the classroom? How would you deal with a tenured teacher who is competent but highly disruptive and destructive to the school culture and faculty morale?

2) *Employment Law Protections*: Are current federal employment discrimination laws adequate, or are additional protections needed? What additional protections (if any) are needed (*e.g.*, protections against discrimination based on sexual orientation; obesity; physical appearance; etc.)? Do current federal or state laws provide any protections in these areas? Could your school district provide needed protections through local policy?

3) *Work place Bullying*: U.S. states are increasingly enacting laws to better protect students from bullying, recognizing the destructive nature of these behaviors and extending protections from physical bullying to the arguably more harmful and destructive emotional abuse associated with bullying. Many nations in Europe now also prohibit bullying in the work place through employment laws. Is work place bullying a significant problem for individuals and institutions? Should U.S. employment laws address work place bullying?

4) *Open Forum*: What other related issues or current events would you like to discuss?

IV. *Suggested Activities*:

1) Review your State's laws governing tenure, dismissal, open records and meetings, and other relevant statutes governing employment and personnel issues in your State.

2) Learn to recognize incidents of work place bullying, emotional abuse, and "academic mobbing" in schools, and discuss what you can do to improve the work place culture for everyone.

3) Read *Getting to Yes*, by Fisher, Ury & Patton. Practice mock negotiations to develop useful negotiations skills.

Chapter 10: Tort Law and other Liability Issues

Tort law is civil law recognizing the plaintiff's legal right to just compensation for damages caused by the defendant. The roots of U.S. tort law can be traced back through English Common Law, and early Germanic Law, Roman Law, and the Law of the Torah. A system of tort law is a necessary foundation for any civil society. The main functions of tort law are to provide:

1) A lawful means of obtaining just compensation for damages; and
2) A deterrent against future injurious conduct.

If citizens could not turn to the courts and tort law to seek just compensation for injuries caused by the wrongful acts and negligence of others, many would take the law into their own hands resulting in additional unnecessary conflict, injury, and an ensuing cycle of retribution in the community. Further, while most people are generally honest and responsible, those that are not are far more likely to conduct themselves honestly and responsibly if they know they will be held financially accountable under tort law for the harms caused by their wrongful or negligent actions.

Because tort law plays an essential role in helping to maintain civil order, tort law developed as civilization developed, serving as a basis for just compensation and as a deterrent against injurious conduct. As societies increased in size and complexity the importance of tort law increased as well. Functional civilizations require mutual inter-reliance and fundamental trust among citizens. In modern societies with millions of inter-reliant citizens, however, citizens cannot know everyone they rely on by name and reputation, as they once did in small communities. Nonetheless, citizens must be able to maintain sufficient trust in others or the social and economic systems stall and collapse.

Tort Law is a Necessary Enforcement Tool for the Social Contract

Modern life requires cars, elevators, supermarkets, restaurants, medical care, etc., and reliance on other people to produce, deliver and maintain needed goods and services safely and responsibly. Imagine a world in which no product or service provider had any responsibility for the damages or injuries they caused. You could have no realistic faith that the brakes on your car were safe; elevators wouldn't fall to the ground; food was safely produced, refrigerated, and cooked; medicine was safe; doctors were qualified and conscientious; etc. Without consequences for wrongful and negligent acts, there would be far more wrongful and negligent acts, and far less social and economic trust.

Under such conditions the social contract and civil society itself would quickly begin to unravel causing immense harm to all. Tort law is the means of enforcing the necessary social contract of mutually responsible conduct, with the compensatory role of tort law acting like the remedial function of contract law, and the deterrent role of tort law acting similar to the deterrent effect of criminal law. The result is that through a just system of tort law, mutual trust is increased, irresponsible conduct is discouraged, and the risks and costs of injuries can be more fairly distributed consistent with rational public policy.

No system is perfect, however, and most everyone has heard horror stories of extreme tort law claims and damage awards. Your chances of falling victim to an unjust tort claim, however, can be greatly reduced if you understand the tort law system and use common sense and prudent preventive measures to avoid unnecessary risks, injuries, and liability. This chapter explains the essential principles of tort law and other relevant liability issues in educational institutions.

Tort Law Generally

The law of torts and contracts are similar, but the tort "contract" is an implied social contract to act reasonably in interactions with others. If you have a legal duty to others, then there is also the implied social contractual obligation of acting reasonably in fulfilling that duty. The civil society "offers" all citizens an opportunity to participate, and everyone "accepts" this general social contract by participating in society. Individuals may also assume higher duties of care by choosing to participate in activities that have a higher potential to harm others if reasonable care is not exercised. For example, all members of the common society have a general duty to refrain from harming others. But if you choose to operate potentially dangerous power equipment around other people, special care is required, and there is a higher duty to protect others around you from foreseeable harms.

A tort is a civil wrong, as opposed to a criminal wrong, where one party has suffered harm because of the injurious conduct of another party. A single wrongful action, however, could serve as the basis for both a prosecution under criminal law, and a civil suit under tort law. For example, if a defendant attacked and injured a victim, the defendant could be prosecuted under criminal laws for assault and battery and face criminal fines and imprisonment. And the victim/plaintiff could file a civil suit under tort law seeking monetary damages for harms caused by the intentional tort of assault and battery. The criminal charge would require the prosecutor to prove the defendant's guilt beyond a reasonable doubt, while the civil law tort suit would only require proof of the plaintiff's tort claim by a preponderance of the evidence. Because the criminal charge requires a higher burden of proof, under the same set of facts the defendant could be found not guilty in the criminal case yet still be held liable for monetary damages to the plaintiff in the tort law suit.

Although some intentional torts are also crimes, this chapter focuses on civil actions for wrongful conduct under tort law, and other liability issues in educational institutions. Potential tort law causes of action include torts resulting from negligence; malpractice; defamation; assault and battery; false imprisonment; invasion of privacy; and intentional infliction of emotional distress.

Tort Law Negligence Claims

Most tort cases concerning schools involve negligence claims. Negligence is the failure to use ordinary care. A legal cause of action arises when negligence results in harm to other people or property. School officials may be either the plaintiff or the defendant in these cases. But generally, a plaintiff student, parent, or community member is seeking monetary damages for some harm that was allegedly caused by the negligence of defendant school officials or those under their supervision.

Part of the explanation for school officials' frequent defendant status is the financial "deep pocket" of larger educational institutions. Schools are often the largest institutions in the community, with relatively substantial insurance coverage and other financial resources to pay monetary damages. If school employees have arguably been negligent, the school district is an attractive legal target.

Plaintiffs will generally name as defendants every school official in the chain from the individual who is alleged to have directly caused the harm, through all intervening supervisors, and up to the heads of the educational institution with control of the "deep pocket" resources and responsibility for policy decisions and general governance of the school. While individual liability is possible under some circumstances, the goal is usually not to obtain damages from individuals, but to obtain compensation for damages from the larger funds available to the educational institution. Even large educational institutions, however, do not have unlimited capacity to pay damage claims. And every dollar paid out in tort liability is one less dollar to fund education, making liability prevention a high priority for educational institutions.

To prevail in a negligence claim, the plaintiff must prove by a preponderance of the evidence that a legal duty to the plaintiff existed, defendant school officials breached that duty, the breach of duty caused the plaintiff's injuries, and there are compensable damages. The plaintiff must prove all four elements of a negligence claim to prevail:

    1) Duty;
    2) Breach of Duty;
    3) Causation (both factual and legal cause); and
    4) Damages.

Establishing the Defendant's Duty to the Plaintiff

Under the U.S. system of tort law the only general duties are to refrain from harming others and to act as a reasonable person under the circumstances. There is, however, no general duty to act affirmatively or render aid to others absent the creation of a legal duty by the defendant's actions or through a special relationship with the plaintiff. While there may be an ethical or moral duty to help others in need of help, these are not legally enforceable duties under tort law.

For example, if you were to see someone laying on their back in the parking lot calling for help, while most people would agree that you should help people in need if you can, there is no legal duty to help. Unless, of course, the reason the person is laying in the parking lot is because you ran over him or otherwise caused his injury. No general duty to render aid exists, but you may acquire a duty to help if you caused the injury; if you offered to help and the plaintiff reasonably relied on that offer of help; or if you somehow made the person's situation worse. But absent actions on your part that cause a legal duty to attach there is no general duty to render aid to persons with whom you have no special relationship.

There is, however, a special duty to help someone with whom you do have a special relationship. For example, parents have a duty to their children; teachers have a duty to students; doctors have a duty to patients; etc. The duties of parents include providing their children with necessary food, shelter, clothing, medical care, education, protection, and adequate parental supervision. Teachers acting *in loco parentis* have a general duty to instruct, reasonably supervise, and protect children from known or reasonably foreseeable dangers while the children are under the teacher's care. School officials also have a duty to reasonably supervise employees

417

and students, keep school property safe, and to protect against or warn of any known or reasonably foreseeable dangers to students, faculty, staff, and visitors on school property.

Those who do choose to voluntarily render aid even when there is no legal duty to do so are generally protected from liability under state "Good Samaritan" laws. Although laws vary among jurisdictions, these laws generally provide immunity from liability where persons voluntarily render aid to others in need of help, the rescuer acted in good faith, and acted reasonably under the circumstances. A few states require witnesses to accidents to render minimal emergency assistance, such as calling for help. But most states leave these matters to the conscience of the individual. Assistance is encouraged with good faith immunity. But most states have not established any general legal duty to render aid to others.

Proving the Defendant's Breach of Duty

Once a duty of care exists for the defendant, the duty is to act as a reasonable person under the circumstances. The defendant's actions are measured against what would be expected from a hypothetical "reasonable person" acting under the circumstances that prevailed at the time of the alleged breach of duty. The reasonable person is a legal fiction created as a standard for measuring whether the defendant met or breached the duty of care.

The Hypothetical Reasonable Person Standard: Did the Defendant Breach the Duty?

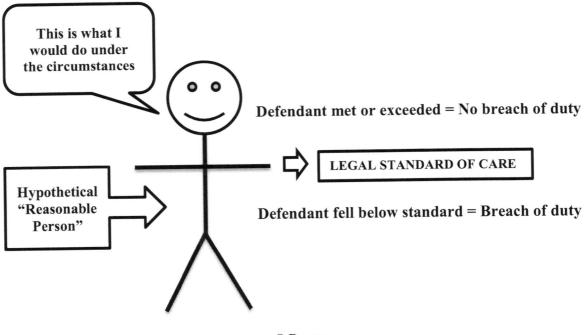

© Dayton

The hypothetical reasonable person is deemed to be an ordinary person in every way, with ordinary intelligence, knowledge, skills, judgment, etc. If the defendant's actions met or exceeded the level of care by the ordinary reasonable person under the circumstances, the defendant did not breach the duty of care and the plaintiff will fail in proving the case.

418

Whether the defendant breached the duty of care must be considered based on the totality of circumstances at the time. When the accident occurred was it raining, icy, or dark? Reasonable people use greater care under adverse conditions. Did the defendant have advance notice of a potential problem? Had a similar incident occurred previously? Reasonable people take sensible precautions to prevent foreseeable dangers. Was the activity in question one that required special care, training, or safety equipment? As the circumstances change, so does the reasonable person's actions and greater care is required under circumstances that present greater potential dangers to others.

Although defendants are generally measured against the objective standard of a reasonable person under the circumstances, in some cases the special abilities of the defendant may also be relevant. Persons with greater training and skills may be held to a higher standard of care, especially if they hold themselves out to the community as having special knowledge and skills in a relevant area. For example, a plaintiff can reasonably expect greater medical knowledge and skills from medical personnel, and greater knowledge and skills related to education and children from professional educators.

In general, while some persons are held to a higher standard because of special abilities, allowing lowered standards of care is disfavored by courts. Nonetheless, persons with disabilities may sometimes be allowed a lowered legal standard if the disability prevented them from doing what someone without the disability could have done under the circumstances. Children may also be held to a lower standard of accountability than adults. In these cases the disability or minority age is viewed as one of the circumstances under which the reasonable person standard is assessed (e.g., what would the reasonable blind person, or child, have done under those circumstances?). Children and persons with disabilities must necessarily engage in regular daily activities like everyone else, and holding them to a standard they cannot possibly meet in doing so may be unjust under some circumstances.

However, the disability or minority age is also a condition that requires extra care in other circumstances. Persons with disabilities or children must not voluntarily engage in potentially dangerous activities that exceed their known limitations, or they may be held to the same legal standard as all other persons engaged in those inherently dangerous activities. For example, children or persons with disabilities that prevent them from safely driving should not drive, as any unqualified driver presents an unnecessary danger to everyone on the road. For public safety reasons, persons unqualified to participate in potentially dangerous activities cannot be granted a lowered standard of care. As with all inherently dangerous activities, all drivers must be qualified and fully accountable or they must not drive.

Courts will also generally balance the foreseeable risks to plaintiffs against the reasonableness and social value of the defendant's actions. We cannot live in a risk free world, but some risks are more reasonable and have greater social value than others. Operating heavy equipment is always potentially dangerous, but it is necessary for farming, building, etc. Choosing to operate heavy equipment while heavily intoxicated, however, greatly increases the danger to others and has no added social value.

To prove a breach of duty the plaintiff must prove by a preponderance of the evidence that the defendant failed to use ordinary care and do what a reasonable person would have done under the circumstances. The conduct of the defendant is measured against the conduct expected from a reasonable person. If the defendant meets or exceeds the standard of the reasonable person, the plaintiff will fail in proving the case.

Proving the Breach of Duty was the Cause of Injury

To prove a negligence claim, proof of two separate and distinct types of causation is required. The defendant's actions must have been: 1) The actual cause (cause in fact) of the plaintiff's injuries; and 2) The proximate (legal cause) of the plaintiff's injuries. These two different elements of causation require independent proof and both elements must be established to prove a claim of negligence.

Cause in fact is established if the plaintiff can prove that the defendant is the factual cause of the plaintiff's injury. For example, if the defendant carelessly dropped a rock and the rock hit the plaintiff, the defendant clearly appears to be the cause in fact of the injury. But the defendant may still be found to be the cause in fact of the injury even if the defendant dropped a rock, the rock hit a board, and the board hit a shelf that then hit the plaintiff. As long as the plaintiff can prove by a preponderance of the evidence that the defendant's failure to exercise reasonable care was either a direct or a substantial cause in the chain of events leading to the injury, and that but for the defendant's actions the injury would not have occurred, the plaintiff has established the defendant's actions as the cause in fact of the injury.

It is not sufficient, however, to prove only cause in fact. The plaintiff must also prove that the defendant's actions were the proximate or legal cause of the injury. The principle question in proving legal cause is whether it was foreseeable that the defendant's actions would cause the plaintiff's injuries. Everyone is expected to act reasonably under the circumstances. But it is unfair to punish defendants just for bad luck or freak accidents that were not foreseeable to a reasonable person. The requirement of establishing legal cause involves a policy decision by the court concerning how far the defendant's potential liability should fairly extend. The plaintiff must prove that it was foreseeable that the defendant's actions could have caused the injury, and that the possible dangers were foreseeable to a degree sufficient to justify liability by the defendant.

It is important to note that negligence is not strict liability. The defendant charged with negligence is only responsible for harms caused by the defendant either directly or as a substantial causative factor, and only when it was reasonably foreseeable that the defendant's actions could have caused the harm under the circumstances. Defendants are not responsible for harms caused by others, or for bizarre events that could not have been reasonably foreseen under the circumstances.

Proving Compensable Damages

Negligence claims require proof of actual damages. These may include present and appropriately calculated future property loss, wage loss, medical expenses, compensation for pain and suffering, etc. Claims must be proven by a preponderance of the evidence, and must not be based on mere speculation about future possibilities. A student athlete may recover, for example, for the losses associated with an injury resulting from a coach's negligence. But whether years later the student athlete would have received a valuable athletic scholarship or made millions of dollars as a professional athlete likely involves speculation that exceeds reasonable bounds of just compensation and liability for the defendant. The speculated events may or may not have happened depending on countless future variables. Mere speculation about future possibilities is not proof of compensable damages.

420

Negligence law is generally intended to compensate the plaintiff for actual, provable damages. Punitive damages are not related to actual damages, but are intended to punish the defendant for outrageous misconduct. Punitive damages are not available in suits involving mere negligence by the defendant. These damages will only be awarded if the plaintiff can prove that the defendant acted recklessly or intentionally in causing serious harm to the plaintiff. Because these damages are intended to punish, punitive damages may be scaled to the financial resources of the defendant, with wealthier defendants being assessed higher punitive damages as lesser damages may be insufficient to punish and deter future misconduct.

As with contract law, there is also a requirement in negligence cases for the plaintiff to reasonably attempt to mitigate damages. If the plaintiff failed to reasonably attempt to mitigate damages, the plaintiff cannot recover for damages resulting from the failure to mitigate. For example, a defendant may be held liable for the costs of a personal injury caused by the defendant's negligent conduct. But the defendant would not be liable for additional injuries caused by an infection resulting from the plaintiff's unreasonable refusal to submit to medical treatment or follow medical advice.

In summary, to establish a prima facie case of negligence the plaintiff must prove:

1) The defendant had a duty to the plaintiff;
2) The defendant breached that duty;
3) The breach was both the cause in fact and legal cause of damages; and
4) There are provable, compensable damages.

Possible Defenses to Negligence Claims

After the plaintiff has established a prima facie case of negligence, the defendant may attempt to rebut the plaintiff's case, attacking the plaintiff's arguments on duty, breach, causation, and damages. The defendant need only successfully rebut one of the essential elements of the plaintiff's case. To prevail, the plaintiff bears the burden of proving all four elements of negligence (duty; breach; causation; and damages) by a preponderance of the evidence. When applicable, the defendant may offer the following defenses or arguments for reductions in potential liability:

Assumption of Risk

We do not live in a risk-free world. Engaging in activities means assuming responsibility for the natural consequences of those activities. Reasonable people weigh the potential risks and benefits before deciding whether to participate in an activity. Contact sports, swimming, skiing, sailing, ocean fishing, sky diving, racing, etc., are potentially hazardous, yet people want to participate in and watch these events. If owners, managers, and administrators were held liability for all foreseeable harms associated with these activities, as potential defendants they would be unlikely to offer these opportunities to anyone, or the costs of participating in or watching these events would become prohibitively high.

Assumption of risk allows potential defendants to shift some of the responsibility for personal safety to persons who choose to participate. This legal doctrine holds that when a plaintiff recognized and understood potential risks associated with the activity, yet voluntarily chose to participate anyway, the plaintiff assumed the reasonable risks associated with participation.

The defendant is still responsible for his or her own negligence, and must act reasonably in providing equipment that is safe, proper safety instructions, warnings of known dangers, etc. But based on assumption of risk by the plaintiff, the defendant is not liable for harms that were reasonably foreseeable as the natural consequences of voluntary participation. For example, a football player may injure a leg in the game or suffer other injuries that are the natural consequences of voluntary participation in a contact sport. The defendant is not liable for reasonable risks voluntarily assumed by the plaintiff.

The risk is not voluntarily assumed, however, when the plaintiff had no reasonable alternative to participation. For example, students assigned to play football as part of a required physical education class are not voluntarily assuming risks in the same way as students who voluntarily play football on an extracurricular team. Accordingly, the level of contact and risk should be adjusted appropriately for the students involved (*e.g.,* "flag football" instead of full contact tackle football). However, all participants, assigned or voluntary, are expected to follow reasonable safety instructions and rules that were adequately explained to them by teachers and coaches. A student does assume the risks associated with a knowing and intentional disregard for safety rules, or other willful misconduct beyond the control of the teacher or coach.

> ### *Having Students Thoroughly Review and Sign a Printed Copy of Safety Rules Helps Prevent Injuries and Documents Safety Precautions*

Defendants will find it difficult, however, to argue assumption of risk by younger children. Younger children's age and inexperience generally makes them less able to recognize and understand risks and consequences. Adult defendants charged with the care and protection of young children cannot shift the consequences of foreseeable harm by claiming assumption of risk when the child was too young to fully understand the risk. Extra care is always required in protecting young children from dangers they do not fully understand. Younger children should not be allowed to participate in inherently dangerous activities until they are old enough to recognize and understand the risks, and they are capable of safely participating. It may also be difficult to shift the consequences of foreseeable harm to adults when the defendant knew the adults were inexperienced or otherwise unable to fully recognize and understand the risks involved in participation in a potentially dangerous activity.

> ### *Proving Assumption of Risk Requires Proving the Plaintiff Recognized, Understood, and Voluntarily Accepted the Reasonable Risks Associated with Participation*

The use of waiver forms and other documents intended to shield defendants from liability through "assumption of risk" may have some utility, but they also have some limitations. Having a parent sign a permission form for a student field trip provides notice to the parent of student participation, and gives school officials evidence that the parent knew about and consented to the child's participation in activities that may involve some reasonably foreseeable risks. These forms do not, however, act as total waivers of liability and responsibility for defendants. Regardless of what the form may say, no waiver form can lawfully waive the defendant's responsibility to use reasonable care in supervising and protecting children from known or reasonably foreseeable harms. Nor do these waiver forms shield defendants from any harms inflicted recklessly, knowingly, or intentionally by the defendant.

It is contrary to rational public policy to allow defendants to waive their responsibilities to act reasonably through fine print exculpatory clauses, especially where parties are in unequal bargaining positions or the notice is constructive and not actual. Printing "by accepting this ticket for admission you agree to waive all claims for liability" in fine print on the back of an admission ticket does not constitute a knowing, voluntary assumption of risk by the recipient. Nor will it allow culpable defendants to escape their legal duty to not harm others and to act as reasonable persons under the circumstances. Waiver forms may be useful in providing notice of participation by children and warnings of reasonable risks, but they are not a license for unreasonable, irresponsible, or wrongful conduct by the defendant.

Plaintiff's Negligence as a Defense

Legal doctrines that may bar or limit recovery from the defendant because of the plaintiff's own negligence include "contributory negligence," "comparative negligence," and the rule of "avoidable consequences." Everyone is expected to use ordinary care in their daily activities, including plaintiffs. Plaintiffs who could have reasonably avoided an injury, but through their own negligent or reckless conduct contributed to their own injury, may be barred from recovering damages from the defendant under the legal doctrine of "contributory negligence." For example, a custodian may have negligently left an electrical cord lying across the hallway. But a plaintiff who trips on the cord and is injured because he was engaged in foolish antics, running backwards, and not looking where he was going may be barred from recovering damages for the injury because his own negligence significantly contributed to the injury.

Even if the plaintiff's negligence is not a total bar to recovering damages from the defendant, it may serve to reduce the extent of the defendant's liability through "comparative negligence." Comparative negligence allows the defendant to offset damages in proportion to negligence attributable to the plaintiff. For example, if it is found that damages totaled $100,000 but that 30% of the injury could be attributed to the plaintiff's own negligence, liability for the defendant is reduced to $70,000. Many jurisdictions bar any recovery, however, if the plaintiff's negligence equaled or exceeded that of the defendant, the so-called "49% rule" as the limit on plaintiff negligence in which any damages may still be recovered from the defendant who must be 51% or more responsible for the injury.

Plaintiffs who failed to reasonably attempt to mitigate damages may be barred from recovery for any reasonably avoidable further damages under the doctrine of "avoidable consequences." The plaintiff may be able to recover damages for injuries caused by the defendant, but the plaintiff must take reasonable actions to mitigate and avoid further damages. Failure to do so may bar recovery for any avoidable consequences of the injury. A plaintiff must make reasonable efforts to attempt to mitigate damages including protecting damaged property from unnecessary further damage, seeking prompt medical care for injuries, etc.

Sovereign Immunity

The English Magna Carte proclaimed that King John was King of England, Lord of Ireland, etc., by the grace of God. Because the King was deemed to be acting under Devine authority, it was held that to question the King or the King's government in a court of law was the legal equivalent of questioning God, and therefore prohibited by law. Under the doctrine of sovereign immunity "the King can do no wrong." Although U.S. law rejected the theory of Devine rights of Kings, with the formation of the new U.S. government the English common law doctrine of sovereign immunity was incorporated into U.S. law to provide government agencies with protections from liability.

More recently, however, while some significant remnants of sovereign immunity remain, absolute sovereign immunity has been modified or abandoned by most jurisdictions. Judges clearly do not believe that federal, state, and local governments are chosen and acting under Devine authority. Instead, elements of sovereign immunity are retained to protect limited government resources for the purposes for which they were allocated.

What would happen, for example, to a small rural school district if a plaintiff's tort liability award exceeded the school district's annual operating budget? Closing down the district's schools and not educating children for that year is not an option. Modern sovereign immunity laws attempt to allow reasonable compensation to injured plaintiffs through available insurance, etc., without exposing school districts to absolute financial ruin from massive tort liability judgments.

The U.S. Constitution still provides States with some protections from suits in federal court. Suing state government in federal court may offer some strategic advantages, but also raises some additional challenges under the Eleventh Amendment. In *Hans v. Louisiana*, 134 U.S. 1 (1890), the U.S. Supreme Court found that the Eleventh Amendment prohibited a citizen from suing the State in federal court without the consent of the State. In *Ex parte Young*, 209 U.S. 123 (1908), however, the United States Supreme Court held that when state officials act unconstitutionally, suits in federal court may proceed regardless of immunity.

Constitutional Torts and 42 U.S.C. § 1983

Tort law is generally governed by state law. But plaintiffs may also sue state officials for a "deprivation of any rights, privileges, or immunities" protected by the U.S. Constitution and federal laws, a "constitutional tort" under 42 U.S.C. § 1983. In the wake of the U.S. Civil War Congress enacted legislation to help secure the rights of all citizens, and in particular citizens subjected to a pattern of deprivations of rights because of their former status as slaves. The Thirteenth Amendment (1865) abolished slavery, and the Fourteenth Amendment (1868) guaranteed equal protection of the laws to all persons. Both amendments also granted Congress power to enforce these provisions through appropriate legislation.

Without real consequences, however, these protections were nothing but words on paper to state and local officials determined to continue patterns of discrimination. In the face of such persistent discrimination by state and local officials Congress determined that citizens needed a lawful means of enforcing rights of federal citizenship, and enacted 42 U.S.C. § 1983 (1871) pursuant to legislative powers granted by the Thirteenth and Fourteenth Amendments. This statute continues to provide a legal basis for holding state officials accountable for deprivations of rights of federal citizenship through monetary damages awarded to plaintiffs. 42 U.S.C. § 1983 declared:

> Every person who, under color of any statute, ordinance, regulation, custom, or usage, of any State or Territory or the District of Columbia, subjects, or causes to be subjected, any citizen of the United States or other person within the jurisdiction thereof to the deprivation of any rights, privileges, or immunities secured by the Constitution and laws,

shall be liable to the party injured in an action at law, suit in equity, or other proper proceeding for redress.

Under 42 U.S.C. § 1983 plaintiffs may seek damages from both the school district and individual school officials. Individual school officials are only denied qualified immunity and held personally liable for damages, however, when they have personally disregarded well established law. In *Wood v. Strickland*, 420 U.S. 308 (1975) the U.S. Supreme Court affirmed that ignorance of the law does not excuse school officials from a duty to comply with the law. School officials are not required to guess what a court will decide the law is in the future when the law is unsettled. But school officials are expected to know and comply with laws that were well established at the time of the events the plaintiff is challenging. School officials who violate well established law may be held personally liable for damages. In addition to monetary damages federal courts may also order injunctive relief, for example, ordering an expelled student or a dismissed teacher reinstated by school officials.

Educational Malpractice

Those who hold themselves out to the community as having special knowledge and skills may be held to a higher standard of care where persons reasonably relied on their promise of professional expertise. Therefore all professionals, doctors, nurses, lawyers, educators, etc., must at least conform to the minimal level of skill and knowledge that is recognized in their profession.

Tort suits against professionals for failure to meet professional standards in practice are called malpractice suits. Malpractice suits require proving the same four elements required in negligence suits (duty; breach; causation; and damages) except that whether there is a duty and whether the defendant breached that duty are judged by standards applicable to professionals engaged in professional practice. Bad results for the plaintiff, however, do not prove malpractice. Professionals cannot always guarantee good outcomes, and they are only required to provide professional services that meet or exceed minimal standards of competence recognized in the profession.

Suits for educational malpractice have generally been unsuccessful, especially concerning the "Johnny can't read cases" in which plaintiffs graduated from high school but were unable to read at a high school level. There is a general duty for educators to use professional level skills in educating students in their classes. But whether they breached that duty can be difficult to prove. Education is far more of an art than a science. There are many schools of thought on educational methods, making it difficult for plaintiffs to clearly define duty and breach of duty in educational malpractice cases.

But even if a plaintiff could establish a breach of duty in a "Johnny can't read" case, showing causation would likely prove fatal to the plaintiff's claim. Defendants need only introduce evidence that the vast majority of students who graduated in Johnny's class were taught to read by the school, and that Johnny was among the few who failed to learn. Who then caused Johnny's failure when most students in the school successfully learned to read? The defendants can argue that Johnny's own negligence caused his failure to learn through a pattern of willful inattention to instruction; lack of effort; failure to ask for help; misbehavior resulting in removals; etc. Plaintiffs' cases are further complicated if the student moved among several school districts, allowing the defendants to further minimize their control and responsibility in Johnny's education.

Successful educational malpractice suits are more likely in very specialized areas such as special education and counseling. In the area of special education, the Individualized Education Plan (IEP) clearly documents the school district's duty, making it much easier to prove a breach of duty, and that the breach was a cause of injury. While it is more likely that a court would order remedial services than monetary damages for a special education student, remedial services can be very costly to a school district.

Counselors should also take care to adequately address situations where there is clear evidence that a student poses a serious danger to the student or others, appropriately addressing and warning of the danger. In *Tarasoff v. Regents*, 551 P.2d 334 (Cal. 1976), the Supreme Court of California recognized a duty for mental health care professionals to warn when there is clear evidence of an intent to harm an identified person, so that at a minimum targets of threats may take appropriate actions to protect themselves. In *Tarasoff*, despite clear evidence of a specific threat, university mental health care professionals failed to warn a targeted victim of the threat from a patient under their care. The patient later killed the targeted victim. The court in *Tarasoff* stated: "We conclude that the public policy favoring protection of the confidential character of patient-psychotherapist communications must yield to the extent to which disclosure is essential to avert danger to others. The protective privilege ends where the public peril begins." Many states have codified the *Tarasoff* principle into state laws. These statutes require counselors and other mental health care professionals to warn of specific dangers to identified persons, whether these are warnings to parents if a minor child threatens to harm him or herself, or warnings of threats to targeted third parties.

Defamation

To defame someone is to unlawfully harm that person's public reputation. Slander is spoken defamation and libel is written defamation, but both are governed under the same laws of defamation. The English Common Law origins of defamation law are complex and archaic. Defamation law is further complicated under U.S. law because of broad protections for free speech under the U.S. and state constitutions, and different standards of law depending on whether the plaintiff is deemed a private or public figure for purposes of defamation. U.S. citizens have a First Amendment right, sometimes further strengthened by a state constitutional right, to express their opinions concerning other people, and especially concerning public officials and other public figures.

It is not enough for a defamation plaintiff to merely prove that the defendant said something negative about the plaintiff. The plaintiff must generally show that the statement was untrue and that there was at least negligence by the defendant concerning the truth when the plaintiff is deemed a private figure. Those plaintiffs who are deemed to be public figures will find it much more difficult to prove a case of defamation because proof of reckless disregard for the truth or malice by the defendant is generally required. U.S. defamation law seeks to balance the individual's right to be free from untrue damaging public statements, with the rights of others to free speech and the public expression of their opinions, especially concerning public figures.

Nonetheless, while there is a broadly protected right to freedom of speech in the U.S., defamation is not protected speech. To establish a prima facie case of defamation, the plaintiff must show that the defendant's alleged defamatory declarations:

1) Contained untrue statements of fact concerning the plaintiff;
2) The statements were communicated to one or more persons other than the plaintiff;
3) The statements caused foreseeable prejudice towards the plaintiff; and
4) There are provable damages to the plaintiff.

As noted above the plaintiff's burden of proof also depends on whether the plaintiff is deemed a public or a private figure. Public officials are generally deemed public figures in defamation suits. According to the U.S. Supreme Court, in *Rosenblatt v. Baer*, 383 U.S. 75 (1966), public officials are those government officials that reasonably appear to the public to have substantial control over governmental affairs. In *Hutchinson v. Proxmire*, 443 U.S. 111 (1979), however, the U.S. Supreme Court noted that the public figure designation does not extend to all public employees. State courts have tended to hold that elected or higher-level appointed public school officials are public figures, including elected school board members, elected or appointed superintendents, and college presidents and deans, and that lower-level appointed school officials such as teachers and staff retain their citizen status as private figures even when they work for public institutions.

Mid-level appointed officials, such as school-level principals, have been a much closer call for courts, with some state courts holding that school principals are public figures and others holding that principals are not public figures under state law. A particular plaintiff's public status may also influence a court's decision concerning whether that individual is deemed a public or a private figure for purposes of defamation. For example, even if principals were generally deemed private figures under applicable state law, a principal that was a former celebrity; a prominent state, national or international figure; an elected official; or otherwise sought and achieved broad public recognition, might still be held to be a public figure in that unique case regardless of the general rule under state law. It is expected that citizens will make statements about public figures, and one of the prices of broad public recognition is that public figures must tolerate more critical comments and opinions from the public than private figures.

Accordingly, to prove a case of defamation plaintiffs that are public figures must meet a higher burden of proof. In *New York Times v. Sullivan*, 376 U.S. 254 (1964) the U.S. Supreme Court required that to prove defamation as a public figure the plaintiff must prove "that the statement was made with actual malice . . . that is with knowledge that it was false or with reckless disregard of whether it was false or not." In contrast plaintiffs that are private figures need only establish by a "preponderance of the evidence that the defendant failed to use ordinary care to determine the truth or falsity" of the statement concerning the plaintiff.

A defamation plaintiff must prove all elements of a defamation claim by a preponderance of the evidence under the applicable standard for a public or private figure. A plaintiff that prevails in a defamation suit may seek monetary damages from the defendant, attorney's fees, and an injunction against the defendant. In cases involving especially malicious behavior by the defendant punitive damages may also be awarded to the plaintiff.

In nearly all jurisdictions, however, truth is an absolute defense to a claim of defamation. Defamation law only protects plaintiffs from untrue statements concerning their character and reputation. True statements of fact are not defamation. The defendant's expression of personal opinion is also not subject to claims of defamation. A defendant's statement that "I do not believe the principal is a nice person" is a statement of personal opinion. But even though it may be cast as a personal opinion, a declarative public statement by the defendant stating "I believe that teacher, Mrs. Smith, is a child molester" is not merely a statement of opinion, but is reasonably understood as based on some underlying facts within the knowledge of the defendant and may be subject to a defamation claim. It is important to remember, however, that good faith reports of suspected child abuse made in compliance with state laws requiring these reports are not defamation. Even if the reports turn out to be unfounded, if the statements were made in good faith and were not communicated beyond official routes of required reporting, good faith reports are protected under state law.

Intentional Torts

Intentional torts are distinguished from the tort of negligence in that the plaintiff must prove intent to cause harm, and not merely negligence in performing a duty. Because of the element of intent, many intentional torts are also crimes. Claims of intentional torts in educational institutions may include assault and battery; false imprisonment; invasion of privacy; and intentional infliction of emotional distress.

Assault and Battery

Assault and battery are often discussed together, because an assault may be followed by a battery if a defendant carries through with a treat. Nonetheless, these two intentional torts are separate and distinct causes of legal action, and depending on the facts, the plaintiff may claim either or both of these intentional torts. An assault occurs when the defendant acts with the intent of causing apprehension of bodily harm or offense by the plaintiff, while battery is the actual and intentional infliction of harmful or offensive bodily contact. School officials may be the plaintiffs or the defendants in these cases.

Proving a prima facie case of assault requires the plaintiff to establish by a preponderance of the evidence that there was an action by the defendant intended to cause apprehension and that it did in fact cause apprehension. For example, a defendant may have pulled out a knife and said "I am going to cut you." If the plaintiff can prove that the defendant's actions were taken with the intent to cause apprehension, and in fact did cause apprehension, the plaintiff has proven a prima facie case of assault and may argue for appropriate damages.

Damages for assault may include compensation for emotional stress caused by the assault, physical injuries resulting from the distress, and other provable damages. Punitive damages may be appropriate where the defendant's actions were sufficiently malicious or outrageous. Defenses may include attempting to rebut any necessary element of the prima facie case of assault, claiming consent to the interaction (*e.g.*, the interaction was part of a game, a play, etc., consented to by the plaintiff), or an appropriate exercise of disciplinary authority (*e.g.*, the teacher threatened physical punishment but the threat was of lawful corporal punishment).

Proving a prima facie case of battery requires the plaintiff to establish by a preponderance of the evidence that there was an action by the defendant intended to inflict harmful or offensive bodily touching and that it did in fact result in this bodily touching. For example, a defendant may have punched the plaintiff, or a defendant may have approached the plaintiff with the intent to touch the plaintiff in an offensive way (*e.g.*, sexual contact or an affront to personal dignity such as ripping clothing, etc.) and in fact did so. The plaintiff has proven a prima facie case and may argue for appropriate damages.

Damages for battery may include compensation for physical injuries, damages to personal property, emotional distress, punitive damages, and other provable damages. Defenses may include attempting to rebut any necessary element of the prima facie case of battery, arguing the defendant's act was not volitional (*e.g.*, caused by mistake, accident, seizure, reflex, etc.) arguing the plaintiff consented to the contact, or the touching was an exercise of self-defense, defense of others, or lawful disciplinary authority. Use of force in defense must not exceed what is reasonably necessary for defense, and the use of force must end when the threat ends. Retaliation is not self-defense.

False Imprisonment

False imprisonment occurs when a plaintiff has been unlawfully confined by the defendant without consent. Proving a prima facie case of false imprisonment requires the plaintiff to establish by a preponderance of the evidence that there was an action by the defendant intended to cause confinement and that it did in fact cause unlawful confinement without the consent of the plaintiff.

Confinement may be caused by physical barriers; physical force; verbal orders or intimidation; or removing of the ability of the plaintiff to physically leave. For example, if the plaintiff can prove that the defendant unlawfully seized the plaintiff's car keys with the intent of confining the plaintiff to the area, and the plaintiff was in fact unable to leave without her car keys, the plaintiff has proven a prima facie case and may argue for appropriate damages.

Damages for false imprisonment may include compensation for any physical injuries resulting from the confinement, damages to personal property, emotional distress, punitive damages, and other provable damages. Defenses may include attempting to rebut any necessary element of the prima facie case of false imprisonment, *e.g.*, presenting evidence that the plaintiff consented to the confinement or failed to leave through a known and reasonable means of leaving, or arguing the defendant's acts were lawful, necessary discipline, self-defense or in defense of others.

Temporary restraint or seclusion of students may be necessary in some cases to protect safety. Nonetheless, when restraint, seclusion, or any use of force is necessary, school officials should be certain not to exceed what is required and lawful under the circumstances; to document the need for their actions and what occurred; and to seek and implement the least severe options sufficient for protecting safety in the school.

Restraint or seclusion of students is potentially dangerous and may be regulated by federal or state laws. Restraint or seclusion should only be used in response to an imminent danger and where less restrictive interventions would prove ineffective in protecting against the imminent danger.

School officials should assure that any school policies concerning the restraint or seclusion of children are in compliance with applicable laws which may prohibit the use of mechanical restraints (*e.g.*, handcuffs, ties, shackles, etc.); chemical restraints (*e.g.*, non-prescribed drugs or other chemicals to alter behavior); physical restraints that restrict breathing; or any other aversive interventions that may endanger health or safety.

If a student is temporarily restrained or secluded for valid safety purposes, the health and safety of the student must be closely monitored. Further, the restrictive conditions should be ended as soon as practicable through disciplinary removal; change in placement; transfer of the student to law enforcement officials; or other appropriate expedited resolutions of the safety risk.

Invasion of Privacy

Everyone has a general right to be left alone and to not be subjected to unreasonable intrusions on their personal privacy. And everyone has a general duty not to invade the privacy of others in unreasonable and unlawful ways. In the U.S., legal causes of action for invasion of privacy have been recognized in four general areas:

1) Invasion into the plaintiff's private life;
2) Public disclosure of the plaintiff's private facts;
3) Misappropriation of the plaintiff's name or likeness; and
4) Presenting the plaintiff in a false and offensive light.

Like most tort actions, establishing a prima facie case of invasion of privacy generally tracks the basic elements of negligence and most other torts: Duty, breach, causation, and damages. There is a general duty to respect other persons' reasonable expectations of privacy. That duty is breached if the defendant's actions in invading the personal privacy of the plaintiff were serious and unreasonable. The defendant's actions must have caused foreseeable harm to the plaintiff. And there must be provable damages which may include serious emotional distress and mental suffering resulting from the invasion of privacy.

An invasion of the plaintiff's private life may occur, for example, if school officials remotely activated cameras on school computers loaned to faculty and students for home use. Publicly disclosing private information acquired through this invasion of privacy, or any other public disclosure of private information, might also constitute a public disclosure of private facts. The unauthorized use of an individual's name or likeness for commercial purposes would constitute a misappropriation of the plaintiff's name or likeness. Further, an unauthorized use of the plaintiff's name or likeness may also constitute presenting the plaintiff in a false light if it wrongfully portrays the plaintiff to the public in a manner that would be highly offensive to the reasonable person (*e.g.*, video of the person eating candy but falsely claiming the "pills" were illegal drugs).

Truth is generally not a defense to a claim of invasion of privacy because in these cases the plaintiff had a right to keep the truth private. But false statements about the plaintiff related to a breach of privacy may also be grounds for a defamation suit. The plaintiff's lawful consent to the breach of privacy generally is a valid defense to a claim of invasion of privacy. In some cases, there may also be First Amendment defenses available, especially to members of the Press reporting on matters of legitimate public concern.

Intentional Infliction of Emotional Distress

It is an unfortunate reality that some troubled individuals are motivated by jealousy, hatred, personal insecurities, a desire for power and control, etc., to intentionally inflict emotional distress on others. And it is not true that "sticks and stones may break my bones, but words will never hurt me." Words can do serious emotional, psychological, and even physical harm to the person targeted for harassment. The tort of intentional infliction of emotional distress provides a remedy for wrongful emotional abuse intentionally inflicted on the plaintiff by the defendant.

With increased awareness of the connection between mental stress and physical health, and broader knowledge of the serious human and institutional consequences of harassment and bullying, U.S. courts are increasingly recognizing the validity of claims of intentional infliction of emotional distress. Nonetheless, the burden of proof for the plaintiff is still very high. The plaintiff must prove that the defendant engaged in extreme and outrageous acts intended to cause foreseeable harm to the plaintiff. Damages may include compensation for the pain and suffering of emotional distress; consequential damages such as lost wages; counseling expenses; medical costs; and punitive damages where the defendant's actions were truly outrageous in nature.

In the U.S. bullying is general thought of as a problem among children. The reality, however, is that bullying and harassment continue to be serious problems in the adult work place. This type of employee misconduct can have devastating impacts on its victims and the common work environment. Victims of work place bullying and harassment may experience increased anxiety, depression, and stress related physical and mental illnesses. Job satisfaction and productivity of the victim, the bully, and others can plummet, as bullying and harassment are so emotionally charged that they can increasingly consume the energy and time that should have been focused on productive work. In extreme cases victims pushed beyond their psychological limits and desperate to end severe and prolonged harassment may ultimately respond with work place violence against the perpetrator and others they believe supported or allowed the abuse.

If work place bullies are not dealt with promptly and appropriately, all employees witnessing these events may lose faith in the ability of institutional administrators to manage a fair, safe, and healthy work environment. A few bad apples can spoil the work place culture for everyone increasing problems with morale, absenteeism, and employee retention. The first employees to leave are often the employees most needed by the institution. Those with the most talents generally have the most alternative employment options. Allowing bullying to continue harms everyone: The direct victim; indirect victims; bystanders; the institution; and even the bully. The bully is eventually the final victim of bullying when consequences ultimately come home to the perpetrator.

Bullies rely on an imbalance in power, either real or perceived. Anti-bullying laws and policies can help to shift the balance of power away from the would-be bully and towards support for a culture of civility. Many developed nations have already established legislation prohibiting work place bullying, harassment, "academic mobbing," and similar forms of employment related misconduct and abuse. Until appropriate legislation is adopted in the U.S., plaintiffs must rely on informal resolutions; administrative interventions; institutional policies; or suits for intentional infliction of emotional distress in more extreme cases. Cyber-bullying and cyber-stalking may also be areas in which courts or legislators may increasingly recognize legal remedies for the intentional infliction of emotional distress.

Other Important Areas of Safety Concern and Potential Liability

The core lesson of tort law is that you must do what a reasonable person would do, thereby avoiding harm, protecting safety, and preventing liability. Recognizing and reasonably addressing potential problems before they become emergencies is the key to safety and liability management. In these areas an ounce of prevention may be worth many pounds of cure. Based on common school safety risks, federal and state laws addressing these risks, and reviews of applicable case law, this section summarizes some important areas of safety concern and potential liability as an aid in recognizing and addressing these problems in schools.

Many of these issues are regulated by specific state laws and local policies. These issues are addressed here generally and in summary as a foundation for further exploration of the applicable laws and policies in your jurisdiction. These are critically important issues to proactively address to promote greater safety and prevent unnecessary liability. It is hoped that the overviews and examples in this section will encourage you to think further about safety concerns in your school; review applicable state laws and local policies; and discuss with colleagues and community members how everyone can work together to improve safety in your school. Avoiding unnecessary liability is a high priority for school officials. But protecting everyone's safety must always be the first priority.

Child Supervision

Courts have consistently held that school officials have a duty to reasonably protect the health and safety of children left in their care. Adequate supervision is a legal duty and a community expectation. It is per se negligence to leave children unsupervised. A responsible adult must be in charge at all times, supervising children from the moment school officials take physical custody until physical custody is transferred back to the parent. If children are not adequately supervised and an assault or injury occurs because of inadequate supervision, school officials may be held liable for negligent supervision and dismissed for neglect of duties.

Adequate supervision includes protecting children from foreseeable dangers. Choking and food allergies are serious but often overlooked dangers until tragedy strikes. If an airway is blocked for more than four minutes, however, serious brain damage or death may result. School officials, classroom teachers, school nurses, and cafeteria personnel must work together to reduce risks associated with choking and food allergies in schools. Younger children are at higher risk of choking, but choking is a serious danger for all persons. Younger children may choke on a toy or other small object, but food is the most common cause of choking for everyone.

Because of the increased risks of choking, children should not be allowed to run or engage in other unsafe physical antics during lunch or snacks. Exerted breathing while chewing and food related pranks greatly increase choking risks. Cafeteria personnel should also avoid serving younger children round, firm foods, such as hot dogs, chunks of meat or cheese, grapes, etc., or serve these foods cut in safer-sized pieces appropriate for younger children. In addition to serving safer foods and providing adequate supervision, school personnel should be trained in administering first-aid to a choking victim, including appropriate techniques for very small children when applicable. A blocked airway is a critical emergency, with only minutes to respond before permanent injury or death occurs.

Serious food allergies may also result in an emergency situation by closing the airway through anaphylactic shock. School officials have a duty to take reasonable precautions to prevent known risks, and to be prepared to respond appropriately to foreseeable emergencies such as a severe allergic reaction. Reasonable accommodations for persons with severe allergies may be required by § 504 and the ADA, but safety is of course the primary concern.

To prevent allergy related emergencies, school officials, parents, and students must work together to reduce risks for persons with severe allergies. Parents and students should be directed to inform school officials of any known and severe allergies. Students with severe food allergies should be warned never to trade lunches with other students or eat anything unless they are certain it is safe, as even traces of some foods can cause serious reactions in hypersensitive persons. Classroom teachers with hypersensitive allergic students should watch to assure that known allergens are not introduced into the classroom if this would result in a serious risk to the allergic student. All school personnel should be trained in recognizing the symptoms of a serious allergic reaction, and in administering first-aid and the school's emergency plan for anaphylactic shock victims. Consistent with applicable laws, epinephrine should be stored and readily available for emergency use.

Personnel Supervision

Courts have held that school officials are responsible for reasonably supervising on-duty personnel. School officials may be held liable for negligent supervision and the on-duty tortious acts of employees under the doctrine of respondeat superior (*i.e.*, the higher authority/supervisor must also answer for the conduct of an employee acting in the scope of employment). In addition to adequate daily supervision of employees, criminal background checks should be conducted on all persons who have access to children in the school, consistent with state laws governing background checks.

If adequate background checks are not conducted, or warning signs concerning employee misconduct go unheeded, school officials may be liable for negligent hiring, supervision, or retention of employees. It is per se negligence to fail to conduct a required criminal background check. Further, consistent with the Court's decisions in *Gebser* and *Franklin* concerning sexual harassment and Title IX, if school officials receive actual notice of sexual harassment they must not react with deliberate indifference or liability under Title IX may result.

Children must be protected from abusers and sexual predators. But school personnel must also protect themselves from situations that could invite false allegations from students and parents. Case law confirms that educators have been subjected to false claims of abuse by students and parents. The personal and professional damage from these false claims can be devastating to the educator, even when later proven false.

To protect children and school personnel, school policies should generally discourage unnecessary physical contact with a child by school personnel, and school personnel should avoid being alone with a child in isolated areas. Whenever possible another person should be present, doors should be left open, etc. Limited physical contact with a child is sometimes appropriate or necessary. Further, school counselors and nurses sometimes require greater privacy in their work with students. But in all circumstances common sense measures can help to better protect school personnel from false allegations and help protect children from abuse.

School Visitors

Public schools are public institutions, but they are not public streets open to everyone. School officials have a legal duty to supervise and control public school buildings and grounds. State laws allow school officials to reasonably decide who does and does not have a legitimate cause for being present on school property. Only checked and approved persons with a legitimate cause to be there should be allowed inside the secured areas of the school. It is essential that school officials have an effective security system for both signing in visitors and signing out children to adults. Consistent with state laws, buildings should be physically secured to limit access by outside persons, and all entryways should have a posted requirement for visitors to first check-in at the designated area before entering the secured areas of the school.

To guard against risks of abduction, abuse, and injury, children should only be released to the custody of parent/guardian authorized and school approved safe, sober, adult pick-up persons.

When in doubt, confirm the identity and valid authorization of the adult seeking to take the child from the school. Even if an unknown person is wearing a uniform or showing official credentials, confirm the person's identity and valid legal authority with a call to an official phone number of the authorizing institution (*e.g..*, the Police Department; Child Protective Services; etc.). For a planned child abduction police uniforms and false credentials can be purchased or fabricated, and an accomplice's phone number can be given for a fraudulent confirmation. School officials should also not rely only on the child identifying the adult (*e.g.*, "that's my Daddy"), as unauthorized non-custodial parents are among the most likely persons to abduct a child.

To guard against theft, vandalism, and inappropriate or unlawful use, unsupervised areas of the school should be secured during school events open to outside visitors. Through postings and/or verbal notices, visitors should be instructed to remain in authorized event areas only. For larger events a school resource officer or other law enforcement officer should be present. Additional law enforcement officers are needed for events with larger crowds or with hard to manage crowds (*e.g.*, events more likely to attract intoxicated persons). For smaller, lower risk events, faculty and staff supervising the event should have an established emergency procedure for contacting law enforcement officers and school officials.

During appropriate times and circumstances visitors are lawfully allowed to enter school property as invitees. School officials have a duty to reasonably protect the safety of these visitors. But visitors have a duty to conduct themselves appropriately and to follow reasonable rules and orders from school officials. If a visitor refuses to do so, school officials may lawfully order the visitor to leave school property. A willful refusal to leave school property when lawfully ordered to do so is a criminal trespass, and may also violate specific state laws governing public school property, making the individual subject to arrest and prosecution. To protect the safety of persons and property school personnel should be instructed to politely and professionally question unknown persons they find in the school or any persons outside of designated event areas. Wandering visitors should be escorted back to the authorized areas, and suspicious persons should be reported to school administrators or law enforcement officers.

School Activities

Some school activities (*e.g.*, contact sports; physical education; chemistry labs; cooking, woodworking, construction, or automotive classes; field trips, etc.) present greater safety risks than more purely academic classroom instruction. Nonetheless, adequate planning, safety precautions, and supervision can help to reduce risks and still allow students the educational benefits of these activities. For all of these activities school officials should assure that instructors are qualified to safely supervise the activity; equipment is appropriate and regularly checked for safety; assigned activities are safe and appropriate for the age and abilities of students; students are properly instructed in documented and adequate safety procedures; and students are adequately supervised to assure safe participation in activities.

Safety equipment and procedures must comply with current standards of practice accepted in the field. Students should know safety rules and practice emergency safety procedures so they know exactly what to do in the event of an emergency. In sports training and physical education classes, coaches and teachers should not push students beyond their individual safe physical limits, especially under hot and humid weather conditions. Students have different levels of physical health and fitness. Uniform exercise assignments may physically overstress some students. When necessary because of individual physical or mental limitations, consistent with § 504, the ADA, and reasonable professional judgment, exercise assignments must be appropriately modified to assure individual student safety. Unreasonably dangerous activities should be prohibited for everyone (*e.g.* javelin throwing; activities that risk neck injuries; etc.). Instructors should be trained in first-aid and necessary first-aid equipment should be stored and available near the area it will most likely be needed.

Locker rooms, weight rooms, and shower areas must be adequately supervised. Access to these areas should be restricted unless authorized and under adult supervision. Students should be instructed that running, roughhousing, and other activities that risk falling or other injuries are strictly prohibited. Further, students should be instructed that they have an affirmative duty to immediately report any misconduct, injuries, or breaches of safety protocols to the supervising teacher.

Field trips can be rewarding experiences for students. But because these events are beyond the secured boundaries of the school they present unique potential dangers. Students must be adequately supervised at all times and strictly prohibited from talking with strangers or leaving the group. Adequate numbers of teachers and parent/chaperones must be present to safely supervise children. Parent/chaperones must be trusted persons who have been cleared through a criminal background check consistent with state law and local policy. Students should be notified that even though they are off-campus for field trips they remain under the lawful authority of school officials at all times during the field trip; they must obey the lawful orders of school officials; students must immediately report any known misconduct, injuries, or breaches of safety protocols to the supervising teacher; the student code of conduct will be strictly enforced to protect student safety; and all alcohol, drugs, weapons, or other contraband are strictly prohibited. If school officials have individualized reasonable suspicion of a violation of the law or school rules by a student, school officials may conduct a reasonable search consistent with the *T.L.O.* standard.

Buildings and Grounds

To enhance safety and avoid liability buildings and grounds should be regularly inspected, identifying and correcting security risks and safety hazards. Periodic checks for school security risks should include inspections of all possible routes of entrance including doors, windows, and roofs, examining whether unauthorized persons could gain access through these areas. Inspectors should attempt to see these areas through the eyes of a potential intruder who may break windows, force weak locks, or remove grates or covers to gain entry.

Among the questions inspectors should ask is what level of security is necessary under current circumstances; are security fences, lighting, cameras, or alarm systems needed; what affordable building or landscaping modifications could enhance security; how can the most security sensitive areas within the school be protected even if an intruder enters the building; how can students and personnel be protected from an intruder; are room numbers clearly marked and is an accurate building map available for emergency personnel if needed; do systems to keep intruders from getting in interfere with the ability of persons to get out in the event of an emergency; and are security measures compatible with daily uses of the school? Moveable classrooms and other outbuildings must be included in inspections, assuring that persons in these units are also safe and that they have an emergency means of communicating with security personnel in the main building.

Buildings and grounds should also be inspected to identify and correct safety hazards such as tripping hazards (*e.g.*, objects in walkways, weather heaved or broken side-walks, exposed drain pipes, cords, cables, rodent holes, tree roots, etc.); fire and electrical safety; sharp or protruding objects; heavy objects that could fall; defective chairs, desks, and other equipment; and dangerous animals (*e.g.*, feral dogs, rabid animals, poisonous snakes, spiders, hornets, fire ants, etc.). Athletic areas should be inspected to assure safety for students and to reduce the risk of injury to spectators from flying baseballs, unsafe seating areas, etc.

Play areas and playground equipment merit special attention as some of the most frequent and severe injuries occur in these areas. Parents think of a playground as a safe haven for their children. But the U.S. Consumer Product Safety Commission found that more than 200,000 U.S. children receive emergency room treatment each year as a result of playground injuries. A third of these injuries are classified as severe, and at least 15 children die each year due to playground injuries, mostly caused by falls to hard surfaces, strangulation by entanglement, or head-entrapment.

Playground safety is an important area of safety and liability concern with rapidly evolving standards. The general rule of tort law is that one must do what a reasonable person would do under the circumstances. As the circumstances change, so does what is reasonable under those circumstances. In decades past a major factor in the design of playground equipment was durability, resulting in playground areas dominated by steel structures embedded in concrete surfaces. Not surprisingly, the playgrounds of our youth would likely fail to meet current safety standards. In retrospect these ultra-durable playgrounds created unnecessary safety risks for children. Child safety and tort law concerns drove dramatic advancements in playground safety standards.

To protect safety and avoid liability play areas and equipment must comply with current safety standards. Outdated and unsafe equipment should be removed and the play area should be regularly inspected to assure proper maintenance of equipment and to guard against preventable safety hazards. In reviewing the play area for safety, it may be helpful to inspect the area not only from the height, view, and mindset of an adult, but also to examine the area from the height and perspective of a child at play, identifying otherwise hidden dangers and likely triggers for child behaviors that could result in injuries.

While out-dated and un-repaired equipment may pose special risks, injuries are not confined to a few aging playgrounds. Safety problems are shockingly widespread. Most playground injuries and deaths could be prevented with safer equipment and play area designs, regular safety inspections, and proper adult supervision of children. Playground safety standards published by the U.S. Consumer Product Safety Commission in its Handbook for Public Playground Safety are available free online.

Every year children are unnecessarily injured or killed by school buses or cars. Children are at special risk because of their small size, unpredictable behavior, and undeveloped abilities to foresee dangers and consequences. School parking lots and traffic flow patterns must be carefully planned to reduce risks of injury as buses and cars pick-up and drop-off children at the school. Never assume that children will watch for vehicles. Drivers must watch for children, and they must be regularly reminded to do so through posted signs, periodic reminders, and cautions from parking lot supervisors. Anyone who drives unsafely on school property should be warned or prohibited from driving on school property before a tragic accident occurs. Bus drivers should be periodically reminded that small children may not be within their view, and they must be absolutely certain all children are safely away from the vehicle before proceeding.

School officials may also consider advocating for stronger state laws and local enforcement governing vehicles passing stopped school buses dropping off children, or speeding in school zones.

Health and Safety Hazards

Students and school personnel spend much of their waking hours at the school. For good or ill the school environment has a significant impact on their health and safety. For this reason school officials must do all they can reasonably do to protect students and personnel from known dangers related to environmental toxins, infectious diseases, etc. School officials must comply with federal and state laws concerning hazardous materials (*e.g.*, asbestos, lead, etc.), storage and use of chemicals, mold control, and any other significant environmental, biological, or other known hazards.

The primary law governing work place safety is the Occupational Safety and Health Act (OSH Act), 29 U.S.C. § 651 (2011). This federal Act is administered by the U.S. Occupational Safety and Health Administration (OSHA). Section 654 (a) (1) of the OSH Act established a general duty for employers to protect employees from known hazards, stating: "Each employer shall furnish to each of his employees employment and a place of employment which are free from recognized hazards." In some states, state laws supplement OSHA safety standards, creating additional safety protections for workers. In all states employees have a "right to know" concerning recognized hazards in the workplace, so that they may take reasonable precautions to protect themselves and others from known dangers such as the presence of potentially harmful levels of chemicals, radiation, bio-hazards, etc.

Modern life would be impossible without chemicals. But even very useful chemicals may create unnecessary health and safety risks when improperly or excessively applied. Children are especially susceptible to environmental toxins, including cleaning chemicals and pesticides. Cleaning chemicals can release harmful vapors that may cause irritation to eyes, noses, and throats; trigger asthma attacks and allergic reactions; and cause long-term health problems resulting from prolonged and repeated exposures. Whenever possible, chemicals should be applied when children are not present, and custodial staff must assure the use of proper ventilation and appropriate safety gear (*i.e.*, respirators; goggles; gloves; etc.).

Many pesticides use neurotoxins to kill pests. While these chemicals may be effective in killing pests, over time repeated exposures may also do serious harm to humans, increasing risks of neurological disorders, cancer, and other serious health problems. Concerning the dangers of pesticides in schools, the U.S. Environmental Protection Agency (EPA) recommends the use of Integrated Pest Management (IPM) in schools. State laws may require the use of IMP in schools.

In using IPM, school officials working with the custodial staff first attempt to use non-toxic means of controlling pests, including sanitation, traps, and other non-toxic methods. If these non-toxic methods prove ineffective, they next use the least-toxic means of controlling pests. If the use of more toxic chemicals is ever necessary these are only used sparingly and at the times most distant from when students and personnel will be present in order to limit human exposure as much as possible. School custodial staff should be trained in the safe use of necessary pesticides and herbicides; only use these products consistent with federal and state laws; and always wear appropriate protective gear during application. Where toxic chemicals have been applied warning signs must be posted in the area consistent with state laws.

Most infectious diseases can be prevented through regular attention to basic hygiene. Hand washing is an essential and inexpensive first line of defense. To protect themselves and others from preventable infections, children should be instructed in the proper method of hand washing and taught that hand washing is essential before eating, after bathroom use, and after contact with any body fluid (*e.g.*, mucous, saliva, blood, etc.). Regular hand washing by all students and personnel should be encouraged by making hand washing facilities available in classrooms and work areas when possible. When this is not possible hand sanitizer should be available. Students should be cautioned not to drink or eat from shared containers, share personal hygiene items, or engage in any activities that result in an exchange of blood or other body fluids.

Cafeteria and custodial staff can help keep everyone healthy through careful attention to hygiene in food preparation, and by regularly and thoroughly cleaning commonly used surfaces, including table tops, desktops, computer keyboards, hand rails, door handles, water fountains, sinks, and bathrooms. Athletic surfaces (*e.g.*, weight training benches; wrestling, gymnastics, and yoga mats; etc.), must be regularly cleaned and sanitized, and all open wounds must be properly treated and dressed before students engage in contact sports or contact with commonly used athletic surfaces.

Universal biological safety precautions must always be used, treating all body fluids as potentially infectious. Disposable protective gloves should be worn, and bio-hazardous materials (*e.g.*, used needles, body fluids, contaminated bandages, etc.) must be safely disposed of in accordance with federal and state laws. Consistent with § 504 and the ADA, persons who pose a significant risk of transmitting a serious communicable disease should be supported with reasonable accommodations in continuing their studies or work from home or a medical facility until they can safely return to the school.

Emergency Planning and Response

When disaster strikes it may be too late to plan a response to effectively protect people and property. Consistent with federal and state laws and local ordinances, school officials must have an emergency management plan ready to respond to the dangers most likely in their areas including fires; storms; earthquakes; floods; chemical and bio-hazards; and attacks by internal or external persons. The U.S. Department of Education's Readiness and Emergency Management for Schools (REMS) Technical Assistance (TA) Center describes four phases of emergency management, and states:

> To ensure that the protocols align with the structure, policies and activities of emergency management and public safety officials, local education agencies and institutions of higher education should be familiar with the four interconnected phases of emergency management: Prevention-Mitigation, Preparedness, Response, and Recovery. These should be incorporated into all school, district, or campus emergency management plans.

The Department defines these as:

> *Prevention-Mitigation*: Identifying all potential hazards and vulnerabilities and reducing the potential damage they can cause;

Preparedness: Collaborating with community partners to develop plans and protocols to prepare for the possibility that the identified hazards, vulnerabilities or emergencies will occur;

Response: Working closely with first responders and community partners to effectively contain and resolve an emergency in, or around, a school or campus; and

Recovery: Teaming with community partners to assist students and staff in the healing process, and restore a healthy and safe learning environment following an emergency event.

Additional information is available through the U.S. Department of Education website, and further assistance can be obtained through state and local officials.

After the Columbine tragedy special concern has been given to preventing and responding to risks from persons within the school, *i.e.*, a potentially dangerous students or personnel. Because some identified behavioral concerns may be manifestations of mental illnesses or other disabilities, it is essential that school officials strike an appropriate balance between respect for the rights of individuals under the IDEA, § 504, and the ADA, and protecting the safety of the community. In cases where the individual clearly poses a safety threat to the community, however, public safety must be the first concern.

The problem, however, is that it is often not clear whether identified behavioral concerns are relatively benign symptoms of mental illnesses; other disabilities; social maladjustment; or a red flag signaling an impending danger. Further, individuals may have pieces of information that do not indicate any eminent danger in isolation, but would indicate a serious danger if all the pieces of the puzzle were seen and understood together.

To address these problems some schools have established a Behavioral Intervention Team (BIT) made up of persons with relevant multi-disciplinary expertise (*e.g.*, a counselor; psychologist; special educator; social worker; health care professional; school lawyer; safety and law enforcement professional; etc.). The BIT seeks to fairly and systematically review reports of behavioral concerns; to help the individual whenever possible by proactively addressing identified needs; and to protect the individual and others in the institution by preventing an imminent danger whenever possible. The BIT can help school officials to make an informed decision concerning whether services are needed or intervention is warranted. Based on the findings of the BIT school officials may determine the individual poses no current threat; merits continued monitoring; needs educational or health services; needs a referral or mandate for counseling; should be reassigned; or should be removed from the school through the disciplinary process or a report to law enforcement officials.

Information Security

Information security concerns include internal control of confidential information, protection from external threats, and mediation and response between the school and legitimate external requests for information. School officials have a duty to keep confidential information protected, including student and employee information protected under FERPA, HIPAA, or other applicable federal or state laws. Confidential paper or electronic files should be maintained in a secured area. There should be a qualified designated person in charge of controlling access to this information and responsible for compliance with applicable federal and state regulations governing confidential information. Generally, when access is granted records should note who was allowed access; for what lawful purpose access was granted; what specifically the individual was permitted access to; and dates and times in and out of the secured area.

School computer systems must be adequately protected both to secure information and to protect the systems from malicious attacks. School Internet systems must be operated with a filtering system in compliance with the CIPA and sufficient to protect children from harmful online materials. Children should also be instructed in Internet safety protocols and taught not to provide personal information, photos, etc., to unknown persons online. Some personal information controlled by the school (*e.g.*, phone numbers; e-mail addresses; home addresses; photos; class or work schedules; etc.) may also need to be protected for personal safety reasons if a student or employee is under government protection; being stalked; threatened; etc.

School officials should appoint qualified designated persons to respond to external requests for information. These persons must be adequately trained in compliance with applicable federal and state laws, and in compliance with school policies consistent with those laws. Similarly, there should be a designated spokesperson for the school trained to respond appropriately and lawfully to questions from members of the Press. Public schools are public institutions that should cooperate with members of the Press in providing information on matters of legitimate public concern. Some information, however, cannot be disclosed (*e.g.* information re: individual student discipline; disability; family or economic status; or details of pending investigations, personnel matters, legal proceedings, etc.).

Potentially sensitive external questions should be referred to the designated school spokesperson and/or to the school attorney. If an unauthorized school official makes an improper, inaccurate, or unlawful statement to the public or the Press, school officials cannot "un-ring the bell." It can be difficult or impossible for school officials and school attorneys to correct the error without unnecessary damage to the public reputation of the school or a pending case.

Compliance with State and Local Law

State laws, local ordinances, and local school policies may address many of the above issues. The State Department of Education, State Professional Organizations, and State School Boards Associations are often good sources for information on state specific laws. The National School Boards Association (NSBA), www.nsba.org is a useful source of information on school law and policy generally, and the NSBA provides links to State School Boards Associations with information on state specific laws and policies. The local Sheriff, Fire Chief, and other local officials may be helpful sources of information concerning compliance with local ordinances and protocols.

Applicable state and local codes may include regulations governing fire safety, health, traffic, construction, and land use and zoning issues. Schools must also be in compliance with applicable rules concerning usage of water, electricity, sewage, and sanitation services. As a state institution, however, public schools may be immune from some local regulations, especially if the issue is expressly regulated by a state statute governing public schools.

It is essential that all school officials read and understand their own school's policies. As obvious as this may seem, if fact many school officials have not read their own school's policies. Improvising may work for a while. But if the school official's failure to follow the school's own policies results in serious consequences or a legal challenge, failure to comply with published school policies may be an act of negligence or insubordination by the school official. The school is unlikely to prevail in a legal challenge when a school official is acting in violation of the school's own valid policies. A periodic review of current local school policies is an important way to assure compliance with applicable school policy and to guard against personal or institutional liability.

Insurance and Risk Management

Insurance serves as an important tool for risk management. Expenses from damage resulting from a fire, for example, could cause financially devastating costs to repair or replace a necessary school facility. And legal liability resulting from an accident or wrongful acts of employees could cost a school district millions of dollars. Insurance policies spread the risks of loss across a larger population, making it possible to compensate for predictable losses without bankrupting any single institution or individual. Commercial insurance companies set insurance premium rates based on calculated rates of group losses and individual risk factors, plus added costs of administration and company profits.

Another form of insurance is self-insurance which allows a larger school district with substantial resources to save the added costs of commercial insurance premiums by setting aside funds sufficient to cover predictable and manageable risks. A school district may decide to purchase commercial insurance to protect against catastrophic losses, but self-insure other more manageable financial risks. If state laws establish limits on legal liability through modified sovereign immunity and state workers' compensation plans, these risks become more predictable and manageable for larger public institutions.

Safety is always the first concern, but school officials also have a duty to protect school resources for educational purposes. State workers' compensation plans generally cover injuries incurred in employment. Employees may receive benefits under these plans, but in exchange they give up the right to a tort law suit against the employer. The employee can receive financial compensation for work related injuries without suing, and employers are protected against unpredictable tort losses in these cases.

Individual educators must also protect themselves and their families from preventable liability losses through reasonable precautions and adequate insurance. Individuals, however, can rarely afford to self-insure and instead purchase necessary insurance from commercial providers. Affordable liability insurance is often available through professional organizations.

Copyright Law and Liability

Article I, Section 8, of the U.S. Constitution states: "The Congress shall have Power . . . To promote the Progress of Science and useful Arts, by securing for limited Times to Authors and Inventors the exclusive Right to their respective Writings and Discoveries." The purpose of Article I, Section 8, of the U.S. Constitution was to encourage the creation of useful intellectual properties by giving private owners public protection of those rights. Without these protections, there would be little financial incentive for the creation of intellectual property, and these works would not be available to contribute to the common good.

Congress may and has, however, extracted a price for this public protection of private property. As a condition of receiving copyright protection authors must allow the "Fair Use" of their works consistent with the fair use test in § 107 of the U.S. Copyright statute:

§ 107. *Limitations on Exclusive Rights: Fair Use*

Notwithstanding [general copyright protections] the fair use of a copyrighted work, including such use by reproduction in copies . . . for purposes such as criticism, comment, news reporting, teaching (including multiple copies for classroom use), scholarship, or research, is not an infringement of copyright. In determining whether the use made of a work in any particular case is a fair use the factors to be considered shall include--

> (1) The purpose and character of the use, including whether such use is of a commercial nature or is for nonprofit educational purposes;
> (2) The nature of the copyrighted work;
> (3) The amount and substantiality of the portion used in relation to the copyrighted work as a whole; and
> (4) The effect of the use upon the potential market for or value of the copyrighted work.

In a suit for copyright infringement a reviewing court weighs the plaintiff's copyright entitlement against the defendant's claim of fair use based on these four factors. Copyrighted works that are within fair use may be lawfully copied and used for educational and other purposes permitted by the statute. Otherwise copyrighted works require lawful purchase or permission which can be efficiently obtained through the Copyright Clearance Center. Educational institutions can mitigate their potential liability for copyright violations by showing a lawful published institutional policy governing fair use of copyrighted materials; evidence that faculty and students were instructed concerning fair use; and by promptly addressing and correcting any valid complaints of copyright infringement.

Chapter Summary

This chapter reviewed tort law, liability, and safety issues. After reading this chapter, please consider the following points in review and for further thought and discussion:

I. *Review Points*:

1) Tort law is civil law recognizing the plaintiff's legal right to just compensation for damages caused by the defendant.

2) The main functions of tort law are to provide:

    1) A lawful means of obtaining just compensation for damages; and
    2) A deterrent against future injurious conduct.

3) The law of torts and contracts are similar, but the tort "contract" is an implied social contract to act reasonably in interactions with others. Tort law is the means of enforcing the necessary social contract of mutually responsible conduct, with the compensatory role of tort law acting like the remedial function of contract law, and the deterrent role of tort law acting similar to the deterrent effect of criminal law.

4) Without consequences for wrongful and negligent acts, there would be far more wrongful and negligent acts, and far less social and economic trust.

5) Potential tort law causes of action include torts resulting from negligence; malpractice; defamation; assault and battery; false imprisonment; invasion of privacy; and intentional infliction of emotional distress.

6) To establish a prima facie case of negligence the plaintiff must prove:

    1) The defendant had a duty to the plaintiff;
    2) The defendant breached that duty;
    3) The breach was both the cause in fact and legal cause of damages; and
    4) There are provable, compensable damages.

7) Teachers have a general duty to instruct, supervise, and protect children from known or reasonably foreseeable dangers. School officials have a general duty to reasonably supervise employees and students; to keep school property safe; and to protect against or warn of any known or reasonably foreseeable dangers to students, faculty, staff, or visitors.

8) To prove a breach of duty the plaintiff must prove by a preponderance of the evidence that the defendant failed to use ordinary care and do what a reasonable person would have done under the circumstances. The conduct of the defendant is measured against the conduct expected from a reasonable person. If the defendant meets or exceeds the standard of the reasonable person, the plaintiff will fail in proving the case.

9) Proof of two separate and distinct types of causation is required. The defendant's actions must have been:

1) The actual cause (cause in fact) of the plaintiff's injuries; and
2) The proximate (legal cause) of the plaintiff's injuries.

These two different elements of causation require independent proof and both elements must be established to prove a claim of negligence.

10) Negligence claims require proof of actual damages. These may include present and appropriately calculated future property loss, wage loss, medical expenses, compensation for pain and suffering, etc. Claims must be proven by a preponderance of the evidence, and must not be based on mere speculation about future possibilities.

11) The defendant may attempt to rebut the plaintiff's case by attacking the plaintiff's arguments on duty, breach, causation, and damages. The state defendant may also offer the following defenses or arguments for reductions in liability: Assumption of risk; plaintiff's negligence; or sovereign immunity.

12) Under 42 U.S.C. § 1983 plaintiffs may also sue state officials for a "deprivation of any rights, privileges, or immunities" protected by the U.S. Constitution and federal laws. Plaintiffs may seek damages from both the school district and individual school officials. Individual school officials are only held personally liable for damages when they have personally disregarded well established law.

13) Successful educational malpractice suits are more likely in very specialized areas such as special education and counseling.

14) In *Tarasoff* the court stated: "We conclude that the public policy favoring protection of the confidential character of patient-psychotherapist communications must yield to the extent to which disclosure is essential to avert danger to others. The protective privilege ends where the public peril begins." Many states have codified the *Tarasoff* principle into state laws. These statutes require counselors and other mental health care professionals to warn of specific dangers to identified persons, whether these are warnings to parents if a minor child threatens to harm him or herself, or warnings of threats to targeted third parties.

15) To establish a prima facie case of defamation, the plaintiff must show that the defendant's alleged defamatory declarations:

1) Contained untrue statements of fact concerning the plaintiff;
2) The statements were communicated to one or more persons other than the plaintiff;
3) The statements caused foreseeable prejudice towards the plaintiff; and
4) There are provable damages to the plaintiff.

The plaintiff's burden of proof also depends on whether the plaintiff is deemed a private or public figure for purposes of defamation. The Court has held that to prove defamation as a public figure the plaintiff must prove "that the statement was made with actual malice . . . that is with knowledge that it was false or with reckless disregard of whether it was false or not." In contrast plaintiffs that are private figures need only establish by a "preponderance of the evidence that the defendant failed to use ordinary care to determine the truth or falsity" of the statement concerning the plaintiff.

16) Intentional torts are distinguished from the tort of negligence in that the plaintiff must prove intent to cause harm, and not merely negligence in performing a duty. Because of the element of intent, many intentional torts are also crimes. Claims of intentional torts in educational institutions may include assault and battery; false imprisonment; invasion of privacy; and intentional infliction of emotional distress.

17) Recognizing and reasonably addressing potential problems before they become emergencies is the key to safety and liability management.

18) It is per se negligence to leave children unsupervised. A responsible adult must be in charge at all times, supervising children from the moment school officials take physical custody until physical custody is transferred back to the parent.

19) School officials are responsible for reasonably supervising on-duty personnel and may be held liable for negligent supervision and the on-duty tortious acts of employees under the doctrine of respondeat superior.

20) School officials have a legal duty to supervise and control public school buildings and grounds. To enhance safety and avoid liability buildings and grounds should be regularly inspected, identifying and correcting security risks and safety hazards.

21) Safety equipment and procedures must comply with current standards of practice accepted in the field. School officials must comply with federal and state laws concerning hazardous materials; storage and use of chemicals; and any other significant environmental, biological, or other known hazards. Consistent with federal and state laws and local ordinances, school officials must have an emergency management plan ready to respond to the dangers most likely in their areas.

22) School officials have a duty to keep confidential information protected. School computer systems must be adequately protected to secure information, and school Internet systems must be operated with a filtering system in compliance with the CIPA.

23) Copyrighted works that are within fair use may be lawfully copied and used for educational and other purposes permitted by the U.S. copyright statute. Otherwise copyrighted works require lawful purchase or permission.

II. *Principles to Practice Tips*:

1) *Duty of Care*: Tort law requires conduct consistent with what a reasonable person would do under the circumstances. When in doubt, err in favor of greater care. Tort law legal duties are only breached by falling below the ordinary standard of care. Extra care protects safety and prevents liability.

2) *Planning and Prevention*: In the areas of safety and liability, an ounce of prevention can be worth many pounds of cure. Prevention is the key to protecting safety and avoiding liability. Time and resources spent now on wise planning and prevention efforts will ultimately save time and resources in the future. Look for potential dangers and correct them before they become emergencies. You may not only save time and resources in the future, you may also save lives.

3) *Professional, Respectful, and Fair Treatment of All Persons*: Accidents and errors are inevitable, but tort law suits are not. It is unnecessary and unwise to admit negligence on behalf of the school district (*e.g.*, "it was our fault; we should have been more careful"). But it is humane and wise to express sincere concern regarding any accident or error, and to offer to help to the degree possible (*e.g.*, "I am very sorry that happened; let's see what we can do to help" is professional, respectful, and fair without admitting negligence on behalf of the school district). Legal fault and whether school officials were in fact negligent can be complex legal questions that may be decided later in a court of law. A voluntary admission of negligence on behalf of yourself and the school district is not a necessary part of treating a mishap sufferer (and potential plaintiff) respectfully, humanely, and fairly after a regrettable occurrence. But kindness, human concern, and an offer to help when possible are always appropriate under unfortunate circumstances. Further, persons treated professionally, respectfully, and fairly by school officials are generally less likely to become plaintiffs than persons further angered by unprofessional, disrespectful, and unfair treatment after an unfortunate incident.

III. *Questions for Discussion*: Please consider these questions and be prepared to discuss:

1) *Judging the Tort Law System*: Good laws establish a just and efficient system of problem resolution. In what ways does the U.S. system of tort law function well as a just and efficient system of problem resolution? In what ways does the system need to be reformed?

2) *Safety First*: What can you do to better protect safety in your school?

3) *Guarding Against Liability Risks*: What can you do to better protect yourself and your school from liability risks?

4) *Open Forum*: What other related issues or current events would you like to discuss?

IV. *Suggested Activities*:

1) Conduct a safety and security inspection of your school, attempting to identify and address potential risks.

2) Conduct a safety and security inspection of the grounds and parking area of your school, attempting to identify and address potential risks.

3) Conduct a safety and security inspection of your play area. Check online for current standards for play area safety and do a field inspection of the play area to assure that:

___ Play equipment meets current safety standards.
___ Ground surfaces have adequate depths and widths of impact safety materials.
___ Play equipment and ground safety materials are non-toxic.
___ Swings are made of soft materials and appropriately located.
___ Play equipment is safely spaced.
___ Elevated areas have adequate guard rails to prevent falling.
___ Hardware is properly tightened and not protruding.
___ There are no sharp edges, splinters, broken glass, etc., in the area.
___ There are no dangerous dogs, wild animals, snakes, spiders, etc., in the area.
___ There are no tripping, strangling, trapping, or pinching hazards.
___ Only authorized persons have access to the play area.
___ Children are adequately supervised.

For a free copy of the U.S. Consumer Product Safety Commission's Handbook for Public Playground Safety, see: http://www.cpsc.gov/cpscpub/pubs/325.pdf

4) Conduct an environmental review of your school. To help in improving the health of the school environment, the EPA has created a "One-Stop Location for Information and Links to School Environmental Health Issues" which can be found at: http://cfpub.epa.gov/schools/index.cfm

5) Review your school's emergency management plan. Additional resources and online training courses from the Department of Education's Readiness and Emergency Management for Schools (REMS) Technical Assistance (TA) Center can be found at: http://rems.ed.gov

Epilogue

Congratulations on completing your voyage through the law, a journey that is certain to both enrich your life and make you a more capable and confident professional. The law impacts every aspect of our lives, so acquiring a strong working knowledge of essential legal principles, policies, and their application in practice is a valuable and noteworthy achievement.

The intellectual ground you have covered is vast, and what you have learned in this book is extensive. Nonetheless, it is certain that you will learn even more in the future, as your understanding of the law is further expanded and enriched through your future experiences. Once a strong working knowledge of the law is acquired, over time this knowledge will continue to expand and you will see new facets, connections, and applications of the law grow in clarity with experience. It is recommended that you periodically review relevant sections of this book, as doing so will reveal new aspects of the law in the light of your new experiences.

It is my most sincere hope that you will find what you have learned life-enriching and highly beneficial both personally and professionally. Further, I hope that this is just the beginning of your journey to greater understanding and mastery of the law.

With very best wishes and hopes for future success.

John Dayton

Appendix

U.S. Constitution (1787)
(Abridged)

We the People of the United States, in Order to form a more perfect Union, establish Justice, insure domestic Tranquility, provide for the common defence, promote the general Welfare, and secure the Blessings of Liberty to ourselves and our Posterity, do ordain and establish this Constitution for the United States of America.

Article I

Section 1

All legislative Powers herein granted shall be vested in a Congress of the United States, which shall consist of a Senate and House of Representatives.

Section 2

The House of Representatives shall be composed of Members chosen every second Year by the People of the several States . . .

No Person shall be a Representative who shall not have attained to the Age of twenty five Years, and been seven Years a Citizen of the United States, and who shall not, when elected, be an Inhabitant of that State in which he shall be chosen . . . The Number of Representatives shall not exceed one for every thirty Thousand, but each State shall have at Least one Representative . . . The House of Representatives shall chuse their Speaker and other Officers; and shall have the sole Power of Impeachment.

Section 3

The Senate of the United States shall be composed of two Senators from each State, chosen . . . for six Years . . .

No Person shall be a Senator who shall not have attained to the Age of thirty Years, and been nine Years a Citizen of the United States, and who shall not, when elected, be an Inhabitant of that State for which he shall be chosen.

The Vice President of the United States shall be President of the Senate, but shall have no Vote, unless they be equally divided . . .

The Senate shall have the sole Power to try all Impeachments. When sitting for that Purpose, they shall be on Oath or Affirmation. When the President of the United States is tried, the Chief Justice shall preside: And no Person shall be convicted without the Concurrence of two thirds of the Members present.

Judgment in Cases of Impeachment shall not extend further than to removal from Office, and disqualification to hold and enjoy any Office of honor, Trust or Profit under the United States: but the Party convicted shall nevertheless be liable and subject to Indictment, Trial, Judgment and Punishment, according to Law . . .

Section 6

The Senators and Representatives shall receive a Compensation for their Services, to be ascertained by Law, and paid out of the Treasury of the United States. They shall in all Cases, except Treason, Felony and Breach of the Peace, be privileged from Arrest during their Attendance at the Session of their respective Houses, and in going to and returning from the same; and for any Speech or Debate in either House, they shall not be questioned in any other Place . . .

Section 7

All Bills for raising Revenue shall originate in the House of Representatives; but the Senate may propose or concur with Amendments as on other Bills.

Every Bill which shall have passed the House of Representatives and the Senate, shall, before it become a Law, be presented to the President of the United States: If he approve he shall sign it, but if not he shall return it, with his Objections to that House in which it shall have originated, who shall . . . proceed to reconsider it. If after such Reconsideration two thirds of that House shall agree to pass the Bill, it shall be sent . . . to the other House, by which it shall likewise be reconsidered, and if approved by two thirds of that House, it shall become a Law . . . If any Bill shall not be returned by the President within ten Days (Sundays excepted) after it shall have been presented to him, the Same shall be a Law, in like Manner as if he had signed it, unless the Congress by their Adjournment prevent its Return, in which Case it shall not be a Law . . .

Section 8

The Congress shall have Power To lay and collect Taxes, Duties, Imposts and Excises, to pay the Debts and provide for the common Defence and general Welfare of the United States; but all Duties, Imposts and Excises shall be uniform throughout the United States;

To borrow Money on the credit of the United States;

To regulate Commerce with foreign Nations, and among the several States, and with the Indian Tribes;

To establish an uniform Rule of Naturalization . . .

To promote the Progress of Science and useful Arts, by securing for limited Times to Authors and Inventors the exclusive Right to their respective Writings and Discoveries;

To constitute Tribunals inferior to the supreme Court . . .

To declare War . . .

To make all Laws which shall be necessary and proper for carrying into Execution the foregoing Powers, and all other Powers vested by this Constitution in the Government of the United States, or in any Department or Officer thereof.

Section 9

. . . The Privilege of the Writ of Habeas Corpus shall not be suspended, unless when in Cases of Rebellion or Invasion the public Safety may require it.

No Bill of Attainder or ex post facto Law shall be passed . . .

No Tax or Duty shall be laid on Articles exported from any State.

No Preference shall be given by any Regulation of Commerce or Revenue to the Ports of one State over those of another; nor shall Vessels bound to, or from, one State, be obliged to enter, clear, or pay Duties in another.

No Money shall be drawn from the Treasury, but in Consequence of Appropriations made by Law; and a regular Statement and Account of the Receipts and Expenditures of all public Money shall be published from time to time.

No Title of Nobility shall be granted by the United States: And no Person holding any Office of Profit or Trust under them, shall, without the Consent of the Congress, accept of any present, Emolument, Office, or Title, of any kind whatever, from any King, Prince, or foreign State.

Section 10

No State shall enter into any Treaty, Alliance, or Confederation; grant Letters of Marque and Reprisal; coin Money; emit Bills of Credit; make any Thing but gold and silver Coin a Tender in Payment of Debts; pass any Bill of Attainder, ex post facto Law, or Law impairing the Obligation of Contracts, or grant any Title of Nobility.

No State shall, without the Consent of the Congress, lay any Imposts or Duties on Imports or Exports, except what may be absolutely necessary for executing it's inspection Laws: and the net

Produce of all Duties and Imposts, laid by any State on Imports or Exports, shall be for the Use of the Treasury of the United States; and all such Laws shall be subject to the Revision and Controul of the Congress.

No State shall, without the Consent of Congress, lay any Duty of Tonnage, keep Troops, or Ships of War in time of Peace, enter into any Agreement or Compact with another State, or with a foreign Power, or engage in War, unless actually invaded, or in such imminent Danger as will not admit of delay.

Article II

Section 1

The executive Power shall be vested in a President of the United States of America. He shall hold his Office during the Term of four Years, and, together with the Vice President, chosen for the same Term, be elected . . .

The President shall, at stated Times, receive for his Services, a Compensation, which shall neither be increased nor diminished during the Period for which he shall have been elected, and he shall not receive within that Period any other Emolument from the United States, or any of them.

Before he enter on the Execution of his Office, he shall take the following Oath or Affirmation:-- "I do solemnly swear (or affirm) that I will faithfully execute the Office of President of the United States, and will to the best of my Ability, preserve, protect and defend the Constitution of the United States."

Section 2

The President shall be Commander in Chief of the Army and Navy of the United States, and of the Militia of the several States, when called into the actual Service of the United States; he may require the Opinion, in writing, of the principal Officer in each of the executive Departments, upon any Subject relating to the Duties of their respective Offices, and he shall have Power to grant Reprieves and Pardons for Offences against the United States, except in Cases of Impeachment.

He shall have Power, by and with the Advice and Consent of the Senate, to make Treaties, provided two thirds of the Senators present concur; and he shall nominate, and by and with the Advice and Consent of the Senate, shall appoint Ambassadors, other public Ministers and Consuls, Judges of the supreme Court, and all other Officers of the United States . . . but the Congress may by Law vest the Appointment of such inferior Officers, as they think proper, in the President alone, in the Courts of Law, or in the Heads of Departments.

The President shall have Power to fill up all Vacancies that may happen during the Recess of the Senate, by granting Commissions which shall expire at the End of their next Session.

Section 3

He shall from time to time give to the Congress Information of the State of the Union, and recommend to their Consideration such Measures as he shall judge necessary and expedient; he may, on extraordinary Occasions, convene both Houses, or either of them, and in Case of Disagreement between them, with Respect to the Time of Adjournment, he may adjourn them to such Time as he shall think proper; he shall receive Ambassadors and other public Ministers; he shall take Care that the Laws be faithfully executed, and shall Commission all the Officers of the United States.

Section 4

The President, Vice President and all civil Officers of the United States, shall be removed from Office on Impeachment for, and Conviction of, Treason, Bribery, or other high Crimes and Misdemeanors.

Article III

Section 1

The judicial Power of the United States shall be vested in one supreme Court, and in such inferior Courts as the Congress may from time to time ordain and establish. The Judges, both of the supreme and inferior Courts, shall hold their Offices during good Behaviour, and shall, at stated Times, receive for their Services a Compensation, which shall not be diminished during their Continuance in Office.

Section 2

The judicial Power shall extend to all Cases, in Law and Equity, arising under this Constitution, the Laws of the United States, and Treaties made, or which shall be made, under their Authority;--to all Cases affecting Ambassadors, other public Ministers and Consuls;--to all Cases of admiralty and maritime Jurisdiction;--to Controversies to which the United States shall be a Party;--to Controversies between two or more States;--between a State and Citizens of another State,--between Citizens of different States,--between Citizens of the same State claiming Lands under Grants of different States, and between a State, or the Citizens thereof, and foreign States, Citizens or Subjects.

In all Cases affecting Ambassadors, other public Ministers and Consuls, and those in which a State shall be Party, the supreme Court shall have original Jurisdiction. In all the other Cases before mentioned, the supreme Court shall have appellate Jurisdiction, both as to Law and Fact, with such Exceptions, and under such Regulations as the Congress shall make.

The Trial of all Crimes, except in Cases of Impeachment, shall be by Jury; and such Trial shall be held in the State where the said Crimes shall have been committed; but when not committed within any State, the Trial shall be at such Place or Places as the Congress may by Law have directed.

Section 3

Treason against the United States, shall consist only in levying War against them, or in adhering to their Enemies, giving them Aid and Comfort. No Person shall be convicted of Treason unless on the Testimony of two Witnesses to the same overt Act, or on Confession in open Court. The Congress shall have Power to declare the Punishment of Treason, but no Attainder of Treason shall work Corruption of Blood, or Forfeiture except during the Life of the Person attainted.

Article IV

Section 1

Full Faith and Credit shall be given in each State to the public Acts, Records, and judicial Proceedings of every other State . . .

Section 2

The Citizens of each State shall be entitled to all Privileges and Immunities of Citizens in the several States . . .

Article V

The Congress, whenever two thirds of both Houses shall deem it necessary, shall propose Amendments to this Constitution, or, on the Application of the Legislatures of two thirds of the several States, shall call a Convention for proposing Amendments, which, in either Case, shall be valid to all Intents and Purposes, as Part of this Constitution, when ratified by the Legislatures of three fourths of the several States, or by Conventions in three fourths thereof, as the one or the other Mode of Ratification may be proposed by the Congress . . .

Article VI

. . . This Constitution, and the Laws of the United States which shall be made in Pursuance thereof; and all Treaties made, or which shall be made, under the Authority of the United States, shall be the supreme Law of the Land; and the Judges in every State shall be bound thereby, any Thing in the Constitution or Laws of any State to the Contrary notwithstanding.

The Senators and Representatives before mentioned, and the Members of the several State Legislatures, and all executive and judicial Officers, both of the United States and of the several States, shall be bound by Oath or Affirmation, to support this Constitution; but no religious Test shall ever be required as a Qualification to any Office or public Trust under the United States . . .

Amendment I (1791)

Congress shall make no law respecting an establishment of religion, or prohibiting the free exercise thereof; or abridging the freedom of speech, or of the press; or the right of the people peaceably to assemble, and to petition the Government for a redress of grievances.

Amendment II (1791)

A well regulated Militia, being necessary to the security of a free State, the right of the people to keep and bear Arms, shall not be infringed.

Amendment III (1791)

No Soldier shall, in time of peace be quartered in any house, without the consent of the Owner, nor in time of war, but in a manner to be prescribed by law.

Amendment IV (1791)

The right of the people to be secure in their persons, houses, papers, and effects, against unreasonable searches and seizures, shall not be violated, and no Warrants shall issue, but upon probable cause, supported by Oath or affirmation, and particularly describing the place to be searched, and the persons or things to be seized.

Amendment V (1791)

No person shall be held to answer for a capital, or otherwise infamous crime, unless on a presentment or indictment of a Grand Jury, except in cases arising in the land or naval forces, or in the Militia, when in actual service in time of War or public danger; nor shall any person be subject for the same offence to be twice put in jeopardy of life or limb; nor shall be compelled in any criminal case to be a witness against himself, nor be deprived of life, liberty, or property, without due process of law; nor shall private property be taken for public use, without just compensation.

Amendment VI (1791)

In all criminal prosecutions, the accused shall enjoy the right to a speedy and public trial, by an impartial jury of the State and district wherein the crime shall have been committed, which district shall have been previously ascertained by law, and to be informed of the nature and cause of the accusation; to be confronted with the witnesses against him; to have compulsory process for obtaining witnesses in his favor, and to have the Assistance of Counsel for his defence.

Amendment VII (1791)

In Suits at common law, where the value in controversy shall exceed twenty dollars, the right of trial by jury shall be preserved, and no fact tried by a jury, shall be otherwise re-examined in any Court of the United States, than according to the rules of the common law.

Amendment VIII (1791)

Excessive bail shall not be required, nor excessive fines imposed, nor cruel and unusual punishments inflicted.

Amendment IX (1791)

The enumeration in the Constitution, of certain rights, shall not be construed to deny or disparage others retained by the people.

Amendment X (1791)

The powers not delegated to the United States by the Constitution, nor prohibited by it to the States, are reserved to the States respectively, or to the people

Amendment XI (1795)

The Judicial power of the United States shall not be construed to extend to any suit in law or equity, commenced or prosecuted against one of the United States by Citizens of another State, or by Citizens or Subjects of any Foreign State . . .

Amendment XIII (1865)

Section 1

Neither slavery nor involuntary servitude, except as a punishment for crime whereof the party shall have been duly convicted, shall exist within the United States, or any place subject to their jurisdiction.

Section 2

Congress shall have power to enforce this article by appropriate legislation.

Amendment XIV (1868)

Section 1

All persons born or naturalized in the United States, and subject to the jurisdiction thereof, are citizens of the United States and of the State wherein they reside. No State shall make or enforce any law which shall abridge the privileges or immunities of citizens of the United States; nor shall any State deprive any person of life, liberty, or property, without due process of law; nor deny to any person within its jurisdiction the equal protection of the laws . . .

Section 5

The Congress shall have the power to enforce, by appropriate legislation, the provisions of this article.

Amendment XV (1870)

Section 1

The right of citizens of the United States to vote shall not be denied or abridged by the United States or by any State on account of race, color, or previous condition of servitude.

Section 2

The Congress shall have power to enforce this article by appropriate legislation . . .

Amendment XIX (1920)

The right of citizens of the United States to vote shall not be denied or abridged by the United States or by any State on account of sex.

Congress shall have power to enforce this article by appropriate legislation . . .

Amendment XXVI (1971)

Section 1

The right of citizens of the United States, who are eighteen years of age or older, to vote shall not be denied or abridged by the United States of by any State on account of age.

Section 2

The Congress shall have power to enforce this article by appropriate legislation . . .

Table of Cases

Index